DICTIONARY OF THE ISRAELI-PALESTINIAN CONFLICT

DICTIONARY OF THE ISRAELI-PALESTINIAN CONFLICT

CULTURE, HISTORY, AND POLITICS

VOLUME 1: A-J

MACMILLAN REFERENCE USA
An Imprint of Thomson Gale, a part of The Thomson Corporation

THOMSON
GALE™

Detroit • New York • San Francisco • San Diego • New Haven, Conn. • Waterville, Maine • London • Munich

Dictionary of the Israeli-Palestinian Conflict: Culture, History, and Politics

Based on *Shalom, Salam: Dictionnaire pour une meilleure approche du conflit israélo-palestinien,* by Claude Faure, ©Librarie Arthème Fayard, 2002.

For more information, contact
Thomson Gale
27500 Drake Rd.
Farmington Hills, MI 48331-3535
Or you can visit our Internet site at
http://www.gale.com

LIBRARY OF CONGRESS CATALOGING-IN-PUBLICATION DATA

Faure, Claude.
[Shalom, salam. English]
Dictionary of the Israeli-Palestinian conflict : culture, history and politics / by Claude Faure.
p. cm.
Includes bibliographical references.
ISBN 0-02-865977-5 (set hardcover : alk. paper)—ISBN 0-02-865978-3 (vol 1)—ISBN 0-02-865979-1 (vol 2)—ISBN 0-02-865996-1 (e-book)
1. Israel—Politics and government—Encyclopedias. 2. Jews—Politics and government—Encyclopedias. 3. Israel—History—Encyclopedias. 4. Arab-Israeli conflict—Encyclopedias. 5. Palestinian Arabs—Politics and government—Encyclopedias. 6. Palestine—History—Encyclopedias. I. Title.

JQ1830.A58F3813 2005
956.9405'03—dc22

2004018641

This title is also available as an e-book.
ISBN 0-02-865996-1
Contact your Thomson Gale sales representative for ordering information.

Printed in the United States of America
10 9 8 7 6 5 4 3 2 1

CONTENTS

EDITORIAL & PRODUCTION STAFF

INTRODUCTION

The conflict that has pitted since 1948 the State of Israel against its Arab neighbors is the direct result of the decision by the United Nations to divide Palestine into two states, one Jewish and the other Arab, but the origins of the conflict have their roots in the history of the Middle East.

When, on 2 November 1917, then-foreign-minister Lord Arthur James Balfour officially declared to Lord Edmond de Rothschild that Great Britain would look favorably upon the creation of a Jewish Homeland in Palestine, he made inevitable the conflict between Arabs and Jews that has lasted the better part of the 20th century and, in the early years of the 21st century, still shows no sign of resolution. Indeed, petroleum, East-West tensions, and, most enduring, the Palestinian people's homelessness have hardened the roots of the conflict and turned the region into a battleground for international economic and political interests.

The Israeli-Palestinian conflict is one of the oldest and most complex in the region. For many years it has had serious international repercussions. The five wars that were fought since 1948 involved, indirectly, the two superpowers, the United States and the then U.S.S.R. The 1978 peace accords between Israel and Egypt, the Palestinian-Israeli "Declaration of Principles" of 1993 (later known as Oslo I), and the Israel-Jordan peace treaty of 1994 are important milestones in the peace process, but the conflict goes on.

While one cannot affirm that the September 2001 terrorist attacks on the United States were caused by the situation in Israel and in the Occupied Territories, it nevertheless remains that stagnating Israeli-Palestinian negotiations may have nourished growing resentment—if not hatred—toward America and resulted in the birth and growth of extremist movements around the world and far beyond the Middle East.

The Israeli-Palestinian conflict has touched and continues to affect masses of persons, famous and anonymous, and of all origins, professions, and ages. It has mobilized and still involves many countries outside the region, especially the United States, Russia, Great Britain, France, as well as political organizations such as the United Nations, the European Community, and the Arab League. All these entities share humanitarian as well as strategic concerns, while they may disagree ideologically or on ways to end the conflict.

The Middle East is a complicated region, where religions, politics, the past, the present, local and international interests, even water, are all intertwined issues. The cradle of the three major monotheistic religions that venerate the same prophets and claim the same holy places, this part of the world also holds natural resources and strategic access to Africa and Asia that only add to the complexity of the situation.

The dictionary is a tool to better understand this multi-faceted reality, unravel the many threads of its history, and penetrate the unique political characteristics of, and at play in, the region. Expanded, both in number of entries and in scope, from its original French version—Fayard's *Shalom, Salam,* by Claude Faure, released in Paris in 2002—and entirely rewritten to answer appropriately the questions of English-reading audiences, the two-volume work offers 1140 cross-referenced definitions. Written with the non-specialist in mind, the *Dictionary of the Israeli-Palestinian Conflict* does not deliver a single point of view, nor does it develop an opinion-based analysis. The work gives voice to the many positions at play through the history of the political parties, the movements, organizations, individuals, wars, peace treaties, and news media that have shaped and been shaped by this fifty-year-old conflict.

The detailed history of events, the contents of negotiations and agreements, the description and explanation of the many United Nations resolutions, and the detailed biographies that appear in this work make it a real tool for student and researcher alike. While the research for the dictionary carries it into 2004, the body of the work aims at providing as wide and deep a background to facilitate understanding of the issues at stake. The timeline of the conflict, which appears at the back of each volume, supports the fully developed and cross-referenced entries. It goes back to the first Zionist Congress (1897) in Basel, Switzerland, and Theodor Herzl's articulation of the long-held dream of a homeland for the Jews and on to the consequences of Israel's decision to build a wall of separation from the occupied territories. Some 110 images and maps help the reader locate and visualize the lands as well as the people involved in the dispute. Rounded up with a bibliography designed to support the readers' interest in further research, the *Dictionary of the Israeli-Palestinian Conflict* provides an exhaustive, un-biased, and easily accessible body of knowledge on a complex and tragic reality.

The efforts of many must be acknowledged: Mr. Claude Faure, who supplied the original idea and the first list of entries in this dictionary. Prof. Philip Mattar, who introduced us to Profs. Rochelle Davis and Neil Caplan, who provided patient guidance, deep knowledge and understanding of the history of the region, and the collegiality necessary to the redevelopment of a dictionary on such a sensitive topic. Their work was facilitated by the thoroughness of the research provided by Dorothy Bauhoff, Justine Ciovacco, Sylvia Engdahl, and Drew Silver, who rewrote and added to the original materials faithfully translated by Philip Beichtmann. Melissa Hill, project editor, deserves much credit for skillfully putting together a complicated project that needed to be done.

Hélène Potter
6 October 2004

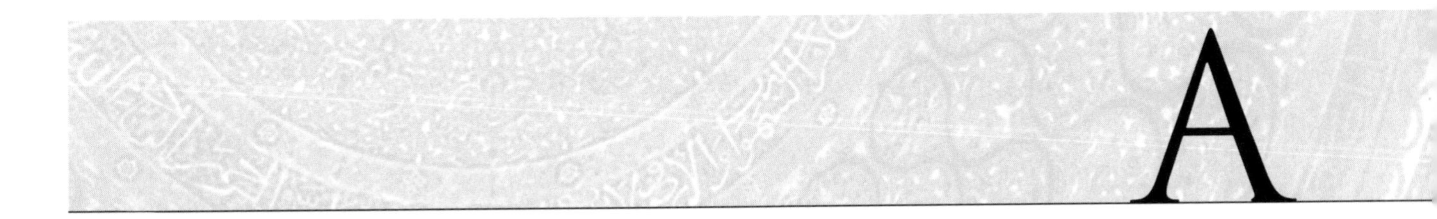

A

Abba: Aramaic term meaning "father, my father." Title conferred on bishops of the Eastern Church.

Abbas: Name of Muhammad's paternal uncle. Died in 652 or 653, when he was around eighty years old. The caliphs of the Abbasid dynasty are his descendants.

SEE ALSO Caliph.

Abbas, Mahmud Rida (Abu Mazin; 1935–): Palestinian political figure. Mahmud Abbas was born in 1935 in Safad, Mandatory Palestine. During the first Arab-Israel War in 1948, he fled to Syria, then joined the Baʿath Party in 1954. Four years later Abbas moved to Qatar, where he worked for the ministry of education for ten years. After joining the Palestinian al-Fatah movement, he was sent to Jordan in 1961, in charge of information in the Palestinian community. After the Jordanian-Palestinian clashes of Black September 1970 he was expelled to Syria, where he joined a small Palestinian group, whose members included Issam Sartawi and Saʿid Hamami, who favored the establishment of a dialogue with the Israelis. In 1971 he was elected to the Central Committee of al-Fatah and, the following year, to the Central Council of the Palestine Liberation Organization (PLO). In 1977 he traveled to Prague, where he met, discreetly, with representatives of the Israel Communist Party. In July 1978 he led the first al-Fatah delegation to Moscow. While in Moscow he wrote a thesis on Zionism that earned him a doctorate in political science.

Three years later Abbas joined the political department of the PLO, under the leadership of Faruq Qaddumi. He was in Tunis, in January 1983, at a meeting between Yasir Arafat and three Israeli figures: Mattityahu Peled, Uri Avnery, and Yaacov Arnon. The following September, at a meeting of the PLO's executive committee, Abbas was reelected to the political department as director of domestic affairs. At the meeting, he proposed the idea of beginning a dialogue with Israel. In May 1988 he was named leader of the Palestinian delegation to the mixed Jordanian-Palestinian Committee for the Occupied Territories, replacing Khalil al-Wazir (Abu Jihad), assassinated the previous month by an Israeli commando. Six months later, on 16 November, after the announcement by the Palestine National Council (PNC) of the "creation of the Palestinian State," Abbas supported the project of reform of the Palestinian Charter to include an official recognition of the State of Israel. In November of the following year he was appointed by Yasir Arafat to lead the Palestinian committee in charge of supervising the Israeli-Arab peace negotiations. On 1 June 1992, while the leader of the PLO was hospitalized in Amman, he joined Faruq Qaddumi and Hani al-Hasan in the triumvirate appointed by Yasir Arafat to direct the PLO in the interim. In March 1993, Arafat placed Abbas in charge of the secret negotiations with Israel in Oslo, Norway, which resulted, the following 13 September, in the signature of the Israeli-Palestinian Declaration of Principles (DOP). In February 1994 he supported Faysal al-Husayni, who was advocating the creation of a Jordanian-Palestinian confederation. Then, in disagreement with Arafat on certain points of the Israeli-Palestinian Agreement, Abbas announced his retirement from political life.

In March 1995, having returned to the West Bank, Abbas was once more asked to lead the Palestinian committee in negotiations with Israel. On 22 May 1996, elected by the executive committee of the PLO to the post of secretary general, he became second in command after Arafat and as such his potential successor. Abbas presided over the Central Elections Committee during the campaign for the January 1996 elections. Between 1997 and 2000, he met often with Israeli, American, and Arab political figures, with whom he tried to advance the Israeli-Palestinian peace negotiations. In the middle of May 2001, in the context of the al-Aqsa Intifada, which had intensified in the Palestinian territories, he traveled to Washington to meet with U.S. secretary of state Colin Powell, with whom he discussed ways of implementing the cease-fire enjoined by the Mitchell Commission. Early in September 2001 he flew to Moscow, a few days after the visit of Israeli prime minister Ariel Sharon.

In April 2003 Arafat appointed Abbas to the newly created post of prime minister. Arafat and the Palestinian Authority (PA) had agreed to this move only under great pressure from the Americans and the Israelis, who were refusing to deal with Arafat. Abbas's tenure was a constant power struggle with Arafat, chiefly over the many security services under Arafat's personal control, though Abbas was also interior minister. As prime minister, Abbas reappointed Saib Erekat as negotiation minister; urged Israel to act on its commitment to the Road Map plan for peace, including an end to the building of illegal settlements in the West Bank; and urged the Israelis and Americans to end their boycott of Arafat. Israel criticized Abbas for his reluctance to use force against militant groups, especially HAMAS, against which Israel was conducting a campaign of assassinations. Abbas was widely regarded among Palestinians as being excessively conciliatory. Facing a no-confidence vote in the Palestine Legislative Council, Abbas resigned from his cabinet posts on 5 September 2003. The next day Israel attempted to assassinate Ahmad Yasin, the nominal leader of HAMAS.

In October 2004, as Arafat's health declined, Abbas appeared to be in the best position to succeed Arafat. Returned to Arafat's favor, he is believed to have been a more honest, if not effective, PNA prime minister than Ahmad Qurai, and had wide, if not deep support at least among the older generation in the PLO. Abbas is known to favor bringing HAMAS and Islamic Jihad into the mainstream of Palestinian politics, something that may not be attractive to those organizations as long as the PLO continues to meet aggressive Israeli policy with attempts to compromise.

SEE ALSO Aqsa, Intifada, al-; Arafat, Yasir; Black September 1970; Erekat, Saib Muhammad; Fatah, al-; HAMAS; Husayni, Faysal al-; Palestine Liberation Organization; Palestinian Islamic Jihad; Qurai, Ahmad Sulayman; Road Map (2002).

ABBASIDS: Second dynasty of Islamic caliphs (750–1258 C.E.), founded by Abu al-Abbas al-Saffah, descendant of Abbas, uncle of the prophet Muhammad and victor over Marwan II at the Battle of the Zab River (Iraq) in 749. After they overturned the Umayyads, the Abbasids transferred their capital from Syria to Baghdad, which they made into a city of great splendor, enriched by Mediterranean and Far Eastern influences. Muslim theology and law made great strides under their reign. However, their far-flung empire was diverse and Baghdad was far from the difficulties experienced by the provinces. The Abbasids ignored the growing power of certain governors, and a few regions even seceded. In 836, the capital of the caliphate was moved to Samarra, a city north of Baghdad. Troubles multiplied and decadence set in, and power had to be shared with the Iranian and the Turkish bureaucratic families. At the end of the tenth century, the Seljuk Turks seized power, leaving the Abbasid caliphs only the semblance of sovereignty. In 1258 the Mongols brought an end to the Abbasid dynasty, sacking Baghdad and its libraries. The survivors of Caliph Abdullah al-Musta'sim's family took refuge in Egypt, where the dynasty became extinct in 1517 with the Ottoman conquest of Egypt.

SEE ALSO Abbas; Caliph; Ottomans; Seljuks; Umayyads.

ABBAYA: A cloak worn in different styles by men and women. It is commonly seen in black in the Persian Gulf states.

Abd (pl. *ibad*): Arabic word meaning "servant, or slave." Abd, followed by one of the ninety-nine names of God (e.g., Abd al-Rahman "the servant of the Merciful One"), is a common man's name in Arabic.

Abd al-Hadi, Awni (1889–1970): Palestinian political figure. Awni Abd al-Hadi was born in Nablus into a prominent landowning family and educated in Beirut, Istanbul, and Paris, where he attended the Sorbonne. A pan-Arab nationalist in Ottoman Palestine and Syria, he was a member of the Decentralization Party and helped organize the secret nationalist society al-Fatat (*al-Jamiʿya al-Arabiyya al-Fatat,* the Young Arab Society, which later evolved into the Istiqlal [Independence] Party) in 1911 and the Arab Nationalist Congress in Paris in 1913. He was secretary to Amir Faysal ibn Hussein al-Hashem, who was then ruling Syria, at the Paris Peace Conference after World War I and worked as an adviser to Faysal's short-lived government, and then after the French expelled Faysal to that of his brother Abdullah I in Transjordan. He was elected to the Arab Executive, the leading Palestinian nationalist organization until 1934, at its congresses in 1922, 1923, and 1928. He favored dialogue with the British and was a member of the Palestinian delegation to the London Conference of 1930. In 1932, his attitude toward the British hardening, he helped to revive the Istiqlal Party as a Palestinian political party opposing British rule and Zionism. Abd al-Hadi became secretary general of the Arab Higher Committee (AHC), formed in 1936 to coordinate the activities of the general strike called that spring, which developed into the Arab Revolt of 1936 through 1939. Deported in 1937 because of his work for the AHC, he remained in exile until 1941, although he was allowed to participate in the London Conference that produced the white paper of 1939. He was given a ministry in the All-Palestine Government formed in the Gaza Strip during the 1948 War but never served in the short-lived and hopeless enterprise. He was the Jordanian ambassador to Egypt from 1951 to 1955 and later a Jordanian government minister and a member of the Jordanian senate. He died in Cairo.

SEE ALSO Abdullah I ibn Hussein; All-Palestine Government; Arab Executive; Arab Higher Committee; Gaza Strip; Istiqlal, al-; Palestine Arab Revolt (1936–1939); White Papers on Palestine.

Abd al-Maguid, Esmat (1924–): Egyptian diplomat. Esmat Abd al-Maguid studied international law in Paris and began his career in foreign affairs in 1950, becoming secretary to the Egyptian ambassador in London, a post that he held until 1954. Back in Cairo he became director (until 1957) of the Bureau of British Affairs in the Foreign Ministry. In this capacity he participated in negotiations on the evacuation of British troops from Egypt. From 1957 to 1961 he was a member of the Egyptian delegation to the United Nations in Geneva. Between 1961 and 1963 he held the position of deputy director of the Legislative Department of the Foreign Ministry, where he became one of the main collaborators of Muhammad Hafiz el-Ismail, vice minister of Foreign Affairs. Between 1963 and 1966 he was chargé d'affaires of the Egyptian embassy in Paris. He then became director of the Department of Cultural Affairs at the Foreign Ministry, and then spokesman for the Egyptian government.

In June 1970, Abd al-Maguid was named Egyptian ambassador in Paris, replacing Muhammad Hafiz el-Ismail, who had become director of Egypt's Intelligence Service. That November, Abd al-Maguid was appointed chargé d'affaires in the government of Mahmud Fawzi. In January 1972 he was named permanent representative of Egypt to the United Nations. On 16 July 1984, Abd al-Maguid was appointed minister of Foreign Affairs, replacing Kamal Hassan Ali, who had become prime minister. On 11 November 1986 Abd al-Maguid was promoted to vice prime minister, in charge of foreign affairs. As such he guided Egyptian diplomacy in its efforts to support the Palestinian cause. On 15 May 1991 he was elected general secretary of the Arab League, an election that marked the return of Egypt to a leadership position in the pan-Arab organization, from which it had been excluded since the Camp David Accords. He was replaced as director of the ministry of Foreign Affairs by Amr Mousa, who, ten years later, succeeded him as head of the Arab League.

SEE ALSO Camp David Accords; League of Arab States; Mousa, Amr Muhammad.

Abd al-Nasir, Jamal

SEE Nasser, Gamal Abdel.

Abd al-Rahim, Tayyib (Abu al-Tayyib; 1945–): Palestinian political figure, born in 1945 in Palestine. Abd al-Rahim is a member of Yasir Arafat's inner circle. A refugee in Egypt, he studied in Cairo, where, in the middle of the 1960s, he was president of the Palestinian Students Union. After earning a degree in economics, in 1969 he became responsible for information at Sawt Filastin (Voice of Palestine), the

Palestinian radio station in Cairo, and was its director from 1973 to 1978. He also participated in the editing of the magazine *Al-Watan*. After having joined the political department of the Palestine Liberation Organization (PLO), he was named the organization's ambassador to China. He was assigned to the Palestinian Mission at Cairo in 1985 and to Yugoslavia between 1987 and 1988. A member of the Palestine National Council (PNC) since 1977, he was elected to the Central Committee of al-Fatah and appointed al-Fatah's representative on the Central Council of the PLO in August 1989. Abd al-Rahim was appointed PLO ambassador to Jordan the following November. In May 1994, in the context of the application of the Oslo Agreements, he became general secretary of the presidency of the Palestinian Authority (PA) and in 1996 he was elected to the Palestinian Legislative Council.

SEE ALSO Arafat, Yasir, al-Fatah; Oslo Accords; Oslo Accords II; Palestine Liberation Organization; Palestine National Council; Palestinian Authority.

ABD AL-SHAFI, HAYDAR (1919–): Palestinian political figure. Born in 1919 in Gaza, Palestine, Haydar Abd al-Shafi received a degree in surgery from the American University of Beirut. He became a doctor of medicine in 1945, after a number of stays in the United States. Close to the Communist Party, he was, in 1945, one of the rare Arabs who supported Resolution 181 of the United Nations on the partition of Palestine. Between 1952 and 1956 he headed the Palestinian Parliament of Gaza, then under Egyptian administration. In 1964, as a member of the Palestine National Council (PNC), he was elected to the First Executive Committee of the Palestine Liberation Organization (PLO). Four years later he attempted, in vain, to restart the activity of the Gaza Parliament. Accused of anti-Israeli activities in 1970, he was expelled by Israeli authorities to Lebanon for a few months.

From 1972 on, favorable to Resolution 242, he became one of the leaders of the nationalist Palestinians in the West Bank. In October of that year he participated in setting up, in the Gaza Strip, the Palestine Red Crescent Society, of which he assumed presidency in 1979. He was an opponent of the Camp David Accords and subsequent peace treaty. Beginning in July 1980 the Israeli authorities barred him, for a period of four years, from leaving Gaza City to go abroad. In 1983 he was elected to the Administrative Council of Bir Zeit University in the West Bank. The Israeli police interrogated him a number of times between 1988 and 1990; he was accused of being one of the leaders of the Intifada. During the Gulf War he opposed the PLO's support for Iraq. In October 1991 he presided over the Palestinian delegation at the Mideast Peace Conference held in Madrid, where he was assisted by Faysal al-Husayni, whose views on the Palestinian question he did not share. He resigned from the delegation in April 1993 but was persuaded to stay. In July 1993, he argued with Yasir Arafat over the concessions Arafat had made in the Oslo Accords concerning Israeli settlements. He was upset as well over Arafat's having conducted the negotiations in secret. Critical of Arafat's autocratic rule of the PLO, Abd al-Shafi demanded, in vain, the creation of a plural leadership. He resigned from the delegation after the Accords were made public.

In May 1994 Abd al-Shafi refused to be part of the Palestinian Authority. In February 1996 he was elected to the Palestinian Legislative Council with the largest vote of any candidate. He resigned his seat in March 1998 (having announced his decision the previous October)—despite the attempts of many deputies to change his mind—declaring that he could not support Arafat's authoritarianism, which he believed was sabotaging the Council. In July 2002 Abd al-Shafi was one of the principal promoters, with Mustafa Barghuthi and Ibrahim Dakkak, of the Palestinian National Initiative, al-Mubadara, which calls for the formation of a "national emergency leadership," democratic elections at all levels, and institutional reform to achieve Palestinian national rights and a "durable, just peace." Considered a voice of public conscience by some, Haydar Abd al-Shafi is a "Palestinian from within" who enjoys the respect of the entire Palestinian population as well as the political class.

SEE ALSO Arafat, Yasir; Camp David Accords; Intifada (1987–1993); Oslo Accords; Palestine National Council; Palestinian Authority.

ABD RABBO, YASIR (Muhammad Abu Bashir; 1944–): Palestinian political figure. Yasir Abd Rabbo was born in 1944 at Hebron. After the War of 1967, he went to Cairo, where he pursued literary studies. As president of the General Union of Palestinian Students in Egypt, he was part of the team guiding the Popular Front for the Liberation of Palestine (PFLP), along with George Habash and Nayif Hawatma. On 21 February 1969, following the congress of Amman, along with Hawatma, he quit the PFLP to found the Democratic Popular Front for the Liberation of Palestine (DPFLP), which was transformed later into the Democratic Front for the Liberation of Palestine (DFLP). As head of the cultural department of this movement and its assistant secretary general, in February 1973 he accompanied Yasir Arafat to Bulgaria and Czechoslovakia. In 1974 he was elected to the executive committee of the Palestine Liberation Organization (PLO), in charge of the department of information.

In 1988 Abd Rabbo participated in the dialogue between the PLO and the U.S. State Department, during which, according to the Americans, he showed himself to be an "open and constructive" interlocutor. In October 1989 he was in Cairo to attempt, by the intermediary of Egyptian authorities, to open a channel of negotiations with the Israelis. In 1990, favoring the policies of rapprochement with Israel recommended by Yasir Arafat, he found himself at loggerheads with Nayif Hawatma, who opposed this approach. In September 1991, with his two assistants, Salih Ra'fat and Muhammad al-Labadi, he quit the DFLP to found his own movement, the Palestinian Democratic Union (PDU), which supported the peace process started at the Madrid Conference in 1991. In May 1994 he became minister of information and culture in the newly formed Palestinian Authority (PA), presided over by Arafat.

In addition to his ministerial duties, Abd Rabbo remained one of the principal figures of the Palestinian delegations that were negotiating with Israel. In October 1998 he participated in the Israeli-Palestinian negotiations that were taking place at Wye Plantation in the United States. In November 1999 he served as head of the delegation responsible for negotiations on the final status of the Palestinian autonomous territories. In March 2000 he met with the U.S. mediator, Dennis Ross, and the head of the Israeli delegation, Oded Eran, in Washington, but in May of that year resigned from the negotiating team when he learned that Arafat had authorized secret Palestinian-Israeli negotiations in Sweden without informing him. When Arafat reorganized the Palestinian Authority administration in 2002, Abd Rabbo refused an invitation to join, but he did accept the position of cabinet affairs minister in the government of Prime Minister Mahmud Abbas in April 2003.

In 2001 Abd Rabbo was a signatory, along with Hanan Ashrawi, Yossi Beilin, Amos Oz, and a number of other prominent Palestinians and Israelis, to the Cairo Declaration of 2001, which called for an end to the Israeli occupation of Palestinian territories and an end to bloodshed. He was the chief Palestinian participant in the unofficial Palestinian-Israeli talks that produced the Geneva Peace Initiative, proposed in 2003 to replace the Oslo Accords as the basis for Palestinian-Israeli peace.

SEE ALSO Arafat, Yasir; Ashrawi, Hanan Daouda; Beilin, Yossi; Democratic Front for the Liberation of Palestine; Geneva Peace Initiative of 2003; Oslo Accords; Palestinian Authority.

ABDULLAH I IBN HUSSEIN (King Abd'allah of Jordan): Second son of Amir Husayn ibn Ali al-Hashimi al-Sharif of Mecca, Abdullah ibn Husayn was born in 1882 in the Hijaz region of Arabia. During the First World War, his father, supported by Great Britain, incited the Arab tribes to revolt against the Ottoman Empire. The British high commissioner in Egypt, Henry MacMahon, persuaded Sharif Husayn to support the creation of a greater Arab kingdom under Hashimite authority. With the help of British captain T. E. Lawrence, Abdullah participated actively in combat and drove the Turks from Hijaz, in November 1917. But in June of the following year Abdullah was driven out of Hijaz by the Wahhabi forces of the al-Sa'ud family, equally supported by the British, obliging him to take refuge in Medina.

In October 1918 Abdullah became king of Iraq while his brother, Faisal, was trying to become amir of Syria. In July 1920, the latter was driven from Damascus by the French. In fury, the Hashimite family considered raising troops for the reconquest of Syria. To placate Faisal, the British, at the Cairo Conference of March 1921, made him amir of Iraq, and Abdullah Amir of Transjordan, which was under their mandate. In May 1923, as amir, Abdullah proclaimed the independence of Transjordan. The following October, his father, Sharif Husayn, driven from Mecca by the Wahhabis, was obliged to seek exile in Cyprus. In February 1928, in the context of the application of the Balfour Declaration, a treaty between Transjordan and Britain stipulated the separation of Palestine from Transjordan. This decision aroused the anger of the Transjordanian tribes and caused conflicts with the British forces. In November 1929, while on a visit to Jerusalem, Abdullah ibn Husayn escaped an assassination attempt. During the Second World War, Transjordan supported the Allies against the Germans. On 22 March 1946, the British Mandate over Transjordan officially ended, and on 25 May, after the proclamation of the accession to rule of the Hashimite Kingdom by the Transjordanian Legislative Council, Abdullah was crowned king of Transjordan.

On 16 November 1947, while the creation of a Jewish state was the subject of intense international negotiations, Abdullah secretly received the envoy of the Jewish Agency, Golda Meir, who tried to convince him to accept guaranteeing the security of the Jewish entity in Palestine in exchange for control over the Arab portion of the country. On 15 May 1948, on the morrow of the creation of the State of Israel, Abdullah joined forces with the Arab countries that attacked the Israeli troops. His Arab Legion took control of the Arab section of Jerusalem. On 16 December, in spite of protests of the Arab League, he prepared to annex the West Bank, at the request of the Palestinian Congress installed in Amman. On 3 April 1949, by signing an armistice treaty with Israel, Abdullah's kingdom gained control of the West Bank and the Arab part of Jerusalem. On 27 February he secretly signed a draft of an Israeli-Jordanian treaty with Israeli prime minister David Ben-Gurion. Accused by the Arab League of wanting to conclude a separate peace with Israel, he had to abandon this project.

On 24 April 1950, after having discharged the Grand Mufti of Jerusalem, Muhammad Amin al-Husayni, Abdullah officially annexed the West Bank and proclaimed the creation of the Hashimite Kingdom of Jordan. A majority of Palestinians immediately accused him of trying to take over their country. On 15 February 1951, the Israeli and Jordanian governments concluded an agreement on measures to be taken to prevent any infiltration into Israel of Palestinian groups acting from Hashimite territory. The following 20 July, Abdullah ibn Husayn was assassinated in Jerusalem by a Palestinian. Talal, Abdullah's older son, was in bad health and held power for a few weeks only, leaving the throne to his son, Hussein, who would reign over Jordan for almost forty-eight years.

SEE ALSO Balfour Declaration; Hussein ibn Talal; Jerusalem; Jewish Agency for Israel; League of Arab States; Meir, Golda; Wahhabis.

ABDULLAH II IBN HUSSEIN (Abdullah II of Jordan; 1962–): King of Jordan. The eldest son of King Hussein of Jordan and his British second wife, Princess Muna (Antoinette Avril Gardiner), Prince Abdullah ibn Hussein was born on 30 January 1962 and was Jordan's crown prince from 1962 to 1965. However, in order to avoid a too-prolonged regency in case of premature death, the king designated his own brother, Hassan ibn Talal, as crown prince, on the condition that Abdullah would become crown prince in case of the accession of Hassan to the throne. In 1980, after studies in England and the United States, Abdullah enrolled in the British Royal Military Academy, Sandhurst, then did graduate studies at Oxford.

KING OF JORDAN. ABDULLAH II IBN HUSSEIN, THE ELDEST SON OF KING HUSSEIN, CONTINUED HIS FATHER'S MODERATE POLICIES AND CLOSE TIES WITH THE UNITED STATES—DESPITE OPPOSITION TO THE 2003 WAR IN IRAQ—AFTER HE ACCEDED TO THE THRONE IN 1999, AT THE AGE OF THIRTY-SEVEN. *(© 2003 Landov LLC. All rights reserved)*

Upon his return to Jordan in 1984 he was assigned to the 40th Armored Brigade. He traveled the following year to the United States and France for military training. In 1986 he was assigned to a Jordanian helicopter platoon. In 1989, after new periods of military and college education in the United States and Great Britain, he was promoted to the rank of commander, then, in January 1993, to the rank of colonel. On 10 June Abdullah married Rania al-Yasin, a Kuwaiti-born Palestinian, with whom, a year later, he had his first child, Hussein. In November 1993, promoted to brigadier general, he took command of the Jordanian Special Forces, then three years later, of the Royal Jordanian Special Operation

Command (RJSOC), merging the Special Forces corps and those of the Royal Guard. On 2 May 1998 he was named major general.

On 25 January 1999, upon his father's return from a stay in the United States, where King Hussein had received treatment for cancer, Abdullah was made crown prince, replacing his uncle Hassan. After the death of his father on 7 February, Abdullah became king of Jordan, under the name of Abdullah II. He designated his brother Hamza—son of King Hussein and Queen Noor—as crown prince. To make himself known on the international political scene, Abdullah traveled extensively that summer, going to Europe, the United States, and Canada. On 26 July, on the morning of the funeral of the king of Morocco, where he also had an opportunity to meet with U.S. president Bill Clinton and Israeli prime minister Ehud Barak, he paid a surprise visit to Damascus, where he was received by President Hafiz al-Asad.

On 5 September Abdullah signed an accord developed at Sharm al-Shaykh (Egypt) between Ehud Barak and Palestinian president Yasir Arafat. This agreement was thought to open the way to negotiations for a final peace settlement between the Palestinians and the Israelis. A few days later King Abdullah visited Kuwait, ending a period of chill in the relations between the two countries that had followed the Gulf War. On 1 November, after his first address to the Jordanian Parliament, Abdullah dedicated himself to pursuing his father's work in favor of peace in the Middle East and a rapprochement with Arab "brother" nations. Domestically, after having warned off Islamist Jordanians opposed to peace with Israel, he announced his intention of continuing the process of democratization begun ten years earlier and to pursue the fight against corruption. On 25 November, in his speech opening the World Conference on Religion and Peace, which took place in Amman, he hardened his tone on Israel, declaring that the latter should renounce its territorial ambitions in the eastern sector of Jerusalem and accept the return of Palestinian refugees in order to attain a durable peace in the Middle East. On 22 August 2000 he made his first official visit to Tel Aviv, where he was received by Prime Minister Barak. Before his trip Abdullah had talked with Arafat and had reaffirmed to him Jordanian support for the Palestinian cause.

The king implicitly gave his support to the U.S. campaign against the Iraqi regime of Saddam Hussein in 2002–2003, but opposed the war, refusing U.S. forces the use of Jordanian airspace. In June 2003 Abdullah hosted the Aqaba Summit, which was intended to work out the means of implementing the Road Map plan put forth that April by the so-called Quartet (United States, European Union, United Nations, Russia). Later the same month the king hosted an extraordinary "global reconciliation" meeting of the World Economic Forum, concerned mainly with the Middle East, at the Dead Sea resort of Southern Shuneh. He met privately with Prime Minister Ariel Sharon in Israel in March 2004 to discuss the problems with the "separation wall" Israel was building around Palestinian areas in the West Bank. Aside from his opposition to the wall as inflammatory, he was concerned that it would eventually cause a mass movement of new Palestinian refugees into Jordan, resulting in economic stress and upsetting the demographic balance between Palestinians and East Bank Jordanians, which already threatens Jordan's political stability. After having canceled an earlier meeting with President George W. Bush to protest American support for Sharon's latest plan for Gaza and the West Bank, Abdullah went to Washington in April 2004. There he was the chosen recipient of the president's apology for the torture committed by U.S. forces against Iraqi prisoners in Baghdad. In May 2004 Abdullah again hosted an extraordinary meeting of the World Economic Forum. The circumstances of Abdullah's rule have largely been shaped by the al-Aqsa Intifada in the Palestinian territories and by the U.S. "war on terror." Concerned mainly with the survival of his regime and heavily dependent on aid from the West, he remains active in his attempts to encourage a political settlement for the Palestine-Israel issue while cooperating with the United States and preserving the peace with Israel.

SEE ALSO Abdullah I ibn Hussein; Aqaba Summit; Bush, George W.; Iraq War; Sharm al-Shaykh Summits.

ABED RABBO, YASSER

SEE Abd Rabbo, Yasir Muhammad.

ABNA' AL-BALAD ("sons of the land," in Arabic): Nationalist Movement of Israeli Arabs who insist they are part of the Palestinian People. Appearing at the beginning of 1970, the movement was started by Muhammad Kiwan in anticipation of the municipal elections in the village of Umm al-Fahm. Its principal leaders are Raja Ighbariyeh, Awad Abdul Fattah, and Ahmad Muhammad.

ABRAHAM (Abram, Ab-Raham, "father of the multitude," in Aramaic and in Hebrew; Sidna Ibrahim, Ibrahim al-Khalil, Abraham "close friend of God," in Arabic): According to Biblical tradition Abraham is considered the first of the Jewish patriarchs to have revealed, in the nineteenth century B.C.E., the existence of One God. Therefore, according to the Bible, Abraham, son of Terah (Terakh), is descended from Shem, eldest son of Noah and of the line of Eber (Heber). A Chaldean (Mesopotamian) shepherd, Abraham left the city of Ur (Haran) under the prompting of God, leading his tribe to Canaan. According to a divine messenger, a "Promised Land" awaited him there, "between the river of Egypt and the great Euphrates," where his tribe, chosen by God, would become a great nation. Abraham settled in Canaan for a time, but, because of the hostility of the Canaanites and difficulties feeding his tribe, he decided to go to Egypt. There, with the consent of his wife, Sarah, who was sterile, he had a son, Ishmael (Hebrew)/Isma'il (Arabic), with Hagar, his Egyptian servant.

Later, at the head of his tribe, he left Egypt to return to the land of Canaan where he settled in the forest of Mambreh, near the city of Hebron. There, his wife Sarah, who, meanwhile, miraculously had given him a son, Isaac (Itzhak, Hebrew; Ishaq, Arabic), asked him to renounce Ishmael. At that moment, God, testing his loyalty, commanded Abraham to sacrifice his son Isaac on Mount Moriah. Before Abraham's determination to obey the divine would lead him to accomplish this, God sent a sign to prevent the execution. Abraham decided then to sacrifice a lamb to the glory of God. After their death, Abraham and Sarah were buried in Hebron, and this city became a Jewish holy place, then a Christian and Muslim one. Traditionally described as the ancestor of the Arabs and the Jews, because he is the father of both Ishmael and Isaac, Abraham is a major personage in the Jewish, Christian, and Muslim religions. The Qur'an depicts him as one of the prophets, builder of the Ka'ba, and Muslims commemorate his willingness to sacrifice his son Isma'il (instead of Isaac of the Biblical story) on the occasion of the festival of *Id al-Adha.* According to some historians, the words *Abarama, Abirami* ("love the father, loved by the father"), inscribed on the Ebla Tablets that predate the Biblical story, designate Abraham; while for others, many elements recounted in Genesis are difficult to place in the period when they were supposed to have occurred (around 1850 B.C.E.).

SEE ALSO Arabs; Bible; Canaan; Hebron; Isaac; Ishmael; Jew; Ka'ba; Patriarchs.

ABRAHAM OFFERING UP HIS SON ISAAC. THIS COLOR LITHOGRAPH, C. 1860S, DEPICTS GOD'S TEST OF ABRAHAM'S LOYALTY, ACCORDING TO THE BIBLE. MUSLIMS BELIEVE IT IS ISMA'IL (ISHMAEL), THE FIRST-BORN SON OF IBRAHIM, WHOM THE TRADITIONAL ANCESTOR OF THE JEWS AND THE ARABS WAS WILLING TO SACRIFICE. *(© Historical Picture Archive/Corbis)*

ABRAMS, ELLIOTT (1948–): Senior director for Near East and North African Affairs, U.S. National Security Council (2002–). Educated at Harvard University, the London School of Economics, and Harvard Law School, Abrams first gained prominence when he served as U.S. president Ronald Reagan's assistant secretary of state for human rights (1981–1985), then as assistant secretary for inter-American affairs (1985–1989). He was indicted by the Iran-Contra special prosecutor for giving false testimony about his role in illicitly raising money for the Contras but pleaded guilty to two lesser offenses of withholding information from Congress. He was pardoned, along with a number of other Iran-Contra defendants, by President George H. W. Bush in 1992. In 2001 President George W. Bush nominated Abrams as senior director for Democracy, Human Rights, and International Operations in the National Security Council, a post Abrams held until 2002, when he was appointed senior director for Near East and North African Affairs. Critics charged that Abrams lacked credentials for the position, arguing that he was cho-

ELLIOTT ABRAMS. PARDONED BY THE FIRST PRESIDENT BUSH FOR HIS ROLE IN THE IRAN-CONTRA AFFAIR, ABRAMS BECAME A SENIOR ADVISER TO PRESIDENT GEORGE W. BUSH ON THE MIDDLE EAST. CRITICS SAID HE WAS APPOINTED FOR HIS NEOCONSERVATIVE SUPPORT FOR ISRAEL'S LIKUD GOVERNMENT. *(AP/Wide World Photos)*

sen only because of his ideology (a criticism that had earlier been leveled when he served in the Reagan administration). He has not been known as an Arab-Israeli specialist but has been thought to favor Likud positions on the Palestinian-Israeli conflict.

SEE ALSO Bush, George H. W.; Bush, George W.; Likud.

ABU (*abu, abi*): Arab term meaning "father of." Many Arabs use this patronymic, which conveys respect, to indicate their status as the father of a first born or of their oldest son. To disguise their identity vis-à-vis the Israeli Security Services, Palestinians use this term to designate each other, even when the parties concerned are not fathers, as was the case with Yasir Arafat, called Abu Ammar.

SEE ALSO Arafat, Yasir.

ABU ALA

SEE Qurai, Ahmad Sulayman.

ABU AL-ABBAS

SEE Zaydan, Muhammad ʿAbbas.

ABU AL-HASAN

SEE Hasan, Hani, al-.

ABU AL-RAGHIB, ALI (1946–): Jordanian political figure. Ali Abu al-Raghib was born in December 1946 in Amman to a wealthy Jordanian family. After earning a civil engineering degree in the United States, Abu al-Raghib was named director of projects at the Ministry of Municipal Affairs, a post he held from 1967 to 1972. Next, he joined the private sector to head a construction company. In 1986 he was elected president of the Association of Jordanian Entrepreneurs; the following year he was elected councilman of the city of Amman. In 1989 he was elected president of the Higher Council of the Federation of Entrepreneurs of the Arab Council of Cooperation. Ali Abu al-Raghib was close to the Jordanian Arab National Democratic Alliance (JANDA); in June of 1991, then-Prime Minister Taher Masri named him director of the Ministry of Industry and Commerce. On 21 November he became minister of Energy and Mining in the cabinet of Zayd bin Shakir, a post to which he was reappointed in May 1993. On 8 January 1995 he was named minister of Commerce and Industry in the bin Shakir government, an office he held until the government resigned in 1996. Elected deputy in 1997, he chaired the Commission on Finance and Economic Affairs of the Chamber of Deputies, playing an important role in the privatization program in Jordan and in finalizing an accord linking Jordan with the European Union.

On 12 December 1999, King Abdullah II appointed him president of the Consultative Economic Council, in charge of supervising economic reforms, and in January 2000 he was placed in charge of creating a zone of economic expansion at Aqaba. On 18 June he became prime minister, replacing Abdul Raouf al-Rawabdeh. On 7 August 2001, while the al-Aqsa Intifada intensified in the Palestinian territories, he met with Yasir Arafat. On 25 October King Abdullah instructed Abu al-Raghib to initiate a ministerial reorganization aiming at the elimination of the Ministry of Information and its replacement by a "Supreme Council for Information," the idea being to liberalize this economic sector. The king also asked Abu al-Raghib to accelerate the program of economic and social reforms set in motion by the government. In October 2003, Abu al-Raghib was removed from office by the king after a long period of deteriorating relations with opposing political factions, particularly the Islamists, who complained of oppressive measures and government by decree.

SEE ALSO Abdullah II ibn Hussein; Bin Shakir, Zayd; Rawabdeh, Abd al-Ra'uf al-.

ABU AMMAR

SEE Arafat, Yasir.

ABU AYAD

SEE Khalaf, Salah.

ABU BASHIR

SEE Abd Rabbo, Yasir.

ABU DAUD

SEE Odeh, Muhammad.

ABU DIS: Name of a suburban neighborhood (village) of East Jerusalem, mentioned frequently between 1995 and 1996 during the negotiations between Palestinians and Israelis. The latter, firmly opposed to Jerusalem becoming the capital of an eventual Palestine State, suggested the city of Abu Dis as a solution. Subsequently, during the course of the intense negotiation that followed, the name of Abu Dis was mentioned regularly, but only to be immediately rejected by most Palestinians. On 9 April 2000, Israeli Prime Minister Ehud Barak announced his government's intentions to annex Jewish neighborhoods in the eastern periphery of Jerusalem in exchange for the transfer of the administration of the localities of Anata and Abu Dis to the Palestinians. A few days later, facing Israeli opposition and the threat of resignation of the SHAS members in his government opposed to such a transfer, Barak rescinded his decision. On 15 May, by a margin of 58 votes for and 48 against, the Knesset approved the transfer to Palestinians of three localities close to Jerusalem, including Abu Dis.

SEE ALSO Barak, Ehud; Knesset; SHAS.

ABUD IYAD

SEE Khalaf, Salah.

ABU FADIL

SEE Dahlan, Muhammad.

ABU HASAN

SEE Hasan, Hani al-.

ABUHATZEIRA, AHARON (1938–): Israeli politician and Knesset member. Born in Morocco, Aharon Abuhatzeira was first elected to the Knesset in 1974 as a member of the National Religious Party. He was reelected in 1977, serving as minister of religious affairs under Menachem Begin. In 1981 Abuhatzeira founded TAMI (Tnu'at Masoret Israel), a political party that sought to advocate for Sephardic Jews, especially those from North Africa. He was elected to the Knesset in 1981 and in 1984 served as a TAMI member, then later joined the Likud and served as minister of labor, welfare, and immigration.

SEE ALSO TAMI.

ABU IYAD

SEE Khalaf, Salah.

ABU JIHAD

SEE Jibril, Ahmad.

ABU JIHAD

SEE Wazir, Khalil al-.

ABU KHALID

SEE Hawatma, Nayif.

ABU LUFT

SEE Qaddumi, Faruq.

ABU MAZIN

SEE Abbas, Mahmud Rida.

ABU MUSA

SEE Musa Muragha, Sa'id.

ABU NIDAL

SEE Banna, Sabri al-.

ABU NIDAL GROUP

SEE Fatah Revolutionary Council.

ABU ODEH

SEE Abu Odeh, Adnan.

ABU ODEH, ADNAN (Abu Udeh, Abu Oudeh, Abu Aoudeh; 1933–): Jordanian political figure. Adnan

Abu Odeh was born in 1933 in Nablus, Mandatory Palestine. Following literature studies in Syria, he taught English in Jordan from 1951 to 1959, then in Kuwait from 1959 to 1964. Upon his return to Jordan in 1965, he joined the Jordanian intelligence service, the General Intelligence Department (GID) headed by Muhammad Rasoul Kilani. On 15 September 1970, when the regime of King Hussein of Jordan was threatened by a Palestinian revolt, Abu Odeh was named minister of culture and information in the new military government of General Daoud. In October 1972 he resigned from his post to become general secretary of the Arab National Union Party. In March 1973 he was named minister of culture and information again, replacing Ma'an Abu Nawar, who had succeeded him at this post one year earlier.

In September 1977 Abu Odeh represented Jordan at the Euro-Arab Conference in Paris. In March 1979 he assumed the functions of interim prime minister. In June he chaired a delegation appointed to raise funds for the inhabitants of territories occupied by Israel; Palestinian Mahmud Abbas (Abu Mazin) was a member of the delegation, and he and Abu Odeh later formed a friendship. In January 1984 Abu Odeh was named minister to the court, in charge of the Royal Cabinet. From then on, Abu Odeh became one of King Hussein of Jordan's principal advisors. In November 1991 he resigned his position as advisor to the king and founded the Party for Progress and Justice in early 1992. A few weeks later, in April 1992, he was appointed Jordanian ambassador to the United Nations, participating as such in some of the negotiations in the Israeli-Arab peace process. In 1995, after having resigned this position, he remained in the United States as a senior fellow of the United States Institute of Peace (1995–1996) to study history and to write.

In May 1998, upon his return to Jordan, he became a member of the Jordanian parliament. In early March 1999 he was appointed minister (chief) of the Royal Court and political advisor to the new king, Abdullah II of Jordan. That same year he published his book, *Jordanians, Palestinians and the Hashimite Kingdom in the Middle East Peace Process,* in which he discussed the injustices suffered by the Palestinians, notably in Jordan, creating a stir in Jordanian political circles. Since leaving his official post in 2000, Abu Odeh has written and consulted extensively on Palestinian-Israeli-Jordanian issues. He is a regular commentator for the *Daily Star,* a Lebanese English-language newspaper with an international readership. In March 2004 he was elected to the board of the International Crisis Group, an independent nongovernmental organization headquartered in Brussels.

SEE ALSO Abdullah II ibn Hussein; Hussein ibn Talal.

ABU RAMI

SEE Rajub, Jibril.

ABU RASHID

SEE Sha'th, Nabil Ali Mohamed.

ABU RA'UF

SEE B'seisso, Atef Fa'iq.

ABU SA'ID

SEE Hasan, Khalid al-.

ABU SHARIF, BASSAM (1946–): Palestinian political leader, born in Jerusalem. In 1948, at the beginning of the Israeli-Palestinian conflict, Bassam Abu Sharif became a refugee in Jordan. After secondary studies in Amman, he traveled to Lebanon to study chemistry at the American University of Beirut. When the Arab-Israel War broke out in June 1967, he returned to Jordan, where he joined the Popular Front for the Liberation of Palestine (PFLP) of George Habash and became associated with Ghassan Kanafani, spokesperson for the PFLP. In October 1970, after the bloody confrontations between the Jordanian Army and Palestinian splinter groups, Abu Sharif returned to Lebanon where, with Kanafani, he became one of the mainstays of the weekly *al-Hadaf,* a PFLP organ. On 8 July 1972 Kanafani was assassinated by the Israelis in a car explosion. On 25 July Abu Sharif escaped an attempt on his life that used a booby-trapped package, but he lost an eye and several fingers. Between 1973 and 1981 he pursued his activities in the PFLP, distancing himself increasingly from the line espoused by Habash. In 1982, when the war in Lebanon intensified, Yasir Arafat asked him to be his spokesperson. In July 1987 Abu Sharif was expelled from the PFLP. A member of the General Union of Writers and Journalists, he became Arafat's media advisor and was sometimes the origin of unexpected press announcements that did not always reflect Arafat's position; for example, in June 1988 an article advocating negotiations between the Israelis and the Palestinians was published in the American press, provoking anger in the radical wing of al-Fatah. That November he escaped another assassination attempt.

In April 1990, shortly before the Gulf War, he supported Iraq. Between 1992 and 1993 he participated indirectly in the conversations that resulted in the Israeli-Palestinian Peace Accords of 13 September 1994, but by the autumn of 1994 he no longer appeared to be among Arafat's close advisors.

SEE ALSO Arab-Israel War (1967); Arafat, Yasir; Fatah, al-; Gulf War (1991); Habash, George; Popular Front for the Liberation of Palestine.

ABU TAYYIB

SEE Natur, Mahmud Ahmad al-.

ABU ZAYYAD, ZAYYAD ALI KHALIL (1940–): Palestinian political figure. Ali Abu Zayyad was born in 1940 in Azariya, near Jerusalem. After obtaining a degree in law from the University of Damascus in 1965, Abu Zayyad worked for the Jordanian department of immigration. He was associated with the newspaper *Al Quds* and edited the Hebrew-language edition of *Al-Fajr* from 1977 to 1983. In 1985 he joined a discussion group that had been started by some Palestinian figures who were favorable to a peace accord with Israel. In 1986 he founded a Hebrew-language bimonthly, *Gesher* (Bridge), intended for a Jewish Israeli readership. In February 1988, at the time of the visit of U.S. secretary of state George Shultz to Israel, Abu Zayyad was part of a Palestinian delegation received by Schultz. In 1990 he was interrogated a number of times by Israeli police, who were suspicious of his political activism.

Abu Zayyad headed the advisory committee of the Palestinian delegation to the Madrid Conference of 1991 and participated in various Israeli-Palestinian negotiations. In 1993 he co-founded with Hillel Schenker the quarterly *Israel-Palestine Journal* and he remains its coeditor as of 2004. In January 1996, he was elected a deputy in the new Palestinian Legislative Council. In 1998 he joined the Palestinian Authority (PA), headed by Yasir Arafat, as minister without portfolio; he became minister for Jerusalem on the death of Faysal al-Husayni in May 2001 and remained in that position until the PA reorganization in 2002.

SEE ALSO Husayni, Faysal al-; Palestinian Authority; Palestinian Legislative Council.

ABU ZUHAYR

SEE Hindi, Amin al-.

ACHILLE LAURO: Name of an Italian passenger-liner hijacked by a commando of the Palestine Liberation Front (PLF) on 8 October 1985 near Alexandria, Egypt. This operation was undertaken in reprisal for an Israeli raid carried out seven days previously on the headquarters of the Palestine Liberation Organization (PLO) in Tunis. The group, consisting of four persons and commanded by Majid al-Malki, was supervised externally by Khalid Abdul Rahim (Petros Floros, Hussein Khalid). During the operation, an American Jewish citizen, Leon Klinghoffer, was killed by one of the terrorists. Meanwhile, the leader of the PLF, Muhammad Zaydan (Abu al-Abbas), who had arrived on the scene, ordered the commando to surrender to Egyptian authorities.

In the night of 10–11 October, American fighter planes intercepted the Egyptian plane carrying members of the commando group and forced it to land at a North American Treaty Organization (NATO) base in Sicily. There, at the end of a face-to-face confrontation between the Italian police forces and the members of a special American unit, on a mission to capture the terrorists, the commando was arrested by the Italian police, while Zaydan was released and left Italy for Belgrade. On 14 October, the United States issued an international arrest warrant against Zaydan. Later a court in Genoa, Italy, sentenced the four hijackers to prison terms of four to nine years.

In January 1986 Zaydan traveled to Iraq via Cairo, Egypt. On 2 July, the Genoa court sentenced the leader of the PLF, in absentia, to life imprisonment. The attorney general had asked for life imprisonment for the leader of the commando as well as for four other Palestinians who had supplied logistical help to the group. On 22 April 1987, Zaydan, as member of the executive committee of the PLO, participated in the Congress of the Palestine National Council (PNC) that was held in Algiers. Indignant, the United States protested officially to the Algerian authorities against his presence. Under American pressure, the leader of the PLO, Yasir Arafat, demanded that Zaydan be expelled from the PLO.

SEE ALSO Arafat, Yasir; Palestine Liberation Front (1977); Palestine Liberation Organization; Palestine National Council.

ACRE (Akka, in Arabic; Akko, in Hebrew): Ancient name of the city of Saint-Jean d'Acre (Palestine).

ACTION ORGANIZATION FOR THE LIBERATION OF PALESTINE (Al-Haya'al-Amila li-Tahrir Filastin): A guerrilla organization created in 1968 by Issam Sartawi, a Palestinian cardiologist. After the 1967 Arab-Israel War, Sartawi returned to the Occupied Territories from the United States, where he had been living, and joined al-Fatah, organizing a group to provide medical care to al-Fatah's guerrilla fighters. After quarreling with Yasir Arafat, he and a handful of militants left al-Fatah and created the Action Organization for the Liberation of Palestine (AOLP), a guerrilla commando, which operated mainly in Jordan. In 1970 the AOLP was the only Palestinian group to support Gamal Abdel Nasser's acceptance of the Rogers Plan, the U.S. proposal to implement United Nations Resolution 242, which would have returned captured land to Egypt and Jordan while ignoring Palestinian national interests. Expelled from Jordan after the Black September confrontations, the members of the AOLP took refuge in Beirut. Sartawi by now had come to favor establishing contacts with Israel, so as to find a solution to the Palestinian problem. Sartawi merged the AOLP into al-Fatah in July 1971 and went on to become an advisor to Arafat on American and European issues, eventually emerging as a leading advocate of mutual compromise with Israel. Sartawi was assassinated by agents of Abu Nidal in Lisbon in April 1983.

SEE ALSO Arafat, Yasir; Fatah, al-; Sartawi, Issam.

ADALAH ("Justice" in Arabic): An independent, nonprofit nongovernmental organization (NGO) providing legal services to Arab citizens of Israel. In its own words, it "works to protect human rights in general, and the rights of the Arab minority in particular." On behalf of individuals, NGOs, and Arab institutions, it brings civil rights and civil liberties cases to Israeli courts, advocates legislation and advises Arab members of the Knesset, makes representations to the Israeli government, provides legal consultation, and works with international legal and human rights organizations. In addition, it publishes reports and trains lawyers and law students in human rights law. Located in the town of Shafa ʿAmr in Galilee, it was founded in 1996 by Hassan Jabareen (trained in law at American and Tel Aviv universities), who remains its director as of 2004.

ADAM: According to Biblical tradition, Adam, created by God, is the ancestor of humanity. The myth of the first man created out of earth by a divinity is found in many Assyro-Babylonian texts. For numerous scholars the Hebrew term *adam,* from *adama,* "earth," seems more a general word than a proper name. The Arabic term for human beings is *bani adam,* "the tribe of Adam."

ADAR: Name of the sixth month of the Hebrew calendar, corresponding to the period between the end of the month of February and the beginning of the month of March. Depending on whether one is or is not in a walled city, the Jewish feast of Purim is celebrated on the thirteenth or fourteenth of Adar. According to Biblical tradition, the seventh of Adar is the birthday of Moses.

SEE ALSO Calendar, Jewish; Moses.

ADF

SEE Arab Deterrent Force.

ADHAN: The Islamic call to prayer; sometimes spelled *azan* in English transliterations of Arabic.

AD HOC LIAISON COMMITTEE

SEE Local Aid Coordination Committee.

AD HOC LIAISON COMMITTEE ON AID TO THE PALESTINIANS

SEE Local Aid Coordination Committee.

ADL

SEE B'nai B'rith.

ADMOR: Hebrew acronym for *adonai morenu verabbenu* ("our lord, our teacher, our guide"). Honorific title Hasidic Jews give their dynastic leaders.

ADNAN: Eponymous ancestor of the Arabs of the northern parts of the Arabian peninsula, among whom two groups may be distinguished: the Rabiʾa and the Mudar. Before Islam, most of the northern tribes were designated by the word "Maʾad," considered to be the name of one of the sons of Adnan, while in fact the Arabs seem to be rather descended from two eponymous ancestors: Qahtan, for the Arabs of the north, and Adnan for those of the south.

ADONAÏ ELOHIM: "My Lord God," in Hebrew. One of the names of God in the Torah.

SEE ALSO Torah.

ADP

SEE Arab Democratic Party.

AEUC

SEE Council of Arab Economic Unity.

AFESD

SEE Arab Fund for Social and Economic Development.

AFPPR

SEE Arab Front for Participation in the Palestine Revolution.

AFWAJ AL-MUQAWAMA AL-LUBNANIYA

SEE AMAL.

AGADAH

SEE Haggadah.

AGHA KHAN: Title given to the imam of the Nisarite (Druze) Isma'ili Shi'ites.

AGHA, ZAKARIYA AL- (Zakaria Agha, Zakariyya al-Agha; 1942–): Palestinian political figure. Born in 1942 at Khan Yunes in the Gaza Strip, Zakariya al-Agha is a medical doctor by training. He was director of public relations at Bir Zeit University in the West Bank, then department head at Al-Ahli Hospital in Gaza; and he has been president of the doctors' union of Gaza since 1985. Close to the Palestinian Communist Party, al-Agha was imprisoned several times by the Israeli authorities between 1975 and 1988. In June 1989 he met with the U.S. ambassador to Israel, who was visiting Gaza. In November 1991 he was part of the Palestinian delegation to the peace conference in Madrid. During the Intifada of 1987–1993 he played an important role in providing medical assistance to the wounded.

A Palestinian from "inside" (one who remained in the territories while the Palestine Liberation Organization [PLO] leadership was in Jordan, Lebanon, or Tunisia) and a Yasir Arafat loyalist, he has been a member of al-Fatah's Central Committee since 1989. In December 1993, Arafat named him al-Fatah representative for the Gaza Strip. He became head of al-Fatah high command in 1994. At the end of May 1994, when Palestinian autonomy was put into place, he joined the Palestinian Authority (PA) as minister of housing, serving until 1996, when he became head of the PLO's Refugee Affairs Department and al-Fatah representative on the PLO executive committee. Al-Agha was the head of the Fatah delegation to the Palestinian all-party talks in Cairo in December 2003, aimed at reaching a united strategy against the Israelis.

SEE ALSO Arafat, Yasir; Fatah, al-.

AGRANAT COMMISSION, ON ARAB-ISRAEL WAR (1973): Established in November 1973 to investigate the reasons for Israel's vulnerability to the surprise attack by Syrian and Egyptian forces on 6 October, the commission, chaired by Chief Justice Simon Agranat, inquired into the responsibility of the Cabinet and the failures of military intelligence. Despite Israel's ability to recoup militarily after the first few days of the war, the initial fighting had incurred heavy losses of manpower and matériel, and Israeli military intelligence was discredited for not having predicted the attack. In addition, the brief war shattered Israel's belief that it was militarily invulnerable and hence its conviction that territories could be held indefinitely. The commission blamed the Israel Defense Forces (IDF) for its flawed assessment of Egyptian military prowess and recommended the removal of the chief of staff, the chief of intelligence, and other high-ranking officers. To the disappointment of many Israelis and the press, the commission called for the dismissal of David Elazar, chief of General Staff, and four other officers, but stopped short of judging Prime Minister Golda Meir and Defense Minister Moshe Dayan, relegating that responsibility to the Knesset via a no-confidence vote and to the public via general elections. The commission's report, issued in April 1974, did, however, lead to a major shake-up of the Labor government, the resignation of Prime Minister Meir, and a new cabinet led by Yitzhak Rabin in June 1974, and it was considered a factor in Labor's defeat in the 1977 Knesset election.

SEE ALSO Agranat, Simon; Arab-Israel War (1973).

AGRANAT, SIMON (1906–1992): Chief justice of the Israeli Supreme Court (1965–1976). Born in Louisville, Kentucky, into a Zionist family, Simon Agranat attended the University of Chicago and its law school. He emigrated to British Mandatory Palestine in 1930, settling in Haifa and entering a private law practice. In 1940 he became the second Jewish magistrate in Haifa, served briefly as chief judge on the Haifa District Court, and was appointed to the Israeli Supreme Court in 1949. He became chief justice in 1965, retiring in 1976 at the mandatory age of 70. By introducing a "rights discourse" into Israel's legal dialogue—attributed by many to his American background—Agranat is considered to have been instrumental in the development of a judicially protected rule of law and an independent judiciary, and to have thus enhanced the status of political and civil liberties in Israel. In the aftermath of the October 1973 ("Yom Kippur") War, he chaired the Agranat Commission of Inquiry, which investigated the failure of Israeli intelligence to anticipate the surprise combined attack by Syrian and Egyptian forces. Criticism of the commission's 1974 report, which fell short of the expectations of many Israelis and much of the press, shadowed Agranat's last two years as chief justice. He died in 1992.

SEE ALSO Agranat Commission, on Arab-Israel War (1973); Arab-Israel War (1973).

AGUDAT ISRAEL (Hebrew, "Association of Israel"): A Jewish ultraorthodox movement founded in 1912 in Katowice, Poland, Agudat Israel was at first a conglomerate of currents, ranging from extreme hostility toward Zionism to a more or less explicit recognition of the religious value inherent in the nationalism advocated by the Zionists. In 1922 the Labor element of the movement seceded to found Po'alei Agudat Israel. Once it became a religious political party, Agudat Israel refused to join the Labor coalitions in power between 1953 and 1976. In 1977 the party decided to support Menachem Begin's right-wing government, which enabled it to have a number of its demands met, all of them of a religious nature. In the elections of 1981, backed up financially by the Lubavitch movement, Agudat Israel won four seats in the Knesset.

Two years later, a split in the party between Sephardi and Ashkenazi members gave rise to a new political formation, the SHAS (Sephardi Torah Guardians) Party. In 1988 a second splintering led to the creation of another religious party, Degel ha-Torah. In the December Knesset elections, Agudat Israel won five seats. With two other religious parties, SHAS and the National Religious Party, it joined the government coalition formed by the Likud and the Labor Party. In 1990 a third splintering of the party resulted in the creation of a new religious organization, Geulat Israel. In November, Agudat Israel joined the government of Yitzhak Shamir, thereby allowing him to consolidate his position in the Knesset with 64 seats of the 120. In exchange, Shamir committed his government to support various proposals in the Knesset for a stricter application of religious laws. However, in the elections of 1992, the party was able to keep only two seats.

In the elections of May 1996, Agudat Israel joined the parliamentary group United Torah Judaism and successfully supported the candidacy of Benjamin Netanyahu. On 18 June, Prime Minister Netanyahu appointed one of the principal leaders of Agudat Israel, Rabbi Menachem Porush, deputy minister for housing. As of 2004, the principal leaders of the party are Menachem Alter, Zeev Feldmann, Shlomo Grinberg, Schmuel Halpert, Menachem Porush, and Avraham Verdiger. In the 2003 elections, United Torah Judaism (the coalition of Agudat Israel and Degel ha-Torah) won five seats.

SEE ALSO Degel ha-Torah; Po'alei Agudat Israel; SHAS; United Torah Judaism Party.

AHALI, AL- (Arabic, "The People"): A Jordanian weekly of the Jordanian People's Democratic Party, this publication speaks also for the Hashd Party, the Transjordanian branch of the Democratic Front for the Liberation of Palestine (DFLP).

SEE ALSO Democratic Front for the Liberation of Palestine; Jordanian People's Democratic Party.

AHC

SEE Arab Higher Committee.

AHD, AL

SEE *Intiqad, al-*.

AHDUT HA-AVODA: A Jewish political organization created in the 1920s, and Marxist in tendency, this movement promoted the coming together of Jews from all over the world in a socialist state, extended by peaceful means over the totality of Greater Israel. In 1930 the movement merged with Ha-Po'el ha-Tza'ir to give birth to the Israel workers' party, MAPAI, led at the time by David Ben-Gurion. In the legislative elections of July 1955, the Ahdut ha-Avoda list won ten seats in the Knesset. In 1968 MAPAI, which comprised Ahdut ha-Avoda and RAFI, decided to merge to found the Israel Labor Party.

SEE ALSO Israel Labor Party; MAPAI; RAFI Party.

AHDUT LEMA'AN ALIYAH ("Union for Aliyah," in Hebrew): Israeli political organization, created in April 1996 in anticipation of the May Knesset elections, when representatives and the prime minister were to be elected for the first time by universal suffrage. A party of immigrants, this organization was led by Ephraim Gur, a Likud deputy who had quit the Labor Party in June 1990, and by Yaacov Feitelson. This organization won no seats in the Knesset in the elections.

SEE ALSO Israel Labor Party; Knesset; Likud.

AHL AL-ABA

SEE Ahl al-Beit.

AHL AL-BEIT (*Ahl al-Bayt,* "People of the House," in Arabic): Arab term used to designate "those of the family of the prophet Muhammad," that is, his daughter, Fatima, his son-in-law, Ali, and their two sons, Hasan and Hussein. This descent is also designated by the term *Ahl al-Aba* ("People of the Cloak").

SEE ALSO Ali; Fatima; Muhammad.

AHL AL-KITAB ("People of the Book," in Arabic): Arab term used to designate those who practice a revealed religion (Judaism, Christianity, and later Zoroastrianism, Hinduism, and even Buddhism) and who are accorded the status of *dhimmi* in a Muslim country. Christians and Jews enjoy a certain reciprocal respect, in the sense that each possesses a portion of the truth to which the three monotheistic religions lay claim.

SEE ALSO Dhimmi.

AHLC

SEE Local Aid Coordination Committee.

AHRAM, AL- (The pyramids): The principal Egyptian Arabic newspaper, *al-Ahram* was started in 1876 by Syrian-Lebanese Christian immigrants to Egypt. Nationalized by the government in 1952, it became an official government newspaper. The first Egyptian editor, Muhammad Hassanein Heikal, assumed the directorship of the paper in 1957. *Al-Ahram* remains a pro-government newspaper, and has had both an English edition (*al-Ahram*) and a French edition (*al-Ahram Hebdo*) since 1994.

AIPAC

SEE American Israel Public Affairs Committee.

AISHA (ʿAʾisha): Daughter of Abu Bakr, Aisha was very young when she married Muhammad. After his death, she contested the designation of the Prophet's successors and opposed Ali, Muhammad's son-in-law, to the point of provoking the rebellion of a group of Muslims against him. In 656, after being defeated at the "Battle of the Camel," she was isolated from power. Respected by the Sunnis, Aisha is criticized by the Shiʿites who reproach her for her opposition to Ali.

SEE ALSO Ali; Shiʿite; Sunni Islam.

AJAMI: Arab term dating back to the Islamic Middle Ages that designates the "non-Arabs," particularly from the east.

AJC

SEE American Jewish Congress.

AKHBAR, AL- (The News, in Arabic): Egyptian daily Arabic-language newspaper.

AKHBARI: Representative of a fundamentalist theological school, inspired by twelfth-century Imami-Shiʿism. Founded in the Middle Ages, it adheres strictly to the traditions of Hadith.

SEE ALSO Hadith.

AKHER KHABAR: Jordanian pro-Palestinian daily newspaper.

AKKAM

SEE Hakham.

ALAMI, MUSA AL- (1897–1984): Palestinian administrator and diplomat. Born in Jerusalem in 1897 into a prominent, wealthy landowning family, Musa al-Alami came into contact with Palestinian nationalists in Damascus, where he was evading the Ottoman draft in 1917–1918. He studied law at Cambridge and in 1925 began working as a legal officer for the British administration in Mandatory Palestine. In 1932 he became private secretary to the high commissioner, whom he lobbied for the political rights and economic interests of the Arab population. He was among a number of prominent Palestinians who met with the Zionist leadership in 1934 and 1936, seeking to find grounds for a compromise; the Palestinian group concluded that no voluntary compromise was possible. Al-Alami was subsequently removed from his job and demoted, following pressure from the World Zionist Organization. In 1936 he publicly supported the General Strike, circulating a petition among Palestinian officials of the Mandatory government that called for limiting Jewish immigration and Zionist land purchases. In 1937 he was fired from the government and went into exile in Beirut, but he was forced by the French to leave for Baghdad in 1939. During this time he was a member of the Palestinian delegation to the London Conference, whose convening he had urged. He was allowed to return to Palestine in 1942.

Al-Alami was the Palestinian delegate to the Alexandria conference at which the creation of the Arab League was agreed upon, and he became the Palestinian representative in the League when it was established in 1945. He headed the League's Information Office in London from 1945 to 1949, and was also responsible for setting up the League's Constructive Scheme, administered by the Arab Higher Committee, a fund that bought land to keep it from being sold to the Zionists and worked to improve conditions in Palestinian villages. After the 1948–1949 War al-Alami returned from London, having lost his home and most of his property. He renamed the Constructive Scheme the Arab Development Society and used it to start a large farm near Jericho in the West Bank with an orphanage and vocational school for refugee children, which he continued to operate until his death in 1984.

SEE ALSO Arab Higher Committee; League of Arab States.

AL-AQSA INTIFADA

SEE Aqsa Intifada, al-.

ALAWITE: According to some scholars, this term comes from the Arab word *alawi,* which means "descendant of Ali"; others contend that it comes from the Turkish *alev,* which means "flame." The Alawite cult seems to be of remote Isma'ili origin, when in the ninth century the Abbasid Dynasty began to decline in Syria and southern Turkey. Its leader, Muhammad ibn Nusair al-Namir, was a Persian contemporary of the Eleventh Shi'ite Imam, Hasan al-Askari, preacher of an extremist faith in Ali. The Alawites, or Nusaris, practiced an initiatory religion that resembled early Gnostic Christianity and Babylonian rites. The Alawite calendar included Sunni, Shi'ite, and Christian holidays. The Alawite faith was characterized by its secret nature: The basic tenets of the faith were in the keeping of a small group of the devout, belonging to the *Majlis al-Shuyur* (Community Council). Attached to a principle of the Trinity identical to that of Christianity, the Alawite faith identified each of its members with a heavenly body, such as the Sun or the Moon, or with an animal.

Historically, the Alawites were divided into five sects—Khamaria, Shamsia, Ghabiya, Murchidiya, and Haidaria; and were grouped into six main tribes—Khayyatium, Shamsin, Raslan, Khalbiyya, Haddadium (Haddadin), and Matura-Nomilatia (Matawira). Treated for decades like traitors or apostates, the Alawite tribes went to live by themselves, isolated from the rest of Syria. They developed, accordingly, a systematic practice of hermeticism and of *taqiya,* which allowed them to say they were close to one or another current, so as to protect themselves from any inquisition, an attitude that engendered suspicion and incredulity in the Muslim community. In 1920 France, which had a mandate over Syria, decided on the creation of an autonomous Alawite territory, and in 1952 the Islamic Jafarite Association gained the Alawites recognition by the Syrian state as Shi'ite Muslims.

SEE ALSO Shi'ite; Taqiya.

MADELEINE ALBRIGHT. PRESIDENT BILL CLINTON'S SECOND-TERM SECRETARY OF STATE LISTENS IN AS PALESTINIAN LEADER YASIR ARAFAT SPEAKS ON THE TELEPHONE WITH THE PRESIDENT IN SEPTEMBER 1999. ALBRIGHT'S MIDDLE EAST VISIT WAS PART OF HER EXTENSIVE BUT ULTIMATELY UNSUCCESSFUL EFFORTS TO ACHIEVE A FINAL PEACE ACCORD BETWEEN ISRAEL AND THE PALESTINIANS. *(© Reuters NewMedia Inc./Corbis)*

ALBRIGHT, MADELEINE (1937–): American political figure. Madeleine Korbel Albright was born in 1937 in Czechoslovakia. Her father, Joseph Korbel, was an eminent Czechoslovakian diplomat. Exiled to the United States in 1949, the family took up residence in Denver, where her father taught political science. A brilliant student, Albright was also developing into a militant Democrat. She taught International Relations for a time at Georgetown University (Washington, D.C.). Between 1976 and 1978 she was an assistant to Democratic senator Edmund Muskie; then, from 1978 to 1981, she was a member of the National Security Council, headed by Zbigniew Brzezinski. In 1984 she supported the vice-presidential campaign of Geraldine Ferraro. Between 1992 and 1994 she was U.S. ambassador to the United Nations.

On 5 December 1996 Albright was named secretary of state in the administration of President Bill Clinton, replacing Warren Christopher, becoming the first woman ever to occupy the post. On 9 September 1997, she paid her first visit to the Middle East in an attempt to restart the Israeli-Palestinian negotiations, which had been stalled since the coming to power of Israeli prime minister Benjamin Netanyahu. From then on, she and assistant Dennis Ross worked on reviving the Israeli-Palestinian peace process. On 23 October 1998, at Wye River, Maryland, she sponsored the signing by Yasir Arafat and Netanyahu of an accord on the withdrawal of the Israel Defense Force (IDF) from the West Bank. On 5 September 1999, after visiting Syria and Lebanon, she traveled to Sharm al-Shaykh, Egypt, where, with Egyptian president Husni Mubarak and King Abdullah II of Jordan, she initialed the Israeli-Palestinian Accord signed by Arafat and Ehud Barak. This agreement, which was reached in the context of the application of the Wye River Agreements, brought a successful conclusion to the many meetings she held, both in Washington and the Middle East.

On 5 December 1999 Albright began another round of visits to the region, while the Israeli-Palestinian negotiations were once more stalled. After a visit to Damascus, she announced that Syrian-Israeli negotiations would resume shortly in Washington, specifying that this would not slow down the Israeli-Palestinian peace process. On 29 June 2000, after a two-day visit to Israel and the Palestinian territories, she won the participation of Israelis and Palestinians in a tripartite summit, organized by the United States, to restart the peace negotiation process, even though Prime Minister Barak no longer had a majority at the Knesset. The summit, held in July at Camp David, Maryland, ended in failure. That December—in the last days of the Clinton administration and during a time of continued political difficulty for Barak—the United States presented what became known as the "Clinton proposals" for renewal of the peace process.

Since leaving her position as secretary of state, Albright has served on various boards promoting ethical foreign investment, was elected to the board of the New York Stock Exchange, and authored *Madam Secretary: A Memoir* (2003). On 23 March 2004 she testified before the National Commission on Terrorist Attacks upon the United States.

SEE ALSO Camp David II Summit; Clinton, William Jefferson; Oslo Accords II ; Sharm al-Shaykh Summits.

ALF

SEE Arab Liberation Front.

AL-FAJR

SEE Fajr, al-.

ALGIERS ARAB SUMMITS: The Algerian capital has frequently welcomed Arab leaders for summits, in the course of which important decisions have been made. On 26 November 1973, meeting in Algiers following the 1973 Arab-Israeli War, the summit recognized the Palestine Liberation Organization (PLO) as the sole representative of the Palestinian people. On 7 June 1988, the special Arab League summit in Algiers expressed its support for the Palestinian uprising in the occupied territories. On 15 November 1988, at the congress of the Palestine National Council in the Algerian capital, Yasir Arafat proclaimed the State of Palestine, with Jerusalem as its capital.

SEE ALSO Arab-Israel War (1973); Palestine National Council.

ALGIERS DECLARATION

SEE Proclamation of the State of Palestine.

AL-HAQ

SEE Haq, al-.

ALI (c. 660–661): Fourth caliph (656–661). The son of Abu Talib, Ali was the cousin of the Prophet Muhammad, whose daughter, Fatima, he married. Father of Hassan and Hussein—the only male descendants of the Prophet—Ali, according to some, should have succeeded Muhammad. After the death of Muhammad, Ali refused to recognize the election of Abu Bakr as caliph. It was only after the assassination of the third caliph, Uthman, that he became caliph himself, in 656. Under pressure from Aisha, the third wife of Muhammad, Governor Muawiyah, a relative of Uthman, denounced the succession, thus provoking an armed conflict. Arbitration resulted in Ali being declared in the wrong. He was assassinated by a Kharijite in the Great Mosque of Kufa, Iraq, in 661.The main schisms within Islam were born from these events. The Shi'ites have become the partisans of Ali, and the Sunnis the heirs of Muawiyah, and later of the Umayyads. Ali's tomb, in Najaf, Iraq, is a Shi'ite pilgrimage site.

SEE ALSO Kharijites; Muhammad; Shi'ite.

ALI, NAJI AL- (1936 or 1937–1987): Palestinian political cartoonist. Naji al-Ali was born in 1936 or 1937 in the village of al-Shajara in the Galilee. His family fled Palestine in 1948, and he grew up in the Ayn al-Hilwa refugee camp in Sidon in southern Lebanon. He was frequently censored and jailed by Lebanese authorities between 1958 and 1963; he was encouraged by the Palestinian writer and journalist Ghassan

Kanafani after the latter discovered his drawings on the walls of a Lebanese jail cell in the late 1950s. Al-Ali studied art in Lebanon and Kuwait in the 1960s. He returned to Lebanon in the early 1970s, working as a political cartoonist for the Beirut newspaper *Al-Safir* and contributing as well to the United Arab Emirates paper *Al-Khalij.* In 1983, after witnessing the massacres at the Sabra and Shatila camps in West Beirut, he felt his life was in danger, and he returned to Kuwait, where he worked for the newspaper *Al-Qabas.* He was expelled from Kuwait in 1985, due to pressure from the Saudi government, and moved to London, where he continued to contribute work to both *Al-Qabas* and *Al-Khalij.*

Naji al-Ali was murdered in London in 1987 by persons unknown, though he had recently been warned by a friend within the Palestine Liberation Organization (PLO) that his life was in danger. At the time, he was the most successful political cartoonist in the Arab world. His work dealt sharply with the life of the common people and in particular with the Palestinian tragedy. He had no factional political affiliation and attacked not only Israel but Arab states and Palestinian institutions for a lack of humanity and the absence of democracy. Despite—or perhaps because of—his popularity, he had many powerful enemies.

SEE ALSO Sabra and Shatila.

ALIYAH. JEWISH REFUGEES ARRIVE IN HAIFA, C. 1945. FROM 1881 UNTIL THE CREATION OF THE STATE OF ISRAEL IN 1948, JEWS RETURNED TO THEIR ANCIENT ROOTS IN SEVERAL WAVES OF IMMIGRATION TO PALESTINE. IN LATER DECADES, ISRAEL BROUGHT IN OR WELCOMED LARGE GROUPS FROM IRAQ, YEMEN, ETHIOPIA, THE SOVIET UNION, AND ELSEWHERE, AS WELL AS JEWS IMMIGRATING INDIVIDUALLY. *(© Hulton-Deutsch Collection/Corbis)*

ALIDES

SEE Ali.

ALIGNMENT PARTY: Israeli political alliance. The Alignment existed from 1969 to 1984 as a combination of the Israel Workers' Party (MAPAI) and the United Workers' Party (MAPAM). The parties retained their independence but shared a common slate for elections to the Knesset, the Histadrut, and local government.

SEE ALSO Histadrut; MAPAI; MAPAM.

ALIM (pl. *ulama*; *ulemas*): Arabic word designating a Muslim scholar.

ALIYAH ("Ascent," in Hebrew): The term evokes the "return to roots" that every "believer" must accomplish, referring to the dispersion (diaspora) of the Jewish people in the year 135 C.E. By extension it designates Jewish emigration to the territory that would become, after 1948, the new State of Israel. The immigrants are called *olim,* and those who immigrated clandestinely *ma'apilim.*

The first waves of Jewish immigration into Palestine took place in the fifteenth century, following persecution suffered by the Jews in Spain and Portugal. New waves of immigration took place between 1882 and 1890, 1904 and 1915, as well as between 1919 and 1923 from Central Europe, contributing to the development of colonies established in Palestine, conforming to the Zionist and socialist ideology advocated by the principal leaders of the international Jewish community. The victory of Nazism in Germany gave rise to a new mass exodus of persons, who sought to escape genocide more than to participate in the renewal of the Land of Zion, hence allowing a move from ideological Zionism to political Zionism. Toward the end of the 1940s and the beginning of the 1950s, Israel organized several operations, named "Flying Carpet" and "Ezra and Nehamiah," to bring in 120,000 Jews from Iraq, and several thousand others from Yemen and North Africa. During the 1970s and 1980s, the "Moses" and "Solomon" operations allowed almost 35,000 Ethiopian Jews to come to Israel. Finally, between 1989 and 1994, American-Soviet détente and the collapse of the Soviet Union led to the arrival in Israel of almost 500,000 Jews of Russian provenance. The word *aliya* is close in meaning to the Arab term *Awliya*.

SEE ALSO Diaspora.

ALIYAH UNION

SEE Ahdut Lemaʿan Aliyah.

ALIYYINS: A group formed at the end of the 1950s by Muhammad Umran, the Aliyyins included Syrian personalities who later became pillars of the regime of Hafiz al-Asad. The name was chosen to reflect its membership of mostly Alawite, and the frequency of "Ali" as a given name among them.

SEE ALSO Alawite; Asad, Hafiz al-.

ALLAH ("God," in Arabic): The root of the word Allah most likely comes from the Arabic *ilah* (God) and from the Aramaic *alaha* (the God). A word close to it, *Al-lat,* designates one of the Meccan divinities (Allat or Hobal) of the Thamuds, whose statue was set up in the Kaʿba with two other divinities, Al-Uzza and Manat. So "Allah" is just the Arabic name for God: Christians and Jews also use the word when speaking or writing Arabic to refer to the monotheistic deity they believe in.

ALLENBY, EDMUND HENRY (1861–1936): English general. Edmund Allenby served first in Africa, notably against the Boers. In 1914, when World War I began, he took command of a cavalry division sent to France, then of the Fifth Corps and Third Army on the Somme. In June 1917 he took command of British forces on the Middle Eastern front. On 9 December in the same year he entered Jerusalem, with, among others, Captain T. E. Lawrence. In the following months, British troops defeated the Turkish-German army of Palestine, notably at Meggido, which led to the capitulation of the Ottoman Empire on 30 October 1918. Named marshal in 1919, then high commissioner in Egypt, Edmund Allenby contributed to the elaboration of a treaty recognizing the independence of Egypt.

SEE ALSO Lawrence, T. E.

EDMUND ALLENBY. THE BRITISH COMMANDER OF THE EGYPTIAN EXPEDITIONARY FORCE ENTERED JERUSALEM IN DECEMBER 1917. THE QUICK CAPTURE OF THE CITY DEMORALIZED TURKISH FORCES AND PLAYED A ROLE IN THE BRITISH ASSUMPTION OF CONTROL OVER PALESTINE AFTER WORLD WAR I.

ALLIANCE FOR EQUALITY: A political movement created in April 1992 at a meeting of some 300 Jews and Palestinian Arabs assembled in Haifa, the Alliance for Equality later became part of the National Democratic Assembly (also known as the Democratic National Alliance [DNA]), a political party founded in 1996, representing primarily Palestinian Israelis. One of its founders, Azmi Bishara, a scholar at the Van Leer Institute in Jerusalem, was elected a member of the Knesset on the DNA ticket in 1996.

SEE ALSO Bishara, Azmi; Democratic National Alliance.

ALLIANCE OF PALESTINIAN FORCES (APF): This Palestinian organization, founded in October 1993, united the Palestinian movements opposed to the Israeli-Palestinian accord signed on 13 September 1993. The APF, supported by Syria and based in Damascus, replaced de facto the Group of Ten and included the Democratic Front for the Liberation of Palestine (DFLP), the Popular Front for the Liberation of Palestine (PFLP), HAMAS, Islamic Jihad, the Palestinian Liberation Front's Yaʿqub faction, the PFLP-GC (General Command), al-Fatah-Intifada, Saʿiqa, the PPSF–Abdul Majid faction, and the

RPCP. The APF thereby became the successor of the Palestinian National Salvation Front (PNSF). Confronted with the political divergences among its members and personnel, the APF proposed no program that could represent an alternative to the political program of Yasir Arafat. On 24 May 1995, this organization called in vain for a reinforcement and extension of the newly founded Palestine Unity Party in the hope of creating a movement of opposition in the Occupied Territories. On 3 November 1996, to spark the APF, HAMAS and Islamic Jihad proposed creating a new organization, the Front for Palestinian National Independence, or National Democratic and Islamic Front, that would exclude the DFLP and the PFLP, against which the two Islamic movements were in ideological opposition.

APF unity was shaken in February 1997, when HAMAS, PFLP, and DFLP announced their decision to accept participation in the "national dialogue" proposed by Arafat, which resulted, nevertheless, in no agreement. In early June 1998, the APF leadership rejected Arafat's proposal inviting some of its members into the Palestine Authority (PA). On 13 December 1998, following the Wye Plantation Accords, which it denounced, the APF called a congress in Damascus in the course of which members officially called for the election of a new Palestine National Council (PNC), as well as for the election of a new executive committee and a new Central Council of the PLO. Differences between the leaders of the DFLP and those of the PFLP-GC became apparent during the meeting. On 9 August the APF declared that it rejected all dialogue with the PA, which, in its view, had lost all legitimacy by renouncing the Palestinian National Charter. The APF has been largely unsuccessful in crafting a coordinated political strategy, and its support from Syria is largely rhetorical.

SEE ALSO Democratic Front for the Liberation of Palestine; Group of Ten; HAMAS; Islamic Jihad; Oslo Accords II; Popular Front for the Liberation of Palestine.

ALLON, YIGAL (1918–1980): Israeli soldier, politician, deputy prime minister. Born Yigal Paicovitch in Kfar Tabor, Palestine, he attended Hebrew University, then studied at St. Anthony's College in Oxford. Beginning in 1937 he served in the Haganah. With Moshe Dayan, he helped create the Palmach, the Haganah's commando unit, attaining the rank of commander in 1945. He Hebraized his name to Allon, meaning "oak," in 1948 to signify the strength of his commitment to Israel. A member of the Knesset during Israel's early years, Allon served as minister of labor from 1961 to 1967, then deputy prime minister from 1966 to 1974. A close adviser to Golda Meir, under whom he served from 1969 to 1974, he created what became known as the Allon Plan, which urged the annexation of the Gaza Strip by Israel and the return to Jordan of about 70 percent of the West Bank, while retaining for Israel the Jordan River valley as a security zone. Though the plan was neither formally adopted nor rejected, it has been cited as the inspiration for the idea of a belt of Jewish settlements along the Jordan.

SEE ALSO Dayan, Moshe; Haganah; Meir, Golda.

ALLON PLAN: Named for its initiator, Yigal Allon (deputy prime minister of Israel, 1969–1974), the Allon Plan linked Israeli security to the development of Jewish civilian settlements. It proposed the creation of a line of agricultural settlements in the Jordan valley to ensure a defensible border between Israel and Jordan. The plan also called for the establishment of additional settlements around Jerusalem and close to the Green Line border as a method of ensuring future territorial changes that would favor Israel. It did not suggest settlement in the rest of the West Bank, already densely populated with Palestinians, which it suggested should become part of an autonomous area under Jordanian administration. Though considered a proposal for minimal settlement, the Allon Plan continues to be cited as the originator of settlement activity linked to Israeli defense and territorial concerns.

SEE ALSO Allon, Yigal; Green Line; Jordan River.

ALL-PALESTINE GOVERNMENT: Approved on 21 September 1948 by the Arab League, the All-Palestine Government was formed by the Arab Higher Committee (AHC) during the 1948–1949 Arab-Israel War, at a time when most of Palestine was already lost. Though the AHC took it seriously, it was backed by Egypt primarily to counter the claim by King Abdullah I of Transjordan to be the true representative of the Palestinians. (Abdullah had concluded a secret agreement with the Jewish Agency in 1947 to split Palestine between them, under which he was to annex those parts not controlled by Israel.) Based in Gaza and entirely under the control of Egypt, the "government" was headed by the mufti of Jerusalem, al-Hajj Amin al-Husayni, as president and Ahmad Hilmi as prime minister. It lasted only a few weeks.

Prior to the war in 1948, the mufti had rejected United Nations (UN) Resolution 181, which provided for partition, and had appealed to the Arab League several times to form a Palestinian govern-

ALL-PALESTINE "GOVERNMENT." FOREIGN MINISTERS OF IRAQ, JORDAN, LEBANON, SYRIA, SAUDI ARABIA, AND EGYPT MEET IN CAIRO IN 1948. THE SHORT-LIVED ENTITY THAT THE ARAB LEAGUE CREATED, HEADED BY THE MUFTI OF JERUSALEM BUT CONTROLLED BY EGYPT, EXISTED PRIMARILY TO COUNTER ANNEXATION CLAIMS BY THE KING OF TRANSJORDAN. *(© Hulton-Deutsch Collection/Corbis)*

ment that could claim all of Palestine after the British left in May 1948. Rivalries between Arab governments, pressure from the British, and the annexationist ambitions of Abdullah had long prevented any sort of unified Arab action on Palestine. Once the war began, the Israelis quickly gained control of even more territory than had been allotted to them in the partition plan, and the UN attempted to mediate a truce. In June the mediator, Count Bernadotte, recommended that the Arab areas be placed under the control—temporarily—of Abdullah. To forestall Abdullah's annexation of these areas, the Arab League voted to create a civil administration for these areas, responsible directly to the League. The mufti rejected this, and the administration was never established. In September, after most of Palestine had been lost and the Arab states were seeking to withdraw their forces without outraging their own people, the League agreed to set up the All-Palestine Government, which claimed the right to rule all of Mandatory Palestine. It had no resources and no territory except for the parts of Gaza then under control of the Egyptian army. It immediately convened a national council and on 1 October issued a Declaration of Independence. Within a week the Egyptian government evacuated the All-Palestine Government to Cairo. No Arab government had recognized it until after it had been withdrawn from Gaza. Except for an office issuing passports to Palestinians living in the Gaza Strip, it ceased to exist. It was officially closed by decree of the Egyptian government in 1959.

SEE ALSO Abdullah I ibn Hussein; Arab Higher Committee; League of Arab States; Resolution 181.

ALONI, SHULAMIT (1929–): Israeli politician and social activist. Born in Tel Aviv, Aloni served in the 1948 Arab-Israel War and later studied law at Hebrew University. During the 1950s and 1960s she became known as an advocate for civil and human rights and for the separation of religion from politics,

ALTALENA. THE CARGO SHIP, WITH WHICH MENACHEM BEGIN'S IRGUN MOVEMENT SMUGGLED ARMS INTO PALESTINE IN VIOLATION OF AN ARAB-ISRAELI TRUCE, BURNS ON 29 JUNE 1948 AT TEL AVIV. DAVID BEN-GURION ORDERED THE PROVISIONAL ISRAELI GOVERNMENT'S ARTILLERY TO FIRE ON THE VESSEL. *(© Hulton-Deutsch Collection/ Corbis)*

writing a weekly column and hosting a popular radio program. Aloni was elected to the Knesset in 1965 and served on various committees before being dropped from the Labor ticket in 1969. She established the Civil Rights movement in 1973 and was reelected to the Knesset, serving until 1999. Yitzhak Rabin appointed her minister of education in 1992, after her party joined with Shinui and MAPAM to form the Meretz Party. Still known as an activist for peace and civil rights, she was awarded the Israel Prize for lifetime achievement in 2000.

SEE ALSO MAPAM; Shinui Party.

AL-QAʿIDA

SEE Bin Ladin, Osama.

AL-SAʿIQA

SEE Saʿiqa, al-.

ALTALENA: Boat chartered by the nationalist Irgun movement, named in honor of Vladimir Jabotinsky's literary pseudonym. On 20 June 1948, the vessel carried 940 volunteers en route to join the Israel Defense Force (IDF), the new Israel army, and several tons of arms recently purchased by the movement.

The *Altalena* penetrated Israeli waters, off Tel Aviv. The ship arrived just hours after a truce between Arabs and Israelis had been implemented by the United Nations. Each side had committed itself not to import arms during the truce. Under pressure from his men, Irgun leader Menachem Begin refused to deliver the weapons cargo to the IDF because, Begin claimed, the arms should go to the new Irgun recruits. David Ben-Gurion, head of the provisional Israeli government, disagreed. He ordered Begin's arrest and the sinking of the *Altalena.* During the night of 21–22 June, Begin started unloading the boat near Kfar Vitkin. During the day, IDF troops surrounded and fired on the men of Irgun, killing six. Begin and his men reembarked on the *Altalena,* sailing toward Tel Aviv, where the beach was crowded with Irgun sympathizers. After a tense standoff of several hours between the men of the *Altalena* and Israeli troops, Ben-Gurion ordered the artillery to fire on the boat. The ship caught on fire and ten members of Irgun were killed. Begin and his men then surrendered. The *Altalena* incident was the source of the reciprocal hatred that marked the many years of confrontation between Begin and Ben-Gurion on the Israeli political scene.

SEE ALSO Begin, Menachem; Irgun; Jabotinsky, Vladimir Ze'ev.

AMAL (Afwaj al-Muqawama al-Lubnaniyya, or the Lebanese Resistance Detachments; in Arabic, *amal* means "hope"): A Lebanese Shiʿite militia, AMAL was officially created in July 1975 by Imam Musa Sadr. Sadr had founded the "Movement of the Disinherited" in 1974, and established AMAL as the armed branch of this organization. Inspired by the al-Daʿwa movement, Musa Sadr advocated the establishment of an independent and democratic republic in Lebanon, one that would protect the interests of the Lebanese Shiʿite community and support the struggle against Zionism. Despite this, AMAL did not engage in fighting at the start of the Lebanese Civil War in 1975. As a result, it lost considerable support, to the Palestine Liberation Organization (PLO) and groups associated with the Lebanese National Movement. AMAL also endorsed Syrian intervention in 1976, which cost it more support. However, the mysterious disappearance of Musa Sadr while in Libya in 1978, which transformed him into a popular Shiʿa symbol (analogous to the Hidden Imam), the success of the Iranian Revolution, and disillusionment with the PLO all contributed to a revival of AMAL's support.

In 1980 Nabi Berri, a lawyer and close associate of Musa Sadr, became leader of AMAL, which then became the chief Shiʿa organization in the country and a major factional political and military force. Following the Israeli invasion of Lebanon in June

1982, a scission appeared in the movement. Husayn al-Musawi, number two in the organization, founded the faction of "Islamic AMAL," which was more radical and aggressive and which sent guerrilla fighters to oppose the Israeli invaders. Progressively, under the impulsion of Musawi and Muhammad Husayn Fadlallah, Iran attempted but failed to gain control over the entire AMAL movement. In February 1985 Berri, who in 1984 had agreed to participate in a national unity government as minister of justice and minister of state for South Lebanon, proclaimed himself "minister of national resistance" and supported sending anti-Israeli commandos to South Lebanon.

In 1985 the Islamic faction of AMAL became part of the newly created Hizbullah. Thereafter AMAL, supported by Syria, and Hizbullah, supported by Iran, attempted to monopolize control over the Lebanese Shi'ite community, with resulting periodic deadly confrontations between their partisans. Despite its formal commitment to the Palestinian cause, there was friction between AMAL and the PLO, and there was occasional fighting between them in South Lebanon. After the PLO had been removed to Tunisia and could no longer protect the refugees, AMAL attacked Palestinian camps in the so-called "War of the Camps" that lasted from 1985 to 1987. After the 1989 Ta'if Accords and the 1990 victory of the Syrian-backed forces over the right-wing Maronite forces, the militias were disbanded (many of the remaining AMAL fighters were absorbed into the Lebanese Army). AMAL was transformed into a political movement, still with the backing of Damascus. After the 1992 elections Berri was elected speaker of the Parliament, a post he still held as of 2004, becoming thereby the principal leader of the Lebanese Shi'ite community. In the 2000 elections AMAL made common cause with Hizbullah and between them won all the constituencies in South Lebanon.

SEE ALSO Berri, Nabi; Hizbullah; Sadr, Musa al-; Ta'if Accords.

AMAN (Agaf Modi'in): The intelligence division of the Israel Defense Force, Aman was created in 1948 under the name of Sherut ha-Modi'in. It was reorganized in 1953, when it was given its current name. The successive directors of Aman have been Israel Beeri (1948–1949), Chaïm Herzog (1949–1950), Benyamin Gibli (1950–1955), Yehoshafat Harkabi (1955–1959), Chaïm Herzog (1959–1961), Meir Amit (1962–1963), Aharon Yariv (1964–1972), Eliahu Zeira (1972–1974), Shlomo Gazit (1974–1979), Yehoshua Saguy (1979–1983), Ehud Barak (1983–1985), Amnon Lipkin-Shahak (1986–1990), Uri Saguy (1990–1995), Moshe Ya'alon (1995–1998), Amos Malka (1998–2001), and Aharon Ze'evi-Farkash (2002–).

SEE ALSO Israel Defense Force.

AMBA (also rendered as *anba* or *ampa*): The Arabic version of the Coptic term *apa,* meaning "father" (from the same Semitic root as the Arabic and Hebrew *abba*). As a title it is given to the members of the hierarchy of the Coptic Church, including bishops, archbishops, and patriarchs.

AM EHAD PARTY (One Nation): An Israeli electoral list, constituted in February 1999, on the initiative of union leaders of the left, anticipating the scheduled elections for the following May. As a result of the elections of 17 May, which saw the victory of the Laborite Ehud Barak as prime minister, this list won two seats in the Knesset, taken by Haim Katz and Amir Peretz. As a labor-oriented organization, it focuses on social welfare and issues related to employment. In the 2003 elections it received 2.8 percent of the vote (three seats in the Knesset).

AMERICAN ISRAEL PUBLIC AFFAIRS COMMITTEE (AIPAC): A Jewish-American association created in 1954 (originally the American Zionist Public Affairs Committee), AIPAC has become a powerful and influential interest group that lobbies the U.S. Congress for pro-Israel legislative initiatives. As a registered lobby, AIPAC is prohibited from directly contributing funds to political candidates; it does supply politicians and government officials with information on Israel and the Middle East. In 2004 the organization claimed 65,000 members and was considered one of the most effective lobbying groups in the United States.

AMERICAN JEWISH COMMITTEE: A Jewish-American association founded in 1906, the American Jewish Committee defined its purpose as the defense of the civil and religious rights of Jews in the United States and around the world. Its goals also include "to strengthen the basic principles of pluralism around the world as the best defense against anti-Semitism and other forms of bigotry; and to enhance the quality of American Jewish life by helping to ensure Jewish continuity and deepen ties between American and Israeli Jews." By 2004 the organization had a membership of 100,000. It was headquartered in New York City, with regional offices across the United States and international offices in Europe and Israel.

SEE ALSO American Jewish Congress.

American Jewish Congress (AJC): A Jewish-American association, the American Jewish Congress was initially created in 1918 to combat anti-Semitism and to address the problems facing Jews in Europe. It was formed after negotiation with the American Jewish Committee; proponents of an alternative organization took issue with the leadership of the Jewish American Committee, whom they perceived as representing only the wealthier sector of the Jewish-American community. It was agreed that the Jewish American Congress would meet for one time only, with one-quarter of its representatives appointed by the American Jewish Committee and three-quarters elected by the Jewish-American community. The Jewish American Congress sent a delegation to the Paris Peace Conference in 1919. Following the conference, it was disbanded.

In 1922 proponents of the AJC formed a second American Jewish Congress, this time as a permanent body. A membership-based organization, the new AJC used public campaigns to promote awareness of issues affecting Jews worldwide and to defend the civil and religious rights of Jews. The AJC, with headquarters in New York and an office in Jerusalem, had fifty thousand members in 2004. It continues to combat anti-Semitism and advocates for Israeli security and peaceful relations with Israel's neighbors.

SEE ALSO American Jewish Committee.

Americans for a Safe Israel: (AFSI) A Jewish American association promoting the development of Israeli-American relations in support of Israeli unity.

AMF

SEE Arab Monetary Fund.

Amir, Yigal (1970–): Convicted assassin of Yitzhak Rabin. Yigal Amir was born in 1970 to a Sephardic Yemenite family in Herzliya. He served in the Golani Brigade of the Israel Defense Force, then attended the law school of Bar-Ilan University. While a student there, Yigal was involved in right-wing demonstrations against the Oslo Accords. On 4 November 1995, following a demonstration in Tel Aviv in support of the peace process, Amir assassinated Prime Minister Rabin with three shots of a pistol. Apprehended at the scene of the crime, he was convicted and sentenced to life imprisonment. In a later trial, he was also convicted of conspiring to commit the murder with his brother Hagai and his friend Dror Adani. Amir expressed no regret for the murder of Rabin, claiming he killed the prime minister to halt the peace process.

SEE ALSO Bar-Ilan University; Rabin, Yitzhak.

Amirav, Moshe: Israeli politician. Moshe Amirav was educated at the Hebrew University of Jerusalem, New York University, and the London School of Economics, where he earned a doctorate in political geography. From 1981 to 1986 he served as director general of the Israel Highway Safety Administration. A member of the Jerusalem City Council from 1989 to 1993, he served during that period as director of engineering, roads, and transport development for the city of Jerusalem. In 1987, while a member of the Likud Party, Amirav initiated a political dialogue with Palestinian intellectual Sari Nusseibeh that was criticized by both camps. In 2000, after the failed Camp David summit, Amirav was appointed adviser to Prime Minister Ehud Barak, continuing to serve in that capacity until Barak left office in 2001. Amirav asserted that sovereignty over Jerusalem, particularly over the Temple Mount, had prevented the Israelis and Palestinians from reaching an agreement at Camp David. He proposed a plan (later described in his book *The Palestinian Struggle over Jerusalem,* 2002) to divide Jerusalem and to establish a "commonwealth of states" to govern the Temple Mount. In 2004 Amirav is a professor of political science and public policy at Haifa University and Beit Berl College.

SEE ALSO Camp David II Summit.

Amishav ("My people return," in Hebrew): Israeli association, created in the 1980s by Rabbi Eliahu Avihail. The purpose of the association is to search for the traces of the ten lost tribes of Israel dispersed in the world.

Amitaï ("Citizens for Honest and Ethical Government," in Hebrew): Israeli association created in 1990 for the purpose of exposing corruption in the Israeli political class. Headquartered in Tel Aviv, this organization works in collaboration with lawyers, journalists, and former members of the intelligence services or the police.

Amman Accords

SEE Jordanian-Palestinian Accord.

Ammar bin Yasir (Ammar ibn Yaser): Companion of the Prophet Muhammad, supporter of Ali. He died in 657 C.E. at the Battle of Siffin, where, in spite of his advanced age (ninety-three years), he was in command of the Kufa infantry.

SEE ALSO Ali; Muhammad.

Amora ("Speaker, interpreter," in Hebrew): Designates sages, whether Babylonian or Palestinian, who participated in the writing of Torah commentaries (Mishna).

SEE ALSO Torah.

ANG

SEE Fatah Revolutionary Council.

Anglo-American Committee of Inquiry: On 13 November 1945, after the end of World War II, Great Britain and the United States announced the formation of a commission in charge of examining the problem of European Jews and of Palestine. The Anglo-American Committee of Inquiry, also known as the Singleton-Hutcheson Commission, first met in January 1946 in Washington, D.C., before traveling to Europe to visit the remains of concentration camps. It then moved to Cairo to conduct hearings with officials of the recently established Arab League, then to Palestine to meet with British military and civil administrators as well as representatives of the Palestinian Arab and Jewish communities. In April 1946 the committee released its report, recommending that 100,000 Jewish displaced persons from Europe be authorized to enter Palestine, and calling for the annulment of the 1940 Land Transfer Regulations restricting Jewish purchase of Arab land. It also called for an indefinite extension of trusteeship, in effect an extension of the British Mandate. It recommended that "Jew shall not dominate Arab and Arab shall not dominate Jew in Palestine" and that "Palestine shall be neither a Jewish nor an Arab state." Shortly afterward, in the summer of 1946, the report was shelved; Britain backed away from adoption of the report, and the United States was unwilling to assist in its implementation. A year later, the United Nations Special Committee on Palestine (UNSCOP) issued a recommendation to partition the disputed land.

SEE ALSO League of Arab States.

ANO

SEE Fatah Revolutionary Council.

Ansar (Arabic, "auxiliary, partisan"): Originally signifying an inhabitant of Medina converted or rallied to the Prophet Muhammad, the term has been used since to designate supporters of the Islamic movement. It is also the name of Israeli detention centers for Palestinians, used during and after the Israeli invasion of Lebanon, notorious as sites of torture.

Ansar Allah ("God's auxiliary," in Arabic): Paramilitary organization formed during the Lebanese Civil War, which began in 1975, in order to counter the influence of the troops of the Palestinian Fatah.

SEE ALSO Fatah, al-.

Anti-Defamation League

SEE B'nai B'rith.

Antisemitism: The term *anti-Semitism* was invented in 1879 by the anti-Jewish German pamphleteer, Wilhelm Marr. Today it refers to the social or even ideological behavior of hatred or rejection of Jews, whether defined as a racial or a religious group. Ancient texts proving the existence of anti-Semitism dating back to Antiquity have caused many scholars to study the deeper reasons of such comportment. The rigorous monotheism and alimentary rules of the Jews, limiting the possibilities for them to maintain full social relations with non-Jews, may have contributed to the rise of anti-Semitisim. Early Christian religious teachings blamed Jews for the crucifixion of Jesus (deicide) and persisted to some extent despite the Vatican ruling, as late as 1965, that Jews were not to blame for Jesus' death. Another Christian accusation was the infamous "blood libel," in which Christians accused Jews of kidnapping a Christian child to obtain blood to bake unleavened bread (matzoh). This fabrication incited anti-Semitism for centuries, resurfacing in recent times even in Islamic societies and on racist Internet web sites.

Antisemitism has played a role in the Israeli-Palestinian conflict, and the conflict itself has led to further entrenchment of anti-Jewish sentiment. Early Zionists linked the creation of an independent Jewish state to the persecution of Jews in Europe and elsewhere, while some Muslims depicted the establishment of the State of Israel as part of a global "Jewish conspiracy." In 2002 and 2003 Egyptian and Lebanese television networks aired several historical-fiction series based on the theme of a worldwide Jewish conspiracy. While the extent of contemporary anti-Semitism in the Middle East is widely debated, there is a tendency among some Palestinian and Arab commentators to include anti-Semitic statements in their criticisms of Israeli policy or military actions. Other Palestinian leaders and intellectuals draw a careful distinction between anti-Zionism and anti-Semitism.

SEE ALSO Jew; Judaism.

ANTONIUS, GEORGE (1891–1942): Palestinian civil servant and intellectual of Lebanese Greek Orthodox background. Antonius was born in 1891 in Alexandria, Egypt, where his father was a successful businessman. He was educated at an elite Anglo-Egyptian private school and at King's College, Cambridge, where he took a degree in engineering in 1913. During World War I, Antonius worked in the British government censorship office in Alexandria, and he was a member of a literary and social circle that included, among others, E. M. Forster and Constantine Cavafy. From 1921 to 1930 Antonius worked for the education department of the British government of Palestine in Jerusalem. While there, he was assigned to assist British diplomats on a number of missions in Arabia, Yemen, and Egypt, for which he was awarded a CBE (commander of the British Empire). Though never ceasing to be an admirer of British and European culture, he became increasingly alienated from imperial rule and sympathetic to the Palestinian cause. He resigned partly out of dissatisfaction with British favoritism toward the Zionist movement.

While working as a Middle East expert for the Institute of Current World Affairs, a U.S. foundation, he cultivated many influential acquaintances in Palestine and elsewhere in the fields of politics, diplomacy, and journalism. He made himself known in the Palestinian community and became an informal advisor to the conservative nationalist leader, the mufti of Jerusalem, Hajj Amin al-Husayni. In 1934 and 1936 he met with Zionist leaders in a failed attempt to convince them to work toward a shared Palestine. In 1936 he supported the Palestinian general strike that preceded the armed insurrection of 1936–1939, and called for limits on Jewish immigration. Antonius was a member of the Palestinian delegation to the London Conference of 1939 and afterward helped to persuade the British to include provisions regarding Jewish immigration and independence in the White Paper of 1939. He died in 1942.

George Antonius is remembered primarily as the author of the classic *The Arab Awakening,* published in 1938. A study of the development of Arab nationalism beginning in the late Ottoman period, it was the first and one of the most influential works on the subject. The work examined the events of World War I and the denial of self-determination by the British and French afterward, and analyzed the current situation in Iraq, Syria, and Palestine. In it Antonius published for the first time the Husayn-McMahon Correspondence of 1915–1916—whose existence the British had denied—detailing British promises to Arab leaders. Antonius opposed the Zionist project of establishing a Jewish state in Palestine, and always hoped for a compromise by which the country could be shared peacefully. His book concludes with these words: ". . . the relief of Jewish distress may not be accomplished at the cost of inflicting a corresponding distress upon an innocent and peaceful population. . . . the logic of facts is inexorable. It shows that no room can be made in Palestine for a second nation except by dislodging or exterminating the nation in possession."

SEE ALSO Husayni, Hajj Amin al-; White Papers on Palestine.

AOLP

SEE Action Organization for the Liberation of Palestine.

AOUN, MICHEL (1935–): Lebanese military and political figure. Michel Aoun was born in September 1935 at Haret Houreik to a lower middle class Maronite family. After choosing a military career in 1955, he began a period of training and study in France and the United States that lasted several years. Promoted to brigadier general at the beginning of 1984, he was named commander in chief of the Lebanese Armed Forces by President Amin Jumayyil in June of that year. This appointment was made during a time when the Lebanese Christian community had been weakened by years of civil war, and also by conflicts among its principal leaders. At forty-nine, Aoun thereby became the youngest commander of the army since Lebanon's independence. As soon as he was appointed, Aoun attempted to assume the leadership of the Christian camp as well. On 22 September 1988, just before the end of his own term, President Jumayyil named him interim prime minister, provoking the anger of Muslim leaders, who demanded that the rule regarding the sharing of power between the Muslims and Christians be observed. Furthermore, then-prime minister Salim al-Hoss refused to resign.

Opposed to the Syrian presence in Lebanon, Aoun declared a "war of liberation against the Syrian

MICHEL AOUN. In 1999, when this photograph was taken, Aoun was Lebanon's military commander, interim prime minister, and self-proclaimed president. The Maronite general's war against Syrian occupation—and a Christian rival—ended in defeat in 1990 and exile to France. *(AP/Wide World Photos)*

occupiers" that raged between March and September of 1989, causing hundreds of deaths. In October, Aoun rejected the Ta'if Accords, which, according to him, only sanctioned the presence of Syrian troops on Lebanese soil. On 7 November, contesting the legitimacy of René Muʿawwad, elected president of the republic two days earlier, Aoun proclaimed himself "president of a free and sovereign Lebanon." After Muʿawwad was assassinated, Aoun also contested the election of his successor, Ilyas al-Hirawi. The new president then discharged Aoun from his posts of commander of the Lebanese army and interim prime minister.

On 30 January 1990, General Aoun launched a military attack of some scope against Samir Geagea, his Christian rival and leader of the Lebanese Forces. The fighting among Christians lasted for a few weeks; 1,046 died and 2,800 were wounded. On 13 October, surrounded by Lebanese and Syrian forces, Aoun sought refuge in the French embassy at Beirut and asked for political asylum. On 19 April 1991, the Lebanese government officially ended General Aoun's tenure. On 27 August, while he was being prosecuted by Lebanese authorities for "rebellion and usurpation of power," Aoun was granted amnesty by President Ilyas al-Hirawi.

Forced into exile, Aoun secretly left Lebanon on 29 August 1991, taking refuge in France, where he started an opposition group, the Lebanese National Movement (LNM). On 18 May 2000, while Israel was on the verge of a final withdrawal from South Lebanon, Aoun suggested that the international community oblige Syria to apply United Nations Resolution 520, requiring the withdrawal of all foreign forces from Lebanon. In 2003, while in France, Aoun agreed to run a candidate in a Lebanese parliamentary election, despite his previous position that no election in Lebanon was legitimate while Syrian influence prevailed. His candidate lost. As of 2003, Aoun remained in exile, continuing to critique the Lebanese government.

SEE ALSO Hoss, Salim al-; Jumayyil, Amin; Lebanese Forces; Resolution 520; Ta'if Accords.

APF

SEE Alliance of Palestinian Forces.

APO

SEE Organization of Arab Palestine.

AQABA, GULF OF: Only 170 kilometers (106 miles) long by 25 kilometers (16 miles) wide, the Gulf of Aqaba separates the Sinai Peninsula from the Arabian coast. Four countries share its northern section: Egypt controls the western shore; Saudi Arabia the eastern shore; Jordan possesses a 25-kilometer corridor along the Gulf in which is located the city of Aqaba (the country's only maritime port); Israel has a 10-kilometer strip that includes the city of Eilat. The Gulf of Aqaba has always been, regionally, of strategic significance. Cargo through the port of Aqaba increased throughout the 1980s, partly as a result of development of the Jordanian port with aid from Iraq, to a high of 18.7 million tons in 1989. Cargo handling fell sharply (to 10 million tons) after the imposition of United Nations (UN) sanctions against Iraq in 1990. The lifting of UN sanctions in 2003 suggested that cargo shipment through the Gulf of Aqaba would again be on the rise.

AQABA SUMMIT: The Aqaba Summit of 4 June 2003, hosted by King Abdullah II of Jordan, was attended by Palestinian prime minister Mahmud Abbas, Israe-

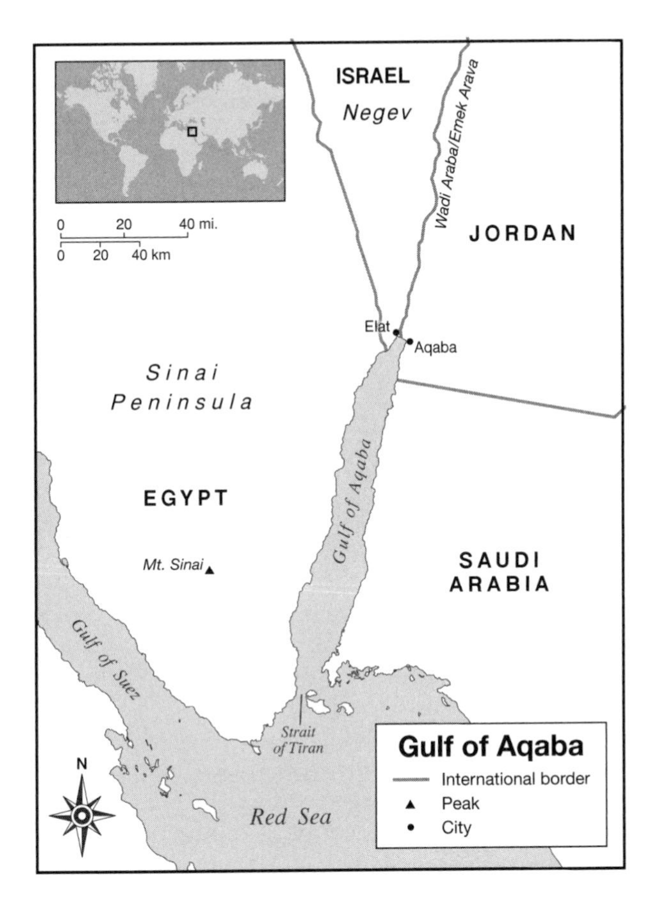

li prime minister Ariel Sharon, and U.S. president George W. Bush. The summit was intended to begin implementation of the "Road Map" for peace, promoted by the Bush administration alongside the United Nations, Russia, and the European Union (the "Quartet"). The Road Map called for an end to the violence that had erupted in September 2000 (the al-Aqsa Intifada) and for negotiations toward the creation of an independent Palestinian state by 2005. At the summit's end, both Abbas and Sharon pledged to implement the plan, with Sharon promising to begin removal of settlement outposts on the West Bank and Abbas calling for an end to violence. HAMAS immediately rejected Abbas's request, and forty thousand Israeli settlers demonstrated against Sharon. Less than a week later, the suicide bombing of a bus in Jerusalem was followed by Israeli air strikes against HAMAS targets.

SEE ALSO Abbas, Mahmud Rida; Aqsa Intifada, al-; Bush, George W.; HAMAS; Sharon, Ariel.

AQEDAH ("binding"): Hebrew term that describes the episode when, according to Biblical tradition, Abraham agreed to sacrifice his son Isaac to God.

SEE ALSO Abraham; Isaac.

AQSA, AL-: The name of the mosque (the Arabic term means "distant, extreme, furthest,") atop Mount Moriah (known to Jews as the Temple Mount) in Jerusalem. It is one of the two main structures in the Haram al-Sharif (Noble Sanctuary). The other is the Dome of the Rock, which encloses what Muslims believe is the site to which the Night Journey of the prophet Muhammad brought him, and from which he was taken to pray with the earlier prophets. The entire precinct is built upon what devout Jews believe to be the site of the Temple of Solomon and the ruins of the Second Temple, of which the Western Wall, or Kotel, is believed to be the remnant.

SEE ALSO Moriah, Mount; Western Wall.

AQSA INTIFADA, AL-: By 2000, virtually no progress had been made in negotiating a settlement between Israel and the Palestinians since the Oslo Accords and 1993 Declaration of Principles. During this time the Israelis continued to build new settlements and roads, confiscate land and water resources, and demolish homes in the territories ostensibly intended to be part of a Palestinian state. Over 200,000 Israeli settlers were in the territories by 2000, not including East Jerusalem and environs, and new construction was increasing each year. Despite the establishment of the Palestinian Authority (PA), the lives of Palestinians in the West Bank and Gaza Strip continued to be controlled by Israel much as they had been under direct occupation. To many Palestinians, it came to seem that under the terms of the Oslo process the PA existed largely to suppress them on behalf of the Israelis, and to use their taxes and international aid to line the leadership's pockets. Anger at the Israelis and frustration with the PA, the Palestine Liberation Organization (PLO), and other established groups continued to grow. In 1996, the situation in Hebron and Israel's opening of a tunnel beneath the al-Aqsa Mosque occasioned the worst violence (four days of rioting, and fifty-eight Palestinians and fifteen Israelis killed) since the Intifada of 1987–1993. In May 2000, on the anniversary of the State of Israel's foundation, during demonstrations in support of Palestinian prisoners, violence broke out in the West Bank during which four Palestinians were killed by the Israel Defense Force (IDF) and hundreds were injured by rubber bullets and live ammunition. In July 2000 the last attempt to reach a "final status" agreement as called for under the 1993 accords failed at Camp David, mainly over the issue of Jerusalem, specifically, according to many Palestinians, over the insistence of Prime Minister Ehud Barak—whose government had narrowly escaped losing power just before he left for Camp David—on maintaining Israeli sovereignty over the Haram al-Sharif (Temple Mount), an important Muslim religious site, which Jews believe to be the site where the temple once stood. As tensions grew, and as Barak's government weakened, the head of the opposition Likud, Ariel Sharon, on 28 September 2000, visited the Haram al-Sharif with one thousand armed Israeli police. The visit was tied to Jewish extremists' calls to destroy the mosque there and rebuild the temple. The next day, after midday prayers at the al-Aqsa Mosque in the Haram, a large, angry protest demonstration took place. Israeli security forces responded with live ammunition, killing seven Palestinians. Demonstrations and spontaneous attacks followed, leading to street fighting and violent IDF responses all over the West Bank and Gaza Strip. This was the beginning of the second Intifada, known as the al-Aqsa Intifada. An enduring image of the uprising was created on 30 September when the IDF shot and killed a twelve-year-old boy clinging to his wounded father at the base of a wall on a street in Gaza. The incident was videotaped and broadcast all over the world. On 12 October, after the lynching of two Israeli soldiers by Palestinians—an incident that followed the lynching of three Palestinians by Israeli settlers—the IDF bombarded PA headquarters in Ramallah and PLO offices in Gaza. On 16 October the United States sponsored a summit conference at Sharm el-Sheikh between Barak and Yasir Arafat, which accomplished little. That month Barak sealed the borders between Israel and the territories, cutting off trade.

As happened during the first uprising, unified coordinating groups arose—the Popular Resistance Committees—which included representatives of various nationalist and Islamic groups. A young Palestinian leadership, mainly associated with al-Fatah—prominent among them was Marwan Barghuthi—formed a number of small groups, in particular the al-Aqsa Martyrs Brigade, the Sabra and Shatila Martyrs Group, and the Popular Army Front–Return Battalions. These and similar formations are known as the *tanzim* (organization).

In February 2001 Ariel Sharon was elected prime minister on a platform of increasing Israeli settlements and refusing to negotiate with the PLO. The result was greater violence, including organized armed attacks by the *tanzim* against Israeli military outposts and settlements (a major difference from the first Intifada), and more severe countermeasures, including an Israeli policy of "targeted reprisals" (assassinations) against individuals declared responsible for attacks. Eventually the Israelis reoccupied the territories, in the process destroying large parts of Jenin, Ramallah, Rafah, Nablus, and other cities and refugee camps. Effectively, Israel and the Palestinians have been in a state of war since late 2000. According to the Israeli human rights group B'Tselem, 2,683 Palestinians, 441 Israelis, and 17 foreign nationals had been killed as of 30 June 2004.

SEE ALSO Aqsa Intifada, al-; Aqsa Martyrs Brigade, al-; Barak, Ehud; Barghuthi, Marwan Hussein al-; Fatah, al-; Gaza Strip; Haram al-Sharif; Hebron; Intifada (1987–1993); Likud; Israel Defense Force; Oslo Accords; Oslo Accords II; Palestine Liberation Organization; Palestine Authority; Sabra and Shatila; Sharon, Ariel; West Bank.

AQSA MARTYRS BRIGADE, AL-: A Palestinian militia that emerged in the West Bank in October 2000, specifically in the Balata refugee camp in Nablus, after the beginning of the al-Aqsa Intifada. Its members (numbers unknown) are believed to be mostly members of al-Fatah, and the group is assumed by some to be under its control, although neither al-Fatah nor Yasir Arafat has acknowledged it, and both have publicly opposed its actions. The group has taken responsibility for a number of attacks, including shootings and suicide bombings, against Israelis; at first the attacks were against soldiers and settlers in the occupied territories, but as the Intifada continued and Israeli tactics became more extreme and destructive (particularly in Jenin and Ramallah), civilians inside Israel were also targeted. The Israelis have accused the Fatah leader Marwan Barghuthi of being the Brigade's leader. They arrested him in 2002, and in May 2004 he was convicted for several killings. It has been speculated that the reason the Brigades are allowed to operate is to ensure that someone connected to the Palestine Liberation Organization (PLO) is seen by the public to be making a forceful response to Israeli repression, so that the PLO might not lose political support to HAMAS and Islamic Jihad, groups that wish to establish an Islamic state.

SEE ALSO Aqsa Intifada, al-; Barghuthi, Marwan Hussein al-; Fatah, al-; HAMAS; Islamic Jihad.

ARAB ALLIANCE FOR PROGRESS AND RENEWAL

SEE Arab Movement for Change.

ARAB COOPERATION COUNCIL (ACC): Organization founded in February 1989, uniting Iraq, Egypt, Jordan, and Yemen. The ACC was destroyed by the Gulf War of 1991, in which members found themselves on opposite sides.

SEE ALSO Gulf War (1991).

Arab Democratic Front

SEE Arab Democratic Party.

Arab Democratic Party (ADP; Hizb al-Democrati al-Arabi; Mifleget Democratit Aravit): An Israeli Arab political entity, created in 1988 by Abdul Wahab Darawshe (former Labor member of Knesset), the ADP advocated the integration of Arabs in Israel, as well as the creation of a Palestinian state alongside the Israeli state. As a result of the elections of 1988, the party won a seat in the Knesset, filled by Darawshe. In the elections of June 1992, the ADP won two seats, filled by Darawshe and Talib al-Sanaa. In June 1993 Darawshe expressed his displeasure over the entry of the Arab member representing Meretz, Walid Tsadik, into the cabinet of Yitzhak Rabin. Darawshe thought the support of the ADP for the Labor Party should have allowed him to expect a portfolio. At the end of November, Darawshe threatened to withdraw his support from the Rabin government but, faced with the risk of ending the peace process by causing the fall of the cabinet of Yitzhak Rabin, he renounced his plan. In January 1994, the ADP proposed to the Knesset that the 1981 law on the annexation of the Golan Heights be abrogated. In September 1994 and February 1996, ADP members of Knesset served as secret envoys between the Israeli government and two Arab countries: Iraq and Yemen.

During April 1996, anticipating Knesset elections, the ADP joined with the Israeli Islamic Movement (IIM) to form a common list, the United Arab List. As a result of the ballot, this bloc won four seats, of which three went to members of the ADP (Darawshe, al-Sanaa, and Tawfiq Khatib). In August 1997, for the first time since the creation of the State of Israel, a delegation of some thirty Israeli Arabs, including ADP members, visited Damascus, where they were welcomed by President Hafiz al-Asad. In the 1999 elections, the United Arab List won five seats in the Knesset, with 3.4 percent of the vote. In 2003, receiving only 2.1 percent of the vote, their representation was reduced to two seats.

SEE ALSO Darawshe, Abdul Wahab; Israeli Islamic Movement; United Arab List.

Arab Deterrent Force (ADF): Armed force constituted in fulfillment of the resolutions of the Riyadh Arab summit (16–18 October 1976) and of Cairo (25–26 October), both convoked for the purpose of ending the war in Lebanon. The Arab Deterrent Force, placed under the control of Lebanese president Elias Sarkis, was responsible for observance of the ceasefire in Lebanon, overseeing security, preserving the sovereignty of the country, and applying the Lebanese-Palestinian Cairo accords of 1969. Because Israel opposed the presence of Arab troops other than Lebanese beyond the Litani River, the ADF was deployed only up to the banks of the Zaharani River. A special fund for financing the ADF, made up of contributions from Arab League members, was set up, by vote, at the Cairo summit. On 6 February 1980, the Lebanese Council of Ministers asked that the ADF be relieved by the Lebanese army. When a withdrawal was announced there was an increase in tensions, which prompted the Lebanese leaders and the Syrians to extend its mandate. Between 6 and 7 March 1980, the ADF units withdrew from Beirut and its suburbs, replaced by the Lebanese army. In September 1982, at the request of the Lebanese president, the ADF mandate was not renewed, which ended its existence.

SEE ALSO League of Arab States.

Arab Executive: Palestinian nationalist umbrella group founded in 1920. It was formed at the third Arab Congress in Haifa with nine members and was expanded in 1928 to include forty-eight. It was primarily a conservative organization of the middle and landowning classes. Its leader, as president from 1920 to 1928 and chairman from 1928 to 1934, was Musa Kazim al-Husayni, a prominent member of a notable family and former mayor of Jerusalem. Through direct appeals to the British government and the League of Nations, the Arab Executive opposed the imposition of British rule, whose formal mandate (written by the British themselves) was founded on the provisions of the Balfour Declaration and accorded privileged status to the Zionists while denying the right to self-determination to the Palestinians (who were referred to in the Mandate only as "non-Jewish communities," although they were 90 percent of the population in 1922). It failed, and the Mandate was officially instituted in 1923. Rallying public support, the committee was more successful in opposing British plans for a legislative council with limited powers and a disproportionately small number of seats allocated to Palestinians; accepting it would have meant accepting the legitimacy of the Zionist project. The failure to prevent the imposition of the Mandate, however, or to penetrate the indifference of the policy makers in the British government, caused dissension among Palestinians, and on the Arab Executive.

In 1928 a sense of crisis grew as Zionist immigration and land purchases (often, it should be said, from members of the Arab Executive or interests with which they were associated) increased and Zionist economic power and organizations grew in strength. The Arab Executive tried to meet the problem by expanding the committee to include representatives of various factions and religious groups. Renewed discussions with British Mandatory officials, however, broke down at the time of the Western Wall disturbances in 1929. Investigations by two British commissions, the Shaw Commission and the Hope-Simpson Commission, into the causes of the violence resulted in an official report, the Passfield White Paper, which in 1930 recommended serious changes to recognize Palestinian rights and redress social and economic problems among Palestinians caused or exacerbated by Zionist activity. Private talks between the Jewish Agency and the British government increased Zionist political strength in Palestine, and the British government's basic commitment to the "Jewish National Home" as part of the Mandate ensured that these recommendations were repudiated.

This chain of events was the beginning of the radicalization of the Palestinian community's opposition to the Zionist project and of the end of its support for the caution, moderation, and deference of the committee's methods, which were those of the Ottoman-era politics in which its members had been schooled. Amid calls for strikes, boycotts, and other such actions, the Arab Executive was seen as increasingly old-fashioned and ineffectual, and it was not able to adapt to the changed conditions. Under pressure, it did sponsor a public demonstration in Haifa in October 1933, in which Musa Kazim al-Husayni was beaten by the police, but it fell apart not long after al-Husayni's death (largely as a result of the beating) in March 1934; it held its last meeting that August. Its position as Palestinian nationalist umbrella group was filled in 1936 by the Arab Higher Committee.

SEE ALSO Arab Higher Committee; Balfour Declaration; British Mandate; Husayni, Musa Kazim al-; Jewish Agency for Israel; Western Wall Disturbances; White Papers on Palestine.

ARAB FUND FOR SOCIAL AND ECONOMIC DEVELOPMENT (AFESD): An Arab regional financial organization participating in the financing of economic and social development projects in the Arab world since 1968. The Arab funds provide subsidies (project loans) to governments, private and public organizations, and institutions. Projects of importance to the Arab world receive priority funding. Development projects include agriculture and rural development, infrastructure and transport, electricity, and water. The organization's mandate is limited to supporting projects of Arab states. AFESD has twenty-two members, with headquarters located in Kuwait.

ARAB HIGHER COMMITTEE (AHC): The Arab Higher Committee was created on 25 April 1936 in Mandatory Palestine by six leading Palestinian political parties to coordinate the general strike that had begun on 15 April. It was led by Hajj Amin al-Husayni, a member of a prominent Palestinian family, mufti of Jerusalem and leader of the Supreme Muslim Council, and it became the chief Palestinian nationalist organization. Its goals were to boycott Jewish businesses, to end Zionist land purchases and Jewish immigration, and to replace British rule with an independent elected national legislature and government. The strike was staged in response to several events: the killing of the resistance leader Izz al-Din al-Qassam by the British; the discovery of clandestine arms shipments to Zionist groups; and a British proposal for a limited legislature in which the minority Zionist community would have been overrepresented. The strike led to an armed revolt, which was met with a military response by the Mandatory authorities. The committee called off the strike on 12 October 1936, and the British government agreed to investigate the causes of the disturbances.

In June 1937 the Peel Commission recommended partition of Palestine between the Arab and Zionist communities, which the AHC rejected. Disputes between the parties represented on the committee led to a partial breakup in July, and after further guerrilla attacks the British outlawed the AHC on 1 October. Four of its members were arrested and deported to the Seychelles Islands, and the rest, including al-Husayni, escaped to neighboring Arab countries, from which they encouraged and attempted to direct the rebellion, which lasted until the spring of 1939. After the White Paper of May 1939 recommended limiting Jewish immigration, the AHC was legalized again.

In November 1945 the committee, with al-Husayni as its head, was reestablished under the auspices of the Arab League and was recognized by Britain as representing the Arabs of Palestine. Factional disputes, however, made it politically ineffective, and it broke into two competing groups. At its meeting in June 1946 at Bludan, Syria, the Arab League dissolved these two groups and established a new AHC, under the leadership of al-Husayni, which it then recognized as the official representative organization of the Palestinians. King Abdullah I of Transjordan, however, who wished to annex much of Palestine to his kingdom and who was secretly cooperating with the Zionists, worked within the League to undermine it. The AHC rejected the partition plan adopted in United Nations Resolution 181 in 1947, and it also rejected the recommendations of the United Nations mediator, Count Bernadotte, in June 1948. In September 1948, with the 1948–1949 War all but lost, the AHC, with the approval of the League, founded the so-called All-Palestine Government in Gaza, which lasted little more than two weeks. It was the last attempt at serious activity by the committee. The AHC continued to exist in name only until the rise of the Palestine Liberation Organization (PLO).

SEE ALSO Abdullah I ibn Hussein; All-Palestine Government; Husayni, Hajj Amin al-; League of Arab States; Resolution 181.

Arab Islamic Liberal Party (HAQ): Name of a Palestinian movement, founded in January 1994 by members of al-Fatah who wanted to counter the radical positions of HAMAS. Its program was "upholding liberal concepts of Islam, linked with Arab ideas, so as to fight religious extremism; the struggle against Zionism, in order to create a Palestinian state that would cohabit with the Hebrew state." In 2004, the HAQ, whose headquarters are located in Jerusalem, is led by Muhammad Said Burani and Khayr Kilani.

SEE ALSO Fatah, al-.

Arab-Israel War (1948): The first conflict between Arab states and the new State of Israel, the Arab-Israel War began as a civil conflict between Palestinian Jews and Arabs following the announcement of the United Nations (UN) plan of November 1947 to partition the country into a Jewish state, an Arab state, and an international enclave in greater Jerusalem. Palestinian Arabs were incensed by the plan, which they considered a violation of their right to self-determination. Palestinian Arab demonstrations against the partition plan and Jewish celebrations in support of it soon erupted into violence, and within a few days armed groups were battling across the country. Arabs attacked Jewish settlements and institutional targets such as the headquarters of the Jewish Agency. Jewish attacks against Palestinians, including the raid on Dayr Yasin, caused a mass flight and the military expulsion of Arab Palestinians from areas seized by Jewish forces. By the end of the British Mandate in May 1948, when British forces left Palestine, Jewish forces had already seized most of the territory allotted to them by the UN partition plan, as well as additional areas.

Israel declared independence on 15 May 1948, and the struggle became an international conflict involving the new Jewish state and the armies of Egypt, Transjordan, Lebanon, Syria, and Iraq, with some involvement by Saudi Arabia and Yemen. Despite the appointment of Amir Abdullah of Transjordan as commander-in-chief, the Arab forces lacked a coordinated military plan and were for the most part poorly trained. By June 1948 both sides accepted a twenty-eight-day truce ordered by the United Nations Security Council, which went into effect on 10 June.

Fighting resumed on 8 July, with Israeli forces taking Arab areas such as Nazareth in Galilee. A second truce of 19 July was broken when Israel tried to break the Egyptian blockade of the Negev. Israel captured Beersheba in October, and by the end of the year Egypt's forces were being isolated and subdued. On 5 January 1949, Egypt agreed to the UN Security Council's request for armistice negotiations, which began on 13 January at Rhodes. The General Armistice was signed on 24 February 1949; an armistice with Lebanon was signed on 23 March, with Jordan on 3 April, and with Syria on 20 July. Iraq did not participate in armistice talks. The agreements established frontiers that remained in effect until the Arab-Israel War of 1967. Israeli territory increased from the 5,400 square miles proposed in the UN partition plan to 8,000 square miles.

Over 4,500 Israeli soldiers and 2,000 civilians were killed in the fighting. Among the Arab regular armies, 2,000 soldiers died. Some estimates place Palestinian deaths as high as 13,000. A large number of Palestinians fled the country; the United Nations estimated the number of Palestinian refugees at over 700,000, over half the Arab population of Mandatory Palestine. Called the *nakba*, or "disaster," by the Palestinians, the loss of the war and the establishment of the State of Israel set in motion a long-term, costly conflict that has yet defied resolution as of 2004.

SEE ALSO British Mandate; Dayr Yasin; General Armistice Agreements; Nakba, al-.

Arab-Israel War (1967) (5 June–10 June 1967): Third major Israeli-Arab war, after the War of 1948 (Israel's "War of Independence"; the *nakba*, or "di-

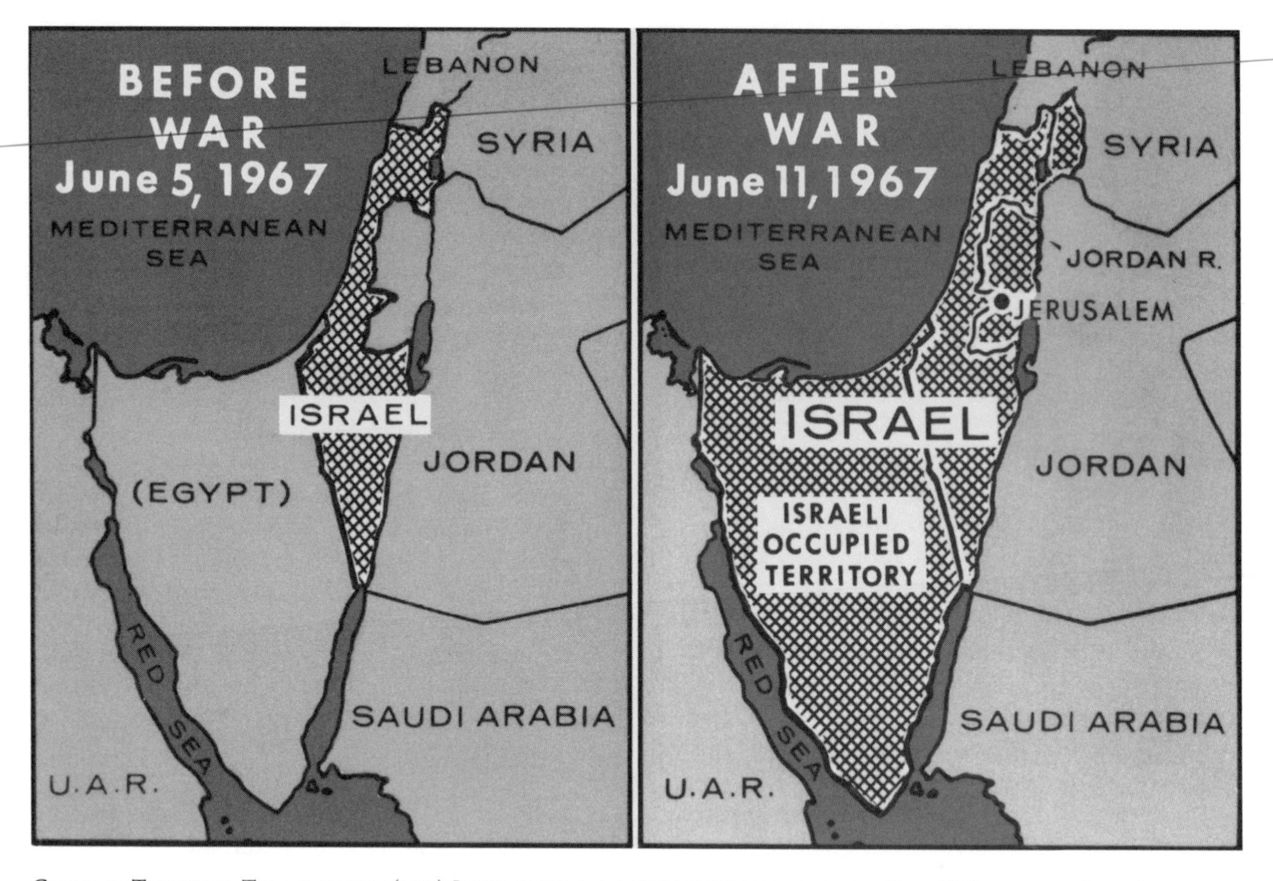

CAPTURED TERRITORY. THE MAPS SHOW (LEFT) ISRAEL AND THE ADJACENT COUNTRIES BEFORE THE JUNE 1967 WAR AND (RIGHT) THE LARGE AMOUNT OF TERRITORY THAT ISRAEL TOOK CONTROL OF DURING THE SIX DAYS OF FIGHTING. *(© Bettmann/Corbis)*

saster," to Palestinians) and the Suez-Sinai War of 1956. On 25 January 1967, the Israeli-Syrian mixed armistice commission convened, after an eight-year hiatus, and published a communiqué according to which the two parties had reached an agreement meant to prevent any hostile or aggressive action. On 7 April, in reprisal for Syrian artillery barrages on kibbutzim in the north of Galilee, Israeli planes conducted a raid on the Golan, in the course of which six Syrian MiGs were downed. On 13 May, Soviet intelligence informed Cairo and Damascus that the Israelis were massing troops on the Syrian frontier. In the context of the Egyptian-Syrian defense pact, Egyptian president Gamal Abdel Nasser decided to mobilize his army. The following day, several Egyptian units left Cairo for the Sinai.

On 15 May, the anniversary date of the founding of Israel, the general staff of the Israel Defense Force (IDF) put on an impressive military parade. The day after, Syrian and Egyptian forces were put on high alert. On 19 May, at the request of the Egyptian government, the United Nations (UN) withdrew its troops, on duty since the end of the Suez-Sinai War of 1956, from Sinai and the Gaza Strip. On 20 May, Israel mobilized a part of its reserves. The next day, Egypt banned Israeli shipping in the Straits of Tiran, leading to a protest on the part of the United States, which declared the blockade of the Gulf of Aqaba illegal. With tension between Egypt and Israel at its apogee, on 25 May, Egyptian, Syrian, and Jordanian army divisions approached their respective frontiers with Israel. On 30 May, before the cameras of Egyptian television, King Hussein of Jordan signed a mutual defense pact with Egypt, according to which the Jordanian army would pass under Egyptian command in case of war. On 2 June, faced with Arab military preparations openly aimed at the Jewish state, Israeli prime minister Levi Eshkol ceded the portfolio of defense to Moshe Dayan. The next day, France and the United States decreed an embargo on arms shipments to the Middle East. On 4 June, Iraq joined the Syrian-Jordanian-Egyptian military alliance.

On the morning of 5 June 1967, Yitzhak Rabin, army chief-of-staff of the IDF, flanked by Generals Ezer Weizman and Haim Bar-Lev, unleashed a simultaneous attack against Egypt and Jordan. In a few hours, Israeli aircraft annihilated practically all of the Egyptian air force, surprised on the ground, and 416 Egyptian, Syrian, and Jordanian planes were destroyed. Sudan, Saudi Arabia, Algeria, and Yemen, in solidarity with the Arab countries, declared war on Israel. Egypt, Syria, Algeria, Yemen, Iraq, and Sudan broke off diplomatic relations with the United States, then with Great Britain. On 6 June, the U.S. ship *Liberty* was attacked by the Israelis, who claimed they had mistaken it for an Egyptian craft. Believing this to be Soviet aggression, U.S. president Lyndon Johnson ordered the U.S. fleet on high alert, while the U.S. Sixth Fleet approached the combat zone. On the same day, the UN Security Council unanimously passed a resolution demanding an immediate cease-fire. The next day, concluding its takeover of the West Bank, which had been under Jordanian control since 1948, Israeli troops, under the command of General Uzi Narkiss, penetrated into East Jerusalem. On the Egyptian front, Israeli troops were closing in on the Suez Canal. On 8 June, the UN Security Council unanimously adopted a resolution, again insisting on an immediate cease-fire. The Soviet Union and countries in its orbit, with the exception of Rumania, broke off diplomatic relations with Israel. Israel then attacked and captured the Golan region, and on 10 June, Syria accepted a cease-fire. Movements of the U.S. Sixth Fleet, misinterpreted by the Soviet general staff, led to a state of high tension between Washington and Moscow, but this scare ended after only a few hours.

The Israeli army had defeated the Egyptian, Jordanian, and Syrian armies in six days, Israel more than tripling its territorial area by the occupation of the West Bank (which included East Jerusalem), a part of the Golan Heights, the Sinai Desert, and the Gaza Strip. Israeli military leaders judged now that they had acquired the strategic "depth" necessary to assure the security of Israel, while the ultra-orthodox movements perceived the victory of the IDF as the messianic expression of political Judaism. On 12 June, in the army's orders of the day, the chief-of-staff, Yitzhak Rabin, saluted the "unification and liberation of Jerusalem," and celebrated the victory of the "sons of light" over those who "wanted to cover the country with darkness." On 14 June, the UN Security Council adopted Resolution 237, recommending Israel respect international conventions concerning the treatment of prisoners of war and the protection of civilians in time of war. On 19 June, U.S. President Lyndon Johnson proposed a peace plan for the Middle East. Four days later, after his meeting with Johnson, Soviet prime minister Alexis Kosygin published a communiqué backing a peace plan in the Middle East, specifying that the "rapid withdrawal of Israeli troops is the key to the reestablishment of peace." On 27 June, the Israeli Knesset voted to annex the Arab part of Jerusalem. On 29 August, the leaders of Arab states, meeting in Khartoum, reaffirmed their will to continue the war against Israel with statements such as "no to peace, no to negotiations, no to recognition of Israel." The oil-producing states decided to aid Egypt financially. On 22 November, the UN Security Council unanimously adopted Resolution 242, requiring Israel to evacuate the occupied territories, in exchange for a cessation of the state of belligerence.

SEE ALSO Egypt; Golan Heights; Hussein ibn Talal; Jordan; Nasser, Gamal Abdel; Resolution 237; Resolution 242; Suez Crisis; Syria.

ARAB-ISRAEL WAR (1973) (6 October–24 October 1973): Fourth major Arab-Israel war. On 12 September 1973, Egyptian president Anwar al-Sadat received King Hussein of Jordan and Syrian president Hafiz al-Asad. During their conversations, an Egyptian-Syrian-Jordanian alliance was sealed. The next day, Israeli and Syrian fighters engaged in aerial combat, in the course of which thirteen Syrian planes were downed. On 3 October, during Ramadan, the Muslim month of fasting, reserve officers in the Syrian army were called up, and two days later, reserve units were mobilized. On 6 October, while the Jewish state was celebrating the religious holiday of Yom Kippur, the Egyptian army crossed the Suez Canal and attacked the Israeli troops stationed along the Bar-Lev Line, along the canal, the frontier between Israel and Egypt since the Arab-Israel War of June 1967. The Syrian army, for its part, retook control of the Golan Heights, occupied by Israel since June 1967. A part of the Israeli air force was rapidly destroyed by Soviet missiles that had been supplied to the Arab armies. For four days Israel seemed in danger of a military defeat.

Israeli defense minister Moshe Dayan and the army general staff of the Israel Defense Force (IDF), commanded by General David ("Dado") Elazar, seconded by General Aharon Yariv, decided to launch a counterattack simultaneously on the Golan and the Egyptian front. Despite belonging to the Syrian-Egyptian military pact, Jordan did not participate in the fighting, which allowed Israel to focus its efforts on fighting only on two fronts. On 12 October, the Soviet Union established an airlift to send supplies to Syria and Egypt. The next day, the U.S. Sixth Fleet, in turn, started an airlift to Israel. On the Syrian front, the IDF advanced, while in the Sinai Desert,

QUNAYTRA. THE TOWN IN THE GOLAN HEIGHTS, WHICH ISRAEL OCCUPIED AFTER THE ARAB-ISRAEL WAR OF 1967, IS MOSTLY IN RUINS SINCE THE 1973 WAR, WHEN IT RETURNED TO SYRIAN CONTROL. THE UNITED NATIONS GENERAL ASSEMBLY CONDEMNED ISRAEL FOR DESTROYING THE TOWN BEFORE ABANDONING IT. SYRIA REFUSED TO REBUILD AND REOCCUPY QUNAYTRA. *(AP/Wide World Photos)*

Egyptian and Israeli forces were engaged in a face-off. On 13 October, some Jordanian-Palestinian reinforcements arrived on the Syrian front, backed up by "Arab international brigades," formed of Moroccan and Iraqi soldiers. The following day, the Egyptian Second and Third Armies launched a large offensive in the Sinai, engaging in a gigantic tank battle against the Israeli forces. On 16 October, much to the surprise of the Israeli general staff, General Ariel Sharon succeeded in establishing a beachhead on the western bank of the Suez Canal.

In Washington and Moscow, serious negotiations were begun to establish a cease-fire, while the U.S. and Soviet airlifts intensified. The following day, the tank battle in the Sinai was at its apogee. The Syrian forces on the Syrian-Israeli front launched a counterattack, while the Arab oil-exporting countries announced a progressive reduction of their exports "until the territories occupied by Israel are liberated and the Palestinian people regains its rights." On 19 October, U.S. president Richard M. Nixon asked Congress to accord a supplementary $2 billion in aid to Israel. The following day, Libya, Algeria, Kuwait, and Saudi Arabia declared an embargo on oil to the United States and the Netherlands.

In the Golan, Israeli troops retook control over some of the terrain, while in the Sinai the Egyptian armies found themselves surrounded by the armored units of the IDF. On 21 October, after many hours of intense fighting, the Israeli "Golani" brigade pushed through the last of the Syrian resistance, taking control of Mount Hermon. On 22 October, the UN Security Council passed Resolution 338, calling for an immediate cease-fire and the application of Resolution 242, and for "negotiations . . . between the parties concerned under appropriate auspices aimed at establishing a just and durable peace in the Middle East." The next day, in spite of the cease-fire demanded by the United Nations, Israeli troops advanced on both sides of the Suez Canal, definitively cutting the Egyptian Third Army from its rear. The UN Security Council adopted Resolution 339, demanding the immediate end of hostilities and the return of the warring parties to the positions they occupied previously. Between 23 and 24 October, a series of misunderstandings between Moscow and Washington created a risk of confrontation between the superpowers, as had occurred in 1967.

On 24 October, the second UN cease-fire was finally implemented. Three days later, the first international observers arrived in Egypt. During the night of 27 to 28 October, Israeli and Egyptian officers met at Kilometer 101 on the Cairo-Suez road, so as to agree on conditions for safe conduct of the Egyptian Third Army, trapped in Sinai. On 6 November, U.S. secretary of state Henry Kissinger arrived in Cairo, where a resumption of U.S-Egyptian diplomatic relations, interrupted since 1967, was announced. On 11 November 1973, at Kilometer 101 on the Cairo-Suez road, Israelis and Egyptians signed a cease-fire, calling for disengagement and separation of their forces. Israeli general Aharon Yariv and Egyptian general Muhammad Gamassi signed this document, as well as the commander-in-chief of the United Nations forces, Ensio Siilasvuo. On 26 November, Algerian president Houari Boumédienne convened an Arab summit in Algiers, after which, two days later, the Arab countries recognized the Palestine Liberation Organization (PLO), over Jordanian objections, as the sole representative of the Palestinian people. On 21 December, a Middle East peace conference opened in Geneva, chaired by the UN and co-chaired by the United States and the Soviet Union.

On 18 January 1974, the Israeli army chief-of-staff, David Elazar, and General Muhammad Gamassi signed an accord stipulating the withdrawal of Israeli forces, within forty days, to approximately 30 kilometers east of the Suez Canal. Five days later, the IDF started to withdraw from the western bank of the canal. On 29 April, when sporadic fighting had broken out again in the Golan Heights, Kissinger began a new series of diplomatic visits in order to obtain the adherence of Syria to the peace plan. On 31 May, at Geneva, the Syrians and Israelis signed an accord of "limited" disengagement of their forces. Israel accepted evacuating the pocket in the Golan it had occupied in October 1973, during the recent war, but refused to cede the territories it had occupied in 1967. Israeli prime minister Golda Meir and her defense minister Moshe Dayan resigned following the report of the Agranat Commission, established to probe the reasons for Israel's vulnerability to surprise attack. The report blamed the IDF's mistaken assessment of Egyptian military strength and recommended the removal of the chief of staff and other high-ranking officers. A new cabinet was formed, led by Yitzhak Rabin, in June 1974. Debate continued in Israel over whether failures in political and military leadership had allowed the Arab armies to surprise the Jewish state and unleash a conflict that caused nearly 2,800 deaths in the ranks of the IDF.

SEE ALSO Agranat Commission, on Arab-Israel War (1973); Asad, Hafiz al-; Dayan, Moshe; Hussein ibn Talal; Meir, Golda; Rabin, Yitzhak; Sadat, Anwar al-.

ARAB-ISRAEL WAR (1982): On 4 June 1982, in reprisal for the attack against Shlomo Argov, the Israeli ambassador in London, Israeli aviation bombarded a number of Palestinian military bases in Lebanon. The assassination attempt, however, has been widely considered a pretext for invasion, as the attacker belonged to the Abu Nidal group, which opposed the Palestine Liberation Organization (PLO), and PLO members were reportedly on the hit list as well. Israel wished to destroy the infrastructure and leadership of the PLO and to install in Lebanon a government led by the Phalange Party (predominantly Maronite Christian), which had allied itself with Israel. On 6 June the general staff of the Israel Defense Force (IDF), headed by General Raphael Eitan and overseen by Defense Minister Ariel Sharon, received the green light from Israeli prime minister Menachem Begin to unleash the "Peace in Galilee" Operation. The invasion of Lebanon, the fifth major Israeli-Arab war, aimed at the definitive neutralization of the Palestinian military bases that had been established there. During this period, Lebanon was in the throes of a civil war, in which Palestinians and Syrians played an active role, while Israel was backing the Phalange.

After brushing aside the "blue helmets" (the United Nations Interim Force in Lebanon, UNIFIL), the IDF neutralized a part of the Syrian air force that had intervened. On 11 June a Syrian-Israeli cease-fire was signed. Two days later, Israeli forces linked up with the Lebanese Christian Phalangist militia. The IDF began a siege of West Beirut, where the Palestinians, supported by the forces of the Lebanese National Movement, were dug in. The pro-Iranian Guardians of the Revolution took up positions in the Baquaa Valley to battle with the Israeli troops. On 3 July nearly 100,000 Israelis demonstrated in Jerusalem for peace. On 11 July the Soviet Union proposed a peace plan for Lebanon. On 25 July, in a document passed to U.S. congressman Paul McCloskey, Yasir Arafat, the head of the PLO, affirmed that he was ready to accept all UN resolutions concerning the Palestine question. On 7 August, U.S. mediator Philip Habib announced the conclusion of an accord al-

Invasion of Lebanon. Israeli troops move into Damour, Lebanon, in June 1982, near the start of the invasion. The Israelis tried to destroy the entrenched Palestine Liberation Organization and place Lebanon under the control of Maronites, but the operation had severe long-term consequences. *(© Webistan/Corbis)*

lowing the militiamen of the PLO to leave Beirut under the protection of an international contingent.

On 23 August, Bashir Jumayyil, the leader of the Phalange and head of Christian forces, was elected president of Lebanon. Six days later, in the framework of the evacuation of the Palestinians from Beirut, Israel lifted its siege of the Lebanese capital. On 30 August, under the protection of a French-Italian force, Yasir Arafat and his partisans left Beirut for Tunis. By 1 September about 14,420 PLO fighters and officials had left West Beirut, and about 3,000 Syrian troops were withdrawn. The same day, U.S. president Ronald Reagan proposed a peace plan. On 9 September, in the course of an Arab League summit in Fes, the Arab states proposed a plan to settle the Israeli-Arab conflict (the Fes Plan).

On 14 September, President Jumayyil was assassinated. The IDF entered Beirut once again, in violation of the truce agreement, claiming it was needed to prevent disorder. From 16 to 18 September, the IDF, under Sharon and Eitan, approved the entry of Phalange forces into the Sabra and Shatila refugee camps. While Israeli soldiers looked on, the Lebanese Christian militia massacred Palestinian refugees; estimates put the numbers between 800 and 1,500 Palestinian and Lebanese civilians, mostly women, children, and older men. At Tel Aviv, 400,000 people demonstrated against this carnage and against the Israeli presence in Lebanon. The United States decided to cut off assistance for the construction of the Israeli bomber, *Lavi.* On 29 September the IDF withdrew from West Beirut, falling back to the south of Lebanon, being replaced in the Lebanese capital by an international military force. On 8 February 1983 the Israeli Kahan Commission, charged with inquiring into the Sabra and Shatila massacres, found that Israeli officials were indirectly responsible for the atrocities. An international commission chaired by Sean MacBride charged that Israel was directly responsible because the camps were under its jurisdiction as an occupying power and because the IDF had facilitated an ally's activities in the camps. Despite the findings of both commissions, no one was prosecuted. Defense Minister Sharon resigned, to be replaced by Moshe Arens, but remained in the cabinet.

On 17 May, the Israelis and Lebanese signed a peace treaty, rejected by Syria. On 23 October in Beirut, two attacks against the buildings where French and U.S. military were housed caused, respectively, 58 and 241 deaths. On 2 November, Yasir Arafat and his last followers fell back on Tripoli, in the north of Lebanon. On 20 December, the head of the PLO and his partisans left Lebanon definitively, to go to Tunisia. On 7 March 1984, under Syrian pressure, the Israeli-Lebanese accord of 17 May of the preceding year was abrogated by Lebanese president Amin Jumayyil. On 4 April, at the behest of Israel, Antoine Lahad, a Maronite and former general of the Lebanese army, took command of the South Lebanon Army (SLA), charged with security in the south of Lebanon.

On 13 September, Labor Party leader Shimon Peres became prime minister of Israel, and Yitzhak Rabin was named defense minister. On 15 January 1985 the Israeli National Unity government announced a plan for a staged withdrawal of IDF troops from South Lebanon, with the exception of a six-mile strip along the Lebanese-Israeli frontier. Called a "security zone," this Lebanese territory was placed under the military command of the SLA of General Lahad, charged with countering the anti-Israeli actions of the Lebanese Hizbullah; nearly 1,200 Israeli soldiers were assigned to accompany the SLA. Sixteen years later, on 1 April 1998, the Israeli government of Benjamin Netanyahu published a communiqué proposing a negotiated military withdrawal from Lebanon, based on UN Security Council Resolution 425. Finally, under the government of Ehud Barak, the Israeli army left Lebanon on 24 May 2000.

SEE ALSO Arafat, Yasir; Barak, Ehud; Israel Defense Force; Jumayyil, Amin; Jumayyil, Bashir; Lahad, Antoine; Palestine Liberation Organization; Phalange; Resolution 425; Sabra and Shatila; Sharon, Ariel; South Lebanon Army.

ARAB LEAGUE

SEE League of Arab States.

ARAB LIBERATION FRONT (ALF; in Arabic, Jabhat al-Tahrir al-Arabiya): A Palestinian movement, the Arab Liberation Front was founded in February 1969 by the Iraqi Baʿth Party to counter the influence of the Syrian Baʿth Party's al-Saʿiqa faction. Founded through the initiative of ʿAbd al-Wahhab al-Kayyali and Abd al-Rahim Ahmad, the ALF—whose slogan was "revolutionary armed struggle to liberate Arab Palestine with Arab blood"—upheld the Palestinian cause in terms of pan-Arabism. ALF forged an alliance with the Command of the Palestinian Armed Struggle (CPAS) in July 1969, then joined with the IPCFL (Islamic-Progressive Common Force of Lebanon) and, between 1974 and 1979, with the Rejection Front. In June 1991 the death of its principal leader, Abd al-Rahim Ahmad, led to a schism in the movement between pro-Iraqi and pro-Arafat currents. Advocating the creation of a Jordanian-Palestinian confederation, the leadership of the ALF opposed the Israeli-Palestinian accord of September 1993 (though it remained in the Palestine Liberation Organization), which prompted the formation of a pro-Arafat faction, taking the name of ALF–General Command. The ALF, backed by Iraq and Sudan, was, at least until the Iraq War of 2003–2004, headquartered in Baghdad, where its main function was to distribute funds to the families of Palestinian "martyrs." Its principal leaders have been Zayd Haydar, Munif al-Razzaz, and ʿAbd al-Wahhab al-Kayyali in the 1970s, Abd al-Rahim Ahmad (1970s–1991), and Mahmud Ismaʾil Rakad Salem. Salem was captured by Israeli forces in 2002.

SEE ALSO Rejection Front.

ARAB MONETARY FUND: Regional organization composed of members of the Arab League. It was founded in 1976 to regulate exchange rates and coordinate monetary policies among members; to promote trade and capital movement between member states; to promote the development of capital markets; and to prepare the development of a common Arab currency. It is based in Abu Dhabi, United Arab Emirates.

SEE ALSO League of Arab States.

ARAB MOVEMENT FOR CHANGE (Arabic: al-Haraka al-Arabiya lil-Taghyeer; Hebrew: ha-Tnua ha-Aravit le-Hitʾhadshut): An Israeli Arab political bloc, the Arab Movement was created on 27 March 1996 by Ahmad Tibi, anticipating the Knesset elections of the following May. Ambitious to become the leader of the Israeli Arab camp, Tibi attempted to constitute a common list with two other parties, the HADASH, a party of the left, and the Arab Democratic Party (ADP), whose head, Abdul Wahab Darawshe, was a staunch opponent of Tibi. After the collapse of these negotiations, Tibi changed the name of his bloc to the Arab Alliance for Progress and Renewal, hoping thereby to obtain the adherence of some members of the ADP and the Israeli Islamic Movement. Finally, on 21 May, Tibi withdrew his candidacy in the Knesset elections, calling on his partisans to vote for the Israel Labor Party. In the 1999 elections, Tibi ran again and was elected for what again became known as the Arab Movement for Change. In the 2001 elections, the AMC had two members, including Tibi. In 2002 Tibi and Azmi Bishara of the Democratic National Alliance (Balad) were prohibited from running in the next election on the grounds that they had supported "terrorists" by denouncing the Israeli assault on Jenin that spring; the Israeli Supreme Court overturned the ban shortly before the election in January 2003. The AMC ran in alliance with HADASH; the two parties won three seats, including one for Tibi and the AMC.

SEE ALSO Arab Democratic Party; Bishara, Azmi; Darawshe, Abdul Wahab; Democratic Front for Peace and Equality; Israeli Islamic Movement.

ARAB NAME: In the Arab tradition—used by Muslims, Christians, and Jews in the Arab world—a person's name contains his or her patrilineal genealogy. In other words, the person's given name is followed by that of his or her father and his father and his father, and so on. This list can often be ended with a family, tribal, or clan name or a *nisba,* a designation of the place the person is originally from. The *ibn* or *bin* (son of) or *bint* (daughter of) is part of this tradition. Palestinian political figure Hanan Ashrawi provides an example of the lineage revealed by the Arab name: "Hanan Daud Khalil Mikhail (Awwad)-Ashrawi is my personal and collective narrative. I am Tenderness, the daughter of David, who is the son of Khalil (Abraham) from the family of Michael (also the name of an ancestor), which is of the clan of Awwad (the one who inevitably returns), which is one of the original seven clans who are the descendants of the seven founding fathers of the town [of Ramallah]."

ARAB NATIONALIST MOVEMENT (ANM; in Arabic, Harakat al-Qawmiyyin al-Arab): A political movement, the Arab Nationalist Movement was created at the beginning of the 1950s at the American University of Beirut. Its founders, among whom were George Habash and Hani al-Hindi, advocated an independent, regional Arab nationalism, socialist in ideology. In 1967, following the Arab defeat in the 1967 War, the ANM was dissolved, giving rise to the Popular Front for the Liberation of Palestine (PFLP), led by Habash.

SEE ALSO Habash, George; Popular Front for the Liberation of Palestine.

ARAB ORGANIZATION FOR HUMAN RIGHTS: Independent Arab international human rights organization, founded in Cyprus in 1983. The Arab Organization for Human Rights (AOHR) seeks to defend the rights of individuals in the Arab world; endeavors, "regardless of political considerations, to obtain release of detained or imprisoned persons, and [seeks] relief and assistance for persons whose freedom is restricted in any way or who are subject to coercion of any kind because of their beliefs and political convictions, or for reasons of race, sex, colour, or language; protest[s] in cases where a fair trial is not guaranteed; provide[s] legal assistance where necessary and possible; call[s] for improvements in conditions of prisoners of conscience; work[s] for amnesty of persons sentenced for political reasons." It offers both legal and financial assistance to families. It is a membership organization and is funded by contributions. The AOHR is affiliated with other nongovernmental organizations, including Amnesty International, Human Rights Watch, the International Commission of Jurists, Middle East Watch, and the International Committee of the Red Cross. Its headquarters are in Cairo, Egypt. Its web site is available at www.aohr.org.

ARAB ORGANIZATION FOR THE RIGHTS OF MAN

SEE Haq, al-.

ARAB ORGANIZATION OF 15 MAY: Palestinian movement, created in November 1978, following a splinter in the Popular Front for the Liberation of Palestine–Special Operations (PFLP-SO) that was provoked by Hussein al-Omari (Abu Ibrahim) after the death of Wadi Haddad. The name of this organization alludes to 15 May 1948, date of the start of the first Israeli-Arab conflict, following the creation of the State of Israel. Backed by Iraq, this movement proposed "pursuing the fight against imperialism, capitalism and Zionism." Responsible for many attacks in the early 1980s, the AO-15 May (or Abu Ibrahim Group) stopped practically all activities toward the end of 1984. Specializing in actions involving booby-trapped briefcases, it was redoubtable for the technical expertise of its operatives. Some of its members joined the al-Fatah of Yasir Arafat, others the Fatah-Intifada of Abu Mussa.

al-Hasan, and Mahmud Abbas to lead the PLO in the interim. Emerging unhurt from this accident, Arafat strengthened his position as uncontested leader of the PLO.

After the Israeli elections of June 1992 in which a Labor government headed by Yitzhak Rabin was returned, Arafat authorized secret talks with the Israelis, which were held in Norway. In February 1993 the formal negotiations that led to the Oslo Accords began; Arafat also kept these secret from most of the PLO leadership. The chief negotiator was Mahmud Abbas. During that spring, finding himself once more severely criticized by his closest collaborators, he was saved from discredit by the intensification of the Intifada in the occupied territories. On 9 September 1993, after months of secret negotiations, Arafat won one of his greatest political victories, recognition of the PLO by Israel, with the signature in Washington, D.C., on 13 September, of an Israeli-Palestinian Declaration of Principles (DOP) on provisional autonomy for the Palestinian territories. On this occasion, Arafat and Rabin exchanged a "historic" televised handshake before the entire world. On 4 May 1994, in Cairo, the two men signed an agreement on the application of Palestinian autonomy. On 1 July, Arafat left Tunis to settle in Gaza, from where he would direct the setting up of the provisional autonomy of the Palestinian territories, guaranteed by the Oslo Accords. That 14 October, together with Yitzhak Rabin and Shimon Peres, Arafat received the Nobel Peace Prize.

In the spring of 1995, Arafat launched an appeal for national dialogue, in a vain effort to gain the support of all the Palestinian factions for the application of the Oslo Accords. On 20 January 1996, with more han 80 percent of the votes, Arafat was elected presilent of the Palestinian Authority (PA), which would e responsible for administering the partial autonony of the Palestinian territories. The results of these ections strengthened his position in the context of gotiations with Israel on the final status of the terories. In May 1996, the coming to power in Israel the leader of Likud, Benjamin Netanyahu, an opnent of the Oslo Accords, led to a stalling of the aeli-Palestinian negotiations for a period of several nths. On 4 May 1999, in the middle of another eli election campaign, Arafat refrained from proming the creation of a Palestinian state, as the Accords entitled him to do, to avoid encouragthe reelection of the leader of Likud. The failure he ground of these agreements affected his crediin the Palestinian population, particularly ng the young of al-Fatah.

On 22 March 2000, Arafat welcomed Pope John Paul II, on pilgrimage to Bethlehem. During the course of the spring and the summer, he traveled to Europe and Asia, around the Middle East, and into Africa. In July, under the sponsorship of the United States, he participated in a mini-summit with Israeli prime minister Ehud Barak (at Camp David), a meeting that was in principle aimed at coming to an agreement on the final status of the occupied territories. The conversations were interrupted because of the obstacle constituted by the question of Jerusalem. The following September, Arafat refrained once more from proclaiming the creation of the Palestinian State, this time not to hamper the actions of the leader of the Israeli government, whose political situation was very fragile.

In September 2000 the al-Aqsa Intifada began. In January 2001, as it intensified and as both the Barak government and the Clinton administration were in their last days, Arafat accepted an invitation to travel to Washington for negotiations aimed at restarting the peace process. These also failed. A few weeks later, the coming to power of Ariel Sharon in Israel and the determination of young Palestinians to continue the Intifada once more blocked the situation. On 15 October 2001, a month after the attacks on the World Trade Center in the United States, while the Intifada was continuing in the occupied territories, Arafat went to London, where he talked with British prime minister Tony Blair, who reaffirmed his support for a "viable Palestinian state." Referring to the American strikes in Afghanistan, the president of the Palestinian Authority declared that they were caused by "a war against terror and not by a war against Arabs, Muslims, or Islam." Divided between the opinions he had expressed publicly and his need for Western backing of the Palestinian cause, Arafat lent his support to the United States for its military operation against the Taliban.

At the beginning of December 2001, as the terrorist acts of HAMAS and Islamic Jihad against Israel were intensifying, Arafat was obliged to withdraw into his offices at Ramallah. The Israeli government decided to isolate him from his popular base by launching military attacks against the political structures of the Palestinian Authority as well as the economic infrastructure of the West Bank and Gaza. With the anti-Israel attacks continuing, the United States lent its support to the government of Ariel Sharon, while threatening to close the PLO offices in Washington. Arafat has essentially been a prisoner in his Ramallah compound (much reduced by Israeli attacks) ever since.

SEE ALSO Arafat, Yasir; Fatah, al-; Intifada (1987–1993); Popular Front for the Liberation of Palestine.

ARAB PALESTINE ORGANIZATION

SEE Organization of Arab Palestine.

ARABS: A Semitic language–speaking people who originated in the Arabian Peninsula, Arabs are referred to in inscriptions of other Middle Eastern cultures as early as the eighth century B.C.E. The word "Arab" may come from *Araba*, a little territory in the southern Hijaz, or from a Semitic root connoting nomadism. Pre-Islamic (to mid-seventh century C.E.) Arabs were adherents of various animistic or idolatrous cults, as well as of Judaism, Zoroastrianism, and Christianity. Starting in the eighth century C.E., successive Arab conquests incorporated most of Western Asia and North Africa, as well as Spain, Sicily, and parts of France, spreading Islam and absorbing indigenous peoples and languages. The Arabs became the teachers of the West, their mastery of astronomy, geography, medicine, and mathematics allowing Europeans to educate themselves in these domains. During almost six centuries, Arab supremacy in scientific, cultural, and political domains made Arabic the most widespread lingua franca in the world.

The Arab empire disintegrated progressively, with the establishment of small independent kingdoms and with the advent of the Turkish Seljuks, who weakened the power of Baghdad. Three centuries later, the Mongols put an end to the Abbasid Caliphate. The Arab-language peoples entered then a period of decline until a movement of renaissance (*al-Nahda*) arose in the nineteenth century. This consciousness had already begun stirring at the time of Napoleon's Egyptian expedition, which made the Arab world aware of the military and technological power of Europe. Reverting to themes that had been current in the thirteenth century, some Arab thinkers thought of an Islamic renaissance as a necessary return to sources. The Arab language, spoken in all Arab countries, though with regional dialects, became the focus of a polemic on Arab identity, culture, and history.

After World War II, pro-independence Arab movements succeeded in prevailing politically, giving birth to new independent states. Today the term "Arab" refers (with a few exceptions) to the peoples of the Arabic-speaking countries, whatever their ethnic origins, and to the Arabs of the diaspora, mainly in Europe and North America. There are twenty-two states in the League of Arab States, with an estimated 290 million inhabitants.

OLD AND NEW. A BEDOUIN MAN RIDES ON A CAMEL WHILE USING A MOBILE TELEPHONE IN ISRAEL IN 1994. EVEN PEOPLE AS FAR REMOVED FROM THE MODERN WORLD AS THESE NOMADIC ARAB DESERT DWELLERS HAVE FOUND THEIR TRADITIONAL LIFESTYLES INCREASINGLY ALTERED BY TECHNOLOGY. *(© Moshe Shai/Corbis)*

SEE ALSO Abbasids; Islam; League of Arab States; Seljuks.

ARAB UNION PARTY: A party formed by Mustafa Khamis in 1996 when he broke from the Popular Front for the Liberation of Palestine–General Command (PFLP–GC). Khamis supported the policies of Yasir Arafat.

SEE ALSO Arafat, Yasir; Popular Front for the Liberation of Palestine.

ARAD, RON: Israeli soldier, born in 1958, who disappeared on 16 October 1986, during an air raid on South Lebanon, when his plane was shot down east of Sayda. He succeeded in ejecting and was taken prisoner by men belonging to the Amal Shi'ite Movement. Despite rumors over the years that he is alive, all trace of him has been lost. He has been reported to be held in Lebanon, by the Hizbullah, or in Iran. Campaigns on his behalf are regularly organized in Israel and Israel's intelligence services have been assigned the mission of finding Arad's place of detention. The kidnapping of Mustafa Dirani, one of the leaders of the AMAL Movement, by an Israeli command on 21 May 1994, aimed at finding out what happened to the Israeli pilot. Additionally, secret emissaries have often attempted to obtain information from the Iranian authorities about the missing airman.

SEE ALSO AMAL; Hizbullah; South Lebanon.

ARAFAT, YASIR (1929–2004): Chairman of al-Fatah and the Palestine Liberation Organization, and president of the Palestinian Authority. Yasir Arafat was born on 24 August 1929 in Jerusalem, Cairo, or the Gaza Strip, depending on which biography is consulted. (Arafat's full given name is Muhammad Abd al-Ra'uf al-Arafat al-Qudwa; "Yasir" is a childhood nickname. He is widely known as *al-lkhityar,* "the Old Man.") His father was a merchant from Gaza and belonged to the Qudwa family, a branch of the Hussayni clan. Bereft of his mother when he was four years old, Arafat was raised in Jerusalem by his maternal uncle, Salim Abu Sa'id. Six years later he returned to Cairo to live with his father, who had married an Egyptian.

While a student he joined the Union of Palestinian Students. In June 1948, during the first conflict between the forces of the new State of Israel and the Arab armies, he joined the ranks of Palestinian groups in Gaza, where he played a modest role. Back in Egypt after the Arab defeat, he became in 1952 secretary general of the Union of Palestinian Students for Egypt and Gaza. In that context, he became friendly with Khalil al-Wazir, Khalid al-Hasan, and Salah Khalaf. Along with these men, who had close ties to the Muslim Brotherhood, Arafat participated in the creation of the newspaper *The Voice of Palestine.* In 1955 he earned a degree in civil engineering from Cairo University, and was inducted into the Egyptian army in 1956 for the duration of the Suez War.

Arafat left Egypt the following year for Kuwait, where he first worked for the Kuwaiti government and later established a construction business, all the while continuing to militate for the Palestinian cause. In December 1959, with al-Wazir, al-Hasan, Khalaf, and Faruq Qaddumi, he founded the Palestinian National Liberation Movement, al-Fatah, whose doctrine called for the liberation of Palestine

YASIR ARAFAT. THE HEAD OF THE PLO SINCE 1969 AND PRESIDENT OF THE PALESTINIAN AUTHORITY SINCE 1996, ARAFAT SURVIVED NUMEROUS MILITARY AND DIPLOMATIC FAILURES. HE WAS AWARDED A NOBEL PEACE PRIZE IN 1995, BUT ISRAELI ATTACKS IN RESPONSE TO THE AL-AQSA INTIFADA MADE HIM ESSENTIALLY A PRISONER IN HIS MUCH-REDUCED COMPOUND IN RAMALLAH. *(AP/ Wide World Photos)*

as distinct from Arab unity, the ostensible goal of the Arab states. In 1962, as soon as Algeria was independent, Arafat initiated contacts with the leaders of the Front de Libération Nationale (FLN), who became supporters of al-Fatah. After much internal debate, al-Fatah on 1 January 1965 mounted its first (failed) attack inside Israel, carried out by al-Asifa (Fatah's military arm) led by Arafat under the *nom de guerre* of Abu Ammar ("[Father of] the Builder").

In 1966, with the cooperation of the Syrian government, al-Fatah launched some small-scale guerrilla attacks into Israel from that country, but Arafat was impatient with the restraints put on him by the Syrians, who jailed him at one point. The defeat of the Arab countries in the war of June 1967 led many Palestinians to join the ranks of al-Fatah. The success of the *fida'iyyun* (along with the Jordanian army) in

containing Israeli troops on 21 March 1968 at Karameh (Jordan) made Arafat the uncontested leader of the Palestinian resistance. On 4 February 1969, Arafat was elected president of the executive committee of the Palestine Liberation Organization (PLO). In October 1970, he became an undesirable in Jordan after the attempt to take power by the principal factions of the Palestinian resistance and the massacres of the Palestinians by Jordanian forces (Black September).

Arafat established himself in Lebanon, where he continued his struggle against Israel. On 26 October 1974 the Arab League, at its summit in Rabat (Morocco), proclaimed the PLO "the only legitimate representative of the Palestinian people." On the following 13 November, invited by the United Nations to speak before the General Assembly, he was acclaimed by the delegates, except for the Israeli representatives, to whom he remarked: "I come carrying an olive branch and the rifle of a fighter for liberty; do not let the branch fall from my hand!" Established in Lebanon for almost fifteen years, the Palestinian resistance would come to constitute a veritable "state within a state," discomfiting the Lebanese and Syrians as much as the Israelis. On 6 June 1982 the Israeli army launched a vast offensive against the Palestinians in Lebanon (Operation "Peace for Galilee"). After a number of confrontations with the Israelis—as well as with Lebanese militias, the Syrians, and other Palestinian factions—and abandoned on all sides, Arafat left Lebanon for the first time on 30 August 1982.

In March 1983, he presided over the Second Session of the Seventh Summit of Non-aligned Countries, which was held in New Delhi, India. At the meeting he also held discussions with Syrian president Hafiz el-Asad, with whom relations had been cold since Arafat's departure from Lebanon. After the Sabra and Shatila massacres in 1982, he returned to Lebanon to stand by his supporters who had remained behind. Weakened militarily, and under powerful international pressure, Arafat agreed to leave Lebanon definitively with the PLO (20 December 1983), and to establish himself in Tunisia. But, in spite of the military defeat he had just suffered and his distance from the Israeli front, Arafat won a diplomatic victory through the approval of his action by the international community. Indeed, even before he left Lebanon, the Congress of the Palestine National Council (PNC), meeting in Algiers in February 1983, reelected him president of the executive committee of the PLO. The fact that elements of the Palestine movement belonged to the Socialist International (SI) allowed the head of the PLO to broach a new diplomatic offensive, centered on the idea of the creation of a Jordanian-Palestinian federation.

On 1 October 1985, Arafat narrowly escaped death when his headquarters in Tunis was bombed by Israeli planes. In April 1988, while the Intifada persisted in the occupied territories, the assassination of Khalid al-Wazir (Abu Jihad), one of his clos
collaborators, in charge of operations in the occu
pied territories, isolated him further from the da
life of the Palestinians "from inside." On 15 Nove
ber 1988, at Arafat's urging, the PNC, meeting in
giers, issued a Proclamation of the State of Palest
with Jerusalem as its capital, and elected Arafa
president. This proclamation was, in part, an att
by Arafat to gain control of the Intifada. The
also voted a reform of the PLO charter, renou
the use of terror and recognizing United N
Resolutions 242 and 338 as a basis for an i
tional peace conference.

On 13 December 1988, Arafat gave a sp
fore the General Assembly of the United
convening in Geneva, Switzerland, especiall
him, in which he confirmed the PLO's re
of Israel's right to exist and declared its ren
of terrorism. These moves put the PLO i
ance with American conditions for d
which Arafat wanted, and the United
prompted to call for a "substantive dia
the PLO. By the beginning of 1990, oppo
Palestinian movement between the "te
Tunis and the Palestinians inside Gaza
Bank had reached a boiling point. C
1990, ten days after Iraq invaded Ku
spite of the opposition of a majority o
of al-Fatah and of the executive co
PLO—Arafat decided to support Ira
days, the PLO and its leader lost the
international community, as well
backing of the Gulf countries. In J
assassination of his friend Salah K
in charge of security for al-Fatah, b
Abu Nidal Group, increased this i
tober, the Madrid Peace Conf
sponsorship of the United Sta
Union, encouraged Arafat to loo
with Israel. Between 21 and 25
meeting of the Revolutionary C
Tunis, Arafat faced severe critic
On 7 April the airplane in w
crashed in the Libyan desert. I
he was hospitalized in Amma
a triumvirate composed of F

containing Israeli troops on 21 March 1968 at Karameh (Jordan) made Arafat the uncontested leader of the Palestinian resistance. On 4 February 1969, Arafat was elected president of the executive committee of the Palestine Liberation Organization (PLO). In October 1970, he became an undesirable in Jordan after the attempt to take power by the principal factions of the Palestinian resistance and the massacres of the Palestinians by Jordanian forces (Black September).

Arafat established himself in Lebanon, where he continued his struggle against Israel. On 26 October 1974 the Arab League, at its summit in Rabat (Morocco), proclaimed the PLO "the only legitimate representative of the Palestinian people." On the following 13 November, invited by the United Nations to speak before the General Assembly, he was acclaimed by the delegates, except for the Israeli representatives, to whom he remarked: "I come carrying an olive branch and the rifle of a fighter for liberty; do not let the branch fall from my hand!" Established in Lebanon for almost fifteen years, the Palestinian resistance would come to constitute a veritable "state within a state," discomfiting the Lebanese and Syrians as much as the Israelis. On 6 June 1982 the Israeli army launched a vast offensive against the Palestinians in Lebanon (Operation "Peace for Galilee"). After a number of confrontations with the Israelis—as well as with Lebanese militias, the Syrians, and other Palestinian factions—and abandoned on all sides, Arafat left Lebanon for the first time on 30 August 1982.

In March 1983, he presided over the Second Session of the Seventh Summit of Non-aligned Countries, which was held in New Delhi, India. At the meeting he also held discussions with Syrian president Hafiz el-Asad, with whom relations had been cold since Arafat's departure from Lebanon. After the Sabra and Shatila massacres in 1982, he returned to Lebanon to stand by his supporters who had remained behind. Weakened militarily, and under powerful international pressure, Arafat agreed to leave Lebanon definitively with the PLO (20 December 1983), and to establish himself in Tunisia. But, in spite of the military defeat he had just suffered and his distance from the Israeli front, Arafat won a diplomatic victory through the approval of his action by the international community. Indeed, even before he left Lebanon, the Congress of the Palestine National Council (PNC), meeting in Algiers in February 1983, reelected him president of the executive committee of the PLO. The fact that elements of the Palestine movement belonged to the Socialist International (SI) allowed the head of the PLO to broach a new diplomatic offensive, centered on the idea of the creation of a Jordanian-Palestinian federation.

On 1 October 1985, Arafat narrowly escaped death when his headquarters in Tunis was bombed by Israeli planes. In April 1988, while the Intifada persisted in the occupied territories, the assassination of Khalid al-Wazir (Abu Jihad), one of his close collaborators, in charge of operations in the occupied territories, isolated him further from the daily life of the Palestinians "from inside." On 15 November 1988, at Arafat's urging, the PNC, meeting in Algiers, issued a Proclamation of the State of Palestine, with Jerusalem as its capital, and elected Arafat its president. This proclamation was, in part, an attempt by Arafat to gain control of the Intifada. The PNC also voted a reform of the PLO charter, renouncing the use of terror and recognizing United Nations Resolutions 242 and 338 as a basis for an international peace conference.

On 13 December 1988, Arafat gave a speech before the General Assembly of the United Nations, convening in Geneva, Switzerland, especially to hear him, in which he confirmed the PLO's recognition of Israel's right to exist and declared its renunciation of terrorism. These moves put the PLO in compliance with American conditions for discussions, which Arafat wanted, and the United States was prompted to call for a "substantive dialogue" with the PLO. By the beginning of 1990, opposition in the Palestinian movement between the "technocrats" in Tunis and the Palestinians inside Gaza and the West Bank had reached a boiling point. On 12 August 1990, ten days after Iraq invaded Kuwait—and in spite of the opposition of a majority of the members of al-Fatah and of the executive committee of the PLO—Arafat decided to support Iraq. In just a few days, the PLO and its leader lost the approval of the international community, as well as the financial backing of the Gulf countries. In January 1991, the assassination of his friend Salah Khalaf (Abu Iyad), in charge of security for al-Fatah, by a member of the Abu Nidal Group, increased this isolation. That October, the Madrid Peace Conference, under the sponsorship of the United States and the Soviet Union, encouraged Arafat to look for a compromise with Israel. Between 21 and 25 March 1992, at the meeting of the Revolutionary Council of al-Fatah in Tunis, Arafat faced severe criticism of his leadership. On 7 April the airplane in which he was traveling crashed in the Libyan desert. Found safe and sound, he was hospitalized in Amman, where he designated a triumvirate composed of Faruq Qaddumi, Khalid al-Hasan, and Mahmud Abbas to lead the PLO in the interim. Emerging unhurt from this accident, Arafat strengthened his position as uncontested leader of the PLO.

After the Israeli elections of June 1992 in which a Labor government headed by Yitzhak Rabin was returned, Arafat authorized secret talks with the Israelis, which were held in Norway. In February 1993 the formal negotiations that led to the Oslo Accords began; Arafat also kept these secret from most of the PLO leadership. The chief negotiator was Mahmud Abbas. During that spring, finding himself once more severely criticized by his closest collaborators, he was saved from discredit by the intensification of the Intifada in the occupied territories. On 9 September 1993, after months of secret negotiations, Arafat won one of his greatest political victories, recognition of the PLO by Israel, with the signature in Washington, D.C., on 13 September, of an Israeli-Palestinian Declaration of Principles (DOP) on provisional autonomy for the Palestinian territories. On this occasion, Arafat and Rabin exchanged a "historic" televised handshake before the entire world. On 4 May 1994, in Cairo, the two men signed an agreement on the application of Palestinian autonomy. On 1 July, Arafat left Tunis to settle in Gaza, from where he would direct the setting up of the provisional autonomy of the Palestinian territories, guaranteed by the Oslo Accords. That 14 October, together with Yitzhak Rabin and Shimon Peres, Arafat received the Nobel Peace Prize.

In the spring of 1995, Arafat launched an appeal for national dialogue, in a vain effort to gain the support of all the Palestinian factions for the application of the Oslo Accords. On 20 January 1996, with more than 80 percent of the votes, Arafat was elected president of the Palestinian Authority (PA), which would be responsible for administering the partial autonomy of the Palestinian territories. The results of these elections strengthened his position in the context of negotiations with Israel on the final status of the territories. In May 1996, the coming to power in Israel of the leader of Likud, Benjamin Netanyahu, an opponent of the Oslo Accords, led to a stalling of the Israeli-Palestinian negotiations for a period of several months. On 4 May 1999, in the middle of another Israeli election campaign, Arafat refrained from proclaiming the creation of a Palestinian state, as the Oslo Accords entitled him to do, to avoid encouraging the reelection of the leader of Likud. The failure on the ground of these agreements affected his credibility in the Palestinian population, particularly among the young of al-Fatah.

On 22 March 2000, Arafat welcomed Pope John Paul II, on pilgrimage to Bethlehem. During the course of the spring and the summer, he traveled to Europe and Asia, around the Middle East, and into Africa. In July, under the sponsorship of the United States, he participated in a mini-summit with Israeli prime minister Ehud Barak (at Camp David), a meeting that was in principle aimed at coming to an agreement on the final status of the occupied territories. The conversations were interrupted because of the obstacle constituted by the question of Jerusalem. The following September, Arafat refrained once more from proclaiming the creation of the Palestinian State, this time not to hamper the actions of the leader of the Israeli government, whose political situation was very fragile.

In September 2000 the al-Aqsa Intifada began. In January 2001, as it intensified and as both the Barak government and the Clinton administration were in their last days, Arafat accepted an invitation to travel to Washington for negotiations aimed at restarting the peace process. These also failed. A few weeks later, the coming to power of Ariel Sharon in Israel and the determination of young Palestinians to continue the Intifada once more blocked the situation. On 15 October 2001, a month after the attacks on the World Trade Center in the United States, while the Intifada was continuing in the occupied territories, Arafat went to London, where he talked with British prime minister Tony Blair, who reaffirmed his support for a "viable Palestinian state." Referring to the American strikes in Afghanistan, the president of the Palestinian Authority declared that they were caused by "a war against terror and not by a war against Arabs, Muslims, or Islam." Divided between the opinions he had expressed publicly and his need for Western backing of the Palestinian cause, Arafat lent his support to the United States for its military operation against the Taliban.

At the beginning of December 2001, as the terrorist acts of HAMAS and Islamic Jihad against Israel were intensifying, Arafat was obliged to withdraw into his offices at Ramallah. The Israeli government decided to isolate him from his popular base by launching military attacks against the political structures of the Palestinian Authority as well as the economic infrastructure of the West Bank and Gaza. With the anti-Israel attacks continuing, the United States lent its support to the government of Ariel Sharon, while threatening to close the PLO offices in Washington. Arafat has essentially been a prisoner in his Ramallah compound (much reduced by Israeli attacks) ever since.

SEE ALSO Arafat, Yasir; Fatah, al-; Intifada (1987–1993); Popular Front for the Liberation of Palestine.

ARAB PALESTINE ORGANIZATION

SEE Organization of Arab Palestine.

ARABS: A Semitic language–speaking people who originated in the Arabian Peninsula, Arabs are referred to in inscriptions of other Middle Eastern cultures as early as the eighth century B.C.E. The word "Arab" may come from *Araba,* a little territory in the southern Hijaz, or from a Semitic root connoting nomadism. Pre-Islamic (to mid-seventh century C.E.) Arabs were adherents of various animistic or idolatrous cults, as well as of Judaism, Zoroastrianism, and Christianity. Starting in the eighth century C.E., successive Arab conquests incorporated most of Western Asia and North Africa, as well as Spain, Sicily, and parts of France, spreading Islam and absorbing indigenous peoples and languages. The Arabs became the teachers of the West, their mastery of astronomy, geography, medicine, and mathematics allowing Europeans to educate themselves in these domains. During almost six centuries, Arab supremacy in scientific, cultural, and political domains made Arabic the most widespread lingua franca in the world.

The Arab empire disintegrated progressively, with the establishment of small independent kingdoms and with the advent of the Turkish Seljuks, who weakened the power of Baghdad. Three centuries later, the Mongols put an end to the Abbasid Caliphate. The Arab-language peoples entered then a period of decline until a movement of renaissance (*al-Nahda*) arose in the nineteenth century. This consciousness had already begun stirring at the time of Napoleon's Egyptian expedition, which made the Arab world aware of the military and technological power of Europe. Reverting to themes that had been current in the thirteenth century, some Arab thinkers thought of an Islamic renaissance as a necessary return to sources. The Arab language, spoken in all Arab countries, though with regional dialects, became the focus of a polemic on Arab identity, culture, and history.

After World War II, pro-independence Arab movements succeeded in prevailing politically, giving birth to new independent states. Today the term "Arab" refers (with a few exceptions) to the peoples of the Arabic-speaking countries, whatever their ethnic origins, and to the Arabs of the diaspora, mainly in Europe and North America. There are twenty-two states in the League of Arab States, with an estimated 290 million inhabitants.

OLD AND NEW. A BEDOUIN MAN RIDES ON A CAMEL WHILE USING A MOBILE TELEPHONE IN ISRAEL IN 1994. EVEN PEOPLE AS FAR REMOVED FROM THE MODERN WORLD AS THESE NOMADIC ARAB DESERT DWELLERS HAVE FOUND THEIR TRADITIONAL LIFESTYLES INCREASINGLY ALTERED BY TECHNOLOGY. *(© Moshe Shai/Corbis)*

SEE ALSO Abbasids; Islam; League of Arab States; Seljuks.

ARAB UNION PARTY: A party formed by Mustafa Khamis in 1996 when he broke from the Popular Front for the Liberation of Palestine–General Command (PFLP–GC). Khamis supported the policies of Yasir Arafat.

SEE ALSO Arafat, Yasir; Popular Front for the Liberation of Palestine.

ARAD, RON: Israeli soldier, born in 1958, who disappeared on 16 October 1986, during an air raid on South Lebanon, when his plane was shot down east of Sayda. He succeeded in ejecting and was taken prisoner by men belonging to the Amal Shiʿite Movement. Despite rumors over the years that he is alive, all trace of him has been lost. He has been reported to be held in Lebanon, by the Hizbullah, or in Iran. Campaigns on his behalf are regularly organized in Israel and Israel's intelligence services have been assigned the mission of finding Arad's place of detention. The kidnapping of Mustafa Dirani, one of the leaders of the AMAL Movement, by an Israeli command on 21 May 1994, aimed at finding out what happened to the Israeli pilot. Additionally, secret emissaries have often attempted to obtain information from the Iranian authorities about the missing airman.

SEE ALSO AMAL; Hizbullah; South Lebanon.

ARAFAT, YASIR (1929–2004): Chairman of al-Fatah and the Palestine Liberation Organization, and president of the Palestinian Authority. Yasir Arafat was born on 24 August 1929 in Jerusalem, Cairo, or the Gaza Strip, depending on which biography is consulted. (Arafat's full given name is Muhammad Abd al-Ra'uf al-Arafat al-Qudwa; "Yasir" is a childhood nickname. He is widely known as *al-lkhityar,* "the Old Man.") His father was a merchant from Gaza and belonged to the Qudwa family, a branch of the Hussayni clan. Bereft of his mother when he was four years old, Arafat was raised in Jerusalem by his maternal uncle, Salim Abu Sa'id. Six years later he returned to Cairo to live with his father, who had married an Egyptian.

YASIR ARAFAT. THE HEAD OF THE PLO SINCE 1969 AND PRESIDENT OF THE PALESTINIAN AUTHORITY SINCE 1996, ARAFAT SURVIVED NUMEROUS MILITARY AND DIPLOMATIC FAILURES. HE WAS AWARDED A NOBEL PEACE PRIZE IN 1995, BUT ISRAELI ATTACKS IN RESPONSE TO THE AL-AQSA INTIFADA MADE HIM ESSENTIALLY A PRISONER IN HIS MUCH-REDUCED COMPOUND IN RAMALLAH. *(AP/ Wide World Photos)*

While a student he joined the Union of Palestinian Students. In June 1948, during the first conflict between the forces of the new State of Israel and the Arab armies, he joined the ranks of Palestinian groups in Gaza, where he played a modest role. Back in Egypt after the Arab defeat, he became in 1952 secretary general of the Union of Palestinian Students for Egypt and Gaza. In that context, he became friendly with Khalil al-Wazir, Khalid al-Hasan, and Salah Khalaf. Along with these men, who had close ties to the Muslim Brotherhood, Arafat participated in the creation of the newspaper *The Voice of Palestine.* In 1955 he earned a degree in civil engineering from Cairo University, and was inducted into the Egyptian army in 1956 for the duration of the Suez War.

Arafat left Egypt the following year for Kuwait, where he first worked for the Kuwaiti government and later established a construction business, all the while continuing to militate for the Palestinian cause. In December 1959, with al-Wazir, al-Hasan, Khalaf, and Faruq Qaddumi, he founded the Palestinian National Liberation Movement, al-Fatah, whose doctrine called for the liberation of Palestine as distinct from Arab unity, the ostensible goal of the Arab states. In 1962, as soon as Algeria was independent, Arafat initiated contacts with the leaders of the Front de Libération Nationale (FLN), who became supporters of al-Fatah. After much internal debate, al-Fatah on 1 January 1965 mounted its first (failed) attack inside Israel, carried out by al-Asifa (Fatah's military arm) led by Arafat under the *nom de guerre* of Abu Ammar ("[Father of] the Builder").

In 1966, with the cooperation of the Syrian government, al-Fatah launched some small-scale guerrilla attacks into Israel from that country, but Arafat was impatient with the restraints put on him by the Syrians, who jailed him at one point. The defeat of the Arab countries in the war of June 1967 led many Palestinians to join the ranks of al-Fatah. The success of the *fida'iyyun* (along with the Jordanian army) in

In mid-October 2004, Arafat's health, which had been slowly deteriorating for some time, became markedly worse. Increasingly weak with an unknown illness, on 29 October he was allowed to leave his compound in Ramallah for the first time since the Israeli assault in 2002 to seek medical help. Helicoptered by the Jordanian government to a waiting plane sent for him by French president Jacques Chirac, he was taken to a military hospital outside Paris specializing in blood disorders. The cause of his illness remained unknown in early November when he lapsed into a coma. He died on 11 November.

SEE ALSO Aqsa Intifada, al-; Barak, Ehud; Black September 1970; Fatah, al-; Gaza Strip; HAMAS; Hasan, Khalid al-; Intifada (1987–1993); Khalaf, Salah; Madrid Conference; Netanyahu, Benjamin; Oslo Accords; Palestine Liberation Organization; Palestinian Authority; Qaddumi, Faruq; Sharon, Ariel; Suez Crisis; Wazir, Khalil al-.

ARAMAIC: Northern Semitic language spoken mainly during antiquity. A language close to Hebrew and Phoenician, Aramaic also resembled Arabic. In its beginnings Aramaic was the language of nomadic tribes—referred to in Akkadian texts under the name of Ahlamou as early as the fourteenth century B.C.E.—who lived in Upper Mesopotamia, then in the territories of contemporary Syria and Lebanon. By the tenth century B.C.E., the Aramaeans had started creating small states, Bit-Adini and Damascus among them, which came into conflict with the Israelites and the Assyrians. In the third century C.E. Aramaic divided into two dialects: Eastern, or Syriac; and Western Aramaic, or the language of the Targum. Aramaic was spoken and written up to the seventh century C.E., when the Aramaeans were conquered and deported by the Arabs. According to Biblical tradition, Shem's son Aram is the eponymous ancestor of the Aramaeans.

ARCHAEOLOGY: Since the nineteenth century, Palestinian archeology has been one of the major preoccupations of Jews, anxious to find in recent discoveries evidence to confirm Biblical writings. Jews and Muslims alike expect to find an answer to the question: "Who are the real inheritors of the Land of Palestine?" Ever since the creation of the State of Israel, archaeological discoveries have been thought by some to grant preemptory rights to descendants of the Biblical Hebrews over the Promised Land. Therefore, archaeology, considered a kind of national sport in Israel, has become a priority issue in national politics—both on the Israeli and on the Palestinian side—and, therefore, also plays an important role in the Israeli-Palestinian conflict.

SEE ALSO Hebrew.

THE SCROLL OF THE RULE. THESE FRAGMENTS—PART OF THE DEAD SEA SCROLLS—WERE WRITTEN IN ARAMAIC, WHICH SERVED AS A COMMON LANGUAGE FOR PEOPLES THROUGHOUT THE ANCIENT MIDDLE EAST (AMONG MANY OTHERS, IT WAS THE LANGUAGE OF JESUS). WITH THE RISE OF ISLAM, IT WAS SUPPLANTED BY ARABIC, THOUGH MODERN FORMS OF ARAMAIC ARE STILL IN USE TODAY. *(© West Semitic Research/Dead Sea Scrolls Foundation/Corbis)*

ARD AL-MUQADDASA, AL-: Arabic term meaning "Holy Land" and used to designate Palestine.

ARENS, MOSHE (1925–): Israeli politician and cabinet minister. Born in Lithuania in 1925, Moshe Arens immigrated to the United States in 1939, then to Israel in 1948. He studied mechanical engineering at the Massachusetts Institute of Technology and aeronautical engineering at the California Institute of Technology. Arens was a professor of aeronautical engineering at Haifa University from 1959 to 1961, then served as vice president for engineering at Israeli Aircraft Industries from 1962 until 1971. First elected to the Knesset in 1974, he served as chairman of the foreign affairs and security committee from 1977 to 1982 and was considered a hawk regarding Israeli security. Arens served as ambassador to the United States from 1982 to 1983, then returned to Israel to replace Ariel Sharon as defense minister. In the National Unity government (1984–1986) Arens served as minister without portfolio, then from 1988 to 1990 was foreign minister. In 1990 he was again appointed minister of defense, serving until 1992, at

MOSHE ARENS. A MEMBER OF THE ISRAELI KNESSET STARTING IN 1977, THE HAWKISH ARENS SERVED IN MANY GOVERNMENT POSTS SINCE THEN, INCLUDING AMBASSADOR TO THE UNITED STATES AND MINISTER OF DEFENSE.

which time he retired from political life. Arens returned to politics in 1999, serving once more as defense minister until 2002.

ARIF, ARIF AL- (1892–1973): Palestinian journalist, bureaucrat, and historian. Born in Jerusalem in 1892 and educated in Istanbul, Arif al-Arif worked briefly in the Ottoman foreign ministry. He served in the Ottoman army in World War I and was a prisoner of war in Siberia for two years. Arif returned to Jerusalem after the war and became editor of the Arab nationalist newspaper, *Suriya al-Janubiyya,* where he advocated Palestinian union with Syria. Sentenced to prison by the British in 1920, he went into exile in Syria and later Transjordan. After being pardoned, he became a civil administrator under the Mandate government and held a number of posts in Palestine and Transjordan. In 1948 the Transjordan government of King Abdullah I made him military governor of Ramallah in the West Bank, and from 1949 to 1955 he was mayor of East Jerusalem. In 1967 he became the director of the Palestinian Archaeological Museum. He died in Jerusalem in 1973. Al-Arif was the author of a number of important histories, including *Ta'rikh Bir al-Sab'a wa Qaba'iliha* (History of Beersheba and its tribes, 1934), *Ta'rikh Ghaza* (History of Gaza, 1934), *al-Mufassal fi Ta'rikh al-Quds* (History of Jerusalem, 1934) and the seven-volume *Ta'rikh al-Nakba* (History of the disaster, 1956–1962).

ARIHA: Arabic name of the city of Jericho.

SEE ALSO Jericho.

ARKAN: Arabic term designating the five obligations (pillars) of the Muslim religion: profession of faith (*shahada*), prayer (*salat*), alms (*zakat*), fasting (*ramadan*), and pilgrimage (*hajj*).

ASABIYA: The phenomenon of social solidarity in the Arab or Muslim community.

ASAD, BASHSHAR AL- (1965–): President of Syria since July 2000. The younger son of Hafiz al-Asad, Bashshar al-Asad was born 11 September 1965 in Damascus. After graduating from the College of Medicine of Damascus University in 1988, he practiced at the Military Hospital of Tekrin until 1992, when he left for Britain to pursue advanced studies in ophthalmology. On 21 January 1994, his older brother Basil, presumed successor of President Hafiz al-Asad, was killed in an automobile accident. At the request of his father, Bashshar returned to Syria. He joined the army as a medical officer with the rank of captain, but soon renounced his career in medicine to undergo military staff and command training in preparation to succeed his father. He became a major in 1995, a lieutenant colonel on graduating the general staff school in 1997, and a full colonel in 1999 when he became a brigade commander in the elite Republican Guard. He became chairman of the Syrian Information Technology Company, from which position he introduced personal computers, the Internet, and cell phones into Syria.

During the last two years of Hafiz al-Asad's life, when his health was failing, "Dr. Bashshar," as he was known, was increasingly involved in political decision making. He was given responsibility for the Lebanese and Golan Heights issues, the latter the principal obstacle to Syrian-Israeli peace, and he moved, with his father's help, to neutralize political support for his uncle, Hafiz al-Asad's brother Rif'at, a major political figure who commanded the loyalty of many within the regime. (On 8 February 1998,

BASHSHAR AL-ASAD. THE BAʿTH PARTY LEADER AND COMMANDER-IN-CHIEF OF THE SYRIAN ARMED FORCES SUCCEEDED HIS FATHER, HAFIZ AL-ASAD, AS PRESIDENT OF SYRIA IN JULY 2000, AT THE AGE OF THIRTY-FOUR. SINCE THEN, HE HAS INSTITUTED LIMITED ECONOMIC, POLITICAL, AND SOCIAL REFORMS IN HIS COUNTRY. *(AP/Wide World Photos)*

Hafiz al-Asad abolished the office of vice president, which Rifʿat had held.) At the same time Bashshar launched a campaign against corruption aimed at certain powerful figures. In late 1999 Bashshar al-Asad undertook a visit to a number of Gulf states and to France, in an effort to become better known on the international scene. On 10 June 2000, the day Hafiz al-Asad died, Parliament reduced from 40 to 34 years the minimum age for the highest office, thereby making possible Bashshar al-Asad's presidency. The next day he was promoted to lieutenant general and named commander-in-chief of the armed forces, and on 20 June he became secretary general of the Baʿth Party. On 27 June, seventeen days after the death of his father, Bashshar al-Asad was designated unanimously by the People's Assembly as candidate for the presidency of the Republic. On 11 July, with more than 97 percent of the votes, he became president.

Desiring to undertake a liberalization of Syrian society without, in so doing, renouncing the attainments of the past, he surrounded himself with advisors of his generation, some of whom had ties to his own family, while others were close collaborators of his father. In the first year of his rule he began an ambitious program of economic and administrative reform and a limited program of political and social liberalization: He suspended emergency laws, released some political prisoners, lightened censorship, allowed the creation of independent political parties and newspapers, and generally ruled Syria with a lighter hand than his father. He has since felt it necessary to be more cautious about alienating the "old guard" in the party and the military. He has made efforts to reinforce Syria's ties with its Arab neighbors, notably Iraq (before the U.S.-Iraq war of 2003), Iran, and the Gulf states, and has made a number of foreign visits, including one to France in June 2001. Bashshar al-Asad has been less inclined to interfere in Lebanon, although Syrian troops remain, and he continues to support the Lebanese Hizbullah, a major Lebanese religious movement/militia/political party regarded by Washington as a terrorist organization. Since the September 2001 attacks on the United States, his regime has supplied useful intelligence information to Washington but opposed the war in Iraq. Syrian relations with Israel have been frozen since the failure of the Wye negotiations and the radicalization of Israeli and American policies toward the Palestinians.

SEE ALSO Asad, Hafiz al-; Baʿth; Syria.

ASAD, HAFIZ AL- (1930–2000): Syrian military figure and head of state, born in October 1930 at Khardaha, an Alawite fief in the north of Syria. Hafiz al-Asad joined the Baʿth Party in 1948. Three years later, after having been president of the Congress of the Syrian Student Union, he entered the Homs Military School where he became friends with Mustafa Tlas, Muhammad Omran, and Saleh Jedid, with whom he formed a clandestine Baʿth Party cell. He graduated a fighter pilot and continued his training in the USSR and Egypt. He was promoted to the rank of general in 1963. On 2 December 1964, a year after the Baʿth Party had taken power in Syria, he became commander of the Syrian Air Force, and he was later elected to the leadership of the National Baʿth Party.

In February 1966, while his friends Nur al-Din al-Atasi and Saleh Jedid were in power, al-Asad became defense minister. His chief of staff was his friend General Tlas. Distancing himself from Jedid's political positions, al-Asad, as the leader of the "military" branch of the Baʿth Party, supported a pragmatic kind of socialism. On 7 September 1966, backed up by his brother Rifʿat, commander of an armored division, and by General Tlas, he thwarted a coup attempt organized by Selim Hatoum. On 24 December al-Asad narrowly escaped an attempt on his life. At the end of the War of 1967, the Israeli Army occupation of the Golan Heights caused a faction in the Syrian Army. Hafiz al-Asad began to broadcast his opposition to the government. Even though a new government had been in power for only a few months, on 20 September 1970 he refused to supply air cover to Syrian armored units that were attempting to come to the rescue of Palestinians who were confronted by Jordanian forces.

On 13 November of the same year, he took power through force following the resignation of the Syrian government. Two days later, Ahmed Khatib became president of the Syrian state, and he named al-Asad prime minister. In February 1971, he was appointed to the People's Council and became secretary general of the Baʿth Party. On 12 March, he was elected president of the Arab Republic of Syria. To lead his country al-Asad would depend on the army, the security services, the Baʿth Party, the Alawite community, and his family clan. He named his brother, Rifʿat, head of the Brigades for the Defense of the Revolution, responsible for the security of the regime. The economic policies that President Asad started carrying out involved nationalizations tinged with realistic socialism, while striving in vain to achieve strategic military parity with Israel. Between 1972 and 1977 he attempted to reestablish relations with Jordan and Saudi Arabia. In October 1973, he backed Egyptian president Anwar al-Sadat in beginning the war with Israel (known as the 1973 War or the Yom Kippur War), which ended with Israel consolidating its occupation of the Golan Heights.

In June 1976, as the civil war just broke out in Lebanon, the intervention of the Syrian Army in that country was approved by the Arab Summit of Cairo. Such support conferred upon al-Asad the right to interfere in Lebanese affairs. In December 1977, he joined the ranks of the Refusal Front, opposed to the Egyptian initiative for peace with Israel. In October 1980, two years after his reelection as president, he signed a treaty of friendship and cooperation with the Soviet Union. In January of 1982 Syrian Intelligence thwarted a coup attempt organized by the Muslim Brotherhood. Rifʿat al-Asad led a merciless repression, causing more than twenty thousand deaths. In November 1983 health problems momentarily removed Hafiz al-Asad from leadership of the country. Government continuity was assured by a triumvirate that included Rifʿat, who tried to seize power. Back in office, Hafiz al-Asad disbanded a number of associations, including Al-Murtada, led by his other brother, Jamil, and he reorganized the command of the special forces, headed by Rifʿat, whom he forced into exile in France in 1984.

In February 1985, Hafiz al-Asad was reelected president of Syria. Henceforward, he pushed his elder son, Basil, to take a prominent place on the political scene, so as to assure his succession. At the same time he undertook a series of political and economic reforms to help make the country more stable and also for the purpose of obtaining developmental aid from the West. In 1990–1991, in the context of the Gulf War, the participation of Syria in the anti-Iraq coalition allowed him to consolidate his place as necessary interlocutor in the Middle East. In November 1991, he accepted an invitation to participate in a peace conference, organized at Madrid. However, his ideas of a global peace, based on the restitution of the territories occupied by Israel, collided with Israeli intransigence. In September 1993, al-Asad denounced the Israeli-Palestinian Declaration of Principles (signed in Washington), arguing that peace with Israel could only be realized in the context of a global agreement with all concerned Arab countries. In 1994, after the accidental death of Basil, he decided to impose his second son, Bashshar al-Asad, as his successor at the head of the country.

On 10 September, two days after Israeli prime minister Yitzhak Rabin proposed a "partial" withdrawal from the Golan Heights, al-Asad affirmed that his country was ready to accept "the objective imperatives of peace" in the Middle East, all the while reiterating his insistence on a total Israeli withdrawal from the Golan. The following October, he received a visit from American president Bill Clinton. Between 1995 and 1997, in an effort to consolidate the future power base for his son, al-Asad proceeded to make new appointments to various ministries. In April 1996, after Israel launched its operation "Grapes of Wrath," he became the principal interlocutor in the negotiations that resulted in a cease-fire between Hizbullah and Israel. On 3 June, he traveled to Egypt, where he met with President Mubarak, at the same time that the leader of Likud had come to power in Israel. On 3 August he received King Hussein of Jordan, making official the restart of Syrian-Jordanian relations that had been interrupted after the peace agreement was signed two years earlier between Jordan and Israel. On 31 July 1997, as regional tension ran high due to the stalling of the Israeli-Palestinian peace process, Hafiz al-Asad made an official visit to Tehran, for the purpose of reinforcing Iranian-Syrian cooperation.

On 8 February 1998, in the context of his succession, he signed a decree abolishing the office of vice president, which had been filled by Rif'at, thus eliminating the potential for a sudden change of regime. On 11 February 1999, as sole candidate to his own succession, he was reelected for a fifth seven-year term. On 5 July, he traveled to Moscow to negotiate new arms contracts for Syria with the Russian authorities. On 25 March 2000, he went to Geneva, where he met with President Clinton, with whom he discussed the Israeli-Arab peace process. On 10 June 2000, Hafiz al-Asad died following a reign of thirty years over an exceptionally stable but economically fragile Syria. On 11 July, Bashshar succeeded him as leader of the Syrian State.

SEE ALSO Alawite; Arab-Israel War (1967); Arab-Israel War (1973); Golan Heights; Grapes of Wrath Operation; Gulf War (1991); Hizbullah; Muslim Brotherhood; Rabin, Yitzhak; Sadat, Anwar al-; Tlas, Mustafa.

ASFUR, HASAN (1950–): Palestinian political figure. Hasan Asfur was born in 1950 at Khan Younis in the Gaza Strip. He studied agriculture in Baghdad, where he earned an engineering degree. Later he went to Moscow to study Marxist philosophy. After the Arab-Israel War of 1967 ("Six-Day War"), he took refuge in Jordan, where he joined the Palestinian Communist Party. In 1979 he rejoined the ranks of the Palestinian resistance in Lebanon and became a member of al-Fatah. Forced to leave by the Israeli invasion of June 1982, he took refuge in Syria for two years. In 1984 Asfur became a member of the Palestinian leadership, headquartered in Tunis, where he was associated with the economic section of the Palestine Liberation Organization (PLO), directed by Ahmad Qurai (Abu Ala). A few years later Asfur was part of the group responsible for negotiations with Israel and participated, alongside Mahmud Abbas, in the secret Palestinian-Israeli negotiations in Oslo, which led to the Israeli-Palestinian agreements signed on 13 September 1993, in Washington, D.C. In June 1994 he was expelled from the Central Committee of the Palestinian People's Party (PPP), after having been named as head of the department responsible for negotiations with Israel. On 1 July of that year, in the framework of the application of autonomy in Palestinian territories, Asfur left Tunis for Gaza, where he became part of Yasir Arafat's entourage. In August 1998 he was named minister without portfolio of the Palestinian Authority (PA), responsible for relations with nongovernmental organizations (NGOs), and in July 1999 minister for NGO Affairs. This position was eliminated in June 2002 when the cabinet was reorganized, but Asfur remained as the head of the PA Commission on NGO Affairs.

SEE ALSO Abbas, Mahmud Rida; Fatah, al-; Palestine Liberation Organization; Palestinian Authority; Qurai, Ahmad Sulayman.

ASHKENAZI: Name used in the Bible to designate Noah's great grandson, and subsequently, in Talmudic writings, Germania, or more exactly, Lotharingia (modern Lorraine). By extension, this term designates a Jew from a European country, principally central Europe.

First inhabiting Flanders and the Rhine Valley, the Ashkenazi Jews emigrated progressively toward eastern Europe, in particular toward Poland. The difference between Ashkenazim and Sephardim, other than their geographic origin, is based mainly on their pronunciation of Hebrew, on their utilization of different forms of a separate language, Yiddish, and in their liturgical rituals and songs. In most countries where there is a Jewish community, there are Ashkenazi synagogues and Sephardic synagogues. The Ashkenazim have become the dominant ethno-cultural group of modern Judaism, and it is they who have propagated the ideals of Zionism. The first waves of immigration into Palestine were comprised mainly of Ashkenazim. One of the main causes for dissension among Israelis is the opposition that exists between Ashkenazim and Sephardim, the latter reproaching the former their control of the country.

SEE ALSO Sephardim.

ASHRAWI, HANAN DAOUDA (1949–): Palestinian academic and political figure. Hanan Ashrawi was born in 1949 in Ramallah. After studying at the American University in Beirut and completing a Ph.D. in the United States, she became a professor of English literature and dean of the Faculty of Letters of Birzeit University (West Bank). In 1970 she founded a support group for Palestinians faced with difficulties with the Israeli administration. Her name became widely known in April 1988, after she participated in a televised debate on the situation in the occupied territories. Because of her opinions and her supposed affiliation with al-Fatah, Ashrawi was questioned several times by Israeli authorities. On 8 May 1991,

Hanan Daouda Ashrawi. The Palestinian activist, who was first elected to the Palestinian Legislative Council in 1996, has spoken out widely on human rights, education, and other issues as they affect Palestinians. *(AP/Wide World Photos)*

she and Faysal al-Husayni met with Douglas Hurd, British secretary of the Foreign Office. The following September she became spokesperson of the Palestinian delegation to the peace process, specifically in charge of relations with Israel. In this capacity, she participated in the Middle East Peace Conference in Madrid, and in the negotiations that followed. On 8 August 1993, along with Faysal al-Husayni and Saib Erekat—who were also opposed to Yasir Arafat's strategy—she threatened to quit her position on the Palestinian delegation. In September, after the signing of the Israeli-Palestinian Declaration of Principles (DOP), she carried out her threat and pledged to devote herself to the defense of human rights in the Palestinian territories.

In May 1994 Ashrawi declined Arafat's offer to join the Palestinian Authority (PA). The following month she founded the Palestinian Independent Commission for Citizens' Rights (PICCR). On 20 January 1996, with the first universal-suffrage Palestinian elections in the autonomous territories, she won a seat as Jerusalem representative on the new Palestinian Legislative Council, where she became president of the Political Committee. The following June, she accepted the portfolio of higher education on the PA. That October, she petitioned European countries to assume a more active role in the peace process in the Middle East. In February 1997, United Nations Educational, Scientific and Cultural Organization (UNESCO) awarded her the Palestine-Hamshari Prize for her book *Palestine Israel: Peace Seen from Inside.* On 6 August 1998, after being named minister of tourism and archeology despite her wish to keep the portfolio of higher education, she quit the PA. Before resigning, she presided over the Bethlehem 2000 Committee.

In 1999, after having retaken her seat on the Palestinian Legislative Council, she started a campaign for "institutional, structural, and political" reform. In parallel, she created a platform designed to promote dialogue between Palestinians and the international community (MIFTAH, the Palestinian Initiative for the Promotion of Global Dialogue and Democracy). In July 2001, at the request of Amr Musa, the secretary general of the League of Arab States, Ashwari accepted the post of information counselor to the organization, one of the new positions created by the League to be held by influential Arab figures.

SEE ALSO Erekat, Saib Muhammad; Husayni, Faysal al-; League of Arab States; Palestinian Authority.

ASHURA: Muslim holiday celebrating the tenth day of the Islamic year (the tenth of Moharram) to commemorate the death of Husayn, grandson of Prophet Muhammad. On this occasion the Shiʿa devote themselves to acts of repentance, while the Sunnis celebrate this anniversary with joy, because for the latter this festival coincides with the meeting of Adam and Eve and the end of the Deluge. At the time of the beginning of Islam, this day was marked by a fast, inspired by Jewish traditions.

SEE ALSO Shiʿite; Sunni Islam.

ASIFA, AL- ("The Storm"): The military branch of al-Fatah.

SEE ALSO Fatah, al-.

ASKIN, AVIGDOR

SEE Kach Party.

ASLAN, ALI SHAKER (1936–): Syrian Alawite, born in 1936 in the Ladhiqiyah region. Ali Aslan chose a military career when he was twenty years old. Trained at the Military Academy of Homs (Syria), he

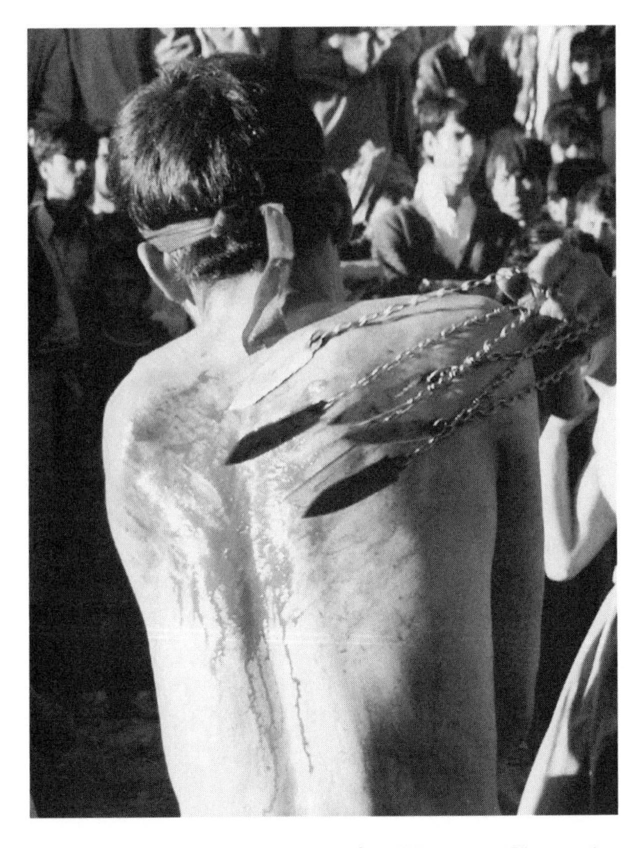

Self-Flagellation Ritual. A Shi'ite Muslim in Kabul, Afghanistan, whips his back with knives attached to chains as an act of repentance on the holiest day for Shi'ites, Ashura, the anniversary of the death of Husayn, grandson of the Prophet Muhammad. *(AP/Wide World Photos)*

studied also in the Soviet Union. In October 1966, he was appointed commander of the Syrian Infantry Eighth Brigade. In November 1970, he supported the military coup that brought Hafiz al-Asad to power in Syria. In 1973, he was designated leader of the First and Fifth Divisions. Two years later, he became chief of the "operations" bureau of the Syrian Army General Staff.

From 1976 to 1979, he was in charge of the Syrian contingent based in Lebanon, supervising the "hundred days war" against the Christian militia of Bashir Jumayyil. Aslan was one of the principal Syrian interlocutors with the Soviet defense minister. In July 1984, promoted to lieutenant general, he was appointed commander of the Army Second Corps. In 1989 he was named assistant chief of staff of the Syrian Army. After he assumed this post, he was considered the true "operational boss" of the Syrian Army. In July 1998, he became army chief of staff, replacing General Hikmat al-Shihabi, who retired after twenty-four years in this position. A member of the Central Committee of the Ba'th Party, with a reputation for intelligence, Ali Aslan was a powerful member of the Ba'th "old guard" and a member of the inner circle of President Hafiz al-Asad. After al-Asad's death in June 2000, Aslan was retained in his post by al-Asad's son and successor, Bashshar al-Asad. In January 2002, he was retired as part of the younger Asad's program of reform.

SEE ALSO Asad, Bashshar al-; Asad, Hafiz al-; Ba'th; Jumayyil, Bashir; Shihabi, Hikmat al-.

Assassins: Possibly from the Arabic *hashshasheen,* designating a smoker of hemp (*hashish,* in Arabic). This name was given in the Middle Ages by the European Crusaders to adepts of the Nizari branch of the Isma'ili sect settled in the Syrian mountains. The members of this Shi'ite sect swore absolute obedience to their leader, Rashid al-Din Sinan, called "The Old Man of the Mountain," who led a revolt against Seljuk power in 1090. This secret society, created by Hasan al-Sabah, included a special group composed of *fida'i,* who are alleged to have used hashish as a stimulant during incantatory rituals or for the accomplishment of dangerous missions.

SEE ALSO Ismaili; Seljuks.

Assefat ha-Nivhrarim

SEE Va'ad Leu'mi.

Association for Islamic Liberation

SEE Islamic Liberation Organization.

Association of Forty: Civic association, founded in 1988, that represents "unrecognized" Palestinian villages in Israel. Unrecognized villages are those the Israeli government does not recognize as legal, even though most of them existed before the establishment of the State of Israel. The government refers to them as "scattered settlements." They lack all basic services and infrastructure, including access roads, water, sewage, electricity, schools, and municipal services. The government has classified them all as "agricultural land"; it has no development planned for them and all construction is illegal. When the inhabitants (who are all Israeli citizens) have attempted to create infrastructure or services for themselves, the government has responded with demolitions and evacuation orders; the residents are considered to have "stolen land from the state." A 1988 survey found 32 unrecognized villages in the north and 117 in the south, largely in the Negev, with a total population of about 75,000. The Association of Forty, founded by a group of residents of the villages (and a number of their Jewish Israeli neighbors), attempts to achieve recognition of these places, to promote the provision of basic services, and to claim full citizenship rights for their inhabitants. They do this through providing legal services, through parliamentary lobbying, and through organizing activities to protest government land confiscations. The association has also helped initiate and plan projects to pave roads and connect villages to water, electricity, and telephone networks, and it has established health clinics and kindergartens. It attempts to publicize the problem of the unrecognized villages through exhibitions and local and international conferences. The association publishes a monthly newspaper, *Sawt al-Qura* (Voice of the villages). The association is a member of al-Ittijah and has worked with other non-governmental organizations. The association maintains a web site at www.assoc40.0rg.

SEE ALSO Ittijah.

ASSYRIANS: Name of an ancient Mesopotamian civilization (1800–600 B.C.E.), also attributed in the nineteenth century to Nestorian Christians living notably in Iraq and Turkey and having Aramaic as their native and liturgical language. Having been subjected to the same genocidal policies as the Armenians at the end of the Ottoman Empire, numbers of them fled to Lebanon, Syria, and Palestine, particularly Jerusalem. The Assyrians in Jerusalem (*Syriani,* in Arabic) have their own church and have enjoyed a long-standing community there.

ATERET COHANIM ("Priests' Crowns," in Hebrew): Israeli association (as well as a yeshiva) created in 1978, politically close to the far right, that upholds the Jewishness of the Arab section of Jerusalem. It is supported by the American association Hashavat Yerushalaim. Since the end of the 1980s, Ateret Cohanim has been buying up numerous buildings in this part of the city, through financing provided by the American billionaire Irving Moskowitz. The association also promotes the project of reconstruction of Solomon's Temple on Haram al-Sharif, which would involve destroying the mosques that are there.

SEE ALSO Haram al-Sharif; Jerusalem.

ATID ("future," in Hebrew): Israeli political organization whose creation was announced on 28 November 1997 by several Likud members who were opposed to the policies of then-prime minister and leader of the party, Benjamin Netanyahu. Officially formed on 11 January 1998, its major leader has been Roni Milo, flanked officially by Beni Begin, Limor Livnat, Dan Meridor, Ron Peer, and Ehud Olmert. The organization's ambition was to become a centrist party. The announcement in December 1998 of early general elections did not allow this project to be realized, since some of its members chose to join the ranks of the new Center Party or to create their own.

SEE ALSO Center Party; Likud; Netanyahu, Benjamin.

AUDEH, MUHAMMAD DAOUD

SEE Odeh, Muhammad.

AV: Eleventh month of the Hebrew calendar, corresponding to the period between the end of July and the beginning of August. The destruction of the Temple of Solomon is commemorated on the ninth of Av (*Tish'a b-Av*).

SEE ALSO Hebrew Calendar.

AVANT-GARDE OF THE PEOPLE'S WAR OF LIBERATION

SEE Saʿiqa, al-.

AVANT-GARDE ORGANIZATION OF POPULAR WAR OF LIBERATION

SEE Saʿiqa, al-.

AVANT-GARDES OF THE CONQUEST

SEE Egyptian Islamic Jihad.

AVNERY, URI (1923–): Israeli writer, politician, and peace activist. Born in 1923 as Helmut Ostermann in Beckum, Germany, Avnery immigrated to Mandatory Palestine when he was ten years old. He joined the Irgun Zvaʾi Le'umi in 1938 but left several years later, opposing its anti-Arab ideology. He fought in the Arab-Israel War of 1948, and later wrote two successful books that were critical of the war. Avnery owned and edited the controversial magazine *ha-Olam ha-Zeh.* In 1965 he established a political party named after the magazine, winning two seats in the Knesset. He served in the Knesset for ten successive years, except for one term.

Following the Arab-Israel War of 1967, Avnery became a prominent leader of the peace movement. He has advocated recognition of the Palestine Liberation Organization (PLO) and the creation of a Palestinian state in the territories occupied by Israel in 1967. In defiance of Israel's ban, he met with PLO representatives (with Sa'id Hamami in London, then Issam Sartawi in Paris) and then with Yasir Arafat. After the Oslo Accords (1993), Avnery founded Gush Shalom (Bloc for Peace). The group campaigns for Israeli withdrawal from the occupied territories, dismantling of Jewish settlements there, and the creation of "two states for two nations." Avnery writes a newspaper column and maintains a web site called "Avnery News."

SEE ALSO Oslo Accords; Sartawi, Issam.

AVODA ZARA ("idolatry," in Hebrew): Idolatry is considered one of the most serious sins in Jewish religious law.

AWDAH, AL- (Arabic, "return"): A term often used by Palestinians as a sign of defiance and hope. There is an al-Awdah mosque in the refugee camp at Rafah, and an al-Awdah hospital in the refugee camp at Jabaliya, both in the Gaza Strip. In January 1992, during the first Intifada, more than 400 alleged sympathizers of HAMAS were expelled by Israel from the occupied territories to the no-man's land beyond the Lebanese border. The Israelis assumed they would proceed into Lebanon and exile, but instead they set up a camp in full view of the world's media and stayed there for months. They named their camp "al-Awdah." A U.S.-based activist group that advocates for Palestinian rights is called Al-Awda: The Palestine Right to Return Coalition.

SEE ALSO HAMAS; Intifada (1987–1993).

AWDAH, AL- (The return): Palestinian weekly magazine, published in East Jerusalem, started in 1982, politically close to the PLO. Run by Raymonda Tawil, who has also headed the Palestinian Press Agency (PPA) and whose daughter, Suha, is married to Yasir Arafat, this newspaper has been the object of much censure by the Israeli authorities.

SEE ALSO Arafat, Yasir; Palestine Liberation Organization; Tawil, Raymonda Hawa.

AWILIYA: Plural of the Arabic word *wali,* which means "friend, dear one." As a Wali Allah, someone is a companion of God. The term has come to designate a saint or holy man. The large number of tombs of *awliya* in Palestine (e.g., Nabi Rubin) have become an important part of folk religion.

AYAT (*Aya,* "divine sign," in Arabic): The verses of the Qur'an.

AYATOLLAH ("designated by God," in Arabic): Highest rank in the Shi'ite hierarchy, which itself is commanded by the Great Ayatollah (*Ayatollah Uzma*).

AYN EL-HILWAH (Ein el-Helweh): A camp for Palestinian refugees in South Lebanon, located 3 kilometers east of the coastal city of Sidon (Sayda). Set up in 1949 by the International Red Cross following the first Palestinian exodus, it became one of the largest and most populated of the Palestinian camps. Until 1952, housing was in tents; then, fabric was replaced with concrete buildings, transforming the camp into a true city. From 1970 on, Ayn el-Hilwah has been one of the most important bastions of Palestinian resistance in Lebanon, and diverse organizations rub shoulders there, some of which are opposed to the peace process. Camp security is the responsibility of Palestinian groups themselves.

SEE ALSO South Lebanon.

AYN JALUT: Locality near contemporary Nazareth where, in September 1260, a battle took place that allowed the Mamluks of Egypt to repulse a Mongol army.

SEE ALSO Mamluks.

AYYAM, AL- (The days): Palestinian daily newspaper, published in Ramallah, considered the mouthpiece of the Palestinian Authority.

SEE ALSO Palestinian Authority.

AZHAR, AL- ("The Brilliant" or "Resplendent," in Arabic): This name is given to the Great Mosque, opened in Cairo in 972, which has since become one of the most important centers of Islamic teaching. In 988 a college was started there to propagate the faith among the Egyptian population. In 1005, the teaching program expanded to include philosophy, astronomy, and chemistry, which enhanced its reputation. In the twelfth century the Mamluks came to power in Egypt and created a university at the mosque for the purpose of training ulema. Al-Azhar served as the main college for religious education among Palestinians, particularly in the nineteenth and twentieth centuries. In 1961, President Gamal Abdel Nasser transformed the religious college into a multidisciplinary university. Directed by the Great Imam Muhammad Sayed Tantaoui in 2004, Al-

Azhar Mosque is the home of a university with fifty-two schools that welcome almost 140,000 students.

SEE ALSO Mamluks.

AZYME Unleavened bread (*matzah*): Used in the Jewish diet.

B

Baal (Semitic, *ba'al*; "master, lord"): Main Canaanite divinity, whose cult is that of fertility, similar to the goddess Astarte (Ashtart, Asherah, Tanit), thought of as the wife of Baal and called also Baalat. Mountain, storm, and rain god for the Phoenicians, Baal represented a great danger for the Israelite head priests and their religion because many of their coreligionists were drawn to his cult. For example, Jews worshipped (especially at Sichem) another Canaanite divinity, Baal Berith (in Hebrew, "master of the covenant"), who presided over compacts between families and individuals. Between 860 and 853 B.C.E., the king of Israel, Ahab, and his wife Jezebel worshipped the god Baal. The main center of the Baal cult was in the Lebanese city of Baalbek. The term *baal* is used in the Bible to designate false gods.

Bab: Arab word meaning "door." In early Shi῾ism this name was given to the highest ranked of the disciples of an Imam.

SEE ALSO Imam.

Babism

SEE Baha᾿i.

Badr Operation: Military operation launched on 6 October 1973 by Egypt and Syria against Israel.

SEE ALSO Arab-Israel War (1973).

Baghdad Pact: A U.S.-sponsored Cold War cooperation accord, the Baghdad Pact was signed on 4 February 1955 at Baghdad between Iraq and Turkey, later joined by other states, such as Great Britain, on 4 April; Pakistan, on 1 July; and Iran, on 23 October. The resulting security organization, officially instituted 15 April 1955, was called the Middle East Treaty Organization (METO). The Baghdad Pact was preceded by the Middle East Defense Organization (MEDO), created in 1950 as the "supreme allied command in the Middle East" and comprising the United States, Great Britain, France, and Turkey. This organization eventually failed because of the refusal of Egypt to join. MEDO was headquartered in the Suez Canal Zone, then controlled by Britain; later, President Gamal Abdel Nasser was determined to keep Egypt nonaligned in the Cold War. A U.S.-Pakistani defense accord had been signed in May 1950, and Turkey had joined the North Atlantic Treaty Organization (NATO) in May 1951. After the disintegration of MEDO, the United States turned toward Iraq and Turkey, but was unable to obtain the adhesion of Syria, Lebanon, or Jordan. A bilateral accord was signed on 2 April 1954 between Turkey and Pakistan, and the Baghdad Pact followed the next year.

On 16 April 1955 the Soviet Union published a communiqué denouncing the Baghdad Pact, which it deemed "aggressive." On 27 September, the Soviet Union, with Czechoslovakia as intermediary, decid-

BAAL WITH A LANCE. THE IMAGE REPRESENTS THE PRIMARY CANAANITE DIVINITY; HIS FERTILITY CULT ATTRACTED MANY ANCIENT ISRAELITES, INCLUDING KING AHAB AND HIS WIFE JEZEBEL. *(© Gianni Dagli Orti/Corbis)*

ed to deliver Soviet armament to Egypt. On 11 February 1957, the Soviet Union shocked the United Nations General Assembly by insisting on a debate on the "danger to peace posed by the U.S. initiative in its foreign policy in the Middle East." On 7 March, the U.S. Congress gave President Dwight D. Eisenhower the right to "use the armed forces" on behalf of any Middle East nation which "asked for help against armed aggression from a country controlled by international Communism." On 19 June, meeting in Ankara, the Iraqi, Iranian, and Turkish prime ministers agreed on a statement that "the policy of President Eisenhower towards the Middle East comports a recognition of the danger posed by Communist aggression and subversion in the area." On 14 July 1958, a coup d'état having overthrown the Iraqi monarchy, the previous accords were rejected by the new government. On 21 August, the United Nations General Assembly, acting on a proposal of countries belonging to the Arab League, passed a resolution stating that the Middle East should not become part of the quarrel between the United States and the Soviet Union. In March 1959 Iraq formally withdrew from the Baghdad Pact; METO was formally replaced on 19 August 1959 by the Central Treaty Organization (CENTO). Iran repudiated CENTO after the Islamic Revolution, withdrawing in March 1979; Pakistan also withdrew, and the organization was dissolved in September of that year.

SEE ALSO Middle East Defense Organization.

BAGOT, JOHN

SEE Glubb, John Bagot.

BAHA'I: Muslim sect, originated in the nineteenth century from a scission that appeared in Twelver Islam, whose credo it is that all religions come from the same divine source. In 1844, in Persia, Mirza Ali Muhammad (called el-Bab), who represented himself as "the door" (*bab*, in Arabic) of divine truth, was recognized by his followers as the Mahdi (Messiah). He was executed by the Persian authorities in 1850, but one of his disciples, Mirza Hosayn Ali Nuri (*Baha'ullah*), took up his message in *The Very Holy Book* (*Kitab-I-Aqdas*). In the letters of invitation that he sent to the principal leaders of European states, Nuri invited them to join with him to "establish universal religion and peace." Later, expelled from Persia, Mirza Hosayn Ali Nuri took refuge in Acre (Palestine), where he died on 29 May 1892. His son, Abdu'l-Baha (Abbas Efendi), succeeded him as the head of the movement until his death in 1921. Baha'ism venerates all the prophets of the great religions and preaches a syncretic religion, which has spread widely, especially to the United States and India. The Baha'i religion enjoys a presence in Israel and its world headquarters is in Haifa, where its founder is buried. The Baha'i calendar is based on the solar year and includes nineteen months of nineteen days each. The Baha'i celebrate their new year (*Nowrouz*) on 21 March.

SEE ALSO Mahdi; Messiah.

BAHURIM: Hebrew term meaning "Yeshiva students."

SEE ALSO Yeshiva.

BAKER PLAN: A five-point plan, presented in November 1989 by U.S. secretary of state James Baker, in an attempt to facilitate an Israeli-Palestinian dialogue. In September, Egypt and Israel had discussed several

JAMES BAKER. THE U.S. SECRETARY OF STATE UNDER THE FIRST PRESIDENT BUSH PROPOSED A FIVE-POINT PLAN IN 1989 FOR DIALOGUE BETWEEN ISRAELI AND PALESTINIAN DELEGATIONS, BUT THE NEW ISRAELI GOVERNMENT OF PRIME MINISTER YITZHAK SHAMIR REJECTED THE INITIATIVE IN MID-1990. *(© Dick Moreno/Corbis)*

peace proposals that foundered over the issue of participation by the Palestine Liberation Organization. Baker's five-point plan proposed that an Israeli delegation conduct a dialogue with a Palestinian delegation in Cairo; that Egypt consult with the Palestinians on all aspects of the dialogue; that Israel attend the dialogue only after a satisfactory list of Palestinians had been established; that Israel's participation would be based on its 14 May initiative regarding elections and negotiations concerning the West Bank and Gaza; and that the foreign ministers of Israel, Egypt, and the United States meet to facilitate the process. Israel's National Unity government fell in March 1990 in a vote of no confidence precipitated by disagreement over the Baker initiative. In June 1990, Prime Minister Yitzhak Shamir formed a new government, which rejected the Baker Plan.

SEE ALSO Gaza Strip; West Bank.

BALAD

SEE Democratic National Alliance.

BALFOUR, ARTHUR JAMES (1848–1930): British political figure, born in Scotland. Elected as a Conservative deputy in 1874, his political beginnings were facilitated by family connections with Lord Salisbury, who entrusted him with the office for Ireland from 1887 to 1892. Leader of the Conservatives in the House of Commons, he was prime minister between 1902 and 1905. In 1917 he was named foreign minister. On 2 November of the same year he wrote a letter to Lord Lionel Walter Rothschild, representing the Jewish Community of Great Britain, in which he proposed the creation of a Jewish national homeland in Palestine, in the name of His Majesty's government.

BALFOUR DECLARATION: A letter dated 2 November 1917, the Balfour Declaration was sent by Lord Ar-

ARTHUR JAMES BALFOUR. IN 1917, THE BRITISH FOREIGN SECRETARY WROTE A HISTORIC LETTER—SUBSEQUENTLY KNOWN AS THE BALFOUR DECLARATION—EXPRESSING HIS GOVERNMENT'S SUPPORT FOR THE CREATION OF A JEWISH NATIONAL HOMELAND IN PALESTINE (WHICH BECAME A BRITISH MANDATE AFTER WORLD WAR I).

thur Balfour, British minister of foreign affairs, to Lord Lionel Walter Rothschild, a Zionist philanthropist and one of the drafters of the declaration, following its revision and approval by the British war cabinet. It stated: "It is my great pleasure to express to you, on behalf of His Majesty's Government, the following declaration of sympathy for the Jewish Zionists' aspirations, which has been submitted to and approved by the Cabinet—'His Majesty's Government looks favorably on the establishment in Palestine of a national homeland for the Jewish people, and will apply all its efforts towards facilitating the realization of this objective, with it being clearly understood that nothing should be done that will prejudice either the civil and religious rights of non-Jewish communities existing in Palestine, or the rights and political status that Jews are accorded in other countries.'—I would be thankful to you for bringing this declaration to the attention of the Zionist Federation."

The Balfour Declaration was motivated by a number of factors. The British cabinet hoped to win the support of British and American Jews, thereby gaining Jewish money for Britain's war effort and benefiting from Jewish pressure on the United States to enter the war. In addition, Liberals like Balfour believed that the West had allowed historical injustices against the Jews and should now assist them, and prominent Jewish intellectuals in Britain were advocating for a Jewish State. The Balfour policy had long-term consequences, particularly for the Palestinians, who in 1917 formed 90 percent of the population but were mentioned only as "non-Jewish communities" in the declaration. British political support allowed the rapid growth of Jewish immigration to Palestine (from a Jewish population of 50,000 in 1917 to over 600,000 in 1947) and ultimately paved the way for the establishment of the State of Israel in 1948 and the departure of about 726,000 Palestinians.

SEE ALSO Balfour, Arthur James; British Mandate; Diaspora.

BANDUNG CONFERENCE: Afro-Asiatic conference of nonaligned countries that took place in Bandung (Indonesia) between 17 and 24 April 1955. This conference marked the political birth of the Third World. Point number two of the final communiqué, affirming the right of people to decide for themselves, treated the Palestinian question in the following terms: "Considering the tension existing in the Middle East, tension that has been caused by the situation in Palestine, and considering the danger this tension constitutes for world peace, the Asiatic and African Conference declares its support for the rights of the Arab people of Palestine and demands the application of the United Nations resolutions on Palestine and the realization of a peaceful solution to the Palestinian problem."

BANNA, HASSAN AL- (1906–1949): Egyptian activist, born in 1906 near Alexandria, and founder of the Muslim Brotherhood (Society of Muslim Brothers), he entered a mystic brotherhood at the age of thirteen. In 1922, when Egypt had just obtained a limited independence from England, he matriculated at a school for primary teachers. In September 1927 he became an instructor at a primary school in Ismailia, the home of the Suez Canal Company and a town with many foreign residents. He spoke publicly against foreign, liberal ways and in March 1928 he started the first chapter of the Society of Muslim Brothers, which advocated establishing a religious state in Egypt. Twenty years later he was supervising some 2,000 chapters of this fraternity all over Egypt, and the distribution of the society's publication all over the Islamic world. After World War II the society established a militia, which participated in the Arab-Israel War of 1948–1949, and committed a number of assassinations and other acts of violence against the Egyptian government. The government banned the Brotherhood in December 1948; the society assassinated the minister who had banned it. Hasan al-Banna was killed by the police a few weeks later, on 12 February 1949.

SEE ALSO Arab-Israel War (1948); Muslim Brotherhood.

BANNA, SABRI AL- (Abu Nidal; 1939–2002?): Terrorist, born in Palestine. Sabri al-Banna came from a wealthy Jaffa family that, in 1948, at the time of the first Israeli-Arab conflict, sought refuge in the Gaza Strip and later went to Nablus in the West Bank. In 1955, he went to Egypt to study to be a technician but never completed his secondary education. He joined the Baʿth Party in Jordan in the mid-1950s and later worked in Saudi Arabia but was expelled in 1967. After the Arab defeat in the Arab-Israel War of June 1967, he joined Yasir Arafat's al-Fatah, where he was associated with the security services, directed by Salah Khalaf.

ABU NIDAL. UNDER THIS NOM DE GUERRE, THE FOUNDER OF A BREAKAWAY ORGANIZATION DEDICATED TO VIOLENT ACTION CARRIED OUT MASS MURDERS, ASSASSINATIONS, AND OTHER TERRORIST ACTS AGAINST ISRAEL AND ITS PERCEIVED SUPPORTERS IN MANY PARTS OF EUROPE AND THE MIDDLE EAST, ESPECIALLY DURING THE 1980S. HE LATER DIED IN IRAQ UNDER QUESTIONABLE CIRCUMSTANCES. *(© Reuters NewMedia Inc./Corbis)*

In 1970, after a stay in Khartoum, Sudan, he became al-Fatah representative in Iraq. In 1974, after the Arab defeat in the Arab-Israel War of 1973, he opposed the "realist" policy of the Palestine Liberation Organization (PLO) and was expelled from Fatah. With the help of Iraq (for whose intelligence service he had been working), he created his own movement. At first called Political Committee for the Palestinian Revolution, this group took the name of Fatah Revolutionary Council (Fatah RC). Supported by Baghdad, the Fatah RC worked for the Iraqi Baʿthists in their feud with the Syrian Baʿthists. It also advocated extreme escalation in the struggle against Israel, and by November had begun carrying out a significant number of attacks directed against Israelis and Westerners as well as against Palestinians it considered too moderate. In claiming credit for these actions, the movement used sometimes the names Black June or Arab Revolutionary Brigades.

Between 1982 and 1987, Abu Nidal organized many terrorist actions, including assassinations and some spectacular mass murders in Paris, Rome, Madrid, Vienna, Istanbul, and elsewhere. In 1982, the attempted assassination of the Israeli ambassador in London became the pretext for Israel's invasion of Lebanon that year (the Israelis publicly blamed the PLO). In 1983, Baghdad, needing American help in fighting the Iran-Iraq War, officially withdrew its support and asked Abu Nidal to leave the country. He went to Syria, which used him to apply pressure on Jordan to keep it from helping the PLO open a dialogue with the United States and Israel. In 1985, with the support of Libya, he tried but failed to forge an alliance with the Fatah-Intifada that would have constituted an opposition front capable of competing with the Fatah of Yasir Arafat.

Syria expelled Abu Nidal in 1986, after which he was received by Colonel Qaddafi in Libya. In 1988, after the Iran-Iraq War, he returned to Baghdad, all the while maintaining a strategic base in Libya. In the summer of 1989, relations with the PLO broke down irremediably, leading to a wave of assassinations involving his associates and those of Yasir Arafat. In

1990, some members of his movement contested his authority and created a faction called Fatah Revolutionary Council–Emergency Command. There followed a succession of internal executions. In January 1991, obliged once more to leave Iraq, Abu Nidal moved to Lebanon, then to Libya. Rejecting the Israeli-Arab peace process delineated by the Madrid Conference of 1991 (without proposing any alternative), Abu Nidal found himself isolated within the Palestinian resistance. In July 1998, weakened by illness and by the maneuvering of his entourage, which aimed at taking over his movement, he left Libya to seek medical care in Egypt. In 1999, Abu Nidal returned to Baghdad. He is reported to have died in August 2002, either a suicide (officially) or at the hands of the Iraqi security services.

SEE ALSO Arab-Israel War (1967); Arab-Israel War (1973); Baʿth; Fatah, al-; Fatah-Intifada; Fatah Revolutionary Council; Fatah Revolutionary Council–Emergency Command; Gaza Strip; Iran Iraq War; Khalaf, Salah; Palestine Liberation Organization.

BAQDASH, KHALID (1912–): Syrian political figure, born to a Kurdish family in Damascus. Khalid Baqdash joined the National Bloc, the main Syrian nationalist organization, in 1929. Later he became a member of the Syrian-Lebanese Communist Party, climbing rapidly to a position of leadership. Having been arrested a number of times by the French authorities, who had a mandate over Syria, Baqdash left Syria for the Soviet Union, where he enrolled in a school that trained party cadres. In 1935, he led the delegation of the Syrian-Lebanese Communist Party to the Seventh Comintern Congress, in Moscow. The following year, the victory of the Popular Front in France allowed him to return to Syria and play an important role in political life there. In 1937, he became secretary general of the Syrian-Lebanese Communist Party, replacing Fu'ad Shemli. For two years the Communist Party expanded rapidly in Syria and Lebanon, until the fall of the Popular Front, which led to the interdiction of the party.

Baqdash reappeared on the political scene in 1941, with the arrival in Syria of the Free French Forces, whom he joined in the fight against fascism. Baqdash acquired international stature after the war. In 1948, he became the Cominform delegate for the Middle East while the Communist Party was banned again in post-independence Syria. The military regimes that followed each other in Damascus strengthened the position of the Syrian Communist Party. Baqdash won a seat in the 1954 elections, thereby becoming Syria's first Communist representative. He quickly became one of his country's principal political figures. In 1958, after the creation of the Syrian-Egyptian union, he strongly opposed "the Nasserian protection." A ban on political parties forced him to leave Syria for an exile of eight years in the Soviet Union, Czechoslovakia, and Bulgaria. The strengthening of the left wing of the Baʿth Party, which had come to power in 1966, allowed him to return to Syria once more, where from then on he played only a secondary role while supporting the regime. In 1972, accused of having concentrated too much power in his hands, his became a minority voice in the political bureau, and two years later he was no longer part of the leadership of the Syrian Communist Party.

SEE ALSO Baʿth; Syria.

BAR: Aramaic word meaning "son of."

SEE ALSO Ibn.

BARAK, EHUD (1942–): Israeli military and political figure; prime minister of Israel (1999–2001). Born Ehud Brog in 1942 in Mandatory Palestine, Barak grew up in Kibbutz Mishmar Ha-Sharon and entered the Israeli Army in 1959. Awarded lieutenant's stripes in 1962, he went on to take commando training in France in 1964. Barak participated in the Arab-Israel War of June 1967 in an armored intelligence unit. Between 1970 and 1973 he commanded the Sayeret Matkal, a unit within the General Staff responsible for special operations. In that capacity, he commanded the neutralizing, on 8 May 1972, of a Palestinian commando unit that had taken over a Sabena airplane and its passengers at Tel Aviv airport. Other members of his group were Benjamin Netanyahu, future prime minister, and Dani Yatom, future head of Mossad.

On the night of 9–10 April 1973, in Beirut, Barak participated in the "Springtime of the Young" operation, conducted in collaboration with Amnon Lipkin-Shahak, whose objective was the elimination of Yasir Arafat, the head of the Palestine Liberation Organization (PLO). Arafat was absent from his supposed location, but three important Palestinian leaders were killed instead. The following July, Barak joined the General Staff of the Israel Defense Force (IDF). He participated in the Arab-Israel War of 1973 at the head of a tank battalion. In October 1974, he joined Aman as deputy-director of military intelligence. In this capacity he participated, in July 1976, in the operation against the terrorists who had hijacked an Air France airliner to Entebbe, Uganda.

EHUD BARAK. AFTER THREE DECADES IN THE ISRAELI MILITARY, INCLUDING COUNTERTERRORISM OPERATIONS AND HIGH-LEVEL PLANNING, BARAK SHIFTED TO POLITICS AND SERVED AS PRIME MINISTER FROM 1999 TO 2001. THE FAILURE OF THE ISRAELI-PALESTINIAN PEACE SUMMIT AT CAMP DAVID IN MID-2000, HOWEVER, SOON ENDED HIS POLITICAL CAREER. *(© Corbis Images)*

Promoted to general at the age of thirty-nine, Barak was appointed head of the planning department of the IDF General Staff in 1982. From April 1983 to September 1985, he headed Aman, where he was replaced, at the end of his command, by his friend Amnon Lipkin-Shahak. Between September 1985 and January 1987, Barak was in command of Israel's central military region. In February 1987, then-Defense Minister Yitzhak Rabin appointed Barak assistant to the army chief of staff, General Dan Shomron. As such, he was involved in the operation that led to the assassination in 1988 of Khalil al-Wazir (Abu Jihad), the second in command of the PLO. On 1 April 1991, Barak was named army chief of staff of the IDF. General Amnon Lipkin-Shahak became his deputy and then replaced him when, in January 1995, Barak resigned from the army to devote himself to politics.

On 16 July 1995, Barak joined the Labor Party; two days later, he was appointed minister of the interior in the government of Yitzhak Rabin. On 23 November 1995, after the assassination of the prime minister, he took over the post of foreign minister in the government of Shimon Peres, a position he retained until May 1996, when the Likud Party came to power. Barak won the leadership of the Labor Party, taking it away from his rival, Shimon Peres, on 3 June 1997. In his capacity as the new Labor Party leader, Barak affirmed that he supported the creation of a Palestinian state, on the condition that the latter be demilitarized and federated with Jordan. According to him, Israel's security did not depend only on its military strength, but also on its economy, prosperity, and national cohesion.

In January 1999, in preparation for early general elections scheduled to take place the following May, the Labor Party chose him as its candidate for the post of prime minister, against his adversary from Likud, Benjamin Netanyahu. Barak put together an electoral list called United Israel (Israel Ahat), with David Levy's Gesher Party and Rabbi Yehuda Amital's Meimad organization. On 17 May, Barak was elected prime minister with 56 percent of the votes cast, against 43 percent for Netanyahu. Barak paid homage to Yitzhak Rabin in his acceptance speech, and then went on to declare: "We expect peace to come not from weakness, but from strength and from a feeling of security; peace will not come at the cost of security, but it is peace that brings security." He promised also to come to a final agreement with the Palestinians, while conserving the unity of Jerusalem and keeping most of the Jewish settlements in the West Bank under Israeli sovereignty. On 6 July 1999, he introduced his government to the Knesset. A unity cabinet, it included 18 members from 8 different political parties. Barak won a vote of confidence with 75 deputies voting for, 29 against, 11 abstentions, and 5 absences. In his inaugural speech, he declared himself determined to take all possible steps to conclude a definitive Israeli-Arab peace, referring to United Nations Resolutions 242 and 338.

On his first official trip abroad, Barak met the principal participants in the peace process, including U.S. president Bill Clinton, Palestinian president Yasir Arafat, Egyptian president Hosni Mubarak, and King Abdullah II ibn Hussein of Jordan. While in Washington, Barak said that he expected to reach a definitive peace settlement with Israel's neighbors within fifteen months. On 5 September, at Sharm el-Sheikh, Egypt, Barak and Arafat signed an accord that was intended to open the way to negotiations on a definitive peace settlement between Palestinians and Israelis. During the ceremony, presided over by

Husni Mubarak, Barak again paid homage to former Israeli prime minister Rabin, and made an appeal to Syrian president Hafiz al-Asad to resume peace negotiations with Israel. On 15 December, Barak returned to Washington, where he met officially with Syrian foreign minister Faruq al-Shara to discuss the resumption of the Israeli-Syrian peace negotiations that had been frozen since the spring of 1996.

On 1 March 2000, Barak suffered his first political reversal when the Knesset adopted the draft of a law aimed at establishing a mandatory enlarged majority in any referendum on a peace agreement with Syria. In April of the same year, he informed the United Nations of Israel's intention to withdraw its troops from South Lebanon before 7 July. On 1 June, while he was attending a ceremony marking the conquest of the Arab part of Jerusalem by Israeli troops, he confirmed his determination to defend the unity of the Holy City, an "inseparable part of the sovereign territory of Israel." On 7 June, he suffered a repudiation by the Knesset, which agreed to hold early general elections, by a vote of 61 in favor and 48 against. Three of the six parties belonging to Barak's governing coalition voted with the opposition. A month later, as Barak was scheduled to leave for Camp David to participate in an Israeli-Palestinian peace summit, the political crisis intensified with the resignation of six of his ministers, who were opposed to the concessions he was about to make to the Palestinians. On 2 August, Foreign Minister David Levy also resigned, confirming the widespread disappointment at the failure of Camp David II to result in a political breakthrough. On 19 December, after having failed to convince Likud to participate in a government of "national emergency," Ehud Barak submitted his resignation to President Moshe Katsav. The February 2001 elections brought Likud leader Ariel Sharon to power. That same month, Barak announced his retirement from the political scene and his resignation from the leadership of the Labor Party. He began a business career, though his frequent commentary on political matters led some to speculate that he might eventually return to politics.

SEE ALSO Camp David II Summit; Labor Party; Likud; Resolution 242; Resolution 338.

BARAKA: Arabic word designating the attribute of holiness and power of benediction belonging to a saint or to a sheik of a fraternity, which is transmitted to his descendants in a chain of succession, *silsilat al-baraka*. The Muslim believer can obtain this attribute by visiting a holy place or a *maqam*. For Jews, *berakhah* is the generic name of all kinds of blessings, whether of human or divine origin.

BARGHUTHI, MARWAN (Barghouthi, Bargouti; 1959–): Palestinian political leader. Born in 1959 in Ramallah (West Bank), Marwan Barghuthi holds a degree in history and political science from Bir Zeit University. He joined al-Fatah at the beginning of the 1980s, along with others of the Palestinian student movement in the Occupied Territories. Barghuthi was arrested and imprisoned several times by Israeli authorities. A professor of history at Bir Zeit University, in the West Bank, he was one of the main leaders in the Ramallah region of the first Intifada, and he was expelled by Israeli authorities in September 1990. Having taken refuge in Jordan, he was very active in the Association of Palestinian Deportees, and he wrote articles for the local press. During his stay in Amman, he maintained some contacts with the local representatives of HAMAS, such as Muhammad Nazal and Ibrahim Ghoshe.

On 5 April 1994, Barghuthi was included in a group of fifty expelled Palestinians who were allowed to return to the Occupied Territories, and he regained his teaching position at Bir Zeit University. A month later, he was elected secretary general of al-Fatah for the West Bank and became an important link between Yasir Arafat and young Palestinians, who tended to be rather hostile to the conciliatory strategies they thought Arafat was advocating toward Israel. A few months later, Barghuthi joined the Revolutionary Council of al-Fatah. In February 1996, elected as representative of Ramallah, he became a member of the new Palestinian Legislative Council (PLC). Beginning at that time, he attempted to lead a "reformist" current within al-Fatah, thereby finding himself in opposition to Hussein al-Sheikh, who supported Arafat's policies. In October of the same year, Barghuthi was part of the PLC delegation received by the Knesset, on the invitation of the Israeli Communist Party, HADASH. In June 1999, displeased with the confrontations between young al-Fatah adherents and the Palestinian police, Arafat threatened to remove Barghuthi from his position in al-Fatah.

In October 2000, at the time of the Israeli-Palestinian clashes in the autonomous territories, Barghuthi appeared to be one of the principal catalysts of the revolt. The beginning of the al-Aqsa Intifada propelled him into the forefront, and he was regarded by the Israelis as the leader of the Tanzim, an armed group linked to al-Fatah. On 6 August 2001, while the growing number of Palestinian attacks resulted in some severe Israeli reprisal operations in the Palestinian territories, he made an appeal for the creation of a Palestinian government of national unity. On 23 September, the Israeli authorities put out an arrest warrant for Barghuthi, for "participation in terrorist activities." In 2002 he was arrested and in May 2004 was convicted in a public trial, whose authority over him he denied. Considered a reformer within al-Fatah, Barghuthi was a supporter of Mahmud Abbas (Abu Mazen).

Barghuthi is popular, especially since his widely admired defiance toward the Israelis during his trial, and has sometimes been mentioned as a possible successor to Arafat. This would be possible only if the Israelis could be convinced to release him, an improbable eventuality without conditions to which the Palestinians would be unlikely to agree.

SEE ALSO Abbas, Mahmud Rida; Aqsa Intifada, al-; Arafat, Yasir; Fatah, al-; Tanzim, al-.

BARGHUTHI, MUSTAFA (1954–): Palestinian physician and human rights activist. Mustafa Barghuthi, a medical doctor trained in Moscow, was for some years a member of the Palestinian People's Party and director of the Union of Palestinian Medical Relief Committees, which has provided health care for 100,000 Palestinians living in rural areas of the Occupied Territories. As of 2004, he is the director of the Health, Development, Information, and Policy Institute in Ramallah, an independent nongovernmental organization established in 1989 to improve the status of Palestinian health care through research, planning, and development. It has also become an advocacy organization for better public policy in regard to such groups as women, children, and the disabled. It provides information and training programs in health care, development policy, and system management. It also publishes the *Palestine Monitor,* an important source of news on political and human rights issues. Barghuthi was one of the principal promoters, with Haydar Abd al-Shafi and Ibrahim Dakkak, of the Palestinian National Initiative (al-Mubadara), an organization that seeks to mobilize Palestinian society for the formation of a "national emergency leadership," democratic elections at all levels, and institutional reform to achieve Palestinian national rights and a "durable, just peace."

SEE ALSO Abd al-Shafi, Haydar; Palestinian People's Party.

BAR-GIORA: Secret organization, constituted in 1907 in Jaffa, Palestine, by a group of Jewish immigrants originally from the Ukrainian city of Gomel. Its principal leaders were David Ben-Gurion and Izhak Ben-Zvi. After organizing a self-defense group, the leaders of Bar-Giora decided to form a veritable army, capable of defending the whole Jewish community in Palestine. This new organization took the name of Hashomer (the Guardian). Through it the leaders of Bar-Giora went on to inculcate a socialist ideology and a feeling of national pride in new immigrants. They called themselves Halutzim ("pioneers").

SEE ALSO Ben-Gurion, David.

BAR-ILAN UNIVERSITY: Orthodox university located in the suburbs of Tel Aviv. Founded in 1955, it was the first religious institution of higher learning established in Israel. In 2003 it had an enrollment of 32,000 students, including those studying at five regional colleges. The university offers undergraduate and graduate degrees in liberal arts, social sciences, and natural sciences. The curriculum includes required courses in religious studies. Yigal Amir, the zealot who assassinated Prime Minister Yitzhak Rabin in November 1995, was a law student there. For some time thereafter, the university wrestled with a tarnished international reputation as a place that fosters and encourages religious and political extremism.

SEE ALSO Rabin, Yitzhak.

BAR-LEV, HAIM (1924–1994): Israeli general and politician. Haim Bar-Lev was born in Vienna, grew up in Yugoslavia, and immigrated to Mandatory Palestine in 1939. He joined the Palmach (the first and elite military group within the Haganah) in 1942 and commanded a battalion in the Arab-Israel War of 1948. Bar-Lev remained in the army, commanding an armored brigade in the Arab-Israel War of 1956, and in 1957 becoming chief of the Armored Corps. After studying economics and business at Columbia University in New York from 1961 to 1963, he returned to Israel. He became chief of military operations in 1964, deputy chief of staff in 1967, and chief of staff in 1968. From 1968 to 1970, Bar-Lev led the Israel Defense Force (IDF) in the war of attrition against Egypt. The Bar-Lev Line, Israel's line of defense along the Suez Canal, was named for him. Bar-Lev retired from the IDF in 1972, then was elected to the Knesset in 1973 and served as minister of commerce and industry until 1977. He was minister of police from 1984 until 1988, then served as Israeli ambassador to the Russian Federation from 1992 until his death in 1994.

BARNAWI, FATIMA AL- (Birnaoui, Fatma; 1942–): Palestinian militant, active in al-Fatah. Fatima al-Barnawi was born in 1942 in Palestine and trained to be a nurse. She was arrested in 1967 by the Israeli police for participation in an anti-Israeli attack and was sentenced to life imprisonment. She was released ten years later and banished to Jordan, where she joined al-Fatah. Barnawi followed Yasir Arafat to Tunisia, after the Palestinian forces were expelled from Lebanon. In July 1994, when the Palestinian Authority was organized, Arafat appointed Barnawi head of the Policewomen, the women's unit of the civil police force (al-Shurta al-Nisaʾiyeh), which had about 300 members.

SEE ALSO Fatah, al-.

BASSIOUNI, MUHAMMAD ABDUL AZIZ (1937–): Egyptian military and diplomatic figure. Between 1968 and 1976, Muhammad Bassiouni was a military attaché in Syria. In 1979 he retired from twenty-six years of service with the rank of general and joined the ministry of foreign affairs. First assigned to Tehran, Iran, where he witnessed the fall of the shah in 1980, he was sent to Israel, where he was chargé d'affaires at the Egyptian Embassy. In 1982 he replaced the head of the Egyptian Mission in Tel Aviv, who was recalled to Cairo after the massacres of Palestinians in the Lebanese refugee camps of Sabra and Shatila. On 12 September 1986, Bassiouni was named Egyptian ambassador to Israel. In November 2000 he was recalled in protest over the Israeli response to the al-Aqsa Intifada and is now serving in the Egyptian legislature.

SEE ALSO Sabra and Shatila.

BAʿTH (Arab Socialist Baʿth Party): Political party created on 7 April 1947 in Damascus by Michel Aflaq, a Greek Orthodox Christian, and Salah al-Bitar. Part of the Arab Renaissance movement born in the 1930s, the Baʿth was also inspired by radical socialism. In March 1954, this organization combined with the Arab Socialist Party of Akram al-Hourani (Hawrani). With its vision of a union of all the Arab states combining into a single nation, the Baʿth ideology spread to Jordan, Iraq, Libya, and Aden.

Because of its support of some local rebellions, the Baʿth was banned in the countries concerned. In March 1954, the movement took advantage of the fall of the Shishakli regime in Syria to get eighteen of its members into parliament, including Akram al-Hourani, who became president of the Syrian National Assembly the following year. In February 1958, the Baʿthists in Syria advocated the creation of the United Arab Republic (UAR), which united Egypt and Syria. The president of the UAR was Gamal Abdel Nasser and the vice president was Akram al-Hourani. In December 1959, disappointed with Nasser's politics, the Syrian Baʿthists broke with him, advocating the secession of Syria from Egypt, which took place in February 1961. On 8 March 1963, a coup d'état carried out by "independent officers" still supporting union with Egypt brought the Baʿth to power in Syria. A month earlier, the Baʿth had carried out the same action in Iraq, overthrowing the Qassem government.

The Syrian Baʿth Party split into two currents: One, socialist and anti-Nasserian, was led by al-Hourani; the other, essentially nationalist, was led by Michel Aflaq. In April 1963, the Tripartite Union was proclaimed, uniting Syria, Egypt, and Iraq. In 1964, a reformist current emerged, consisting essentially of violently anticommunist and old guard military. In March 1969, the Syrian army denounced the pro-Soviet policies of the government. On 13 November, General Hafiz al-Asad took power in Syria and immediately undertook a reorganization of the party, becoming its secretary general in the elections of February 1971. The following year, six political parties joined with the Baʿth in a coalition, the National Progressive Front (NPF). The Baʿth Party became one of the principal pillars of the regime of President Hafiz al-Asad. On 18 June 2000, after he died, his son and successor, Bashshar al-Asad, was elected secretary general of the Baʿth Party. Twelve new members were elected to its command, including Prime Minister Muhammad Miro and Foreign Affairs Minister Faruk al-Shara. Among those leaving were Vice President Abdul Halim Khaddam and Defense Minister Mustafa Tlas. Members of the command also were members of the Central Committee, which comprised many army and security service leaders. Among them were loyal friends of the new Syrian president, such as his brother, Maher al-Asad, head of the Presidential Guard; General Safi, commander of the Syrian Brigade in Lebanon; Colonel Tlas, son of General Mustafa Tlas; and General Aslan, army chief of staff. The Baʿth is also known as the Arab Reform Movement, the Resurgence Movement, and the Socialist Party of Arab Resurrection.

SEE ALSO Asad, Bashshar al-; Asad, Hafiz al-; Nasser, Gamal Abdel.

BATIN: Arab term used to signify the esoteric and hidden side of things, in contrast to the word *dhahir*. By extension, this word is used to mean that it is not enough simply to observe religious rules outwardly, but one must be utterly sincere in one's faith in order to be a true Muslim.

BATINIANS: Name used in the Middle Ages to designate Ismaili Shi'ites.

SEE ALSO Ismaili.

BAYAH: Arab term to used to designate the oath of allegiance sworn by believers to the Prophet Muhammad or his successor(s). By extension, it means the obedience of subjects to their king.

SEE ALSO Muhammad.

BAYT (Bait, Beit, Beth): Arab word meaning "house, city, place." Also exists in Hebrew, as "Beit."

BAYT AL-ATIQ ("ancient place or house," in Arabic): One of the honorific names of Mecca.

SEE ALSO Mecca.

BAYT AL-HARAM ("sacred city," in Arabic): One of the honorific names of Mecca.

SEE ALSO Mecca.

BAYT ALLAH ("house of God," in Arabic): One of the honorific names of Mecca.

SEE ALSO Mecca.

BAYT AL-MAQDIS ("holy house," in Arabic): One of the honorific names for Jerusalem.

SEE ALSO Jerusalem.

BAYT LAHM

SEE Bethlehem.

BAZ, OSAMA AL- (1931–): Egyptian political figure, born in Cairo. With law degrees from the University of Cairo and Harvard, Osama al-Baz became a public prosecutor in 1953. Two years later he joined the Egyptian ministry of foreign affairs. In 1958 he became director of the cabinet of Sami Sharaf, who was responsible for the security of then-President Gamal Abdel Nasser. In March 1975, while Husni Mubarak was vice president, he was named director of the cabinet of the foreign minister, and then first undersecretary of state in the foreign ministry. In November 1977, as a member of the presidential cabinet, he was director of political affairs. In October 1981, after Mubarak came to power, al-Baz became one of the closest advisors of the new Egyptian head of state. In 1983, he headed the Egyptian delegation to the United Nations. In this capacity, al-Baz participated in numerous negotiations touching on sensitive issues, such as the Palestinian question, Sudan, and Islamic terrorism. In August 2001, during the intensification of the Intifada in the Occupied Territories, he traveled to Washington to discuss possible ways of restarting the Israeli-Palestinian negotiations, which had been stalled for several months.

SEE ALSO Aqsa Intifada, al-; Mubarak, Husni; Nasser, Gamal Abdel.

BEDOUIN (*al-Bad'n* and *al-ruhhal*): Arab word for "desert nomads."

BEERSHEBA: In Hebrew called B'er Sheva, and in Arabic, Bir al-Sabi, the city of Beersheba is located in the northern Negev. In Biblical times Beersheba marked Palestine's southern limit. The Ottoman Empire made it the administrative center for the Bedouin tribes of the Negev in 1901. After creation of the State of Israel in 1948, new immigrants expanded its population. One of Israel's largest cities, it is an industrial center for porcelain, chemicals, and textiles. Ben-Gurion University of the Negev is located there, as is the Negev Institute for Arid Zone Research. In 2002 the population was estimated at 182,000. On 31 August 2004 two Palestinian suicide bombers detonated explosives on two municipal buses in Beersheba, leaving sixteen Israelis dead and over eighty wounded. This first suicide bombing in Beersheba, located near the southern edge of Israel's planned but unfinished security barrier, raised concerns about a possible shift in location for Palestinian militant activity to southern Israel.

BEGIN, MENACHEM (1913–1992): Israeli political figure, prime minister of Israel (1977–1983). Menachem Begin was born in 1913 in Poland. Trained as a lawyer, he attracted notice at the World Congress of Betar (1938) in Warsaw, Poland, for his oratorical skills. Begin went to Palestine in 1942 with the Free Polish Army, from which he was demobilized at the end of that year. In December 1943 he took command of the extremist group, Irgun Zva'i Le'umi (IZL). Until the creation of the State of Israel in 1948, the Irgun was engaged in a campaign of attacks against British officials and institutions as well as Arabs in Palestine. The Irgun was responsible for, among others, the attack on the King David Hotel in Jerusalem, which caused 91 deaths, and the massacre of some 100 inhabitants of the Arab village of Deir Yasin.

MENACHEM BEGIN. HEAD OF THE NATIONALIST AND VIOLENT IRGUN IN THE 1940S. HE FOUNDED TWO RIGHT-WING POLITICAL PARTIES, HERUT (IN 1948) AND LIKUD (IN 1973), AND WAS ISRAEL'S FIRST NON-LABOR PRIME MINISTER, FROM 1977 TO 1983. HIS LEGACY INCLUDED A HISTORIC PEACE TREATY WITH PRESIDENT ANWAR AL-SADAT OF EGYPT—AS WELL AS AN INVASION OF LEBANON AND SUPPORT FOR ISRAELI SETTLEMENTS IN THE OCCUPIED TERRITORIES. *(© Hulton-Deutsch Collection/Corbis)*

On 2 June 1948, after the creation of the State of Israel, Begin proclaimed the allegiance of the Irgun to the new Jewish state, which allowed his militants to join the new Israeli army, the Israel Defense Force (IDF). Nevertheless, on 21 June, Begin refused to surrender to the latter a shipment of arms belonging to his movement. Prime Minister David Ben-Gurion ordered cannons to be fired on the *Altalena,* the ship that was transporting the arms. This incident formed the basis of an undying hatred between the two men.

In the autumn of 1948, after his movement had been disbanded, Begin founded the ultranationalist party Herut, advocate of a "Greater Israel." In the first Israeli parliamentary elections, in January 1949, Herut obtained fourteen seats in the Knesset. In the 1950s, after losing six of these seats, the leaders of Herut tried to capture the Sephardi vote, which was going mostly to Labor. In April 1965, Begin decided to ally his party with the Liberal Party, forming the Gahal parliamentary group, which accounted for twenty-six members of parliament. On 1 June, just before the Arab-Israel War of 1967, he joined the Labor government of Levi Eshkol as minister without portfolio. After the war, Begin left the government, while a few Gahal members stayed on until August 1970, when Prime Minister Golda Meir accepted the American Rogers Plan, which provided for a negotiated solution to the Israeli-Arab conflict. During the spring of 1973, with Ariel Sharon and Yitzhak Shamir, he formed Likud, a new parliamentary block of the right. Leader of the right since 1948, Begin led Likud to parliamentary victory in May 1977—ending thirty years of Labor hegemony—and became prime minister.

As soon as Begin took office, he initiated secret negotiations with Egypt that eventually led to the Camp David Summit of September 1978 and a peace treaty in March 1979. At the same time, Begin advocated the development of Jewish settlements in the occupied territories. On 14 August 1977 he decided to extend Israeli jurisdiction over the Gaza Strip and the West Bank. In December 1977 he stated he was in favor of administrative autonomy for the West Bank and the Gaza Strip, while firmly insisting on Israeli sovereignty in these territories. With Foreign Minister Moshe Dayan, Begin took a series of steps toward reconciliation with his Arab neighbors. As a result, Begin's position weakened within his own party, as well as within the Likud parliamentary bloc. In November 1977, Begin was host to Egyptian president Anwar al-Sadat on the latter's extraordinary visit to Israel. On 17 September 1978, the Camp David Accords were signed. On 26 March 1979, Begin signed a peace treaty with Egypt, the first one concluded between Israel and an Arab country. On 27 October 1979, Begin, together with President Sadat, was awarded the Nobel Peace Prize. There was, however, a wave of international protests when Begin pressured the Knesset, in July 1980, into adopting a law that decreed Jerusalem "the eternal capital of Israel."

That same month, after Likud narrowly won the parliamentary elections, Begin started his second term as prime minister of a government of national unity. Toughening his policies, he annexed the Golan Heights in December 1981; then on 6 June 1982, under pressure from Defense Minister Ariel Sharon, he gave the green light to the invasion of Lebanon (called Operation Peace for Galilee). The massacres at the Palestinian camps of Sabra and Shatila by the

Lebanese Phalange militia, while the IDF looked on, stirred up national and international protest. On 19 September 1983, weakened physically by illness and politically damaged by economic difficulties and by the Lebanese crisis, Begin resigned his post as prime minister and leader of Herut, replaced in both of these functions by his friend Yitzhak Shamir. From that moment until his death on 9 March 1992, Begin remained out of the public eye.

SEE ALSO Altalena; Arab-Israel War (1982); Camp David Accords; Dayan, Moshe; Herut Party; Irgun; Meir, Golda; Sabra and Shatila; Sadat, Anwar al-; Shamir, Yitzhak.

BEGIN, ZE'EV BENJAMIN (Benny) (1943–): Israeli politician. The son of the late prime minister Menachem Begin, Benjamin "Benny" Begin was born in Jerusalem in 1943. He was educated at the Hebrew University of Jerusalem and then at Colorado State University, where he received a doctoral degree in geology. He served in the Armored Corps from 1960 to 1963 and later volunteered for additional military service (1975–1976). Begin worked as a geologist for the Geological Survey of Israel (1965–1988), heading the environmental and mapping divisions. In 1989 he was appointed head of the research institute of the College of Judea and Samaria. Begin was a member of the Knesset from 1988 to 1999. A member of the Likud Party, he served on the Foreign Affairs and Defense Committee, for which he chaired a subcommittee on national defense. He served briefly (June 1996–January 1997) as minister of science.

BEILIN, YOSSI (1948–): Israeli political figure. Yossi Beilin was born in 1948 in Israel. Between 1969 and 1977, he worked as a journalist at the leftist daily, *Davar*. During this time he earned a degree in Hebrew literature and a doctorate in political science. In 1977 he joined the Israel Labor Party, where he became one of the main advisors of Shimon Peres. Four years later, he became spokesperson of the Labor Party, a post he kept for almost three years. Within the party he belonged to the leftist current that promoted the struggle against social inequality, supported the opening of a dialogue with the Palestine Liberation Organization (PLO), and advocated the creation of an Israeli-Jordanian-Palestinian economic confederation.

Between 1984 and 1986, Beilin was government secretary in the cabinet of Peres. In 1986, when a new prime minister came in, as specified in the agreement between Labor and Likud, Beilin was named director general of the foreign ministry, headed by Peres. Two years later, elected a member of Knesset, he became deputy minister of finance and the economy in the national unity government of Yitzhak Shamir, a position he kept until 1990. In June of 1992, the Labor Party emerged a victor in the Knesset elections, and Beilin was reelected. In July he was named deputy minister of foreign affairs in the government of Yitzhak Rabin, Peres holding the title of foreign minister. With the support of the latter, Beilin undertook secret negotiations with the Palestinians that led to the signing of an Israeli-Palestinian peace agreement (the Oslo Accords), in Washington, D.C., on 13 September 1993.

On 18 July 1995, Beilin was named minister of economy and planning in the Rabin government. That November, after Rabin's assassination, Beilin stayed on in the government led by Peres, but as minister without portfolio, responsible for the peace process. In May 1996, the Labor Party suffered a serious setback in the Knesset elections, losing to Benjamin Netanyahu's Likud. In December, Beilin announced his candidacy for the leadership of the Labor Party, running against Ehud Barak, who won the election to this post. Beilin came in second with 29 percent of the votes. Between 1996 and 1998 he took numerous steps to restart the peace process that had been stalled since Netanyahu had come to power. During Labor's electoral campaign of May 1999, Beilin was in charge of contacts with the Palestinians and Israeli Arabs. On 6 July, after the electoral victory of the Left, he became minister of justice in the Barak government.

On 11 July 2000, Beilin was part of the Israeli delegation at the Camp David negotiations with the Palestinians. On 21 July, during these discussions, he publicly denounced the "myth of a united Jerusalem recognized as capital of Israel" by the international community. In December, he went to Jordan to meet with King Abdullah II ibn Hussein, with whom he discussed ways of rekindling the peace process. Following the disappointment caused by Barak's defeat by Ariel Sharon in the election for prime minister in February 2001, Beilin became active in the opposition to the new Likud policies. He participated that summer in a demonstration in Tel Aviv protesting the military escalation engineered by the Sharon government in an attempt to suppress the al-Aqsa Intifada in the Palestinian territories. Later that summer Beilin traveled to Egypt, where he met with Egyptian foreign minister Ahmed Maher, with whom he discussed the Israeli-Palestinian situation. Along with Palestinian Yasir Abd Rabbo, Beilin led the group of Palestinians and Israelis that created the Geneva

Peace Initiative of 2003, an unofficial proposal for a solution to the Israeli-Palestinian conflict.

SEE ALSO Abd Rabbo, Yasir; Aqsa Intifada, al-; Geneva Peace Initiative of 2003; Oslo Accords.

BEIT

SEE Bayt.

BEIT AL-MAQDESS

SEE Bayt al-Maqdis.

BEIT DIN (*beth din;* "house of the law," in Hebrew): Rabbinical tribunal.

BEN-AMI, SHLOMO (1943–): Israeli political figure. Born in 1943 in Morocco, Shlomo Ben-Ami emigrated to Israel in 1955. After earning degrees in history and literature, he became a professor at Tel Aviv University. In 1976 he became director of the Officers' Training College at the Israel Defense Force Military School. Between 1980 and 1982 he taught at Oxford University. After returning to Israel he was named, in 1987, Israel's ambassador to Spain. In October 1991, Ben-Ami was part of the Israeli delegation to the Middle East Peace Conference held in Madrid, Spain. He resigned his post as ambassador a short while later to return to Israel, where he taught history once more.

As a Labor Party candidate, Ben-Ami won a seat in the May 1996 elections to the Knesset. On 7 February 1997, he announced he would run against Ehud Barak for the position of secretary general of the party. Barak won. Within the Labor Party, Ben-Ami was considered one of the leaders of the moderate wing, approving the creation of a Palestinian state. On 7 July 1999, he joined the Barak government as minister for internal security. In May 2000 he engaged in secret conversations with Palestinian leaders in an effort to prepare for the Israeli-Palestinian negotiations that were to take place the following month at Camp David. On 10 August, as Barak's cabinet stood weakened by the resignation of a number of his ministers, Ben-Ami was appointed foreign minister for a period of three months, replacing David Levy, while still keeping his portfolio as minister for internal security. At the end of the same month, he began a European tour in connection with Israeli-Palestinian negotiations for a definitive peace.

On 26 September 2000, Ben-Ami participated in a secret meeting in Washington, D.C., with Palestinian leaders. Under the guidance of U.S. emissary Dennis Ross, this meeting lasted three days but failed to conclude in an agreement to restart the peace process between Israelis and Palestinians. Ben-Ami resigned his ministerial functions in March 2001, after Barak was defeated by Likud leader Ariel Sharon.

SEE ALSO Barak, Ehud; Camp David II Summit; Israel Labor Party; Ross, Dennis B.

BEN ELIEZER, BENYAMIN (1936–): Israeli military and political figure, also known as Fouad, born in Iraq. After immigrating to Israel in 1949, Benyamin ben Eliezer joined the Israeli Army in 1955, intending to make a career in the military. Attached to an elite unit, he participated in military operations in the 1956 Suez-Sinai War and in the Arab-Israel War of June 1967. In March 1978, he commanded one of the larger units participating in the invasion of South Lebanon, which was in reprisal for an attack near Tel Aviv by a Palestinian commando from Lebanon. Between 1978 and 1981 he was in command of the central military region of Israel. In 1983, Ben Eliezer became coordinator of Israeli activities in the Occupied Territories. In 1984, having retired with the rank of general, he joined the centrist party, Yad, created by Ezer Weizman. Elected to the Knesset that same year, he became a member of the foreign affairs and defense committee, where he advocated dialogue with the Arabs and territorial compromise with the Palestinians. In 1988, along with Weizman, he joined the ranks of the Labor Party and was elected to the Knesset.

In February 1992, in the context of the Israeli-Arab peace process, which had started at the time of the Madrid Conference, Ben Eliezer came out against the dismantling of Jewish settlements in the occupied territories. That July, he participated actively in the election campaign of the Labor candidate, Yitzhak Rabin. On 11 July, he was named minister of housing and social development in the Rabin government. On 4 March 1993, he held an informational conference for ambassadors from the European Union, during which he stated his support for the principle of a "united Jerusalem, as capital of Israel; and of the Jordan Valley, as a natural security frontier," thereby confirming his support of the "hawk" camp of the Labor Party. He survived the cabinet reshuffle of May 1993, keeping his post of minister of housing. He traveled discreetly to Tunis in early December, where he met with Palestine Liberation Organization leaders. At the same time, Rabin entrusted him with secret missions to certain Iraqi leaders. During the summer of 1995, his name was cited in the press in connection with massacres of Arab soldiers perpetrated by an Israeli unit to which he belonged during the fighting in the 1956 Sinai-Suez War and 1967 Arab-Israel War. After the assassination of Yitzhak Rabin in November 1995, Ben Eliezer remained minister of housing in the new cabinet headed by Shimon Peres. In February 1996, he took over the Labor Party's electoral campaign in preparation for the elections to be held the following May, when the prime minister and Knesset members were to be chosen for the first time by separate ballot. The vote gave thirty-four seats to the Labor Party and twenty-two to Likud, whose leader, Benjamin Netanyahu, was elected prime minister. Ben Eliezer won reelection, thereby consolidating his position in the Labor Party. On 17 May 1999, Labor Party leader Ehud Barak was elected prime minister. That July Ben Eliezer was appointed minister of communications.

In February 2001, in anticipation of the upcoming election of a new prime minister, he declared himself in favor of the participation of Labor in a government of national unity, even if the latter included movements of the extreme right. The following March, Ben Eliezer and six other Labor members, including Peres, joined the cabinet of Ariel Sharon. He took on the ministry of defense. When the Intifada intensified in the Occupied Territories, he approved of and supported the reprisal operations ordered by Sharon. In September of that same year, Ben Eliezer was defeated in the election for the post of secretary general of the Labor Party by Avraham Burg, whom he accused of electoral fraud. In late December, after months of legal proceedings and battles, Ben Eliezer was elected secretary general of the Israel Labor Party in a vote where participation was very low.

SEE ALSO Aqsa Intifada, al-; Arab-Israel War (1967); Barak, Ehud; Madrid Conference; Netanyahu, Benjamin; Peres, Shimon; Rabin, Yitzhak; Sharon, Ariel; Suez Crisis; Weizman, Ezer; Yad.

BEN-GURION, DAVID (Born Gruen, Gryn; 1886–1973): Israeli political figure, born in Plonsk, Poland (then part of the Russian Empire). In 1905, David Ben-Gurion joined the ranks of the Zionist-Socialist movement, Poalei Zion (Workers of Zion), of which he became the leader. He moved to Palestine in 1906. Deported by the Turkish authorities in 1915, he came to the United States where, as a spokesperson for Zionism, he attempted to unify the diverse socialist tendencies of the movement. Back in Palestine in 1920, he continued his work of unifying the diverse labor movements. In 1921, along with Golda Meir and Izhak Ben-Zvi, he created the Workers' Union, Histadrut, of which he became the secretary general. In 1930, he participated in the foundation of the Zionist Workers Party, MAPAI, and became its head. On 24 July 1933, Ben-Gurion became director of the political department of the Jewish Agency, the administrative link between the Jewish community and British authorities, who had a mandate over Palestine. In 1934, MAPAI won 42.3 percent of the votes in the Elected Assembly of the Yishuv (Jewish community of Palestine), thereby becoming its principal political bloc. In liaison with Chaim Weizmann, Ben-Gurion intensified his activities within the Jewish Agency.

In October 1944, confronted by the decision of the British to stop all Jewish immigration by the end of the year, Ben-Gurion decided, in his capacity as president of the Jewish Agency, to cease all collaboration with the British authorities. Although determined to fight for the Zionist cause, he was opposed to the extremist methods of certain Jewish militias. On 14 May 1948, a few hours before the expiration of the British Mandate, Ben-Gurion proclaimed the creation of the State of Israel, and he became its prime minister and defense minister. In this capacity, he supervised the defense of the State of Israel during the first Israeli-Arab War of 1948–49. After the Knesset elections of February 1949, MAPAI was confirmed as the leading political party of Israel, with 46 seats out of the 120. On 14 December 1949, Ben-Gurion announced the transfer of the Israeli capital to Jerusalem. In 1951, in spite of the disapproval of his entourage and of a majority of political figures, he decided to strengthen ties between Israel and the Germany of Chancellor Konrad Adenauer, thereby obtaining financial and technical aid as indemnification for Nazi crimes.

In 1953, leaving his post to Moshe Sharett, he resigned from the government to retire to Sde Boker, a kibbutz in the Negev Desert. In February 1955, he reassumed the post of defense minister, and in November he again became prime minister. In October 1956, backed by France and Great Britain, Ben-Gurion made the decision to involve his country in the Suez-Sinai War. The failure of this expedition, for reasons having to do with the international political situation, persuaded him to strengthen the Israeli Army and to initiate secret contacts with certain Arab leaders. On 31 January 1959, the findings of the commission of inquiry on the Lavon Affair having led to his resignation from the government, Ben-Gurion was obliged also to leave his post as secretary general of Histadrut. Knesset elections held in 1961 showed a weakening of his party, but he succeeded,

DAVID BEN-GURION. A ZIONIST LEADER EVEN BEFORE HE IMMIGRATED TO PALESTINE IN 1906, BEN-GURION (CENTER) SHAPED THE DEVELOPMENT, CREATION, AND EARLY YEARS OF THE STATE OF ISRAEL MORE THAN ANYONE ELSE. HE WAS ISRAEL'S FIRST PRIME MINISTER AND DEFENSE MINISTER, FROM 1948 TO 1953, AND RETURNED TO POWER FROM 1955 TO 1963. IN THIS PICTURE, HE IS SHOWN REVIEWING THE TROOPS WITH GENERAL MOSHE DAYAN. *(© Photograph by Hans Pinn. Government Press Office [GPO] of Israel)*

on 1 November 1961, in forming a new government that, in spite of the weakness of its parliamentary base, showed itself to be fairly stable. On 16 June 1963, a scission in MAPAI, caused in part by the Lavon Affair, led him to resign suddenly, after having designated Levi Eshkol as his successor. In spite of his retirement from government, Ben-Gurion remained the principal leader of his party, supported by such rising stars of MAPAI as Shimon Peres and Moshe Dayan. In November 1964, he resigned from the central committee of MAPAI to create a new political organization, the RAFI Party, which led to his being expelled from MAPAI. From 1965 to 1969 he occupied a seat in the Knesset. In 1968, RAFI united with MAPAI and Ahdut ha-Avoda to form the Israeli Labor Party. In the parliamentary elections of 1969, Ben-Gurion headed a "state list" that won only four seats in the Knesset. Ben-Gurion retired from the Knesset in 1970 and moved back to his kibbutz, where he died. He is considered the founder of the State of Israel.

SEE ALSO Ahdut ha-Avoda; Dayan, Moshe; Histadrut; Israel Labor Party; Jewish Agency for Israel; Lavon Affair; MAPAI; Meir, Golda; Peres, Shimon; RAFI Party; Weizmann, Chaim; Zionism.

BEN SHAKIR, ZAYD (Zeid Ben Shaker, 1934–): Jordanian military figure, related to a cousin of King Abdullah of Jordan. With degrees from Sandhurst Military Academy (England) and the Command and General Staff College at Fort Leavenworth, Kansas, Zayd Ben Shakir was named commander of the Jordanian Sixth Armored Brigade (1966). He participated in the Arab-Israel War of 1967 and a year later in the battle of al-Karameh, where he helped the Fedayeen against the Israelis. He was called back to Jordan from London by King Hussein in the autumn of

1968 to help the government deal with the deteriorating situation inside the kingdom. In September 1970, he directed operations against Palestinian groups who were trying to take power (Black September). In 1972, he was named army chief of staff, then in 1976 commander-in-chief of the Jordanian armed forces. Promoted to marshal in 1987, he resigned from the army and, the following year, became head of the royal house and counselor for military affairs to King Hussein. In 1989, he was named prime minister and defense minister. During his mandate, legislative elections took place in Jordan for the first time in twenty-two years. He resigned his post in 1990 but assumed it again in November 1991, remaining prime minister until May 1993. On 5 January 1995, he was named head of the Jordanian government for the third time before being replaced by Abdul Karim Kabariti in February 1996.

SEE ALSO Abdullah II ibn Hussein; Arab-Israel War (1967); Black September 1970.

BEN-ZVI, IZHAK (1884–1963): Zionist leader, second president of Israel (1952–1963). Born in Poltava, Ukraine, in 1884, Izhak Ben-Zvi was involved in the Zionist movement from an early age. He was one of the founders of the Poʿalei Ziyyon Party in Palestine, editing the party's newspaper and opening a small school in Jerusalem. In 1908 Ben-Zvi went to Constantinople with his friend David Ben-Gurion to study law; at the outbreak of World War I they returned to Palestine but were expelled by Ottoman authorities. They immigrated to the United States, where they lectured in support of the Zionist movement.

Ben-Zvi returned to Palestine as a soldier in the Jewish Legion. He maintained a commitment to Labor Zionism throughout his political career, eventually providing a link between British authorities and Labor Zionist leadership. He was elected to the Jerusalem municipality several times and served as a member, and later chair, of the Vaʿad Leʾumi (National Council). Ben-Zvi served as president of Israel from 1952 until his death in 1963.

SEE ALSO Ben-Gurion, David.

BERLIN SUMMIT: At a meeting in Berlin on 26 March 1999, the member countries of the European Union published a text on Israeli-Palestinian relations, according to which the European Union: "1) Reaffirms its support for a negotiated solution, reflecting the principle of 'exchange of the territories against peace' and guaranteeing the collective and individual security of the Israeli and Palestinian people; welcomes in this context the decision of the Palestinian National Council nullifying the particulars of their charter that called for the destruction of Israel, while reaffirming their commitment to live in peace with Israel; is concerned by the current impasse in the peace process, calling on all parties to apply fully and immediately the Wye River memorandum. 2) Calls on the parties to reaffirm their commitment to the basic principles established in the framework of Madrid, Oslo, and subsequent agreements, in accord with Security Council Resolutions 242 and 338; urges the parties to agree on an extension of the interim period, as was established in the Oslo accord. 3) Calls for, in particular, a prompt restart of negotiations on final status in the upcoming months on an accelerated basis, which should lead to a rapid settlement, not be prolonged indefinitely; expresses its conviction that it should be possible to conclude the negotiations within a year's time, while declaring its willingness to facilitate these negotiations. 4) Urges the parties to refrain from activities that anticipate the result of these negotiations on a final status, or any activities contrary to international law, including any settlement activity, and to eliminate provocation and violence. 5) Reaffirms the permanent and unrestricted right of the Palestinians to self-determination, including the option of a state; desires the prompt respect of this right; calls on the parties to make an effort of good will to find a negotiated solution based on existing accords, without prejudice to this right, which is not subject to cancellation; expresses its conviction that the creation of a viable and peaceful democratic Palestinian state, based on existing accords and through negotiations, would be the best guarantee of Israel's security and the acceptance of Israel as an equal partner in the region; declares its willingness to consider recognizing a Palestinian state, when the time comes, on the basis of the above-mentioned principles. 6) Calls for a prompt restart of negotiations on the Syrian and Lebanese wings of the peace process, resulting in an application of Security Council Resolutions 242, 338, and 425."

SEE ALSO Madrid Conference; Oslo Accords; Oslo Accords II; Resolution 242; Resolution 338.

BERNADOTTE, FOLKE (1895–1948): Nephew of King Gustave V of Sweden, Count Folke Bernadotte af Wisborg was born in Stockholm. At the beginning of 1945, as president of the Swedish Red Cross, Count Bernadotte succeeded in negotiating with the German authorities for the liberation of almost 30,000 prisoners from concentration camps. On 28 April, he participated in negotiations that concluded in the surrender of Germany. On 29 May 1948, in the framework of the end of the British Mandate in Palestine and of the fighting that erupted upon the proclamation of the creation of the State of Israel, the United Nations (UN) General Assembly designated him as mediator in Palestine, to be assisted by Ralph S. Bunche. Bernadotte obtained a truce in Israeli-Arab fighting, and on 28 June he proposed a plan suggesting the constitution of a federated "Greater Palestine" incorporating the West Bank and including two autonomous states, one Jewish and the other Arab. His project reduced the portion allowed to Jews in the UN plan of November 1947. Rejected by both parties, this proposition led to a resumption of combat. On 16 September 1948, Count Bernadotte's "Progress Report" to the United Nations advocated the "right to return" of Arabs who had been expelled from their land and the establishment of an international status for Jerusalem, which provoked the anger of Jewish extremists. The next day, along with one of his assistants, the French Colonel André Pierre Sérot, he was assassinated by Meshulam Makover and other members of the Stern Gang (LEHI). On 18 September, nearly 200 members of or sympathizers with this small group were arrested. Two days later, both the Stern Gang and Irgun were banned.

Nabi Mustafa Berri. The Lebanese cofounder of the Amal militia in 1975, Berri advocated an alliance with Syria and opposed both the Israeli occupation of South Lebanon and the influence of Palestinian groups in his country. He served in ministerial posts and became the president of the Lebanese Parliament in 1992. *(AP/Wide World Photos)*

Berri, Nabi (1938–): Lebanese political figure. A Shiʿite Muslim, Nabi Mustafa Berri was born in 1938 in Freetown, Sierra Leone, into a family of merchants originally from Tibnin in southern Lebanon. Berri's family returned to Lebanon in 1948, and in 1963 he was elected president of the Student Union at the Lebanese University of Beirut, where the Baʿth Party held a majority. Between 1964 and 1965 he studied law at the Sorbonne in Paris, then settled in Detroit. In 1972 he returned to Sierra Leone, then back to Lebanon, where he started practicing law.

In 1973 Berri joined the ranks of the Movement of the Disinherited, founded by Imam Musa Sadr, where he advocated an alliance with Syria. During the summer of 1975, while the civil war that was to last for fifteen years was just starting, he joined with Musa Sadr in creating the AMAL militia, whose purpose was the defense of the Shiʿa community against the attacks from other Lebanese militias. Between 1975 and 1978 he represented the pro-Syrian current of the movement and, taking the side of Damascus, participated in the overthrow of alliances that had been formed between AMAL and the Palestinian movements. In April 1980, two years after the mysterious disappearance of Musa Sadr in Libya, Berri succeeded Husayn al-Husayni, who had run AMAL in the interim. In June 1982, after the Israeli invasion of Lebanon, an Islamic current appeared in the movement, which Berri fought until there was a break that gave rise to Hizbullah.

In February 1984 the conflict pitting the Shiʿite and Druze communities against President Amin Jumayyil propelled Berri to a prominent place on the political scene, and he became one of Lebanon's "warlords." That summer he joined the national unity government led by Rashid Karame, in the capacity of minister of state and minister of justice for South Lebanon, while advocating an alliance with the Syrians. On 6 October, he accompanied the Lebanese prime minister to the United Nations to plead the cause of South Lebanon. On 6 February 1985, Berri declared himself to be "minister of national resistance" and supported sending anti-Israeli commandos to South Lebanon. From then on, in an effort to counter the influence of Hizbullah, he committed AMAL to resistance to the Israeli occupier.

On 27 March 1989, Berri was reelected president of AMAL. That November, as a supporter of the Ta'if Accords that had just been signed, he was appointed minister of housing, electricity, and hydraulic power in the cabinet of national unity led by Salim al-Hoss. A fervent partisan of Syria, he opposed the "war of liberation" that General Michel Aoun had just launched that December against the Syrian forces in Lebanon. Aoun's Maronite forces were defeated in October 1990, effectively ending the civil war, and the militias were disbanded. AMAL became a political movement. On 31 August 1991, along with Muhammad Beydoun, housing minister and AMAL member, Berri threatened to resign from the government in protest against a visit Lebanese prime minister Omar Karame had just paid to Libya, where Imam Musa Sadr had disappeared in 1978. On 20 October 1992, Berri was elected president of the Lebanese Parliament, with 105 of the 125 votes that were cast. He was reelected to this post four years later, and again in 2000, after legislative elections saw the victory of Rafiq Hariri.

SEE ALSO AMAL; Arab-Israel War (1982); Shi'ite.

BETA ISRAEL (*beth-Israel;* "of the house of Israel," in Hebrew): The various tribes of Israel dispersed all over the world.

BETAR (B'rith Trumpeldor): Jewish extremist movement founded in 1923 by Vladimir Ze'ev Jabotinsky in Riga, Latvia, for the training of the future cadres of revisionist Zionism. Betar's program was built around an intense political and paramilitary education. Once transformed into a veritable militia, the movement was integrated into the Herut Party of Menachem Begin. Betar is likewise the name of the fortress from which Bar Kochba directed the revolt against the Roman legions in Palestine, in 135 C.E.

SEE ALSO Begin, Menachem; Herut; Jabotinsky, Vladimir Ze'ev.

BETHLEHEM (Bayt Lahm): An Arab city in the West Bank, Bethlehem is located five and a half miles (eight kilometers) south of Jerusalem. According to the Gospels, it was the birthplace of Jesus. In the fourth century, Constantine built the Basilica of the Nativity there, over the grotto that is traditionally considered the site of Jesus' birth. Since then, the church has become a place of Christian pilgrimage. It is situated near the tomb of Rachel, a Jewish holy place.

Bethlehem had a population that was mostly Christian until 1948. In 1944 its population was less than 9,000; in 1948 it was 14,000; by 2003 it was estimated to be 27,000, about half Christian and half Muslim. An additional 25,000 people live in the adjacent towns of Bayt Jala and Bayt Sahur. Three nearby refugee camps established in 1948—Dheisheh, Aida, and Bayt Jibrin—are home to another 20,000 people. Bethlehem is also the site of Bethlehem University, a Roman Catholic institution that was founded as a secondary school in 1893 and became a university in 1973.

Bethlehem is located in a Palestinian autonomous zone, under the Oslo Accords. In April and May 2002, the Church of the Nativity was the site of a five-week-long siege by Israeli forces who were seeking to apprehend a group of militants they accused of being terrorists, who had taken refuge there from the Israel Defense Force (IDF). The incident ended with a deal that allowed the men to leave the country. In June, like other West Bank cities, Bethlehem was reoccupied by the Israelis and placed under military control, with 24-hour curfews. Although Bethlehem is a regional center of trade, its local economy is heavily dependent on tourism, which has been greatly reduced since 2001 by the ongoing al-Aqsa Intifada and Israeli military activity. When the Israeli separation wall is completed, it will run just to the north of Bethlehem, cutting the city off from Jerusalem.

SEE ALSO Aqsa Intifada, al-; Bethlehem University; Oslo Accords.

BETHLEHEM UNIVERSITY: Founded in 1973, Bethlehem University is a Roman Catholic, Vatican-sponsored Palestinian university, created in cooperation with the De La Salle Brothers, a religious order that has established schools in Turkey, Lebanon, Jordan, Egypt, and other countries. In 2002 the university had an enrollment of more than two thousand students (of whom 70 percent were Muslim), with faculties in art, business administration, education, nursing, science, and hotel management. It also housed a United Nations Educational, Scientific, and Cultural Organization (UNESCO) Biotechnology Center and an environmental research facility. The university was closed by Israeli military authorities from 1987–1990, during the first Intifada. In April and May 2002, during the the al-Aqsa Intifada, the university was shut down several times as Israeli forces entered Bethlehem and besieged the Church of the Nativity in pursuit of Palestinian militants who had taken refuge there. In June, the Israelis re-

Bethlehem. In the place where the Bible says Jesus was born, now an Arab town in the West Bank just a few miles outside Jerusalem, an Israeli tank and armored vehicle patrol Paul VI Street in early 2002. *(AP/Wide World Photos)*

occupied the city, and the university was shut down until the military occupation ended a year later.

SEE ALSO Aqsa Intifada, al-; Bethlehem; Intifada (1987–1993).

Bevin, Ernest (1881–1951): British political figure. Ernest Bevin's career started at a young age in the union movement, where he demonstrated his organizational skills, in particular during a stevedore strike in 1920. In 1937 he became chairman of the general council of Trades Union Congress. In 1940 he was elected to the House of Commons and joined a government coalition formed by Winston Churchill, as minister of labor and national service. He participated in the Potsdam Conference (July–August 1945). The Labor election victory in 1945 allowed him to become secretary of state for foreign affairs, in charge, among other matters, of the Palestine dossier.

Bevin played an active role in the formation of British policy concerning Palestine, and it was he who announced in November 1945 the formation of the Anglo-American Committee of Inquiry on Palestine, composed of six prominent Americans and six prominent Britons. Bevin pursued a policy that followed the one outlined in the British White Paper of 1939, restricting the number of Jewish immigrants from Europe to Palestine. The committee's report, issued in April 1946, recommended the authorization of the immigration of 100,000 European Jews and the annulment of land regulations restricting Jewish purchase of Arab land. Despite British pledges to adopt the committee's recommendations if they were unanimous, within a few months Britain backed away from adopting the report. In April 1947, Bevin announced that the British government had decided to lay the Palestine problem before the United Nations. An antisemitic comment regarding Jews "always wanting to push to the head of the queue" has been said to reveal his purported impa-

Ernest Bevin. A longtime British labor leader, Bevin was the country's secretary of state for foreign affairs after World War II. In that post, he tried to slow the pace of postwar Jewish immigration to Palestine and then turned over the fate of the British mandate to the United Nations.

tience with Zionist pressure for postwar immigration. In March 1951, his health declining, Bevin resigned his position. He died a month later.

see also White Papers on Palestine.

Bibigate: Political scandal uncovered in 1997 that touched Israeli prime minister Benjamin Netanyahu, known as Bibi. On 10 January 1997, Israeli lawyer Roni Bar-On was appointed legal adviser to the government. Two days later, under pressure from political figures, he resigned. On 22 January, Israeli television's channel 1 revealed that Arye Deri, head of the ultra-orthodox party SHAS, had threatened Netanyahu that his party would vote against the 15 January 1997 Hebron Protocol unless he named Roni Bar-On as legal adviser. According to the television report, Deri hoped that with this appointment he would obtain clemency from the ministry of justice in an affair that had been under investigation for several months. The scandal made headlines in all Israeli newspapers and led to a judicial inquiry that created the Bibigate scandal, the first time in the history of Israel that a prime minister was investigated by his own police. Several cabinet members raised the possibility of resigning should Netanyahu be found guilty. On 15 April, the Israeli police recommended indictment of the prime minister, his justice minister, and others for "abuse of confidence and prevarication." Deri's indictment was also recommended, for "blackmail." On 20 April, the charges against the Israeli prime minister and his close associates were dismissed and on 15 June the Israeli Supreme Court declined to prosecute Netanyahu, for "lack of proof."

see also Deri, Arye; Netanyahu, Benjamin; SHAS.

Bible (from the Greek *biblia*, meaning "books"): Ensemble of writings presented as being divinely inspired. The Hebrew Bible (*TaNaKh,* in Hebrew) is comprised of three sections: Torah (Pentateuch), Nevi'im (Prophets), and Ketuvim (Holy Writings). Originating with Moses in the desert around the thirteenth century B.C.E., the Bible developed in Palestine principally through oral transmission, in tandem with the evolution of the Jewish people. It began with the creation of the world, and went on to recount relations between God and humankind. Considered the book of the people of Israel, the Bible designated, by extension, the written law of the Jewish people. This sacred work included, among others, the Book of Joshua, which told the story of the conquest of Canaan; that of Samuel, which recounted the history of the Hebrew people up to the time they came to be ruled by royalty; and the Book of Kings, which recalled the history of the Kingdom of Solomon and the destruction of the Kingdom of Israel in 722 B.C.E.

The Hebrew Bible corresponds to the Old Testament of the Christians, the latter not recognizing the same texts as the Jews. Most of the Bible was composed in Hebrew, with some passages in Aramaic. In many of its stories, Biblical literature is based on real material elements, though the marvelous sometimes prevails. For example, the episode of Moses and the burning bush could be a description of fraxinella, a desert plant that bursts into flame easily in very hot weather. Likewise the tale of the "plagues," visited on the Egyptians because of the refusal of Pharaoh to allow the Hebrews to leave, could be a description of natural events.

The Zionist movement of the late nineteenth and early twentieth century, which sought to establish a national homeland for Jews in Palestine, drew upon the Biblical notion of Eretz Yisrael, the "Promised Land" pledged by God to his chosen people. Adherents of the Greater Land of Israel movement, founded after the Arab-Israel War of 1967, who oppose ceding sovereignty of Occupied Territories, base their conception of Eretz Yisrael on the definition of a Biblical Promised Land.

SEE ALSO Eretz Yisrael.

BILADI, BILADI (My country, my country): The Palestinian national anthem, by Ibrahim Hefeth Touqan, Muhammad Salim Flayfel, and Ahmad Salim Flayfel.

BILU: Acronym for *Beit Ya'acov Lekhou Venelekha* (House of Jacob, let us arise and go!, in Hebrew). First modern Jewish movement for the agricultural colonizing of Palestine, founded in Kharkov in 1882. By extension, the plural, *biluim*, designated the first Jewish colonists, of Russian origin, who settled in Palestine.

BIN LADIN, OSAMA (Usama bin Ladin, ibn Laden; 1957–): Saudi Islamist militant, born in Saudi Arabia to one of the richest families in the kingdom, owners of an important conglomerate of construction companies. At the beginning of the 1980s, after studies in economics and theology that put him in contact with various Islamic groups, Osama bin Laden joined the ranks of the Islamic Legion, which had been formed by Prince Turki ibn Abdelaziz Faisal, head of Saudi security services. This small group was concerned with helping the Afghan people in their struggle against the Soviet Army. Prince Turki was also one of the leaders of the World Islamic League. Bin Laden created al-Qaʿida in 1986 with Ayman al-Zawahri, leader of the Egyptian Islamic Jihad, under the cover of the Islamic Salvation Foundation. In the organization, bin Laden was responsible for recruiting, financing, and arming volunteers from different Arab countries. In Peshawar, Pakistan, he benefited indirectly from the material help that the American Central Intelligence Agency (CIA) was providing to the Afghan rebels, which was being delivered through the Pakistani special services, or ISI. In 1991, having been back in Saudi Arabia for a year, he openly expressed his opposition to the pro-American policies of the Saudi rulers, thereby identifying with the fundamentalism espoused by Sheikhs Sfar al-Hawli and Salman al-Awdah, founders of the Islamic Resurgence Movement. At the time of the Gulf War, he accused the Saudi regime of having "profaned the land of Islam" by welcoming U.S. troops there.

OSAMA MUHAMMAD BIN LADIN. THE MOST PROMINENT ISLAMIST MILITANT OF HIS ERA (SHOWN IN A 1998 PHOTOGRAPH), HE CO-FOUNDED AL-QAʿIDA IN 1986 AND LED IT INTO THE TWENTY-FIRST CENTURY. STARTING IN THE MID-1990S, HE APPROVED OR INSPIRED NUMEROUS ATTACKS ON AMERICAN AND ALLIED TARGETS IN THE MIDDLE EAST, AFRICA, AND EUROPE, THE MOST SPECTACULAR AND DEADLY OF WHICH WAS THE BOMBING OF THE WORLD TRADE CENTER IN NEW YORK AND THE PENTAGON IN WASHINGTON, D.C., ON 11 SEPTEMBER 2001. *(AP/Wide World Photos)*

In the autumn of 1991, he decided on exile in Sudan, where he created a number of commercial enterprises, from which a share of the profits went to finance Islamic Jihad through the Sudanese Islamic al-Shamal Bank, in which he was a major stockholder. In 1992, he was suspected of supporting the militias that were harassing American troops in Somalia. Two years later, in April 1994, he was officially stripped of Saudi nationality. In the summer of 1996 he was suspected of having financed two anti-American attacks in Saudi Arabia: that of 13 November, in Riyad, on a building where American advisors were staying, and that of 27 June, in Khobar, against a U.S. military base. In autumn 1996, he left Khartoum under pressure from Sudanese authorities, first going to Pakistan, then to Afghanistan, where he became a mainstay of the Taliban regime. On 23 February 1998, at Peshawar, with several leaders of the Jihad, he established the World Islamic Front for

Holy War against Jews and Crusaders, a sort of federated movement of extremist groups. On 6 June, in an interview given to the American network ABC, he upheld the start of an open war against Americans, who, he specified, "whether civilian or military, are all targets of a fatwa." On the following 7 August, a double attack against the American embassies in Nairobi, Kenya, and Dar es-Salaam, Tanzania, cost the lives of 258 people, including 12 Americans. U.S. intelligence agencies accused bin Laden of having ordered these attacks. On 20 August, in spite of missile strikes against camps at Khost, in the Afghan province of Paktia, which were thought to be harboring his followers, the Americans failed to dislodge him.

An international hunt was initiated for networks that he was believed to control. In September, one of his financiers, Mamdouh Mahmud Salim, a Sudanese national, was arrested in Bavaria, Germany. In October 1999, the U.S. government requested bin Laden's extradition from the Afghan government, which was led by the Taliban and underwritten by Saudi Arabia. The Federal Bureau of Investigation (FBI) offered a reward of $5 million for his capture. On 17 February 2001, fourteen of his partisans were indicted for terrorist activities by the Jordanian authorities. On 5 February a trial of four men accused of belonging to his network and of being responsible for terrorist actions on American soil opened in New York City. On 13 September, two days after the suicide attack on the New York World Trade Center and on the Pentagon in Washington, D.C., which caused several thousand deaths, the FBI, suspecting bin Laden of being responsible, renewed its offer of $5 million for his capture. The next day, with the support of Congress, the Bush administration started to prepare a military operation directed against the Taliban regime in Kabul. On 18 September, the United Nations Security Council demanded "the immediate and unconditional surrender of Osama bin Laden" from the Afghan government. On 19 September the council of Afghan *ulemas* asked him to leave Afghanistan of his own accord. On 23 September, U.S. secretary of state Colin Powell announced that the United States was ready to offer a reward of $25 million for information leading to his capture. On 25 September, Saudi Arabia broke off diplomatic relations with the Taliban regime. Three days later, Saudi Arabia authorized the United States to use its military bases in the operation against Afghanistan. On 7 October, Operation Enduring Freedom started with the first U.S. aerial strikes on Afghanistan. Bin Laden went into the mountains on the Pakistan border that fall. He escaped a major American assault on an al-Qa'ida base at Tora Bora in December and could not be located, although he was seen thereafter on several videotaped messages that he sent to Arabic-language broadcasters.

SEE ALSO Gulf War (1991); International Islamic Front; Islamic Jihad; World Islamic Front for Holy War against Jews and Crusaders; Zawahri, Ayman Muhammad al-.

BIN SHAKIR, ZAYD (Zeid Ben Shaker; 1934–): Jordanian military figure, a distant cousin and childhood friend of King Hussein of Jordan. Born in September 1934, Zayd bin Shakir earned degrees from Sandhurst Military Academy (England) and the Command and General Staff College at Fort Leavenworth, Kansas. He was named commander of the Jordanian 6th Armored Brigade in 1966. He participated in the Arab-Israel War of 1967, then, a year later, in the battle of al-Karameh, where he helped the Fedayeen against the Israelis. He was called back to Jordan from London by King Hussein in the autumn of 1968 to help the government in dealing with the deteriorating situation within the kingdom. In September 1970, bin Shakir directed operations against Palestinian groups who were trying to take power ("Black September"). In 1972 he was named army chief of staff, then in 1976 commander-in-chief of the Jordanian Armed Forces.

Promoted to marshal in 1987, bin Shakir resigned from the army and, the following year, became head of the royal court and counselor to King Hussein for military affairs. In 1989 he was named prime minister and defense minister. During his mandate, legislative elections took place in Jordan for the first time in twenty-two years. He resigned his post in 1990, but assumed it again in November 1991, remaining prime minister until May 1993. On 5 January 1995 he was named head of the Jordanian government for the third time, before being replaced by Abdul Karim Kabariti in February 1996. On bin Shakir's retirement, King Hussein awarded him the title of prince. Since the accession in 1999 of King Abdullah II ibn Hussein, who served under him in the army, bin Shakir has been an informal advisor to the king.

SEE ALSO Abdullah II ibn Hussein; Hussein ibn Talal.

BIO

SEE League of Arab States.

BIRKAT MOSHE: Israeli Religious College in Maale Adoumim that since 1993 has been training the new generation of "religious warriors" ready to sacrifice their lives in defense of Israel. Most of these students, a majority of whom are right wing, wound up in elite units of the Israel Defense Force. One of the college deans, Nahum Rabinovitch, was among the rabbis who in 1994 authored an appeal to Israeli soldiers for disobedience in the event the Israeli Army was ordered to withdraw from the Occupied Territories.

SEE ALSO Israel Defense Force.

BIR ZEIT UNIVERSITY: Palestinian university located near the town of Birzeit, south of Ramallah, about twelve miles north of Jerusalem in the West Bank. Founded in 1924 as an elementary school for girls, it became a secondary school for boys and girls in 1930. In the 1950s and 1960s postsecondary courses were added and the school became exclusively a two-year postsecondary institution in 1967. In 1975 it became a four-year undergraduate university. Graduate programs were first introduced in 1977. Because of its location and circumstances, the Bir Zeit student body (now about 6,000) has always been highly active in Palestinian politics and anti-Israeli resistance. Student groups affiliated with Palestine Liberation Organization member groups such as Fatah have claimed the loyalties of many students. An Islamist current has also appeared, as it has in the larger society. Israeli authorities have regarded the campus as a dangerous center of militant activity and have shut the school down numerous times since 1973. In 1974 the president of the university, Hanna Nasir, was deported and not allowed to return until 1993, after the Oslo Accords. In the 1990s the university suffered from strict Israeli censorship and foreign faculty members were required to sign loyalty oaths, resulting in some deportations. During the first Intifada, Bir Zeit remained closed from 1988 to 1992, and during the al-Aqsa Intifada classes continue to be disrupted by closures, curfews, and Israeli military activity.

SEE ALSO Aqsa Intifada, al-; Fatah, al-; Intifada (1987–1993); Oslo Accords; Palestine Liberation Organization; West Bank.

BISHARA, AZMI (Beshara, Bichara; 1956–): Palestinian Israeli. Born in 1956 in Nazareth, the son of a union leader, Azmi Bishara joined the leftist party HADASH while he was a student at Hebrew University. In 1974 he created the National Committee of Arab High School Students. In 1985 he was awarded a doctorate in philosophy from Humboldt University in East Berlin. He went on to become a professor at Bir Zeit University in the West Bank, where he taught philosophy and political history. Between 1988 and 1991 he was also associated with the Van Leer Institute, a prestigious research center in Jerusalem.

Running on the HADASH list in the parliamentary elections of 29 May 1991, Bishara won a seat in the Knesset. In April 1992, advocating equality between Jews and Arabs, he founded a movement called the Alliance for Equality. He was reelected in May 1996, running again on the HADASH list, which won five seats in the Knesset. At the end of the following December, he announced he would run for the post of prime minister in the 2000 elections. The first Arab candidate for the post, Bishara ran against Benjamin Netanyahu, Ehud Barak, Yitzhak Mordechai, and Benny Begin. He also headed the electoral list of his party, Balad (National Democratic Assembly), with Ahmad Tibi of the Arab Movement for Change (AMC) in second place. The main themes of his campaign were "identity" demands of the Arab Israelis who wanted to be better integrated into Israeli society. But on 14 May, just before the vote in the general elections, Bishara withdrew his candidacy for the post of prime minister, urging his supporters to cast their ballots for the Israel Labor Party. Balad won two seats in the Knesset, one of which was allotted to Bishara.

In November 2000 he went to Damascus, where he held talks with President Bashshar al-Asad. One of the results of this visit was the organization of a trip that allowed Arab-Israeli families to see their relatives who were refugees in Syria. In June 2001 the Knesset opened an inquiry about Bishara, following remarks he had made that were thought to be anti-Israeli, on the occasion of Syrian president Hafiz al-Asad's death. Two months later the same charges were leveled against another Arab-Israeli representative in the Knesset, Taleb al-Sanaa. On 7 November 2001 the Knesset lifted the parliamentary immunity of Azmi Bishara, accusing him of incitement to terrorism and organizing travel to Syria, a country at war with Israel.

In 2002 Bishara and Ahmad Tibi were barred from running in the next election on the grounds that they had supported "terrorists" by denouncing the Israeli assault on Jenin that spring, but the Israeli Supreme Court overturned the ban shortly before the election in January 2003. Both Tibi and Bishara were returned to the Knesset.

SEE ALSO Asad, Bashshar al-; Asad, Hafiz al-; Democratic Front for Peace and Equality; Tibi, Ahmad.

Bitahon ("security," in Hebrew): Generic term used to describe a permanent preoccupation of Israelis, who fear for their lives and the survival of the State of Israel. More existential than physical, this malaise is still widespread in Israeli society, in spite of the Israeli-Arab peace process begun in 1991.

Black Hand

see Qassam, Izz al-Din al-.

Black June

see Fatah Revolutionary Council.

Black Panthers: Name of an armed branch of al-Fatah.

see also Fatah, al-.

Black Panthers: Israeli political and protest movement created in the 1970s by the leaders of the Sephardi community in their struggle for equal rights. Working against the Laborites, in power since 1948, their activity enabled the advent to power of Menachem Begin and the Likud Party in 1977.

see also Begin, Menachem; Sephardim.

Black September 13 Brigades: A Palestinian movement, the Black September 13 Brigades was created on 27 October 1993 by Lieutenant Colonel Munir Hasan al-Maqdah, al-Fatah military commander at the Ain al-Hilwa (Lebanon) camp, who opposed the Israeli-Palestinian accord of the preceding 13 September. The principal cause of his opposition was the exclusion, from this accord, of the question of the refugees from 1948. While the Alliance of Palestine Forces (APF) made efforts to rally al-Maqdah to its cause, the latter, on his side, tried vainly to obtain the backing of important al-Fatah leaders, such as the brothers Hani and Khalid al-Hasan. The principal members of this movement, in addition to Maqdah, were Abu Khalid al-Arkoub, Jamal Qudsi, and Ali Hussein Fahoud. Black September 13, with the Lebanese Hizbullah, carried out attacks against Israeli forces in south Lebanon in 1995. Since then, Maqdah has been involved in supporting the Hizbullah and the al-Aqsa Martyrs Brigades. Though effectively out of PLO or al-Fatah control since 1993, Maqdah was not formally relieved of his position as al-Fatah commander at Ain al-Hilwa until June 2003.

see also Ayn el-Hilwah; Fatah, al-; Hasan, Hani al-; Hasan, Khalid al-.

Black September 1970: Name given by the Palestinians to the events of September 1970 in Jordan, when the fighters of the Palestine Liberation Organization (PLO) were attacked by the Jordanian army. In ten days of bloody fighting, more than 4,000 people died. Black September was the result of a series of events that began with the defeat of the Arab armies in the Arab-Israel War of 1967, which discredited all Arab governments and particularly disillusioned the Palestinians. The occupation by Israel of the West Bank, which had previously been controlled by Jordan, caused more than 250,000 Palestinians (many already displaced by the 1948-1949 War) to flee to Jordan, and it deprived both them and Jordan of the benefits of the West Bank economy, causing a recession. There was then extensive growth in Jordan of Palestinian organizations and institutions, both social and military, amounting almost to a separate government. The Jordanian government at this point was too weak to prevent this, and there was already hostility to the Jordanian royal house by certain Palestinian movements, such as the Popular Front for the Liberation of Palestine (PFLP), many of whose members were of Jordanian origin.

In 1970, during the war of attrition, Egypt's unsuccessful campaign to drive Israel back from the Suez Canal, U.S. secretary of state William Rogers, who had proposed the rejected Rogers Plan in 1969, offered a modified proposal calling for a ninety-day truce while a cease-fire between Israel and the Arab states was negotiated by United Nations mediator Gunnar Jarring. This was accepted by Egypt, Jordan, and Israel—and unanimously opposed by the PLO. The cease-fire took effect on 7 August. On 16 September 1970, King Hussein formed a military government, and the following day, the Jordanian army undertook its campaign of violent repression of the Palestinians, which lasted until a truce was negotiated by President Gamal Abdel Nasser of Egypt. Fighting broke out again in July 1971; after the Jordanians suppressed it, they expelled the Palestinian organizations from the country *en masse*. These organizations regrouped in Lebanon.

see also Hussein ibn Talal; Nasser, Gamal Abdel; Palestine Liberation Organization; Popular Front for the Liberation of Palestine; Rogers Plan.

Black September Organization: A Palestinian terrorist splinter group, the Black September Organization was formed with the more or less tacit cooperation of the leadership of al-Fatah, after the expulsion of the Palestinian resistance fighters from Jordan in July 1971. This expulsion followed their defeat in the virtual civil war that started in "Black September"

1970. The group's purpose was to avenge the *fida'iyyun* killed during the fighting and to convince Palestinians that a serious fight could be made against their enemies, including Arab governments. The founders of this group, members of al-Fatah, were Muhammad al-Najjar (Abu Yussef), Salah Khalaf (Abu Iyad), Ali Hasan Salameh (Abu Hasan), and Mohammed Daud Odeh (Abu Daud).

On 28 November 1971 a commando of the Black September assassinated the Jordanian prime minister, Wasfi al-Tall, on a visit to Cairo. This was the group's first operation. The following 15 December, it mounted an attack on the Jordanian ambassador to Great Britain, who was seriously wounded. On 5 September 1972, Black September executed a dramatic operation at the Olympic Games in Munich, taking Israeli athletes hostage and demanding the release of 236 Palestinians imprisoned in Israel. After Israeli authorities refused to yield to the blackmail, the German police intervened to try to free the hostages. In the course of the assault, five terrorists and eleven Israeli athletes were killed. A few days later, the Israeli prime minister ordered Mossad to eliminate all the Palestinians who, directly or indirectly, participated in the operation.

On 25 January 1973, in Madrid, a commando of Black September assassinated Baruch Cohen, a member of Israeli special services. The following March, eight members of Black September occupied the embassy of Saudi Arabia, in Khartoum, taking five diplomats hostage, including two Americans and one Belgian. The terrorists demanded the liberation of some fifteen Palestinians imprisoned in Jordan, among whom was Mohammed Daud Odeh, arrested a few days earlier while preparing an attack against King Hussein of Jordan. They also demanded the liberation of Sirhan Sirhan, the assassin of Robert Kennedy. Two days later, having killed the ambassador of the United States, Cleo Noel, the Belgian chargé d'affaires, Guy Eid, and the head of the section of U.S. interests in Sudan, George Curtis Moore, the eight hostage takers surrendered to the Sudanese police. This operation led to a chill in the relations of certain Arab countries with the Palestinian movement and also blocked the attempts Yasir Arafat was making to approach the Americans and the Europeans.

Concurrently, between November 1972 and June 1973, in reprisal for the Munich bloodbath, seven Palestinian leaders believed by the Israelis to be part of Black September were assassinated by the Israeli Mossad. During July 1973, the Mossad team that was assigned this mission killed a Moroccan waiter in Norway, having confused him with Ali Hasan Salameh. At the year's end, after Arafat decided to dissolve Black September, Salah Khalaf took it over, for the purpose of moving its members into the various security services under his charge. In the spring of 1974 a new unit, Force 17, was formed, to assure the personal security of Arafat and to carry out certain missions. It was placed under the command of Ali Hasan Salameh, who appealed to former members of Black September to help organize Force 17. During the following month of October, although the group had been theoretically dissolved, a Black September commando was arrested by the Moroccan police, suspected of preparing an attack on King Hussein of Jordan at the Arab summit that was to be held in Rabat. This arrest led to tension in the relations between the king of Morocco and Arafat.

After the effective dissolution of Black September, some members of the group joined al-Fatah security services, directed by Salah Khalaf, and others joined the Popular Front for the Liberation of Palestine–Special Operations (PFLP–SO) of Wadi' Haddad. Between 1975 and 1978, Ali Hasan al-Salama, nicknamed the "Red Prince," served as liaison to the CIA agent in Beirut, Robert Ames. Thereby the Palestinian organization was able to transmit information to the U.S. intelligence services, in the interests of the security of U.S. citizens in Lebanon. On 22 January, al-Salama was killed in Beirut, in a car bombing carried out by Mossad, with the complicity of Sylvia Raphael, who was supposed to have lured the Red Prince into the trap. Six years later, she was assassinated by a Force 17 commando.

SEE ALSO Black September 1970; Fatah, al-; Mossad.

BLUE LINE: Geographic line marking the frontier between Lebanon and Israel, fixed by the terms of the armistice signed between these two countries on 23 March 1949. This frontier was confirmed by the United Nations in May 2000, after the definitive withdrawal of Israeli troops from South Lebanon. The Shebaa Farms area, which is claimed by Lebanon, remains occupied by Israel pending a settlement with Syria over the Golan Heights.

B'NAI AKIVA (Bene Akiva, Bnei Akiba): Israel youth association, affiliated with the National Religious Party.

B'NAI BRAK: City in the Tel Aviv suburbs, which, along with Jerusalem, has become one of the principal Jewish ultra-Orthodox centers. It is the capital of the *haredim* and has the largest *yeshivot*; life there is markedly removed from the secular world.

SEE ALSO Haredi; Ultra Orthodox; Yeshiva.

B'NAI B'RITH (*Bene Berith,* "sons of the covenant," in Hebrew): Association founded in 1843 in the United States for the purpose of helping new Jewish immigrants. In time, B'nai B'rith turned to the defense of human rights and the struggle against antisemitism and racism. In 1913, its leaders formed the Anti-Defamation League, whose goal was to protect the rights and status of Jews as well as to develop inter-confessional relations. Having become a group with considerable influence, B'nai B'rith is one of the nongovernmental organizations represented at the United Nations, United Nations Educational, Scientific, and Cultural Organization (UNESCO), and the European Council.

BOUEIZ, FARES NOUHAD (1955–): Lebanese political figure. Fares Boueiz was born in 1955 in Lebanon into a Maronite family of distinction. Very early on, he became active in the ranks of the National Unity Party of Raymond Eddé. In November 1989 his father-in-law, Elias Hrawi, president of the Republic of Lebanon, appointed him special counselor to the presidency. In this capacity he traveled frequently to Damascus, where he established good relations with the Syrian leaders. In December he was named foreign minister in the government of Omar Karamé; then in June 1991, he was appointed to parliament as a replacement for a deputy from Kesrouan who had died. In October 1991 he led the Lebanese delegation to the Madrid Conference on the Middle East.

On 27 August 1992, along with other ministers, Boueiz opposed the holding of legislative elections, which were nevertheless held, although characterized by a high rate of abstention. After his reelection as deputy, he was once more named foreign minister in October 1992 in the government of Rafiq al-Hariri. The cabinet reshuffle of 25 May 1995 left him at his post. Boueiz left the government in November 1998, after the resignation of the Hariri cabinet. In June 2003, with Rafiq al-Hariri once again prime minister (since 2000), Bouiez was appointed minister of environment.

SEE ALSO Eddé, Raymond; Hariri, Rafiq Baha'uddin al-.

BOUTROS-GHALI, BOUTROS (1922–): Egyptian political figure. Boutros Boutros-Ghali was born in November 1922 in Cairo to an old Coptic family that produced several highly placed officials in the Egyptian state. His grandfather, Boutros Pasha, prime minister between 1908 and 1910, was assassinated by an Egyptian nationalist who blamed him for the abandonment of Sudan to England (1899). After brilliant studies in law and economics in Cairo and Paris, Boutros-Ghali embarked on a career in journalism and university teaching. Between 1953 and 1977 he was professor of political science at Cairo University. At the same time, he was doing research at the International Law Academy, in The Hague, Holland. As a visiting professor, he taught at many European, African, and Arab universities. He was also responsible for editing a political and economics magazine, *al-Ahram al-Iqtisadi* (Economic al-Ahram), associated with the Egyptian newspaper *al-Ahram.*

BOUTROS BOUTROS-GHALI. AN EGYPTIAN OFFICIAL WHO SUPPORTED PRESIDENT ANWAR AL-SADAT'S EFFORTS TOWARD PEACE WITH ISRAEL IN THE LATE 1970S, HE BECAME SECRETARY GENERAL OF THE UNITED NATIONS IN 1992 AND SERVED UNTIL THE UNITED STATES IN 1995 OPPOSED A SECOND TERM FOR HIM. *(AP/Wide World Photos)*

Backing the policy adopted by President Anwar al-Sadat, Boutros-Ghali joined the Arab Socialist Union, becoming a member of its political bureau. On 27 October 1977 he was named minister without portfolio. That November, when both the foreign affairs minister and the minister of state for foreign affairs resigned in protest against President Sadat's upcoming trip to Israel, Boutros-Ghali was named interim foreign minister. In this capacity, two days later, he accompanied Sadat on his historic visit to Jerusalem. On 24 December, just before Egyptian-Israeli peace parleys were to begin, he was named minister of state for foreign affairs, becoming thereby the principal deputy to the new foreign minister, Muhammad Ibrahim Kamel.

During the following months, Boutros-Ghali visited a number of foreign leaders, particularly in nonaligned countries, to obtain their support for Sadat's initiative. In September 1978, at the time of the Camp David negotiations, he was again named interim foreign minister, following Kamel's resignation. He retained his post in the February 1979 cabinet reshuffle that saw Prime Minister Mustafa Khalil take on the portfolio of foreign minister. At the time of the implementation of the Camp David Accords, Boutros-Ghali participated in various delegations responsible for negotiating specifics, in particular those relating to the Palestinian territories. He was named president of the Egyptian committee responsible for the normalization of Egyptian-Israeli relations. Parallel to his actions conducted in the context of the Egyptian-Israeli peace process, Boutros-Ghali played a key role in promoting the development of relations between Egypt with African countries. On 5 September 1985 he was confirmed in his post as Egypt's minister of state for foreign affairs. On 1 January 1992 he took office as secretary general of the United Nations, replacing Javier Perez de Cuellar. His attempt to win a second five-year term was vetoed by the United States in 1995.

SEE ALSO Camp David Accords; Sadat, Anwar al-.

BOYCOTT OF ISRAEL OFFICE

SEE League of Arab States.

BRIGADES OF THE PALESTINIAN ISLAMIC JIHAD

SEE Palestinian Islamic Jihad.

BRITISH MANDATE: Following the Allied defeat of the Ottoman army in 1918 and the Paris Peace Settlements of 1919, Britain and France assumed control over much of the former Ottoman Empire. On 24 July 1922, confirming the San Remo accords of 1920, the League of Nations entrusted Great Britain with the mission of administration and development of Palestine. Referring to Article 22 of the League of Nations Charter and the Balfour Declaration, and recognizing "the historical connection of the Jewish people with Palestine," the League urged Great Britain to facilitate the establishment in that country of a Jewish national home. The British government published a White Paper (Command Paper 1700) in which it drew "attention to the fact that the terms of the [Balfour] Declaration . . . do not contemplate that Palestine as a whole should be converted into a Jewish National Home, but that such a Home should be founded *in Palestine*." After serving a five-year term, the first high commissioner in Palestine, Herbert Samuel, was replaced in 1925 by Lord Plumer. An organization, the Jewish Agency for Israel, was constituted to represent the Jewish people with the British authorities and international organizations, and the headquarters of the British high commissioner was situated in Jerusalem.

Arab nationalists mobilized against the British and the Jews, leading to bloody confrontations between the communities in 1920, 1921, 1929, and 1933; Jewish underground activities against the British and against the Arabs took place in the late 1930s and 1940s by groups such as the Irgun Zva'i Le'umi. In April 1936, bloody riots broke out between Jews and Arabs, as well as between Arabs and the British. The intervention of Arab rulers of Iraq and Transjordan allowed a return to calm after several months of confrontations. On 22 June 1937, faced with this situation, the Palestine Royal Commission concluded that it was necessary to divide Palestine into two states, one Jewish and the other Arab. The following October, a general insurrection spread to Palestine. Playing on the enmity between the great Arab families, such as the Husayni and the Nashashibi, the British authorities attempted to retake control of the situation.

In March 1938 the Woodhead Commission was formed in response to dissension within the British government over the partition plan for Palestine. The Arab and Jewish positions proved irreconcilable, and the commission's report, issued on 9 November 1939, stated that two independent states would be impracticable, in terms of both finances and administration. It called as well for a conference to negotiate a compromise. The St. James Round Table Conference, which included the Jewish Agency, Arab governments, and Palestinian Arabs, met in London

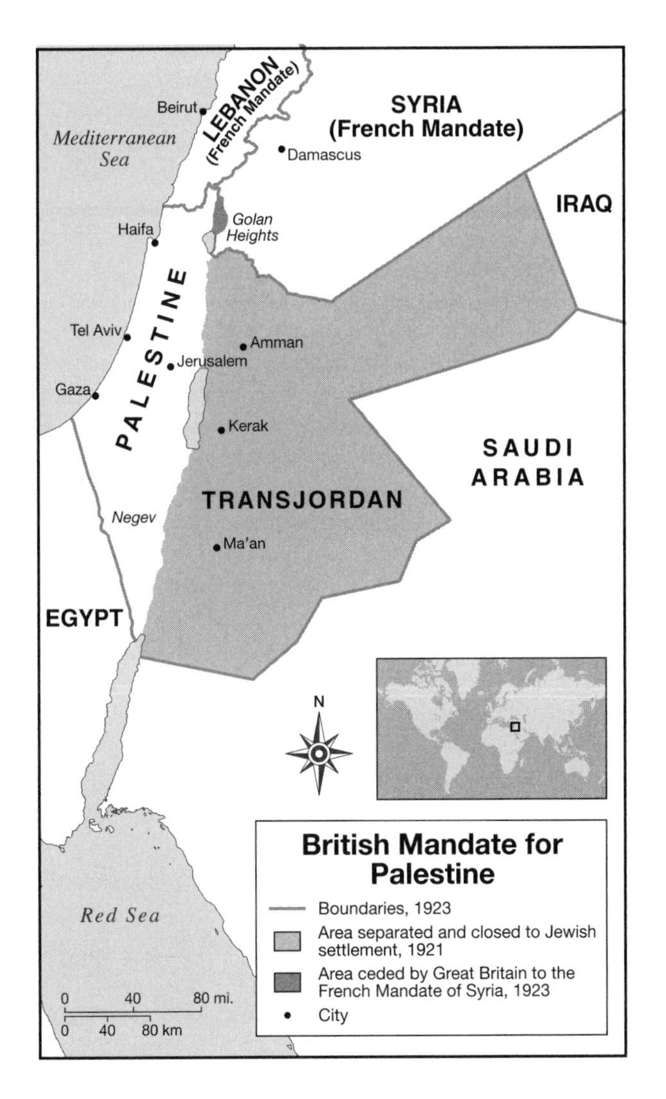

in February and March 1939 but ended in deadlock. The British government then issued the MacDonald White Paper of 17 May 1939, in which it repudiated partition and proposed the creation of self-governing institutions over a ten-year period. It limited Jewish immigration to 75,000 over five years and restricted Jewish purchase of land in some parts of Palestine. The White Paper met with negative reactions on both sides. The Zionists viewed it as a harsh reversal of the Balfour Declaration and the partition proposal, and were incensed by its immigration restrictions, which were imposed at the moment that European Jews were attempting to flee Nazi persecution in Europe. The Palestinians, though they welcomed restriction of Jewish immigration and land purchase, were skeptical that London would fulfill its promises. Apart from the immigration restrictions, the MacDonald White Paper remained largely unimplemented.

Following the Holocaust and World War II, the crucial problem of the placement and treatment of Jewish survivors added an element of urgency to discussions of Jewish immigration to Palestine. The United States called for the admission of 100,000 Jews into Palestine. Britain offered to convene an Anglo-American Committee of Inquiry (AAC) to seek a solution to the Arab-Jewish conflict and to the plight of the European Jewish refugees. The AAC met in January 1946; its recommendations, issued three months later, included the immigration of 100,000 Jews to Palestine, the annulment of restrictions against Jewish purchase of land, and the indefinite extension of trusteeship (essentially the British Mandate system) in Palestine. The AAC's report was shelved just a few months afterward; the British backed away from its adoption, and the United States was not willing to assist in its implementation.

On 14 January 1947 the British prime minister, Ernest Bevin, decided to relinquish the British Mandate over Palestine to the United Nations (UN). On 29 November the UN voted for a partition of Palestine between two states: one Jewish and the other Arab. Arab demonstrations against the UN plan and Jewish celebrations in support of it turned to violent clashes, and Jewish and Arab forces were soon battling throughout the country. The British Mandate over Palestine expired on 14 May 1948. By that time Jewish forces had seized most of the territory allocated to the Jewish state by the UN partition plan as well as land beyond those proposed borders. On 19 May 1948 David Ben-Gurion declared the independence of the new State of Israel. The Arab-Israeli War became an international conflict between the Jewish state and the armies of Egypt, Transjordan, Syria, Lebanon, and Iraq, with some involvement by Saudi Arabia and Yemen.

SEE ALSO Anglo-American Committee of Inquiry; Arab-Israel War (1948); Balfour Declaration; Ben-Gurion, David; Bevin, Ernest; Jewish Agency for Israel; Palestine Arab Revolt (1936–1939); White Papers on Palestine.

BRIT SHALOM: Founded in 1925, Brit Shalom (Covenant of Peace) was a Jewish organization that promoted binationalism, asserting that Palestine belonged to both Palestinian Arabs and Jews, and that both were entitled to national self-determination. Among its founders were Judah Magnes, president of the Hebrew University of Jerusalem, and Arthur

Ruppin, head of the Palestine Office of the World Zionist Organization. In 1942 Magnes and other Brit Shalom members created the Ihud (Union) Association, which presented its ideas for a binational government in Palestine to the Anglo-American Committee of Inquiry in 1946, and then to the United Nations Special Committee on Palestine in 1947. Ihud proposed dividing Palestine into districts, which would have a large degree of autonomy, with two national committees, Jewish and Arab, and a federal executive and legislature. Although Brit Shalom ultimately became a marginal group, in 2001 a new organization, Brit Shalom/Tahalof Essalam (the Jewish-Palestinian Alliance for Peace), was founded. The organization promotes the ideals of full and equal rights for the Arab citizens of Israel, the rejection of violence, and the renewal of a dialogue aimed at creating a lasting peace between Israelis and Palestinians.

SEE ALSO Anglo-American Committee of Inquiry; Magnes, Judah.

B'SEISSO, ATEF FA'IQ (Abu Raouf; 1946–1992): Palestinian militant, born in Gaza, Palestine. In 1971, Atef B'seisso joined the ranks of Black September, which was led by Salah Khalaf (Abu Iyad). In September 1973, he was arrested in Ostia, Italy, along with four other Palestinians, among whom was Amin al-Hindi (Abu Zuhayr), while they were preparing an attack against the Israeli airline El Al. A few days later, the group was set free. After going to Lebanon, B'seisso was named head of the civil arm of Fatah's security forces headed by Khalaf. In 1983, he was assigned to East Berlin as representative of the Palestinian Liberation Organization's security council, in charge of relations with East German special services. In August 1989, he was elected to al-Fatah's revolutionary council, where he collaborated closely with Khalaf in the organization's security council. In 1991, after the assassination of Khalaf and Hayel Abdul Hamid (Abu al-Houl), he became part of the leadership of Fatah's security council, along with al-Hindi. In his new duties, B'seisso had numerous contacts with leaders of Arab and Western special services. In October 1991, he went to Madrid to organize security for the Palestinian delegation at the Middle East peace conference. The following year, he was assassinated in front of his hotel, in Paris, France. According to some investigators, the Mossad (the Israeli intelligence agency) may have been behind the murder because of B'seisso's suspected participation in the massacre of Israeli athletes in the Munich Olympic Games of 1972. According to others, he was the victim of a settling of scores within the Palestinian leadership.

SEE ALSO Black September Organization; Fatah, al-; Hindi, Amin al-; Khalaf, Salah.

B'TSELEM: A human rights organization, B'Tselem, or the Israeli Center for Human Rights, was founded in 1989 by a group of academics, journalists, attorneys, and members of the Knesset. In Hebrew, *B'Tselem* means "in the image of," a reference to the Biblical assertion that humans were created in the image of God. B'Tselem focuses on human rights violations by Israeli authorities in the Occupied Territories, addressing what it calls the "phenomenon of denial prevalent among the Israeli public." It regularly publishes reports on its findings; the reports include allegations of torture, shootings by security forces, restriction on movement, and expropriation of land. B'Tselem distributes printed material to the public, holds press conferences, participates in protests in the occupied territories, and provides information to members of the Knesset.

SEE ALSO Peace Now.

BURG, AVRAHAM (1955–): Israeli political figure. Born in 1955 in Jerusalem, Avraham Burg is the son of the leader of the National Religious Party, Yosef Burg, who joined the government of Menachem Begin as minister of the interior in August 1981. The following year, after completing his military service, Avraham Burg participated in forming a small group, "Soldiers Against Silence," that called for an investigation of the circumstances surrounding the Sabra and Shatila massacres. Shortly afterward, he joined the ranks of Peace Now, where he spoke in favor of Israeli-Arab peace and the creation of a Palestinian state. In 1984, having joined the Israel Labor Party, he became advisor to Prime Minister Shimon Peres on issues related to the diaspora. In 1986, he was named director of the Center for Judaism and Tolerance.

During the summer of 1988, Avraham Burg was elected Labor Party member of Knesset and was appointed chairman of its education committee. Confirming his reputation as an orator, he became one of the principal figures in the party and a leader of its "dove" wing. In the Knesset, his fight for tolerance and for the creation of an Israeli constitution attracted notice. In the parliamentary elections of June 1992, he ranked third on the Labor Party list, after

Yitzhak Rabin and Shimon Peres. Within the Labor Party, he belonged to the renewal tendency, along with Yossi Beilin, Yael Dayan, and Nawaf Massalha. On 15 February 1995 Burg was elected chairman of the executive committee of the Jewish Agency for Israel, the state organization in charge of immigration to Israel and relations with the diaspora. A few months later he launched an international inquiry to restore to their rightful owners or their descendants the Jewish assets seized during World War II and deposited in Swiss banks.

In June 1999 Burg was reelected to his Knesset seat and was chosen speaker of the Knesset; while the head of the Labor Party, Ehud Barak, was elected prime minister. On 4 September 2000, his selection as head of the Labor Party was contested by his adversary, Benyamin Ben-Eliezer, leading to the initiation of an internal inquiry procedure. He was invited, shortly thereafter, to the European Parliament in Strasbourg, France, along with the president of the Palestinian Legislative Council, Ahmad Qurai. There, Burg spoke on the subject of the Israeli-Palestinian peace process, recommending the resumption of negotiations. Affirming that "religious fundamentalism" was the common enemy of both the Palestinians and Israelis, he came out in favor of shared "sovereignty" of the three religions (Jewish, Christian, and Muslim) in Jerusalem, and for the creation of a Palestinian state. That year, Burg was finally bested by Ben-Eliezer for the leadership of the Labor Party, in an election where participation was particularly low. In 2003 Burg was re-elected to the Knesset on the Labor Party list. Since that time, he has written several critiques of Israeli policy regarding the Israeli-Palestinian conflict.

SEE ALSO Barak, Ehud; Beilin, Yossi; Ben-Eliezer, Benyamin; Israel Labor Party; Peace Now.

BURNS, WILLIAM (1957–): American diplomat. Born in 1957, William Burns earned degrees in history and international relations. Between 1982 and 1984 he was a political advisor attached to the United States Embassy in Jordan. He came to be appreciated by the Jordanian leaders for his seriousness, pragmatism, and profound knowledge of the issues. Between 1995 and 1996 he was spokesperson for the U.S. State Department for Middle Eastern Affairs. In August 1998 he was named United States ambassador to Jordan. In this capacity, Burns participated in numerous negotiations between Palestinians and Israelis, including those at the Wye Plantation. On 21 May 2001, Secretary of State Colin Powell appointed him special emissary for the Near East, in charge of negotiating the application of the Mitchell report recommendations with Palestinian and Israeli leaders. Burns traveled to the West Bank, where he met with Yasir Arafat, then on to Israel, where he was received by Ariel Sharon. That June, Burns was named assistant secretary of state for Near Eastern affairs. William Burns is the author of *Economic Aid and American Policy toward Egypt, 1955–1981.*

SEE ALSO Oslo Accords II.

BUSH, GEORGE H. W. (1924–): U.S. president (1989–1993). George H. W. Bush served in World War II as a naval combat pilot. He graduated from Yale University, then moved to Texas, where he worked as an oil executive. He was elected to the House of Representatives, and later served as director of the Central Intelligence Agency, U.S. ambassador to the United Nations, and vice president under Ronald Reagan. As president he continued the first official U.S. dialogue with the Palestine Liberation Organization, which had begun in December 1998, shortly before Bush took office, and which continued until June 1990. Jointly with President Gorbachev, he convened the Madrid Conference in October 1991, the first formal Arab-Israeli peace negotiations since the 1979 Israel-Egypt treaty. The talks, presided over by the United States and the Soviet Union, included Palestinians for the first time, as part of a joint Jordanian-Palestinian delegation.

SEE ALSO Madrid Conference.

BUSH, GEORGE W. (1946–): U.S. president (2001–). The son of George H. W. Bush, George W. Bush graduated from Yale University and Harvard University. He worked in the petroleum industry, and he later served as governor of Texas (1995–2001). He was elected U.S. president as a result of the controversial elections of November 2000; his opponent, Albert Gore, received more popular votes than Bush, but the Supreme Court intervened to resolve the disputed Florida electoral vote in Bush's favor. The Bush administration's involvement in the Middle East centered around counter-terrorism policies following the attacks of 11 September 2001; Bush ordered the invasion of Afghanistan in October 2001 and launched a war against Iraq's Saddam Hussein in March 2003, toppling the Hussein government. After some initial hesitation, he also followed the efforts of his predecessor, Bill Clinton, to forge an Israeli-Palestinian peace. He became the first U.S.

PRESIDENTS BUSH. GEORGE W. BUSH (RIGHT) AND HIS FATHER, GEORGE H. W. BUSH, EACH MADE SOME EFFORTS TOWARD ISRAELI-PALESTINIAN PEACE WHILE PRESIDENT. IN 1991, THE FIRST PRESIDENT BUSH (AND HIS SOVIET COUNTERPART) CONVENED THE FIRST FACE-TO-FACE ARAB-ISRAELI PEACE TALKS IN MORE THAN A DECADE, WITH PALESTINIAN DELEGATES INCLUDED FOR THE FIRST TIME. THE SECOND PRESIDENT BUSH GENERALLY PRAISED PRIME MINISTER ARIEL SHARON OF ISRAEL AND SHUNNED PALESTINIAN LEADER YASIR ARAFAT, BUT HE ALSO OPENLY SUPPORTED THE RAPID CREATION OF A PALESTINIAN STATE AS PART OF HIS "ROAD MAP" FOR PEACE. *(AP/Wide World Photos)*

president to call openly for the creation of a Palestinian state, though his administration refused to deal with Palestinian Authority leader Yasir Arafat. At the same time, Bush called Israeli prime minister Ariel Sharon a "man of peace." The Bush administration, forming a "Quartet" along with the United Nations, Russia, and the European Union, developed a "Road Map" for peace that was presented at the Aqaba Summit in June 2003.

SEE ALSO Aqaba Summit; Arafat, Yasir; Clinton, William Jefferson; Hussein, Saddam.

Caliph (from the Arab word *khalifa,* deputy, successor): Muslim ruler and head of the Muslim community. The first Caliphs and successors to Muhammad were Abu Bakr al-Siddiq (632–635), Omar ibn al-Khattab (635–644), Othman ibn Affan (645–656), and Ali ibn Abi Talib (656–661). Some Muslim historians question the claim of Abu Bakr to the title of Caliph, since it was not until the reign of Omar ibn al-Khattab that the "commander of believers" was designated by the title of *khalifat rasûl Allâh* (successor to God's messenger). The Caliphate has been in dispute throughout history, with multiple claims to authority. Therefore, historians distinguish between the Eastern Caliphate, the Umayyad Caliphate of Cordoba, the Fatimid Caliphate of North Africa, and the Ottoman Caliphate.

see also Fatimids; Ottomans; Umayyads.

Cambon

see Cambon Declaration.

Cambon Declaration: Statement made on 4 June 1917 by then-French Foreign Minister Jules Cambon. The declaration expressed the "sympathy" of France for the Zionist cause, described as a "renaissance, under the aegis of the world powers, of Jewish nationality on this land [of Palestine] from which the people of Israel had been driven."

Camp David

see Camp David Accords.

Camp David II

see Camp David II Summit.

Camp David II Summit: Unsuccessful Israeli-Palestinian negotiations that took place at the U.S. presidential retreat at Camp David, Maryland, from 11 to 24 July 2000, sponsored by President Bill Clinton, assisted by his secretary of state, Madeleine Albright. The summit brought together the Palestinian president, Yasir Arafat, with the Israeli prime minister, Ehud Barak, at a time when both were in a weakened position within their own camps. The Americans deliberately chose the symbolic site of Camp David, where the Israeli-Egyptian peace accords of 1978 were negotiated.

No official documents were exchanged as a result of the summit, so most knowledge of the proceedings comes from media accounts and interviews with some participants. There were several areas of disagreement. Israel reportedly was willing to relinquish some Palestinian villages and neighborhoods to the Palestinian Authority (PA), but was unwilling to give up East Jerusalem and the Old City. The Palestinians were reported to have proposed that East Jerusalem become the capital of the new Palestinian state and that Israel relinquish territory gained during the

Arab-Israel War of 1967. The right of return was reportedly another insurmountable issue. The Palestinians asserted that 3.7 million Palestinian refugees should either be allowed to return to their homes in Israel or should receive compensation. Israel rejected both alternatives, contending that the return would threaten the identity of the Jewish state. Concerning the question of Jewish settlements, Israel proposed the annexation of 10 percent of West Bank territory, where the majority of the settlements were located, with the remaining 90 percent of the territory going to the Palestinians. The Palestinians objected to the size of the proposed annexation and called for an equal amount of territory in Israel. No agreement could be reached.

At the conclusion of the summit, the two leaders, Israeli and Palestinian, presented the following principles for future negotiation: "1) The two parties agree that the object of their negotiations is to put an end to decades of conflict and realize a just and durable peace; 2) The two parties commit themselves to pursue their efforts to conclude, as soon as possible, an accord on all questions relating to a permanent status; 3) The two parties agree that negotiations based on UN Resolutions 242 and 338 are the only means of coming to an agreement, and they commit themselves to creating the conditions for being able to negotiate without pressure, intimidation or the threat of violence; 4) The two parties agree on the importance of avoiding unilateral initiatives and that their divergences can only be resolved on the basis of the good faith of each; 5) The two parties agree that the United States will remain a vital partner in the peace process, and that they will stay in close contact with President Clinton and Secretary of State Albright."

In December 2000 the United States presented a proposal, called the Clinton Plan, to guide a resumption of the negotiation process, and talks began in Taba, Egypt. Time ran out, however, as Clinton left office in January 2001 and Barak lost to Ariel Sharon in the Israeli elections in February.

SEE ALSO Albright, Madeleine; Arafat, Yasir; Barak, Ehud; Clinton, William Jefferson; Clinton Plan.

CAMP DAVID ACCORDS: The signing of these accords, in September 1978, resulted from the American desire to establish durable peace in the Middle East and from a process of negotiations started between the Israeli government, led by Menachem Begin, and Egyptian President Anwar al-Sadat. Immediately upon his coming to power in Israel, in June 1977, Menachem Begin, leader of Israeli right-wing party Herut, made a number of gestures toward the Arab countries in an attempt to resolve the Arab–Israeli contentions arising from the 1967 Arab-Israel War as well as the 1973 war. His Labor Party foreign minister, Moshe Dayan, participated in numerous secret meetings with Arab leaders, while U.S. secretary of state Henry Kissinger tried to convince the Israelis and Egyptians of the need to come to a peace agreement. These steps concluded, on 9 November 1977, in the historic trip of President Sadat to Israel, which in turn brought about, in early December, the creation of a Refusal Front uniting Arab countries opposed to a negotiated peace with Israel.

A year later, after intense negotiations under the supervision of then-U.S. president Jimmy Carter, Begin and Sadat signed two general agreements at Camp David on 17 September 1978. The first defined the basis of a solution to the Israeli-Egyptian conflict: restitution of the Egyptian territories occupied by Israel in exchange for a peace treaty. The second, which concerned the Palestinian question, stipulated that any solution must take into account "the recognition of the legitimate rights of the Palestine people" and specified that the latter would exercise full and complete autonomy within a five-year period. At the end of this period, Egypt, Jordan, and Palestinian delegates would negotiate the final status of the territories with Israel. However, the Palestinians in the territories, overwhelmingly supporting the Palestine Liberation Organization in this matter, rejected the accord, about which they had not been consulted. On 27 October 1978, the Nobel Peace Prize was awarded jointly to Sadat and Begin. On 26 March 1979, in spite of the Palestinian rejection, Egypt and Israel signed a peace agreement ending thirty years of belligerence. Following the signing, the member countries of the Arab League transferred the headquarters of the organization from Cairo, Egypt, to Tunis. Eighteen Arab countries recalled their ambassadors from Cairo. On 6 October 1981, President Sadat was assassinated in Cairo. On 25 April 1982, with the dismantling of the last Jewish colonies, Egypt reestablished sovereignty over the whole of its territory, including the Sinai.

SEE ALSO Arab-Israel War (1967); Arab-Israel War (1973); Begin, Menachem; Dayan, Moshe; Herut Party; League of Arab States; Palestine Liberation Organization; Sadat, Anwar al-.

CANAAN: Name of Phoenicia-Palestine before the coming of the Hebrews, who, led by Abraham around 1790 B.C.E., saw this as the land promised to

HISTORIC MOMENT. PRESIDENT ANWAR AL-SADAT (LEFT) OF EGYPT AND PRIME MINISTER MENACHEM BEGIN OF ISRAEL FLANK PRESIDENT JIMMY CARTER ON 26 MARCH 1979 AT THE WHITE HOUSE, AS THEY LISTEN TO THE THREE COUNTRIES' NATIONAL ANTHEMS BEFORE SIGNING A PEACE TREATY BASED ON THE CAMP DAVID ACCORDS OF 1978. *(© Wally McNamee/Corbis)*

them by God. The name *Canaan* comes from the word *kinahu,* which means a region where the population has mastered the technique of purple dyeing. According to Biblical tradition, the Israelites established themselves in the land of Canaan after leaving Egypt twice: the first time led by Abraham, around 1800 B.C.E., the second by Moses, five hundred years later. From this later date, the Hebrews lived there in stable settlements until the breakup of the Kingdom of Judah. Many cities were built in the natural highlands of the country, including Megiddo, Hebron, Sh'khem (Nablus), Gezer, and Salem (Jerusalem, Urusalimu). Although they had sworn loyalty to the religion of Moses, some Hebrews borrowed religious customs from the Canaanites, even worshipping their gods, such as Baal and Astarte. Toward the year 1004 B.C.E., David conquered the city of Salem, inhabited by the Jebuseans, and under the name of Jerusalem made it the capital of the kingdom of Israel. The reign of Solomon (968–928 B.C.E.) marked the apogee of Israelite royalty, exemplified by the construction of the Temple, which housed the Ark of the Covenant. According to the Bible, Canaan was the son of Shem and the eponymous ancestor of the Canaanites.

SEE ALSO Abraham; Baal; Bible; Hebrews; Hebron; Israelite; Jerusalem; Moses.

CANAANISM: Movement created by a small group of Jewish artists and intellectuals in 1942 within the revisionist current of Vladimir Jabotinsky.

SEE ALSO Jabotinsky, Vladimir Ze'ev.

CARLOS

SEE Ramirez, Ilyich Sanchez.

CATHOLIC (from the Greek *katholikos,* universal): Person associated with Catholicism or professing a faith in accord with the doctrine and practices of the Roman Catholic Church, based on the principles taught by Jesus Christ and transmitted by the Apostles. There were approximately 50,000 Catholics living in the Occupied Territories in 2002. In Israel, Roman Catholics are mostly guest workers.

SEE ALSO Christianity; Jesus; Roman Catholic Church.

CEASEFIRE SURVEILLANCE COMMITTEE: Organization created on 26 April 1996, following the Israeli military intervention in South Lebanon (Operation "Grapes of Wrath") against Hizbullah, which, according to Human Rights Watch, killed 154 people and wounded 351. The Ceasefire Surveillance Committee was made up of representatives of the United States, Israel, Lebanon, Syria, and France and was responsible for overseeing the agreement that ended the fighting, which required the belligerents to refrain from firing on civilians on both sides of the border and from launching operations from zones populated by civilians. On 11 February 2000, Israel withdrew from the committee, leading to its de facto suspension.

SEE ALSO Hizbullah; South Lebanon.

CEDMENA: Conference on the Economic Development of the Middle East and North Africa.

CENTER PARTY (Mifleget ha-Merkaz): An Israeli political entity, the Center Party was created on 25 January 1999 under the impetus of Yitzhak Mordechai, former defense minister, who had resigned from the Netanyahu government and was a dissident from the Likud Party. Among the main leaders of this party were Amnon Lipkin-Shahak, former chief of the general staff of the Israel Defense Force; Dan Meridor, former finance minister, who had resigned from the Netanyahu government and was also a dissident from Likud; and Roni Milo, former mayor of Tel Aviv and former Likud member. A few days later, they were joined by Dalia Rabin-Pelosoff, the daughter of former prime minister Yitzhak Rabin, and by Uri Savir. Formed in anticipation of the general elections of May 1999, this party declared itself in favor of the creation of a Palestinian entity, and of a territorial compromise on the Golan Heights, under certain conditions for protecting the security of Israel. Their official stand on the Golan Heights issue demonstrated the party's ability to reconcile divergent views. Mordechai was designated as candidate for the post of prime minister, to run against Benjamin Netanyahu, Ehud Barak, Benny Begin, and Azmi Bishara. On 14 May, just before the vote, Mordechai announced the withdrawal of his candidacy and asked his supporters to vote in favor Barak, the candidate of the Labor Party.

On 18 May, as a result of the elections, in which Barak emerged the victor, the Center Party won six seats in the Knesset and agreed to join Barak's governing coalition. The Center Party received many votes from supporters of the Third Way. Two leaders of the Center Party joined Barak's cabinet: Mordechai, as deputy prime minister and transport minister, and Lipkin-Shahak, as minister of tourism. On 28 May 2000, implicated in a sexual harassment scandal, Mordechai resigned his ministerial duties and his post as president of the Center Party. Early elections for the post of prime minister took place on 6 February 2001 and resulted in the victory of Ariel Sharon, the head of Likud. A few days later, the number of deputies of the Center Party fell to five, after the departure of Rabin-Pelosoff, who created her own party, the New Way, and then, the following month, joined the Sharon government as deputy minister of defense. Two leaders of the Center Party, Meridor and Milo, joined Sharon's national unity government in August 2001 and were respectively named minister without portfolio, in charge of strategic affairs, and minister of regional cooperation, effectively dismantling the Center Party, which received only 0.1 percent of the vote in the 2003 elections.

SEE ALSO Lipkin-Shahak, Amnon; Likud; Meridor, Dan; Milo, Roni; Mordechai, Yitzhak; Rabin-Pelosoff, Dalia; Savir, Uri; Sharon, Ariel.

CENTO

SEE Baghdad Pact.

CENTRAL COUNCIL OF THE PLO

SEE Palestine Liberation Organization.

CHABAD

SEE Lubavitcher Hasidim.

CHAI VE-KAYAM ("alive and well," in Hebrew): Israeli ultranationalist, extremist movement, founded at the end of the 1970s. This splinter group advocated the "divorce of Judaism from exile and from Western culture" and the creation of a "truly Jewish state" by invoking a revolutionary messianism meant to "update the Torah as the normative guide of the Jewish people." Its members have made a number of attempts to blow up Muslim religious edifices in Jerusalem on the Haram al-Sharif.

President of Lebanon. Camille Chamoun (right), who was elected in 1952, converses with King Hussein of Jordan in December 1955. Chamoun was forced out of power three years later as a result of the 1958 Lebanese Civil War, but he remained influential politically until the end of 1976. *(© Bettmann/Corbis)*

see also Haram al-Sharif.

Challah: Egg-loaf bread consumed by Jews, especially during the Shabbat.

see also Shabbat.

Chamoun, Camille (1900–1987): President of the Republic of Lebanon (1952–1958). Camille Chamoun was born in 1900 at Dayr al-Qamar, in southern Mount Lebanon. Between 1916 and 1918, his family was forced into exile because of his father's pro-French sympathies. After he obtained a law degree, Chamoun worked in journalism, then was admitted to the bar in 1925. Elected representative of the Mount Lebanon area in 1934, he joined the ranks of the Destourian Bloc and became finance minister in 1938. During World War II he advocated the abolition of the French mandate over Lebanon. After Lebanon gained independence in 1943, Chamoun served as minister of the interior. From 1944 to 1947, he was ambassador of Lebanon in London, and also headed the Lebanese delegation at the United Nations, where he supported the cause of the Palestinians. In 1947 he was again named finance minister, and in April of the following year, represented his country at the Arab League.

After the legislative elections of 1951, Chamoun joined the ranks of the Socialist and Nationalist Front. On 2 September 1952, he was elected president of the Republic of Lebanon, following the withdrawal of his rival, Hamid Franjiyya. During his tenure, Chamoun modified the electoral districting in Lebanon, so as to lessen the influence of feudal holdovers. Internationally, he supported the Baghdad Pact without joining it, disapproved of the nationalization of the Suez Canal by Egyptian president Gamel Abdel Nasser, and was a partisan of the Eisenhower Doctrine. His rigging of the Parliamentary elections of 1957 led Chamoun's rivals to rebel against him in what has since become known as the 1958 Lebanese Civil War. Chamoun was allowed to stay in office until the end of his term—September

1958—but was not allowed to run for a second mandate.

Replaced in the presidency by Fouad Chehab, Chamoun retook his deputy's seat. In 1959 he founded the National Liberal Party (NLP), which maintained support for his political line. A determined opponent of President Chehab, the NLP formed an alliance with the Phalange of Pierre Jumayyil and the National Bloc of Raymond Eddé. During the summer of 1968, the coalition NLP-Phalange-National Bloc came out on top in the legislative elections. In 1970 Chamoun backed the election to the presidency of his adversary, Sulayman Franjiyya (Hamid's brother). Reelected to the Chamber in 1972, Chamoun became minister of the interior in the Karame government in July 1975.

During the Civil War of 1975–1976, Chamoun played a significant role as leader of the National Liberal Party, participating in political and military fighting on the Maronite fronts. On 17 June 1976, he was named foreign minister. Three months later he was appointed interim prime minister and was assigned the joined portfolios of foreign affairs and defense, up to the month of December. At that time he was accused by his enemies of being in favor of an alliance of the Lebanese Christian camp with Israel, while within his own party he found himself at odds with other Maronite leaders. In December 1976, Chamoun resigned from his positions. In July 1980, after bloody confrontations, the Lebanese Forces defeated NLP's militia, headed by his son Dany. Chamoun participated in the Government of National Unity formed in 1984, but his influence on national politics was negligible. He died in 1987.

SEE ALSO Chamoun, Dory; Eddé, Raymond; Franjiyya, Sulayman; Phalange.

CHAMOUN, DORI (1931–): Lebanese political figure. Born in November 1931 at Dayr al-Qamar, Lebanon, Dori Chamoun is the son of the former Lebanese president Camille Chamoun, and the brother of Dany Chamoun (who was assassinated, along with his wife and two of his children on 21 October 1990). With a degree in commercial law, Dori Chamoun was a businessman until the mid-1970s. In 1975 he became secretary general of the National Liberal Party (NLP), a rightist party founded by his father. In September 1978, along with Bashir Jumayyil, he opened the office of the American Lebanese League in Washington, whose purpose was to organize the support of the U.S.-based Lebanese community in the struggle against the Syrian presence in Lebanon. On 2 September 1985 he became president of the NLP. Between 1986 and 1990 he returned to business, leaving his post as head of the NLP to his brother Dany.

In May 1991, after his brother was assassinated, Dori Chamoun was reelected president of the NLP. In June 1998 he became a town councillor of his native city, Dayr al-Qamar. In April 2001 Chamoun helped to found the Qornet Shehwan Gathering (named after the Maronite monastery in which the founding meetings had been held), a coalition of Christian political groups that oppose the government and the Syrian presence in Lebanon. Qornet Shehwan formally advocates judiciary reform and the elimination of corruption, and has made gestures toward the Druze and other non-Christian Lebanese factions; generally, however, it has not managed to rise above its Maronite factionalist origins. It is understood to be dominated by its more right-wing elements. For the elections of May 2004, Qornet Shehwan formed a unified electoral list with the backing of such groups as the Lebanese Forces and the Phalange Party opposition.

SEE ALSO Chamoun, Camille; Jumayyil, Bashir.

CHARISMATIC: In Christianity, this term means a spiritual movement based on the conviction that the Holy Spirit continues to grant spiritual gifts (charismas) to believers.

CHRIST

SEE Christianity.

CHRISTIANITY: A religion based on the teachings of Jesus of Nazareth, a Jew who preached in Judea in the first century C.E. and was crucified by Roman authorities. His followers, who believed that he rose from the dead, considered him the Messiah of the Jews, son of God, and redeemer of humankind. The Greek *christos,* which means "the anointed one," is a translation of "Messiah." For the Jews, according to the Talmud, Jesus was a rabbi who desired to modify the religious practices of his time. He was neither Messiah nor prophet. The first apostles never denied their Jewish origins, and they always affirmed their opposition to idolatry. Around 45 C.E. some of the apostles, notably Paul, began to preach to the Gentiles of the Middle East. By the fourth century, Christianity had become the official religion of the Roman Empire. Though censuses in the Middle East, particularly concerning religious affiliation, are unreliable at best, estimates have put the number of Christians in the Middle East at the turn of the twenty-first century at 8 to 12 million. Among the Palestinian population of Israel, by the 1990s Christians accounted for approximately 13 percent.

SEE ALSO Gentile; Messiah.

CHRISTOPHER, WARREN (1925–): U.S. politician, secretary of state (1993–1996). Warren Christopher was born in October 1925 in North Dakota. In 1959 he became president of the Lawyer's Guild of Los Angeles and also an advisor to the governor of California, Edmund Brown. In 1965, following the Watts riots in California, President Lyndon B. Johnson appointed him to head a commission of inquiry. Between 1967 and 1969 Christopher was assistant attorney general in the federal department of justice. During his tenure he headed, among others, commissions charged with inquiry into the Detroit riots and the assassination of Dr. Martin Luther King, Jr.

From 1977 to 1981 Christopher was deputy secretary of state, second to Cyrus Vance. During his time in office, he won, in March 1978, the lifting of the embargo on the northern part of Cyprus, occupied by the Turkish Army. The government of Ankara had threatened to withdraw from the North Atlantic Treaty Organization (NATO) if the embargo was kept in place. In January 1981 he negotiated successfully the release of the American hostages who had been held more than a year in Tehran. He withdrew from the State Department to become head of the law firm of O'Meleveny & Meyers. On 6 November 1992, with lawyer Vernon Jordan, he was appointed by President-elect Bill Clinton to preside over a governmental transition team.

In January 1993, Christopher became secretary of state in the Clinton administration. He devoted a major portion of his activity to the peace process in the Middle East. In August 1993, he visited Jordan, Israel, and Syria. In December of the same year, after having been to Rome, Brussels, and Geneva in the context of the European Security Conference, he traveled to Israel, along with Edward Djerejian and Dennis Ross. In the course of the following year, he took a number of trips to the Middle East, in an effort to organize direct negotiations between Israelis and Syrians, as well as to meet with local political leaders involved in the peace process. At the end of January 1996, he attempted, in vain, to get the Israeli-Syrian negotiations held at the Wye Plantation in the United States to move forward. In April, when Israel launched its operation "Grapes of Wrath" in Lebanon, Christopher shuttled back and forth between Damascus and Tel Aviv to obtain a cease-fire between Hizbullah and the Israel Defense Force. In December 1996, Christopher resigned his position as secretary of state; he was replaced by Madeleine Albright, the first woman to hold this office, in January 1997. Christopher served as advisor to Vice-President Al Gore, the Democratic candidate for president, in the 2000 campaign. Christopher is the author of *In the Stream of History: Shaping Foreign Policy for a New Era* (1998) and *Chances of a Lifetime* (2001).

SEE ALSO Albright, Madeleine; Clinton, William Jefferson; Djerejian, Edward; Ross, Dennis B.

CIRCASSIANS: Originally from the Black Sea area, some Circassians and Chechens (all Muslim) emigrated to the Ottoman Empire in the middle of the nineteenth century, when tsarist troops invaded their lands. Since they were famous for their abilities as warriors and scouts, Sultan Abdul Hamid inducted them into units responsible for the Syrian and Palestinian frontiers. Small groups still live in Syria, Jordan, and Israel. In Israel, as a non-Arab minority, they are required to serve in the military and are generally incorporated into units in charge of border security.

CIRCUMCISION (*khitan,* in Arabic; *britmilah,* in Hebrew): Removal of the foreskin. Arab-Bedouin and Semitic custom practiced on boys. Circumcision was originally an initiation rite whose goal was mainly hygienic. Jews perform it on the eighth day after birth so as to commemorate the covenant between their people and God. Muslims circumcise their sons at a variety of ages, depending on the region. Every 1 January, the Catholic Church celebrates the circumcision of Christ.

SEE ALSO Covenant.

CITIZENS' RIGHTS MOVEMENT

SEE Movement for Civil Rights and Peace.

CLINTON, WILLIAM JEFFERSON (1946–): U.S. president (1993–2001). Born in Hope, Arkansas, Bill Clinton received a bachelor's degree from Georgetown University and a law degree from Yale. He was elected governor of Arkansas in 1978, losing a reelection bid in 1980 before returning for five successive terms from 1982 to 1993. After assuming the U.S. presidency in 1993, Clinton found himself thrust into Middle Eastern affairs, and during his presidency he devoted more attention to the Arab-Israeli peace process than any previous U.S. president. Although his administration was not directly involved

CIRCASSIAN REFUGEES. THIS ILLUSTRATION DEPICTS A FEW OF THE MUSLIMS WHO FLED TO THE OTTOMAN EMPIRE IN THE MID-NINETEENTH CENTURY WHEN RUSSIAN TROOPS INVADED THEIR HOMELAND AROUND THE BLACK SEA. SOME CIRCASSIANS STILL LIVE IN SYRIA, JORDAN, AND ISRAEL. *(© Bettmann/Corbis)*

in the secret talks in Oslo in 1993 between Israel and the Palestine Liberation Organization (PLO), the resulting Oslo Accord was signed on the White House lawn, where Clinton urged the now-famous handshake between Israeli prime minister Yitzhak Rabin and PLO chairman Yasir Arafat—the first public demonstration of civilities between two high-ranking Israeli and Palestinian leaders. At the same time, Clinton became the first sitting U.S. president to publicly meet with Arafat on U.S. soil.

After Rabin's assassination in November 1995, the Clinton administration's desire to salvage the peace process was hindered by the resumption of violence between both sides under Rabin's successor, Benjamin Netanyahu. Nevertheless, Clinton continued the role of "broker" for peace, inviting Netanyahu and Arafat to Wye River, Maryland, in October 1998 and persuading them to negotiate further Israeli redeployments from the West Bank. Later that year, he became the first U.S. president to visit the Palestinian Authority. Clinton's most memorable effort to achieve a lasting Israeli-Palestinian agreement occurred in the last year of his presidency, in July 2000, when he hosted Arafat and Israeli prime minister Ehud Barak at the Camp David Summit at the presidential retreat in Maryland. The negotiations were unsuccessful. Following the failed summit, Clinton in December 2000 presented his "parameters" as a guide for reaching a lasting peace agreement. Despite these efforts, Clinton left the presidency in January 2001 having failed to achieve a peace settlement.

SEE ALSO Arafat, Yasir; Barak, Ehud; Camp David II Summit; Clinton Plan; Netanyahu, Benjamin; Rabin, Yitzhak; Oslo Accords II.

CLINTON PLAN: Parameters for Israeli-Palestinian peace agreement proposed by U.S. president Bill Clinton in December 2000, following the failed Camp David Summit of July 2000. Clinton had invited Israeli prime minister Ehud Barak and Palestinian Authority chairman Yasir Arafat to the presidential

Bill Clinton. This U.S. president spent more time than any other striving to be a broker for Israeli-Palestinian peace, from the Oslo Accords handshake on the White House lawn between Prime Minister Yitzhak Rabin and Palestinian leader Yasir Arafat to the failed Camp David talks in mid-2000.

retreat at Camp David, Maryland, to build on earlier negotiations that had led to the Oslo Accords of 1993. The summit failed, each side blaming the other for its failure. There were several obstacles to agreement. The Palestinians opposed Israeli annexation of settlement blocks in the West Bank, and the Israelis refused to accede sovereignty over East Jerusalem. The Palestinians also argued that any settlement would have to acknowledge the future of refugees; the Israelis claimed that allowing a right of return to Israel proper would jeopardize Israel's Jewish identity.

Following the failure of the summit, Clinton put forward his "parameters," in December of that year, as a guide toward reaching an agreement. The proposal included Palestinian sovereignty over Gaza and the vast majority of the West Bank, along with the incorporation into Israel of "settlement blocks," in effect returning to the Palestinians most of the territory taken by Israel in the Arab-Israel War of 1967; a limited right of return for Palestinian refugees; security guarantees for both sides; and Jerusalem as an open and undivided city, functioning as cultural and political center for both Israelis and Palestinians. The Clinton Plan rekindled some hope of breaking the impasse and helped the parties to return briefly to negotiations at Taba, Egypt, in early 2001.

SEE ALSO Camp David II Summit.

Cohen (pl. *cohanim*): Name, sometimes altered to *kahane* or *kahn,* given to Temple priests. By extension, refers to a Jew linked to that role through a family tradition expressed by this patronymic.

Cohen, Ge'ula (1925–): Israeli politician and former LEHI radio announcer. A leading figure in the radio broadcasts of Lohamei Herut Yisrael (LEHI), Cohen was one of nineteen LEHI members arrested when the British seized LEHI's radio transmitter on 19 February 1946 as part of a campaign against Jewish terrorist groups. Though sentenced to nineteen years in prison, she escaped and resumed illegal broadcasts. Her work as a journalist in Israel included advocacy for Soviet Jewry. In 1970 Cohen joined the Likud Party. She was elected to the Knesset in 1973, serving through 1992, first as a member of Likud and then as a member of the Tehiya, a party that she helped found. After Tehiya's defeat in the 1992 elections, she rejoined Likud. She has been a prominent opponent to the Israeli-Egyptian peace agreement and is associated with the ideology of a Greater Israel. Cohen received the Israel Prize in 2001.

Cohen, Raanan (1941–): Former Knesset member and minister of labor and social welfare. Born in 1941 in Iraq, Raanan Cohen immigrated to Israel in 1951. He received a doctoral degree in Middle Eastern studies from Tel Aviv University and was secretary of the Young Guard of the Labor Party in B'nei Brak from 1961 to 1970. He later served as chairman of the Arab and Druze Branch of the Labor Party (1975–1986) and as chairman of the Elections Branch of the Labor Party (1986–1992). First elected to the Knesset in 1988, Cohen served on the Finance, Foreign Affairs and Defense, and State Control committees, and he was secretary-general of the Israel Labor Party from 1998 until 2002. In August 2000 Cohen was appointed as minister of labor and social welfare, then in March 2001 as minister without portfolio. He resigned from that post and from the Knesset in August 2002.

Committee of Six on Palestine: Structure connected to the Organization of the Islamic Conference

(OIC), created at the Twelfth Islamic Conference of Foreign Ministers, held in Baghdad between 1 and 5 June 1981. The committee—originally composed of the foreign ministers of Pakistan, Senegal, Malaysia, and Guinea plus the OIC secretary general—was responsible for seeking to implement sanctions against Israel that had been adopted by the OIC at previous summit and foreign ministers' meetings. The committee continues to be active and includes the foreign minister of the Palestinian Authority as the sixth member.

SEE ALSO Organization of the Islamic Conference; Palestinian Authority.

COPTIC CHRISTIAN. A MONK STUDIES IN THE COPTIC MONASTERY IN WADI AL-NATRUM, EGYPT. COPTIC MONKS FLEEING PERSECUTION IN IRAQ AND SYRIA DURING THE EIGHTH CENTURY BUILT MANY MONASTERIES IN THIS AREA. COPTS IN EGYPT HAD PRIVILEGED STATUS FOR MUCH OF THE EIGHTEENTH AND NINETEENTH CENTURIES, BUT THE RISE OF ISLAMISM IN THE 1980S INCREASED DISCRIMINATION AND VIOLENCE AGAINST THEM. *(© Johannes Armineh/Corbis-Sygma)*

COMMUNIST ACTION ORGANIZATION (LEBANON)

SEE Organization of Communist Action of Lebanon.

CONSTANCY FRONT

SEE Rejection Front.

COOPERATION COUNCIL FOR ARAB STATES OF THE GULF

SEE Gulf Cooperation Council.

COPT: Name given by the Arabs to all the inhabitants of Egypt at the time of the Muslim conquest of 641. The word was transposed from the Greek *aiguptoï*, meaning Egyptian, which was itself formed from the Egyptian hieroglyphic *Het Ka-Ptah* (Castle of the Spirit of Ptah), the nickname of Memphis, the Pharaonic capital. Subsequently this word came to designate only Monophysite Christians of Egypt and later Ethiopia who believe in the union of the divine and the human in Christ. The Copts of Egypt are the descendents of the ancient Egyptian population that converted to Christianity around the first century C.E. and separated from the Catholic Church after the Council of Chalcedon, in 432. The evangelist Mark, who introduced Christianity into Egypt, is considered the father of the Coptic Church. After the Arab-Muslim conquest of 639 to 641, the Copts had the status of *dhimmis*, and over the following centuries numerous conversions to Islam led to a decrease in their numbers.

The Copts make up the largest Christian community of the Middle East and represent 7 to 10 percent of the Egyptian population. The coming to power of Muhammad Ali in 1805 and the modernization of Egypt allowed Copts to accede to high administrative positions for the first time since the Islamic conquest. In 1804, the naming of Cyril IV as patriarch gave new impetus to the Coptic Church. The arrival of the English in 1882 consolidated the position of the Copts, on whom the British administration depended; for example, Boutros Pasha Ghali, finance minister, foreign minister, and prime minister, became the first great Coptic statesman of Egypt. The Copts retained their privileged status once Egypt won its independence in 1922. It became normal to have Coptic ministers in the government. Nevertheless, although they account for a substantial portion of the Egyptian economy, the majority of the Copt community, as non-Muslims, are treated like second-class citizens. In the 1980s, while Islamism was growing in Egypt, the number of deadly incidents pitting Coptic communities against Muslim fundamentalists increased dramatically. In 1992, fourteen Copts were killed by members of the Jamiʿa al-Islamiyya. On 31 December 1999, at al-Qusayr, a quarrel between a Muslim customer and a Coptic merchant degenerated into a street battle that resulted in some thirty Coptic deaths. In November 2000, a Copt, Mounir Abdul Nour, became head of the opposition in the Egyptian parliament although Copts are underrepresented in that forum.

Outside Egypt, the Coptic Church is present in Sudan and Ethiopia. The principal Coptic saints are Athanasius, Anthony, and Pakem, the name of the latter deriving from the Egyptian hieroglyphic *Pa Kem* (son of the god Kem). The Coptic liturgical year reflects the main Egyptian seasons: flood, sowing, and harvest. The Copts practice circumcision. In

1899, at the initiative of Pope Leon XIII, a Coptic patriarchy was founded in Jerusalem and included approximately one hundred families. Since 1971, the church has been headed by Pope Shenouda III. Until 706, Coptic was the language spoken by this community. Replaced by Arabic, Coptic became a dead language, utilized only in the liturgy and called Bohairic.

SEE ALSO Christianity; Dhimmi; Jamiʿa al-Islamiyya, al-; Monophysite.

COPTIC CALENDAR: This calendar began in the year 284 to commemorate the accession of Emperor Diocletian and as a result of the persecutions perpetrated by the Romans on the Coptic community in Egypt. The calendar's first day corresponded to 29 August in the Julian calendar and to 11 September in the Gregorian calendar, the day when the Copts celebrate the Festival of Martyrs.

SEE ALSO Gregorian Calendar; Julian Calendar.

CORRECTIVE MOVEMENT: Movement within al-Fatah to create a new leadership for it and the Palestine Liberation Organization (PLO) that would be more favorable to Jordan and Jordanian influence in the West Bank. It was launched in 1986 by Colonel ʿAtallah ʿAtallah, former head of al-Fatah's military intelligence in Lebanon, and was sponsored by King Hussein. ʿAtallah had resigned from al-Fatah in 1985 after being removed from its central committee because of his performance in Lebanon after the Israeli invasion of 1982 and the PLO's subsequent withdrawal. In February 1986 King Hussein, unhappy with the PLO leadership, suspended Jordan's cooperation with the PLO in its approach to Israel, which it had formally agreed to the previous year. In March he altered the composition of the Jordanian parliament, increasing the number of West Bank seats. When al-Fatah objected to this as compromising its status as the sole representative of the Palestinians, Hussein closed its offices in Jordan and deported a number of its officials. In April, he induced ʿAtallah to launch his internal rebellion. In 1986 and 1987, based in Amman and disposing of official support from Saudi as well as Jordanian authorities, the corrective movement attempted to unite al-Fatah dissidents into a group that could compete with Yasir Arafat's supporters. ʿAtallah had his supporters elect him "caretaker" chairman of the PLO in Jordan, which allowed Hussein to give him control of PLO assets. He then attempted to help Hussein increase his influence on the West Bank, acting as a go-between with local leaders. Ultimately he had little support or credibility among Palestinians and was abandoned by his Jordanian patron.

SEE ALSO Arafat, Yasir; Fatah, al-; Hussein ibn Talal; Palestine Liberation Organization; West Bank.

COUNCIL OF ARAB ECONOMIC UNITY (CAEU; in Arabic, *al-Jamʿiyyah al-ʾArabiyyah Lil-wihdah al-Iqtisadiyyah*): A specialized institution of the League of Arab States, the Council was created in 1957 to promote the progressive economic integration of its member states. In 1964, with the Arab Economic Unity Agreement, the Council established an Arab Common Market, whose membership now formally includes Egypt, Iraq, Jordan, Kuwait, Libya, Mauritania, Palestine, Somalia, Sudan, Syria, and Yemen.

SEE ALSO League of Arab States.

COUNCIL OF COOPERATION OF ARAB STATES OF THE GULF

SEE Gulf Cooperation Council.

COUNCIL OF GULF COOPERATION:

SEE Gulf Cooperation Council.

COVENANT: Principal foundation of Judaism, based on three principles: a direct relation with God; revelation; and the royalty of God. According to Biblical tradition, the first true covenant was concluded between God and Abraham, based on the divine promise that the latter's people, "elect of God," would soon dwell in a "Promised Land." This first covenant (*b'ritt,* in Hebrew), sealed by the circumcision (practiced also by the Egyptians) of Abraham, was renewed by Abraham' descendants, Isaac and Jacob. The second covenant is that of Sinai, between God and Moses, with the transmission of the Ten Commandments (*asseret ha-dibrot,* in Hebrew), and the renewed assurance of a "Promised Land." According to the sacred texts, this covenant is temporary, for it prepares the way for the "New Covenant," which would be materialized with the coming of the Messiah.

SEE ALSO Abraham; Isaac; Jacob (Biblical); Messiah; Moses.

DA (Demokratia v'Aliyah; Hebrew, meaning "democracy and immigration"): Israeli political bloc of the center-left, founded in February 1992 by Yuri Kocharovski to further the interests of Jewish immigrants from the Soviet Union. This movement is not represented in the Knesset.

DA'AM

SEE Organization for Democratic Action.

DAHIR: Muslim term designating the apparent or literal meaning of things, particularly religious interpretations, as opposed to the word *batin.*

SEE ALSO Batin.

DAHLAN, MUHAMMAD (Abu Fadil; 1960–): Palestinian leader, born in 1961 in the refugee camp of Khan Yunis in the Gaza Strip. At the beginning of the 1980s, Muhammad Dahlan became active in the al-Fatah youth movement (Shabibat al-Fatah) and was imprisoned by the Israelis. In December 1987, he was deported to Lebanon by the Israeli authorities. Later, Dahlan moved to Iraq, where he met Khalil al-Wazir (Abu Jihad), the head of Palestine Liberation Organization (PLO) security, who appointed him to oversee the Intifada in the Gaza Strip, in liaison with the Fatah Hawks. In 1989, Dahlan went to Tunis to work with PLO security, where, between 1990 and 1993, he was responsible for communications between the Unified National Command of the Uprising (UNCU) and the activists of the Intifada. In this capacity he became one of Yasir Arafat's advisors for Gaza Strip affairs.

In October 1993, following the Israeli-Palestinian Declaration of Principles signed on 13 September, Dahlan joined the Palestinian delegation to the Taba (Egypt) negotiations as a member of the security affairs commission. In December, Israeli authorities allowed him to return to the Palestinian territories. At the end of December, accompanied by Jibril Rajub, he went to Rome to meet General Shahak, Israeli army chief of staff, and Jacques Neria, advisor to the Israeli prime minister. The four jointly elaborated a plan for coordinating Israeli and Palestinian security services in the general context of the application of autonomy in the occupied territories. In June 1994, Dahlan was named head of the Palestinian preventive security services in Gaza, while Rajub obtained the same post in the West Bank. Dahlan participated in numerous negotiations with Israeli and American heads of security services, who appreciated his intelligence and his determination to counteract extremist Palestinian groups.

In July of 2000, Dahlan took part in the Israeli-Palestinian negotiations at the U.S. presidential retreat at Camp David, Maryland. On the following 26 September, accompanied by Saib Erekat, he met secretly with Shlomo Ben-Ami in Washington, D.C., to discuss steps to restart the peace process. In the autumn, while the Intifada was intensifying in the Palestinian territories, Dahlan—torn between his personal convictions and his security duties in the Gaza Strip—attempted to channel widespread resentment into a coherent movement. On 21 November 2000, Ariel Sharon, the head of the Israeli Likud Party, accused Dahlan of responsibility for an attack on Jewish settlers in Gaza and called for his removal. After Sharon took office as prime minister, an attempt was made on Dahlan's life. Dahlan was one of the key people who ran the Palestinian Authority (PA) government during Arafat's captivity in Ramallah in March–May 2002, and he was security chief in the short-lived PA administration of Prime Minister Mahmud Abbas. Dahlan is on record as favoring reform in the Palestinian Authority, including consolidation of PA security services. Although he has been regarded as a potential successor of Arafat, he has said, "As long as the Israelis are against Arafat, I'm with him." Dahlan, an ally of Mahmud Abbas, general secretary of the PLO returned to Arafat's favor, would perhaps succeed Arafat in tandem with the older Abbas. However, he would probably not be acceptable to HAMAS, which opposes PLO policies but has not attacked it while Arafat has been in power. In early 2004, Dahlan was reported to have been maneuvering to take charge of security in the West Bank as well as in Gaza, pitting him directly against Jibril Rajub, but he denied that this was true.

SEE ALSO Abbas, Mahmud Rida; Arafat, Yasir; Ben-Ami, Shlomo; Erekat, Saib; Fatah, al-; HAMAS; Intifada (1987–1993); National Unified Uprising Command; Rajub, Jibril; Sharon, Ariel; Wazir, Khalil al-.

DALET

SEE Dalet Plan.

DALET PLAN: Prepared in March 1948 by Colonel Yigal Yadin, this plan involved preparations for a number of actions against the Palestinian Arabs so as to "guarantee the security of the Jewish defense network." In effect the plan was a revised version of Haganah's contingency plan, devised in 1947, for defending the future Jewish state. According to Haganah, the plan was defensive in nature, though pro-Palestinian historians disagree, contending that the plan was the basis for the subsequent expulsion of Palestinians by Israeli forces.

SEE ALSO Arab-Israel War (1948); Haganah.

DAMASCUS DECLARATION

SEE Gulf Cooperation Council.

DAR AL-HARB: Arabic term, literally "house (or abode) of war"; in classical Islamic jurisprudence it designated a country without an Islamic government, in which "Islam is not the established religion, where the ruler is not a Muslim, and where there exists no mechanism by which political or military leaders may seek the counsel of Islamic religious specialists" (*Encyclopedia of Islam and the Muslim World*, 2003, p. 169). In these circumstances, the Muslim community could declare a holy war to establish an Islamic government, but there was little agreement about when this was permissible.

SEE ALSO Dar al-Islam.

DARAWSHE, ABDUL WAHAB (1943–): Palestinian Israeli politician. Abdul Wahab Darawshe was born in 1943 in the village of Iksal in the Galilee. After graduating from Haifa University, he worked as a teacher. Darawshe was first elected to the Knesset in 1984 as a member of the Israel Labor Party, but he left Labor in January 1988 to protest the violent military response to the Intifada that had begun in the Occupied Territories in late 1987. Later in 1988, in association with members of local Arab councils, heads of religious communities, businessmen, and intellectuals, he established the Arab Democratic Party and was elected to the Knesset on its list in November.

Darawshe is regarded as a moderate whose primary political goals are peace between Palestinians and Israeli Jews, and equal rights for the Palestinian citizens of Israel. In October 1992, Darawshe went to Tunis to meet with Yasir Arafat, encouraging him to seek negotiations with Israel; in response, the Likud Party attempted to have Darawshe's parliamentary immunity lifted so he could be charged under antiterrorist laws. In 1997 he helped to arrange a meeting between Ariel Sharon, then a cabinet minister, and Mahmud Abbas, Arafat's deputy. In October 1998 he was among a group of Arab members of the Knesset who met with Egyptian president Husni Mubarak to discuss the peace process. The next year, Darawshe attempted to form an alliance with other Israeli Arab political parties in order to present a united list in the forthcoming elections, but was unable to do so.

In 1999, Darawshe resigned from the Knesset, but he has remained active in efforts to bring about peace negotiations. Late in 2001, in an attempt to stem the ongoing violence related to the al-Aqsa Intifada, he arranged for Israeli president Moshe Katsav to speak before the Palestinian parliament to express his "regrets" over the violence, after which all parties would be asked to agree to a cease-fire while Israel and the Palestinian Authority negotiated a "final status" agreement as envisioned in the Oslo Accords; the event was vetoed by Prime Minister Sharon. Darawshe is also a member of the International Alliance for Arab-Israeli Peace (the Copenhagen Group), which brings together prominent private citizens of Israel (both Jewish and Palestinian), Jordan, and Egypt.

SEE ALSO Abbas, Mahmud Rida; Aqsa Intifada, al-; Arab Democratic Party; Arafat, Yasir; Sharon, Ariel.

DARWAZA, IZZAT MUHAMMAD (also Darwazeh; 1889–1975): Palestinian pan-Arab nationalist politician and writer from Nablus. Izzat Darwaza became involved in politics while employed in the local Ottoman administration before World War I. He helped to organize the first Arab Congress of 1913, held in Paris, and after the war was an advocate for Palestinian inclusion in an independent Greater Syria. He helped to organize several Palestinian organizations, including the Society of Palestinian Youth, an armed anti-Zionist group. In 1932 he helped to establish the Istiqlal (Independence) Party, a political grouping aimed to appeal to youth, whose program was pro-independence and anti-Zionist. During the 1936–1939 Revolt, Darwaza organized guerrilla activity from Damascus on behalf of the Arab Higher Committee. He was elected delegate from Nablus to the fourth and seventh Palestinian National Congresses in the 1920s, was appointed general administrator of the Waqf in the 1930s, and served for a year on a reorganized Arab Higher Committee in 1947. He was the author of numerous articles and books dealing with Arab nationalist politics and the threat of Zionism to Arab interests.

SEE ALSO Arab Higher Committee; Waqf.

DARWISH, MAHMUD (1942–): Palestinian writer and poet. Born in 1942 at al-Birwa near Acre in Galilee, Mahmud Darwish fled with his landowning family to Lebanon in 1948, at the time of the first Israeli-Arab war; they returned clandestinely two years later. Since they had been away during the Arab census conducted by the Israelis after the end of hostilities, they lacked proper state identification and were considered "present-absent aliens" in Israeli terminology. Their native village having been destroyed, they settled in the village of Deir el-Assad as "internal refugees."

After secondary studies in Nazareth, Darwish participated in the formation of an Arab nationalist movement, "al-Ard" (the Land), with other young intellectuals, among whom was poet Samih al-Qasim. Darwish then joined the ranks of the Israeli Communist Party, RAKAH. Between 1960 and 1967, he was a journalist for the cultural magazine *al-Jadid* and the weekly *al-Ittihad,* press organs of RAKAH. Israeli authorities jailed him repeatedly, mainly for traveling as an "alien" without a permit, and placed him under house arrest from 1968 to 1970. In 1969, Darwish won the Lotus Prize, awarded by the Union of Afro-Asian Writers.

Between 1970 and 1971, Darwish chose exile and lived in Moscow, then in Cairo, where he worked at the daily *al-Ahram.* A year later he was in Lebanon, where he edited a Palestinian monthly, *Shu'un Filistiniyya.* In September 1972, he was elected to the secretariat of the Congress of Palestinian Journalists and Writers. Three years later, he was named head of the Center of Palestinian Research, replacing Anis Sayegh. In a few months' time, Darwish was widely regarded as al-Fatah's roaming ambassador. In 1982 he became editor of the Palestinian literary review *al-Karmil,* and the following year he won the Lenin Prize. In April 1984, living in Paris, he was elected president of the Federation of Palestinian Writers and Journalists. He traveled many times to Tunis, where the Palestine Liberation Organization (PLO) headquarters was located. In November of that year, he participated in the Seventeenth Congress of the Palestine National Council (PNC). In April 1987 he was elected to the executive committee of the PLO, as president of the high committee on culture, patrimony, and information. On 18 September of that year, he attended the Congress of the Union of Palestinian Writers and Journalists, which was held in Baghdad. In 1987, inspired by the Intifada in the Palestinian territories, he published a poem, "Those Who Pass Between Fleeting Worlds" ("It is time for you to be gone. / Live wherever you like, but do not live among us . . . ."), that provoked the ire of many Israelis, who called him "the terrorist poet." Darwish was the author of the Algiers Declaration, the proclamation of a Palestinian state, in 1988.

On 23 August 1993, disagreeing with the turn the Israeli-Palestinian peace process was taking, he resigned from the executive committee of the PLO, while reaffirming his support for a peace treaty with Israel. Three years later, with permission from Israeli authorities, he decided to relocate the offices of *al-*

Karmil (which, almost uniquely in the Arab world, publishes Israeli writing in translation) to Ramallah. In 2001, Darwish was awarded the (American) Lannan Foundation Prize for Cultural Freedom. One of the most popular poets in the Arab world, he has published numerous books of poetry and prose, and his work has been translated worldwide. In 2000, Israeli education minister Yossi Sarid proposed publishing some Darwish poems, translated into Hebrew, in Israeli school textbooks; the proposal met with opposition, and Prime Minister Ehud Barak vetoed the idea.

SEE ALSO Ahram, al-; Ittihad, al-.

DASH: Israeli political party, centrist in tendency, which surfaced at the time of the 1977 Knesset elections through the initiative of Professor Yigael Yadin. Dash ran its campaign advocating change, and the party won fifteen seats. In June 1977, after much debate, delay, and a very close vote, the leadership of the party threw its support to the right-wing coalition government of Menachem Begin. In November 1978, a split in this bloc led to a majority of its members rallying to Likud. The rest, under the leadership of Meir Amit, participated in constituting a new party, Shinui.

SEE ALSO Begin, Menachem; Likud; Shinui Party.

DAVAR (The word, in Hebrew): Israel's daily Labor newspaper, founded in 1925 and considered the mouthpiece of the Histadrut union. In October 1995, in an effort to demarcate itself from the Israel Labor Party, the leadership of the newspaper started to use a new name, *Davar Rishon.* The paper disappeared in 1996.

SEE ALSO Histadrut; Israel Labor Party.

DAʿWA (*daawa*): Arab word meaning invocation, call. Originally this term was used to designate political or religious propaganda delivered by a prophet. In the Middle Ages, the word was used by movements, often clandestine, that wanted to take power to further a political program but knew they needed religious justification to gain support. The term is used to suggest Islamic proselytism in general.

DAʿWA, AL- (al-Daʿwa al-Islamiyya, "Islamic Call"): An Iraqi Shiʿite party, al-Daʿwa was founded in 1957 by Muhammad Baqir al-Sadr and Monteza al-Askar, with the semi-official financial support of Iran. In 1958, after the fall of the Iraqi monarchy, al-Daʿwa opposed the Communist forces present in Iraq, while dissociating itself from other Islamic parties. In 1963, after the Baʿth Party came to power, al-Daʿwa went underground. The leaders of the movement sent many Lebanese, who had come to study at Najaf, back to their homeland with the mission of propagating the ideas of al-Daʿwa there.

In 1974, Muhammad Baqir al-Sadr issued a fatwa forbidding religious students to adhere to any political party, accentuating the isolation of the movement. In 1979 the Iranian Islamic Revolution caused al-Daʿwa to come forward and recognize Imam Ruhollah Khomeini as the sole head of the "Islamic nation." The following year, when the Iran-Iraq War broke out, the headquarters of the movement was transferred to Teheran. Muhammad Baqir al-Sadr was arrested by the Iraqi authorities and executed. Al-Daʿwa joined the Supreme Council of the Islamic Revolution in Iraq (SCIRI), a gathering of the Iraqi opposition. In 1982 a Lebanese branch of the movement was created under the impetus of Shaykh Muhammad Husayn Fadlallah.

SEE ALSO Fadlallah, Shaykh Muhammad Husayn; Hizb al-Daʿwa al-Islamiyya; Iran-Iraq War.

DAʿWA AL-ISLAMIYYA, AL- ("Islamic Call," in Arabic): Iraqi Shiʿite party founded in 1957 by Muhammad Baqr al-Sadr and Monteza al-Askar, with the semiofficial financial support of Iran. In 1958, after the fall of the Iraqi monarchy, Al-Daʿwa opposed the Communist forces present in Iraq while disassociating itself from other Islamic parties. In 1963, after the Baʿth Party came to power, al-Daʿwa went underground. The leaders of the movement sent many Lebanese, who had come to study in at Najaf, Iraq, back to their homeland with the mission of propagating the ideas of al-Daʿwa there. In 1974, a fatwa was issued by Muhammad Baqir al-Sadr forbidding religious students to adhere to any political party, accentuating the isolation of the movement. In 1979, the Iranian Islamic Revolution caused al-Daʿwa to abandon clandestine status. Its leaders recognized Imam Khomeini as the sole head of the Islamic nation. The following year, when the Iraq-Iran war broke out, the headquarters of the movement was transferred to Teheran. Al-Sadr was arrested by the Iraqi authorities and executed. Al-Daʿwa joined the Supreme Council of the Islamic Revolution in Iraq, a gathering of the Iraqi opposition. In 1982, a Lebanese branch of the movement was created under the impetus of Shaykh Muhammad Husayn Fadlallah.

SEE ALSO Baʿth; Fadlallah, Shaykh Muhammad Husayn; Fatwa; Hizb al-Daʿwa al-Islamiyya.

DAYAN, MOSHE (1914–1981): Israeli military and political figure, born in Kibbutz Deganiah, Palestine. Moshe Dayan joined the Haganah in 1932. Arrested by the British forces in 1939, he was sentenced to ten years of hard labor. In 1941, after the Allies released him from prison, Dayan joined the ranks of the Jewish Brigade, which was merged into the British Army for the duration of World War II. In this unit he fought against the French Vichy forces in Syria. He lost his left eye in one of these confrontations. In 1948, as an officer of Haganah, he fought in the first Israeli-Arab war, Israel's "war of independence," in the course of which he was noted for both his courage and his gifts as a strategist. In 1950, he was made a general in Israel's new army and given the command of the southern and northern regions. Dayan became Israel Defense Force (IDF) chief of staff in December 1953 and led the Israeli Army during the Suez-Sinai War, where he demonstrated his extraordinary tactical talents.

In 1958, he quit the army and entered politics. He joined the MAPAI Party under David Ben-Gurion and became agriculture minister in 1959, a position from which he resigned in 1964. The following year, along with Ben-Gurion and Shimon Peres, he participated in the creation of a MAPAI splinter party, RAFI, and won a seat in the Knesset. On 2 June 1967, as the Arab threat escalated, Dayan was named defense minister in the National Unity government headed by Levi Eshkol. Already a hero of the 1956 Suez campaign, Dayan became a legend with Israel's victory in the 1967 Arab-Israel War when the IDF defeated the Arab armies and quadrupled the territory of Israel. In 1968, he joined the Israel Labor Party, which had just been formed through a merger of MAPAI with Ahdut ha-Avoda, Po'alei Zion, and RAFI. In March 1969, he became defense minister in the government of Golda Meir. Although he supported Israeli sovereignty over the Occupied Territories, Dayan was aware that this situation could not last forever.

On 19 April 1974, revelations that Israeli intelligence and political personnel had been caught unprepared led Dayan and others to resign. In June 1977, after three years out of politics, he returned to government, joining the cabinet of right-wing prime minister Menachem Begin as foreign minister, provoking anger in the Labor Party leadership. The Begin government initiated contacts with certain Arab countries, in which Dayan participated, which led to the Israeli-Egyptian peace accord of March 1979. In October 1979, disappointed by the turn the peace accords with Egypt had taken, especially on the

MOSHE DAYAN. THE LEGENDARY ISRAELI DEFENSE MINISTER DURING THE ARAB-ISRAEL WAR OF JUNE 1967, SEEN HERE IN HEBRON AFTER ISRAELI FORCES TOOK CONTROL OF THE RELIGIOUSLY IMPORTANT CITY, HAD A LONG, DISTINCTIVE MILITARY CAREER, INCLUDING CHIEF OF STAFF OF THE ARMED FORCES FOR SEVERAL YEARS IN THE MID-1950S. HE ALSO WAS A MEMBER OF THE KNESSET AND A MINISTER IN SEVERAL ISRAELI GOVERNMENTS UNTIL 1979. *(© David Rubinger/Corbis)*

Palestinian question, he resigned his position to devote himself to his passion, archeology. He died two years later in Tel Aviv.

SEE ALSO Ahdut ha-Avoda; Arab-Israel War (1967); Begin, Menachem; Ben-Gurion, David; Haganah; Israel Defense Force; Israel Labor Party; MAPAI; Meir, Golda; Peres, Shimon; RAFI; Suez Crisis.

DAYAN, YAEL (1939–): Israeli writer and activist. Born in 1939 at Nahalal, in British Mandatory Palestine, Yael Dayan is the daughter of the late General Moshe Dayan. In 1959, barely twenty years old, she published her first novel, *New Face in the Mirror*. Between 1965 and 1980, while continuing to write, she was a journalist at *Yediot Aharonot*. At the time of the Arab-Israel War of 1967, she became a spokesperson for the Israel Defense Force (IDF). In 1984, as a member of the Israel Labor Party, she ran for the first time in the Knesset elections. In 1985 she published a book about her father.

In June 1992, Yael Dayan won a seat in the Knesset, the first of her three terms. She belonged to the reformist wing of the Labor Party. As a feminist and a defender of the rights of sexual minorities, she missed no chance at lambasting the champions of religious orthodoxy in the Knesset. A member of the Peace Now movement, Dayan favored peace with the Palestinians and the creation of a Jordanian-Palestinian confederation, and she was one of the Knesset members who agitated for the abrogation of the law banning all contact with the Palestine Liberation Organization (PLO). In August 1992, on a visit to The Hague, Netherlands, she met with Nabil Shaʿath, one of Yasir Arafat's political advisors. She acknowledged the contact a few days later. On 29 January 1993, ten days after the abrogation of the law forbidding all contact with the PLO, she went to Tunis, where she was welcomed by Arafat, provoking the ire of Israeli prime minister Yitzhak Rabin. After returning to Jerusalem, she spoke publicly of her hope that top Israeli leaders would follow in her footsteps, so as to "understand, learn and listen." Since then Dayan has devoted a major part of her time to activities in support of Israeli-Palestinian peace. In the 2003 elections, she was not included on the Labor Party list; she joined the Meretz Party list of candidates but was not reelected.

SEE ALSO Dayan, Moshe; Peace Now.

DAYR YASIN: An Arab village of 600 to 800 inhabitants, Dayr Yasin is located on the periphery of the suburbs west of Jerusalem. On 9 April 1948, on the eve of the creation of the State of Israel, a Jewish commando—consisting of members of the extremist organizations Irgun and the Stern Gang (Lohamei Herut Yisrael, or LEHI)—attacked the villagers of Dayr Yasin. Surprised by the resistance of some of the inhabitants, the commando leaders asked for help from the Haganah, which sent in one of its Palmach brigades ("shock" brigades, or *Plugot Mahatz* in Hebrew). The brigade put a rapid end to the fighting and retreated, leaving behind the men of Irgun and the Stern Gang, who unleashed a massacre of the villagers, killing at least 100 of them. The survivors were expelled.

Dayr Yasin played a huge role in the decision of Palestinians to flee from their homes, fearing similar massacres in their own villages. Since then, Dayr Yasin has become one of the symbols of the martyrs of the Palestinian resistance. (The village has been renamed Givat Shaul-Bet by the Israeli authorities.) The Dayr Yasin Remembered Committee works to keep the memory of the event alive by building a memorial and supporting a "just and durable resolution" to the Palestinian-Israeli conflict. The committee maintains a web site at www.deiryassin.org.

SEE ALSO Haganah; Irgun.

DEAD SEA SCROLLS: In April 1947, Mohammed el-Dib, a young Bedouin from the Ta'amireh tribe, by chance discovered a number of manuscript scrolls in a grotto near the Qumran ruins, an Essenian site around 30 kilometers from Bethlehem and Jerusalem. Three of these scrolls were purchased by Professor E. L. Sukenik on behalf of the Hebrew University of Jerusalem, and four others by the Syrian Jacobite Convent of Saint Mark, also in Jerusalem. The latter were transported to the United States. In February 1949, Count Lippens, United Nations observer in Israel, opened the way to the exploration of the Qumran site. Father Roland de Vaux, head of the French Biblical and Archeological School of Jerusalem, and G. Lankester Harding, in charge of Jordanian antiquities, were named to direct the digs. Between 1949 and 1958, nearly 800 manuscripts were exhumed, and Jordanian authorities appealed to the international community to finance a study of the documents. On its side, the Vatican entrusted Father de Vaux with deciphering the documents, which were placed in the Rockefeller Museum in East Jerusalem, under Jordanian control. In 1961, the Jordanian state declared all the manuscripts in the Palestinian Archeological Museum of Jerusalem to be national property. Five years later, the entire museum became national property of Jordan.

In the 1967 Arab-Israel War, the Israeli army occupied East Jerusalem, taking over the museum and its holdings. From then on, Israeli authorities administered the Palestinian Archeological Museum. The team of Father de Vaux was authorized to continue its research but limited other scholars' access to the manuscripts, provoking ire in the international scientific community. Photos of original documents were sent to the United States (Claremont and Cincinnati) and to Great Britain. Ten years later, a portion of the documents kept at Claremont were entrusted to the Huntington Library in Virginia, where they remained for years without being studied seriously. There was some conjecture that access to the manuscripts was being limited because they contained information on Jesus and his adherence to the sect of Essenians, which would raise questions about

THE MANUAL OF DISCIPLINE. ONE OF THE HISTORICALLY AND RELIGIOUSLY IMPORTANT DEAD SEA SCROLLS, THIS TEXT IS DISPLAYED AT THE SHRINE OF THE BOOK, PART OF THE ISRAEL MUSEUM IN JERUSALEM. *(© Bettmann/Corbis)*

his divine nature. For Father de Vaux, however, the "Master of Justice" described in these manuscripts had nothing to do with Jesus.

The international scientific community was shocked that translations of the texts, whose study had been underway for many years, had not yet been published. According to a former member of the committee, John Marco Allegro, some of the manuscripts, particularly the Copper Scroll, intimated the existence of a fabulous treasure, that of the Temple of Solomon, the Ark of the Covenant, and the Tables of the Law, which would lead to censure on the part of Israeli authorities. On 22 September 1991, the Huntington Library, in Virginia, decided to make all the copies of the manuscripts in its keeping available to the public and to publish a photocopy edition. During the following October, Israeli authorities permitted access to all manuscripts in its collections, including the unpublished ones.

SEE ALSO Arab-Israel War (1967); Essenes; Jesus.

DECALOGUE: According to Biblical tradition, this was the ensemble of the Ten Commandments (*asseret ha-dibrot,* in Hebrew) given by God to Moses on Mount Sinai. The Decalogue is the moral basis for Jewish, as well as Christian, life.

SEE ALSO Christianity; Moses.

DEGEL HA-TORAH (Torah Banner): An ultra-orthodox Israeli political party, Degel ha-Torah was created before the Knesset elections of 1988 by Rabbi Eliezer Menachem Schach, a dissident in the Agudat Israel Party. Representing the non-Hasidic Ashkenazi current and opposed to the Lubavitch movement, Degel ha-Torah won two seats in the Knesset that year. Between 1988 and 1994, in an attempt to obtain subsidies for its institutions, Degel ha-Torah backed the governments in power, left as well as right. In the Knesset elections of 1992, it formed a common list with Agudat Israel; then, in anticipation of the elections of 1996, it constituted a new list with Agudat Israel and Poʿalei Agudat Israel and again won two seats in the Knesset, which were taken by Rabbis Avraham Ravitz and Moshe Gaoni. Principal figures in the movement were Eliezer Menachem Schach, Chaim Epstein, Moshe Gaoni, Chaim Miller, and Avraham Ravitz. In the 2003 elections Degel ha-Torah formed a list with Agudat Israel as Yahadut ha-Torah, or United Torah Judaism, which won five seats in the Knesset.

SEE ALSO Agudat Israel; Poʿalei Agudat Israel; Schach, Eliezer.

DEHAMSHE, ABDULMALIK (1943–): Israeli-Arab politician, born in Kfar Kana. He is a lawyer and former president of the Israeli League of Human Rights. Abdulmalik Dehamshe was arrested in 1971 and sentenced to ten years in jail for belonging to al-Fatah. An atheist at the time, he became a practicing Muslim during his detention. Freed in 1978 and readmitted to the Israeli bar, he became one of the main leaders of the Israeli Arab Movement. At the beginning of the 1980s, he was responsible for the protection of the HAMAS leader Ismaʿil Ahmad Yasin. In April 1996, he joined with the Arab Democratic Party in creating a common list, the United Arab List, for the parliamentary elections scheduled for that spring. In the elections of 29 May 1996, Dehamshe won a seat, thus becoming the first Islamist to sit in the Knesset. In the general elections of May 1999, the United Arab List won five seats, one of which was taken by Dehamshe. In October 2000, with the Intifada raging in the Occupied Territories, he failed to convince other Israeli-Arab leaders to form a single electoral list. In 2003, Dehamshe was still a member of the Knesset representing the United Arab List.

SEE ALSO Aqsa Intifada, al-; Arab Democratic Party; Fatah, al-; HAMAS; Knesset; United Arab List; Yasin, Ahmad Isma'il.

DEMOCRATIC ALLIANCE

SEE Democratic Front for the Liberation of Palestine.

DEMOCRATIC FRONT FOR PEACE AND EQUALITY (HADASH): Israeli political bloc, formed in 1977 by a union of a number of smaller parties of the left. Created following a schism in the Communist camp, HADASH, in which RAKAH was the dominant party, it favored the creation of a Palestinian state, and supported human rights and the creation of a socialist system in Israel. This bloc, which had about 2,000 members, the vast majority of whom were Arabs, won four seats in the Knesset in 1981 and 1988. In the elections of May 1991, the Arab bloc of Azmi Bishara, the Democratic National Alliance (Balad), had a list in common with HADASH and won five seats. At various Knesset sessions, HADASH has been backed by Arab groups, such as the Arab Democratic Party (ADP). In the May 1999 elections, HADASH obtained only three seats. This failure revealed the loss of influence of the movement among the Arab population of Israel as well as the broadening of the possible political representation for Arabs, including the Arab Democratic Party and an Islamic party. On the following 14 June, the secretary general of the party, Muhammad Baraki, was one of the candidates for the speakership of the Knesset. As of 2004, the principal figures in HADASH are: Muhammad Baraki (secretary general), Tamar Gozansky, Salah Salim, Hashim Mahamid, Ahmad Saad, Meir Wilner, and Neila Zayyad.

SEE ALSO Arab Democratic Party; Bishara, Azmi; Democratic National Alliance; RAKAH.

DEMOCRATIC FRONT FOR THE LIBERATION OF PALESTINE (DFLP; al-Jabha al-Dimuqratiya li-Tahrir Filastin): Palestinian movement, formed on 21 February 1969, after a split in the Popular Front for the Liberation of Palestine (PFLP). Originally Marxist-Leninist in allegiance, the DFLP, formerly called PDFLP (Popular Democratic Front for the Liberation of Palestine), was created through the impetus of Nayif Hawatma and Yasir Abd Rabbo, who had fallen out with George Habash, head of the PFLP. This movement advocated an extreme left program, recommending active struggle against "conservative Arab regimes and the State of Israel." Through the 1970s it evolved toward democratic socialism and in favor of a secular Palestinian state. Striving to prioritize Palestinian unity over ideological quarrels, the DFLP often served as an intermediary between the Palestine Liberation Organization (PLO) and the Rejection Front. The DFLP was also one of the first Palestinian groups to establish contact with Israeli leftist parties, while still supporting armed struggle against Israel. In 1978, at the time of the Iraqi-Iranian conflict, the DFLP broke its ties with Baghdad to support the Khomeini revolution.

In 1983 the movement formed a joint political-military command with the PFLP, and in March 1984, it attempted to constitute an opposition front to al-Fatah by creating the Democratic Alliance, which was composed of the DFLP, the PFLP, the Palestine Communist Party (PCP), and a part of the Palestine Liberation Front (PLF); but within several months, personality conflicts and ideological differences had dissolved this union. The DFLP and the PFLP decided to consolidate their activity in a unified command. Within the DFLP, an armed group called the "Red Star" was formed, charged with carrying out military actions on behalf of the front against Israel. In 1990 a fracture surfaced in the movement, caused in part by the internal crisis in the Soviet Union. The following year, the DFLP came out against the peace process that had started in Madrid, arguing that other Palestinian movements had not been consulted on the program advocated by the PLO in the negotiations.

Serious differences emerged between the head of the DFLP, Nayif Hawatma, and his second in command, Yasir Abd Rabbo, who favored a rapprochement with Yasir Arafat. Having quit the DFLP, Abd Rabbo founded a dissident movement, the Palestinian Democratic Union (PDU or FIDA), which backed the policies of al-Fatah. Following the signing of the Israeli-Palestinian accord of 13 September 1993, the DFLP and the PFLP decided to withdraw from the executive committee of the PLO, and appealed to "all national and Islamic forces and Palestinian notables to come together in a coalition to bring about the failure of this accord." A few days later, the two movements joined with the Palestinian opposition front, the Alliance of Palestinian Forces (APF). In August 1994, hoping to make their opposition to the Israeli-Palestinian accord more effective, the DFLP and the PFLP announced, once more, the creation of a joint military command. In May 1995, the partisans of Arafat tried vainly to provoke a split in the DFLP. Differing with the other parties within the APF, the DFLP distanced itself from it, in an attempt to become a political force in the Palestinian autonomous territories, while still maintaining its opposition to the Oslo Accords.

On 19 February, Taysir Khalid, one of the principal lieutenants of the DFLP, expressed a wish to have his movement participate in negotiations with Israel on a definitive status for the Palestinian territories. In February 1999, at the funeral of King Hussein of Jordan, Hawatma shook hands with the president of Israel, Ezer Weizman. In August 1999 meetings took place in Cairo between the leaders of the DFLP, the PFLP, and al-Fatah, in an attempt to coordinate a common strategy in the context of negotiations on the final status of the Palestinian territories. In October 2000, a month after the start of the al-Aqsa Intifada in the Palestinian territories, the head of the DFLP called on his militants to support the uprising but not to resort to the use of arms against Israel. At the end of April 2001, while the Intifada was intensifying, the leadership of the front launched an appeal for general mobilization and the formation of a "national emergency organization," uniting all Palestinian forces and responsible for coordinating the actions of the Intifada, in parallel with negotiations with the Israelis. On 24 August, the DFLP claimed credit for a raid in the Gaza Strip, in the course of which three Israeli soldiers were killed. In early 2004, Hawatma held discussions with members of the Israeli Meretz Party with a view to promoting a two-state solution, and called for an end to attacks on civilians. The DFLP, whose headquarters is in Damascus, is well established in Jordan, the West Bank, and in Lebanon. As of 2004, its principal leaders are: Nayif Hawatma (secretary general), Qays Abdul Hakim (assistant), Ramzi Rabah, Qays Samarra'i' (Abu Leila), and Taysir Khalid.

SEE ALSO Abd Rabbo, Yasir; Afarat, Yasir; Fatah, al-; Habash, George; Hawatma, Nayif; Palestine Liberation Organization; Palestinian Democratic Union; Popular Front for the Liberation of Palestine.

DEMOCRATIC NATIONAL ALLIANCE (DNA; al-Tajammu' al-Dimuqrati al-Watani): An Israeli Arab political group, the Democratic National Alliance was created in February 1999, in anticipation of the upcoming (May) parliamentary elections, piggy-backed with the election of the prime minister—an election in which, for the first time, an Arab, Azmi Bishara, founder of the Democratic National Alliance, was a candidate. The creation of the DNA is to be seen in the context of the demands of the Israeli Arabs. Just before the elections, Bishara withdrew and asked his supporters to support the candidacy of Ehud Barak, the leader of the Labor Party. On 18 May 1999, following the elections, the Democratic National Alliance found itself with two seats in the Knesset, which were taken by Azmi Bishara and Ahmad Tibi.

SEE ALSO Bishara, Azmi; Tibi, Ahmad.

DEMOKRATIA V'ALIYAH

SEE DA.

DEREKH HA-SHLISHI

SEE Third Way.

DERI, ARYE (1959–): Former Knesset member and minister of Internal Affairs. Born in Morocco in 1959, Arye Deri was educated at the Porat Yosef Talmudic College and the Hebron Talmudic College in Jerusalem. He was a founding member and secretary (1981–1983) of the Maale Amos settlement and in 1984 a founding member of the SHAS (Sephardi Torah Guardians) Party. He held various posts, including senior adviser to the minister of the interior (1985), secretary-general of the SHAS Party (from 1985), secretary-general of the Internal Affairs Ministry (from 1986), and minister of the interior. As the leader of SHAS, Deri formed a close alliance with Benjamin Netanyahu. In 1999 Deri was charged and convicted of using the Interior Ministry in the 1980s to illegally direct government funds to SHAS Party projects in local municipalities, personally receiving $155,000 in bribes. He began a four-year prison sentence in September 2000 but was granted early release in 2003. Some SHAS supporters continued to claim that Deri had been wrongfully accused and convicted.

SEE ALSO SHAS.

DESERT FOX: A joint U.S.-British bombing and cruise missile campaign against Iraq over three days in December 1998, occasioned by the reluctance of the Iraqi government of Saddam Hussein to cooperate fully with UNSCOM, the United Nations team of weapons inspectors.

DESERT SHIELD OPERATION

SEE Gulf War (1991).

DESERT STORM OPERATION

SEE Gulf War (1991).

Devekut: Hebrew term designating a secret Hasidic rite during which the participants enter into ecstasy while chanting Aramaic phrases. A few days before the assassination of Yitzhak Rabin, a ceremony of this sort was organized to obtain a "punishment" for Rabin's "treason."

SEE ALSO Eyal; Pulsa Denura; Rabin, Yitzhak.

DFLP

SEE Democratic Front for the Liberation of Palestine.

Dhikr (*Zikr*): Arabic term describing "the reminder, the evocation" of the various names of God during a religious ceremony, particularly in Sufi groups. Dhikr occurs under the supervision of a shaykh. It is thought to penetrate the chanter with a portion of the divine spirit conveyed in each of God's names.

SEE ALSO Shaykh.

Dhimmi ("protégé," in Arabic): Status particular to monotheistic non-Muslims and Zoroastrians, from whom was asked the payment of a special tribute, the *jiziya*, and that they not serve in the army in exchange for the "protection" of Islam in countries they inhabited.

SEE ALSO Christianity; Jew.

Diaspora (from the Greek *diaspora*, meaning "dispersion"): Term used to designate the dispersion of the Jewish people, whose first real exile outside Palestine dates from 70 C.E.; the word refers as well to any national or religious community living abroad as a result of voluntary or forced migration. By 2004 the Jewish diaspora outside Israel numbered around 8 million persons, of whom approximately 6 million live in the United States. The Palestinian diaspora, living outside the Gaza Strip and the West Bank, numbered around 3.8 million persons, most of whom are in states neighboring Israel, particularly Jordan (1.6 million), Lebanon (370,000), and Syria (400,000). Some Palestinian sources assert that the population of the Palestinian diaspora is closer to 6.5 million, and that official figures do not reflect those Palestinians who are not registered as refugees. The Palestinian exile dates from 1948, following the creation of the State of Israel.

Din ("sentence," in Hebrew): A religious or secular decision, often made by jurisprudence. The Arabic term *din* means religion. Two ancient Jewish religious decrees, "Din Mosser" and "Din Rodef," proposing stern measures to be taken against any person who has betrayed the Jewish people or put them in danger, are sometimes sanctioned by extremist movements.

Diwan: Arabic word meaning council, often used for the governmental chambers or councils. The term also is used to describe a communal house in Palestinian villages and refugee camps, usually for a particular tribe or part of a tribe.

Djerejian, Edward (1939–): A U.S. diplomat, born in 1939, Edward Djerejian is an eminent Arabist, considered one of the best American specialists on the Middle East. After joining the State Department in 1962, he was posted to Lebanon (1965–1969), then to Morocco (1969–1972), in the capacity of chargé d'affaires. Between 1984 and 1986, he was head of the U.S. mission in the Kingdom of Jordan, then from 1986 to 1987, spokesperson for Ronald Reagan's White House. From 1989 to 1991 Djerejian was U.S. ambassador to Syria, where he was appreciated for his profound knowledge of the Lebanese situation. He participated in the Middle East peace conference held in Madrid. While in Damascus, he maintained very good relations with Syrian foreign minister Faruk al-Shara. From 1991 to 1993 he was undersecretary of state for the Middle East. In December 1993 he was named U.S. ambassador to Israel by Bill Clinton. Djerejian resigned his post in 1994, feeling that he was shut out of the Israeli-Arab peace negotiations. Upon his return to the United States, he was hired by the Rice Institute in Houston, Texas, to head the James A. Baker III Institute for Public Policy. In 2003 Djerejian was invited by Colin Powell, secretary of state under President George W. Bush, to chair the Advisory Group on Public Diplomacy in the Arab and Muslim World, a panel assembled at the request of Congress to study the efficacy of U.S. diplomacy and to recommend policy initiatives. The group published its first report in October 2003.

Dor Shalom (Hebrew, meaning "peace generation"): Israeli pacifist movement, founded in the spring of 1996 under the leadership of Yuval Rabin, son of Prime Minister Yitzhak Rabin, who had been assassinated in November 1995. The movement emphasizes volunteerism and social action to address polarization within Israeli society. Its initiatives include ecological clean-up programs, toy drives, and educational programs for Arab and Israeli children.

DOUBA, ALI ISSA IBRAHIM (called Abu Firas; 1933–): Syrian military officer, Alawite, born at Karfis, in the Matawira tribe. Ali Douba entered the army in 1955 and five years later became the deputy head of internal security in Damascus. He was a military attaché in Great Britain between 1964 and 1966, and in Bulgaria between 1967 and 1968. He returned to Syria and became the head of military intelligence for the Latakia region. In November 1970, as head of military intelligence for the city of Damascus, he supported Hafiz al-Asad's coup d'état. In 1971, he was deputy to the head of army intelligence, Hikmat al-Shihabi. Three years later he was made head of this department. Elected to the central committee of the Baʿth Party in 1978, he was promoted to general in 1981. In December 1983, when President Hafiz al-Asad was ill, Douba was a member of the committee responsible for governing the state in the interim. In 1985, the Syrian president put him in charge of the Lebanon dossier, along with al-Shihabi and Ghazi Kanaan. In June 1987, he escaped an assassination attempt. Named lieutenant general in 1993, he became assistant to al-Shihabi, who was now the army chief of staff, while remaining in charge of military intelligence. General Douba was one of the most influential figures in al-Asad's regime. At the beginning of 2000, increasingly marginalized as Bashshar al-Asad, the son of the president, prepared to take power, he retired from his position as head of Syrian military intelligence and was replaced by his deputy, Hassan Khalil.

SEE ALSO Asad, Bashshar al-; Asad, Hafiz al-; Shihabi, Hikmat al-.

DRUZE: The Druze religion was founded in the eleventh century by followers of Caliph Hakim ibn Amr Allah. Its origins are in the Egyptian Ismaʿili sect, which derives from monotheistic Islam combined with Greek philosophy and other influences. Its tenets include reincarnation and the transmigration of souls, and it recognizes as prophets or persons of great esteem (in addition to those of the Qurʾan) such diverse figures as Hermes, Jethro (Moses' father-in-law), Jesus, and John the Baptist, and the philosophers Pythagoras, Plato, and Plotinus. In the fifteenth century, Jamal al-Din ʿAbda-llah al-Tannoukhi was supposed to have compiled the existing Druze religious texts into six volumes, known under the name of "Wisdom Epistles" (*Rasaʾil al-Hikma*), which constitute the basis of Druze doctrine. The mysteries of the Druze religion are secret; the Druze do not proselytize and have been essentially a closed community almost since the beginning.

DRUZE REBELS. A DRUZE SHAYKH (CENTER) TALKS WITH TWO FOLLOWERS OF KAMAL JUMBLATT'S PROGRESSIVE SOCIALIST PARTY, WHICH FOUGHT IN 1958 FOR SOCIAL AND POLITICAL REFORMS FOR ALL SECTS IN LEBANON. TODAY, DRUZE LIVE IN PARTS OF LEBANON AND SYRIA, AS WELL AS IN ISRAEL, WHERE THEY ARE A PRIVILEGED—BUT NOT PROSPEROUS—MINORITY. *(© Hulton-Deutsch Collection/Corbis)*

Historically, the Druze community has practiced dissimulation (*kitaman*), meaning in practice that the Druze adopt local customs and are loyal to the established state.

The Druze settled in the mountains of the Shuf region of Lebanon, where they became, along with the Maronites, the dominant people in the Lebanese mountains. Currently, the Druze live in the Metn, Kesrouan, Shuf, and Hermon regions in Lebanon, in the Hauran and the Golan Heights in Syria, and in parts of Jordan, as well as in the Galilee in Israel. The opposition of the Druze to Sunni orthodoxy inclines them toward lay Lebanese parties, such as the Progressive Socialist Party. Bloody conflicts between the Druze and Christian communities were rife during the Lebanese Civil War (1975–1990). On 4 August 2001, with the visit of Monseigneur Sfeir to the fief of Druze leader Walid Jumblatt, there was a reconciliation between the two communities. The great Druze communities of Lebanon are represented by the Jumblatt and Shahab families.

In Israel, the Druze number around 100,000 (plus another 18,000 in the Golan), mainly in rural areas in the Galilee, and are officially considered non-Arab. As supporters of the state, Druze serve in the Israel Defense Force (IDF). Though a privileged minority in Israel, their status has not increased their prosperity, and the use made of them by the IDF during the 1982 Israeli invasion of Lebanon, in alliance with Maronite forces and in opposition to Lebanese Druze forces, has created some conflict within the Israeli Druze community between the younger and the more conservative older generations.

SEE ALSO Ismaili; Jumblatt, Walid Kamal; Maronites; Sfeir, Nasrallah.

DRUZE INITIATIVE COMMITTEE (Lajnat al-Muhadarat al-Durziya): Israeli leftist Druze organization, opposed to all collaboration of the Druze community with Israeli authorities. It opposes the conscription of Druze into the Israel Defense Force and actively assists conscientious objectors. The committee participates in various activities with international and Israeli peace organizations.

DUNAM: Turkish measuring unit, corresponding to one tenth of a hectare.

Eagles of the Palestinian Revolution

SEE Saʿiqa, al-.

Eastern Christians: Religious community including Melkites, Maronites, and Assyrians.

SEE ALSO Assyrians; Maronites; Melkites.

Eastern Orthodox Church: A descendant of the Byzantine Church, the Eastern Orthodox Church consists of a group of autonomous Christian churches that share doctrine and liturgy. The Eastern Orthodox Church issued from the great schism of 1054, when it formally split from the Roman Catholic Church. Orthodox churches in the Middle East include: the Russian, the Balkan, and the Greek; the churches of Antioch, Alexandria, Jerusalem, and the See of Constantinople (now Istanbul); and the Nestorian and Monophysite churches. The long-established presence of the Eastern Orthodox Church (as well as purchases made from the Georgians in the sixteenth to eighteenth centuries) earned it control over many religious sites in Palestine during the Ottoman Empire and up unto the present.

SEE ALSO Christianity.

Eban, Abba (1915–2002): Israeli foreign minister, born Audrey Salomon, in South Africa. Abba Eban studied eastern languages at Cambridge, and during World War II organized the recruitment of volunteers to join the Jewish brigade of the British army. Eban was the newly created State of Israel's first representative to the United Nations. In 1950, he became Israel's first ambassador to the United States, and in 1953 he was elected vice president of the U.N. General Assembly. In 1959, he joined the Israel Labor Party, MAPAI, which he went on to represent in the Knesset. In December of the same year he joined the government of David Ben-Gurion as minister without portfolio. The following year he was named minister of education and culture. In June 1963, he became deputy prime minister in the cabinet of Levi Eshkol. From June 1966 to May 1974, he was foreign minister, succeeding Golda Meir. After the 1967 Arab-Israel War, he helped formulate United Nations (UN) Resolution 242. At the foreign ministry his moderate positions clashed with the intransigence of Prime Minister Meir. When Yitzhak Rabin became head of the government, Eban resigned. Between 1984 and 1988, he was chairman of the Knesset foreign affairs and defense committee, where he advocated the development of a dialogue with the Palestinians. In June 1988, shunted aside by certain Labor Party leaders, he no longer figured on its list for the Knesset elections. Eban is the author of a number of works dealing with Jewish history and Israel. He died in Tel Aviv.

Abba Eban. A Labor Party moderate, Eban was an Israeli public official during his nation's first four decades. His many posts included first representative to the United Nations and first ambassador to the United States, as well as deputy prime minister and foreign minister in the 1960s and 1970s. A prolific author, he was an articulate spokesman for Israel who often appeared on American television.

see also Arab-Israel War (1967); Ben-Gurion, David; MAPAI; Meir, Golda; Rabin, Yitzhak; Resolution 242.

Echud

see Yad.

Edah Haredit: Ultra-Orthodox independent Jewish community. Anti-Zionist and hostile to the State of Israel, it rejects all participation in Israeli political life.

Eddé, Raymond (1913–2000): Lebanese Maronite Christian politician, born in Alexandria, Egypt. Son of Émile Eddé, president of Lebanon between 1936 and 1941, Raymond Eddé studied law, then entered politics in 1943. Six years later, he became *amid* (president) of the National Bloc, succeeding his father, who had just died. As soon as he took office, he voiced his opposition to President Beshara al-Khoury, the legality of whose election he contested. In opposition to the new president were also Camille Chamoun, Abdelhamid Karamé, Hamid Franjiya, and Kamal Jumblatt. In 1951, with Chamoun and Jumblatt, Eddé created the Lebanese National Socialist Front. In 1956, when he had been representing the town of Jubayl for three years, he succeeded in getting a bank secrecy law passed that would turn Lebanon into an important financial center. Concurrently, he supported the campaign advocating the adoption of civil marriage. In July 1958, he was defeated in the presidential elections by Fu'ad Shahab. In spite of this setback, he asserted himself as one of the principal leaders of the Christian camp. In October, he joined the "people's salvation" cabinet, where he held the interior, foreign affairs, labor, and transportation portfolios. In 1964, he suffered his second political defeat in the legislative elections, losing his deputy's seat, but he won it back the following year in partial elections. Opposed to Shahabism, he participated in a tripartite alliance with Pierre Jumayyil and Chamoun. In October 1968, he became minister of public works and agriculture, but he resigned three months later, following the Israeli raid on the Beirut airport, against which the Lebanese military put up no resistance. Advocating Lebanese unity, he asked for a United Nations force for South Lebanon, which he saw as the only way for Lebanon to avoid growing polarization.

In November 1969, he opposed the agreement between the Lebanese government and the Palestinian *fida'iyyun,* arguing that it gave Israel a pretext for nullifying the Israeli-Lebanese armistice agreement signed in 1949. Condemning the action of the Maronite militias, Eddé was regarded as a traitor to his own group. In August 1970, he opposed the candidacy of the Shahabist Elias Sarkis and supported Suleiman Franjiya in the presidential election, but four years later he dissented from the latter's policies and in October 1974, along with former prime ministers, created an anti-Franjiya bloc. In 1976, he escaped several assassination attempts. In July, opposing the entry of the Syrian army into Lebanon, he founded the National Union Front. In December, condemning the Phalangists' actions, refusing to take a position in intra-Lebanese fighting, and rejecting all plans to partition Lebanon, he decided on exile in France. From Paris, Eddé continued to speak for human rights and democracy in Lebanon. In 1990, in spite of the end of the civil war, he refused to return to Beirut, opposing the Ta'if Accords, which he thought only sanctioned the Syrian presence in Lebanon. He died in Paris in 2000.

SEE ALSO Chamoun, Camille; Jumblatt, Kamal; Phalange; Ta'if Accord.

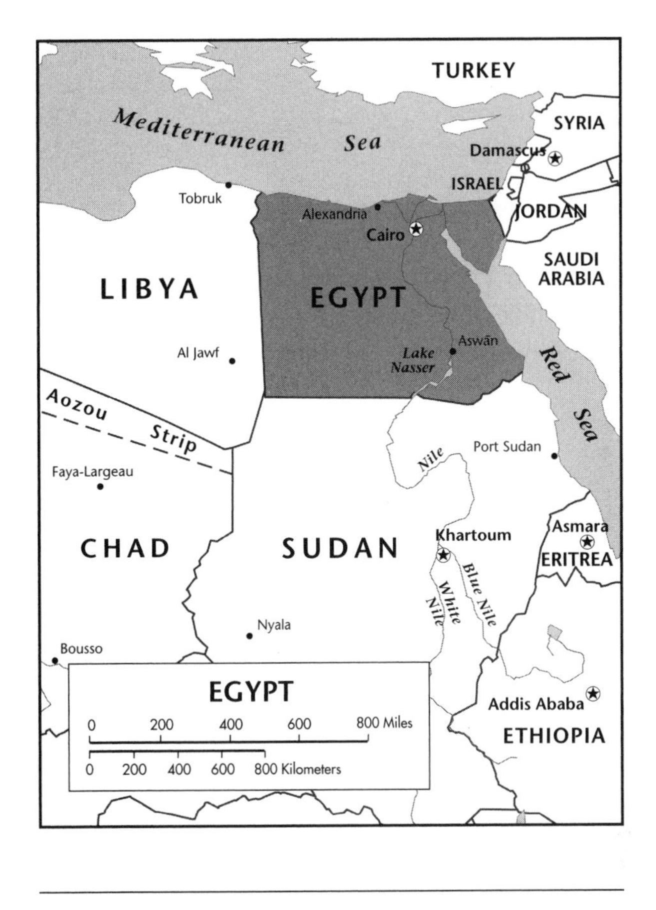

EGYPT: Previously a semiautonomous Ottoman province, Egypt was from 1882 to the early 1950s essentially, though never formally, a British colony whose control the British considered crucial because of the Suez Canal. In 1914, when the Ottoman Empire entered World War I on the side of the Germans, Britain declared Egypt a protectorate, and in 1922 a form of home rule under the Ottoman/Egyptian monarchy (the royal family was Albanian in origin). Hostility to foreign rule (which had been building since European interventions over Egypt's foreign debt in the 1870s and British occupation in 1882), dissatisfaction with social conditions, and later outrage at the ongoing establishment of a European/Zionist settler state in Palestine under imperial protection led to a widespread, although divided, nationalist movement with both religious and secular components.

From the time of the Balfour Declaration in 1917, Egyptian political parties—ranging from the Wafd, the largest secular nationalist party between the wars, to the Communists, to the Muslim Brotherhood—rallied their followers over the cause of the Palestinians. Some, especially the Muslim Brothers, supplied money and volunteers for anti-Zionist actions in Palestine, including strikes, the Arab Revolt of 1936–1939, and the Arab-Israel War of 1948–1949. Egypt was the main advocate for the Palestinians in the League of Arab States after its creation in 1945.

The disaster of the 1948 war, which left the Gaza Strip, with roughly a quarter of a million Palestinian refugees, under Egyptian control, severely weakened the government and discredited most of the existing political parties. A coup d'état in 1952 by a group of young military officers led by Gamal Abdel Nasser led to the abolition of the monarchy and the declaration of a republic in 1953. Political parties, except for an officially approved group, were disbanded, and a thorough program of social, economic, and political reform was undertaken. In 1956, under a new constitution, Nasser became president.

After 1949, under both monarchy and republic, Egypt formally supported the Palestinian cause but in practice refrained from conflict with Israel and even participated in secret negotiations for a compromise settlement; resources were devoted mainly to the domestic economy. But the Lavon Affair in 1954 and Israeli attacks on Gaza in 1954 and 1955 convinced Nasser that the Egyptian armed forces had to be built up. His refusal to join the Baghdad Pact or take sides in the Cold War—in 1955 Egypt joined the Nonaligned Movement—as well as Egyptian aid to the Algerian nationalists then in revolt against French rule, made it impossible to obtain Western arms and prevented an agreement in ongoing negotiations with Britain over its occupation of the Suez Canal zone, which continued under a 1936 treaty. Nasser concluded an arms deal with Czechoslovakia, then a Soviet satellite; the United States withdrew its offer to finance the Aswan High Dam, an important economic project. Nasser's response was to seize and nationalize the Suez Canal. Although he offered financial compensation, the British and French attempted to break him militarily and colluded with Israel to provoke the Suez-Sinai War of October 1956, which ended, mostly because of American pressure, in humiliation for the British and French; in their withdrawal; and in the increased status of Egypt in the world, especially among Arabs. Also under American pressure, the Israelis withdrew from the Sinai, destroying roads and military installations as they left.

In 1958, partly as a result of the popularity of Nasser's Arab nationalism, Syria and Egypt created the United Arab Republic (UAR), with Nasser at its head. Political differences with the Syrians led to the dissolution of the UAR in 1961. In 1962, Egypt also became involved in a civil war in North Yemen, where a coup d'état had overthrown the Saudi-supported monarchy. This conflict was a drain on Egyptian resources for several years.

In 1964, Egypt, along with Syria and Iraq, sponsored the Arab League's creation of the Palestine Liberation Organization (PLO) as a means to channel—and keep under control—the activities of Palestinian nationalists. Under its leader Ahmad Shuqayri, it was largely beholden to Egypt for material support. Shuqayri, however, indulged in extremely belligerent rhetoric, to the detriment of Palestinian as well as Egyptian interests, particularly in the months before the 1967 war with Israel. In 1966, Egypt entered into a mutual defense treaty with Syria.

In the spring of 1967, the Israelis began massing troops along the Egyptian border. Nasser moved troops into the area, requested the removal of the United Nations Emergency Force, which had guarded the border since 1956, and blockaded the Straits of Tiran. Egypt and Jordan then signed a mutual defense treaty. These acts were the culmination of a long period of tension and provocation that led to the Arab-Israel War of 1967, which ended disastrously for all the Arab state participants and for the Palestinians. The Arab armies were routed and Israel was left in possession of the Syrian Golan Heights and the Sinai Peninsula, as well as the remainder of what had been Palestine under the British Mandate, including the Gaza Strip and the West Bank; hundreds of thousands of new Palestinian refugees were created. Nasser's government and international prestige were undermined, and the PLO began to distance itself from Egypt, beginning with the resignation of Shuqayri. Nasser resigned, but his resignation was refused by the National Assembly. He negotiated a ceasefire in the Black September conflict between Jordan and the PLO shortly before he died in 1970.

His successor, Anwar al-Sadat, was less interested in pan-Arab unity than Nasser and worked to reorient Egypt toward the United States. He signed the Egyptian-Soviet Friendship Treaty, which originated during the Nasser regime, but expelled Soviet military advisors in 1972. (He reconciled with the Soviet Union early in 1973 and military aid resumed.) Frustrated by the Israeli refusal to negotiate the return of Israeli-occupied territory, Egypt and Syria launched the Arab-Israel War of 1973, in which Sadat achieved two objectives: showing that Egyptian armed forces were capable of fighting well against the Israelis and provoking the Americans to step in to mediate a peace settlement. Sadat agreed to an Israeli proposal to seek a treaty under U.S., rather than UN, auspices, and concluded agreements in 1974 and 1975 dealing with disengagement in the Sinai. He sought American aid and investment and abrogated the Egyptian-Soviet Friendship Treaty in 1976, when the Soviets refused to delay repayment of Egyptian debts. These moves toward a separate peace constituted a break with the Arab world. Sadat signed the Camp David Accords in 1978 and the subsequent peace treaty in 1979. These agreements proved extremely unpopular both with Egyptians and with other Arabs. Members of the Arab League severed diplomatic relations; Egypt was suspended from the League and from the Organization of the Islamic Conference. There was immense popular opposition to the treaty, with its perceived capitulation on the Palestinian issue, as well as to Sadat's economic liberalization, which brought great hardship to the lower and middle classes (he reduced food subsidies and abolished price controls, largely at the behest of the World Bank; there were riots in 1977, which the army suppressed violently). To retain political control, Sadat governed in an increasingly autocratic and repressive manner, largely by decree and through rigged referenda. He outlawed strikes, imposed censorship, tolerated corruption, repressed Palestinian political and economic activity in Egypt, attempted to undermine the PLO, and jailed political opponents. When Sadat was assassinated in 1981 by a group belonging to Eyptian Islamic Jihad, he was barely mourned; indeed his death was celebrated throughout the Arab world.

His successor, Husni Mubarak, sought to placate popular discontent, but without losing political control. He moderated Sadat's most repressive measures and harshest economic policies, legalized political parties, and loosened censorship. He did not repudiate the peace treaty and he maintained good relations with the United States. Like Sadat, he aided Iraq (also being helped by the United States) in the Iran-Iraq War, which began in 1980. In April 1982, in accord with the peace treaty, Israel withdrew from the Sinai. In June 1982, Israel invaded Lebanon in Operation Peace for Galilee, a move that might not have been possible without the treaty, which limited Egypt's military presence in the Sinai and inserted a multinational force between Egypt and the Israelis. Mubarak withdrew Egypt's ambassador from Israel but did not break relations. When the PLO was expelled from Lebanon in 1983, however, Mubarak did assist it (although he did not accept any PLO fighters into Egypt) and publicly met with its leader, Yasir Arafat; Mubarak was subsequently a frequent intermediary between the PLO and the United States. This was the beginning of Egypt's reacceptance into the Arab World. In 1984, Jordan, another ally of Iraq and the United States, resumed diplomatic relations. In 1989, Egypt joined the Arab Cooperation Council, a group of Arab countries that had aided Iraq during its war with Iran, and later the same year was allowed to rejoin the League of Arab States. In 1990, with a majority of the League, Egypt condemned the Iraqi invasion of Kuwait and the next year joined the American-led coalition in the Gulf War, although Mubarak would not allow Egyptian troops to be used inside Iraq.

The Palestinian cause remained popular in Egypt, and after the Intifada broke out in late 1987 large public demonstrations took place, some of which became violent. These were organized by student, labor, political, and religious groups. Islamist groups particularly condemned both the Egyptian government and the PLO for compromising with the Israelis, and increasingly unpopular government economic policies contributed to the opposition. Through the 1990s, militant groups like Islamic Jihad and al-Jamiʿa al-Islamiyya campaigned against the government; they attempted to assassinate Mubarak in Addis Ababa in 1995 and for several years carried on a violent campaign aimed at foreign residents and tourists, which resulted in many deaths and elicited armed repression.

Mubarak condemned the harsh Israeli response to the Intifada but at no time threatened to abandon the peace treaty. He recognized the Proclamation of the State of Palestine in 1988, but his opposition to Iraq's occupation of Kuwait strained relations with the PLO, which supported Iraq. After the Gulf War, however, Mubarak continued to advocate negotiations and supported both the Madrid Conference and the Oslo Accords.

In the opening years of the twenty-first century, Mubarak's government remains in power through undemocratic means, and its main fear is the political strength of the Islamists. Although the more violent groups of the 1990s have subsided, the officially outlawed Muslim Brotherhood is increasingly popular, especially since the start of the Palestinians' al-Aqsa Intifada in 2000. With the increasing radicalization of the Israeli and American policies and of organized Palestinian responses to them, Egyptian influence in the Palestinian-Israeli dispute has waned. Constrained by his determination to maintain Egypt's relation with the United States (Egypt is the second largest recipient of U.S. aid in the world; Israel is the first), there is little Mubarak can do either to help the Palestinians or to restrain the Israelis. Although he offered Egypt's support after the 11 September 2001 attacks on the United States, his opposition to the American war in Iraq in 2003 was ignored, as was his urging that the Bush administration become more involved in seeking a negotiated settlement of the Israeli-Palestinian issue.

SEE ALSO Aqsa Intifada, al-; Arab Cooperation Council; Arab-Israel War (1967); Arab-Israel War (1973); Arab-Israel War (1982); Arafat, Yasir Muhammad; Baghdad Pact; Balfour Declaration; Black September 1970; Camp David Accords; Eyptian Islamic Jihad; Gaza Strip; Golan Heights; Gulf War (1991); Intifada (1987–1993); Iran-Iraq War; Iraq; Jamiʿa al-Islamiyya, al-; Lavon Affair; League of Arab States; Madrid Conference; Muslim Brotherhood; Nasser, Gamal Abdel; Mubarak, Husni; Organization of the Islamic Conference; Oslo Accords; Oslo Accords II; Palestine Arab Revolt (1936–1939); Palestine Liberation Organization; Proclamation of the State of Palestine; Sadat, Anwar al-; Suez Crisis; United Arab Republic; United Nations Emergency Force; Wafd; West Bank.

EGYPTIAN ISLAMIC GROUP

SEE Jamiʿa al-Islamiyya, al-.

EGYPTIAN ISLAMIC JIHAD: Islamist extremist movement, created at the end of 1976 by former members of the Islamic Liberation Organization. Formed under the initiative of Ali al-Maghrebi, it was partially dismantled by Egyptian authorities in 1978. A few members who escaped from persecution decided to continue the activities of the group, organizing anti-Christian operations in the south of Egypt. In 1979, Lieutenant Colonel Abud al-Zumur joined the movement and became one of its main leaders, along with the ideologue Abdul Salam Faraj. The latter, author of the tract *Al Farida al-Gha'iba* (The hidden imperative), recommended a program of action meant to establish an Islamic state, while commanding a jihad against the regime in place in Cairo. On 6 October 1981, a movement commando assassinated President Anwar al-Sadat during a military parade commemorating the 1973 Arab-Israel War. Two days later, the jihad cell of Upper Egypt staged riots, causing the deaths of almost two hundred people. Many movement members were arrested and imprisoned for a few months. Some of them left Egypt to join the Afghan resistance against the Soviet army. In April 1982, Abdul Salam Faraj, along with the members of the commando that assassinated Sadat, were executed. After the death of President Sadat, the movement was banned, but in 1987 Mahmud Sayyed Jaballah was accused of having reconstituted it and was sentenced to prison. Reorganizing, the Egyptian Islamic Jihad carried out new attacks, principally against Egyptian political figures and security heads, as well as against foreign tourists in Egypt. Repressed by Egyptian authorities, some of these militants settled in Pakistan and in Europe.

Between 1989 and 1991 the movement was seemingly led by Ayman Muhammad al-Zawahri. (In 1992, after Zawahri was expelled from the movement, he formed his own organization, which he named Tala'i al-Fatah [Avant-Garde of the Conquest], an appellation that was already attached to an armed branch of the Jihad. Zawahri, then based in Pakistan, took credit for the attack on 19 November 1995 on the Egyptian embassy in Islamabad.) In February 1998, Egyptian Islamic Jihad joined the World Islamic Front for Holy War against Jews and Crusaders (Front of Liberation of the Holy Sites of Islam), known as al-Qa'ida, whose main leader was Osama Bin Ladin, and with which al-Jamaʿa al-Islamiyya was also affiliated. On 18 April 1999, at a trial of 107 people accused of belonging to the Jihad, the Egyptian high military court tried the principal leaders, including Zawahri, in absentia and sentenced them to death. In 1997 some former Jihad members formed the Islah (Reform) Party and in 1999 others, including Muhammad Ali Sulayman, Raʿafat Ibrahim Nasr, Amin al-Demiri, and Sabri Ahmad Muhammad, created the Shariʿa Party. These parties have thus far been refused permission to contest elections, since parties based on religion are banned under Egypt's constitution).

SEE ALSO Arab-Israel War (1973); Bin Ladin, Osama; Islamic Liberation Organization; Jamaʿa al-Islamiyya, al-; Sadat, Anwar al-.

EGYPTIAN REVOLUTION MOVEMENT (Harakat Thawrat Misr, in Arabic): This Egyptian movement, Nasserite in leaning, surfaced in 1984 and conducted several operations against Israeli and American figures in Cairo. The son and a nephew of former president Gamal Abdel Nasser were suspected of having belonged to it. The arrest of its principal members effectively neutralized the movement, whose activities ceased toward the end of the 1980s. An "Egyptian Revolution" appears among the terrorist organizations listed by the U.S. government, but little information is available on the group.

SEE ALSO Nasser, Gamal Abdel.

EID AL-ADHA

SEE ʿId al-Adha.

EID AL-FITR

SEE ʿId al-Fitr.

ELDAD, ISRAEL (1910–1996): Israeli activist. Born in Galicia, Eldad received a Ph.D. from the University of Vienna and graduated from the Vienna Rabbinical Seminary. In 1941 he immigrated to Palestine under the British Mandate and became a leader of the Stern Gang (Lohamei Herut Yisrael, LEHI), a militant Zionist group. He was arrested by the British in 1944. After the creation of Israel in 1948 and Prime Minister David Ben-Gurion's dissolution of LEHI in September of that year, Eldad remained an advocate for a Greater Israel that would encompass the land between the Nile and Euphrates Rivers. He edited the journal *Sulam* and lectured at the Haifa Technion until Ben-Gurion, in response to Eldad's inflammatory remarks, ordered his dismissal from his teaching post. He became a columnist for Israel's daily newspaper *Haaretz* and was considered a champion of the extreme right. He continued to write for various publications until his death.

SEE ALSO Ben-Gurion, David; Lohamei Herut Yisrael.

ELEM (immigration for the good of the state, in Hebrew): Israeli political group, formed in March 1981 by immigrants of Soviet origin to defend their rights and facilitate their integration into Israeli society. One of their principal leaders was Yuli Nudelman.

EL-HAMISHMAR (The guardian, in Hebrew): Israeli daily newspaper, founded in 1943, considered the organ of MAPAM. Closed in March 1995.

SEE ALSO: MAPAM.

ELON, BENYAMIN (BENNY) (1954–): member of Knesset. Born in Jerusalem in 1954, Elon studied at Yeshivat Merkaz Harav and served as a chaplain in the Israel Defense Force (IDF). He was a Jewish Agency emissary to the United States from 1983 to 1985. On his return to Israel, he taught at the Ateret Cohanim Center in Jerusalem and in 1990 founded Yeshivat Beit Orot. In 1996 he was elected to the

Knesset on the Moledet list, serving since that time on various committees, including the Constitution, Law and Justice Committee and the Committee for Foreign Workers. In October 2001, following the death of tourism minister Rehavam Ze'evi, Elon was appointed minister of tourism. A member of the National Unity Party, he has been a staunch supporter of the Gush Emunim and West Bank settlements.

SEE ALSO Gush Emunim.

EL-SARRAJ, EYAD

SEE Sarraj, Eyad, el-.

EMIR (Amir): Title adopted by sovereigns, often translated as prince. Their jurisdictions are called emirates.

EMUNAT HAKHAKHAMIM: Hebrew term designating the absolute obedience practicing Jews owe their religious superiors.

ENDURING FREEDOM OPERATION: Code name of the U.S. military operation launched on 7 October 2001 against Afghanistan.

SEE ALSO Bin Ladin, Osama.

ENTEBBE: City in Uganda, the scene of an Israeli hostage rescue operation. On 27 June 1976, Air France Flight 139 was hijacked en route from Tel Aviv to Paris by two German nationals and two Palestinians, first to Benghazi, Libya, and then to Entebbe Airport. At Entebbe, the hijackers were joined by a second team. The non-Jewish passengers were released, and 101 Jewish passengers were held hostage. Israel, though appearing to begin negotiations with the hijackers and with Ugandan president Idi Amin, prepared for a military rescue. On the night of 3–4 July, four Hercules transport jets carrying 150 Israeli commandos flew from Sharm al-Shayk to Entebbe, evading detection. The paratroopers stormed the terminal where the hostages were being held, killing all eight hijackers and several Ugandan soldiers. Three hostages and the commander of the mission, Lieutenant Colonel Yonatan Netanyahu (brother of the future prime minister), were killed. The rescue operation was generally praised in the West but was condemned by Arab and African countries and the Soviet Union.

EPIPHANY: Christian holiday, celebrated on the twelfth day of Christmas, commemorating the recognition by the Three Wise Men (Melchior, Balthazar, and Gaspar) of the Messiah in Jesus.

SEE ALSO Jesus; Messiah.

EREKAT, SAIB MUHAMMAD (Erakat, Arakat; 1955–): Palestinian activist and negotiator, born in Jericho. Saib Erekat earned a degree in political science at San Francisco State University in the United States and a Ph.D. at Bradford College in Great Britain. A professor at al-Najah University of Nablus, on the West Bank, he was also in charge of public relations there between 1982 and 1986. He has been an editorialist for the daily *al-Quds* since 1982 and has published several works on the Palestinian question. He is close to al-Fatah and has backed the political line of the Palestine Liberation Organization. He was vice-chair of the Palestinian delegation led by Haydar Abd al-Shafi to the Madrid peace conference in 1991. His involvement in various Israeli-Palestinian meetings only began in August 1992, because until then the Israelis would not accept him as a negotiator. He threatened to resign a year later, along with two other members of the Palestinian delegation, Faysal al-Husayni and Hanan Ashwari, to protest the Oslo Accords, which were negotiated without their knowledge. In January 1994 Erekat replaced al-Shafi as the head of the Palestinian delegation negotiating with Israel. At the end of the following May, as the Palestinian territories were becoming autonomous, he was named minister for local government in the Palestinian Authority (PA), led by Yasir Arafat, while retaining his responsibilities in the Palestinian commission in charge of negotiations with Israel. On 28 September 1995 he participated in signing the provisional Israeli-Palestinian accord on the West Bank and the Gaza Strip (the second Oslo Accords).

Although he is close to Arafat, Erekat has spoken out against corruption in the PA and has fallen out with Arafat more than once. In 1999 Arafat dismissed him from the Wye Plantation negotiations; he was named negotiations minister in the cabinet of Mahmud Abbas when the latter became PA prime minister in 2003, but he resigned after two weeks, when he was excluded from meetings between Abbas and Ariel Sharon. Erekat has participated in a number of delegations charged with restarting peace talks between Israelis and Palestinians, but with little result. He also participated, unofficially, in the discussions that over two years produced the Geneva Accord of November 2003. This unofficial agreement, negotiated with political figures of the Israeli left and endorsed by such international figures as former U.S. president Jimmy Carter, was meant to prod the PA, the Israeli government, and the United States into some constructive movement toward serious negotiations but met with a reception ranging from polite indifference in Washington to enraged condemnation in Israel, and gained little support among Palestinian political factions. In April 2004, shortly after President George W. Bush committed the United States to support the Sharon government's plan to evacuate Gaza while permanently incorporating Israeli settlements in the West Bank, Erekat published a commentary in the *Washington Post,* noting that "President Bush apparently has taken my job. . . . Israel is now negotiating peace with the United States—not with the Palestinians. . . . we are farther away from a permanent peace than we have ever been."

SEE ALSO Abbas, Mahmud Rida; Arafat, Yasir Muhammad; Ashrawi, Hanan Daouda; Fatah, al-; Geneva Peace Initiative of 2003; Husayni, Faysal al-; Oslo Accords; Oslo Accords II; Palestinian Authority; Palestine Liberation Organization; Quds; al-; Sharon, Ariel; Oslo Accords II.

ERETZ YISRAEL (Hebrew, meaning "land of Israel"): Expression used to designate the land of Israel, as it was promised by God to the Jewish people, according to Biblical tradition. Geographically this territory corresponds to the Kingdom of Solomon, which extended from Dan, north of Tiberias, to Beersheba in the south. After the creation of the State of Israel in May 1948, this notion of a "Greater Israel" became the central theme of the political program of Israeli nationalist extremist movements. To them, Eretz Yisrael stretches from the Jordan River to the Mediterranean.

ESHKOL, LEVI (1895–1969): Labor Party leader and prime minister of Israel, 1963–1969. Eshkol Levi was born in Kiev, Ukraine, and settled in Palestine in 1914, serving in the Jewish Legion from 1918 to 1920. During the British Mandate (1922–1948), he became active in labor politics and Zionism, and for three years headed the settlement department of the Palestine office in Berlin during Nazi rule, organizing immigration and transfer of funds, the "Ha'avarah," from Germany to Palestine. He also served as chief financial administrator of the Haganah.

After 1948, Eshkol held various positions in the Israeli government, including director general of the ministry of defense, minister of agriculture, and minister of finance. In 1963, following David Ben-Gurion's retirement and at his recommendation, Eshkol assumed the post of prime minister as well as that of defense minister; he later lost favor with Ben-Gurion, particularly over the Lavon Affair. During the 1967 War, Eshkol continued as prime minister but relinquished the ministry of defense to Moshe Dayan. He established a National Unity government, including the right-wing Gahal bloc, which was retained in the 1969 elections but ended with Gahal's departure from the coalition in 1970. Eshkol died in February 1969 of a heart attack while in office. Golda Meir succeeded him as prime minister.

SEE ALSO Arab-Israel War (1967); Dayan, Moshe; Galal Party; Haganah; Lavon Affair.

ESSENES (from the Hebrew *'esah,* council or party): A Jewish sect, existing between the second and first centuries C.E., whose adepts devoted their lives to the study of religious texts, sharing their possessions, and observing a strict discipline. The Essene movement represented a scission in Judaism, a response by some pious Jews to the influence of Hellenistic culture. The prime cause of this scission was the luxury of sacerdotal ceremonies, which was denounced by many, but another reason was the rivalry between the Pharisees and the Sadducees. The Essenes (also called "the pious") settled in a desert area in the north of Palestine, away from the corruptions of the Temple in Jerusalem. The Dead Sea Scrolls, which were discovered at Qumran in April 1947, are believed to be relics of the Essenes.

SEE ALSO Dead Sea Scrolls.

EXECUTIVE COMMITTEE OF THE PLO

SEE Palestinian Liberation Organization.

EXILES

SEE Muhajirun, al-.

EXODUS: Name of an American boat chartered in July 1947 by Mossad Beth to transport Jewish emigrants to Palestine. Under its original name *President Warfield,* the ship left Sète, France, on 11 July with 4,554 passengers on board, officially heading toward Columbia. When the boat reached high seas, the captain changed its name to *Exodus 47* and altered course toward Palestine. On 18 July, *Exodus* was stopped by the British navy outside of Haifa and seized by the port authorities. The passengers, undesirables in the eyes of the British authorities, were divided into three ships that took them back to Europe. On 29 July, they arrived in France, at Port-de-Bouc, where the passengers refused to debark, except for 130 aged or ill people. On 22 August, the British authorities obliged the boats to pursue their route toward Hamburg, where, on 8 September, the odyssey of the passengers of the *Exodus* ended.

EYAL ("ram," in Hebrew; Jewish National Organization; Jewish Combat Organization): Name of an Israeli ultranationalist splinter group created in April 1991 by Avishai Raviv. Associated with the older ultra-Orthodox Kach Party, the movement has been responsible for several anti-Palestinian attacks, and also has been suspected of assassinating Jews accused of treason by its leaders. On 22 September 1995, Israeli television filmed the members of Eyal, their heads hooded, in the process of swearing on a pistol and a Bible and accusing Prime Minister Yitzhak Rabin of treason. On the following 4 November, Yigal Amir, an Israeli Jew close to Eyal, assassinated Yitzhak Rabin. Brought before a magistrate, he declared that he was "inspired by God." During the investigation, unconfirmed rumors circulated that Eyal was created by Shin Beth to penetrate Israeli extremist milieux. The organization receives financial backing from Jewish extremist groups in the United States.

SEE ALSO Kach Party.

EZRA AND NEHEMIAH OPERATIONS: Code name for a number of operations organized by the Israeli authorities between the end of the 1940s and the middle of the 1950s, bringing almost 180,000 Jews from Morocco, Yemen, and Iraq to Israel. Also known under the code name of Flying Carpet Operation.

INTERRUPTED EXODUS. PASSENGERS LEAVE THE DAMAGED EXODUS 47 UNDER THE WATCH OF BRITISH SOLDIERS IN THE PORT OF HAIFA, PALESTINE, IN 1947. MORE THAN 4,500 WOULD-BE JEWISH IMMIGRANTS WERE FORCED TO RETURN TO EUROPE ON THREE OTHER SHIPS, AND THEY ENDED UP IN HAMBURG.

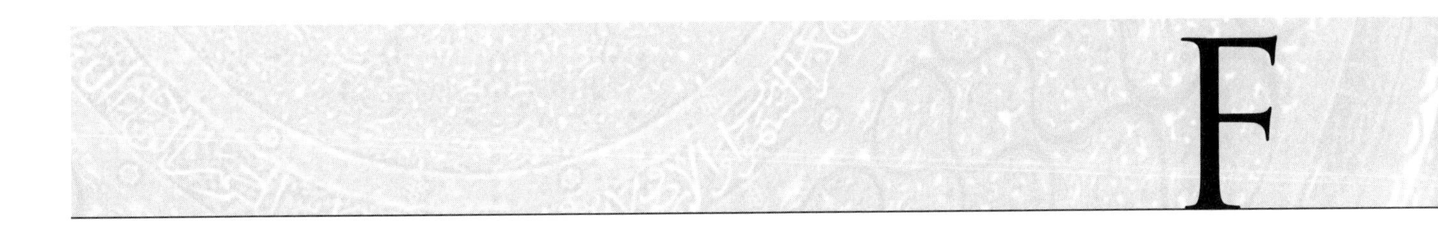

FADLALLAH, SHAYKH MUHAMMAD HUSAYN (1935–): Prominent Shiʿite Muslim scholar and spiritual head of the Hizbullah movement in Lebanon. Fadlallah was born in Najaf, Iraq, and studied with Ayatollah al-Khuʾi, whose representative in Lebanon he later became. In Najaf he also met Baqir al-Sadr, who recommended that he combine his religious beliefs and training with political and social activism. Following further studies in Qom, Iran, Fadlallah went to Lebanon in 1966 at the invitation of the *ulama* and Usrat al-Taʾkhi (family of fraternity). He settled in Nabʿah, an impoverished community at the periphery of Beirut, where he created youth organizations and free clinics. After the destruction of Nabʿah in 1976, during the civil war, Fadlallah moved to southern Lebanon with other Shiʿite refugees. He founded the Islamic Legislative Institute, responsible for the training of *ulama.* In 1982, after a schism developed within AMAL, Fadlallah called for all movements to embrace his program for an Islamic revolution in Lebanon, on the model of Ayatollah Ruhollah Khomeini's successful overthrow of the Shah in Iran. Hizbullah was established in 1982 and by 1987 was the second most important Shiʿa political group in Lebanon, after AMAL. Fadlallah became its leader. After the death of Ayatollah Khomeini, an intense power struggle developed within the leadership of the Iranian government and Muhammad Fadlallah found himself opposing Ayatollah Ali Khameneʾi for presidency of the Marjaʿiya, a Shiʿite clerical magisterium. Shaykh Fadlallah vigorously advocated resistance to the Israeli occupation of South Lebanon, denounced Yasir Arafat's willingness to negotiate with Israel, and rejected the accords signed between Israel and the Palestine Liberation Organization, claiming that the concept of land for peace was a betrayal of Palestinians.

Fadlallah's positions on internal affairs are moderate and distinguish him from other Shiʿa *ulama.* Differences include his commitment to social and charitable organizations and to women's participation in public life. Although his status increased, especially among radicals, when Ayatollah Khomeini allowed him to collect *khums* (religious tax) from his followers in 1982, Fadlallah's views have changed and he now calls for a multicultural Lebanon instead of an Islamic republic. Fadlallah, who is referred to as Ayatollah Fadlallah, denounced the terrorist attacks of 11 September 2001, describing them as "barbaric crimes" that "do not serve those who carry them out, but rather the victims who will reap the sympathy of the whole world. . . . Islamists who live according to the human value of Islam could not commit such crimes."

SEE ALSO Alim; AMAL; Hizbullah; Land for Peace.

FAHD PLAN: Named after the Saudi Crown Prince (since June 1982, King) Fahd ibn Abdelazziz, who

HIZBULLAH LEADER. SHAYKH MUHAMMAD HUSAYN FADLALLAH, THE SPIRITUAL HEAD OF THE HIZBULLAH MOVEMENT IN LEBANON, HAS TAKEN A HARD LINE AGAINST PEACE WITH ISRAEL, BUT HE IS MORE MODERATE ON INTERNAL AFFAIRS IN HIS COUNTRY, AND HE CONDEMNED THE TERRORIST ATTACKS AGAINST THE UNITED STATES ON 11 SEPTEMBER 2001. *(AP/Wide World Photos)*

proposed a resolution of the Israeli-Palestinian conflict. Presented to the Arab League on 7 August 1981, the Fahd Plan was based on the provisions of United Nations resolutions 242 and 338 and consisted of eight points: 1) Israeli retreat from the totality of the Arab territories occupied in 1967, including East Jerusalem; 2) dismantling of all Israeli settlements outside Israel's 1967 borders; 3) guarantee of religious freedom; 4) recognition of the right of return of the Palestinian people and to indemnity for any Palestinians not desiring to return to their country; 5) placing the West Bank and Gaza Strip under UN authority for a short transitional period; 6) creation of a Palestinian state, with East Jerusalem as its capital; 7) recognition of the right to live in peace for every state in the region (in other words, an implicit recognition of Israel by all Arab states); 8) a guarantee by the United Nations or several member states that these principles would be executed. The plan was met without enthusiasm by most Arab states but promoted by the pro-American King Hassan II of Morocco and by King Fahd, and it was formally adopted by the League of Arab States at its summit meeting in Fez, Morocco, in September 1982, where it became known as the Fez Initiative. It was rejected by Israel but remained the official position of the Arab League states until the Madrid Conference of 1991.

SEE ALSO League of Arab States; Madrid Conference.

FAHUM, KHALID AL- (1923–): Palestinian political figure, born in Nazareth. In 1948, at the time of the first Israeli-Arab conflict, Khalid Fahum left Palestine to seek refuge in Syria, where between 1949 and 1955 he taught political science. In 1959 he left Damascus for Egypt, where he joined the Ministry of Culture of the new United Arab Republic, which he represented as cultural attaché in Washington until 1962. An independent member of al-Fatah, he joined the Palestine Liberation Organization (PLO) in the movement's early days, serving on the executive committee from 1964 to 1970, and as head of propaganda and planning. On 13 July 1971 he was elected chairman of the Palestine National Council (PNC). In 1972 Fahum headed a mission to Cairo to reconcile the differences between Egyptian President Anwar al-Sadat and the PLO. That same year, he accompanied Yasir Arafat to the Soviet Union. In 1976, at the time of the break between Syria and the PLO, he sided with Damascus, where he was seen as Arafat's eventual successor. Criticized by most of the leadership of the PLO, he was nevertheless reelected head the PNC in 1977. His pro-Syrian stand enabled him to help negotiate the withdrawal of Palestinian guerrillas from West Beirut in 1982. The PLO's evacuation of Lebanon and the crisis that followed within the organization led to Fahum's removal from the PNC's leadership. In 1984 he joined a challenge to Arafat's leadership, which was backed by Syria. Arafat prevailed and Fahum, who also opposed the project of a Jordanian-Palestinian confederation, left the PNC to found the Palestinian National Salvation Front, with Syrian backing. The new organization's purpose was to unite the various movements that opposed Arafat's policies. Still coordinating the opposition's efforts, Fahum resumed dialogue with Arafat in 1999 and engineered Arafat's rapprochement with Syria in 2001.

SEE ALSO Arafat, Yasir Muhammad; Fatah, al-; Palestine Liberation Organization; Palestine National Council; Palestinian National

Salvation Front; Sadat, Anwar al-; Syria; United Arab Republic.

FAJR, AL- (Arabic, meaning "dawn"): Palestinian daily newspaper, started in 1974, close to the center of the Palestine Liberation Organization (PLO). Between 1973 and 1986, *al-Fajr,* with headquarters in Jerusalem, was closed several times by Israeli authorities, and it was also the object of bombing attacks. Its first editor, Yusif (Joseph) Nasr, was kidnapped and assassinated. In July of 1993, confronted by financial difficulties, *al-Fajr* was obliged to stop publishing for a period. The newspaper has been under the leadership of Hanna Siniora, and had a distribution of 3,000 to 5,000 copies a day in 2001.

FAKIH

SEE Faqih.

FALASHAS: Term that comes from the Amharic word *falâsi,* meaning exiles, strangers. It designates black Jews settled in Ethiopia, who, according to Biblical tradition, are the descendents of followers of Menelik (heir of Solomon and the Queen of Sheba) to Ethiopia. Therefore, the Falashas would belong to the tribe of Dan, exiled to Cush in 722 B.C.E. According to some scholars, Falashas are descended from Himyarite proselytes who converted the indigenous inhabitants of the mountains of Ethiopia. Other hypotheses take the Falashas for Abyssinians converted in the second century C.E. by missionaries from the Jewish communities of Egypt. The word *Falasha* having a pejorative connotation, the latter prefer to be called "sons of the house of Israel" (*Bene Beta Israel,* in Hebrew).

Toward the end of the 1960s, the Falashas became the scapegoats of great feudal lords in Ethiopia, who had been ruined through the central government's confiscation of their lands. In 1973, Israel's chief rabbi, Ovadia Yosef, recognized the Falashas as "full" Jews, thereby enabling them to benefit from the "right of return." In October 1981, at the funeral ceremonies of Egyptian President Anwar al-Sadat, Israeli Prime Minister Menachem Begin discussed the fate of the Ethiopian Falashas with Sudanese President Jaafar al-Nimeiry. Between 1982 and 1983, a few hundred Falashas succeeded in leaving Ethiopia for Sudan. From there, through Operation Brothers, the Israelis were able to slip them secretly into Israel. Between 1984 and 1994, the Israeli authorities recommenced two such operations, called Solomon and Moses, with the participation of the U.S. ambassador to Sudan, Hume Horan, and others. In the end, nearly 22,000 Falashas were able to go to Israel between 1984 and 1991.

FALASHMURAS: Hebrew term designating Jews exiled to Ethiopia and converted to Christianity by Protestant missionaries in exchange for arable land, as opposed to the Falashas, who had none.

SEE ALSO Falashas.

FAQIH (pl., *fuqaha*): Arabic term designating specialists in the interpretation of Muslim law (*fiqh*).

FATAH, AL- (Palestinian Liberation Movement; Fateh, Fath; conquest, in Arabic): Palestinian political movement that surfaced in the late 1950s among students in Gaza and Egypt. The acronym FATAH comes from the first letters, in reverse order, of the Arab words *Harakat al-Tahrir al-Filastiniya,* or Palestinian Liberation Movement. Al-Fatah was officially created on 10 December 1959 in Kuwait. Its founders include Yasir Arafat, Salah Khalaf, Khalid al-Hasan, Faruq Qaddumi, and Khalil al-Wazir. Formed for the purpose of liberating occupied Palestine, the motto of al-Fatah was "Arab unity through the liberation of Palestine," a phrase conveying a degree of opposition to the dominant thinking in Arab countries that supported the Palestinian cause, for whom Arab unity was a precondition to the liberation of Palestine. The political program of al-Fatah specified: 1) "There is no other way to liberate the homeland than armed struggle"; 2) revolutionary action should be independent of parties and states and should be carried out, as a first step, by the Palestinian peoples themselves; and 3) the objective is the total recuperation of a unified and Arab Palestine. The governing organs of al-Fatah were the Central Committee, the Revolutionary Council, the General Congress, and the Council of Security. At the time of its creation, al-Fatah counted around 300 members, of whom two-thirds had belonged to the Egyptian Muslim Brotherhood. Al-Fatah had a military wing, al-Assifa ("the storm," in Arabic), which made itself known on 1 January 1965 in a radio announcement by Abu Ammar (Yasir Arafat) claiming responsibility for an action on Israeli soil. The first countries to recognize al-Fatah were Algeria, Syria, and Saudi Arabia.

In April 1966 Qaddumi was elected secretary general of al-Fatah. After the Arab defeat of June 1967, Fatah, backed by radical splinter groups that were starting up among the Palestinians, advocated armed struggle against Israel. Guerrilla actions multiplied, leading to Israeli reprisals, particularly in Jordan. The ranks of al-Fatah increased greatly in 1968 after the victory of the *fida'iyyun* over an Israeli unit in a confrontation that took place on 21 March in al-Karama, Jordan. The Battle of al-Karama symbolized the desire of the *fida'iyyun* to persist in the struggle against Israel, in spite of the defeat in the Arab-Israel War. On 15 April Yasir Arafat was named spokesperson for al-Fatah, which became the most important and best organized faction of the Palestine Liberation Organization (PLO). Al-Fatah took control of the PLO in 1969, with Arafat's election as head of the executive committee. Al-Fatah advocated the creation of a "secular and democratic" Palestinian state, where Jews, Christians, and Muslims would all have equal rights. In the course of a few months, the movement was transformed into a veritable national liberation party, in spite of the 1970 Jordanian-Palestinian confrontations of Black September, which caused many divisions. The leadership of al-Fatah was not able to counter the desire of some of its members to revenge the massacre of Palestinians by the Jordanian army. Thus the Black September group was born, which carried out several spectacular attacks, in particular the November 1971 assassination of Jordanian Prime Minister Wasfi al-Tell, and the September 1972 attack on Israeli athletes at the Munich Olympics.

Forced back into Lebanon, al-Fatah once more found itself divided by the differing policies of its various leaders in the Lebanese conflict, in the course of which Palestinians fought against Christians, then Syrians, then Shi'ites, and finally among themselves. An armed group within the movement, Suqur al-Fatah ("Falcons of Fatah," in Arabic), drew its most radical members. On 22 June 1973 al-Fatah Secretary General Qaddumi became head of the political department of the PLO. At year's end, after the 1973 Arab-Israel War, which saw the consolidation of the Israeli occupation of the West Bank and Gaza, al-Fatah became resigned to the creation of a Palestinian state "on a liberated portion of the occupied territories." In the autumn of 1974, Sabri al-Banna (Abu Nidal), who belonged to the radical wing, quit al-Fatah to form his own movement, the Fatah Revolutionary Council. The new group made itself known through terrorist action in the West as well as in the Arab world. Under the name Abu Nidal Group, the movement also assassinated al-Fatah cadres. In April 1979 the leadership of al-Fatah failed to convince the Popular Front for the Liberation of Palestine to merge with al-Fatah.

Over the years, al-Fatah became impossible to ignore and its adversaries started calling South Lebanon "Fatahland." On 6 June 1982 Israel launched an invasion of Lebanon, Operation Peace for Galilee, allegedly against Palestinian splinter groups in Lebanon, resulting in the destruction of a portion of the political system of al-Fatah and the PLO. The expulsion of the Palestinians to Tunisia the following year magnified a rupture that had already existed in al-Fatah, some of whose cadres decided to join the opposition in the Palestinian National Salvation Front. On 29 November 1984, in spite of differences in the Palestinian movement, Arafat was reelected president of the PLO executive committee. Distant from the front in Israel, al-Fatah launched a political offensive that led to the recognition of the PLO by the socialist countries of that time, and to wider recognition by the United Nations, consolidating the position of al-Fatah and Arafat among the Palestinians. After December 1987, the outbreak of the Intifada in the Occupied Territories allowed al-Fatah to tighten its ties with the Palestinian populations of the West Bank and the Gaza Strip. A National Unified Uprising Command (NUUC) was constituted by various local committees in the Occupied Territories. The NUUC was linked to the western section of al-Fatah, overseen by the council of security headed by Salah Khalaf (Abu Iyad), who was then in Tunis. The NUUC included local representatives from al-Fatah, the Palestine Communist Party, the Democratic Front for the Liberation of Palestine, and the Popular Front for the Liberation of Palestine. Arafat's proclamation of a Palestinian state, on 15 November 1988, strengthened the position of al-Fatah in the Palestine National Council and injected enthusiasm into the uprising in the Occupied Territories. At the Fifth General Congress of al-Fatah in Tunis between 3 and 10 August 1989, the leadership of the movement reaffirmed its commitment to continue the struggle for "the liberation of the homeland," while also taking a position favorable to pursuing a dialogue with "Israeli democratic elements that reprove the occupation and support the inalienable rights of the Palestinian people," notably the right of return, the right to self-determination, and the right to a Palestinian state.

During the night of 14–15 January 1991, Salah Khalaf was assassinated in Tunis by his bodyguard, an agent of Abu Nidal's al-Fatah Revolutionary Council. The death of one of al-Fatah's principal leaders, who was also considered the second most important leader of the PLO, was a great blow to Arafat and the whole Palestinian movement. In April 1992, while hospitalized following an airplane crash in the Libyan desert, Arafat designated three leaders of al-Fatah—Faruq Qaddumi, Mahmud Abbas, and

Khalid al-Hasan—to head the organization in the interim. Arafat's support of Iraq during the 1990–1991 Gulf Crisis led to a reduction of financial aid from Saudi Arabia. Having negotiated a preliminary Israeli-Palestinian declaration of principles in September 1993, which caused much criticism in the Arab world, Fatah was again shaken by serious internal dissension. Arafat's leadership style was criticized by many Fatah and PLO cadres. Nevertheless, Fatah remained the major Palestinian political force in the territories, in spite of the opposition between the "Tunisians" (Fatah members who went to Tunis during the PLO exile) and "internal" Palestinians, who remained in the territories. Young people who participated in the Intifada reproached the leaders in Tunis with being insufficiently involved in resistance actions. After 1994, with the autonomy of the Palestinian territories, the unity of the Palestinian movements under the banner of Fatah was progressively de-emphasized in favor of the overall policies of the Palestinian Authority, headed by the leader of Fatah, Yasir Arafat. A radical current, opposed to the Oslo Accords, surfaced within the movement, to which flocked former members of the Falcons and the Black Panthers. One of the splinter groups allied with this tendency took the name Abu Reesh Brigade, after a Palestinian killed in the Intifada. On 15 March 1994 a Fatah delegation led by Soufian Abu Zayyad was received for the first time at the Knesset by the parliamentary Labor bloc. In the course of the year, although an Islamist influence surfaced in Fatah, the nationalist mainstream made efforts to strengthen its appeal to the young of the movement (Shabibat Fatah, in Arabic), whose principal leader, Marwan Barghuthi, was named secretary general of Fatah for the West Bank. On 21 January 1996, after the first Palestinian universal suffrage elections, Fatah became the majority party of the new Palestinian Legislative Council and the principal proponent of the policies of the Palestinian Authority (PA). That July, Jamal al-Shobaki was appointed secretary general of the Revolutionary Council of Fatah and Qaddumi was reelected to the leadership of the central committee. On 10 September 1996 Fatah became a member of the Socialist International. In December Ahmad Halas was named secretary general of Fatah for the Gaza Strip. In the spring of 1999 the leadership of the movement undertook a reorganization of its administration in the Palestinian territories to counter HAMAS, which was backed by elements within Fatah. They focused special attention on Palestinian refugee camps in Lebanon and Jordan. The two regional administrations of the Gaza Strip and the West Bank were placed under the authority of a high committee, headed by Faysal al-Husayni, Zakariya al-Agha, and Hakam Balʿawi. After the outbreak of the al-Aqsa Intifada in October 2000, Fatah strove to take charge of the uprising in order to avoid the PA being outpaced by radical elements. Concurrently, some Fatah cadres tried persuading the opposition to support Arafat's policies and also persuading the leaders of Arab countries to make the case for the Palestinian cause before the international community. In 2001 the membership of Fatah was estimated at 21,000.

SEE ALSO AMAL; Aqsa Intifada, al-; Arab-Israel War (1967); Arab-Israel War (1973); Arab-Israel War (1982); Arafat, Yasir Muhammad; Banna, Sabri al-; Barghuthi, Marwan Hussein al-; Black Panthers; Democratic Front for the Liberation of Palestine; Fatah Revolutionary Council; Fedaʾi; Gulf War (1991); Hasan, Khalid al-; Husayni, Faysal al-; Intifada, 1987–1993; Khalaf, Salah; Knesset; Muslim Brotherhood; Oslo Accords; Oslo Accords II; Palestine Communist Party; Palestine Liberation Organization; Palestine National Council; Palestinian Authority; Palestinian Legislative Council; Palestinian National Salvation Front; Popular Front for the Liberation of Palestine; Qaddumi, Faruq; Right of Return; Wazir, Khalil al-.

FATAH-ABU MUSA

SEE Fatah-Intifada.

FATAH-FORCES OF THE BLACK SEPTEMBER 13TH BRIGADES: Palestinian movement created on 27 October 1993 by Lieutenant Colonel Munir Hasan al-Maqdah, Fatah representative at the Ain el-Helweh camp in Lebanon and opponent of the Israeli-Palestinian accord of the preceding 13 September. The principal cause of his opposition was that accord did not address the question of the refugees from 1948. While the Alliance of Palestinian Forces made efforts to rally al-Maqdah to its cause, the latter tried vainly to obtain the backing of important Fatah leaders, including the brothers Hani and Khalid al-Hasan. The principal members of this movement, in addition to Maqdah, are Abu Khalid al-Arkoub, Jamal Qudsi, and Ali Hussein Fahoud. Black September 13 carried out numerous attacks against Israeli occupation forces in south Lebanon in the summer of 1995, some in coordination with Hizbullah.

SEE ALSO Alliance of Palestinian Forces; Fatah, al-; Hasan, Hani al-; Hasan, Khalid al-.

Fatah-Intifada (Abu Musa Group; Fatah—Temporary Command): Palestinian movement that surfaced in Lebanon in June 1982. Fatah-Intifada emerged from a scission in al-Fatah after Yasir Arafat announced to his close collaborators his intention of withdrawing his troops from Lebanon. Headed by Colonel Saʿid Musa Muragha (called Abu Musa) and Khalid al-Amiah (Abu Khalid), Fatah-Intifada opposed any agreement with Israel and advocated the continuation of armed struggle to regain all of Palestine. On 6 November 1983 its secretary general was excluded from the military command of the Palestine Liberation Organization (PLO) and accused of conspiring against Yasir Arafat's authority. Twelve days later, General Khadra, commander-in-chief of the Palestine Liberation Army in Syria, decided to leave the PLO to join the Fatah-Intifada. In 1985 the Fatah-Intifada merged with the Palestinian National Salvation Front after failed efforts to ally itself with the Fatah Revolutionary Council of Abu Nidal. In May 1988 the movement participated in joint operations in Lebanon with the Popular Front for the Liberation of Palestine—General Command against Arafat partisans. Fatah-Intifada was backed by Syria and had its headquarters in Damascus. It also received financial support from Iran, and to a lesser extent from Libya. At the end of the 1980s, as the Israeli-Arab peace process evolved, the movement became less influential among Palestinians. Opposed to the Israeli-Palestinian accord signed in September 1993, Fatah-Intifada joined the ranks of the Alliance of Palestinian Forces. In October 2000, during violent confrontations between the Israeli army and Palestinians in the Palestinian territories, the movement claimed responsibility for several anti-Israel actions in the name of the Forces of Chief Martyr Umar al-Mukhtar, a Libyan nationalist who fought against Italian colonization of Libya.

SEE ALSO Alliance of Palestinian Forces (APF); Arafat, Yasir Muhammad; Fatah, al-; Fatah Revolutionary Council; Palestine Liberation Army; Palestine Liberation Organization; Palestinian National Salvation Front; Popular Front for the Liberation of Palestine—General Command.

Fatah Revolutionary Council (Fatah—RC; Black June; Abu Nidal Organization; Arab Revolutionary Brigades; Revolutionary Muslim Socialist Organization; Abu Nidal Group): Radical Palestinian movement, Marxist in inspiration, created in January 1974. The Fatah—RC was born of a scission in al-Fatah, provoked by differences over policies toward Israel after the failure of the 1973 Arab-Israel War. Opposing all compromise with Israel, Fatah—RC advocated the pursuit of armed struggle until all of Palestine was restored. The founder of Fatah—RC, Sabri al-Banna (Abu Nidal), one of the leaders of the Iraqi branch of Fatah, was a fierce adversary of Yasir Arafat, the head of the Palestine Liberation Organization (PLO). At first influenced by Iraq, the Fatah—RC became independent in 1983, when Iraqi authorities expelled its members who had settled in Baghdad. This was due not only to the intervention of the PLO, but also to Iraq's hope of gaining the support of Western powers and Saudi Arabia in its war with Iran. In 1985, backed by Libya, Abu Nidal proposed, vainly, an alliance with the Fatah-Intifada for the purpose of constituting the Nationalist Alliance and creating a strong opposition movement among Palestinians. In 1988 Abu Nidal returned to settle officially in Baghdad, although he kept his operational headquarters in Libya. During the summer of 1989 relations between the Fatah—RC and the PLO were definitively broken off, which led to a wave of bloody score-settling between members of the Fatah—RC and Arafat partisans. In October 1989 a dispute involving Atif Abu Bakr and Abdul Rahman Issa surfaced, leading to the formation of the Fatah Revolutionary Council—Emergency Command.

The Fatah—RC was responsible for numerous attacks on Israeli, Western, and Arab targets, including the assassination of Yusuf al-Sibaʿyi, editor of the Egyptian newspaper *Al-Ahram,* in Cyprus in February 1978; the attack of Rue des Rosiers in Paris in 1982; the attempted assassination of the Israeli ambassador in London on 12 April 1983; the attacks on the Vienna and Rome airports in December 1985; the attack on an Istanbul synagogue in September 1986; the attack on the ship *City of Poros* in July 1988; and the assassination of the first secretary of the Jordanian embassy in Lebanon in January 1994. The Fatah—RC was also responsible for the assassination of several Fatah leaders, including Issam Sartawi in Portugal in April 1983 and Salah Khalaf in Tunisia in January 1991. As the Israeli-Palestinian peace process evolved, countries supporting the Fatah—RC reduced their aid, which led to fewer actions. In January 1991, forced to leave Iraq, the Fatah—RC regrouped at Mar Elias, in Lebanon. In April 1992 a difference between Ayyash al-Jakiri and Abu Nidal led to the creation of a new faction, the Popular Liberation Force. In March 1993 a second scission, initiated by Abu Nidal's nephew, Abdul Karim al-Banna (Abu Issam), resulted in the formation of Fatah—RC—Dissidents, headquartered in Baghdad. In April 1995 Fatah—RC—Dissidents merged with Fatah—

RC—Emergency Command. Abu Nidal, reportedly after several years of poor health, died in Baghdad in August 2002. The other principal leaders of Fatah—RC were Abdulaziz Muhammad Jawad, Muhammad Wasfi Hanoun, and Ali al-Farrah (Abu Kamal).

SEE ALSO Ahram, al-; Arab-Israel War (1973); Arafat, Yasir Muhammad; Banna, Sabri al-; Fatah-Intifada; Palestine Liberation Organization.

FATAH REVOLUTIONARY COUNCIL—EMERGENCY COMMAND

SEE Fatah Revolutionary Council.

FATAH SECURITY COUNCIL: Internal group within Fatah, responsible for coordinating the activity of the various security organizations of the Palestine Liberation Organization; also called Unified Security Management (*al-Amn al-Muwahhad,* or *Jihaz al-Amn al-Qawmi al-Filastini,* in Arabic). Presided over by Yasir Arafat, this institution was headed for a long time by Salah Khalaf (Abu Iyad), flanked by Hakam Balʿawi (Abu Marwan) and Hayil Abdul Hamid (Abu el-Houl). The Western Department of Fatah, responsible for armed actions in the Palestinian territories, worked in close collaboration with the Fatah Security Council. For this reason, the leaders of two Fatah departments, Khalaf and Khalil al-Wazir (Abu Jihad), became priority targets of Israel's special services. After the assassination of Khalaf in January 1991, leadership of the Security Council passed to a group of four—Amin al-Hindi, Tariq Abu Rajab, Hakam Balʿawi, and Atef B'seisso—supervised by Arafat. In 1994, during the application of Palestinian autonomy guaranteed by the Oslo Accords, the components of the Fatah Security Council were merged into new security organizations under the control of Arafat and officially overseen by the Palestinian Authority.

SEE ALSO Arafat, Yasir Muhammad; Bʾseisso, Atef Faʾiq; Fatah, al-; Hindi, Amin al-; Khalaf, Salah; Oslo Accords; Wazir, Khalil Ibrahim al- (Abu Jihad).

FATAH—TEMPORARY COMMAND

SEE Fatah-Intifada.

FATIHA ("opening," in Arabic): Title of the first chapter (*sura*) of the Qurʾan.

SEE ALSO Qurʾan.

FATIMA: Daughter of the prophet Muhammad and of Khadija. Fatima married Ali, by whom she had two sons, Hasan and Husayn. The Shiʿa regard Fatima with particular reverence, calling her *al-Azhar* (the Brilliant). Her name is the eponym of the Fatimid dynasty.

SEE ALSO Ali; Fatimids; Muhammad; Shiʿite.

FATIMIDS: Shiʿite dynasty of caliphs who trace their origins to Fatima, the daughter of Muhammad. The greatest power in the Muslim world in the eleventh and twelfth centuries in the Maghrib, the Levant, and Egypt, it also enjoyed considerable cultural and artistic influence. The Fatimid Caliphat was proclaimed in 909 by Ubaydullah. Between 953 and 975, the Caliph al-Muʿizz conquered the entire Maghrib and a part of Sicily. In 972 he moved his capital in North Africa to Cairo. The Fatimid Empire, which stretched theoretically from the Hijaz to the Atlantic, was fragile, because it was divided into many pieces. In 1072, the Fatimids lost Syria and Jerusalem, conquered by the Seljuks. In 1153, Ashqelon, the last Fatimid bastion in Syria, was taken by the Crusaders. In 1168, the Fatimid capital, Al-Fustat (Old Cairo), threatened by the Crusaders, was burned by its own inhabitants. Three years later, Saladin abolished the Fatimid dynasty, returning rule to Sunni hands and allegiance to the Abbasids.

SEE ALSO Abbasids.

FATWA (response, opinion, in Arabic): A formal legal opinion issued by an Islamic jurist (*mufti*).

FEDAʾI (he who gives his life for a cause, in Arabic): In contemporary terms, fedaʾi and the plural, fedaʾiyan (commonly written *fedayeen*) designate Palestinian and Palestine Liberation Organization (PLO) fighters in general.

SEE ALSO Palestine Liberation Organization.

FEDAʾIYAN

SEE Fedaʾi.

FEZ PLAN

SEE Fahd Plan.

FIDA

SEE Palestinian Democratic Union.

FILASTIN: Palestine, in Arabic.

***FILASTIN*:** Arabic-language newspaper founded as a biweekly in Jaffa in 1911 and appearing as a daily beginning in 1929. Published by a Christian Arab family, it was strongly nationalist and anti-Zionist. For a while during World War I the paper was shut down by the Ottoman authorities. Publication was also interrupted by the 1948 War, after which it resumed publication in Jordanian-controlled East Jerusalem. *Filastin* ceased publication in 1967.

SEE ALSO Ottomans.

FILASTIN AL-THAWRA (*Palestine of the Revolution*): Official Palestine Liberation Organization (PLO) Arabic-language weekly, created in Beirut in 1972. The current editor in chief, Ahmad Abd al-Rahman, was in the 1970s identified with the Soviet Group, a leftist faction that appeared within the PLO in 1973. Having moderated his position, he later became the head of Fatah's information department, a member of its central committee, and the Palestinian Authority cabinet secretary.

SEE ALSO Fatah, al-; Palestine Liberation Organization; Palestinian Authority.

FILASTINUNA: Palestinian monthly, an organ of Yasir Arafat's al-Fatah, published from 1959 to 1964.

SEE ALSO Arafat, Yasir Muhammad; Fatah, al-.

FIQH: Jurisprudence, the science of Islamic religious law.

FIR

SEE Islamic Revolutionary Front.

FITNA: Arabic term for sedition, or schism, designating the crisis, under the Caliph Ali, that led to the division of the Islamic community.

SEE ALSO Ali.

FITR (*iftar*): Arabic word meaning *breaking the fast.* It refers to the meal eaten after sunset each evening during the month of Ramadan. Ramadan concludes with the Feast of Fastbreaking (*'Id al-Fitr* or *al-'Id al-Saghir,* the Little Feast).

SEE ALSO Ramadan.

FLYING CARPET OPERATION

SEE Ezra and Nehemiah Operations.

FORCE 17 (*Quwat Saba'tasher*): Palestinian security service established in 1974 and placed under the leadership of Ali Hassan Salameh (Abu al-Hassan, nicknamed "the Red Prince"), one of the principal figures of the Black September group. A commando unit with unquestioned loyalty to Palestine Liberation Organization (PLO) leader Yasir Arafat, the group is said to have taken its name from Salameh's Beirut telephone extension. Created by the Fatah Security Council, Force 17 replaced the Black September group, which had been dissolved by the head of the PLO. It was mainly responsible for Arafat's security and that of his close collaborators, as well as for particular missions connected directly to the PLO leader. Force 17 was also placed in charge of security for PLO representatives abroad. Salameh was assassinated in January 1979 in Beirut by an Israeli commando. He was succeeded in February at the head of the organization by Sa'ad Sayel (Abu Walid), who was himself assassinated in September 1982 by a Syrian commando. Force 17, supervised by Salah Khalaf (Abu Iyad) and Khalil al-Wazir, then passed to the command of Mahmud Ahmad al-Natour (Abu Tayib). During the 1980s the organization carried out numerous attacks on Israeli interests and on Palestinian opponents. On 25 September 1985 a commando comprised of two Palestinians and a Briton assassinated three Israeli vacationers who were Mossad members; one of them was Sylvia Raphael, who was considered to be responsible for the death of Salameh. In November 1987, in Jerusalem, two Israelis who were presumed to belong to Shin Bet were killed by a commando who was believed to have been dispatched by Force 17. In 1994, as part of the creation of the Palestinian Authority, Force 17 was merged into the newly created Presidential Security Force, or Presidential Guard (al-Amn al-Ri'asa), one of the many security forces controlled directly by Yasir Arafat. At the end of 1996 Faisal Abu Shaqra took over the leadership of the organization. The Presidential Guard is officially charged with intelligence, counterterrorism, and protecting Arafat and other prominent Palestinian officials; according to Israeli sources, who continue to refer to it as Force 17, it has been engaged in violent anti-Israeli activities since the beginning of the al-Aqsa Intifada in 2000, and at least one of its senior officers has been assassinated by the Israelis.

SEE ALSO Aqsa Intifada, al-; Arafat, Yasir Muhammad; Black September 1970; Fatah Security Council; Khalaf, Salah; Palestine Liberation Organization; Shin Bet.

FRANJIYYA, SULAYMAN (1910–1992): Lebanese Maronite political figure, president of the republic from 1970 to 1976. Sulayman Franjiyyaa was born in

Zgharta and studied with the Marist Brothers and in the College of Antoura. He embarked in the silk business and entered politics in 1959, after his elder brother, Hamid, suffered a stroke and was unable to continue a promising career. In 1960 he was elected to parliament for the first time, and he became one of the leaders of the center bloc. On 1 August 1960 he was appointed minister of communications in the government of Saib Salem. In May 1961 he was given the additional portfolio of agriculture. In 1964 he was reelected deputy. In 1968, after having been again elected to parliament, he became minister of the interior. In the course of the year, the portfolio of the economy was also given to him. On 17 August 1970 he was chosen president of the Lebanese Republic, by a one-vote margin, over his rival, Elias Sarkis. Between 1970 and 1973, Franjiyya strove to solve Lebanon's internal problems and come to the aid of the Palestinian movement. He backed the creation of the al-Marada militia to defend his fief of Zgharta against the attacks of the Lebanese Phalangists.

On 10 April an Israeli operation in central Beirut against three Palestinian leaders brought about a break between the Lebanese president and the Palestinian leadership, which reproached him for not having prevented the action. In November 1974 Franjiyya was mandated by the Arab countries to speak for the Palestinian cause at the United Nations. On 13 April 1975 an incident involving Palestinians and Christians led to the start of a civil war in Lebanon. Judging that only the Syrian army could reestablish order, he supported the appeal that was made to Syria. In September 1976, Sarkis succeeded him to the presidency of the republic. Having returned to his constituency at Zgharta he found himself at odds with other Maronite leaders of the Lebanese Forces. In June 1978 his son, Tony, and his son's family were assassinated by the Phalangists. Franjiyya broke with the Maronite leaders to join with Walid Jumblatt, head of the Progressive Socialist Party and of the National Movement. In July 1983, along with Jumblatt and Rashid Karame, he helped found the National Salvation Front, formed to oppose the policies of Amin Jumayyil.

SEE ALSO Jumayyil, Amin; Jumblatt, Walid Kamal; Karame, Rashid; Lebanese Forces; Phalange.

FREEDOM FOREVER OPERATION

SEE Enduring Freedom Operation.

FRONT FOR THE ISLAMIC SALVATION OF PALESTINE

SEE Islamic Front for the Salvation of Palestine.

FRONT OF OCCUPIED PALESTINE: Movement formed in Lebanon at the end of 1987, with Iranian impetus, after the beginning of the first Intifada in the Palestinian territories. Iranian leaders hoped it would constitute, along with Hizbullah, an armed front in the north of Israel. A victim of internal dissensions, the movement, headed by Saʿid Ghassem, lasted only a few months. Toward the end of 1990, Iran made a similar attempt with the founding of the Islamic Revolutionary Front.

SEE ALSO Hizbullah; Intifada (1987–1993); Islamic Revolutionary Front.

FUHUD AL-ASWAD-AL (Black Panthers, in Arabic): Name of the armed branch of al-Fatah.

SEE ALSO Fatah, al-.

FUNDAMENTALISM : A literal adherence to the tenets of a religion or belief system; fundamentalism also implies an opposition to all development or evolution in religion. On the level of political doctrine, fundamentalism favors an intransigent conservatism. This word surfaced for the first time in Spain, at the end of the nineteenth century, referring to a political-religious party.

GAHAL Party: Gush Herut Liberalim,"The Bloc of Herut and the Liberals," in Hebrew. Israeli Parliamentary coalition constituted in 1965 by an alliance of the Herut and Liberal parties. In July 1973, GAHAL allied itself with three small rightist groups to form the Parliamentary block of Likud.

SEE ALSO Herut Party; Likud.

Galilee: Region in the north of Israel, situated between Lake Tiberias (also known as the Sea of Galilee or the Kinneret) to the east, the Mediterranean Sea to the west, and Lebanon to the north.

SEE ALSO Israel.

Galut: Word of Aramaic origin, meaning "exile," "dispersion," "diaspora"; used to designate Jews living outside of Israel, emphasizing Jewish dispersion as a curse.

Gamaʿa: Arabic word, transliterated in Egyptian pronunciation, meaning "group, association". Identical to the word *Jamaʿa.*

Gamaʿa al-Islamiyya, al-

SEE Jamiʿa al-Islamiyya, al-.

Gamaʿa al-Islamiyya Libnaniyyia, al-

SEE Jamiʿa al-Islamiyya Libnaniyyia al-.

Gaza (City): Largest city of the Gaza Strip. In the 1948 War it came under the control of Egypt. Its prewar population of 65,000 absorbed many of the 200,000 to 250,000 refugees who came into the Gaza Strip; in 2004 the city's population was more than 400,000, an unknown number of whom are refugees. (Refugees comprise over 78 percent of the 1.3 million population of the Gaza Strip as a whole.) Since the 1967 War, which caused 100,000 Palestinian refugees to leave the Gaza Strip, mostly for Jordan, it has been under the control of Israel, either through direct military occupation or through control of settlement and military zones outside the "autonomous" areas under the Palestinian Authority (set up in 1994). The city and its surrounding refugee camps, like the Gaza Strip as a whole, are centers for political unrest and anti-Israel activity, particularly since the first Intifada began in 1987. HAMAS is headquartered there. Gaza, which has a port, is the commercial center of the region, but the economy has been crippled by Israeli border closures and other measures, and it is estimated that more than half the working-age population is unemployed.

SEE ALSO Arab-Israeli War (1948); Gaza Strip; HAMAS; Intifada (1987–1983); Palestinian Authority.

Gaza Community Mental Health Program (GCMHP): A private, nonprofit Palestinian organization founded in 1990 to provide "comprehensive community mental health services to the population of the Gaza Strip, including therapy, training, and research." It has clinics in Gaza City, Jabaliya, Khan Younis, and Dayr al-Balah and provides services to children and adults, including psychological counseling and therapy, occupational therapy, and rehabilitation, with an emphasis on the most vulnerable groups, such as children and the survivors of torture. It also provides some auxiliary medical services and operates public awareness programs. The GCMHP is privately funded and is operated by a board of directors whose chair in 2004 was Dr. Ayad El Sarraj. It has an international board of advisors

SEE ALSO Gaza Strip.

GAZA-JERICHO FIRST OPTION: Phrase utilized to designate the accord on limited autonomy for the Gaza Strip and the zone of Jericho, concluded between Israeli and Palestinian negotiators on 28 August 1993 as part of the Oslo Accords and signed on 13 September 1993 in Washington by Israel and the Palestine Liberation Organization.

SEE ALSO Gaza Strip; Oslo Accords; Oslo Accords II; Palestine Liberation Organization.

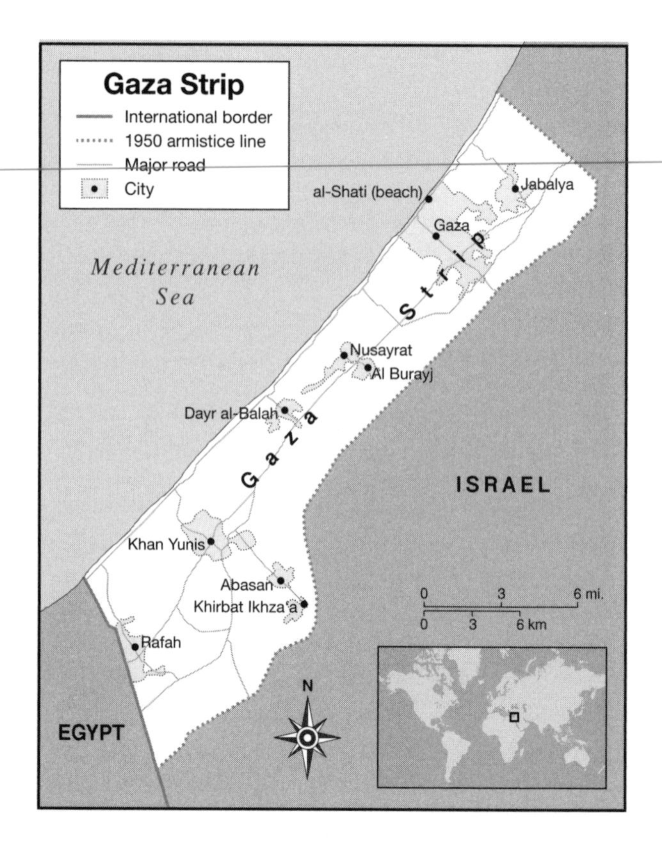

GAZA STRIP: Territory about 28 miles long and from 4 to 8 miles wide (230 square miles) along the Mediterranean coast between the Egyptian Sinai Desert and the southern frontier of Israel. It contains the cities of Gaza, Khan Younis, and Rafah, as well as eight refugee camps and twenty-five Israeli settlements and military areas. The Gaza Strip is one of the most densely populated regions of the world. In 2003 its population was estimated at 1,330,000 Palestinians and 5,000 Israeli settlers. The settlers and military areas occupy about 40 percent of the land. Along with the rest of Palestine, this area was under British control from 1918 and was part of the British Mandate from 1922 to 1948. After the creation of the State of Israel and the Arab-Israel War of 1948–1949, the area came to be called the Gaza Strip and fell under Egyptian administration but was given an autonomous status. Before 1948 the Gaza Strip had around 70,000 inhabitants; during and after the war it absorbed 250,000 Palestinian refugees. It became the scene of numerous frontier incidents between Egypt and Israel caused by anti-Israel operations mounted by Palestinian groups. At the time of the Suez-Sinai War of October 1956, the inhabitants of the Gaza Strip experienced their first occupation by the Israel Defense Force (IDF), which led to a renaissance of Palestine nationalism. Israeli troops occupied Gaza until March 1957, when United Nations forces took over and were themselves later replaced by an Egyptian regiment. During the War of June 1967, the Israeli Army reoccupied the Gaza Strip, which by then was home to 360,000 people. The Israeli government placed the area under its definitive control, encouraging the building of Jewish settlements and expelling about 40,000 people from Gaza, mostly to the West Bank.

From 1967 to 1971 the Palestinian resistance struggled against the Israeli occupation. Numerous Palestinian activists were imprisoned by the Israeli authorities or were exiled to Lebanon. Political figures in Gaza and the West Bank (also occupied by Israel) formed a Palestinian National Front that advocated the creation of a Palestinian state in the occupied territories. From May 1979, as required by the Camp David Accords, Egypt and Israel started negotiating the autonomy of the West Bank and the Gaza Strip. These talks were not successful because of the opposition of most Gazans, and the Palestine Liberation Organization, to the Camp David Accords. Both President Anwar al-Sadat of Egypt and the Israeli government imposed sanctions on the Gazans for their opposition. In April 1980 the Egyptian president proposed that autonomy first be applied in the Gaza Strip. The Israelis placed it under a civilian administration in 1981. The departure of Palestinian forces from Lebanon in 1982 and frictions within Fatah thwarted any lingering impulse to revolt on the part of the Palestinians from within for several years. In 1987, however, not only was HAMAS born in the Gaza Strip, but that December the first Intifada began. The "war of stones" against the IDF lasted almost six years. In March 1993 the Israelis closed Gaza to the outside world, which resulted in an economic decline. This closure has remained in effect, either in full or in part, ever since. In 1994, during the application of the Oslo Accords, approximately 60 percent of the Gaza Strip and a part of the West Bank attained administrative autonomy under the Palestinian Authority (PA) led by Yasir Arafat. Some security matters remained under Israeli control. The stalling of the Israeli-Palestinian negotiations on the final status of the Palestinian territories caused new waves of anti-Israel attacks, as well as a further increase in unemployment, which affected more than half the population. The al-Aqsa Intifada, which began in 2000, worsened the situation. The Israelis responded by carrying out planned assassinations and an increasingly intense program of intimidation by military means. In May and June 2004 the Israelis invaded in force, particularly in the refugee camp at Rafah. Under the pretext of looking for tunnels under the Egyptian border and increasing open security areas near the border, they killed dozens of people and destroyed hundreds of houses.

In 2004 Ariel Sharon's government was promoting a plan that would involve Israeli evacuation of the Gaza Strip and the abandonment of the settlements there but whose acceptance by the PA would entail implicit Palestinian recognition of Israel's right to unlimited settlement and unilateral determination of borders in the West Bank. In October 2004 the Knesset voted to back Sharon's plan to remove Israeli troops, as well as twenty-one settlements from Gaza and four small settlements from the northern part of the West Bank. The vote—sixty-seven for, forty-five against, and seven abstentions—marked the first time in twenty years that the parliament had favored the withdrawal of Jewish settlers from the region. Fearing an extended delay in the start of the withdrawal process, Sharon rejected his Likud Party's call for a referendum on leaving Gaza, thereby splitting the ruling Likud and creating turmoil in the political landscape.

SEE ALSO Aqsa Intifada, al-; Arab-Israel War (1967); Arafat, Yasir Muhammad; British Mandate; Camp David Accords; Fatah, al-; HAMAS; Intifada (1987–1993); Israel Defense Force; Oslo Accords; Oslo Accords II; Palestine Liberation Organization; Palestine Authority; Palestinian National Front; Sadat, Anwar al-; Sharon, Ariel; Suez Crisis; West Bank.

GCC

SEE Gulf Cooperation Council.

GEAGEA, SAMIR (al-Hakim, "the Doctor," in Arabic): Lebanese political figure, Christian Maronite, born in October 1952 at Bsharri in Lebanon into a family of farmers. In 1969, Samir Geagea enrolled in the Youth of the Kata'ib Party of Pierre Jumayyil. From 1972 to 1976, he undertook studies in medicine, interrupted by the civil war that began in Lebanon. Between 1977 and 1982, as the head of an armed militia of Kata'ib, Geagea took part in numerous battles against the Palestinian *fida'iyyun* and Syrian troops, as well as in actions meant to reestablish the authority of the Lebanese Forces (LF)—an integration of various Lebanese Christian militias with a joint command council that was formed to achieve political independence from the traditional Maronite Catholic (Christian) leaders—in areas where it was challenged by others in the Christian camp.

On 12 March 1985, Geagea was dismissed from his post in the Kata'ib organization for insubordination. With the backing of Elie Hobeika, Geagea became head of the military leadership of the LF, whose chief was the president of the Lebanese state, Amin Jumayyil. A year later, on 15 January 1986, having supplanted Elie Hobeika, Geagea took over the military command of the LF as chairman of its executive committee, thereby becoming one of the principal Christian leaders. At the beginning of October 1988, he obliged Jumayyil to leave Lebanon for France. In March 1989, Geagea backed General Michel Aoun, who had launched a "war of liberation against the Syrian invader." Aoun then rebelled against Geagea. In November 1990, Geagea was named a minister of state, without portfolio, in the government of Omar Karame, but he resigned a few days later. In February 1982, he traveled to the United States, where he met with many influential figures in the Lebanese community. A few weeks later, having returned to Lebanon, Geagea attempted to remove Georges Saade from the presidency of the Kata'ib Party in order to take his place. On the following 1 July, Karim Pakradouni was elected secretary general of the party, putting an end to the hopes of Geagea. After being arrested in February 1994, Geagea was indicted for political assassinations on 21 April. In June 1999, he was sentenced to life imprisonment for the assassination of Lebanese Prime Minister Rashid Karame. This was his fourth life sentence, after those following the assassinations of Elias Zayek and Dany Chamoun, as well as the attempted assassination of the defense minister, Michel Murr.

SEE ALSO Aoun, Michel; Hobeika, Elie; Karame, Rashid; Kata'ib; Lebanese Forces.

GEMARA

SEE Talmud.

GEMAYEL, AMIN

SEE Jumayyil, Amin.

GEMAYEL, BASHIR

SEE Jumayyil, Bashir.

GENERAL ARMISTICE AGREEMENTS, 1949: By January 1949 all Arab belligerents in the 1948–1949 War were ready to accept the United Nations Security Council's call for a general truce. The first to accept formally was Egypt, on 5 January. Negotiations began on 13 January in Rhodes, under the supervision of UN undersecretary Ralph Bunche. Egypt signed a General Armistice Agreement with Israel on 24 February 1949, followed on 23 March by Lebanon, on 3 April by Jordan, and on 20 July by Syria. Iraq, which has no common border with Israel, refused to negotiate. These agreements established the border between Israel and its neighbors, including the Green Line between Israel and the West Bank, which lasted until the June 1967 War

SEE ALSO Arab-Israel War (1967); Green Line; West Bank.

GENERAL UNION OF PALESTINE STUDENTS (GUPS): Palestinian association created in November 1959 in Cairo to promote the political program of Fatah among Palestinian youth. It is headquartered in Ramallah. Like the other Palestinian General Unions, it is part of the Palestine Liberation Organization (PLO) and is represented on its governing body, the Palestine National Council. Its main focus is on the Palestinian national struggle. The GUPS is a member of the International Union of Students. It has more than a hundred branches around the world and a membership that GUPS estimates at 100,000. Many leaders of the PLO have belonged to the GUPS, including Yasir Arafat, Hani al-Hasan, Faysal al-Husseini, Salah Khalaf, Leila Shahid, and Ibrahim Souss.

SEE ALSO Arafat, Yasir Muhammad; Fatah, al-; Hasan, Hani al-; Husayni, Faysal al-; Khalaf, Salah; Shahid, Leila Mounib; Palestine Liberation Organization; Palestine National Council.

GENERAL UNION OF PALESTINIAN TEACHERS (GUPT): The quasi-official Palestinian teachers' union, headquartered in Ramallah. Like the other Palestinian General Unions, it is part of the Palestine Liberation Organization (PLO) and is represented on the PLO's governing body, the Palestine National Council. Like all such officially sponsored civic organizations, its primary focus is the Palestinian national struggle. It is affiliated with the international organization Education International in Brussels and maintains relations with teachers' unions around the world. The GUPT works with refugees in camps in and out of Palestine. It is the largest Palestinian teachers' organization, but independent teachers' unions not under control of the Palestine Authority (PA) do exist, and their relationship with the PA has been extremely contentious.

SEE ALSO Palestine Liberation Organization; Palestine National Council.

GENERAL UNION OF PALESTINIAN WOMEN (GUPW): Organization created in 1965 within the Palestine Liberation Organization (PLO). It is the umbrella group for Palestinian women's organizations in Palestine and abroad, including refugees. It is headquartered in Ramallah. Like the other Palestinian General Unions, it is represented on the PLO's governing body, the Palestine National Council, and its main focus is the Palestinian national struggle. The GUPW organizes women toward this end, and also toward the goal of raising the Palestinian women' status; it maintains relations with women's organizations in other countries and has established homes for orphans as well as vocational training centers, nurseries, and kindergartens in refugee camps. It has also organized literacy campaigns and training programs in such subjects as first aid and civil defense

SEE ALSO Palestine Liberation Organization; Palestine National Council.

GENERAL UNION OF PALESTINIAN WORKERS (GUPWo): Organization created in 1963 in Cairo by exiled Palestinian trade unionists. It is part of the Palestine Liberation Organization (PLO) and like the other Palestinian General Unions is represented on the PLO's governing body, the Palestine National Council. Its main focus is the Palestinian national

1949 Armistice. As United Nations mediator Ralph Bunche (second from left at far end of table) and his associates watch, Israeli representative Rafael Eytan (at right) signs the armistice agreement between Israel and Egypt on the Greek island of Rhodes, 1 March 1949. By July, three similar agreements between Israel and Lebanon, Jordan, and Syria had been signed, ending their 1948–1949 war. *(© Bettmann/Corbis)*

struggle. It has branches in both Arab and non-Arab countries and represents those associated with the main organizations within the PLO. In the 1970s it trained and supported *fida'iyyun* who fought in the 1973 Arab-Israel War and in the Lebanese Civil War's factional fighting from 1975 to 1990. Although in theory it represents all Palestinian workers, independent unions not under Palestine Authority (PA) control do exist, and they have a more contentious relationship with the PA.

SEE ALSO Arab-Israel War (1973); Palestine Authority; Palestine Liberation Organization; Palestine National Council.

General Union of Palestinian Writers and Journalists (GUPWJ): A quasi-official organization of individual writers and journalists both in and outside Palestine. It has chapters in several foreign countries and is part of the Palestine Liberation Organization (PLO). Like the other Palestinian General Unions, it is represented on the PLO's governing body, the Palestine National Council. It does not function as a trade union but as an association whose main focus is the national struggle.

SEE ALSO Palestine Liberation Organization; Palestine National Council.

Geneva Peace Conference: Peace Conference in the Middle East that took place in Geneva, Switzerland, from 21 to 22 December 1973, under the aegis of the United Nations and the sponsorship of the United States and the Soviet Union. Gathering the foreign ministers of Egypt, Israel, Jordan, the United States, and the Soviet Union, the conference met to find a solution to the Israeli-Arab conflict in general and to sort out the consequences of the Yom Kippur

War of 1973 in particular. Several encounters took place after this first meeting; then the Geneva Conference was reconvened on 31 May 1974, for the signing of a Syrian-Israeli accord on the disengagement of Israeli forces from the Golan Heights. On 4 September 1975, a second disengagement agreement was signed in Geneva, between Egypt and Israel. These accords would be followed by those of Camp David (September 1978), then by the Israeli-Egyptian Peace Treaty (March 1979).

SEE ALSO Arab-Israel War (1973); Camp David Accords; Golan Heights.

GENEVA PEACE INITIATIVE OF 2003: An unofficial agreement meant to serve as a template for a possible settlement of the Palestine-Israel dispute. It was negotiated, under the sponsorship of the Swiss government, by a group of prominent Palestinians and Israelis including former cabinet ministers, active politicians, and private citizens following the failure of peace talks at Camp David. The Palestinian delegation was led by Yasser Abed Rabbo, former minister of information in the Palestine Authority; the Israeli delegation was led by Yossi Beilin, a former Israeli justice minister. The initiative was signed in Jordan on 12 October 2003 and launched in an attention-getting public ceremony in Geneva that was attended by former U.S. president Jimmy Carter and others on 1 December 2003. The agreement provides for a sovereign, demilitarized Palestinian state on 97.5 percent of the territory of the West Bank and Gaza Strip and secure borders for Israel based on the 1967 border; for shared jurisdiction over Jerusalem; for Palestinian sovereignty over the Temple Mount and Israeli sovereignty over the Western Wall; for almost all Israeli settlements in Palestinian territory to be evacuated; for the remaining settlements to be incorporated into Israel, for which equivalent amounts of territory would be ceded to Palestine as compensation; for a Palestinian-administered access corridor to be established between the West Bank and Gaza; and for Palestinian refugees to give up their right of return to areas within the borders of Israel, in return for which they would receive financial compensation from Israel for their property and their refugee status. (The initiative provides that some refugees could apply to return to Israel, which could accept them at its "sovereign discretion.") The agreement would replace all previous agreements and United Nations resolutions. The initiative was rejected outright by the Israeli government and has not proved popular with Israelis. It was publicly praised by Yasir Arafat but neither Arafat nor any official or quasi-official body, party, or group endorsed it, and it was condemned by many. The most objectionable aspect, for Palestinians, is the cession of the right of return. There are currently 3.8 to 4.1 million Palestinians with the official status of refugees.

SEE ALSO Abd Rabbo, Yasir; Arafat, Yasir Muhammad; Beilin; Yossi; Gaza Strip; Palestine Authority; West Bank.

GESHER "BRIDGE" PARTY: Israeli political party, founded in February 1996 by Likud dissident David Levy, in anticipation of the Knesset elections of the following May. The centrist Gesher conceived of itself as a conduit between underprivileged Israeli social strata and a political ideal that would result from a synthesis of the Likud and Israel Labor Party programs. In March 1996, on the advice of Ariel Sharon, Levy accepted an alliance with Likud and Tsomet to present a common list, headed by Likud leader Benjamin Netanyahu. A few Gesher members, opposing this alliance, decided to found their own group, Israel Hadashah. As a result of the vote of 19 May 1996, Gesher took five seats in the Knesset. The Israeli right had won: David Levy joined the government of Netanyahu as foreign minister, while David Magen became finance minister. During the next few months, some party members decided to join Likud. On 22 March 1999, preparing for the general elections to be held in May of the same year, in which Likud was not favored, Gesher allied itself with the Labor Party and Meimad to create a "One Israel" electoral coalition (*Israel Ehad*). On 18 May, after the vote, this new block had obtained twenty-six deputy seats, two of which belonged to Gesher. On 6 July, Levy became Foreign Minister in the government of Ehud Barak. Principal leaders of Gesher: David Levy, Yehuda Lancry, David Magen, Yacov Berdugo, Maxime Levy, and Michael Kleiner.

SEE ALSO Barak Ehud; Israel Labor Party; Levy, David; Likud; Meimad; Netanyahu, Benjamin; Sharon, Ariel.

GEULAT ISRAEL (Hebrew, "Israel's Redemption"): Orthodox religious Israeli party, created in 1990, following a scission in Agudat Israel. Its founder, Rabbi Eliezer Mizrachi, was close to the Lubavitch.

SEE ALSO Agudat Israel; Lubavitcher Hasidim.

GHETTO: A word designating the foundries of the Cannaregio quarter of Venice, where in 1516 Jews coming from Germany were allowed to settle. In 1555, an encyclical from Pope Paul IV used the term to mean closed and separate neighborhoods where Jews would be obliged to dwell. By extension, the word "ghetto" has come to mean any place where a community lives apart from the rest of the population.

GIMLA'EI ISRAEL PARTY (Party of the Retired): Israeli political group formed in 1996 under the leadership of Nava Arad, member of the Israel Labor Party, in anticipation of Knesset elections for the following May. Essentially meant to attract the attention of Israeli authorities to the rights of retired people, it won no seats in these elections and disbanded soon after.

SEE ALSO Israel Labor Party.

GIVAT SHAUL BET

SEE Dayr Yasin.

GLUBB, JOHN BAGOT [Pasha] (1897–1986): British general born in Lancashire in April 1897, and died in 1986. A scholarship student at Cheltenham College, Glubb joined the British army in 1914. After serving in World War I he became an engineer, then an administrator in Arabia and Iraq, where he was in charge of a mobile Bedouin unit. In the early 1930s his skill at camel-back guerrilla warfare sent him to Transjordan. He was assigned to Colonel Frederick Peake, founder of the Arab Legion. Between 1936 and 1939, at the head of the Bedouin troops in the Desert Patrol Force, Glubb prevented the Arab revolt in Palestine from spreading to Transjordan. In April 1939, he took command of the Arab Legion, which fought brilliantly on the side of the Allies in Syria and Iraq during World War II. In 1946 King Abdullah made him a Jordanian citizen. In May 1948, during the first Israeli-Arab conflict, he entered Jerusalem at the head of the Arab Legion, thereby allowing Transjordan to maintain control of the Arab section of the Holy City. On 1 March 1956, urged by public opinion and his Arab neighbors, King Hussein of Jordan decided on a break with him, relieving him of his command. Glubb then retired to Sussex to devote himself to writing. He published twenty-two books, including *A Soldier with the Arabs*.

SEE ALSO Hussein ibn Talal.

GLUBB, PASHA

SEE Glubb, John Bagot.

GOLAH: Hebrew equivalent of the Aramaic word *galut*, used to designate the Diaspora.

SEE ALSO Diaspora; Galut.

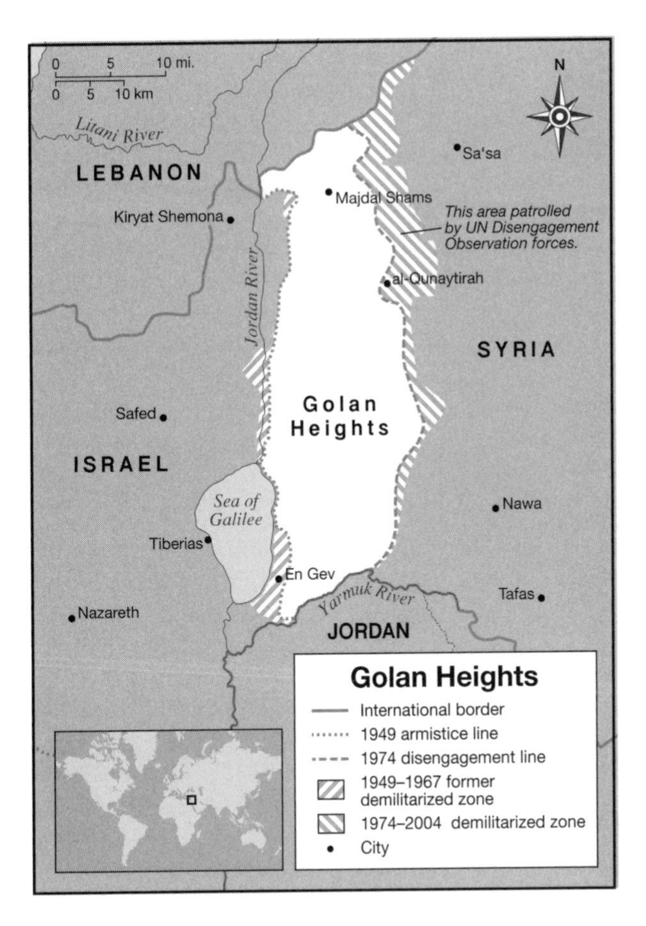

GOLAN

SEE Golan Heights.

GOLAN HEIGHTS (al-Jolan, in Arabic): Plateau of approximately 646 square miles in southwestern Syria, overlooking the Syrian Hawran Plain to the east and the Israeli Plains of Galilee to the southwest. On 3 February 1922 the Newcombe-Paulet (Anglo-French) agreement drew the frontier between Syria and Palestine east of the Jordan River and the Lake of Tiberias. The accord was finalized on 23 July 1923, making the Golan Heights part of Syria. Three years later, France and Great Britain, powers with mandates over Syria and Palestine, came to an agreement allowing France access to the lake. In 1934, the Council of the League of Nations ratified the accords on a 29-square-mile frontier separating the Syrian Golan from Palestine.

On 20 July 1949, as a result of the first Israeli-Arab conflict, the armistice agreement drew a new frontier between Syria and the new State of Israel, which followed the north shore of the Lake of Tiberias, the south shore being part of a newly constituted demilitarized zone. By 1967 approximately 130,000 Syrians lived in 139 villages and 61 farms in the Golan. On 10 June, at the time of the 1967 Arab-Israel War, the Israel Defense Force (IDF) moved into the Golan, forcing out most of the Syrian population. In spite of UN Security Council Resolution 242 demanding that Israel withdraw from all the occupied territories, the IDF remained in place. On 19 June 1967 the Israeli government, headed by Levi Eshkol, sent a secret communication to the United States recognizing "Syrian sovereignty over the Golan Heights," and announcing its readiness to "withdraw to the ceasefire line, in exchange for peace, based on internationally recognized frontiers and taking account of Israel's security needs."

In October 1973 a Syrian attempt to recapture the Golan Heights from Israel led to a further Israeli incursion, adding an additional 197 square miles to the lands occupied by the IDF, a new pocket theoretically divided from the zone conquered in 1967 by a Violet Line. On 31 May 1974 an Israeli-Syrian disengagement agreement allowed Syria to recuperate everything it lost in October 1973, as well as a little piece of the territory conquered in 1967—a total of 256 square miles of land. Since then, a UN force of 1,250 soldiers, known as United Nations Disengagement and Observer Force (UNDOF), has been stationed in the Golan and is responsible for overseeing the ceasefire and supervising a "limited weaponry" zone that is 28 miles long and 3 miles wide.

On 14 December 1981 the Israeli government headed by Menahem Begin pressured the Knesset to vote for a law annexing the Golan Heights. Three days later, the UN Security Council voted unanimously, except for Israel and the United States, to adopt Resolution 497 declaring the Israeli decision invalid. The Israeli government ignored the resolution. Between the end of the 1960s and the middle of the 1980s Israel pursued a policy of colonizing the Golan, although it was not able to attract large numbers of settlers to these colonies. The Arab population of the Golan Heights, which is chiefly Druze, has never stopped opposing Israeli administration. Druze in the Golan do not serve in the Israeli army as the Druze from inside Israel do, and they do not follow the same religious leaders as the Druze inside Israel.

In addition to wanting authority over the settlements already in place in the Golan, both the Israelis and Syrians want control of the Golan because of its military significance. Mount Hermon in the north overlooks southern Lebanon and parts of southern Syria and northern Israel. In the east, volcanic hills overlook Galilee in the west and Damascus to the east. In the west, the Golan overlooks a thriving Israeli metropolitan area. The Golan is also important for its water, particularly because the headwaters of the Jordan River lie in Mount Hermon. The presence of the IDF in the Golan also allows Israel to control access to the Lake of Tiberias as well as two tributaries of the Jordan. This ensemble of resources supplies almost a third of the water needs of the Jewish state.

During the peace process launched in Madrid in 1991, Syria demanded that Israel conform to UN Resolution 242 and evacuate the Golan, withdrawing behind the line the was in place before 6 June 1967. This would leave Israel with access to the lake only from the west and the south. On 16 February 1993 Israeli prime minister Yitzhak Rabin launched an appeal to Damascus, declaring himself ready for "territorial compromise" on the Golan Heights. During the Majdal Shams First Plan, Rabin proposed a "partial" withdrawal from the Golan, spread out over three years. From his point of view, a few divergences with Damascus needed to be worked out: the Israeli line of withdrawal in the Golan Heights, the schedule of this retreat, security arrangements, and the connection between the retreat and normalization of relations.

Between 1994 and 1996 secret Israeli-Syrian negotiations, followed by semiofficial negotiations, took place in the United States, but they were interrupted in 1996 when Likud came to power in Israel. The new Israeli prime minister, Benjamin Netanyahu, said he favored negotiations with Syria but opposed the return of the Golan Heights to Syria. On 4 January 1999 the Israeli Knesset adopted a bill submitting any restitution of an annexed territory to a double approbation: an absolute majority in the Israeli parliament (61 out of the 120) and in a popular referendum.

On the following 15 December, in Washington, new Israeli prime minister Ehud Barak met with Syrian Foreign Minister Faruq al-Shara in an attempt to restart the Israeli-Syrian negotiations, which had been stalled for almost four years. The day before, the Knesset had approved restarting the negotiations by only 47 votes of the full 120, seven members of Barak's majority having voted with the opposition, and the orthodox SHAS Party, which had joined the government, having abstained. On 1 March 2000, by 60 votes to 53, the Knesset passed a draft bill sponsored by Likud for the purpose of enlarging the voter base in view of acquiring a majority in a referendum on a peace accord with Syria.

On the following 22 May the UN Security Council decided that the Shebaa Farms, claimed by Lebanon at the time of the Israeli withdrawal from South Lebanon, was part of the Golan. On 6 August new Syrian President Bashar al-Asad received the U.S. envoy, Edward Walter, who had been asked by President George W. Bush to try to restart the Israeli-Syrian discussions.

Since the Israeli invasion of the Golan Heights, the UN Security Council has regularly extended the mandate of the UNDOF, which is camped between the Israeli and Syrian armies. By 2003 about 16,000 Syrians, mostly the Druze, remained in five Arab villages. The Druze account for many of these Syrians in part because Israeli leadership believes they are more amenable to Israeli rule. Meanwhile, more than thirty-five Jewish settlements have been created in the Golan, with an estimated population of 15,000.

SEE ALSO Arab-Israel War (1948); Arab-Israel War (1967); Asad, Bashar al-; Barak, Ehud; Begin, Menahem; Eshkol, Levi; Galilee; Israel Defense Force; Knesset; Likud; Madrid Conference; Majdal Shams First Plan; Netanyahu, Benjamin; Rabin, Yitzhak; Resolution 242; Resolution 497; SHAS; Shebaa Farms.

GOSHEN (*Gessen*): "Land of the Hebrews," territory situated near the Nile Delta and given by a pharaoh (king of Egypt) to the tribe of Joseph (Yossef, in Hebrew; Yusef, in Arabic), as recounted in the Hebrew Bible, which has been reconstructed as possibly taking place around the sixteenth century B.C.E. According to the Biblical narrative, Joseph, the son of Jacob, was sold into slavery to nomads by his brothers and ended up in Egypt, where he became one of the pharaoh's advisors. To reward his sage counsels, the pharaoh gave the "land of Goshen" to Joseph and his family. So, the clan of Jacob (Israel), which had been dwelling in Canaan, where famine was raging, emigrated to Egypt. Toward 1580 B.C.E., the Egyptian people rebelled against their occupiers, the Hyksos—a Hebrew dynasty that invaded Egypt in 1710 B.C.E. and ruled for more than a century. The Hebrews, having come to terms with the Hyksos, were persecuted by the different pharaohs who followed, until around 1300 B.C.E., when the Biblical narrative notes that Moses arrived on the scene, thereby allowing the Hebrew people to leave Egypt for "the promised land."

SEE ALSO Canaan; Jacob (Biblical); Moses.

GRAPES OF WRATH OPERATION: On 11 April 1996, Israeli Prime Minister Shimon Peres gave the green light to the "Grapes of Wrath" operation. Its goal was to neutralize the Lebanese Hizbullah so as to oblige them to cease their rocket-propelled grenade attacks against populated areas in northern Israel. This operation was launched in the middle of the Israeli election campaign, at the time when the Israelis were preparing for the first time to elect their prime minister by direct ballot, separate from their members of the Knesset. Between 11 and 17 April, there was significant fighting in Lebanon, particularly in the south of the country, which was evacuated by most of the population. Israeli air and naval forces' targets included roads and an electricity station north of Beirut, while the Hizbullah continued daily Katyusha rocket attacks.

On 18 April, Israeli artillery shelled the village of Qana, placed under the protection of United Nations Interim Forces in Lebanon, causing the death of 102 civilians and provoking great outrage. On 20 April, U.S. Secretary of State Warren Christopher went to Damascus to talk with the Syrian leaders and the Russian, French, and Italian foreign ministers who had been sent there. On 23 April, the UN Security Council passed Resolution 1052, demanding an immediate halt to hostilities. Four days later a ceasefire was declared between Israel and the Hizbullah, putting an end to the Grapes of Wrath operation. A group comprised of representatives of the United States, France, Lebanon, Syria, and Israel was put in charge of surveillance of the observance of this accord. On 7 May 1996, a report to the Security Council assigned Israel responsibility for the massacre at Qana, provoking objections in Washington and Tel Aviv.

SEE ALSO Christopher, Warren; Hizbullah; Peres, Shimon; Resolution 1052; United Nations Interim Forces in Lebanon.

GREATER ISRAEL (Hebrew, *Eretz Yisrael [Hashlema]*): The phrase *Eretz Yisrael* is biblical in origin and refers in that context to various parts of the region that were under Jewish sovereignty at different times. Under the British Mandate, *Eretz Yisrael* (Land of Israel) was used as the Hebrew name for Palestine. After 1948 David Ben-Gurion used the term *Medinat Israel* (State of Israel), but other Israeli politicians, including Menachem Begin, continued to speak of *Eretz Yisrael* to suggest an allegiance to the larger historic (biblical) Israel, or the "Greater Israel." After the 1967 Arab-Israel War, the Greater Land of Israel (*Eretz Yisrael Hashelema*) movement developed; its adherents opposed ceding sovereignty over newly conquered territories and began a settlement campaign in disputed areas. The right-wing Herut Party, prior to 1973, continually evoked the notion of a Greater Israel through its emphasis on Jewish control of the territory of *Eretz Yisrael* and its opposition to ceding sovereignty over disputed areas. In 1973 Herut became the senior partner of the Likud bloc.

SEE ALSO Arab-Israel War (1967); Begin, Menachem; British Mandate; Gurion, David Ben-; Herut Party; Likud.

GREEK CATHOLIC CHURCH: Refers to the Christians known as Melkites. The word *Melkite* comes from the Syrian and Arabic words for *king* and was originally used to refer to those within the ancient patriarchates of Alexandria, Antioch, and Jerusalem who accepted Christianity as professed by the Byzantine emperor. Early on, Melkite followers were centered in modern-day Syria and Lebanon, but they later immigrated to Palestine and Egypt. These Arabic-speaking Christians of the Middle East are now part of the Church of Rome but have their own patriarch and still observe Byzantine rituals. The Melkite Church has three major seminaries, including the Holy Savior Seminary in Beit Sahour, Israel, which serves dioceses in Israel, the West Bank, Gaza, and Jordan. Melkites make up the second largest Catholic community in the Middle East, after the Maronites.

SEE ALSO Christianity; Maronites; Melkites.

GREEK ORTHODOX CHURCH

SEE Eastern Orthodox Church.

GREEN LINE: Israeli-Jordanian armistice line of 3 April 1949, separating Israel from the West Bank (including East Jerusalem), implicitly recognized as the frontier of Israel by the 1967 UN Security Council Resolution 242. Delimiting territories under Israeli control and those under Arab control, the Green Line was the frontier claimed by the Palestinians to demarcate the Palestinian state that was to have come into existence as a result of the Oslo Accords and Declaration of Principles. The Israelis preempted this claim by annexing East Jerusalem and later proposed that the frontier be further redefined to take account of Jewish settlements on the Palestinian side. Final status negotiations failed as part of the Camp David Summit of 2000, and the Oslo peace process has become moot.

SEE ALSO Camp David II Summit; Oslo Accords; Oslo Accords II; Resolution 242; West Bank.

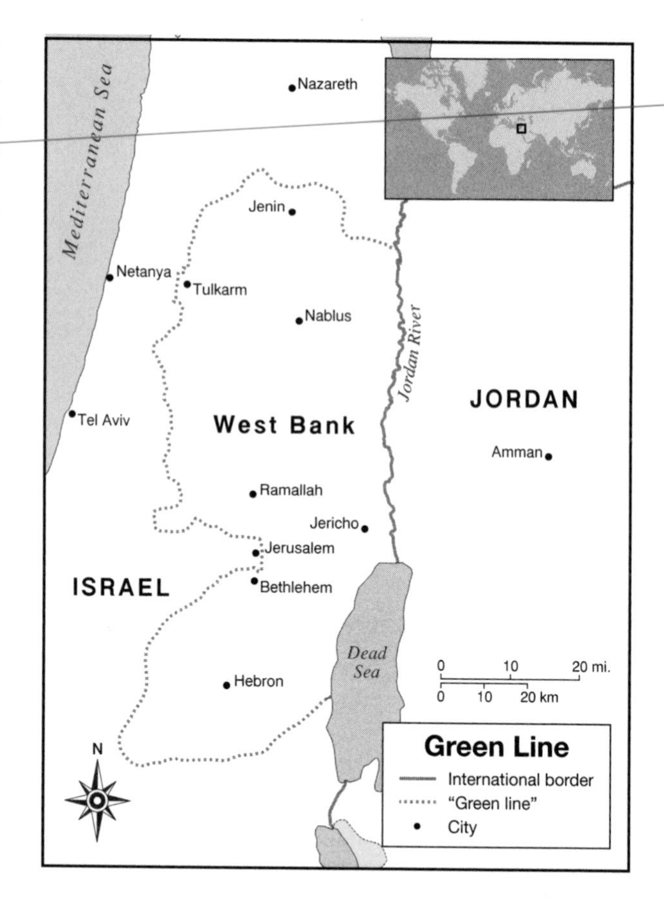

GREGORIAN CALENDAR: Currently in use, the name of this calendar comes from Pope Gregory XIII, who reformed the Julian calendar in 1582. The Julian year was 365 days and 6 hours. By the sixteenth century the total surplus time had displaced the vernal equinox to 11 March 11 from 21 March, the date adopted in the fourth century. Pope Gregory XIII fixed the problem, by removing ten days in the year 1582 and proclaiming that thereafter an extra day would be added every four years (leap year). In 1582, the lag of the Julian calendar in relation to the sun was ten days. Hence, 4 October 1582 was followed by 15 October to correct the disparity. The reform was adopted almost immediately in most Roman Catholic countries but more gradually in Protestant countries. It wasn't adopted in England and her colonies in America until 3 September 1752. While the year there until 1752 began on 25 March, the changeover to 1 January as New Year's Day was also effected that year.

GROUP OF TEN: Ensemble of Palestinian movements opposed to the peace process that had been launched in November 1991 at the Madrid Conference. Created in September 1992, the Group of Ten brought together the Democratic Front for the Liberation of Palestine, the Popular Front for the Liberation of Palestine, the Yacoub Faction of the Palestine Liberation Front, the Palestinian Popular Struggle Front, the Popular Front for the Liberation of Palestine-General Command, HAMAS, Palestinian Islamic Jihad, al-Saʿiqa, Fatah-Intifada, and the Palestinian Revolutionary Communist Party. The goal was to replace the Palestinian National Salvation Front, established in 1985, but ideological differences and personality conflicts in the leadership prevented the Group of Ten from ever constituting a united Palestinian opposition front and presenting an alternative to the policies of Fatah and Yasir Arafat. In October 1993 the Group of Ten was dissolved, to be replaced by the Alliance of Palestinian Forces.

SEE ALSO Alliance of Palestinian Forces (APF); Democratic Front for the Liberation of Palestine; Fatah, al-; Fatah-Intifada; HAMAS; Palestinian National Salvation Front; Palestinian Revolutionary Communist Party; Popular Front for the Liberation of Palestine; Popular Front for the Liberation of Palestine–General Command; Saʿiqa, al-.

GUARDIANS OF CEDARS (Lebanese, *Hiras al-Arz,*): An extreme right-wing Lebanese Maronite nationalist militia founded in 1975 by Etienne Saqr (Abu Arz, b. 1937), a former Lebanese government security officer. Saqr was influenced by the work of the Lebanese poet Saʿid Aql, who promoted a nationalist ideology called Lebanonism, which claimed direct Lebanese descent from the Phoenicians with little input from Muslim or Arab cultural sources, going so far as to devise a Latin alphabet for what he called the Lebanese language. During the civil war of 1975 to 1990, Saqr allied the Guardians (estimated to number about 500) with other Maronite political militias, especially the Phalange, and with Israel, against both Lebanese Muslim groups and the Palestinians. A number of Guardians also joined the Israeli-sponsored South Lebanon Army in 1978. After the civil war ended, the Guardians disarmed, but unlike a number of other such groups declined to transform themselves into a more conventional political party, remaining a very small, highly ideological movement with close ties to the Israelis. In 2000, after the Israeli withdrawal from Lebanon, Saqr was forced to flee into Israel, having been sentenced to death by a Lebanese court on charges relating to his Israeli connections. He was condemned to death a second time in 2001 on new, related charges. The Guardians' stated purposes include to rid the country of Syrians, Palestinians, and "uncivilized" Iranians who "seek the destruction of Lebanon's cultural identity"; to forbid foreigners to own property; to ban political parties "that imported their ideologies . . . from outside Lebanon"; to sign a peace treaty with Israel; to withdraw Lebanon from the Arab League and "eliminate the quality that designates Lebanon an Arab country"; to replace the Arabic with the Lebanese alphabet devised by Saʿid Aql; and to liberate it from the "defacement that was caused by the Arabic."

SEE ALSO South Lebanon Army.

GUARDIANS OF THE REVOLUTION

SEE Pasdaran.

GÜLBENKIAN, CALOUSTE (1869–1955): A businessman, very adept in the oil sector, nicknamed "the King of Oil," and "Mister 5%," born in 1869 in Scutari, near Istanbul, and died in July 1955. Calouste Gülbenkian, a naturalized Englishman, was an engineer by education. He contributed to the merging of Royal Dutch, belonging to Henry Deterding, with Shell, of Marcus Samuel, while attempting to keep U.S. oil companies out of the Middle East. Gülbenkian used his Turkish connections to join the two corporations with Turkish Petroleum Company, in which he held a 5% interest. At the July 1928 oil conference in Oostend, Belgium, he traced the famous "Red Line" on a map of the Middle East, which delineated the former Ottoman oil-rich territories now controlled by Turkish Petroleum. In this zone, the different societies were supposed to exploit oil resources together, and to act in concert in case of the discovery of new deposits. On 27 September 1928, the first oil cartel was founded with the signature at Achnacarry, Scotland, of an accord on the oil trade between Royal Dutch Shell, Standard Oil of New Jersey, and the Anglo-Persian Oil Company.

GULF COOPERATION COUNCIL: Arab organization, officially the Cooperation Council for the Arab States of the Gulf (Majlis al-Ta'awan li Dual al-Khalij al-Arabiya), including Saudi Arabia, Oman, Kuwait, Qatar, Bahrain, and the United Arab Emirates, created on 26 May 1981. The headquarters of the Gulf Cooperation Council (GCC) is in Riyadh, Saudi Arabia. The group is a mutual protection organization of Arab monarchies, controlled by the Saudis, and its purposes are to strengthen cooperation and promote integration and coordination among the members in economic and military affairs, particularly in security matters, both external and internal. It was first proposed by Saudi Arabia in 1979 after an armed revolt in Mecca and was created less than a year after the beginning of the Iran-Iraq War (1980–1988). Previous efforts to create such international institutions often failed; an example of this is the attempt to establish a free-trade zone, beginning in August 1964, through the Council of Arab Economic Unity, an organ of the League of Arab States. These failures were mainly due to the concerns of smaller nations about preserving their autonomy in the face of the great regional powers that were competing against each other for leadership. However, the Camp David Accords, followed by the expulsion of Egypt from the Arab League and the conflict between Iran and Iraq, with the light it shed on the vulnerability of countries in the area, prompted countries in the region to strengthen their ties. In 1982 the council failed in an attempt to mediate a truce in the Iran-Iraq War. In 1986, however, the war inspired the council to create a common defense force, which was deployed at the Saudi border with Kuwait when Iraq invaded Kuwait in August 1990, although it did not intervene. In December 1990 the GCC demanded that Iraq withdraw from Kuwait; its troops were subsequently part of the American-international coalition that ejected Iraq in the Gulf War of 1991. On 6 March 1991, after the war, the foreign ministers of Syria, Egypt, and the GCC states pronounced in favor of maintaining an "Arab peace force" in the Gulf. The Damascus Declaration signed at this meeting also called for improving economic cooperation among Arab states. At the same time, a majority of GCC members opposed an immediate resumption of contacts with countries that had supported Iraq during the Gulf crisis. The members suspended all aid to the Palestine Liberation Organization (PLO) as long as Yasir Arafat, who had supported Iraq, was its head. The council also declared in favor of a "just and global peace" in Palestine/Israel based on the principle of "land for peace." Member states participated in the Madrid Conference, begun in November 1991. Two member states, the Sultanate of Oman and the Emirate of Qatar, initiated relations with Israel.

In 1993, after the signing of the Oslo Accords, member states resumed relations with, and aid to, the PLO. On 12 March 1995, in spite of the reservations of Oman and Qatar, the GCC published a communiqué declaring that it was necessary to maintain international sanctions against Iraq as long as that country had not fulfilled all of its obligations under UN Resolution 687. On 28 June 1998 the members of the GCC denounced Israel's intention of expanding the geographical boundaries of Jerusalem. On 19 May 1999 the leaders of the GCC countries met in Saudi Arabia to discuss the Middle East peace process and rapprochement with Iran. Six days later President Muhammad Khatami made an official visit to Saudi Arabia, the first by an Iranian leader since the Islamic revolution of 1979. On 14 November 1999, the defense ministers of the GCC member countries announced the strengthening of defense agreements between their states. In December 2001 the members agreed to establish a customs union among their countries, which began in 2003, and a common market with a single currency by 2010. The GCC did not take an official position on the American-British war in Iraq that began in 2003, although the member states were not in favor. In December 2002 the Saudi foreign minister urged the United States not to launch the war unilaterally, and in January 2003 the council encouraged Russia in its diplomatic efforts to prevent the war. However, all member countries, particularly Kuwait, gave logistical assistance by opening bases, staging areas, ports, and territorial waters to US and British troops and supplies.

Member states of the GCC hold 45 percent of the world oil reserves and 15 percent of the natural gas. The GCC maintains a permanent mission at the European Union and in 2004 was negotiating the creation of a free trade zone with the European Union.

SEE ALSO Arafat, Yasir; Camp David Accords; Council of Arab Economic Unity; Gulf War (1991); Iran-Iraq War (1980–1988); League of Arab States; Oslo Accords; Oslo Accords II; Palestine Liberation Organization.

GULF CRISIS (1990–1991)

SEE Gulf War (1991).

GULF WAR (1980–1988)

SEE Iran-Iraq War.

GULF WAR (1991) (Second Gulf War): War waged from 16 January to 28 February 1991 by an American-led coalition against Iraq after Iraq's invasion and occupation of Kuwait in August 1990. The war was the culmination of the Gulf Crisis, which began in July 1990 when the price of oil fell to $11 a barrel, severely reducing Iraq's income. Iraq, which was heavily in debt to Kuwait and the other Gulf states as a result of the Iran-Iraq War of 1980 through 1988, blamed the low price on overproduction by Kuwait and the United Arab Emirates and demanded compensation in the form of debt forgiveness, the cession of Kuwait's Rumailiya oil fields (to which

Iraq had a longstanding but internationally unrecognized claim), and the leasing of two Kuwaiti islands at the head of the Persian Gulf for use as an oil port. The Kuwaitis refused, even as Iraqi president Saddam Hussein massed troops on the border. On 2 August 1990 Iraq invaded and occupied all of Kuwait. The administration of U.S. President George H. W. Bush determined to force Iraq out, despite the long friendly relationship between American military and intelligence agencies and Saddam Hussein's regime, especially during the Iran-Iraq War, when the United States had supplied Iraq with weapons, equipment, and intelligence and protected it from international censure over its behavior in the war and its assaults on its Kurdish population. On 2 August, the same day as the invasion, the UN Security Council condemned Iraq and demanded that it withdraw. On 3 August Arab League foreign ministers did the same (the Palestine Liberation Organization [PLO] and Jordan abstained) but also called for an Arab summit where a negotiated settlement could be reached, while rejecting intervention by any outside party. On 4 August the Organization of the Islamic Conference condemned Iraq (again the PLO abstained). On 6 August the Security Council passed a resolution imposing sanctions on Iraq. The Gulf states, including Saudi Arabia, asked the United States for military protection. On 10 August the Arab League repeated its condemnation of Iraq (with only the PLO and Iraq opposed) and reversed its position on foreign intervention by supporting the Gulf states' request for American help.

AIR RAID. AN IRAQI WOMAN AND HER BROTHER STAND INSIDE THEIR BASRA HOME, DESTROYED BY AERIAL BOMBING DURING THE FIRST GULF WAR (ALSO KNOWN AS DESERT STORM). A COALITION LED BY THE UNITED STATES QUICKLY EXPELLED IRAQI FORCES FROM KUWAIT AND COMPELLED IRAQI LEADER SADDAM HUSSEIN TO AGREE TO TERMS. *(© Reuters NewMedia Inc./Corbis)*

Saddam Hussein responded by declaring a *jihad* to free Mecca from the Saudis. On 12 August Saddam Hussein proposed that Iraq's withdrawal from Kuwait be linked to Israel's withdrawal from the occupied territories, an occupation that was also in violation of UN Security Council resolutions. After several months of political maneuvering and failed attempts at negotiation by various parties, the United States obtained UN approval and assembled a military coalition that included some twenty-nine countries, including several Arab states, although the bulk of the forces were American. These were gathered in the Gulf area with the clear intention of attacking the Iraqis in Kuwait and expelling them. Russia, which opposed a war, attempted to mediate but was unsuccessful. The United States launched its military offensive (Operation Desert Storm) on 16 January 1991 with a warplane and cruise missile attack on military installations, infrastructure (transportation, water, gas, and electricity distribution networks), and population centers in Iraq that went on continuously for five and a half weeks. On 21 February Saddam Hussein agreed to the latest Russian plan for a truce; Bush rejected it. The Iraqis announced that they were withdrawing from Kuwait and began to pull out, setting fire to Kuwaiti oil wells as they moved toward the border. Bush ordered a ground attack into Kuwait on 24 February. The Iraqi forces, already in retreat, were driven out of Kuwait City and mostly destroyed from the air on the "highway of death" as their retreat was blocked. A ceasefire was declared on 28 February. Approximately 545,000 troops were involved in the war on the Iraqi side and 700,000 on the US-coalition side. Approximately 80,000 air sorties were flown and more than 200 cruise missiles fired by the coalition. The Iraqi air force was not a factor. Iraq launched perhaps a dozen Scud missiles at Israel, with negligible results; at the request of the United States, Israel did not retaliate. Total casualties, including civilian casualties, are unknown but in the tens of thousands; Iraqi military deaths are estimated at 100,000; total coalition deaths were 376. About 600 Kuwaitis were killed. On 3 April 1991 the UN Security Council made the lifting of sanctions conditional on the elimination of all Iraqi weapons of mass destruction and the surveillance of factories that had the potential to replace them. A war of attrition started between the United States and Iraq that lasted until the Iraq War of 2003. Iraqi deaths attributable to sanctions between 1991 and 2003 are estimated at anywhere from 500,000 to a million.

The war was a disaster for the PLO and for the Palestinians. Some Palestinians supported Iraq, or at least appreciated Saddam Hussein's rhetorical aggressiveness toward Israel; some, especially in Kuwait, condemned the invasion (including the Fatah and PLO representatives there); most are believed to have been neutral. Yasir Arafat and the PLO adopted an equivocal position intended to be seen as neutrality but which effectively supported, and was seen by the world as supporting, Saddam Hussein and Iraq. (The PLO was virtually alone in refusing to condemn the Iraqi invasion and occupation of Kuwait.) The practical results of this position were the persecution, expulsion, and impoverishment of the large Palestinian community in Kuwait—about 350,000 before the war and 30,000 after. The earnings of this community had supported many family members in the territories and the camps, and the PLO had collected taxes from it for the Palestine National Fund. Many of these Palestinians fled to Jordan, which suffered severe economic losses. The PLO also lost financial aid from the Arab states (mainly the Gulf states), which had supported Palestinian civic and social institutions and aid to the needy, and lost Arab diplomatic support in international affairs. Blanket curfews and border closings imposed by Israel on the occupied territories created social and economic havoc, and the PLO was nearly destroyed, leaving the Palestinian community increasingly vulnerable.

SEE ALSO Arafat, Yasir; Fatah, al-; Hussein, Saddam; Iran-Iraq War (1980–1988); Jihad; League of Arab States; Palestine Liberation Organization; Palestine National Fund.

GULF WAR (2003)

SEE Iraq War (2003).

GUPS

SEE General Union of Palestinian Students.

GUPT

SEE General Union of Palestinian Teachers.

HEBRON VIOLENCE. JEWISH SETTLERS FIRE ON PALESTINIANS IN THE WEST BANK TOWN IN DECEMBER 1993, IN RESPONSE TO THE STONING OF RABBI MOSHE LEVINGER'S CAR. THE SMALL GROUP OF JEWISH RESIDENTS IN HEBRON BELONG TO THE EXTREME NATIONALIST GUSH EMUNIM MOVEMENT, WHICH ADVOCATES JEWISH SETTLEMENT THROUGHOUT THE WEST BANK AND GAZA STRIP BECAUSE OF THE LAND'S ANCIENT RELIGIOUS SIGNIFICANCE. *(AP/Wide World Photos)*

GUPW

SEE General Union of Palestinian Women.

GUPWJ

SEE General Union of Palestinian Writers and Journalists.

GUPWo

SEE General Union of Palestinian Workers.

GUR: One of the greatest of Hasidic dynasties, founded by Isaac Meyer Rothenberg Alter. It is the keystone of the Agudat Israel Party.

SEE ALSO Agudat Israel.

GURION, DAVID BEN

SEE Ben-Gurion, David.

GUSH EMUNIM ("Bloc of the Faithful", in Hebrew): Israeli extremist movement, founded in February

1974 by Rabbis Moshe Levinger and Chaim Druckmann. Starting up after a scission in the National Religious Party, where this current had been in existence since 1968, this organization mixed religious fundamentalism and fanatical nationalism, appointing itself the mission of colonizing the Arab territories that had just been reoccupied after the Yom Kippur War. Many settlers saw a messianic sign in the victory of the 1967 War and wanted to reawaken an enthusiasm that had somewhat subsided. Gush Emunim came into its own with the 1977 victory of Likud but withdrew its support in 1979, after the Israeli-Egyptian peace accord implied land restitution. In May 1984, anticipating the Knesset elections, Gush Emunim joined with the extremist nationalist party ha-Tehiya, which allowed them to win five seats. Internal dissension between moderates and religious ultranationalists weakened the Gush Emunim-Tehiya alliance, leading to the departure of many members, who decided to start new movements like Meimad, Oz Ve-Shalom, and Netivot Shalom. As a result of the elections of June 1988, occurring in the shadow of the Intifada, Gush Emunim obtained no seats, while ha-Tehiya held on to three. The principal leader of this movement, Rabbi Levinger, is also the spiritual guide of the extremist settlers who have taken up residence in Hebron.

SEE ALSO Arab-Israel War (1967); Arab-Israel War (1973); ha-Tehiyah; Hebron; Intifada (1987–1993); Likud; Meimad; National Religious Party.

GUSH HERUT-LIBERALIM

SEE GAHAL Party.

HAARETZ ("the Land," in Hebrew): Independent Israeli daily, left-leaning, founded in 1919. Considered the oldest of the Israeli dailies, the influential *Haaretz* has belonged to the Schocken family since 1939. Its views on the Israeli-Palestinian conflict tend to represent the political agenda of the Meretz Party. As of 2003, the newspaper, under publisher Amos Schocken, was selling 50,000 copies per weekday. Though the daily is not a leader among Israeli media, its English-language Web site attracts large numbers of Jews outside of Israel, particularly in America.

SEE ALSO Meretz Party.

HABASH, GEORGE (al-Hakim, "the Doctor"; 1925–): Palestinian political figure born in Lydda, Palestine, to a Greek Orthodox family. In July 1948, after the start of the first Israeli-Palestinian conflict, the Habash family took refuge in Lebanon. After studying at the Orthodox College in Jerusalem and the American University in Beirut, Habash went on to study medicine. In 1948 he joined the Syrian People's Party. In 1951 he graduated from medical school at the top of his class. In October 1952, in Beirut, with his fellow students Hani al-Hindi, Ahmad al-Khatib, Bassel al-Kobeissi, and Wadi' Haddad, he founded the Arab Nationalist Movement (ANM), which was Nasserist in inspiration and agitated against Zionism and for the liberation of Palestine. Having become a pediatrician, he and Haddad opened a clinic in Amman, where he treated the Palestinian refugee population for free. In August 1956 he ran for office unsuccessfully in the Jordanian legislative elections. He was questioned a number of times about his political activism, and the Jordanian authorities expelled him to Damascus, where he continued to advocate the ideas of the ANM.

He arrived in Damascus when Egypt and Syria were forming the United Arab Republic. In 1963, when relations between Ba'thists and Nasserists were deteriorating, he left Damascus for Beirut. In April 1964, after the national conference of the ANM, he created a regional command for Palestine, supervising the planning of armed actions. In December 1967, after the Arab defeat in the 1967 War, he dissolved the ANM in order to found the Popular Front for the Liberation of Palestine (PFLP), into which the Palestine Liberation Front (PLF) of Ahmad Jibril merged. Habash was named secretary general of the PFLP. He was imprisoned in Damascus in March 1968 and freed eight months later by a PFLP commando, led by his friend Haddad. However, while he was incarcerated a number of his close associates began to compete for leadership of the PFLP. Two of his assistants resigned in order to create their own movements: Ahmad Jibril, in 1968, founded the Popular Front for the Liberation of Palestine—General Command, and Nayif Hawatmeh created of the Popular Democratic Front for the Liberation of Palestine (DFLP). On his return to Jordan, Habash came up

George Habash. A cofounder of the Arab Nationalist Movement in 1952, he replaced it with the Popular Front for the Liberation of Palestine after the 1967 Arab-Israel War (and, later, other groups). Habash took a hard line against peace with Israel and also—disastrously—waged war against the monarchy in Jordan in 1970. *(AP/Wide World Photos)*

against the hostility of the Hashimite monarchy, whose abolition he was advocating. In June 1970 PFLP guerrillas entered Amman and fought with the Jordanian army, which was unable to defeat them decisively. A truce was reached, with the PFLP remaining in place in the capital. In August Habash made a virtual declaration of war on King Hussein, demanding the installation of a "national democratic regime" in Jordan. Between 6 and 9 September a PFLP commando hijacked three civilian airliners to the Jordanian desert, destroying them after the passengers were evacuated. On 16 September the king formed a military government and the next day launched an attack against Palestinian refugee camps in Jordan. This was the beginning of Black September 1970. After ten days a ceasefire was arranged by President Gamal Abdel Nasser, but when fighting flared up again the following summer all Palestinian resistance organizations were expelled from the country and went to Lebanon, ending the virtual civil war in Jordan.

In September 1974, opposing a negotiated solution to the Palestinian problem, Habash quit the PLO Executive Committee to join the Rejection Front, in which he became the principal figure. Between 1975 and 1978, opposing Syrian meddling in the Lebanese Civil War, he advised rapprochement with al-Fatah. In 1980 he suffered a serious stroke that incapacitated him for months. In September 1982, evicted from Lebanon along with other Palestinian organizations, he left Beirut at the head of his troops to set up his base in Damascus. In June 1983 he announced the constitution of a common military and political command linking the PFLP and Nayif Hawatmeh's DFLP. The following year, in order to oppose the policies of al-Fatah, he participated in founding the Democratic Alliance, which gathered together the PFLP, the DFLP, and the PLF. In April 1987, after the Democratic Alliance was dissolved, putting the unity of Palestinian forces before ideological differences, he rejoined the PLO Executive Committee, as did the DFLP leadership. In 1989 illness prevented him from completely fulfilling his duties as the head of the movement and a struggle for succession started between Ahmed Yamani and Salah Salah. On 17 September 1990, for the first time in more than twenty years, he returned to Amman, accompanied by Hawatmeh, and both of them were received by King Hussein. In February 1991 he was in Paris for cancer treatment; in Paris his presence caused an international outcry. On 19 September 1993, opposing the Israeli-Palestinian accord that was scheduled to be signed three days later, he and Hawatmeh announced their resignation from the PLO Executive Committee. A few days later, the two movements joined the Palestinian opposition, the Alliance of Palestinian Forces (APF). In August 1994, to consolidate his position in the APF and toughen the organization's opposition to the Oslo Accords, the PFLP announced its resignation from the PLO Central Council. In April 2000 Habash resigned from the leadership of the PFLP. In July he was replaced by Mustafa al-Zabri (Abu Ali Mustafa), who was assassinated by the Israelis in Ramallah in 2001. Habash, in ill health, lives in Damascus.

SEE ALSO Alliance of Palestinian Forces (APF); Arab-Israel War (1967); Arab Nationalist Movement; Black September 1970; Fatah, al-; Hussein ibn Talal; Jibril, Ahmad; Nasser, Gamal Abdel; Popular Front for the Liberation of Palestine; Popular Front for the Liberation of Palestine—General Command; Rejection Front.

Haganah. David Ben-Gurion, who would become the first Israeli prime minister, meets with soldiers of the Jewish paramilitary organization before the creation of the State of Israel. The well-trained defensive group was replaced by the Israel Defense Force in 1948. *(© Bettmann/Corbis)*

Habashis

see Ahbash, al-.

HADASH

see Democratic Front for Peace and Equality.

Hadith: Arab word used to designate a collection of the words and acts of the prophet Muhammad, functioning as commentaries complementing the teaching of the Qur'an.

see also Muhammad; Qur'an.

Hafradah ("separation," in Hebrew): A concept favored by many Israelis, involving a separation between the State of Israel and the Palestinian territories. The partisans of this project believe that "a small country at peace is better than a big country at war."

Haganah:("defense", in Hebrew) Name of the military wing of the Jewish leadership in Mandatory Palestine. This paramilitary organization was created in 1920 for the purpose of protecting Jewish colonies against the actions of Arabs opposed to their expansion. So as to avoid possible excesses, the movement established a rule of "self-restraint" (*havlagah*), according to which the Haganah would restrict itself to defensive actions. Within the Haganah, the "Rekhesh" section was in charge of procuring the necessary weaponry. Between 1936 and 1941, benefiting from the experience of certain British officers, the Haganah produced some particularly well-trained reconnaissance units. The latter served as a nucleus for the constitution of the Jewish Brigade during World War II. In 1948, the Haganah was dissolved, with many of its members joining the ranks of the new Israeli army, the Israel Defense Force (Tsahal).

see also Israel Defense Force

Remembering the Exodus. As happens on the first night of Passover every year in Jewish homes all over the world, a family in San Francisco, California, reads aloud from the Haggadah, the story of the Hebrew people's exodus from ancient Egypt, during the seder meal in 1989. *(© Roger Ressmeyer/Corbis)*

Hagarines: Term used by Christians in the Middle Ages to designate Arabs and Muslims in general. It derives from the tradition that Arabs descend from Ishmael, son of Abraham and his servant Hagar. The term itself derives from the Arabic *Muhajirun,* those who accompanied Muhammad on his *hijra* from Mecca. The word *hijra* is based on the Arabic root H-J-R, from which also comes the Arabic name of Hagar.

see also Abraham; Hijra; Ishmael; Muhajirun, al-.

Haggadah (Haggada, aggadah; "tale", in Hebrew): Ritual reading, during the "seder" meal on the first night of Passover, of the story of the flight from Egypt of the Hebrew people. By extension, designates a non-juridical interpretation of the Jewish law which is read as a kind of instruction during the Passover feast. The Haggadah, whose provenance is the classical rabbinical period, figures in two texts: the Talmud and the Midrash.

see also Talmud.

Hag ha-Matzot ("the Feast of Unleavened Bread," in Hebrew): One of the names for Pesach (Passover), celebrating the liberation of the Jewish people from Egypt.

Haifa: A major city in northwest historic Palestine, located on the Bay of Haifa on the Mediterranean coast, now Israel's third largest city. As part of the Ottoman Empire, Haifa was populated predominantly by Muslim and Christian Palestinians until Jews began to settle there in the late nineteenth century. Under the British Mandate (1917–1948), Haifa expanded, especially after 1933, when a deep-water port was opened. In 1922 its population was recorded as 25,000, of whom 6,000 were Jews and 18,000 Palestinians. By 1944, as a result of growth and increased Jewish immigration, it had about 66,000 Jews and 62,000 Palestinians. During the Arab-Israel War of 1948, Arab and Israeli forces

HAIFA. This view of the northwestern Israeli port city, a major industrial center, looks westward to the Bay of Haifa. The third-largest city in Israel, Haifa has a small Palestinian population and is also the world center of the Baha'i religion. *(© David Rubinger/Corbis)*

fought for control of the city. After the war, only 3,000 Palestinians remained, the rest having been expelled by Israeli forces; many of them fled to Lebanon. Present-day Haifa is Israel's principal port and a major industrial and commercial center. Its population in 2001 was over 270,000, of whom 10 percent were Palestinians.

SEE ALSO British Mandate; Ottomans.

HAIFA, UNIVERSITY OF: A public liberal arts university, established in 1963. Considered one of the leading institutions of higher learning in Israel, it has promoted innovative studies on topics such as the attitudes of Arabs toward Israelis and of Israelis toward Arabs. As of 2004, a total of 13,000 students were enrolled in the university's undergraduate and graduate programs.

HA-IHUD HA-LE'UMI

SEE National Union Party.

HAJJ (Hadj): Arab word for the pilgrimage that every Muslim must make once in his or her life. Accomplished in the twelfth month of the Islamic calendar (*dhû al-hijja*), it consists of a ritual visit to the holy sites in Mecca. The pilgrimage confers upon the person who completes it the title of *hajj* or *hajja* (for a woman), which is added to his or her name. The lesser pilgrimage to Mecca (umra) can be accomplished anytime in the year and does not require the fulfillment of any particular ritual obligations.

SEE ALSO Islamic Calendar; Umra

HAKHAM: Hebrew word meaning "wise man," and likely the origin of the Arabic word meaning "rabbi."

HAKHAM BASHI: (association of two words, Arabic and Turkish) Title of the Chief Rabbi, under the Ottoman Empire. In Jewish tradition this word designates a master of the law.

PILGRIMAGE TO MECCA. MUSLIM MEN PRAY WITH UPRAISED HANDS ON THE MOUNTAIN OF MERCY IN MECCA, SAUDI ARABIA. THE HAJJ IS ONE OF THE ESSENTIAL ACTIONS EXPECTED OF EACH MUSLIM DURING HIS OR HER LIFETIME. *(AP/Wide World Photos)*

HAKIM, AL-

SEE Habash, George.

HALAKHAH (halakha): Legal religious code that has regulated the life of Jews since the post-Biblical epoch, gathering the ensemble of precepts and practical commandments of the religious law, from an orthodox perspective. With roots in the Bible, the authority of the Halakhah is based on the Talmud. In order to allow Jews to locate what they are looking for in the arcana of the Halakhah, succinct and practical résumés were composed in the first centuries of our era. The *Shulhan Arukh*, composed by Joseph Karo in the sixteenth century, is a later codification that has since been the most authoritative.

SEE ALSO Bible; Talmud.

HALAL ("lawful," in Arabic): Describes everything that conforms to the prescriptions of Islam. In the matter of food, this word describes the animals allowable for consumption, as well as the ritual slaughter of those animals. The Muslim religion forbids the consumption of pork and alcohol.

HALUKKA (Haluqa): (Hebrew word meaning "division" or "distribution") referring to the charitable funds received for needy Jews in Palestine and later in Israel from Diaspora Jews. The word also translates as "partition," referring to the British and UN plans of 1937 and 1947 respectively.

HALUTZ: Hebrew word used to designate the Jewish pioneer phenomenon in Palestine.

HALUTZIM: Hebrew word designating "pioneers," or the first Jews who immigrated to and settled in Palestine in the 1880s and afterwards.

HAMAS: Informal name of the Islamic Resistance Movement (Harakat al-Muqawima al-Islamiya), formed from its acronym in Arabic. *HAMAS* is an Arabic word meaning "fervor" or "zeal." HAMAS was founded in the Gaza Strip on 14 December 1987 by Shaykh Ahmad Yasin with Abdullah Darwish, Abd al-Aziz Rantisi, Salah Shahada, and Ahmad Shama, Palestinian followers of the Muslim Brotherhood. Constituted a few days after the start of the first Intifada, it proposed fighting for the liberation of Palestine and the re-Islamization of Palestinian society. According to its charter, published in 1988, HAMAS sanctioned armed struggle against Israel only in Palestinian territory and proscribed inter-Palestinian armed conflict. Its leadership was composed of a board of directors (*Mudiriya*), a consultative council (*Majlis al-Shura*), and departments (*Shaaba*) or bureaus (*Maktab*). The political bureau (*al-Maktab al-siyassi*) was headed by a general secretary, and the military bureau (*al-Maktab al-askari*) supervised the operations of the armed branch (*al-Jinah al-musallah*), called the Izz al-Din al-Qassam Brigade after a martyr of the revolt of the 1930s. HAMAS combined resistance to Israel with significant social action (such as charities) among the Palestinian population. At first Israeli authorities were not opposed to it, hoping that HAMAS would weaken the Palestine Liberation Organization (PLO). In 1988, the western sector of al-Fatah, led by Khalil al-Wazir (Abu Jihad), in charge of operations in the occupied territories, tried unsuccessfully to mount joint actions with HAMAS and Islamic Jihad. On 29 September 1989, the Israeli authorities declared HAMAS illegal. On 14 December 1990, the third anniversary of its creation, it claimed responsibility for its first attack, the assassination of three Israeli soldiers in Haifa. On 12 January 1991, HAMAS launched a general appeal for holy war to the population of the West Bank and Gaza Strip.

At the end of the 1991 Gulf War, while preparations for the Madrid Conference for peace in the Middle East were underway, the HAMAS leadership came out categorically against any negotiated settlement with Israel. In September 1992 HAMAS published a tract expressing a hardening of its position toward the Israeli-Palestinian peace process. On 13 December a commando kidnapped an Israeli border guard. When Israel refused to exchange the guard for Shaykh Ahmad Yasin, who had been sentenced to life in prison, the border guard was killed, which led to the arrest of 1,223 people by the Israeli authorities and the expulsion to Lebanon of 415 sympathizers or members of the Palestinian Islamic Jihad and HAMAS. During this exile, negotiations were begun for a rapprochement between the PLO and HAMAS, but they were fruitless. In November 1993, resolutely opposed to the Israeli-Palestinian accords of the previous 13 September, HAMAS joined the vanguard of those who comprised the Palestinian opposition in Damascus, the Alliance of Palestinian Forces (APF). In April 1994, in response to the assassination of twenty-nine Palestinians by a Jewish colonist in Hebron the preceding 25 February, HAMAS undertook a series of deadly suicide attacks in Israel. In June 1994, with the establishment of the Palestinian Authority (PA) in the Gaza Strip, a difficult cohabitation began between the two organizations. Although rejecting the Israeli-Palestinian accord, HAMAS nevertheless recognized the PA, which among other functions had taken responsibility for suppressing anti-Israeli militancy. Because of its charity work, HAMAS enjoyed the support of a large part of the Palestinian population, even if the majority of the population opposed the terrorist tactics HAMAS was using, such as suicide bombings. Many members of the movement were arrested by the Israeli and Palestinian police forces and two leaders of the armed section were assassinated by Israeli services.

Would-Be Suicide Bombers. HAMAS militants take part in an anti-Israeli demonstration at a southern Lebanese refugee camp in December 2001. The event marked the fourteenth anniversary of the founding of HAMAS, also called the Islamic Resistance Movement, by Islamists dedicated to holy war against Israel. *(AP/Wide World Photos)*

On 25 July 1995 one of the main leaders of the political section of HAMAS, Abu Musa Marzouq, was arrested in the United States. In the autumn, faced with the prospect of presidential elections in January 1996 and not wanting to accept the Oslo Accords, HAMAS refused to engage in the electoral process. Two splinter groups that favored electoral participation but represented only themselves were formed: the Islamic National Way and the Islamic Front for the Salvation of Palestine. In October 1997

Shaykh Yasin was freed from prison as part of a deal to return two Israeli agents who had been caught in Jordan trying to assassinate a HAMAS leader. Shaykh Yasin returned to Gaza, where he gave a speech advocating struggle against Israel and inviting Yasir Arafat to join "the resistance front." Between 1998 and 1999, under the pressure of Israeli authorities, who demanded that harsher measures be taken against HAMAS, the Palestinian police regularly interrogated many of its leaders and militants. In 1998 the PA arrested some HAMAS leaders over their criticism of the Wye River Accords. At the end of August 1999, when the Jordanian authorities decided to close the offices of HAMAS in Jordan and issue warrants for the arrest of its representatives, several of them went underground. On 22 September Khalid Mishʿal and Ibrahim Ghusha were arrested by the Jordanian police and Abu Musa Marzouq, who had returned to Amman, was expelled to Iran. HAMAS attended a national meeting of opposition groups with the PA in October 1999 but later severely criticized it for participating in the Camp David talks of July 2000. At the same time, however, Shaykh Yasin announced that if the Israelis stopped attacking Palestinian civilians HAMAS would stop attacking Israeli civilians and that if the Israelis pulled out of the West Bank and Gaza Strip HAMAS would observe a truce. With the outbreak of the al-Aqsa Intifada in the Palestinian territories in October 2000, HAMAS and the PA reconciled. In November 2000 HAMAS joined the resistance committees through which national and Islamic forces coordinated their local actions. HAMAS intensified its campaign of suicide bombings against Israeli civilians, leading to many Israeli reprisal operations. In 2002 Israel reoccupied the West Bank Palestinian "autonomous" areas. On 22 March 2004, after a failed attempt the previous September, Israel succeeded in assassinating Shaykh Yasin in a missile attack. He was succeeded by Abd al-Aziz Rantisi, who had survived an assassination attempt the previous June. Israel assassinated him on 17 April 2004. His successor's name has not been announced. In June 2004 it was reported that Ismail Hanyeh, a HAMAS leader, announced that HAMAS would stop resisting the Israeli occupation in the Gaza Strip if Israel withdrew from the areas it had been besieging for the previous two months.

HAMAS has offices in many countries, including Iran, Jordan, Sudan, Lebanon, and Syria. Originally financed mainly by its members and others who wished to contribute to its charitable activities, it received substantial aid from the Gulf states during and after the Gulf Crisis of 1990 and 1991, when those states withdrew their aid from the PLO. Although it is Sunni, HAMAS has been financed largely by Shiʿite Iran since 1991, when Iran sponsored an international conference, meant to contrast with the Madrid Conference, to support a Palestinian Islamic revolution.

SEE ALSO Alliance of Palestinian Forces (APF); Aqsa Intifada, al-; Fatah, al-; Gaza Strip; Gulf War (1991); Intifada (1987–1993); Islamic Jihad; Islamic National Way Movement; Madrid Conference; Muslim Brotherhood; Oslo Accords; Oslo Accords II; Palestine Liberation Organization; Palestinian Authority; Palestinian Islamic Jihad; Qassam, Izz al-Din al-; Rantisi, Abd al-Aziz; Wazir, Khalil al- (Abu Jihad); West Bank; Yasin, Ahmad Ismaʿil.

HANUKKAH ("inauguration," in Hebrew): Jewish Festival of Lights, which celebrates the purification of the Temple after the victory of the Maccabees over the Hellenistic Syrians. Beginning on 25 Kislev, the day of the winter solstice, Hanukkah commemorates the inauguration of the temple built to replace the one that had been dedicated to the glory of Zeus by the Syrians, under the reign of Antiochus IV in 164 B.C.E. This holiday takes place during the period between the end of November and the end of December, and lasts eight days. The word *hanukkiyah* refers to the Jewish nine-branch candelabra, returned to the Temple after the Maccabean victory.

HA-POʿEL HA-MIZRACHI ("Eastern worker", in Hebrew): Name of a Zionist religious bloc, with a working-class orientation, created in 1922. In 1956 Ha-Poʿel ha-Mizrachi became an Israeli political party and merged with the Mizrachi Party to form the National Religious Party.

SEE ALSO Mizrachi; National Religious Party

HAQ

SEE Arab Islamic Liberal Party.

HAQ, AL-: Important Palestinian nonpartisan human rights and legal assistance organization in the West Bank, founded in 1979 by Raja Shehadeh and Jonathan Kuttab. The organization's name is usually given as "Law in the Service of Man"; the Arabic word *haq* signifies "fairness," "justice," "law," and "truth.") Originally focused on Israeli legal structures and behavior in the occupied territories, since the establishment of the Palestinian Authority in 1994 it also takes official Palestinian activity within its purview. Its primary activities are monitoring and documenting human rights violations, including war crimes; providing free legal services to the Palestinian community; producing reports and analyses on human rights issues; disseminating information on human rights principles; and intervening to stop or prevent abuses. Al-Haq is headquartered in Ramallah and affiliated with the International Commission of Jurists in Geneva. It has an informal relationship with many international nongovernmental organizations as well as a consultative status with the United Nations Economic and Social Council. It receives its funding from private foundations, human rights and social justice organizations, and individual contributors.

SEE ALSO Occupied Territories; Palestinian Authority; West Bank.

HARAAM: Arabic word designating whatever is illicit, prohibited or forbidden by Islam, such as alcohol, pork, or pre-marital sex.

HARAKA AL-ISLAMIYA AL-MUJAHIDA AL-FILASTINIYA, AL-

SEE Palestinian Islamic Combat Movement.

HARAKA AL-ISLAMIYA LI-TAHRIR FILASTIN, AL-

SEE Islamic Movement for the Liberation of Palestine.

HARAKAT AL-JIHAD AL-ISLAMI AL FILASTIN

SEE Palestinian Islamic Jihad.

HARAKAT AL-MUHAJARUN

SEE -Muhajarun, al-.

HARAKAT AL-MUJAHADA AL-ISLAMIYYA AL-FILASTINIYA

SEE Palestinian Islamic Combat Movement.

HARAKAT AL-MUQAWAMA AL-ISLAMIYA

SEE HAMAS.

HARAKAT AL-NAFIR AL-ISLAMI

SEE Hizbullah-Palestine.

HARAKAT AL-NAHDA AL-ISLAMIYYA

SEE Islamic Renaissance Movement.

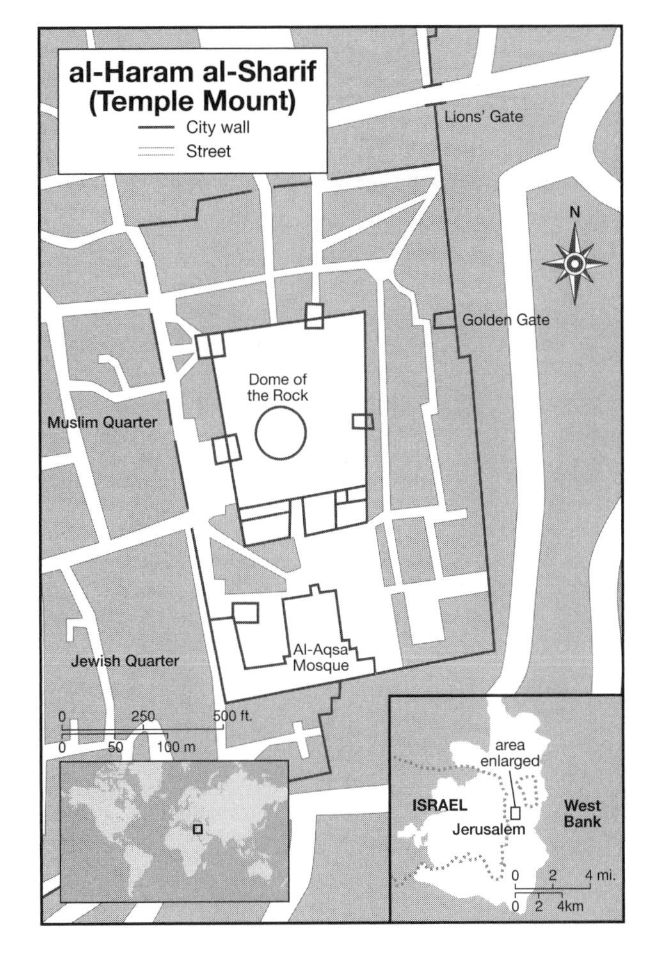

HARAKAT AL-QAWMIYYIN AL-ARAB

SEE Arab Nationalist Movement.

HARAKAT AL-TAHRIR AL-WATANI AL-FILASTINI

SEE Fatah, al-.

HARAKAT AL-TAHRIR AL-WATANI AL FILASTIN AL-MAJLIS AL-THAWRI

SEE Fatah, al-Revolutionary Council.

HARAM: Arabic word for a holy or sanctified area, as in Haram al-Sharif (Noble Sanctuary) in Jerusalem, site of the al-Aqsa mosque and the Dome of the Rock. In more colloquial usage, the word may mean "precinct" or "enclosed area," and thus may be used to refer to the *haram* of the university or of the house.

SEE ALSO Aqsa, al-; Haram al-Sharif.

HARAM AL-SHARIF (Noble Sanctuary): Walled precinct atop a hill in East Jerusalem (called Mount Mo-

Dome of the Rock. This late-seventh-century mosque on the Noble Sanctuary—to Jews, the Temple Mount—is believed to have been built over the site, holy to Jews and Muslims, where Abraham prepared to sacrifice Isaac, where the Temple of Solomon and then the Second Temple stood, and where the Prophet Muhammad ascended to heaven. *(© The Art Archive/Dagli Orti)*

riah in the Bible, known to Jews today as the Temple Mount [Har ha-Bayit]). Mount Moriah is, by tradition, the place where Abraham prepared Isaac for sacrifice upon a rock. The two main structures in the precinct are the al-Aqsa mosque and the Dome of the Rock, enclosing the Rock of Abraham, which Muslims believe is the place to which the Night Journey of the Prophet Muhammad brought him and from which he was taken to receive a message from God and pray with the earlier prophets. The Dome of the Rock replaced an earlier structure, the Mosque of Omar, and is sometimes referred to by that name. It is the third holiest site in Islam, built upon what is thought to be the site of the Temple of Solomon and the Second Temple, or Temple of Herod, of which the Western Wall, or Kotel, is believed by devout Jews to be the remnant. The proximity of these Islamic and Jewish holy sites has led to much conflict between the two communities. After the June 1967 War, when East Jerusalem came under Israeli control, an agreement was reached between Israelis and Palestinians limiting access to the Sanctuary to Muslims. Control of the Sanctuary in matters of worship is in the hands of the Waqf, an organization responsible for the administration of Muslim religious property, while access to it is controlled by Israeli police. Jewish extremist groups frequently demand the right to enter the site; some of them advocate razing the mosques and other buildings to make way for a reconstruction of the Temple of Solomon, destroyed by the Babylonians in 586 B.C.E.. On 28 September 2000 a visit to the site by Ariel Sharon, head of Likud, accompanied by a company of Israeli soldiers, provoked the anger of Muslims and set off the al-Aqsa Intifada in the Palestinian territories. On 29 July 2001 the symbolic laying of the first stone of the proposed new temple further provoked Muslim anger.

see also Aqsa, al-; Aqsa Intifada, al-; Arab-Israel War (1967); Likud; Sharon, Ariel; Waqf; Western Wall.

Haredi (pl. haredim): Hebrew word meaning "God-fearing," and which designates, in practice, ultra-orthodox Jews. The Haredim believe that Jewish sovereignty in Israel will only be established with the arrival of the Messiah (*Mashiah*, in Hebrew).

see also Messiah.

Harel, Isser (1912–2003): Founder of Israel's intelligence community, second and most powerful head of Mossad. Born Isser Halperin in Russia, he immigrated with his family in 1931 to mandatory Palestine. During World War II he served in the Haganah and with the British coast guard. Appointed secretary of the Jewish department of the Haganah's intelligence service in 1944, he oversaw counterespionage efforts and operations against dissident Jewish underground groups such as Lohamei Herut Yisrael (LEHI). His success in these efforts led to his appointment as head of the new General Security Service (Shin Bet, or Shabak) in 1948. In 1953 he was appointed head of the Mossad, supervising all Israeli intelligence agencies. Often criticized for the extensive internal surveillance he maintained, he also developed an effective international intelligence operations network. He is credited with uncovering several Soviet spies, including Yisrael Beer, and with orchestrating the capture of Adolph Eichmann in Argentina in 1960. He left office in 1963 after a dispute with David Ben-Gurion. After a brief stint as Levi Eshkol's intelligence coordinator in 1965 and 1966, he won a seat in the eighth Knesset on the RAFI Party list.

see also British Mandate; Haganah; Lohamei Herut Yisrael; Mossad; RAFI Party; Shin Bet.

Ha-Remishimah ha-Mitkadement le-Shalom

see Progressive List for Peace.

Ha-Reshimah ha-Aravit ha-Me'uhedet

see Unified Arab List.

HARIRI, RAFIQ AL- (1944–): Lebanese political figure, born in Sidon into a working-class family. In 1966, leaving Beirut Arab University after only a year, Hariri emigrated to Saudi Arabia, where he pursued a business career that made him one of the wealthiest people in the Middle East. He obtained Saudi nationality in 1978. He worked for five years as a teacher and accountant in a construction company before founding his own construction business, Siconest, in partnership with the French firm Oger in 1970. Siconest thrived in the 1970s oil boom and Hariri bought out his partner in 1978. In 1980 he opened a Lebanese branch of Oger International, which became the largest construction firm in the Middle East. He also became director of the Lebanese Bank of Commerce, the Mediterranean Bank, and the Saudi Bank, as well as the principal shareholder in the Saudi-Lebanese Bank and the Mediterranean Investors Group. In 1987 he was authorized by the French minister of economy to buy parts of the French banks Suez and Paribas. In August 1992 he merged two smaller French banks to create the French Bank of the Orient. He also controls insurance, engineering, computer, advertising, and broadcasting businesses, the last being especially important to his political career, and his political party publishes a newspaper.

In Lebanon, Hariri used money as an entrée to public life. He created the Islamic Institute for Higher Education, now known as the Hariri Foundation, in 1979; it gives grants to Lebanese students both in Lebanon and abroad. During the 1980s and 1990s he spent freely on many Lebanese and Syrian politicians and political groups (he is reported to have built a palace and given it to President Hafiz al-Asad). In September 1983 he served as an intermediary between Saudi leaders and the Druze leader Walid Jumblatt; six days later, during the Ta'if negotiations, he was a Saudi mediator, which was the beginning of his career in Lebanese politics proper. When the civil war of 1975 through 1990 ended, he promoted a project to reconstruct central Beirut, which had been destroyed by the Israeli siege in 1982 and by the ongoing civil war. On 22 October 1992, after the fall of the Rashid Solh regime, he was appointed prime minister, largely on the basis of his international financial connections, leading to a speedy revaluation of the Lebanese pound in international markets. He backed the creation, in May 1994, of the Solidere Civil Land Society, of which he is the main shareholder. This entity, financed mainly through international borrowing by the Lebanese government, controls a massive program of reconstruction and development of central Beirut (sometimes known as Haririgrad), with the work executed mostly through Hariri's companies and plentiful fees for intermediaries and subcontractors. Several parliamentarians have accused him of mixing politics and business.

In May 1995 he resigned and was reelected to the office of prime minister. In the legislative elections of September 1996, his party won the majority of the seats in Beirut, to the detriment of a portion of the Sunni bourgeoisie traditionally elected there. On 7 November 1996 he was again chosen to form a government. On 27 November 1998, after the election of Émile Lahoud as president of the republic, he resigned from his position as prime minister and was replaced by Selim al-Hoss. Determined to make a political comeback, he created his own party, al-Mustaqbal. In the Lebanese legislative elections of 3 September 2000, his list, which included Christian and Druze leaders, won eighteen of the nineteen seats for the city of Beirut, making him the principal leader of the Lebanese opposition. On 23 October he was named prime minister with the support of 106 of the 128 deputies in the Lebanese parliament. On 6 November, after five days of debate marked by the question of the Syrian presence in Lebanon, parliament gave its approval to his government's declaration of general policy. With thirty ministries, the cabinet of Rafiq Hariri represented all Lebanese parliamentary tendencies except for Hizbullah and General Michel Aoun. Hariri resigned from his post on 15 April 2003 but was asked to form another government the next day. His largest ongoing problem has been the economic consequences of the Lebanese government's debt.

SEE ALSO Aoun, Michel; Asad, Hafiz al-; Hizbullah; Hoss, Selim al-; Jumblatt, Walid Kamal.

HASAN, HANI AL- (Abu Hasan, Abu Tariq; 1937–): Palestinian political figure born in Haifa, Palestine, brother of Khalid al-Hasan. Having become a refugee in Lebanon in 1948, at the time of the first Arab-Israeli conflict, Hani al-Hasan studied in Lebanon and then in Germany, where he obtained a degree in engineering. He was elected president of the General Union of Palestinian Students in Europe in 1958. A member of Fatah since its formation in 1959, he joined the *fida'iyyun* in Jordan and became the movement spokesperson. Between 1969 and 1973, as a refugee in Lebanon, he served in the political section of the Palestine Liberation Organization (PLO), where among other responsibilities he was in charge of relations with China and Romania. In July 1976, in the midst of the Lebanese crisis, he attempted in vain to persuade Yasir Arafat to accept Syrian help. In 1979, after being named to the Fatah's central committee, he became PLO ambassador to Iran, where he remained until 1981. Between 1982 and 1987 he was PLO representative in Jordan and a political advisor to Arafat. During this period he also was a roving ambassador to a number of countries, including Morocco, Egypt, and France. In May 1989 he became the head of a committee responsible for contacts between the PLO leadership and France, a body created after Arafat's Paris visit. After September 1990, in spite of his loyalty to Arafat, he openly expressed his opposition to Arafat's policies and his manner of directing the movement. During the Gulf crisis he was against the PLO siding with Iraq and became one of the leaders of the opposition in Fatah. In July 1991 Arafat relieved him of leadership of the committee on relations with France, and al-Hasan was put in charge of overseeing the activities of Fatah in Jordan. Opposed to the Israel-Palestinian accord of 13 September 1993 because of form but not its basic principle, he declined the post of ambassador to Jordan. Hasan returned to the Gaza Strip in 1995 and became Arafat's chief diplomatic advisor. He was appointed interior minister of the Palestinian Authority in October 2002 but left the cabinet in April 2003. He remains on the central committee of Fatah.

SEE ALSO Arafat, Yasir; Fatah, al-; Gaza Strip; General Union of Palestinian Students; Hasan, Khalid al-; Palestine Liberation Organization; Palestinian Authority.

HASAN, KHALID AL- (Abu Said; 1928–1994): Palestinian political figure and brother of Hani al-Hasan, born in Haifa, Palestine. Khalid al-Hasan became a refugee in Lebanon in 1948, during the first Arab-Israeli conflict. Between 1949 and 1951, as a student at the American University of Beirut, he took part in the activities of the Islamic Liberation Party before going to Kuwait, where in 1959, with Yasir Arafat, he participated in the creation of Fatah, taking responsibility for information and propaganda and becoming the movement's main ideologue. His activities in Arab countries, in particular Saudi Arabia, allowed Fatah, and afterwards the Palestine Liberation Organization (PLO), to obtain significant financial support. Between 1960 and 1967 he was a member of the City Council of Kuwait City and from 1968 to 1974 he was head of the PLO's political department. Opposed to terrorist tactics, he found himself often at odds with Arafat, who recommended armed action; he also reproached Arafat for his alliance with the Palestinian left.

As president of the foreign relations commission of the Palestinian National Council (PNC), in November 1988 he met with three Jewish American leaders to whom he explained the tenor of the PNC resolution on the creation of the Palestinian state and recognition of the Jewish state. In 1991, during the Gulf War, he distanced himself from Arafat's pro-Iraqi position. In September 1993, favoring the creation of a Jordanian-Palestinian federation, he criticized the tenor of the Israeli-Palestinian accords signed in Washington, particularly on the fate of Palestinian refugees. He withdrew from political activity because of illness and died in Rabat.

SEE ALSO Arafat, Yasir; Fatah, al-; Hasan, Hani al-; Islamic Liberation Party; Palestine Liberation Organization.

HASHD

SEE Jordanian People's Democratic Party.

HASHIM, AL-: The ruling family of Jordan. The al-Hashim dynasty (also referred to as Hashimis, or Hashimites) has borne this name for a millennium, and from it sprang the sharifs of Mecca, guardians of the holy sites of Islam. The dynasty claims descent from Ali Hashim, great-grandfather of the prophet Muhammad. The Hashimites ruled in the Hijaz (western Arabian Peninsula) from the twelfth century until 1925, when the Saudis conquered the province and expelled them. In return for their help against the Ottomans in World War I—the Arab Revolt against the Turks was led by Husayn ibn Ali al-Hashim, king of Hijaz and sharif of Mecca—the British installed as king of Iraq in 1921 a Hashimite prince, Faysal ibn Hussein, Sharif Hussein's son. Faysal had ruled Syria in 1920 until he was dislodged by the French; he and his descendants reigned in Iraq until the regime was overthrown in 1958. The British allowed another of Sharif Husayn's sons, Abdullah ibn Hussein (Abdullah I), to become emir of Transjordan (after 1946 the Hashimite Kingdom of Jordan) on condition that he accept the British Mandate and not attempt to restore his brother to the throne in Syria.

SEE ALSO Abdullah I ibn Hussein; British Mandate.

HASHIMITE

SEE Hashim, al-.

HASHEM, AL-

SEE Hashim, al-.

HA-SHOMER HA-TZAʿIR: A socialist-Zionist youth movement, ha-Shomer ha-Tzaʿir was founded in 1913, unifying the Zionist youth organizations in Poland and Galicia into one movement. Its name, which means "Young Guardian," was also the name of the largest of the existing youth organizations as well as that of a Jewish militia organization in Palestine. The new organization placed emphasis on settlement, and in 1919 ha-Shomer ha-Tzaʿir sent its first group of settlers to Palestine. By 1924 its membership was more than 10,000. In the 1920s and 1930s it developed a Marxist-Zionist ideology, and many of its members envisioned a socialist Palestine that would work with the Soviet Union to bring about a worldwide workers' revolution. By 1940 ha-Shomer ha-Tzaʿir had grown to a membership of over 70,000 with thirty-nine kibbutzim in Palestine.

Because it had favored the creation of a binational Arab-Jewish state in Palestine, ha-Shomer ha-Tzaʿir had little influence on the politics of the Zionist movement in Palestine preceding the creation of the State of Israel in 1948. That year, when several socialist factions joined together to form MAPAM, or the United Workers' Party, ha-Shomer ha-Tzaʿir became its youth movement. It has remained active primarily as an educational movement.

SEE ALSO MAPAM.

HASID

SEE Hasidism

HASIDISM: Jewish pietist movement, born in the eighteenth century in the Ukraine and Poland, under the impetus of Israel ben Eliezer, called "Baal Shem Tov." Hasidism taught that man should unite with God through meditation, contemplation, study and respect for the ascetic life. It was inspired by the Kabbalah, but in practice it was in opposition to the hermetic doctrine from which it emerged, which was meant for an intellectual elite. The founder of Hasidism and his companions were opposed to religious austerity, emphasizing joy and fervor of prayer. The ideas and doctrine of this movement came into conflict with the traditional rabbinate, whose principal leader was Eliahu ben Shlomo, called the Gaon of Vilna. The Hasidim believed in the sanctity of the earth itself, and so lived there without accepting the political authority of the state. Hasidism accorded priority to the religious fervor of the chant over intellectual knowledge of the Torah, also considering dancing as a prayer and as a way of achieving spiritual ecstasy and elevation. Gradually, through various migratory waves, this movement developed in Europe, North America, and Israel.

SEE ALSO Kabbalah; Torah.

HASSAN OF JORDAN (1947–): Royal prince and former crown prince (1965–1999) of Jordan. Hassan ibn Talal al-Hashem is the son of King Talal and the younger brother of King Hussein. He has a degree in history and economics from Oxford University. On 1 April 1965 King Hussein designated him crown prince of the Hashimite kingdom in place of King Hussein's son, Abdullah, who was three years old. In 1968, while studying in England, Hassan married the daughter of the Pakistani ambassador to London. When he returned to his country, King Hussein assigned him economic and administrative duties. In July 1970 he founded the Jordan Scientific Academy and two years later a commercial bank, the Housing Bank. He also participated in establishing the Century Corporation Industry Group. In June 1976 King Hussein entrusted him with reorganizing the Jordanian administration. In 1980 he founded the Academy for Research on Islamic Civilization and then the Arab Forum (al-Muntada al-Arabi). In April 1989, while he was in charge of the regency during his brother's absence, his success in dealing with five days of rioting strengthened his credibility among the Jordanian people. Between 1992 and 1997 his involvement in the affairs of his country became more and more noticeable. He participated in Jordanian-Israeli peace negotiations, as well as in various conferences on economic development in the Middle East.

In July 1998 King Hussein was hospitalized in the United States; during that time he gave Hassan control of the regency, which Jordanians saw as a transfer of power. Hassan's direct interference in certain internal matters led to conflicts with a number of highly placed Jordanian leaders. On 23 January 1999, after returning from the United States, King Hussein stripped Hassan of the titles of prince regent and crown prince, giving them to his eldest son, Prince Abdullah, who succeeded him as Abdullah II on 7 February. Hassan holds no official position. He is the chairman of a think tank called the Arab Thought Forum and is involved with the World Conference on Religions for Peace, a private group based in New York. In early 2004 he was rumored to have ambitions to restore the Hashimite dynasty

CROWN PRINCE, NOT KING. THE YOUNGER BROTHER OF KING HUSSEIN OF JORDAN, HASSAN IBN TALAL (SHOWN IN A 1996 PHOTOGRAPH) WAS THE CROWN PRINCE OF THE HASHEMITE KINGDOM FROM 1965 TO 1999. THEN KING HUSSEIN GAVE HASSAN'S TITLES TO PRINCE ABDULLAH, THE KING'S ELDEST SON, WHO SUCCEEDED TO THE THRONE WHEN HUSSEIN DIED TWO WEEKS LATER. *(AP/Wide World Photos)*

to the throne of Iraq, with himself as king, but he has denied this.

SEE ALSO Hashim, al-; Hussein ibn Talal; Talal ibn Abdullah.

HA-TEHIYAH("National Renaissance"): Ultranationalist Israeli party created in October 1979 by dissidents from Herut under the impetus of Ge'ula Cohen and Moshe Samir. This group resulted from a split in the Israeli right, following the Israeli-Egyptian peace accord of the previous year. Ha-Tehiyah advocated maintaining an Israeli presence in all of the occupied territories, even Sinai. In July 1980, Cohen proposed a draft bill on the city of Jerusalem, "united city and eternal capital of Israel," for which she succeeded in gaining the support of Prime Minister Menachem Begin. As a result of the elections of July 1981, ha-Tehiyah won three seats, allowing the government of Begin to enjoy a narrow majority in the Knesset. In October 1983, Professor Yuval Ne'eman was named science minister in the government of Yitzhak Shamir. The following month ha-Tehiyah allied itself for a few months with the new extremist block of General Eitan, Tzomet. In February 1984, Cohen proposed restricting the election of the members of Knesset to Israelis who had done their military service, which consequently would have disqualified the Arab members of the Knesset. As a result of the elections of July 1984, Ha-Tehiyah, allied to the extremist settlers' movement, Gush Emunim, strengthened its position, winning five seats. However, dissension between religious and nonreligious ultranationalists in the movement weakened the Tehiyah-Gush Emunim alliance. Anticipating that the elections of June 1988 would be held in the shadow of the Intifada, the program of ha-Tehiyah proposed: 1) "Peace against peace, without ceding an inch of ground; 2) Augmenting the number of settlements, so as to assure their security; 3) Israeli sovereignty over the West Bank and the Gaza Strip." In the elections ha-Tehiyah won only three seats, many militants having preferred to support Tzomet. In June 1990, backed by the deputies of Likud and those of the far right, Prime Minister Yitzhak Shamir decided to form a new cabinet, in which Professor Ne'eman was again science minister. Six months later, Ne'eman resigned after the Israeli government announced its intention of starting negotiations with the Palestinians. In April 1992, preparing for the Knesset elections of the following June, ha-Tehiyah joined with the extreme right party Moledet. The electoral defeat of the Israeli right led to the disappearance of ha-Tehiyah from the political stage, most of its members joining the ranks of Tzomet or the Likud.

SEE ALSO Begin, Menachem; Cohen, Geʾula; Gush Emunim; Herut; Intifada (1987–1993); Likud; Moledet; Ne'eman, Yuval; Shamir, Yitzhak; Tzomet Party.

HA-TIKVA (*Ha Tikvah*; "The Hope", in Hebrew): National anthem of the State of Israel.

HA-TSOFEH (*The Observer,* "The Scout," in Hebrew): Israeli daily created in 1938, considered the organ of the National Religious Party.

SEE ALSO National Religious Party.

HA-TZOHAR (Hebrew acronym for "Revisionist Zionists"): Radical Jewish movement, founded in 1925. This political party (also known as the Union of Zionist-Revisionists) was founded in Paris by Vladimir Jabotinsky and a group of mostly Russian Zionists who sought a return to the original aims of Zionism with principles espoused by Theodor Herzl. The union's platform actually reflected Jabotinsky's ideology: the future establishment of a Jewish state on both sides of the Jordan River under Jewish sovereignty. In advance of that, a colonization regime would be set up to create the conditions necessary to achieve a demographic Jewish majority, considered a prerequisite for a state.

The movement grew rapidly—particularly in Poland and other parts of Eastern Europe—and by the end of the 1920s the union was the major opposition party, becoming the party of the Zionist Right or even Zionist fascism. One major point of controversy with official Zionism was the union's "independent diplomacy," which was expressed primarily to obtain the support of European countries, particularly Poland, to pressure Britain in the Mandate Council of the League of Nations in Geneva. The movement's growth in popularity brought about many points of contention between the revisionists and "official" followers of Zionism. These differences were often expressed in acts of violence until 1933 when the moderates dropped out of the union and founded a small independent party called the Jewish State Party. Beginning in the mid-1930s, the union began legal and illegal efforts to encourage a mass emigration of 700,000 to 1.5 million Jews from Europe to Palestine within a ten-year period.

SEE ALSO British Mandate; Herzl, Theodor; Jabotinsky, Vladimir Ze᾽ev.

HAWARI, COLONEL

SEE Hawari Group.

HAWARI GROUP: Palestinian group created in February 1979 by the central committee of Fatah in order to take charge of some of the Fatah leadership's security needs and carry out special operations. Rising out of differences in Force 17 and placed under the command of Abdullah Abd al-Hamid Labib (Colonel Hawari), this splinter group was controlled directly by Yasir Arafat and benefited from Iraqi help. It is known to have carried out several terrorist attacks in the 1980s, including exploding a bomb on an American airliner in 1986, killing four people. After it was expelled from Tunisia in 1987, it lost its operational capacities, then disappeared in June 1991 after the death of its leader.

SEE ALSO Arafat, Yasir; Fatah, al-; Force 17.

HAWATMA, NAYIF (Abu al-Nuf; 1935–): Palestinian political figure, born in as-Salt, Jordan, to a Greek Orthodox family. In 1954, while enrolled at Cairo University's Faculty of Medicine, Hawatma joined the Nasserist Arab Nationalist Movement (ANM) of George Habash, who was a friend of his. He returned to Jordan in 1956, during the Suez War, but fled the country in 1957 after participating in anti-regime activities, for which he was sentenced to death in absentia. In 1958 he took part in factional fighting in Lebanon, then fled to Iraq, where a Hashimite king had just been overthrown, and became the head of the Iraqi branch of the ANM. Imprisoned in July 1962 in Baghdad, he was liberated in February 1963, at the time of the Ba῾thist coup d'état, only to be expelled two months later to South Yemen, where he participated, with the Liberation Front, in the struggle against the British presence. In 1967, after an amnesty had been declared, he returned to Jordan. In January 1968, after the Arab defeat in the 1967 War, he participated, with George Habash and Ahmad Jibril, in the creation of the Popular Front for the Liberation of Palestine (PFLP), within which, along with Ibrahim Mohsen, he represented the Marxist current. In February 1969 he quit the PFLP to found, with Yasir Abd Rabbo, the Democratic Popular Front for the Liberation of Palestine, known after August 1974 as the Democratic Front for the Liberation of Palestine (DFLP). This new organization became part of the Palestine Liberation Organization (PLO) and followed a political line at the far left of the Palestinian spectrum.

In January 1970 his movement established its first contacts with leftist Israeli parties, including Matzpen. His intention was to begin a dialogue based on the provisions of United Nations (UN) Security Council Resolution 242. In June 1970 Hawatma was elected to the PLO's central committee. Advocating the abolition of the Hashimite regime, the DFLP participated, along with the PFLP, in battles with the Jordanian army in August and September 1970 and July 1971. After their expulsion from Jordan, Hawatma and his organization settled in Lebanon, where from August 1973 he espoused the creation of a Palestinian state in the West Bank and Gaza, alongside the Israeli state. Accused of capitulating to Israel, he was the object of two assassination attempts. He stayed in contact with leaders of the Israeli left and recommended an alliance with Arab Communist Parties. From 1975 on he favored a rapprochement with Syria, and in 1977, after the visit of Egyptian President Anwar al-Sadat to Israel, he joined the Rejection Front. In 1978 he broke ties with Baghdad after having sided with Tehran in the Iraq-Iran conflict. Backed by the Soviet Union, he became more strident in his opposition in the PLO. In March

1984, along with George Habash, he founded the Palestinian Democratic Alliance, which united the DFLP, PFLP, Palestine Communist Party, and a part of the Palestine Liberation Front in an attempt to counter the influence of Fatah in the Palestine movements. The project failed rapidly as personality conflicts took priority over political purposes. In April 1987, after the dissolution of the Democratic Alliance, he decided that the DFLP would rejoin the PLO executive committee, as the PFLP had done. On 17 September, accompanied by Habash, he went to Jordan, where he hadn't been for twenty years; there the two men were received by King Hussein. This reconciliation, facilitated by the Gulf crisis, allowed the resumption of relations between the DFLP, the PFLP, and Jordan.

Hawatma opposed the Madrid Conference of October 1991, and the DFLP was torn between his partisans and Yasir Abd Rabbo's, who favored the peace process. Abd Rabbo and his followers broke from the DFLP to create a new organization, the Palestinian Democratic Union. On 10 September 1993 Hawatma opposed the Israeli-Palestinian accord, which was to be signed three days later, and he and Habash announced their resignation from the PLO executive committee. In October both took their organizations into opposition in the Alliance of Palestinian Forces. On 25 October 1999, after meeting with Yasir Arafat in Cairo, Hawatma announced his support for the peace process. In an interview, he declared that the struggle of the DFLP was at once "political and diplomatic." In April 2001, while the al-Aqsa Intifada was developing in the Palestinian territories, the leadership of the DFLP launched an appeal for a general mobilization of the Palestinian people and armed resistance against Israel. It took credit for a raid on an Israeli post in the Gaza Strip but in general, in contrast to its earlier years, the DFLP has not been very active. It is much reduced in size and is believed to have about 500 members. In early 2002 Palestinian Authority security began, under Israeli pressure, to round up the members of the DFLP, PFLP, and other groups, leading to public protests against Arafat, but after Israeli attacks in Jenin and Ramallah these groups called for unity among Palestinian political factions. Hawatma has published a number of books and articles on Palestine and the resistance.

SEE ALSO Abd Rabbo, Yasir; Alliance of Palestinian Forces (APF); Aqsa Intifada, al-; Arab-Israel War (1967); Arab Nationalist Movement; Arafat, Yasir; Ba'th; Black September; Democratic Front for the Liberation of Palestine; Habash, George; Hashim, al-; Gaza Strip; Madrid Conference; Matzpen; Palestine Communist Party; Palestine Liberation Organization; Palestinian Democratic Union; Popular Front for the Liberation of Palestine; Rejection Front; Resolution 242; Sadat, Anwar al-; Suez Crisis; West Bank.

HAY'A AL-AMILA LI-TAHRIR FILASTIN AL-

SEE Arab Organization for the Liberation of Palestine.

HAYAT, AL- ("life", in Arabic): Lebanese newspaper, founded in 1946. Its editor in chief, Kamil Mruweh, was assassinated in 1966. The newspaper ceased publication from 1975 to 1988 and resurfaced in 1989. Financed by Saudi sponsors, *al-Hayat* is published in Beirut, Cairo, London, Paris, and New York. It can be found online at http://www.daralhayat.com

HEBREW: A Semitic language whose origin, according to Biblical tradition, is Shem, Noah's second son, whose descendents populated the Middle East. Along with Phoenician, and Ugaritic, Hebrew constitutes the Canaanite branch, an evolved form of the language used by the inhabitants of the Land of Canaan before the arrival of the Israelites. A dead language for many centuries, Hebrew became once more a spoken language due to the efforts of Eliezar ben Yehuda (Yitzhak Perlman) in the nineteenth century. Hebrew is the official language of the State of Israel. The most ancient known Hebrew inscription is from the Gezer calendar of 950 B.C.E.

SEE ALSO Canaan.

HEBREW CALENDAR: Israelite time began on the day of Creation, set by tradition on 7 October 3760 B.C.E., a lag of 3760 years in relation to the Gregorian calendar. The Hebrew calendar was established definitively in the fifth century C.E., during the talmudic epoch. The Israelite year is a compromise between the lunar year and the solar year, its duration varying within a cycle of 19 years, which includes 12 common years of 12 months (29/30 days) and 7 embolismic years, each having an extra month of 30 days.

SEE ALSO Gregorian Calendar; Talmud.

HEBREWS: Early name of a Semitic people of the ancient East, descended from the line of Abraham, whose ancestors today define themselves as "Jews". Hebrew may have come from the word *habirou*, or *habiru*, designating tribes who left Egypt for the Canaanite kingdoms after the death of Amenophis IV (Ikhnaton, 1334/1334 B.C.), or from the word *ibrim*, designating "those beyond the sons of Abraham." In certain Hebrew writings the name of Abraham appears sometimes under that of the *ibri* (sons of Eber), which also could be the source of the word "Hebrew."

HEBREW UNIVERSITY OF JERUSALEM: Israeli university. Opened in 1925 on Mount Scopus, the university's creation as a Jewish institution teaching in Hebrew was considered a major cultural accomplishment among Zionists. By 1947 over a thousand students were enrolled. After the Arab-Israel War of 1948, the Mount Scopus campus was on the Jordanian side of a divided Jerusalem and a new campus was created at Givat Ram in western Jerusalem; other campuses were later added, including the Hadassah medical school at Ein Kerem. After the 1967 War, the Mount Scopus campus was rebuilt as the university's main campus. On 31 July 2002 a bombing of the student cafeteria killed nine and wounded several dozen others. In 2003 nearly 23,000 students, including both Arab and Jewish Israelis, were enrolled in a range of advanced degree programs.

SEE ALSO Arab-Israel War (1967).

HEBRON: Ancient Canaanite city of Judea, now part of the West Bank, where Jewish, Christian, and Muslim traditions situate the burial place of Abraham, Isaac, Jacob, Sarah, Rebekah, and Leah. The site is known to Jews as the Cave (or Tomb) of the Patriarchs (*Mearath ha-Makhpela,* in Hebrew) and to Muslims as the Sanctuary of Abraham the Friend (*al-Haram al-Ibrahimi al-Khalil,* in Arabic) or the Ibrahim Mosque. The Arabic name for the city is *al-Khalil*; the Hebrew is *Hevron*; both mean "friend," a reference to Abraham, who in sacred Muslim literature is known as "the Friend of God" or "the Friend of the Merciful" (*al-Khalil al-Rahman*). For Jews, Hebron—which in the Bible was called Qiryat Arba (City of the Four) before the time of Abraham—is one of the four holy cities of Eretz Yisrael, along with Jerusalem, Safed, and Tiberias. According to Biblical tradition, on the death of King Saul, toward 1010 B.C.E., David was proclaimed King of Israel in Hebron, which became his first capital. The original structure enclosing the cave was built by King Herod the Great (r. 37–4 B.C.E.). The Byzantine rulers made it into a church, and when the Muslims conquered Hebron in 636 C.E. they rebuilt it as a mosque. In 1100 Crusaders took over the city and expelled the Jews. They destroyed the mosque and the Synagogue of the Caves, building in their place a church dedicated to Saint Abraham. In 1187, after the victory of Saladin over the Crusaders, the mosque was reconstructed. In 1267, a Mamluk sultan, Baybars I, declared that Jews would no longer be allowed to visit the tomb of Abraham. This interdiction stayed in effect until June 1967.

A Jewish community remained in Hebron and in 1516 the area came under the rule of the Ottomans, who welcomed to their empire many of the Jews who had been expelled from Spain in 1492. In the sixteenth century many Sephardic Jewish families settled in Hebron and the city became a center of Jewish learning. For three centuries, except for the sacking of the city by the Egyptians in 1834, the pace of life in Hebron was slow, and Palestine as a whole was something of a backwater.

Once Zionist settlement began in the 1880s, and especially after World War I, relations between the Jewish and Arab communities became increasingly tense. On 24 August 1929, following the riots over the Western Wall in Jerusalem, Arabs massacred sixty-seven Jews in Hebron, destroying their synagogue and schools. (The city had only one British policeman.) The remaining Jews, many of whom had been protected by their Arab neighbors, fled. Two years later, thirty-five Jewish families returned, but on 23 April 1936, after months of rising tension and the beginning of a Palestinian general strike (called in reaction to the discovery of Zionist arms shipments into the country), British authorities decided to evacuate them. After the departure of the British and the 1948 War, Jordan inherited control of the West Bank, but as a result of the 1967 War, Israel occupied the area.

A messianic interpretation of the conquest of Palestinian territory among ultra-Orthodox Jews encouraged the development of Jewish settlement, and in 1968 the first extremist settlers, under the leadership of Rabbi Moshe Levinger, moved into the center of Hebron, registering at a hotel and declaring themselves a new Jewish community. The Israeli government removed them to a disused army camp outside the city, which in 1972 they were allowed to convert to a permanent settlement, Qiryat Arba, where in 1974 the Gush Emunim movement was born. These armed extremists demanded the right to live anywhere they chose in "Greater Israel."

In 1979 Gush Emunim started a permanent settlement in the ancient Jewish quarter in the heart of the city and refused to leave. They engaged in a standoff with the government and the next year, after

CLASH IN HEBRON. A PALESTINIAN POLICEMAN CONFRONTS A YOUTH THROWING ROCKS AT ISRAELI SOLDIERS IN THE WEST BANK TOWN. HOLY TO JEWS AND MUSLIMS AS THE TRADITIONAL BURIAL SITE OF THE FIRST THREE GENERATIONS OF PATRIARCHS—ABRAHAM, ISAAC, AND JACOB—HEBRON HAS SEEN VIOLENCE BETWEEN ARABS AND JEWS FOR SEVENTY-FIVE YEARS. *(AP/Wide World Photos)*

six yeshiva students returning from the Tomb of the Patriarchs were killed by Palestinians, the settlement was officially recognized. Since that time the presence of these 400 armed settlers, their deliberately provocative behavior, and their desire, of which they make no secret, to expel the Arabs (an estimated population of 137,000 in 2003)—as well as the Israel Defense Force's (IDF) frequent disruption of the city—have led to violent reactions on the part of the Palestinians, followed by severe Israeli reprisals. Toward the end of 1979, a group of settlers from Qiryat Arba and other settlements formed a clandestine militia, which in June 1980 carried out bomb attacks on three West Bank Palestinian mayors. In 1983 this splinter group killed four students of the Islamic College of Hebron. On 25 February 1994, during the Israeli-Palestinian peace process, which had started in Madrid in 1991, an American Jewish settler, Baruch Goldstein, from Qiryat Arba, killed twenty-nine Palestinians worshipping at the Ibrahim Mosque and wounded sixty others before he was beaten to death while reloading his rifle. An official commission found that he had acted alone and condemned his action; his grave has become a shrine for the Jewish settler movement.

In May 1994 the United Nations deployed an unarmed observer unit called the Temporary International Presence in Hebron (TIPH) to try to calm the situation, but its mandate was allowed to run out that August. On 28 September 1995 Israelis and Palestinians signed the second Oslo Accords, dealing with the extension of Palestinian autonomy to the West Bank and providing for the partial withdrawal of Israeli troops from the city of Hebron. The accord led to a wave of violent protests, organized by Israeli settlers and ultra-Orthodox Israelis, followed on 4 November 1995 by the assassination of Israeli Prime Minister Yitzhak Rabin by a Jewish extremist. Israeli-

Palestinian negotiations were suspended. In May 1996 a new TIPH was constituted and deployed; it was reorganized by treaty in 1997. In June 1996 the new Israeli prime minister, Benjamin Netanyahu, declared his lack of confidence in the Oslo Accords. A group of ultranationalist rabbis launched an appeal to Israeli soldiers to disobey any order to withdraw from Hebron. On 15 January 1997, after many months of negotiation, an accord on the city of Hebron was finally signed between the Israelis and Palestinians, providing for the withdrawal of the IDF from four-fifths of the city, with the Jewish inhabitants remaining under the authority of Israel. This accord included a "protocol on the redeployment of the Israeli army in Hebron," a memorandum on the commitments of both parties to future negotiations, and a letter of guarantee by the U.S. Secretary of State Warren Christopher. In the course of the preliminary discussions leading to this accord, the Israeli prime minister insisted that the notion of reciprocity be the basis of future commitments. On 18 January the Israeli army began its withdrawal from Hebron, and the next day Yasir Arafat proclaimed the liberation of the city. Two days later, hundreds of Jewish settlers demonstrated against the retreat of the IDF.

Obstructions of the Israeli-Palestinian peace process and the development of the al-Aqsa Intifada in September 2000 resulted in the non-application of the Hebron accords and in many deadly confrontations between the Jewish and Palestinian communities. In March 2002, two TIPH observers were killed by Palestinians, and TIPH discontinued patrols in the Jewish quarter because of confrontations with settlers. In November 2002, twelve Israeli soldiers were killed in an attack by Palestine Islamic Jihad, and in August 2003 a suicide bombing killed twenty-three. In 2004, 400 to 600 Jews lived in more than twenty settlements in Hebron, and about 6,000 lived outside the city in Qiryat Arba. The Palestinian population was approximately 16,500 in 1922, 80,000 in 1990, and 137,000 in the city and surrounding villages in 2003.

SEE ALSO Abraham; Aqsa Intifada, al-; Arab-Israel War (1967); Arafat, Yasir; Eretz Yisrael; Greater Israel; Gush Emunim; Isaac; Jacob (Biblical); Judea and Samaria; Netanyahu, Benjamin; Oslo Accords II; Palestinian Islamic Jihad; Rabin, Yitzhak; Saladin; West Bank; Western Wall.

HEBRON ACCORDS

SEE Hebron.

HEGIRA

SEE Hijra.

HEGIRA CALENDAR

SEE Islamic Calendar.

HEREM: Hebrew word meaning "banned."

HERUT PARTY ("liberty", in Hebrew): Israeli political party, founded in 1948 by Menachem Begin, until then head of Irgun. Herut advocated the creation of a Jewish state and picked as its slogan "God has chosen us to rule." In the first Knesset elections, in January 1949, Herut obtained 11.5 percent of the votes, becoming the fourth largest party, with fourteen seats in the Knesset, whereas the MAPAI (Labor) won forty-six seats. Between 1953 and 1959, after losing six seats in 1951, Herut strove to gain some of the Sephardic vote, which had tended to favor MAPAI; it won seventeen seats in the Knesset and MAPAI won forty-seven. In April 1965, in order to pose a more effective opposition to Labor, Herut allied itself with the Liberal Party, which had separated from the General Zionists to form a parliamentary bloc, the GAHAL, which had twenty-six seats under its control. In 1966 Begin was reproached for weakening the party and on 1 June 1967, just before the 1967 War, he joined the Labor-led government of Levi Eshkol as minister without portfolio. Several other members of GAHAL also joined Eshkol's cabinet. In October 1969, with twenty-six seats in the Knesset, as opposed to fifty-six for the Labor bloc, six members of the GAHAL bloc entered the Labor government of Golda Meir. Among them, Ezer Weizman, in transportation, was the first general to have joined a rightist party. In August 1970 Begin and his GAHAL allies resigned their positions as soon as the government's acceptance of the Rogers Plan was announced.

During the spring of 1973, Likud ("Consolidation"), a coalition of the Israel right, was constituted under Ariel Sharon, Menachem Begin, and Yitzhak Shamir, and led by Begin. It united Herut, the Liberal Party, the Free Center, and the Movement for Greater Israel. During August 1976, after the death of his brother in the Israeli raid on Entebbe, Benjamin Netanyahu joined Herut. At the year's end, in anticipation of the coming elections, Sharon resigned from the Likud coalition to create his own political group, Shlomzion. In May of the following year, the Likud bloc won the legislative elections with forty-three seats against the Labor

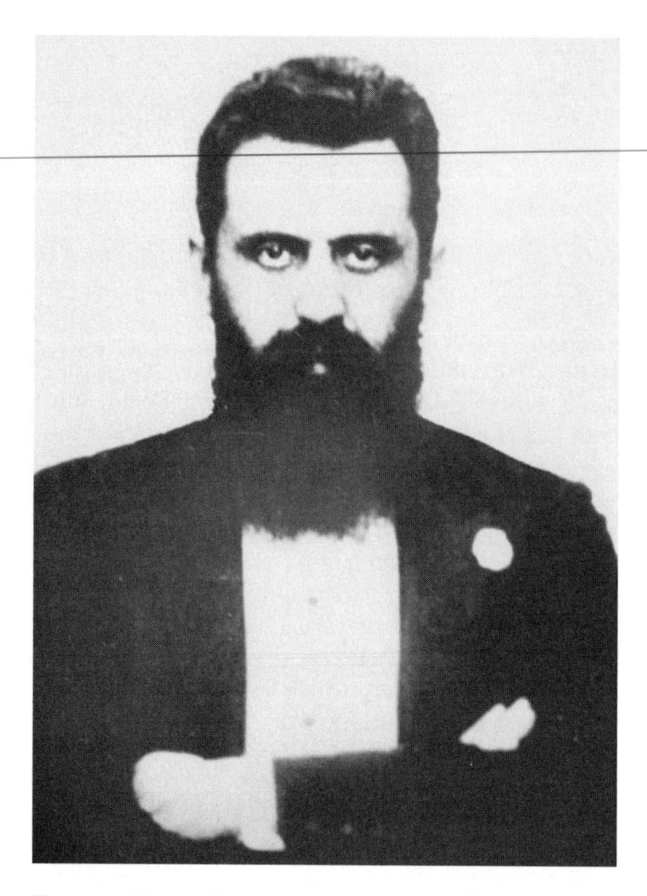

THEODOR HERZL. THE FOUNDER OF POLITICAL ZIONISM, HERZL WROTE A GROUNDBREAKING BOOK IN 1896, THEN ESTABLISHED A WORLDWIDE ZIONIST ORGANIZATION AND A FUND TO BUY LAND IN PALESTINE FROM THE OTTOMAN EMPIRE AND SUPPORT IMMIGRATION TO ESTABLISH A JEWISH HOMELAND THERE. IN JUST EIGHT YEARS, HERZL LAID THE FOUNDATION FOR WHAT BECAME THE STATE OF ISRAEL FORTY-FOUR YEARS AFTER HIS DEATH.

Party's thirty-two. Sharon's group, with two seats, joined with the Likud coalition. Since 1977 Herut has existed as the senior partner of the Likud coalition, and the Herut/Likud bloc has formed the basis of most Israeli governments since then.

SEE ALSO Arab-Israel War (1967); Begin, Menachem; Irgun; Likud; Netanyahu, Benjamin; Rogers Plan; Shamir, Yitzhak; Sharon, Ariel; Weizman, Ezer.

HERZL, THEODOR (1860–1904): Born in Budapest in May 1860, died in Austria in 1904. Theodor Herzl, journalist and writer, is considered the founder of political Zionism. In 1894, as a correspondent in Paris, then literary contributor to the Neue Freie Presse, he was struck by the anti-Semitism that the Dreyfus affair brought to light, posing questions about the assimilation of the Jews. In his 1896 book *The Jewish State,* he propounded his conception of Zionism, proposing the creation of a state that would allow Jews to live with dignity and in security. The following year he organized a meeting of the First Zionist Congress at Basel, in the course of which a strategy aimed at the purchase of land in Palestine was adopted. The project launched by Herzl was supported by Russian Jews who had been victims of pogroms, but met resistance from German and French Jews, who were better integrated into their countries. Theodor Herzl first turned to the Ottoman Sultan in Constantinople, so as to persuade him to "restore" a part of Palestine to the Jews. On 17 June 1901, the Sultan received him and informed him of his intention of extending special protection to the Jews, who he envisaged settling in Turkish territory, in exchange for their creating a fund that would be used to pay off the Turkish debt. A Jewish National Fund was established to finance Jewish emigration to Palestine. In 1902 Theodor Herzl published a utopian novel, *Altneuland* (Old-New Land), in which he depicted a new society where technological advances would allow the resolution of social conflicts. In May 1903, the British minister of colonies, Joseph Chamberlain, proposed Uganda as a place for a Jewish homeland. On 23 August of the same year, the British proposition was rejected by the Zionist Congress. On 3 July 1904, Theodor Herzl died in Austria, and David Wolffson succeeded him at the head of the organization.

SEE ALSO Zionism.

HERZOG, CHAIM (1918–1997): Israeli military and political figure born in 1918, in Belfast (Ireland), died in 1997. In 1936, Chaim Herzog came to Israel, where he joined up with the Haganah. Two years later he returned to Great Britain to study law. At the outbreak of World War II he enlisted in the British Army, where he served as an officer in the intelligence service. In 1946 he married Ora Ambash, whose sister was the wife of Abba Eban. He finished his legal studies in Palestine and became the head of the security section of the Jewish Agency. At the time of the first Arab-Israel war in 1948, he was assigned to the Israeli intelligence services. Two years later he was named military attaché to the Israeli embassy in Washington. In 1957 he returned to Israel and became commander of the Central military region. After three years as commander Herzog was promoted to the rank of general and became head of the Aman (Israeli military intelligence service). Two years later, he resigned from the army to start a law career and then a political one. In 1965 he joined the

CHAIM HERZOG. AN IMPORTANT EARLY FIGURE IN ISRAELI MILITARY INTELLIGENCE AND COMMAND, HERZOG WAS THE FIRST MILITARY GOVERNOR OF THE OCCUPIED WEST BANK AND THEN THE ISRAELI AMBASSADOR TO THE UNITED NATIONS. HE CULMINATED HIS CAREER WITH TWO ELECTIONS IN THE 1980S AS PRESIDENT OF ISRAEL.

RAFI Party, along with David Ben-Gurion and Shimon Peres. In June, during the 1967 War, he became the leading military commentator on Israel's national radio, Kol Israel. After the war's end, he resumed his service in the Israel Defense Force to become the first military governor of the occupied West Bank. In 1969 he quit the army for a career in the Israel Labor Party. In 1975 he was named Israeli ambassador to the United Nations. In 1983, two years after having been elected Member of Knesset on the Labor ticket, he was a candidate to succeed Yitzhak Navon as the president of the Jewish state. Much to everyone's surprise, he was elected to the presidency, partly owing to the backing of the Sephardi party, TAMI. In 1988 he was reelected for a second term. Herzog died in Apri1 1997, at the age of 79. For many Israelis he remains "the president of the Jewish people" because of the great efforts he made to tighten the ties between the Diaspora and the Jewish state.

SEE ALSO Aman; Arab-Israel War (1967); Ben-Gurion, David; Diaspora; Eban, Abba; Haganah; Israel Defense Force; Israel Labor Party; Jewish Agency for Israel; Peres, Shimon; RAFI Party; TAMI; West Bank.

HESHVAN: Name of the second month of the Hebrew calendar, corresponding to the end of October and the beginning of November.

SEE ALSO Hebrew Calendar.

HEZBALLAH

SEE Hizbullah.

HEZBOLLAH

SEE Hizbullah.

HIBBAT ZION: The first international Zionist organization, Hibbat Zion was founded in 1884 by Leo Pinsker, a Russian doctor practicing in Odessa, following the Russian pogroms of 1881 and 1882. Pinsker argued that Jews of the Diaspora were not safe in their adopted homes and asserted that liberation could be achieved only by establishing a national homeland in Palestine. His organization consisted of Jewish traditionalists as well as secular nationalists from Eastern Europe. This mixed membership created internal differences. At the bidding of its orthodox members, Hibbat Zion offered financial aid to settlers in Palestine only if they agreed to observe Judaism and its traditions. Secular nationalists like Pinsker were troubled by this policy, and differences continued to plague the organization. It did manage to establish a few colonies, including Petah Tikvah, and it is thought to have influenced the growth of other Zionist groups in Eastern Europe.

HIJAB: Traditional scarf worn by Muslim women to cover their hair.

HIJAZ: Coastal, mountainous region of the Red Sea located in Saudi Arabia, stretching north to south, and toward the interior of the country. The principal cities of the Hijaz are Mecca and Medina, holy sites of Islam; Jeddah, Ta'if, and Yanbu.

HIJRA ("migration", in Arabic): The voyage of prophet Muhammad from Mecca to Medina in July 622 (12 *rabi al-awwal*) to escape the hostility of the Meccans. The word has also been interpreted to mean "breaking old ties," that is, marking the break between the time of ignorance and the time of knowledge. Muhammad's *hijra* marks the beginning of the Muslim calendar; thus Muslim dates are referred to as *hijri* years, or A.H. (anno hegirae).

SEE ALSO Muhammad.

HILONI: Hebrew word utilized to designate a secular Jew.

HILULA: Hebrew word used to designate a pilgrimage to the tomb of a Jewish sage.

HINDI, AMIN AL- (Abu Zuhayr; 1939–): Palestinian activist, born in Gaza, Palestine. Between 1968 and 1972 Amin al-Hindi was secretary of the Palestinian Student Union in Berlin, where he was a student. After joining Fatah, he was assigned to the security services, headed by Salah Khalaf. At the end of 1972 he joined the radical Iqab group, backed by Libya and considered a branch of the Black September Organization. In September 1973, while participating in preparations for an attack on an Israeli El Al plane, he was arrested in Ostia, Italy, with four other Palestinians, among whom was Atef Bseisso. The five were freed a few weeks later by the Italian authorities. On 5 November 1975 he was sent by Yasir Arafat to King Hassan II of Morocco with a message of support on the question of the Moroccan Sahara. Two years later al-Hindi became the leader of the organization section of Fatah, maintaining contacts with Cuban, East German, Yugoslavian, and other information services. In 1981 he was elected to the Fatah revolutionary council and became one of Khalaf's principal assistants. In 1982 he followed Arafat into exile in Tunis, where he kept his post in al-Fatah's unified security leadership. In February 1991, after the assassinations of Khalaf and of Hayel Abdul Hamid, he became interim head of security services under Arafat's direct control and was often in touch with significant Arab and European security figures. On 17 September 1993, during the application of the Israeli-Palestinian accords on partial autonomy of the Palestinian territories, Arafat named him head of the Palestinian foreign intelligence service. In 2004 he headed the General Intelligence Service in the Gaza Strip and held the rank of major general. He has been proposed as Palestinian Authority interior minister if and when Israel withdraws from Gaza.

SEE ALSO Arafat, Yasir; Black September Organization; Fatah, al-; Gaza Strip; Iqab; Khalaf, Salah; Palestinian Authority.

HISTADRUT: Israeli federation of labor; in full, ha-Histadrut ha-Klalit shel ha-Ovdim ha-Irvriim be-Eretz-Yisrael (General Organization of the Jewish Workers in Eretz Yisrael). Constituted in 1920, this union has been linked, ever since its start, to the Israel Labor Party and controls a large portion of the Israeli economy. The Histadrut functions as an umbrella organization for trade unions and has played a significant role in the development of Israeli agriculture, in the marketing of food and other products, in construction and housing, in insurance, in health, and in social services. Approximately three-quarters of all wage earners in Israel are Histradut members. About forty trade unions are affiliated with the organization, with approximately 85 percent of the Israeli labor force covered by labor agreements negotiated by Histadrut.

In the 1920s its major role was to help develop the Jewish economy; to this end it founded Bank Hapoalim (Workers' Bank) and developed a wide range of economic enterprises, including construction and industrial companies. Its financial enterprises were successful until the 1980s, when many Histradut companies and affiliates faced serious financial difficulties. The government provided financial assistance and stipulated changes in management. The Labor Party subsequently distanced itself from the Histradut bureaucracy, which it considered an electoral liability.

SEE ALSO Israel Labor Party.

HIZB AL-DAʿWA AL-ISLAMIYYA (Islamic Appeal Party, in Arabic): Lebanese Shiʿite movement that surfaced at the end of 1979 to spread the Iranian Islamic revolution. Better known simply as al-Daʿwa, it issued from the Iraqi al-Daʿwa, founded in 1957. Starting in 1970, Iraqi Shiʿite religious leaders sent their followers to Lebanon to teach the fundamentals of their movement. After the Iranian revolution of 1979, Shiʿite proselytism was directed by Tehran through the intermediary of its Syrian representative, the Hojatolislam Ali Akbar Mohtashemi. The Lebanese branch of al-Daʿwa, headed by Shaykh Muhammad Husayn Fadlallah, one of the highest Lebanese Shiʿite dignitaries, advocated an Islamic republic in Lebanon. In 1981 Ayatollah Khomeini recommended dissolving al-Daʿwa, considering the party system a Western phenomenon. The members of the movement joined AMAL to found, in February 1985, the Lebanese Hizbullah.

SEE ALSO Hizbullah.

HIZBALLAH

SEE Hizbullah.

HIZB'ALLAH

SEE Hizbullah.

Histadrut Meeting. Golda Meir (center, standing) speaks in 1946 at the headquarters of Histadrut, which was founded in 1920 to organize economic activities of Jewish workers. It has become an umbrella organization affiliated with about forty trade unions, affecting 85 percent of Israeli workers. *(© Photograph by Zoltan Kluger. Government Press Office [GPO] of Israel)*

Hizbollah

see Hizbullah.

Hizbullah (Hizb Allah, "Party of God", in Arabic): Lebanese Shiʿite Islamist movement, officially constituted in February 1985 but with roots reaching back to the beginning of the 1980s. After the Israeli invasion of Lebanon in June 1982, a group encouraged by Ali Akbar Mohtashemi, the revolutionary Iranian government's ambassador in Syria, and led by Hussein Moussawi, formed a faction within AMAL, a Shiʿite group that had come under Syrian influence and become, in the Moussawi group's opinion, too conservative. This new group was known as the Islamic AMAL Faction. Three years later, under the guidance of Shaykh Muhammad Husayn Fadlallah, the leader of the disbanded Iranian-backed Hizb al-Daʿwa al-Islamiya (Islamic Appeal Party), this faction separated from AMAL to form Hizbullah. Fadlallah became its spiritual mentor, and the movement was swollen by the influx of the revolutionary guards (*pasdaran*) of Subhi Tufayli. Backed by Iran, Hizbullah advocated an Islamic regime in Lebanon and active resistance against the Israeli invasion and occupation of South Lebanon. Concurrently it set up a charity system that was much appreciated by the Lebanese Shiʿite population.

Between 1982 and 1988, in addition to fighting the Israelis, Hizbullah and its predecessor organizations also attacked Western troops. A multinational force had been deployed to protect the withdrawing Palestine Liberation Organization (PLO) in 1982 and it was brought back after the assassination of Bashir Jumayyil and the Israeli/Phalange massacre at Sabra and Shatila in September 1982. In 1983 American and French troops intervened in the ongoing civil war in favor of the Lebanese army, which was actually a partisan Maronite force. Hizbullah (under the name Islamic Jihad) is believed to have been responsible for suicide bombings that killed 241 American and 56 French soldiers in October 1983 and also kidnapped dozens of foreign nationals, especially

Americans, to hold as hostages. Ransoms were paid in exchange for some of these, and others were executed. Some of these acts were meant to discourage further American assistance to Iraq in the Iran-Iraq War (1980–1988). They had no such effect, although one ransom paid by the administration of U.S. President Ronald Reagan took the form of weapons sold to Iran for use against Iraq—part of what became known as the Iran-Contra scandal. (Israel was known to be supplying weapons to Iran at the same time.) Between 1985 and 1989, Hizbullah also fought frequently with the Syrian-backed AMAL and maintained a constant state of high tension in South Lebanon through repeated attacks by the Islamic Resistance Army (al-Muqawama al-Islamiya al-Mussalaha), its military wing, against the South Lebanon Army (SLA), an Israeli proxy, and through firing regular salvos of rockets into the north of Galilee. These actions were sometimes coordinated with the Popular Front for the Liberation of Palestine—General Command. In August 1989 Hizbullah's leader in South Lebanon, Abdul Karim Obeid, was kidnapped by an Israeli commando; he was released in February 2004, along with Mustafa Dirani, who was captured in 1994.

In 1990, with the end of the Lebanese Civil War, Hizbullah refused to join the national government, believing that the government was not committed to expelling the Israelis and that Shiʿites continued to be discriminated against, as they had been in the past. Although all Lebanese militias were to disarm under the Taʾif Accord, Hizbullah refused and the government was not strong enough to force it to. Hizbullah did, however, confine its military activity to fighting Israel and the SLA in the south. In the meantime, dissension developed within the movement as a consequence of internal power struggles in Tehran. In 1986 two currents appeared in Hizbullah, a minority headed by Hassan Nasrallah, siding with Ali Akbar Mohtashemi, Hizbullah's original Iranian patron and now the former Iranian minister of the interior; and the majority led by Subhi Tufayli and Abbas al-Moussawi favoring the Iranian president, Ali Akhbar Hashemi Rafsanjani. During October 1989 members close to Fadlallah were dismissed from their positions because of conflict between Fadlallah and Ayatollah Ali Khamenehi, the successor to Ayatollah Khomeini, who had died in June. In November, Tufayli became secretary general of Hizbullah, which led to divisions between his followers and Fadlallah's. Hoping to take control of the movement, Syria attempted to amplify these dissensions. In 1991 Tufayli lost the leadership of the movement to Moussawi, who was assassinated on 16 February 1992 by an Israeli commando. The post of secretary general was filled by Hassan Nasrallah, who favored active involvement in Lebanese politics. He succeeded to the extent of having eight Hizbullah-backed candidates (including two Sunnis and two Christians) elected to the Lebanese parliament in 1992, the first general election since before the civil war. In July 1993 a Hizbullah attack killed two Israel Defense Force (IDF) soldiers and the Israelis responded with a week's bombardment that killed 139 Lebanese and left 250,000 homeless.

In January 1994 confrontations in Baalbek between the Tufayli and Nasrallah factions clearly revealed the internal divisions in the movement. Tufayli opposed the integration of Hizbullah into Lebanese politics, advocating struggle against Israel even if the latter were to withdraw from South Lebanon. In 1996, in response to more Hizbullah rocketing of the Galilee, the Israelis launched Operation Grapes of Wrath against targets near Beirut and in South Lebanon, including a United Nations base where 100 Palestinian refugees were killed; 400,000 Lebanese were left homeless. In November 1997, anticipating an Israeli retreat from South Lebanon and preparing to participate in Lebanese political life, Hizbullah's leadership launched an appeal to Lebanese of all confessions to join with them in a broad-based national resistance. New recruits were inducted into a unit formed especially for them, the Lebanese National Resistance Brigade.

Attacks against Israel were especially heavy in 1997 and 1998. In February 1998, accused of wanting to divide the movement, Tufayli was expelled from Hizbullah. In May 1999 Ehud Barak won the prime ministerial election in Israel by promising to withdraw the IDF from Lebanon. On 13 January 2000 Israel freed twenty-seven Lebanese, including twelve Hizbullah members, who had been detained for months in SLA prisons. On 30 January the second-in-command of the SLA, Colonel Aki Hashem, was killed in a Hizbullah bombing. Between 17 and 20 May 2000, after Israel had officially informed the United Nations of its decision to withdraw its troops from South Lebanon before 7 July, intense artillery duels occurred between Hizbullah forces and the IDF. On 21 May, weakened by many desertions, the SLA abandoned a number of positions, which were immediately occupied by the Hizbullah. In the 2000 parliamentary elections, Hizbullah and AMAL ran a combined list of candidates and won the majority of the constituencies in the south and the Beqaa Valley.

In October 2000 the leadership of Hizbullah claimed responsibility for the kidnapping in Switzerland of an Israeli reserve officer, who was later used in a prisoner exchange with Israel. On 7 August 2001 the advisory council of the movement reelected Shaykh Nasrallah as secretary general of Hizbullah. Shaykh Naim Qassem was also reelected assistant secretary general, Hassan Khalil political counselor, Ibrahim Amin al-Sayed head of the political section, and Muhammad Yazbek director of religious affairs. Hashem Saffieddin was named head of the executive council, Jawad Noureddin director of coordination of resistance activities, and Nabil Qawuk leader of the movement for South Lebanon. Hizbullah has continued to attack Israel with rockets and artillery, both in the Shabaa Farms area of southern Lebanon, which it still occupies, and across the border, occasionally provoking a severe response. Hizbullah continues to receive support from Iran and Syria, which sees it as almost the only group that has had any success against Israel, and it has become the major Shi'ite political and social organization in southern Lebanon.

SEE ALSO AMAL; Barak, Ehud; Fadlallah, Shaykh Muhammad Husayn; Grapes of Wrath Operation; Iran-Iraq War; Jumayyil, Bashir; Maronites; Palestine Liberation Organization; Phalange; Popular Front for the Liberation of Palestine—General Command; Sabra and Shatila; South Lebanon; South Lebanon Army; Tufayli, Subhi Ali al-.

HIZBULLAH-PALESTINE (Hizb Allah-Filistin): Palestinian Islamic movement, created in Lebanon in August 1989 following dissension in the Palestinian Islamic Jihad (PIJ) between Fathi Shiqaqi and Ahmad Hassan Muhanna. Benefiting from Iranian help, the Palestinian Hizbullah set up its base in Lebanon. After a few military operations against Israeli soldiers in South Lebanon, carried out between 1990 and 1992, the movement ceased activity in the autumn of 1992, most of its members rejoining either the Lebanese Hizbullah or the PIJ. The movement has sometimes been called Harakat al-Nafir al-Islami (Islamic Mobilization Movement).

SEE ALSO Palestinian Islamic Jihad; Shiqaqi, Fathi.

HOBEIKA, ELIE (1956–2002): Lebanese Maronite politician, born in the Kesrouan, Lebanon. After studying business, Elie Hobeika entered a career in banking. In 1976, when the civil war broke out, he joined the Lebanese Forces, the militia of the Maronite Phalange. Four years later, after attracting notice for his intelligence and organizational abilities, he was entrusted by Bashir Jumayyil, leader of the Phalange, with the direction the Lebanese Forces' intelligence services. In 1983, at the time of the inquest into the Sabra and Shatila massacres, he was named as one of those responsible for this operation, which had been carried out by the Christian militia against the Palestinians. On 11 May 1985, backed by Samir Geagea, he was called upon to head the executive committee of the Lebanese Forces. On 28 December, to end the war between the militias, he concluded an accord with the leaders of AMAL and the Progressive Socialist Party, which made his ties to Damascus apparent and led to discontent among the principal leaders of the Christian community. Under pressure from the latter, on 15 January 1986 he resigned his command of the Lebanese Forces and was replaced by Geagea. On the following 28 January, Hobeika declared his support for the ex-president Sulayman Franjiyya, who was demanding the resignation of President Jumayyil.

On 27 September, in a militia called Movement of 9 May, his partisans tried and failed to take control of a portion Beirut's Christian suburbs. On 30 December 1990 he became minister of state in charge of refugees in the national unity government led by Omar Karamé. In February 1991 he founded a small party, Al-Waad, and was elected a deputy. On 30 October 1992 he joined the cabinet of Rafiq Hariri. In December 1998, after Emile Lahoud became president and Hariri refused to form a new cabinet, he resigned his minister's post. Although he planned to run for the presidency, Hobeika was defeated in the legislative elections of September 2000. His part in the Sabra and Shatila massacres caught up with him and he was forced to withdraw from politics. He was assassinated in a car-bombing in Beirut. A Lebanese group opposing Syria's continued grip on the country claimed responsibility, calling Hobeika a traitor for his allegiance to Damascus, but its claim was never confirmed. Speculation also centered on Syria, which may have objected to Hobeika's known cooperation with the CIA, and on Israel, since on the day before his assassination Hobeika had agreed to testify in a war crimes case brought against Ariel Sharon in Belgium over the Sabra and Shatila massaces.

SEE ALSO AMAL; Franjiyya, Sulayman; Geagea, Samir; Hariri, Rafiq Baha'uddin al-; Jumayyil, Bashir; Lebanese Forces; Phalange; Sabra and Shatila; Sharon, Ariel.

HOJATOLISLAM (hojjat al-islam): An honorific accorded to a respected Shi'a cleric. The word means "reason, proof of Islam"; by extension, it designates

CHURCH OF THE HOLY SEPULCHRE. PRIESTS STAND OUTSIDE THE CHURCH IN JERUSALEM THAT WAS BUILT OVER THE TRADITIONAL SITE OF THE CRUCIFIXION AND RESURRECTION OF JESUS CHRIST. THE CHURCH, WHICH DRAWS CHRISTIAN PILGRIMS FROM AROUND THE WORLD, IS DIVIDED INTO SEVERAL AREAS CONTROLLED BY DIFFERENT CHRISTIAN DENOMINATIONS. *(© Paul A. Souders/Corbis)*

one who is capable and worthy of explicating the religion.

SEE ALSO Shiʿa.

HOLOCAUST: Designates the persecutions and extermination systems of which Jews were the victims in Europe, dominated by the Nazi regime during World War II. The roots of the word go back to religious sacrifices practiced in ancient Israel B.C.E., during which an animal victim was consumed by fire. Most Israelis and many Jews prefer to use the word Shoah to describe the extermination of the Jews during World War II, since the word holocaust implies an idea of sacrifice to a higher being.

SEE ALSO Shoah.

HOLY SEPULCHER: Constructed in 326, during the reign of the Emperor Constantine, this building in Jerusalem was meant to protect the tomb of Christ. The structure was originally made up of a group of churches but Constantine gave orders for it to be made into an architectural monument. The original cave and much of the structure were carved away and broken down by Muslim ruler al-Hakim in 1009 as part of a plan to destroy the Christian sanctuary and Christianity itself. The structure was rebuilt between 1030 and 1048 by order of Byzantine Emperor Monomachus. On 27 November 1095 Pope Urban II called for a crusade to protect the Holy Sepulcher. An army of Crusaders occupied Jerusalem on 15 July and seven days later Godfrey de Bouillon took the title Defender of the Holy Sepulcher.

In 1149 Crusaders combined the remaining structures into a Romanesque church with a two-story façade, giving the structure its current architectural form. The building's interior includes a rotunda, which is modeled after the Pantheon, and an Orthodox cathedral. The former houses a shrine covering the tomb of Christ. Several Christian denominations have chapels within the shrine and regularly guard their areas. Roman Catholic, Greek Orthodox, and Armenian Orthodox groups share the control of the shrine, although Ethiopian, Egyptian Coptic, and Syrian churches also are present. The Muslim Nuseibeh and Joudeh families were given the sole key to the church by the Arab conqueror Saladin in the twelfth century, ensuring that no one sect could take control of the shrine. In June 1999 the leaders of all of the denominations agreed to install a new door in the church in order to provide a safe and orderly exit for the millions of pilgrims who were expected to visit the following year.

SEE ALSO Christianity.

HOLY WAR: Armed struggle undertaken in the name of God, accompanied by promises of spiritual rewards. In current Western discourse, the Arabic term *jihad* (struggle) is sometimes taken to have this meaning exclusively, although in Islam the word most often refers to the struggle to create a more just social order (the "lesser jihad"), or the personal struggle with the self to be a better Muslim (the "greater jihad").

SEE ALSO Jihad.

HOSS, SALIM AL- (1929–): Lebanese Sunni Muslim political figure. Salim Hoss was born into a middle-class family in Beirut. After obtaining a degree in economics from the American University of Beirut, then a doctorate in economics at Indiana University in the United States, he taught economics at the American University of Beirut for about ten years. Between 1964 and 1966 he was a financial advisor in Kuwait and in 1967 he was named president of the Central Bank of Lebanon's commission on bank inspection. During this time he formed a friendship with Elias Sarkis, director of the Central Bank, and then became his advisor when Sarkis was elected president. In September 1976 he was named prime minister, holding the portfolios of commerce, industry, oil, and intelligence. As prime minister in the midst of the civil war (1975–1990), he made efforts to apply an "Arab solution", recommended at the Cairo summit. After the resumption of fighting between the militias and the Syrian army, and then the Israeli invasion of 1978, he formed a third national unity cabinet. On 25 October 1980, unable to master the internal situation in Lebanon, he resigned his position as prime minister and was replaced by Shafiq Wassan.

In 1984 he joined the government of Prime Minister Rashid Karame as social affairs minister. After Karame's assassination, President Amin Jumayyil asked him to form a new government. On 22 September 1988 Jumayyil replaced him with General Michel Aoun at the head of a military government consisting of generals. Hoss refused to step down, and for a time Lebanon had two prime ministers. He resigned in the autumn of 1989, and on 13 November he was asked by the new president of the Republic, René Mu'awwad, to form a new national unity government. On 31 December 1990 he was replaced by Omar Karame. In the legislative elections of 1992, he headed the opposition list to the government's candidates. Elected representative for Beirut, he formed a "Bloc for Salvation and Change," which attracted some influential people and aggressively challenged the economic policies of the new prime minister, Rafiq Hariri. In 1996 he suffered a setback in the legislative elections, leading him to join with the National Assembly, which united six prominent figures of the opposition. Hoss again became prime minister on 2 December 1998, after General Emile Lahhud was elected president and Hariri refused to form a new government. For the first time, the great feudal barons and warlords were left out of a new cabinet. As soon as he assumed his duties, he began a reform of the Lebanese public service through a purge of cadres suspected of corruption. Hoss has won respect for his abilities as a manager, but the Sunni community reproached him for his self-effacing manner as prime minister, which worked to the benefit of the republic's presidency. On 17 October 2000 the victory of Hariri's party in the legislative elections prompted Hoss to step down as prime minister and Hariri became prime minister again.

SEE ALSO Aoun, Michel; Hariri, Rafiq; Jumayyil, Amin; Karame, Rashid; Lahhud, Emile.

HOVEVEI ZION

SEE Hibbat Zion.

HURRIYAH, AL- ("Liberty"): Palestinian weekly publication, started in 1960 by the Democratic Front for the Liberation of Palestine. Published in Beirut and available online in Arabic at http://www.alhourriah.org.

SEE ALSO Democratic Front for the Liberation of Palestine.

HUSAYN, ABDULLAH IBN

SEE Abdullah II ibn Hussein.

HUSAYNI, FAYSAL AL- (Husseini, Feisal; 1940–2001): Palestinian politician. Faysal al-Husayni was born in Baghdad into the prominent and influential Husayni family. His father, Abd al-Qadir al-Husayni, a Palestinian nationalist leader, was killed in combat on 9 April 1948 at the Battle of al-Qastal, just before the proclamation of the State of Israel. His grandfather, Musa Kazim al-Husayni, was one of the leaders of the Arab struggle against the British occupation. His great-uncle was Hajj Amin al-Husayni. After his father's death, he was raised by his uncle's family. In 1958, after studying science in Baghdad, he enrolled in the University of Cairo, where he was acquainted briefly with Yasir Arafat, whom he replaced as head of the Palestinian Students Union. In May 1964, while living in Jerusalem, he joined the newly created Palestine Liberation Organization (PLO). In 1966 he underwent military training in a Palestinian camp in Syria. In 1967, after returning to Israel, he was imprisoned for a number of months by Israeli authorities. In 1979, as a member of the Supreme Islamic Council of Jerusalem, he founded the Arab Studies Society in East Jerusalem. Between 1982 and 1987 he was under sentence of house arrest and then accused of being an underground leader of Fatah and again imprisoned. On 12 September 1987 he was sentenced to six months of detention for having had contact with a Likud leader, Moshe Amirav. On 30 July 1988 he was sentenced to six months in prison after the Israelis occupied his office and found a document dealing with the creation of an independent Palestinian state and the formation of a government-in-exile. When this document was published it provoked a controversy in Israel.

In March 1989 he was able for the first time to obtain an exit visa from Israel to travel to London and New York to attend a peace conference. On 29 July he was invited to speak by Israel Labor Party authorities and proposed negotiations between Israelis and Palestinians. On 23 January 1990, after the intervention of the U.S. ambassador to Israel, he was released from confinement by Israeli authorities. In mid-April, after being questioned a number of times by Israeli authorities, he participated in a conference in Brussels, where he was the invited guest of the Jewish Lay Community Center. On 27 June, he attended an Israeli-Palestinian meeting in Stockholm organized by Swedish authorities. After this meeting, he went to the United States, where he pleaded the Palestinian cause before influential American figures. In March 1991 he met three times with U.S. Secretary of State James Baker. On 8 May, accompanied by Hanan Ashrawi, he had discussions with Douglas Hurd, the British foreign secretary, in London. In the course of the summer, his popularity rose in the Palestinian territory.

On 28 October, in spite of Israeli reluctance, he was named to head the Palestinian delegation's commission of orientation for the Middle East peace conference in Madrid. However, Israel refused to allow Palestinian inhabitants of East Jerusalem and PLO members in the delegation, and he did not participate directly. This did not prevent him, in the two years that followed, from being one of the principal negotiators of the peace process that had started in Madrid. Between March and April 1993, he met many times with heads of state and government leaders involved in these discussions. On 26 March he was in Washington with Ashrawi to try to restart the peace process. During his stay, he had a one-on-one conversation with the secretary of state, Warren Christopher. On 9 April Israel officially accepted him as part the Palestinian delegation at peace negotiations. On 8 June he was received by the Amir of Qatar in an attempt to end the stalemate in relations between the emirate and the PLO, which had been broken off at the time of the Gulf War.

On 8 August, disapproving of the parallel negotiations in which the leadership of the PLO was engaged, he, Ashwari, and Saib Erekat, principal negotiators in the peace process, threatened to resign from the Palestinian delegation. On 4 May 1994 he declined to go to Cairo for the signing of the Israeli-Palestinian accord on the application of Palestinian autonomy in order to express his opposition to its content. At the end of the month, after much negotiating, he joined the Palestinian Authority (PA) as minister-without-portfolio in charge of the Jerusalem question. His offices were in Orient House in East Jerusalem, which had been built in the nineteenth century by a member of the Husayni family and was the headquarters of the PA representatives in Jerusalem and considered by Palestinians the seat of their future national government. Israel, which had annexed East Jerusalem and considered it Israeli territory, disputed their right to be there. A majority of the inhabitants of the occupied territories considered Faysal al-Husayni a leader of Palestinian nationalism. He favored the constitution of a Palestinian state, integrated into a Jordanian-Palestinian confederation. He died in Kuwait of a heart attack. In August 2001 Israeli authorities seized Orient House, closing the Arab Studies Society and the PA offices and seizing all archives, documents, and property.

SEE ALSO Arafat, Yasir; Ashrawi, Hanan Daouda; Christopher, Warren; Erekat, Saib Muhammad; Fatah, al-; Husayni, Hajj Amin al-; Israel Labor Party; Likud; Orient House;

Palestine Liberation Organization; Palestinian Authority.

HUSAYNI, HAJJ AMIN AL- (1895–1974): Mufti (Islamic jurist) of Jerusalem and Palestinian nationalist leader. Hajj Amin al-Husayni was born in Jerusalem into one of Palestine's most prominent landholding families. He attended al-Azhar University for a year and, briefly, the Dar al-Daʿwa wa al-Irshad (House of Prayer and Guidance), run by Rashid Rida, a pan-Islamic reformer, which were both in Cairo; he also attended the Military Academy in Istanbul. During World War I, al-Husayni served in the Turkish army, from which he deserted in 1916 to join the Arab Revolt under Husayn ibn Ali al-Hashem, sharif of Mecca.

In 1919, as president of the nationalist Arab Club (al-Nadi al-Arabi), he supported the creation of a Greater Syria, to be ruled by Amir (later King) Faysal ibn Husayn al-Hashem, a son of Sharif Husayn. From February to April 1920 he helped to organize several protests, the last of which turned into an anti-Zionist riot that ended in the deaths of five Jews and four Arabs. Sentenced in absentia to ten years of hard labor, he fled first to Damascus, Syria, where he worked for the Arab nationalist government of Amir (later King) Faysal, and then, when Faysal was expelled by the French, to Transjordan. He was pardoned in April 1921 by the British high commissioner, who appointed him mufti of Jerusalem, succeeding his brother Kamal, who had died. (Their father had also held the position.)

MUFTI OF JERUSALEM. HAJJ AMIN AL-HUSAYNI (SHOWN IN A 1938 PHOTOGRAPH) ROSE TO PROMINENCE AS A PALESTINIAN NATIONALIST LEADER IN THE EARLY 1920S. OPPOSED TO BRITISH RULE IN THE MIDDLE EAST AND THE ESTABLISHMENT OF A JEWISH STATE IN PALESTINE, HE ASSOCIATED HIMSELF WITH NAZI GERMANY DURING WORLD WAR II. HUSAYNI'S INFLUENCE DECLINED OVER THE NEXT TWO DECADES. *(© UPI/Bettmann/Corbis)*

In 1922 Hajj Amin al-Husayni (*Hajj* is an honorific designating someone who has made the pilgrimage to Mecca) was named president of the newly established Supreme Muslim Council of Palestine, a position that gave him control of Muslim religious institutions and made him a prominent and influential public figure. He opposed British proposals for a Palestinian legislative council and warned of Zionist plans for Palestine but in the 1920s was not active in political opposition. In 1929, when violence broke out over the Western Wall, he attempted to pacify the angry Palestinians and helped the Mandate government try to restore peace. He also, however, publicly opposed British policy on Zionist immigration and land purchases and tried to persuade the British to change it. Late in 1929 he participated in negotiations with the British over a compromise political settlement, but it was rejected by Zionist leaders. In this period he became the most visible Palestinian political leader and was in frequent discussions with the British. In 1931, as president of the World Islamic Congress, he organized an Islamic conference in Jerusalem to generate anti-Zionist feeling among Arabs and Muslims outside Palestine, but it was had little effect on the British.

In April 1936, at the beginning of a Palestinian general strike called after the discovery that Zionists were smuggling arms into the country, he organized the Arab Higher Committee (AHC), an ad hoc coalition of political leaders that took over direction of the strike. The AHC sought to defend Palestinian interests against the increasing power of Zionist institutions by boycotting Jewish businesses and demanding an end to Zionist land purchases and Jewish immigration, and ultimately by replacing British rule with an independent elected Palestinian government. Taking this position meant that al-Husayni could no longer conciliate the British; the Palestinian community would no longer allow it, and the strike was escalating into a popular armed revolt against the British rule and British policies, which favored the Zionist project. The AHC rejected the recommendation of the Peel Commission in June 1937 that Palestine be partitioned between the Arab and Zionist communities. In October the British outlawed the AHC. Four committee members were arrested and the rest escaped the country. Al-Husayni fled to Beirut, where he continued to organize the rebellion, which lasted until the spring of 1939. Although the White Paper of May 1939 recommended limiting Jewish immigration and proposed an unpartitioned, independent Palestine with an Arab majority, al-Husayni, no longer trusting the British, rejected it, as did the Zionists.

After the start of World War II, he escaped to Iraq, where he became involved in the nationalist resistance to de facto British rule there. He also began receiving financial assistance from the Germans, to whom he represented himself as the head of the pan-Arab movement, and engaged in diplomatic discussions with them, which produced nothing concrete. After a nationalist coup in Iraq in April 1941, the British government of Winston Churchill sent in a team recruited from the outlawed Zionist group Irgun to assassinate al-Husayni; the attempt failed, but when British troops overthrew the new regime in May he fled to Iran, where he was given asylum by Reza Shah. In June, after the Germans invaded the Soviet Union, both the Russians and the British invaded Iran; Reza Shah was forced to abdicate and al-Husayni went into hiding. Eventually he escaped through Turkey and Italy, where he met with Benito Mussolini, to Germany, where he was received by Adolf Hitler. Hitler, whose beliefs about Arabs were comparable to his beliefs about Jews, gave him assurances of his support for Arab and Palestinian independence in return for Arab help against the British, although he would not make his support public. Al-Husayni conducted propaganda broadcasts and attempted to recruit for a German-Arab Legion, which the Germans wanted to send to the Eastern Front rather than the Middle East.

After the war, he went to Switzerland but was refused asylum and handed himself over to the French, who could not decide what to do with him. The French were not anxious to be seen punishing him, since he was still popular in the Middle East. The British proposed deporting him to the Seychelles, but the French would not agree. In May 1946 he escaped from the house near Paris, where he was interned, and went to Cairo, where he was given asylum by King Faruq. From Cairo he attempted to revive his political influence in Palestine with the help of his cousin Jamal al-Husayni, who was attempting from his own exile to revive the Arab Higher Committee, and of his nephew Abd al-Qadir al-Husayni, who led a Palestinian militia. He could do little without the help of the League of Arab States, which had in effect become the strongest force in Palestinian politics, the only Arab political grouping that could potentially match the strength of the Zionist government, the Jewish Agency for Israel. But the league was a creature of the Arab governments and was not united over Palestine. Al-Husayni and Palestinian nationalism had supporters in the league, but all moves for Palestinian independence were opposed by Amir Abdullah of Transjordan (Abdullah I), who wanted to annex Palestinian territory to his country and was secretly working with the Jewish Agency toward this end. Abdullah refused to deal with al-Husayni, as did the Jewish Agency.

In 1946 the Arab League created a new Arab Higher Committee to represent Palestinians, with al-Husayni as chairman, but it proved ineffective. The paramilitary forces under its nominal control were uncoordinated and no match for the Haganah, and the league would not agree to allow the committee to form a shadow government. Al-Husayni rejected United Nations (UN) Security Council Resolution 181 partitioning Palestine and on 1 December 1947 launched an appeal for a general strike among the Palestinians. In April 1948 his nephew Abd al-Qadir al-Husayni was killed in the Battle of al-Qastal against a Jewish militia. In September 1948, after most of Palestine was already lost to the State of Israel, the Arab League allowed the AHC to set up an All-Palestine Government based in Gaza with al-Husayni as president. It lasted for only a few weeks, in the few square miles controlled by the Egyptian army. Stripped by Abdullah of his title of mufti of Jerusalem, al-Husayni became active in Syria and Egypt, trying to recapture a position as leader of the Palestinian people. In 1951 he became spiritual head of the Muslim Congress of Karachi, Pakistan. The same year, he was suspected of having ordered the assassination of Abdullah by a Palestinian in Jerusalem on 20 July. Between 1952 and 1959, he undertook multiple initiatives in Arab capitals in the name of the moribund Arab Higher Committee. In April 1955 he participated in the Bandung Conference, where he denounced Israel's expansionist policies. His public agitation made some Arab leaders uncomfortable and he was obliged to take refuge in Lebanon in 1959, where he found himself for all practical purposes under house arrest. In June 1962 he was named president of the World Islamic Congress, and in November he led a delegation of the Arab Higher Committee to Algiers. In 1964, with the creation of the Palestine Liberation Organization, he found himself definitively excluded from Palestinian political affairs. He died in Beirut.

SEE ALSO Abdullah I ibn Hussein; Arab Higher Committee; British Mandate; Haganah; Husayni, Jamal al-; Irgun; Jordan; League of Arab States; Western Wall.

HUSAYNI, JAMAL AL- (1892–1982): Palestinian politician. Jamal al-Husayni was born in Jerusalem into a prominent Palestinian family and educated at the Anglican St. George's School and the American University of Beirut. From 1920 to 1934 he was secretary general of the Arab Executive, a committee of notables, chaired by his cousin Musa Kazim al-Husayni, which was the most visible political organization advocating for the Palestinian cause, mostly through petitions and delegations; in its later years it was generally regarded as conservative and inadequate in the face of rising Palestinian anger and increasing political crisis. In 1930 he was a member of a delegation sent by his cousin Hajj Amin al-Husayni, the mufti of Jerusalem, to London to plead the Palestinian position on Zionism and British rule. In 1935 al-Husayni became the president of the Palestine Arab Party, controlled by the Husayni family, and the editor of the party's newspaper, *al-Liwa*. In 1936 he joined the Arab Higher Committee (AHC), chaired by Hajj Amin, which came into existence to coordinate the activities of the general strike organized to protest Zionist activities and British support for them and which attempted to get control of what became an armed uprising against the British and the Zionists. When the British banned the AHC in 1937 al-Husayni joined Hajj Amin in exile in Lebanon, where they attempted to continue coordinating the uprising until it was crushed in 1939.

In 1939 Jamal al-Husayni was allowed to travel to London as the head of the Palestinian delegation to the London Conference. After the start of World War II he went to Iraq, and in 1941 to Iran, where he was arrested by the British in 1942 and deported to Southern Rhodesia (now Zimbabwe). From there he attempted to revive the AHC but found no support from other political factions. In 1946 he returned to Palestine and worked with the newly constituted Arab Higher Committee created by the Arab League in 1946; he became foreign minister in the All-Palestine Government that lasted through September and October 1948 in the Egyptian-controlled Gaza Strip. He later went to Saudi Arabia, where he was an advisor to King Saʿud from 1953 to 1964. He died in Beirut.

SEE ALSO All-Palestine Government; Arab Higher Committee; Gaza Strip; Husayni, Hajj Amin al-.

HUSAYNI, MUSA KAZIM AL- (1853–1934): Palestinian political figure. Musa Kazim al-Husayni was born in Jerusalem into one of Palestine's most prominent families; since the mid-nineteenth century the mayors and muftis of Jerusalem had usually been members of the Husayni family. Educated in Istanbul, he served the Ottomans in numerous administrative positions in several countries. He was a leading member of the Palestinian Muslim-Christian Association in 1918 and 1919 and in 1918 was appointed mayor of Jerusalem by the British, succeeding his late brother Husayn. He was removed from this office in April 1920 for protesting British support for the Zionist project and for publicly supporting the Arab government of Amir Faysal in Syria when the French were moving to impose their League of Nations Mandate there. He was elected president of the Arab Executive in December 1920, at its founding in Haifa. He became chairman in 1928. He followed a course of cautious, moderate, and largely deferential protest, in the style of Ottoman politics in which he and his colleagues on the committee had been schooled; nevertheless, the Arab Executive was the most important Palestinian nationalist organization of its time. In August 1921 he led a delegation to London to argue against the Balfour Declaration, for suspending Zionist immigration, and for establishing a democratic representative government. He later opposed, with more success, the British effort to impose a legislative council that would have had only limited authority and would have allocated the Palestinians only 43 percent of the seats. In 1928, as Zionist organizations were becoming stronger and Jewish immigration was increasing, the Arab Executive was expanded to encompass a greater range of Palestinian political opinion in an attempt to strengthen it. Its influence declined, however, after the Western Wall disturbances of 1929, in which many Jews and Palestinians were killed.

In 1930 he again led a delegation to London to argue against British policies. Once again they were refused, but two British commissions of inquiry did result in the Passfield White Paper, which recommended substantial changes, including suspension of Zionist land purchases. However, Zionist political influence in London and strength in Palestine were great enough to prevent these recommendations from being followed, and Palestinian politics—which through the 1920s had been evolving toward an openness to mass public opinion and the importance of popular action—became radicalized. Husayni and his colleagues on the Arab Executive found it difficult to adapt their strategy to this situation. Under pressure, the Arab Executive sponsored a demonstration in Haifa in October 1933, protesting British support for Zionism and led by Husayni. It was broken up by the police and Husayni was beaten. He never recovered and died the next year. The Arab Executive dissolved in 1934. Musa Kazim al-Husayni was the father of Abd al-Qadir al-Husayni (1908–1948), a military leader and hero of the 1948 War.

SEE ALSO Arab Executive; Balfour Declaration; White Papers on Palestine.

HUSSEIN, SADDAM (Husayn; 1937–): Head of the Iraqi state from 1979 to 2003; Sunni Muslim. Saddam Hussein was born in Auja, near Tikrit. He joined the Baʿth Party in 1956 and was arrested several times in 1958 and 1959 for his political activities against the Iraqi regime. In July 1958 General Abdal Karim Qassim took power in Baghdad, relying on the backing of the communists and banning parties favorable to Egypt, among which was the Baʿth. On 7 October 1959 Hussein participated in an assassination attempt against General Qassim. A few weeks later, after having avoided a death sentence, he left Iraq to take refuge in Syria, and then in Egypt, where he studied law. In March 1963 he returned to Iraq, where the Baʿth Party had taken power on 8 February and named General Abd al-Salam Arif as the head of the National Council of the Revolution. On the following 17 November, General Arif seized all power in Iraq, pushing aside the Baʿthist leaders, who were imprisoned for nearly two years. After his release from prison, Hussein was elected, in September 1966, assistant secretary general of the Baʿth Party. Adhering to the Egyptian-Jordanian mutual defense pact, on 5 June 1967 Iraq joined in the 1967 War against Israel. The conflict ended with the defeat of the Arab armies and Israeli occupation of Sinai, the Golan, the West Bank, and the Gaza Strip. One year later, a coup d'état overthrew the regime of General Arif, who was replaced by General Ahmad Hassan al-Bakr. A new government was formed, controlled by the Baʿth Party, within which Saddam Hussein proceeded to violently purge the principal leaders and strengthen the position of the party in the Iraqi army.

During the Israel-Palestinian conflict, the Iraqi government supplied significant material help to the Palestinians. On 9 November 1969 Saddam Hussein was named vice president of the Command Council of the Revolution, becoming the second most important figure in the state. In June 1972 he supervised the nationalization of the Iraq Petroleum Company, a Western-owned consortium that held a monopoly on the extraction of oil in Iraq. In October 1973, during the 1973 War, Iraq supported Egypt and Syria against Israel. The Arab armies were again defeated. In 1979, after the success of the Iranian revolution, Hussein, over Bakr's objections, confronted Shiʿa dissidence in Iraq directly. In July 1979 he forced Bakr to resign and had himself elected secretary general of the Baʿth Party, president of the Command Council of the Revolution and president of Iraq. The next day he was promoted to marshal of the Iraqi Army. To make himself an important player in the region, he strengthened his support for the Palestinian cause and tried to replace Egyptian President Anwar al-Sadat, who was in a weak position following his peace initiative with Israel, as the leader of the Arab camp. Three months after he came to power, Hussein began to question the validity of the treaty of Algiers, which was signed on 6 March 1975 and fixed the frontier between Iran and Iraq in the Shatt al-Arab.

On 20 June 1980 the Baʿth Party won the majority of seats in parliament in the first Iraqi legislative elections for over twenty years. On 22 September, supported massively by most of the Arab and Western countries, Hussein attacked Iran. During the conflict, the two countries also fought in Lebanon through the intermediaries of Lebanese militias and Palestinian movements. On 18 July 1988, after eight years of war, in the course of which both Iraq and Iran used chemical weapons a number of times, Iran was obliged to agree to a ceasefire. Hussein presented himself as the winner in the war, but it left Iraq in difficult economic straits, not least through its debts to Kuwait.

Two years later, on 19 July 1990, at a meeting of the Organization of Petroleum Exporting Countries (OPEC) in Riyadh, Iraq demanded that Kuwait and the United Arab Emirates stay within their oil production quotas. According to Iraq, these two OPEC members, by exceeding their quotas, were impoverishing the Iraqi people. On 2 August Iraqi armies invaded Kuwait. In the eyes of the West—and the Americans in particular—by annexing this country Iraq was doubling its oil reserves and would therefore become the world's second largest oil exporter in the world, behind Saudi Arabia. A majority of Arab countries voted the next day in the Arab League for a resolution condemning Iraq; the Palestine Liberation Organization, Jordan, Yemen, Mauritania, and Sudan abstained; Libya's representative did not attend the meeting; only Iraq voted against the resolution. The Arab League supported negotiation to resolve the crisis and opposed outside intervention but changed its position a week later to support the Gulf states' right to call for outside help in self-defense. During this crisis Hussein presented himself as a new Saladin, "ready to stand up against the Zionist occupier of Palestine." This was appreciated by some Palestinians, who were frustrated at Arab timidity in the face of Israel and who also had good reason to resent the treatment of Palestinians in Kuwait, but the linkage of Hussein's aggression with the Palestinian issue was not generally accepted.

The United States and its allies built up a huge military force in Saudi Arabia over the next several months, and on 29 November the UN Security Council authorized the use of force against Iraq. The Gulf War of 1991 was launched on 16 January and concluded on 28 February—a long campaign of air and missile bombardment followed by only four days of ground fighting—with the rout of the Iraqi army. During these hostilities, Iraq launched a number of SCUD missiles at Israel. At the request of the United States, Israel did not respond. Following the end of the war, the United States undertook to organize, with the participation of the Soviet Union, the Madrid Conference on peace in the Middle East to begin a peace process between Israel and its Arab neighbors, as well as between Israel and the Palestinians.

The Iraqi defeat was total. The army, until then thought to be one of the world's mightiest, was decimated, and the civilian infrastructure—electricity distribution grids, communications, water, sanitation—was deliberately destroyed. Iraq was not occupied but was isolated and subject to the oversight of the U.S. and British military. From 1991 to 2003, Iraq was subject to a regime of weapons inspections and dismantling, military overflights, restrictions on use of its own airspace, the virtual separation of the Kurdish region in the north of the country, and a severe trade embargo (modified somewhat in 1996), which caused great economic damage and much physical suffering. The purpose of all this was to enforce UN resolutions regarding Iraqi armaments and particularly "weapons of mass destruction" (WMDs)—specifically chemical and nuclear weapons. Iraq essentially complied with the resolutions by 1994 and Hussein spent the next nine years campaigning for an end to the embargo. A crisis arose in 1997 when the new chief of the UN Special Commission (UNSCOM) in charge of disarming Iraq became convinced that Hussein was withholding information about chemical weapons. The dispute was mediated by the UN secretary general, but in late 1998 UNSCOM pulled out of Iraq at the urging of the United States, which that December launched, with Britain, the aerial bombing campaign known as Operation Desert Fox. The result was that in 1999 Saddam Hussein refused to allow the inspectors back under a new UN resolution. He also attempted to develop support in the Arab world by sending assistance to the Palestinians in the al-Aqsa Intifada that began in September 2000, paying compensation to the families of those who had attacked Israelis as suicide bombers.

After the terrorist attacks in the United States on 11 September 2001, the George W. Bush administration engaged in a propaganda campaign, despite a lack of evidence, associating Iraq and Saddam Hussein personally with the attacks and claiming that he had built up stockpiles of weapons of mass destruction in contravention of UN resolutions. After months of building public sentiment for an attack, despite the lack of support from most of the world (except for Britain) and despite Hussein's grudging delivery of all requested information about Iraqi arms programs and their destruction, and his acceptance of last-minute conditions, the Iraq War of 2003 was launched on 20 March. Iraq's shattered economy, weak military, and lack of weapons of mass destruction ensured that the war ended quickly, on 16 April. The occupation of Iraq by U.S. and British forces, however, and the concomitant armed resistance by various factions, continue. Saddam Hussein disappeared from Baghdad some time in April or May and was captured in a rural hideout in December

SEE ALSO Aqsa Intifada, al-; Arab-Israel War (1967); Arab-Israel War (1973); Baʿth; Desert Fox; Gaza Strip; Gulf War (1991); Iraq War; Madrid Conference; Organization of Petroleum Exporting Countries; Palestine Liberation Organization; Sadat, Anwar al-; Saladin; West Bank.

HUSSEIN IBN TALAL (1935–1999): King of Jordan from 1952 to 1999. Hussein ibn Talal al-Hashem was the son of King Talal and grandson of King Abdullah I, of the al-Hashim dynasty, which claims descent from Ali Hashim, great-grandfather of the prophet Muhammad. Hussein was educated at Victoria College in Alexandria, at Harrow in Britain, and at the

British military academy Sandhurst. On 20 July 1951 he was at his grandfather's side in Jerusalem when the latter was assassinated by a Palestinian. On 11 August of the following year, he became King of Jordan, replacing his father Talal, who was removed because of mental illness. A regency council exercised power until Hussein reached eighteen and formally acceded to the throne in May 1953. At the same time, another British-supported Hashimite monarch, Hussein's cousin Faysal II, was beginning his reign in Iraq.

Hussein inherited a kingdom that was supported financially by Britain. Jordan's army (then called the Arab Legion) was paid for by Britain and commanded and partly staffed by British officers, and its security arrangements were governed by a Jordanian-British treaty signed in 1948. The political situation at the time Hussein came to power was shaped by resentment of Britain; anti-Hashimite sentiment and Nasserist-Arab nationalism (the Egyptian revolution had overthrown a British-associated monarchy in 1952); the presence of Palestinians in the kingdom (half to two-thirds of the population was Palestinian, including more than 800,000 refugees from the 1948 War); and the continuing Palestine crisis, including frequent Israeli incursions into the West Bank. In 1954 major public unrest occurred when general elections were rigged by the Hashimite government. In 1955, under public pressure, the king could not sign on to the Baghdad Pact, initiated by Britain and the United States, and in March 1956 he dismissed the British commander of the Arab Legion and changed its name. This resulted in strained relations with Britain, but British aid did not stop. In October 1956, shortly before the Suez War, Hussein allowed honest elections to take place, which resulted in the installation of a left-leaning nationalist government.

British collaboration with Israel in the attack on Egypt inspired the end of Jordan's subordinate relationship with Britain. In January 1957 Jordan entered the Arab Solidarity Agreement with Egypt, Saudi Arabia, and Syria, which provided for military cooperation as well as financial assistance to Jordan. In March the government canceled its 1948 treaty with Britain and negotiated a new one, under which Britain ended its subsidies, turned over its bases, and withdrew its troops. All this was done with Hussein's acquiescence and the support of public opinion. Believing that his Nasserist government was planning to abolish the monarchy, however, Hussein dismissed it in April 1957. After a coup d'état by the Nasserist army commander was squelched, the newly appointed conservative government dissolved parliament and banned political parties.

From this time on Hussein took the lead in governing the country himself. The Arab Solidarity Pact having fallen apart almost immediately, the king, claiming to be menaced by communism, requested and received aid from the United States. In return for this aid he allowed American and British intelligence agencies to operate freely in Jordan, and they in turn helped him against his domestic and foreign opposition. In February 1958, as a conservative counterweight to the United Arab Republic created by Egypt and Syria, he and his cousin Faysal II decided to unite their two countries. Five months later this federation, the Arab Union, failed when the Iraqi monarchy was overthrown and Faysal assassinated. Fearing similar events in Jordan, Hussein's government declared martial law, the United States began supplying Jordan with oil, and Britain sent in troops. On 10 November 1958, while flying to Switzerland, Hussein escaped an assassination attempt when a Syrian plane tried to force his down. In August 1960 Hussein's prime minister was assassinated in his office; the plot was traced to Syria.

On 25 May 1961, having divorced his first wife, Hussein married Antonia Avril Gardiner (renamed Princess Muna), daughter of a British officer, with whom he had his first son, Prince Abdullah. In 1965, to avoid a long regency in the event of his death while Abdullah was still a child, Hussein designated his brother Hassan crown prince.

In 1967, with regional tension rising, Jordan joined Egypt and Syria in a mutual defense pact. As a result of the June 1967 War, Hussein found himself confronted by the loss of the West Bank and East Jerusalem and by a second massive influx of Palestinian refugees. On 16 February 1968, following new reprisals by the Israeli army in Jordanian territory, he condemned armed actions by the Palestinian resistance. Palestinian-Jordanian tensions increased, with much fighting between the Jordanian army and Palestinian organizations, which were trying to bring down the Hashimite regime. The situation culminated in what has come to be known as Black September 1970, when Hussein installed a military government and the army launched a massive attack on the Palestinian fighters, killing some 4,000 of them in ten days and defeating a Syrian force that had been sent to help them, until a truce was negotiated by Egyptian president Gamal Abdel Nasser at the behest of the Arab League. After renewed fighting in July 1971 the Palestine Liberation Organization (PLO) and other groups were expelled to Lebanon and all the Palestinian civil organizations that had made up the Palestinian state-within-a-state were shut down.

In November 1971 Hussein's prime minister, Wasfi al-Tal, who was visiting Cairo, was assassinated by the Palestinian group Black September. On 15 March 1972 King Hussein announced a plan for a Jordanian-Palestinian federation with the West Bank, to be called the United Arab Kingdom. This was rejected the next month by the Palestine National Council (PNC). During the following November, Jordanian security services uncovered a conspiracy organized by Jordanian officers to overthrow the king. During the October 1973 War, under the influence of the United States, Jordan did not open a third front to assist the Egyptian and Syrian armies in the struggle against Israel, although it did send two armored brigades to fight with the Syrians. On 26 October 1974 King Hussein opposed the decision of the Arab League summit, meeting in Rabat, recognizing the PLO as "sole and legitimate representative of the Palestinian people" and supporting an independent Palestinian state in liberated territory. Hussein accepted the decision, however, and dissolved parliament, half of whose constituencies were in the West Bank. He also maintained Jordanian civil and administrative ties to the West Bank.

In February 1977 Hussein met with a delegation from the PLO and the next month, in Cairo, he reconciled with the head of the PLO, Yasir Arafat. On 8 June of the following year, just before his fourth marriage to the Arab-American Lisa Halaby (renamed Queen Noor), he named his son Ali, whose mother, Hussein's third wife Alia Tuqan, had died in a helicopter accident in 1977, as second crown prince. In 1978 he declined to participate in the Camp David negotiations between Israel and Egypt or to endorse the 1979 peace treaty. From 1980 to 1988 he supported Baghdad in the Iran-Iraq War, which allowed his kingdom to benefit from trade with Iraq. In 1981 he negotiated an arms deal with the Soviet Union. In 1984 Hussein allowed parliament to reopen and began dealing with Egypt again, despite the Arab League ban that had been imposed after the 1979 treaty.

In 1985 Hussein allowed the PNC to meet in Amman. He came to an agreement with the PLO regarding a coordinated approach to a Palestinian-Israeli settlement but differences developed, partly over the loyalties of expatriate Palestinians with Jordanian citizenship, and it was abandoned by 1987. In December 1987 the Intifada began in the occupied territories and in July 1988, fearing the violence would spill across the Jordan River, Hussein renounced all legal and administrative claims and responsibilities in the West Bank, canceling the Jordanian citizenship of all West Bank Palestinians. This gave the PLO complete responsibility for Palestinian interests, enhancing its international status.

During the Gulf Crisis of 1990 to 1991, Hussein did not support the Iraqi invasion of Kuwait but refused to join the anti-Iraq coalition. At the Arab League on 3 August 1990, Jordan abstained from voting on the resolution condemning Iraq, but Hussein did support the League's position that the crisis should be resolved by negotiation under Arab auspices rather than by foreign intervention. When the Arab League modified this position a week later, approving the Gulf states' right to self-defense and implicitly approving the use of outside forces, Jordan voted in favor but expressed "reservations"—in effect remaining neutral. In October 1991, when the end of the Gulf War led to the organization of the Madrid Conference on Middle East peace, Hussein agreed to the PLO's inclusion in the Jordanian delegation since the Israelis refused to deal with it directly. On 26 October 1994, a year after the Israeli-Palestinian Declaration of Principles in Washington, King Hussein signed a peace treaty with Israel that was opposed by some Jordanians, ending forty-six years of belligerence between the two countries.

In February 1996 his previously friendly relations with Iraq changed when he authorized an Iraqi opposition group to open an office of in the Jordanian capital. On 5 June 1996, after a Likud government that opposed the Oslo Accords came to power in Israel, he organized, with Yasir Arafat and Husni Mubarak, a mini-summit to reaffirm his support for the Israeli-Palestinian peace process. On 3 August he resumed Syrian-Jordanian relations, which had been interrupted by the Israeli-Jordanian peace accord. On 6 August he met with the new Israeli prime minister, Benjamin Netanyahu, confirming his own role in Israeli-Arab negotiations. Five days later he was in Saudi Arabia for the resumption of Jordanian-Saudi relations, interrupted since the Gulf War. On 15 October he met Arafat in Jericho to show his support in the stalemated negotiations with Israel. On 12 January 1997 he helped break the stalemate when he obtained an accord on the redeployment of Israeli troops in Hebron. In August 1998, his health worsening, Hussein delegated most of his power to his brother Hassan and left for medical treatment in the United States. Returning to Amman in January 1999, he stripped his brother of the title of crown prince and gave it to his son Abdullah, to whom he also accorded the regency. He died the next month.

SEE ALSO Abdullah I ibn Hussein; Arab-Israel War (1967); Arab-Israel War (1973); Arafat, Yasir; Baghdad Pact; Black September 1970; Black September Organization; Camp David Accords; Gulf War (1991); Hashim, al-; Hassan of Jordan; Hebron; Intifada (1987–1993); Iran-Iraq War; League of Arab States; Madrid Conference; Mubarak, Husni; Muhammad; Nasser, Gamal Abdel; Netanyahu, Benjamin; Occupied Territories; Oslo Accords; Oslo Accords II; Palestine Liberation Organization; Palestine National Council; Suez Crisis; Talal ibn Abdullah; West Bank.

HUSSEIN OF JORDAN

SEE Hussein ibn Talal.

HUT, SHAFIQ AL- (1932–): Palestinian political figure and writer. Shafiq al-Hut was born in Jaffa and fled Palestine for Lebanon with his family in 1948, when the State of Israel was created. In 1953 he received a degree in biology from the American University of Beirut and taught for a while before being fired for Nasserist activities. In 1958 he joined the Lebanese weekly, *al-Hawadith* (Events) and later contributed to another weekly, *al-Muharrir* (the Editor). In 1961 he founded a group of intellectuals called the Palestine Liberation Front (PLF; not to be confused with the guerrilla group of the same name founded in 1977). The PLF (later called the PLF—Path of Return or PLF—PR) recruited for the Palestine Liberation Army. In 1964 al-Hut participated in the first meeting of the Palestine National Council, at which the Palestine Liberation Organization (PLO) was organized. He became its Lebanon representative.

In 1966 he became a member of the PLO's executive committee and joined the opposition to Ahmad Shuqayri, the first chairman of the PLO, who resigned six months after the June 1967 War. In 1967 al-Hut declared in favor of the creation of a Palestinian state in the West Bank. Between 1967 and 1969 he traveled widely on behalf of the PLO in the republics of the Soviet Union. In 1968 he left the PLF—PR, which was then absorbed into Fatah. During the summer of 1970 he opposed the new policy direction of the PLO, now led by Yasir Arafat, and was temporarily relieved of his functions as PLO representative in Lebanon, but he assumed them again a few weeks later. In June 1974 he was reelected to the PLO executive committee, taking the place of the poet Kamal Nasser, who had been assassinated two months earlier in Lebanon by the Israelis. He is said to have been offered Nasser's job as PLO spokesman but to have declined it. In November 1974 he was part of the Palestinian delegation, led by Arafat, to the UN General Assembly. From that time on, al-Hut was closely allied with Arafat and his Fatah organization (although he never joined), and participated in numerous negotiations concerning Palestinian interests.

In August 1975 he went to Japan to negotiate the opening of a PLO office in Tokyo. As the PLO's representative in Beirut during the Lebanese Civil War, he was the object of a number of assassination attempts, including one orchestrated by al-Saiʿqa in 1976. In April 1979 he was in Washington to participate in discussions at the Institute for Policy Studies, and in March 1980 he led a Palestinian delegation to the Council of Europe. In May 1985 he was elected to the PLO central council. Between 1986 and 1992 he participated in numerous negotiations, including those concerning the fate of Palestinian refugees in Lebanon. He opposed the Oslo Accords, and in September 1993 a few days after the signing of the Israeli-Palestinian Declaration of Principles in Washington he resigned from all his PLO positions. He remains in Beirut, with no organizational affiliation, working with various Palestinian groups there and in Damascus.

SEE ALSO Arab-Israel War (1967); Arafat, Yasir Muhammad; Fatah, al-; Oslo Accords; Oslo Accords II; Palestine Liberation Army; Palestine Liberation Organization; Saʿiqa, al-; West Bank.

IAF

SEE Islamic Action Front.

IBLIS: Arabic, meaning "Satan" or *shaytan*.

IBN: Arabic word meaning "son of." Equivalent to the Hebrew *ben*.

IBN LADEN, OUSSAMA

SEE Bin Ladin, Osama.

ICO

SEE Organization of the Islamic Conference.

'ID: "celebration," in Arabic (sometimes rendered as *eid.*)

'ID AL-ADHA: Muslim celebration, called the "Feast of the Sacrifice," which marks the end of the pilgrimage to Mecca. Called also 'Id al-Kebir ("Large Feast") in the Maghrib, or Kurban Baïram ("Great Festival") in Turkey, this holiday occurs on the tenth of the month of Dhu al-Hijja. This ceremony commemorates the action of Ibrahim (Abraham), who, obeying the injunctions of God, was ready to sacrifice his son, Ishmael (Isaac), to him.

SEE ALSO Abraham; Ishmael.

'ID AL-FITR: Muslim holiday concluding the period of fast of the month of Ramadan. Called also 'Id al-Saghir ("Little Feast"), it is celebrated on the first of the month of Shawwal.

SEE ALSO Ramadan.

'ID AL-KEBIR

SEE 'Id al-Adha.

'ID AL-SAGHIR

SEE 'Id al-Fitr.

IDB

SEE Islamic Development Bank.

IDF

SEE Israel Defense Force.

IFF

SEE Qassam.

IFTAR

SEE *Fitr*.

IHRAM: Arab word used to designate the sacred state any Muslim must be in before going on a pilgrimage.

By extension, it designates also the ritual apparel of the pilgrim.

SEE ALSO Muslim.

IIM

SEE Israeli Islamic Movement.

ILO

SEE Islamic Liberation Organization.

ILP

SEE Islamic Liberation Party.

ILP

SEE Israel Labor Party.

IMAM: A Muslim prayer leader. During the prayer the imam conducts and regulates the general rhythm of the collective prayer. For the Sunnis, the imam is only one among others exercising this function. Recognizable for his competence in religious studies, the imam, sometimes under the name of a *khatib,* also functions as a preacher.

SEE ALSO Sunni Islam.

IMAN: Arabic word meaning faith or belief.

INDEPENDENT NASSERITE MOVEMENT (INM): Lebanese Sunni political organization, created in 1958 by young students opposed to the pro-Western policies of Camille Chamoun. Backed by Egypt, its moments of glory were under the leadership of Ibrahim Koleilat, between 1975 and 1980, when it was allied with the Palestinian Fatah, while retaining its own armed branch, al-Murabitun (the Sentinels). In 1982, the invasion of Lebanon by Israel forced the Murabitun and the INM to go underground. In June 1983, a split in the group gave rise to the Independent Lebanese National Alliance, under the leadership of Samir Sabbagh, former assistant to Ibrahim Koleilat. In December 1986, a new rift led to the creation of the National Independent Movement, headed by Samir Sabbagh. Weakened by much dissidence, the INM then waned in influence in the Lebanese political arena.

SEE ALSO Fatah, al-.

INDYK, MARTIN (1951–): Former U.S. Ambassador to Israel (1995–1997 and 1999–2001), Martin Indyk grew up in Australia where he earned a degree in economics and a doctorate in international relations. In 1978, he was an advisor to the Australian secret service. In 1982, after he had been living in the United States for two years, he joined the American Israel Public Affairs Committee (AIPAC), a U.S. lobby promoting the interests of Israel within the U.S. administration.

Between 1983 and 1993, while executive director of AIPAC, Indyk headed the Washington Institute for Near East Policy, to which Dennis Ross also belonged. Members of a "group of presidential studies," both played an important role at the time of the crisis brought on by the collapse of the Soviet Union, becoming the principal crafters of the Israeli-Arab peace process that was launched in Madrid in November 1991. In 1988, Indyk supported the candidacy of Michael Dukakis for the presidency of the United States. The following year, with Dennis Ross, he was part of a group of advisors on the Middle East for President George H. W. Bush. During the presidential election campaign of 1992, Indyk was one of the consultants of candidate Bill Clinton on questions having to do with Arabs. In January 1993, after Clinton had been elected to the White House, Indyk obtained U.S. citizenship, and a few days later, he was named director of the Department of the Middle East and Southeast Asia of the National Security Council (NSC), replacing Richard Haas.

Along with Dennis Ross and Daniel Kurtzer, he became one of the principal architects of U.S. policy in the Middle East. In February 1995, succeeding Edward Djerejian, he was named U.S. ambassador to Israel, the first Jew to hold this post. This nomination led to unease in the Arab community, which feared that the policies advocated by the new U.S. ambassador would be too partial to Israel. In November 1997, having returned to Washington, Indyk became assistant secretary for the Middle East in the State Department under Madeleine Albright, while Dennis Ross was special coordinator for the peace process in the Middle East. In October 1999, Indyk was again named U.S. ambassador to Israel, replacing Edward Walker. On 21 September 2000, he was suddenly recalled to Washington for supposed "violation of security rules"; he returned to Israel a few weeks later. On this occasion, the Israeli press recalled that he had often been attacked by the Israeli right, who reproached him for his close ties with the Labor Party. On 12 July 2001, he resigned his post as ambassador to Israel, to be replaced by Daniel Kurtzer. In 2001 Indyk joined the Brookings Institution as senior fellow in the Foreign Policy Studies Program.

Martin Indyk. The U.S. ambassador to Israel visits Metulla in northern Israel in May 2000. After Israel unconditionally withdrew most of its forces from the southernmost part of Lebanon, eighteen years after invading and occupying it, Indyk announced the release of 50 million in U.S. military aid to improve Israeli security along that border. *(AP/Wide World Photos)*

SEE ALSO Albright, Madeleine; American Israel Public Affairs Committee; Djerejian, Edward; Ross, Dennis B.

Infitah: In Arabic, "opening up." The word was used by Egyptian President Anwar al-Sadat to designate the program of economic liberalization that he instituted in 1974, among whose provisions was the opening up of the country to greater foreign investment.

SEE ALSO Sadat, Anwar al-.

INSP

SEE Islamic National Salvation Party.

International Alliance for Arab-Israel Peace: An unofficial organization of prominent citizens, sometimes known as the Copenhagen Group, founded in January 1997 at Copenhagen to promote a just resolution to the Israel-Palestine issue. It holds public meetings and conferences, lobbies governments, monitors the human rights situation, and attempts to mobilize public opinion for its broad goals. The founding membership consisted of sixty representatives of a broad range of political opinion (from the DFLP to Likud) from Israel, Egypt, Jordan, and Palestine. The original founding committee consisted of David Kimche of Israel, Lutfi al-Khuli of Egypt, Ihsan Shurdom of Jordan, and Sari Nusseibeh of Palestine.

SEE ALSO Democratic Front for the Liberation of Palestine; Likud.

International Islamic Front: Loose coalition of radical Islamic groups created in August 1990 in Saudi Arabia and led by Osama Bin Ladin. Among the member organizations of this front were the Egyptian Islamic Jihad and al-Jamiʿa al-Islamiyya, the Jordanian Army of Muhammad, the Kashmiri Harkut al-Ansar (Partisans' Movement), and the Saudi Muhajirun (Exiles, Migrants). (This last was founded by Shaykh Omar bin Bakri Muhammad, who later established himself in London.)

In February 1998, Osama Bin Ladin issued a public statement calling for attacks on all Americans and announced the creation of a new World Islamic Front for Holy War against Jews and Crusaders. This umbrella organization included among its members the Egyptian Islamic Jihad and al-Jamiʿa al-Islamiyya, the Kashmiri Harkut al-Ansar, the Pakistani Jamiat ul-Ulema (Scholars' Group), and the Bangladeshi Islamic Jihad. The Islamic Army for the Liberation of the Holy Places, which claimed credit for the simultaneous attacks of 7 August 1998 against the American embassies in Nairobi and Dar es-Salaam, is understood to be this same group, also known as al-Qaʿida ("the Base").

SEE ALSO Bin Ladin, Osama; Egyptian Islamic Jihad; Jamiʿa al-Islamiyya, al-; World Islamic Front for Holy War against Jews and Crusaders.

INTIFADA (1987–1993): In 1987 the Israeli occupation of the West Bank and Gaza Strip had endured for twenty years. In 1967, the Israelis captured (among other places) the West Bank from Jordan and the Gaza Strip from Egypt, both of which were all that remained of former historic Palestine, and both had large Palestinian populations of refugees and indigenous residents.

During that time, under both Labor and Likud governments, Palestinians had been subjected to humiliating occupation policies—known to Israelis as the "Iron Fist"—designed to prevent the possibility of collective political action. Israeli authorities acted to suppress Palestinian political, social, and economic activity and institution-building by means of school and university closings, press censorship, curfews, control of travel, arbitrary arrests, deportations, home demolitions, limited access to markets and other restrictions on trade, border closings, destruction of agricultural property such as orchards and olive groves, and general harassment. Israel also established numerous permanent settlements in the territories, confiscated land and other property, took control of water resources, and established a physical infrastructure of roads and public works for the use of Israelis only. Israel also annexed and formally incorporated East Jerusalem and surrounding areas. The effect of these policies was not only to impoverish Palestinians and severely damage Palestinian society, but to establish "facts on the ground" that would make it difficult for any future Israeli government to agree to withdraw from the territories. At the same time, the Palestinian issue seemed to be disappearing from the official consciousness of the Arab world; the Arab League summit of November 1987 in Amman devoted almost no attention to it (the Iran-Iraq War was the primary issue).

When the cumulative humiliation, anger, and frustration of the Palestinians came to a head beginning in December 1987 in the popular rebellion against the occupation that came to be known as the (first) Intifada ("uprising"; literally "shaking off"), the intensity of the outrage was almost uncontainable. The Intifada began on 8 December 1987 in the Jabalya refugee camp in the Gaza Strip. Four Palestinians were killed and seven injured by an Israel Defense Force (IDF) truck that crashed into a line of cars at a border checkpoint. That evening a demonstration involving thousands arose spontaneously and continued over several days. Protests arose and spread rapidly in the West Bank and in East Jerusalem. There were clashes with the IDF, which responded with tear gas and live ammunition against stone-throwing demonstrators, mostly young and many of them children (this early phase became known as "the war of stones"), killing twenty-four of them by the end of December.

Neighborhood committees were soon organized, taking upon themselves the responsibility to provide social services, including health care and schooling, as well as to carry out acts of resistance. These began to coordinate their activities through a national structure, the Unified National Leadership of the Uprising (UNLU), which incorporated local members of Fatah, the Palestinian Communist Party (PCP), the Popular Front for the Liberation of Palestine (PFLP), and the Democratic Front for the Liberation of Palestine (DFLP). These new leaders, mostly young and having grown up under the occupation, became known as "Palestinians from inside." The established leadership of the Palestine Liberation Organization (PLO), then in exile in Tunis—"Palestinians from outside"—was surprised by these developments but soon began to provide assistance to (and attempted to exercise some control over) the spontaneous, populist movement of resistance.

In January 1988, members of the Muslim Brotherhood in Gaza organized the Islamic Resistance Movement (Harakat al-Muqawama al-Islamiyya, or HAMAS), which worked independently of the UNLU. The UNLU and HAMAS operated by means, at first, of anonymously printed leaflets (*bayanat*), and then of electronically distributed texts that were reproduced and distributed locally, with instructions and directives. Most called for nonviolent acts of civil

Palestinian Refugees. The First Intifada began in one of the refugee camps in the Gaza Strip in December 1987, in response to Israeli policies in the occupied West Bank and Gaza. By the time the outbursts of nonviolent civil disobedience and violent acts ended six years later, at least 1,200 Palestinians and 170 Israelis had been killed. *(© Peter Turnley/Corbis)*

disobedience, including boycotts, withholding of labor and taxes, general strikes, and demonstrations. As Israeli responses increased in severity, however, violence was often the result. Administrative measures included university closings, increased numbers of house demolitions, confiscation and destruction of agricultural land in the name of "security," mass arrests, curfews sometimes lasting for as much as a week at a time, and other forms of collective punishment. The IDF, encouraged publicly by the government to "break their bones," attacked demonstrators with beatings, tear gassings, and use of both rubber bullets and live ammunition. Palestinians were also attacked by armed settlers (it is estimated that about three hundred were killed by settlers, rather than by the IDF, during the Intifada). As the Intifada wore on, economic damage increased for both sides, and violence became more widespread, not only between Israelis and Palestinians but among Palestinians themselves. Fighters attacked the IDF; suspected collaborators were killed; rival factions fought among themselves. Islamic groups became prominent in Palestinian affairs for the first time. After the first four years, the Intifada was less coherent, but the disorder threatened both sides.

Yasir Arafat had been suggesting for some time that he was willing to negotiate a compromise solution to the Palestinian issue, but the Israelis had been unresponsive, instead pursuing policies intended to achieve permanent possession of the territories, with apparent success: by 1987 the Palestinian population seemed helpless to resist, the occupation was not disrupting Israeli society, and the PLO had been severely weakened by the IDF and its Lebanese proxies during the early 1980s. The Intifada, however, brought the message that suppression of Palestinian national feeling could not continue indefinitely, or at least not without an unacceptably high price. Images of the Intifada, particularly those of Palestinian adolescents confronting armed Israeli soldiers with stones, had a significant impact on public opinion, both Israeli and international. Though the Intifada provoked extreme responses—some, particularly among the settlers, revived the idea of deportation ("transfer") of all Palestinians—Israeli public opinion shifted in the direction of negotiations. In July 1988, King Hussein renounced all of Jordan's legal and administrative claims and responsibilities in the West Bank (including canceling the Jordanian citizenship of all West Bank Palestinians), thus leaving the PLO as the only institution with a plausible claim to represent Palestinian interests.

In November 1988, at the urging of Arafat, the Palestine National Council (PNC), meeting in Algiers, adopted a program favoring a peaceful settlement with Israel, based on UN Resolutions 181 and 242. Arafat was proposing Palestinian statehood in the West Bank and Gaza—the two-state solution. He reiterated this position before the UN General Assembly in Geneva the next month, explicitly accepting coexistence with Israel. The dangerous conditions represented by the Intifada and the Gulf War of 1991 led to the Madrid Conference on Middle East Peace. The Israelis continued to refuse to talk directly with Arafat or other representatives of the PLO, but shortly after the June 1992 Israeli elections a new government led by Yitzhak Rabin, elected on a platform of "land for peace," began the secret negotiations with it that led to the Oslo Accords. The Intifada began to die down around the time of the signing of the Declaration of Principles in Washington, D.C., in September 1993. Estimates of casualties vary by source; according to B'tselem, the Israeli human rights organization, from 8 December 1987 to 13 September 1993, 1205 Palestinians and 172 Israelis were killed; about 175,000 Palestinians were arrested.

SEE ALSO Arafat, Yasir; Democratic Front for the Liberation of Palestine; Fatah, al-; Gaza Strip; Gulf War (1991); HAMAS; Hussein ibn Talal; Iran-Iraq War; League of Arab States; Madrid Conference; Oslo Accords; Palestine National Council; Palestinian Communist Party; Rabin, Yitzhak; Resolution 181; Resolution 242; West Bank.

INTIFADA 2000

SEE Aqsa Intifada, al-.

INTIQAD, AL- (Critique): Weekly Arabic-language newspaper published by Hizbullah in Beirut since 2002. Previously called *al-Ahd* (The Covenant), published between 1984 and 2002.

IQAB ("punishment, sanction," in Arabic): Palestinian radical group, constituted in 1973 by members of the Black September movement. Libyan special services supported it in the hope of revenge for the Libyan Airlines Boeing airplane that was shot down over Sinai on 21 February 1973 by the Israeli air force. On 5 September 1973, five Palestinian members of this group, among whom were Amin al-Hindi and Atef Bseisso, were arrested in Italy while they were preparing an attack against an Israeli airliner. On 17 December, a commando of this splinter group carried out an attack on a Pan Am plane in the Rome airport, which caused thirty-four deaths. In 1975, after Black September was disbanded, Iqab was dissolved in its turn, its members joining the Palestinian security services, headed by Salah Khalaf.

SEE ALSO Black September Organization; Bseisso, Atef Fa'iq; Hindi, Amin al-; Khalaf, Salah.

IRAN-IRAQ WAR: Also known as the first Gulf War, a long, extremely costly, and inconclusive conflict fought from 1980 to 1988. In 1980 Iran was in an isolated and weakened condition as a result of the 1979 Islamic revolution. Its leader, Ayatollah Khomeini, had proclaimed a policy of exporting its Shiʿite Islamic ideology, an implicit threat to the Baʿthist state in Iraq, a secular, Sunni-dominated regime that kept itself in power partly by suppressing its Shiʿa majority.

The war began as a dispute over territory that was to have been returned to Iraq under the terms of a 1975 border treaty between the two countries. On 10 September 1980, Iraq took control of the disputed territory, and on 17 September renounced the 1975 treaty and claimed Iraqi sovereignty over the entire Shatt al-Arab, the estuary at the head of the Persian Gulf. On 22 September Iraq launched a full-scale invasion of Iran, including an aerial bombing campaign against military and economic targets. By November Iraq occupied some 10,000 square miles of Iran, including the city of Khorramshahr. Iraq offered to negotiate but Iran refused as long as Iraq occupied any of its territory. There was a stalemate until March 1982; between then and June 1982, the Iranians rallied and pushed the Iraqi forces back to their own borders. Again Iraq offered to negotiate, but this time Khomeini refused until Saddam Hussein was removed from office. In July 1982 Iranian forces began a series of offensives into Iraqi territory, including an unsuccessful attempt to take Basra. Over the next several years fighting moved back and forth and evolved into a World War I–style war of attrition, of defensive trench warfare, and of massive assaults of "human waves" that produced huge casualties. Both sides bombed civilians, and there is evidence that both sides used chemical weapons, although only Iraq did so on a large scale. Each side also attacked oil tankers in the Gulf carrying oil from the other's ports. Air attacks continued throughout the war, although by the later stages Iran's air force was seriously degraded.

Throughout the war, Iraq had the support of most Arab states, the Gulf states in particular (to which it became seriously indebted, a factor in the origin of the Gulf War of 1991), the Soviet Union, and the United States, which in the later stages of the war supplied it with weapons and intelligence, and which actually carried out naval strikes on its behalf in the Persian Gulf. The Iranians were supported by Syria, Libya, North Korea, and China (and received covert weapons shipments from the United States as well). In August 1988, after years of stalemate, with little territory gained by either side, both sides accepted a UN-sponsored truce. Estimates of the dead vary from 500,000 to 1,500,000, roughly two-thirds of them Iranian. In August 1990, at the same time that his armies were occupying Kuwait, Saddam Hussein agreed to honor the international boundary negotiated in 1975. Prisoner exchanges were still being negotiated as late as 2003.

SEE ALSO Gulf War (1991).

IRAQ: Iraq was under Ottoman rule before World War I. It was created as a state in 1921 by the British, who had arranged in 1919 to receive a League of Nations mandate to govern it. Previously known to Europeans as Mesopotamia, the new state comprised the Ottoman provinces of Mosul, Baghdad, and Basra. After violently suppressing (with, among other strategies, the first systematic campaign of aerial bombing of a civilian population) a 1920 nationalist revolt—one that contributed to the unification of the country—the British appointed as king Amir Faysal ibn Husayn al-Hashim, former king of Syria, son of Sharif Husayn of Mecca, and brother of Amir Abdullah I of Transjordan, who were leaders of the Arab Revolt against the Ottomans during the war. He died in 1933 and was succeeded by his son Ghazi, and after Ghazi's death in 1939 by his grandson Faysal II. A regent, Amir Abd al-Ilah al-Hashim, ruled in Faysal's place until he came of age in 1953.

The British ended the mandate in 1932 and Iraq became officially independent. Under the Anglo-Iraqi Treaty of 1930, however, Britain remained in control of Iraqi foreign policy and British troops were stationed on Iraqi soil. In 1941 a nationalist Iraqi government led by Rashid Ali Gailani staged a revolt against the British that was short-lived but suppressed only with great force. A new treaty with the British (which the government was forced to repudiate), as well as shortages, high prices, and the absence of popular elections, contributed to a revolt in 1948. The defeat of the Arab armies in the 1948 War, and particularly the poor performance of the ill-trained, ill-equipped Iraqi troops, exacerbated the public's anger. The war also caused economic problems. The expense, including allocations for Palestinian refugees, was crushing; the oil pipeline to Haifa was cut; and anti-Jewish sentiment led most of the Jewish community of 120,000, who had mainly been engaged in urban commerce, to emigrate by the early 1950s. Riots and protests broke out again in 1952; the government responded with heavy repression, declaring martial law, closing newspapers, and banning political parties, forcing the opposition underground.

The government was led by the British favorite Nuri al-Saʿid (prime minister seven times from 1930 to 1958), a former army officer and defense minister, with the help of the British-installed regent Abd al-Ilah. In 1955 Saʿid led Iraq into the Baghdad Pact, a Cold War, anti-Nasser alliance sponsored by Britain and the United States, prompting a call from Nasser for the Iraqi army to overthrow the monarchy; in 1956 Saʿid refused to condemn the aggression of Britain, France, and Israel in the Suez War, adversely affecting Iraq's relations with the Arab world. In 1957 he endorsed the Eisenhower Doctrine, a U.S. policy justifying U.S. intervention anywhere on anti-communist grounds. In July 1958, five months after King Hussein of Jordan, working with Abd al-Ilah, proposed to unite Iraq and Jordan into a pro-Western, anti-Nasser federation called the Arab Union, a coup d'état overthrew both the government and the monarchy. Saʿid was executed along with the king, Abd al-Ilah, and much of the royal family.

The coup was carried out by a military group formed in 1956, the Free Officers, containing both Iraqi nationalists and Nasserist pan-Arab nationalists. They were led by Brigadier Abd al-Karim al-Qasim and Colonel Abd al-Salim Arif. After the coup an internal dispute broke out about whether Iraq should join Egypt and Syria in the United Arab Republic (UAR); the Nasserists lost the argument. The new government pulled Iraq out of the Baghdad Pact and followed a policy of Cold War nonalignment. Qasim's government freed communist prisoners, suppressed the Baʿth Party, legalized trade unions, and instituted land reform, educational reform, and partial nationalization of oil. In 1959 an armed rebellion began among the Kurdish population in the northern part of the country, which has continued on and off ever since. Also in 1956 the Ba'th attempted to assassinate Qasim (the assassin was Saddam Hussein). In 1960 Qasim participated in founding the Organization of Petroleum Exporting Countries. In 1961 he threatened Kuwait, which had just become independent, claiming it as part of Iraq. Intervention by the Arab League (and secret payments by Kuwait) ended the crisis.

In February 1963 Qasim's government was overthrown and Qasim executed in a violent coup d'état carried out by the Ba'th in alliance with a group of military officers led by the former Free Officer Abd al-Salam Arif, who had been removed from the government, jailed, and sentenced to death for treason after losing the UAR argument (he was pardoned by Qasim in 1962). Arif became president. The Ba'th, using lists supplied by the American Central Intelligence Agency (CIA), systematically murdered suspected communists, leftists, and intellectuals. In November Arif expelled the Ba'thists, who were internally divided, from the government. He continued a policy of economic nationalization and revived the idea of unification with Egypt. After he was killed in a plane crash in 1966, his brother Abd al-Rahman Arif took his place, continuing the same policies but dropping preparations to unite with Egypt. Arif kept Iraq out of the 1967 War with Israel, and the regime's standing suffered as a result.

With political opposition building and street demonstrations demanding elections, the Ba'th Party, in alliance with some military officers, took power in a bloodless coup in July 1968; two weeks later the Ba'th expelled the non-Ba'thists from the government. The leader of the coup and the president of the Revolutionary Command Council was General Ahmad Hassan Bakr. His chief instrument behind the scenes was his cousin Saddam Hussein, who had been largely responsible for reorganizing and strengthening the Ba'th since 1963. Bakr and Hussein spent the next several years consolidating the Ba'th's power, which included the creation of a huge domestic intelligence apparatus; by the mid-1970s Hussein was clearly the one in charge. During this time he put down an uprising by the Kurds (1974) and negotiated a treaty dealing with an outstanding border dispute with Iran (1975). After Egypt became isolated in the Arab world as a result of the Camp David Accords of November 1978, Hussein hosted the Arab League summit in Baghdad that denounced Egypt. He also took advantage of the situation by improving Iraq's relations with Syria and Jordan. In 1979 Bakr resigned and Hussein took the position of president.

In 1980 Iran was isolated and weak as a result of the 1979 Islamic revolution. Its leader, Ayatollah Ruhollah Khomeini, had proclaimed a policy of exporting its Shi'a Islamist ideology, an implicit threat to the secular, Sunni-dominated Ba'thist regime in Iraq, which kept itself in power partly by suppressing the country's Shi'a majority. In April 1980 members of the Shi'a Islamist al-Da'wa, supported by Iran, attempted to assassinate the Iraqi foreign minister, Tariq Aziz, and were suspected of another attempted assassination. The government responded by deporting thousands of Iranian Shi'as. In the summer, Hussein had a leading Shi'a cleric, Ayatollah Muhammad Baqr al-Sadr, executed. Skirmishes took place over border territory that was to have been returned to Iraq under the terms of the 1975 treaty. On 10 September 1980, Iraq took control of the disputed territory, and on 17 September renounced the treaty and claimed Iraqi sovereignty over the entire Shatt al-Arab, the waterway that drains the Tigris and Euphrates rivers into the Persian Gulf. On 22 September Iraq launched a full-scale invasion of Iran, beginning the Iran-Iraq War of 1980 to 1988.

During the war, the Iraqi regime had the financial assistance of Gulf oil states that feared the influence of the Iranian revolution among their own Shi'a populations; it also received arms, equipment, and intelligence from the United States and its allies, as well as diplomatic assistance in blocking any international censure of Iraq for its conduct of the war. The war killed as many as 500,000 Iraqis and up to 1 million Iranians. After it was over, the regime attacked the Kurds, who had renewed their revolt with the assistance of the Iranians; during this period a chemical attack, which became infamous, on the Kurdish civilian population took place.

In July 1990, as the regime struggled to recover from the war, the price of oil fell to as low as $11 a barrel, severely damaging the Iraqi economy. Iraq was heavily in debt as a result of the war, and Saddam Hussein blamed the low price on deliberate overproduction by Kuwait and the United Arab Emirates. He demanded compensation in the form of debt forgiveness, the cession of Kuwait's Rumailiya oil fields (to which Iraq maintained the claim put forward by Abd al-Karim al-Qasim in 1961), and the leasing of two Kuwaiti islands at the head of the Persian Gulf for use as an oil port. The Kuwaitis refused. On 2 August 1990 Iraq invaded and occupied Kuwait. This led to the Gulf War of 1991, in which an international force including some Arab states and led by the

United States forced Iraq out of Kuwait and destroyed Iraq's military and much of the country's infrastructure. At its end, the Kurds revolted again, as did the Shiʿas of Basra province. Hundreds of thousands of Kurds fled into Turkey until the United States and Britain imposed a "no-fly" zone over the Kurdish areas of the north to protect the Kurds from retaliation and allow them to set up an autonomous government, which still exists. The Shiʿas of the south, however, were bloodily suppressed, with American acquiescence, and thousands were killed. After the war the United Nations, at American urging, instituted an arms inspection/destruction program as well as a set of economic sanctions (first imposed in August 1990) that crippled the Iraqi economy until it was destroyed altogether in the next war, in 2003.

Throughout the 1990s, the sanctions imposed on Iraq combined with the destruction of the war caused widespread destitution, food shortages, and rising public health problems, which particularly affected children. Iraq balked at complying with the requirements of the weapons inspection regime, and the United States and Britain, which carried out military overflights every day, bombed the country on three occasions in 1993, 1996, and 1998. Iraq had essentially complied with the resolutions by 1994 and Saddam Hussein spent the next nine years campaigning for an end to the embargo. A crisis arose in 1997 when the new chief of the UN Special Commission (UNSCOM) in charge of disarming Iraq became convinced that Saddam Hussein was withholding information about chemical weapons. The dispute was mediated by the UN secretary general, but in late 1998 UNSCOM pulled out of Iraq at the urging of the United States but without the permission of the Security Council; that December the United States and Britain launched the aerial bombing campaign Operation Desert Fox. As a result, in 1999 Hussein refused to allow the inspectors back under a new UN resolution. He attempted to develop support in the Arab world by sending assistance to the Palestinians in the al-Aqsa Intifada that began in September 2000, including compensation for the families of those who had attacked Israelis as suicide bombers.

After the terrorist attacks in the United States on 11 September 2001, the Bush administration engaged in a propaganda campaign associating them with Iraq and with Saddam Hussein personally, claiming, despite a lack of evidence, that he had built up stockpiles of weapons of mass destruction in contravention of UN resolutions. After months of building public sentiment for an attack, the Gulf War of 2003 was launched on 20 March, despite a lack of support from most of the world, despite Hussein's grudging delivery of all requested information about Iraqi arms programs and their destruction, and despite Hussein's acceptance of last-minute conditions. Iraq's shattered economy, weak military, and lack of weapons of mass destruction ensured that the war was over by 16 April. The occupation of Iraq by US and British forces, however, and the increasing level of armed resistance by various factions, continue. Saddam Hussein disappeared from Baghdad some time in April or May and was captured in a rural hideout in December. From April 2003 until June 2004, Iraq was ruled directly by US occupation authorities; in June 2004 a US-appointed interim "Iraqi" government took over.

The 2004 population of Iraq was about 24 million, of whom 78 percent were Arab, 18 percent Kurdish, and 4 percent other. About 96 percent of Iraqis were Muslim (62 percent Shiʿa and 34 percent Sunni) and 3 percent Christian (Chaldean Catholic, Nestorian, and Greek Orthodox).

SEE ALSO Abdullah I ibn Hussein; Aqsa Intifada, al-; Arab-Israel War (1967); Baghdad Pact; Camp David Accords; Daʿwa, al-; Desert Fox; Gulf War (1991); Hussein ibn Talal; Iran-Iraq War; Iraq War; League of Arab States; Organization of Petroleum Exporting Countries; Ottomans; Suez Crisis; United Arab Republic.

IRAQ WAR: War fought by a largely Anglo-American force in March and April 2003, leading to the overthrow of the Baʿthist regime of Saddam Hussein and the indefinite occupation of the country by the Americans and the British. The war was preceded by an extended diplomatic crisis over whether or not Iraq was complying with the disarmament regime imposed on it by the United Nations at the end of the Gulf War of 1991. Both the crisis and the war were driven by American claims that Iraq had, in violation of UN resolutions, maintained "stockpiles" of weapons of mass destruction, both chemical and nuclear, and that it was an immediate threat to its neighbors and the United States; that it engaged in proliferation of such weapons to terrorists and "rogue states"; and that it had "ties" to the al-Qaʿida organization of Osama bin Ladin that was responsible for the terrorist attacks in the United States on 11 September 2001.

All of these claims proved to be untrue. They generated little credence or support among the world's governments, and the buildup to war during

2002 inspired the largest popular protest demonstrations in history. The claims were refuted by UN arms inspectors before the war, and no evidence could be found to sustain them after Iraq was occupied. The war did fit, however, with the strategic plans of the U.S. administration of George W. Bush, based upon effective American control of Middle East and Central Asian petroleum resources and the strategic needs of its ally, Israel (for which some of the most important American strategic planners have also worked), and had been planned even before Bush took office in 2001. The United States is currently engaged in building no fewer than fourteen permanent bases for its forces to occupy, when and if it is able to overcome the current armed resistance to its presence.

SEE ALSO Bin Ladin, Osama; Bush, George W.; Gulf War (1991); Hussein, Saddam; International Islamic Front.

IRGUN (IZL, Irgun Zvai Le'umi; National military organization, in Hebrew): Nationalist extremist Jewish movement that surfaced in Palestine in spring 1931 after a scission in Haganah between political and military figures. Its principal founder, Avraham Tehomi, resigned from the Haganah in April 1931 to create the National Haganah, or Haganah B, along with nineteen other officers. In August of 1933, inspired by the revisionist ideas of Vladimir Jabotinsky and backed by the religious party Mizrachi, the movement decided to reply in kind to Arab attacks, taking as a slogan *Rak kach* ("only this way," in Hebrew). In 1936, the leadership of Haganah B strongly criticized the policies of the British in Palestine, which it considered pro-Arab. The British authorities accepted increased Jewish participation in police duties. David Ben-Gurion asked the semiofficial Haganah to exercise *havlagah* ("restraint," in Hebrew), that is to say cease all terrorist activity.

In April 1937, a scission surfaced in the movement between the partisans and the adversaries of *havlagah,* as well as between the revisionists and diverse political tendencies in the organization. Tehomi and his supporters decided to rejoin the Haganah and those who embraced the hard line, headed by David Raziel and Avraham ("Ya'ir") Stern, created their own movement, the Irgun. On 14 November 1937 a commando of the latter group killed eight Arabs in the Jewish quarter of Jerusalem, which led to such a vigorous repression on the part of British authorities that the Irgun decided to cease all violent actions until June, when Shlomo Ben-Yosef, a member of Betar close to the Irgun, was hanged.

Between 4 July and 26 August 1938, the Irgun organized a wave of anti-Arab attacks that caused more than 100 deaths. On 11 September at the Betar World Congress in Warsaw, Menachem Begin attracted notice with his advocacy of armed struggle. In May 1939, the Irgun, under the guidance of Avraham Stern, resumed attacks on the British and Arabs. In September 1940, a scission caused by Jabotinsky's death led to two currents surfacing in the Irgun: one, under the impetus of David Raziel, favoring an alliance with the British against Nazi Germany; the other, headed by Avraham Stern, favoring struggle against British forces in Palestine. Stern quit the Irgun to form his own movement, the Lohamei Herut Yisrael (LEHI). In May of 1941, David Raziel was killed in the course of a mission in Iraq. Yaacov Meridor replaced him as the head of the Irgun but was not able to supply the impetus necessary for the organization to survive.

In December 1943, Begin, after being demobilized from the Polish army, took command of the Irgun. On 2 February 1944 he published a communiqué calling for the Jewish people to struggle against the British forces present in Palestine. Although his program was similar to LEHI's, Begin was not successful in rallying its members to his party. In October 1945 the Irgun, LEHI, and Haganah decided to coordinate their actions against the British authorities, creating a united front, the United Hebrew Resistance (Tnuat ha-Meri ha-Ivri), under the control of Committee X of the Haganah.

On 17 June 1946, Irgun and Palmach units blew up ten of the eleven bridges linking Palestine and Transjordan. On 29 June the British authorities started Operation Agatha, during which a number of members of the United Resistance were arrested along with leaders of the Jewish Agency and a significant quantity of arms and documents were seized. The captured documents were stored at the headquarters of the British army at the King David Hotel in Jerusalem. On 22 July an Irgun commando led by Israel Levy blew up part of the hotel, killing ninety-one people. Confronted with the traumatized reaction of the Jewish community, the United Hebrew Resistance was disbanded, although the Irgun continued the struggle against the British forces.

Between December 1946 and August 1947, the Irgun's attacks were responsible for the deaths of many British soldiers, shocking the British public. British leaders branded the Irgun leaders, including Begin, terrorists and threatened to hang them. At the end of August 1947 the United Nations proposed partitioning Palestine into two independent states,

Jewish and Arab. The Irgun, thinking its battle had been won, directed its operations solely against the Arabs. On 9 April 1948, accompanied by men from LEHI, an Irgun commando attacked the Arab village of Deir Yassin, massacring more than 100 of its 750 villagers. The following May the Irgun recognized the authority of David Ben-Gurion's provisional government while warning against renouncing all of Greater Israel.

The *Altalena* incident on 21 June 1948, in which the eponymous ship carrying Irgun arms to Israel was sunk by gunfire ordered by Ben-Gurion, marked the end of the Irgun, most of whose members joined the new Israeli army, the Israel Defense Force. Begin, after creating the nationalist Herut Party, became prime minister in 1977.

SEE ALSO *Altalena*; Begin, Menachem; Ben-Gurion, David; Betar; Haganah; Herut Party; Israel Defense Force; Jabotinsky, Vladimir; Lohamei Herut Yisrael; Meridor, Yaacov; Mizrachi; Palmah.

ISA: Arabic word used for Jesus. In Islam, he is recognized as a prophet but not as the son of God.

SEE ALSO Jesus.

ISAAC (Ishaq, in Arabic): Son of the prophet Abraham and his wife, Sarah. Because the latter was sterile, the birth of Isaac is considered an expression of the divine will to provide a descendant for the first prophet of God. According to the Hebrew Bible, God, wanting to test Abraham's faith, asked him to sacrifice Isaac. Seeing that Abraham was ready to do so, God intervened and Abraham sacrificed a ram in place of his son. Followers of the Qur'an believe Isaac's half-brother, Ishmael (Isma'il, in Arabic), was the sacrificial son. The Jews consider Isaac the first of their lineage, whereas Ishmael is thought of as the ancestor of the Arabs.

SEE ALSO Abraham; Ishmael; Qur'an.

ISHMAEL (Isma'il, in Arabic): Son of the prophet Abraham and his Egyptian servant Hagar. Abraham's wife, Sarah, after having miraculously given birth to Isaac (Ishaq, in Arabic) in spite of persistent sterility, was jealous of this older son. In response to Sarah's demand, Abraham disassociated himself from Hagar and her son. Although Jews, Christians, and Muslims agree that Abraham showed his faith in God by sacrificing his beloved only son when asked to, they disagree on the identity of the child. The Bible states that this child was Isaac. Followers of Qur'an believe Ishmael was the sacrificial son, although the Qur'an does not give the child's name. Muslims note that the Bible supports their belief by saying that Abraham offered his only son, and Ishmael was Abraham's only son for more than thirteen years, which would make it impossible for Isaac to be the son he sacrificed. A popular tradition recorded in the Bible makes Ishmael the ancestor of the Arabs of the desert (Ishmaelites). Islamic tradition also recognizes Ishmael as ancestor of the Arabs, while his half-brother Isaac is considered the ancestor of the Jews.

SEE ALSO Abraham; Isaac; Qur'an.

ISLAM: Arabic word formed from the root *salam* (peace), meaning submission or reconciliation (to the will of God). Founded in Arabia in the 7th century, Islam is the religion professed by the prophet Muhammad. Muslims believe that God revealed himself to Muhammad through oral communications which he received while meditating on Mount Hira, near Mecca, through the intermediary of the archangel Djabra'il (Djibril, Gabriel). These revelations were written down during Muhammad's life, and later collected in the Qur'an, the entire corpus of revelations. Muhammad was charged with the task of transmitting the message to humankind, based on the unity of God, and to become thereby an Arab prophet of the God of Abraham and Moses.

In preaching this message, Muhammad struggled for almost twenty years with the reigning polytheism of the region. Confronted by Meccan hostility, he and his supporters left Mecca for Medina on 16 July 622. This date was considered subsequently to mark the beginning of the Muslim era: the hijra (immigration or exile). In 630, after many months of fighting, the Muslim community took Mecca, where they destroyed the many idols in the Ka'ba, built by Abraham, leaving only the Black Stone in place. After the death of the prophet Muhammad in 632, Islamic rule spread, in a little over a century, from Samarkand (Uzbekistan) to Andalusia.

In the Muslim religion, the believer is alone with Allah, without the intermediary of any clergy, the imam being there only to direct the collective prayer. Five "pillars of Islam" define what it means to be a Muslim: *shahada* (profession of monotheistic faith), *salat* (prayer in the direction of Mecca), *sawm* (fasting during the period of Ramadan), *zakat* (charity obligation), and the *hajj* (pilgrimage to Mecca during the 12th lunar month).

THE PROPHET MUHAMMAD. THIS MINIATURE FROM THE SIXTEENTH CENTURY DEPICTS THE FOUNDER OF ISLAM MOUNTED ON HIS STEED, BURAQ, AS HE ASCENDS TO PARADISE. IN THE QUR'AN THE PROPHET JOURNEYS IN ONE NIGHT TO THE "FAR DISTANT PLACE OF WORSHIP," MEANING JERUSALEM, AND CONTINUES ON TO THE HEAVENS. *The Granger Collection, New York. Reproduced by permission.*

As it evolved throughout history Islam, like all other religions, has known division and dissidence (*fitna*), reflecting a diversity of doctrinal opinions and juridical options. Consequently, Sunnism and Shi'ism have become the two principal components of Islam.

Finally, Islam defines itself as a religion and project of community life based on a double source: the laws revealed in the Qur'an and the practices instituted by the prophet Muhammad recorded in the Sunna (the sayings and practices of the Prophet).

SEE ALSO Abraham; Hijra; Ka'ba; Mecca; Moses; Muhammad; Shi'a; Sunna.

ISLAMIC ACTION FRONT (IAF): Jordanian branch of the Muslim Brotherhood, transformed into a political party on 8 December 1992, as allowed by the Jordanian law of the preceding 6 July. In the Jordanian legislative elections of 1993, the IAF won thirteen seats in the House of Deputies, and on 8 November of the following year it obtained sixteen (out of a total of eighty seats). In the summer of 1997, a reformist current surfaced in the party, headed by Majid al-Nasser. In the following December, several members of this current were elected to the party's consultative council (*shura*). In the parliamentary election in June 2003, the IAF won twenty seats (out of a total of 104). The IAF, which is the principal Islamist entity in Jordan, was opposed to the Jordanian-Israeli peace accord and to normalization of relations between Jordan and Israel. It also opposed the Iraq War of 2003 and the subsequent occupation of Iraq by American and British forces. The IAF has a general secretariat, an executive committee of seventeen members, a consultative council of 120 members, and local sections. The Secretary General of the IAF in 2004 was Shaykh Hamza Mansur.

SEE ALSO Iraq War; Muslim Brotherhood.

ISLAMIC ARMY FOR THE LIBERATION OF THE HOLY PLACES (al-Jaish el-Islami li-Tahrir al-Muqadasat, in Arabic): This movement claimed responsibility for the attacks of 7 August 1998 carried out simultaneously against the American embassies in Nairobi (Kenya) and Dar es-Salaam (Tanzania). This small group is thought to have joined the International Islamic Front constituted in 1990.

SEE ALSO International Islamic Front.

ISLAMIC AVANT-GARDE

SEE Shiqaqi, Fathi.

ISLAMIC CALENDAR: Based on a cycle of twelve lunar months, the Islamic calendar alternates months of twenty-nine and thirty days to make a year of 354 or 355 days. In the Islamic calendar, the twenty-four-hour day starts at sunset. The Muslim era began on 16 July 622 C.E., according to some, 16 or 24 September, according to others, presumed dates of the beginning of the prophet Muhammad's Hijra to Medina. The month of Ramadan can last twenty-nine or thirty days, and, in relation to the solar calendar, the date moves back every year by eleven days. The first month of the Hijri calendar is Muharram, followed by the months of Safar, Rabi al-Awwal, Rabi al-Thanni, Jumâda al-oula, Jumâda al-Thânnyia, Rajab,

Shabân, Ramadhan, Shawâl, Dhû al-Qa'da and Dhû al-Hijja.

SEE ALSO Hijra; Muhammad; Ramadan.

ISLAMIC CONFERENCE

SEE Organization of the Islamic Conference.

ISLAMIC CONFERENCE ORGANIZATION

SEE Organization of the Islamic Conference.

ISLAMIC DEVELOPMENT BANK (IDB): Specialized institution of the Organization of the Islamic Conference, created in 1974 to contribute to the economic development of member states according to the principles of *Shari'a*.

SEE ALSO Organization of the Islamic Conference; Shari'a.

ISLAMIC FIGHTING FORCE

SEE Qassam.

ISLAMIC JIHAD: A movement of loosely associated extreme Islamists (known as *jihadis*) in the Muslim world. There are many tendencies in the movement—Sunni, Shi'a, pro-Iranian, pro-Egyptian, pro-Saudi. Islamic Jihad in Lebanon is Shi'ite; in Egypt and Palestine, Sunni. The Sunni groups are influenced by the Saudi Wahhabi movement. All jihadis advocate a return to the "genuine Islam" of the prophet Muhammad, with the Qu'ran and *Shari'a* as the foundation for state and society. The modern Islamic movement arose at the beginning of the 1970s, after the Arab defeat in the June 1967 Arab-Israel war, an event that encouraged millenial interpretations among both Muslims and ultra-orthodox Jews.

The creation of the Organization of the Islamic Conference (OIC) by Saudi Arabia in September 1969 reflected this reality in the Muslim world. The OIC proposed the establishment of an "Islamic nation" according to the strictest laws of the Muslim religion, while favoring "Islamic orthodoxy." This institution also participated in the re-Islamization of society by building schools and mosques and by opening Islamic banks. Backed by Saudi Arabia, Islamist political activity revived in countries where it had been harshly repressed, such as Egypt and Syria. After the Arab-Israel War of 1973, Muslims in many countries, disappointed by the ineffective, secular, nominally socialist politics of so many Muslim countries, turned toward Saudi Arabia and Wahhabism. The proclamation of an Islamic republic in Iran, even though Shi'ite (a minority within Islam), confirmed for the Islamist faithful the value of practicing jihad as "holy war." Resorting to terrorism to achieve their ends, jihadis have been responsible for the deaths of hundreds of people (among them Egyptian president Anwar al-Sadat in 1981). At the beginning of the 1980s, many jihadis joined the ranks of the Afghan resistance against the Soviet army. Some of them, called "Afghans," upon returning to their native countries placed the technical expertise they acquired during this conflict (1979–1989) at the disposal of extremist movements in their own countries.

SEE ALSO Arab-Israel War (1967); Muhammad; Organization of the Islamic Conference; Sadat, Anwar al-.

ISLAMIC JIHAD, EGYPTIAN

SEE Egyptian Islamic Jihad.

ISLAMIC JIHAD, PALESTINIAN

SEE Palestinian Islamic Jihad.

ISLAMIC LIBERAL PARTY

SEE Arab Islamic Liberal Party.

ISLAMIC LIBERATION ORGANIZATION: Palestinian movement (Munazamat al-Tahrir al-Islamiya, in Arabic), founded in 1971 by Salah Sarriya, Fatah member and dissident of the Islamic Liberation Party (ILP). Following the Arab defeat of June 1967, Salah Sarriya went to Egypt, where, with a few members of the Muslim confraternities, he created a number of underground Islamic cells. On 18 April 1974, he attempted a coup in Heliopolis, so as to take power in Egypt and proclaim the foundation of an Egyptian Islamic state. The attack on the military barracks failed, at a cost of around forty deaths, and Salah Sarriya was captured, then hanged in November 1976, along with Talal Ansari, head of a cell of the movement at the University of Alexandria. The death of Sarriya resulted in the disappearance of his movement. In 1977, some of his followers participated in the creation of the Egyptian Islamic Jihad.

SEE ALSO Arab-Israel War (1967); Fatah, al-; Islamic Liberation Party.

ISLAMIC LIBERATION PARTY (ILP): Organization (Hizb al-Tahrir al-Islami, in Arabic) created in November 1952 in Jerusalem by Shaykh Taqi al-Din al-

Nabhani (1909–1979), who broke with the Muslim Brotherhood because of its links with the Jordanian Hashemite government. Nabhani was an Islamic court judge in Jerusalem and a former associate of the mufti of Jerusalem, Hajj Amin al-Husayni.

The ILP advocated the establishment of a new caliphate in the Islamic world, opposing both pan-Arabism and nationalist ideas of the left. Because of its opposition to the Hashemite regime, it was soon banned in Jordan, and Nabhani fled to Lebanon in 1953. ILP members were implicated in a number of coup attempts in Jordan (1969), Egypt (1974), and Tunisia (1985). The general ideas of the ILP were adopted by Shaykh Asad Bayud Tamimi, one of the founders of the Palestinian Islamic Jihad. In June 1993, several members of the ILP were questioned by the Jordanian police, accused of having attempted to assassinate King Hussein. In August 1994, the ILP sponsored an Islamic conference in London attended by representatives of HAMAS, the Algerian Armed Islamic Group, and Hizbullah. Today the Islamic Liberation Party exists in Britain, where it is legal—its British branch was founded in 1986 by Shaykh Omar Bakri Muhammad—and illegally in a number of Arab and non-Arab Islamic countries; most of its members are now said to be Central Asian. In 2003 it was banned in Russia, where the government accused it of association with Islamic fighters in Chechnya, and it has been accused of terrorist activities in Uzbekistan, although there is no evidence that it has ever been involved in violence or terrorism. In 2004 a group of twenty-six Islamists, including five Britons, were jailed for attempting to revive the party in Egypt.

SEE ALSO Hizbullah; Husayni, Hajj Amin al-; Hussein ibn Talal; Muslim Brotherhood; Palestinian Islamic Jihad.

ISLAMIC MOVEMENT FOR THE LIBERATION OF PALESTINE (al-Haraka al-Islamiyya il-Tahrir Filastin, in Arabic): Movement created at the beginning of the 1980s by Shaykh Jabir Abdallah Ammar, member of Fatah, with the approval of the latter, desirous of taking control of a part of the Islamist current that had appeared among the Palestinians since the victory of the Iranian revolution.

SEE ALSO Fatah, al-; Palestinian Islamic Jihad.

ISLAMIC NATIONAL SALVATION PARTY (Hizb al-Khalas al-Watani al-Islami, in Arabic): Created in Gaza, on 19 March 1996, so as to realize "Palestinian national unity," this Palestinian entity attracted influential figures from the Muslim Brotherhood. The INSP made a point of distinguishing itself from HAMAS, in that its political program provided for no form of armed resistance. Its main leaders were Fu'ad Nahal (president), Ismael Abu Shanab, Fikr Abdul Latif (spokesperson), and Ahmad Mahmud Bahar.

SEE ALSO HAMAS; Muslim Brotherhood.

ISLAMIC NATIONAL UNION: Palestinian Islamic movement (al-Ittihad al-Watani al-Islami, in Arabic), created in February 1996 by Khadr ʿAttiya Muhjaz, a dissident of the Islamic National Way Movement. This party united former members or sympathizers of HAMAS, opposed to the utilization of violence. Its founder, Muhjaz, a member of the Muslim Brotherhood, was a poet and preacher much appreciated in the Gaza Strip.

SEE ALSO HAMAS; Islamic National Way Movement; Muslim Brotherhood.

ISLAMIC NATIONAL WAY MOVEMENT (Harakat al-Masar al-Watani al-Islami, in Arabic): Palestinian Islamic movement, created in August 1995 in the Gaza Strip by a former member of HAMAS, Mahmud Abu Dan, who had resigned from it in 1991 to join the Fatah of Yasir Arafat. Favorable to the Oslo Accords, some think that this movement was founded at the request of the leader of Fatah, so as to attempt to attract the moderates and malcontents of HAMAS. At the beginning of 1996, one of its leaders, Khadr Attiya Muhjaz, separated from it to found his own party, the Islamic National Union.

SEE ALSO Fatah, al-; Gaza Strip; HAMAS; Islamic National Union; Oslo Accords.

ISLAMIC RESISTANCE MOVEMENT

SEE HAMAS.

ISLAMIC SALVATION FOUNDATION

SEE Bin Ladin, Osama

ISLAMIC UNIFICATION MOVEMENT (IUM): Lebanese organization (Harakat al-Tawhid al-Islami, in Arabic) uniting anti-Syrian Islamic movements. The IUM surfaced in 1984 after the dissolution of the Islamic Union Front (IUF) of Khalil al-Akkawi. It was organized by Shaykh Said Shaʿaban (d. 1998), former member of the Lebanese Islamic Group (Jamiʿa al-Islamiyya Libnaniyya) and professor of Arab literature at Tripoli since 1964, who had followed a course of religious studies abroad, particularly in Egypt and Iraq.

The IUM proposed liberating Lebanon from all foreign occupation, in view of creating an Islamic republic. Between 1984 and 1987 the movement went underground, participating in the fighting against Syrian forces present in Lebanon; then it returned to the Lebanese political arena in 1988. Two years later, a pro-Syrian current, headed by Malik Allush, appeared in the IUM. Since 1991, the leadership of the IUM has benefited from financial help from Tehran, and has become more conciliatory toward Syria. Opposing the Israeli-Palestinian accord of 13 September 1993, the IUM was very involved in the struggle against the Israeli presence in South Lebanon, which ended with an Israeli pullout in 2000. Since then it has focused on its current leader, who is Bilal Sha'aban. A faction called Islamic Unification Group—Leadership Council is headed by Hashim Minqara, who was imprisoned by the Syrians from 1986 to 2000.

ISLAMIC VANGUARD

SEE Shiqaqi, Fathi.

ISLAMISM: Ideology that calls for 1) the practice of Islam to be returned to its sources (*salaf*) in the "true religion," and 2) the organization and regulation of society and the state by Qur'an and *shari'a*. In many Arab countries, where political expression is often heavily repressed by the state, Islamism is a way of challenging social or political power. This current surfaced at the end of the nineteenth century, at a time when most Muslim countries were controlled by European powers. Consequently "Islamic reformism," initiated by Jamal al-din al-Afghani, was having a significant impact by the beginning of the twentieth century. The first modern Islamist movement was the Muslim Brotherhood, which began in Egypt in 1928.

SEE ALSO Muslim Brotherhood.

ISLAMIST: Embodying or acting upon an ideology of Islamism.

SEE ALSO Islamism.

ISRA': According to Qur'anic tradition, in 622 or 623 C.E., after having fallen asleep, the Prophet Muhammad made a voyage (*isra'*), known as the Night Journey, from Medina to Jerusalem, straddling a mare named Buraq, which had a woman's head and a peacock's tail.

Arriving at the Rock of Abraham in what is now the Noble Sanctuary (Haram al-Sharif) on the hill known to Jews as the Temple Mount, he tied up Buraq at the wall, which Jews currently refer to as the Wailing Wall and which Muslims call the Wall of Buraq. Muhammad then ascended to the heavens (*mi'raj*) where God made a revelation to him, and where he prayed together with the prophets and patriarchs. Muslims commemorate the nocturnal ascension of Muhammad on the 27th of the month of Rajab. The revelation associated with it (Surat al-Isra, Sura 17) reads: "Glory be to him who took His slave [Muhammad] on a journey by night, / From the Holy Mosque to the Furthest Mosque, / The precincts of which We have blessed, / That We might show him some of Our signs. / He is the All-Hearing, the All-Seeing." The al-Aqsa (Furthest) Mosque in the Haram al-Sharif was built to commemorate the Night Journey and named after the reference to "the Furthest Mosque" in the Qur'anic verse.

SEE ALSO Muhammad.

ISRAEL: Hebrew word meaning "Let God rule." According to Biblical tradition, this name designates Jacob, son of Isaac, as well as the twelve tribes whose eponyms are the sons of Jacob that comprise the Jewish people. Grandson of Abraham, Jacob took the name of Israel, which also means "strong against God," as a result of a nocturnal combat against an angel at the ford of Jabbok. For some, the name comes from the Hebrew verb *saro* ("struggle") or *sar el* ("God's minister"), or even from *yachar el* ("in the right before God"). This name is also used to designate one kingdom, which had nineteen kings between 930 and 722 B.C.E., from Jeroboam to Hosea, of the two kingdoms that issued from that of Solomon. The first archaeological trace of the name of Israel was found on the Egyptian Merenptah stele, which dates from around 1230 B.C.E.

SEE ALSO Abraham; Isaac; Jacob.

ISRAEL, STATE OF (Medinat Yisrael, in Hebrew): Middle East land bordered by the Mediterranean on the west, Lebanon on the north, Syria and Jordan on the east, the Red Sea on the south, and Egypt on the southwest. The country's length is 270 miles (435 km) from north to south; at its widest it is 67 miles (108 km). On 15 May 1948, a few hours before the expiration of the British mandate, the creation of the State of Israel was proclaimed by David Ben-Gurion, who read its "Declaration of Independence." This decision was made after the United Nations had passed, on 29 November 1947, Resolution 181, recommending the partition of Palestine into two independent states, one Jewish and the other Arab, and after Great Britain had announced its decision to turn its mandate over Palestine back to the United Nations. The declaration sparked clashes between Jewish and Arab Palestinians, leading to the first of the five Arab-Israel wars, in which the armies of neighboring Arab states entered the former mandate lands. Four armistice agreements in 1949 were negotiated between Israel and Egypt, Jordan, Lebanon, and Syria, though no peace treaties were signed. Arab Palestinians fled the country in great numbers; though there are no official figures, the United Nations estimated that over 700,000 Palestinians—over half the Arab population of Mandatory Palestine—became refugees.

The State of Israel, recognized by the principal world powers, has been rejected since its beginnings by the Palestinians, who had lived in this land for centuries, and by the ensemble of neighboring Arab countries. Following the Arab-Israel War of 1967, Israel occupied territory equal to more than three times its previous area; the new territories included the Golan Heights, the Sinai Peninsula, part of the West Bank, some of the Gaza Strip, and East Jerusalem. UN Security Council Resolution 242 called for Israel's withdrawal from the newly occupied territories, which has yet to be negotiated, and which remains at the center of negotiations for a peaceful resolution of the Israeli-Palestinian conflict.

Between 1948 and the 1990s, more than 2 million Jews migrated to Israel, many fleeing persecution in their own countries. There was a massive migration of Jews from the Soviet Union in the late 1980s and 1990s, and Soviet Jews became the largest ethnic group in Israel in the twenty-first century. In 2003 the population of Israel was 6.7 million. The Arab community represented 19 percent of the population; of these, 77 percent were Muslim, 13 percent Christian, and 10 percent Druze.

SEE ALSO Arab-Israel War (1948); Arab-Israel War (1967); Ben-Gurion, David; British Mandate; Resolution 181; Resolution 242.

ISRAEL AHAT

SEE One Israel.

ISRAELI-ARAB PEACE PROCESS: For significant dates please refer to the Arab-Israeli Conflict timeline located in the appendix.

SEE ALSO Aqsa Intifada, al-; Arab-Israel War (1948); Arab-Israel War (1967); Arab-Israel War (1973); Arab Revolt; Arafat, Yasir; Balfour Declaration; Barak, Ehud; Begin, Menachem; Black September; Bush, George H. W.; Camp David Accords; Camp David II Summit; Clinton, William Jefferson; Egypt; Fahd Plan; Golan Heights; Gulf War (1991); Haram al-Sharif; Hussein ibn Talal; Intifada (1987–1993); Lebanon; League of Arab States; Likud; Madrid Conference; Nasser, Gamal Abdel; Netanyahu, Benjamin; Oslo Accords; Oslo Accords II; Ottomans; Palestine Liberation Organization; Palestine National Council; Resolution 181; Resolution 194; Resolution 242; Resolution 338; Road Map (2002); Rogers Plan; Sharm al-Shaykh Summits; Sykes-Picot Agreement; Syria.

ISRAEL BE-ALIYAH (Israel with Immigration): Israeli political party, founded in June 1995 by Anatoly (Natan) Sharansky to defend the social rights of immigrants from Russia. Its political platform, published on the following 1 November, affirmed the "inalienable right of the people of Israel over the land of Israel, from the Mediterranean to the Jordan, including all of the West Bank"; and rejected the creation of a Palestinian state, but envisaged autonomy for the occupied territories.

As a result of the elections of 29 May 1996, the party obtained seven seats in the Knesset, with Anatoly Sharansky being named minister of commerce and industry in the government of Benjamin Netanyahu. In 1997 a police investigation revealed that Israel be-Aliyah had received financing from Grishka Lerner, presumed head of the Russian mafia in Israel. Between 1997 and 1998, Israel be-Aliyah lost some of the support of the community that had come from Russia, which reproached its leader for positions it thought too moderate. On 18 May 1999, as a result of the elections, which saw the victory of Ehud Barak, Israel be-Aliyah won six seats. On 6 July, Sharansky became minister of the interior, and Marina Solodkin became deputy minister of immigrant absorption in Barak's cabinet. In December the leadership of the party threatened the government with withdrawing its support in case of negotiations on the Israeli retreat from the Golan Heights. In February 2001, the party supported the leader of Likud, Ariel Sharon, for the post of prime minister, against Ehud Barak, who lost the elections. On the following 7 March, Sharansky became minister of housing and construction in Sharon' cabinet. The main figures in the party are Sharansky, Yuli Edelstein, Roman Bronfman, Vera Golavensky, Solodkin, Yuri Stern, and Felix Aushrenko. The party supports a democratized Palestinian Authority as an essential element of the peace process. In the 2003 elections, it received 2.2 percent of the vote and two seats in the Knesset.

SEE ALSO Barak, Ehud; Knesset; Likud; Netanyahu, Benjamin; Sharansky, Natan; Sharon, Ariel.

ISRAEL BEITEINU ("Israel is our home," in Hebrew): Israeli political party of the right, founded on 3 January 1999 by Avigdor Lieberman, former chief of staff of Prime Minister Benjamin Netanyahu. Constituted for the scheduled Knesset elections of the following 17 May, the party proposed rallying the votes of Russian immigrants to Israel to Benjamin Netanyahu, taking some that would have gone to Israel be-Aliyah. This ultranationalist grouping advocated a "Greater Israel," with a "strong" government. On 18 May, as a result of the ballot, it won four seats in the Knesset, while the head of the Israel Labor Party, Ehud Barak, was elected prime minister.

On 7 March, 2001, Avigdor Lieberman became minister of infrastructure in the government of Ariel Sharon, head of Likud. Israel Beiteinu formed a coalition—the National Union—with two other right-wing parties: Moledet and Tekumah. The National Union advocates the voluntary transfer of Arabs from the West Bank and Gaza to other Arab countries, and it opposes concessions to the Palestinian Authority and the creation of a Palestinian state. In the 2003 elections the National Union received 5.5 percent of the vote and won seven seats in the Knesset.

SEE ALSO Greater Israel; Lieberman, Avigdor; Netanyahu, Benjamin; Sharon, Ariel.

ISRAEL COMMITTEE AGAINST HOUSE DEMOLITIONS (ICAHD): A self-described nonviolent, direct-action group, the Israel Committee Against House Demolitions was established to oppose the Israeli demolition of Palestinian houses in the occupied territories. It opposes as well the expansion of Jewish settlements in the occupied territories and policies of "closure" and "separation." ICAHD describes its activities as resistance and protest, including attempts by its members to physically block bulldozers sent to demolish homes; dissemination of information to the Israeli public and the international community; and the provision of support to Palestinian families, particularly in dealing with Israeli authorities. ICAHD maintains a web site (http://www.icahd.org) where it posts information about Israeli demolition in the occupied territories, which it claims destroyed as many as 4,500 Palestinian homes during the al-Aqsa Intifada. ICAHD supports the peace process and the creation of a Palestinian state.

SEE ALSO Aqsa Intifada, al-; Occupied Territories.

ISRAEL COMMUNIST PARTY (MAKI) (Miflagah Komunistit Yisraelit): Israeli Communist party, founded in the mid-1960s, following a split within the RAKAH (Reshima Komunistit Hadashah, "New Communist List") party over differences between Communism and Zionism. Representing a mostly Zionist current, MAKI advocated that Israel evacuate the quasi-totality of the occupied territories, as well as negotiate a solution with the Palestinians. In 1973, this party disappeared from the political scene after merging with the T'helet-Adom (the "Blue-Red" movement) to form Moked.

SEE ALSO Moked.

ISRAEL DEFENSE FORCE (IDF; in Hebrew, Tsahal: Ts'va Haganah L'Israel): Successor to the self-defense militias of the Jewish community of Palestine, under the British mandate, the Israel Defense Force (IDF) was officially created on 26 May 1948. The army plays an important role in Israel, not only in matters of defense but also in politics and daily life. Israelis are obliged to serve in the army for relatively long terms: three years for men and two for women. In the course of five wars, the IDF has forged a reputation of invincibility, attributable to the determination of its soldiers as well as to the excellence of its matériel. Handicapped strategically because of its small size, Israel has been confronted with a permanent security problem. Having to choose between a lasting war and an uncertain peace, the Israeli military leaders have made every effort to maintain a technical and technological advantage over the neighboring Arab states as well as those in the "second circle," such as Iraq and Iran. Furthermore, the efficacy of the IDF has been based on its capacity to evaluate dangers as well as the rapidity of its response. In 1949 Israel received $100 million in U.S. aid; beginning in 1951, the country has received annual aid from the United States, beginning at $35 million in 1951 and reaching nearly $3 billion annually by 2004, of which $2.1 billion were for defense.

SEE ALSO Haganah.

ISRAEL EHAD

SEE One Israel.

ISRAELI ARABS

SEE Palestinian Israelis.

ISRAELI ARMY

SEE Israel Defense Force.

ISRAELI ISLAMIC MOVEMENT (IIM): Israeli political organization, founded in 1983 by Shaykh Abdallah Nimr Darwish, to propagate Islam in the Israeli Arab community. The IIM also supported the creation of a Palestinian state, alongside the State of Israel. In September 1995, Shaykh Attaf Qatif proposed creating an "Islamic Group." In April 1996, in the context of the Knesset elections for the following May, the movement allied with the Arab Democratic Party (ADP) to constitute a common list, the United Arab List. Four members of the United Arab List won Knesset seats in the vote. Three—Tawfiq Khatib, Talib al-Sanaʿa and Abdul Wahab Darawshe—were members of the ADP, and Abdul Malik Dahamshe of the IIM became the first Islamist to sit in the Knesset.

The candidates of the Israeli Islamic Movement once more joined the United Arab List in May 1999, winning five Knesset seats, two of which went to the IIM in the elections that saw the victory of Ehud Barak, the leader of the Labor Party. In February 2001, in the elections for prime minister, with the head of the Labor Party, Ehud Barak, running against the head of Likud, Ariel Sharon, the leadership of the IIM recommended abstention.

Principal members of the Israeli Islamic Movement are: Shaykh Abdallah Nimr Darwish, Abdul Malik Dahamshe, Ibrahim Sarsur, Shaykh Attaf Qatif, Kamel Khatib and Ibrahim Darwish.

SEE ALSO Arab Democratic Party; Israeli Arabs; Knesset; United Arab List.

ISRAELI-JORDANIAN ACCORDS: On 25 July 1994 in Washington, Israeli Prime Minister Yitzhak Rabin and King Hussein of Jordan signed an accord ending forty-six years of war between their two countries. The accord came after the conclusion of the Jordanian-Israeli Agenda, signed in 1993 also in Washington, which itself followed the signing of the Israeli-Palestinian Declaration of Principles. On 8 August the frontier post of Arava (Araba, in Arabic) between Israel and Jordan was opened, in the presence of the Crown Prince Hassan of Jordan, Israeli Prime Minister Yitzhak Rabin, Israeli Foreign Minister Shimon Peres, and U.S. Secretary of State Warren Christopher. On 25 October the Israeli Knesset ratified the peace treaty with Jordan by a vote of 105 in favor to 3 against, with 6 abstentions. The next day, under the sponsorship of the United States and the Soviet Union, the peace treaty between Israel and Jordan was signed in the Desert of Arava (Wadi Araba) at the Jordanian-Israeli border. Through this accord Jordan took back most of the 147 square miles between the Red Sea and the Dead Sea that Israel had annexed in 1948.

SEE ALSO Christopher, Warren; Hassan of Jordan; Hussein ibn Talal; Knesset; Peres, Shimon; Rabin, Yitzhak.

ISRAELI-LEBANESE WAR

SEE Arab-Israel War (1982).

ISRAELI NEW LEFT

SEE Siah.

ISRAELI-PALESTINIAN ACCORDS

SEE Oslo Accords.

ISRAELI-PALESTINIAN MUTUAL RECOGNITION: On 9 September 1993, in the framework of the peace process started openly two years earlier at the Madrid Conference and pursued secretly in Oslo, Yasir Arafat, chairman of the Palestine Liberation Organization (PLO), and Israeli Prime Minister Yitzhak Rabin addressed letters to each other in which the PLO recognized the State of Israel and the Israelis recognized the PLO as the legitimate representative of the Palestinian people. The former had been demanded by the Israeli government, which reproached the PLO for its 1968 charter denying Israel's right to exist. These letters were a formal prelude to the Declaration of Principles (DOP) signed 13 September 1993 in Washington—the culmination of the Oslo Accords.

SEE ALSO Arafat, Yasir Muhammad; Madrid Conference; Oslo Accords; Palestine Liberation Organization; Rabin, Yitzhak.

ISRAELI PALESTINIANS

SEE Palestinian Israelis.

ISRAELI PRIME MINISTERS: David Ben-Gurion (1948–1953), Moshe Sharett (1953–1955), David Ben-Gurion (1955–1963), Levi Eshkol (1963–1969), Golda Meir (1969–1974), Yitzhak Rabin (1974–1977), Menachem Begin (1977–1983), Yitzhak Shamir (1983–1984), Shimon Peres (1984–1986), Yitzhak Shamir (1986–1992), Yitzhak Rabin (1992–1995), Shimon Peres (1995–1996), Benjamin Netanyahu (1996–1999), Ehud Barak (1999–2001), Ariel Sharon (2001–).

SEE ALSO Barak, Ehud; Begin, Menachem; Ben-Gurion, David; Eshkol, Levi; Meir, Golda; Netanyahu, Benjamin; Peres, Shimon; Rabin, Yitzhak; Sharett, Moshe; Shamir, Yitzhak; Sharon, Ariel.

ISRAELI SETTLEMENTS

SEE Settlements.

ISRAELI-SYRIAN NEGOTIATIONS (1949)

SEE General Armistice Agreements, 1949.

ISRAELI-SYRIAN NEGOTIATIONS, 1994–2000: In 1991 the Syrian government of President Hafiz al-Asad agreed to join the Madrid Conference on Middle East Peace on receiving assurances that Israel was willing to discuss the status of the Golan Heights in the subsequent bilateral talks that were projected as part of a Madrid peace process.

At the beginning of 1994, Israeli prime minister Yitzhak Rabin undertook secret contacts with the Damascus authorities with a view to starting negotiations on an eventual peace accord. His plan, called "Majdal Shams First," was based on a partial withdrawal from the Golan Heights, to be spread over a period of three years. Negotiations began later that year between the Israeli and Syrian ambassadors in Washington, Itamar Rabinovich and Walid al-Moualem. U.S. president Bill Clinton and Secretary of State Warren Christopher also took an engaged interest in these talks and supported them in their own dealings with Rabin and Asad. Meetings between the two countries' military chiefs were also held in December 1994 and June 1995. In all talks, the Syrians made clear that a complete withdrawal from the Golan was a prerequisite for peace. For the Israelis, extensive, but not complete, withdrawal was acceptable, and only as part of an overall peace agreement, with negotiations addressing these four points: the extent of Israeli withdrawal; the schedule for this withdrawal; the linkage of stages of withdrawal with normalization of relations; and permanent security arrangements. Rabin also made clear that any treaty that included withdrawal would have to be subject to a referendum in Israel, where the status of Israeli settlements, which would have to be removed from any returned territory, was a major political issue.

In late 1995 the Syrians relaxed their position somewhat, and additional meetings at the ambassadorial level were held in December 1995 and January 1996 at the Wye Plantation in Maryland. In February and March 1996 there was a series of suicide bombings in Israel carried out by Islamist fanatics, and Prime Minister Shimon Peres (who had taken office after Rabin was assassinated in November 1995 by a Jewish fanatic) then broke off the Syrian negotiations. The reason was ostensibly that Syria would not condemn the attacks, but critics blamed his move on electoral posturing, having more to do with the strong challenge Peres faced in the upcoming Israeli elections from Benjamin Netanyahu, whose Likud opposed any Israeli withdrawal from occupied land. Netanyahu won, and there were no further negotiations while he was in office. (Netanyahu did publicly offer to restart talks if Syria negotiated without preconditions, understanding that Syria could not agree to this.) In 1999, a new Israeli Labor prime minister, Ehud Barak, who had won office that May on a promise to withdraw Israeli forces from Lebanon, began the Syrian talks anew. On 15 December he and Syrian Foreign Minister Faruk al-Shara met officially at a summit meeting hosted by President Clinton in Washington. Bilateral talks under American auspices were then held in Shepherdstown, West Virginia, from 3 to 11 January 2000; no agreement could be reached.

On the following 26 March, Clinton met with Asad at Geneva and gave him Barak's latest proposal; Asad rejected it because it involved Israel's retaining sovereignty over part of the disputed territory, in this case a strip of land north of Lake Tiberias. This was effectively the end of the negotiations.

SEE ALSO Asad, Hafiz al-; Barak, Ehud; Golan Heights; Likud; Madrid Conference; Majdal Shams First Plan; Netanyahu, Benjamin; Peres, Shimon; Rabin, Yitzhak; Shara, Faruk al-

ISRAELITE: A descendant of Israel, belonging to the Jewish community and religion. This word is used for whatever relates to Biblical Israel and its people. Around 1200 B.C.E. the Hebrews settled between Jerusalem and Nablus (Sh'khem), in the land of Canaan. Allying with the B'nai Jacob (Sons of Jacob), whose authority they recognized, they lay the basis of a confederation and from then on were called Israelites. A century later, at war with the Canaanites, the Israelites formed the first military kingdom of Israel, ruled by King Saul (around 1020 B.C.E.). Taking advantage of the weakness of Egypt and Assyria, Saul's successors, David and Solomon, turned Israel into an even stronger regional power.

SEE ALSO Canaan; Jacob (Biblical).

ISRAEL LABOR PARTY (in Hebrew, Mifleget ha-Avodah): The Israel Labor Party (ILP) was created

in 1968 with the merger of the leftist parties MAPAI, RAFI, and Ahdut ha-Avodah Poʿalei Zion. MAPAI, in fact, effectively governed the State of Israel from 1948 to 1977, when the Labor Party lost the elections to the Likud. Among Labor's major figures were David Ben-Gurion, Moshe Sharett, Golda Meir, Shimon Peres, Moshe Dayan, Yigal Allon, Shulamit Aloni, Abba Eban, Gad Yaacobi, and Yossi Sarid. In 1969, Labor won by the widest margin of any party in Israeli history, obtaining 56 of the 120 seats in the Knesset.

In 1973, when Golda Meir was heading the government, a split surfaced in the party, leading to the departure of Shulamit Aloni, Raanan Cohen, and Yossi Sarid, who decided to create their own group, the Citizens' Rights Movement (RATZ). Under pressure from the right, reinforced by the formation of the Likud, the Labor Party adopted a nationalist rhetoric. On 3 June 1974, Yitzhak Rabin, former chief of staff of the Israel Defense Force, having joined the Labor Party, succeeded Meir as prime minister, and Shimon Peres was named defense minister. In the eyes of Israelis, the Labor Party was confirming its reputation as the party of "rich Ashkenazim," while the Likud was looking like the party of the "discriminated-against Sephardim." On 19 April 1977, Shimon Peres was elected head of the party. In the Knesset elections of the following May, the Israeli electorate voted for Likud, favoring security-oriented policies, to the detriment of Labor. The responsibility for the loss was hotly debated. Rabin's difficulties in 1977 over an allegedly illegal bank account belonging to his wife were considered by some to be linked to Labor's defeat, while others attributed the loss to the "colorless" Peres. With 43 seats in the Knesset, the Likud became the principal political bloc, ahead of the Labor Party, which won only 32. Many Labor votes apparently went to a new centrist party, the Dash. Shimon Peres was replaced as head of the party, on 28 May 1978, by Haim Bar-Lev.

Two currents surfaced in the Labor Party: the "hawks," headed by Yitzhak Rabin, and the "doves," led by Shimon Peres. On 18 December 1980, by an overwhelming majority, the latter was again designated as "unquestionably" leader of the ILP. As a result of the Knesset elections of June 1981, the Labor Party obtained 47 seats, behind Likud, which had 48, obliging the two blocs to unite to form a government coalition, to be led, alternating every two years, by the heads of the two parties. On 26 November, Haim Bar-Lev, backed by Shimon Peres, was reelected secretary-general of the ILP, with 63 percent of the votes, against his adversary, Eliahu Speiser, supported by Yitzhak Rabin. As a result of the elections of July 1984, the Labor Party won 44 seats in the Knesset, ahead of Likud, which obtained 41. In spite of the weakening of Likud, only 34.9 percent of the votes went to the ILP, while some of the votes lost by the right went to the extreme right.

Between 1984 and 1986, succeeding Menachem Begin, Shimon Peres was the prime minister of the Labor-Likud National Unity government, while Yitzhak Rabin was defense minister. One of the main goals Peres set for himself was the economic recovery of the country, which was experiencing an inflation rate of 400 percent. In October 1986, following the rotation agreement, Peres ceded his place as prime minister to Yitzhak Shamir, leader of Likud. As a result of the elections of November 1988, which took place while the first Intifada was raging in the Palestinian territories, the ILP won 39 seats, behind Likud, which won 40. At this time, in the context of the Israeli-Palestinian conflict, the main elements in the Labor Party program were no return to the frontiers of 1967, with part of the occupied territories being kept for security reasons and with a demilitarization of evacuated areas; a resolution of the Palestinian problem by the creation of a Jordanian-Palestinian entity, including regions of high-density Palestinian population in the West Bank and the Gaza Strip; acceptance of negotiation with a Jordanian-Palestinian delegation, to be included in the context of an international conference; the creation of an Israeli constitution; opposition to any form of discrimination against Israeli Arabs; and the separation of religion and the state.

Between 1988 and 1992 the leader of Likud, Shamir, was prime minister, with no change in the Knesset during this period. On 15 March 1990, the left succeeded in obtaining the censure of the government, by a Knesset vote of 60 to 55. On the following 11 June, after Shimon Peres did not succeed in forming a government, Shamir formed a new cabinet. In February 1992, Peres being again blamed for the electoral failures of 1988 and June 1990, Yitzhak Rabin was elected to lead the Labor Party. As a result of the elections of the following June, the Labor Party obtained 34.8 percent of the votes, against 24.9 percent for Likud. Rabin became prime minister. The portfolio of the foreign ministry was accorded to Peres, the latter becoming the architect of peace negotiations with Arabs and Palestinians, with the support of Rabin. On 24 March 1993, Ezer Weizman, a member of the Labor Party, was elected president of Israel. On the following 13 September in Washington, Rabin and Yasir Arafat signed an accord on principles, opening the way to a definitive Israeli-Palestinian agreement. As a result of the municipal elections of the following November, Labor and Likud shared between them the twenty largest cities in Israel. In 1994 many propositions were submitted to the central committee of the party advocating the creation of a new political bloc uniting all the parties of the left.

On 25 June 1994 the government of Yitzhak Rabin signed an accord with Jordan, ending the state of war between the two countries. On 16 February the Laborite Avraham Burg, son of Yosef Burg, former head of the National Religious Party (NRP), was elected head of the Jewish Agency, a para-governmental organization in charge of immigration to Israel. In the course of the following July, the former chief of staff of the Israel Defense Force, Ehud Barak, joined the ILP, to be named, two days later, interior minister in the government of Rabin. During the fall, the ILP was the target of much criticism by Likud and the ultra-orthodox movements, while there were a number of splits in the party itself. Several Labor deputies joined the Third Way. The leadership of the party attempted to get Haim Ramon, head of the Histadrut, to rejoin it. On 5 October, the Knesset approved, by 61 votes against 59, the accord on the extension of Palestinian autonomy. On 12 October, Prime Minister Rabin admitted he was concerned about the violence of the attacks against his peace policies with the Palestinians. On 4 November 1995, Rabin was assassinated by an Israeli extremist.

On 21 November, after being designated as interim head of government and the ILP, Shimon Peres was sworn in as prime minister by the Knesset. Like his predecessor, he combined the functions of prime minister and defense minister. The foreign ministry portfolio was accorded to Ehud Barak, and that of the interior to Chaim Ramon. Yossi Beilin obtained the post of minister without portfolio, responsible for the peace process. In anticipation of the Knesset elections of May 1996, three currents surfaced in the ILP, respectively led by Haim Ramon, Ehud Barak, and Shimon Peres. Apart from the mainstream there was also a reformist current, which included Haim Ramon, Avraham Burg, Yossi Beilin, Haggai Merom, Nawaf Massalha, Amir Peretz, Shlomo Avital, and Yael Dayan. On 30 May 1996, as a result of the elections, the ILP won 34 seats in the Knesset against 32 for the Likud, while the leader of the latter party, Benjamin Netanyahu, was elected prime minister. Many differences surfaced in the ILP. Once more blamed for the electoral failure, Peres was excluded from the party leadership and replaced, provisionally, by Nissim Zvili. On 3 June 1997, the ILP organized the election for the new post of chairman of the party, for which four candidates were jostling: Barak, Beilin, Shlomo Ben-Ami, and Ephraim Sneh. With 50 percent of the votes, Barak was elected chairman of the ILP, ahead of Beilin, who obtained only 29 percent. On the following 28 December, Raanan Cohen was elected secretary-general, replacing Nissim Zvili, who had resigned his post six months earlier.

Weakened by divisions and power struggles, the Labor Party became mired increasingly in certain positions that displeased the electorate, particularly in the social domain and concerning the peace process. In October 1998 the ILP published its program, which emphasized a social pact, proposed by Barak, to encourage understanding between religious and secular Israelis. On 14 January 1999, anticipating the general elections of the following May, the leadership of the party named Barak to head the list, as candidate for the post of prime minister, with Shimon Peres in second position. With the Gesher and Meimad parties, Barak constituted an electoral list called "One Israel." During the election campaign, several party figures, such as Nissim Zvili, quit the ILP to join the Center Party. On 18 June, Barak was elected prime minister, defeating Benjamin Netanyahu by a margin of 56.7 percent to 43.3 percent. The electoral list of Labor Party-Gesher-Meimad won only 26 seats in the Knesset, of which 23 were ILP. On 6 July 1999, Barak presented his government, composed of 18 members from 8 different parties. The foreign ministry was accorded to David Levy, head of the Gesher party, flanked by deputy minister Nawaf Massalha, Israeli Arab and member of the Labor Party. Finance and public security were respectively assigned to Avraham Shohat and Ben-Ami of the ILP, while the portfolio of regional development was given to Peres. On 5 September, at Sharm al-Shaykh, after many encounters, Barak and Yasir Arafat signed an accord, meant to open the way to negotiations on a definitive peace between Palestinians and Israelis. On 24 May 2000, Barak gave the green light to the evacuation of South Lebanon by the IDF, ending eighteen years of occupation. At the beginning of July, Barak lost his majority in the Knesset; then his foreign minister, David Levy, quit just before an Israeli-Palestinian summit to be held in Washington, and in which Barak was supposed to participate. On 31 July, surprising everyone, Peres lost the election for the presidency of Israel against his rival, Moshe Katsav, causing consternation in the ILP.

During the fall of 2000, the al-Aqsa Intifada, which had begun at the end of September, intensified in the Palestinian territories. Barak was not able to negotiate a return to calm with the Palestinian leaders. The members of Knesset rejected a motion to dissolve the Knesset and accepted the organization of elections for the post of prime minister. On 20 December, Peres decided to become a candidate for prime minister, but could not obtain the necessary approval of 10 deputies. On 6 February 2001, Barak was defeated by Ariel Sharon, who obtained 62.5 percent of the votes. The Labor alliance remained the leading political bloc, with 26 seats, against 19 of the Likud. On 20 February, Barak decided to quit politics and resign from the presidency of the ILP. Some Laborites favored joining a government coalition with Likud, but several ILP leaders opposed this project. Finally, on 27 February, the central committee of the party voted, in majority, to participate in a cabinet of national unity, designating seven of its members to join the government of Sharon, among whom were the Laborites Shimon Peres, Benyamin Ben-Eliezer, and Raanan Cohen, becoming respectively foreign minister, defense minister, and minister without portfolio. The following 4 September, Avraham Burg was elected to head the Labor Party, against his adversary, Benyamin Ben-Eliezer, who contested this election, claiming electoral fraud. While waiting for the decisions of the juridical commission, the party was placed under committee leadership, overseen by Peres and by the secretary-general, Raanan Cohen. Three months later, at the end of December, Ben-Eliezer was officially elected head of the party, after a ballot in which participation was low. In October 2002, Peres and other members of the Labor Party resigned from the Sharon government.

In November 2002, Amram Mitzna, former mayor of Haifa, was elected head of the Labor Party. Mitzna, a "dovish" former army general and a favorite of the peace movement, resigned in May 2003, three months after leading Labor to its worst election defeat. In June 2003, the party once again chose elder statesman Peres as its leader. Under Peres, it was again conceivable that Labor might move toward a coalition with Likud. In July 2004 the Sharon government sought to formally widen its shaky governing coalition, after barely surviving three no-confidence motions in the Knessset, asking Labor as well as United Torah Judaism to begin coalition talks. It was anticipated that Labor would press for a swifter pullout from the Gaza Strip and for direct talks with the Palestinians.

SEE ALSO Barak, Ehud; Begin, Menachem; Beilin, Yossi; Ben-Ami, Shlomo; Ben-Gurion, David; Cohen, Raanan; Likud; Meir, Golda; Peres, Shimon; Rabin, Yitzhak.

ISSA: ("Jesus," in Arabic.) The name is derived from the Greek *Iesous,* which in turn is derived from the Aramaic *Yeshua,* which is a form of the Hebrew *Yehoshua.* (The name *Jesus* is an anglicized version of the Latin *Iesus,* which in turn derived from the Greek.) Muslims believe that Jesus was a prophet, and that his teachings were genuine revelations from God, but not that he was divine.

ISTIQLAL, AL- (Independence): Weekly newspaper, created in 1994, of the Palestinian Islamic Jihad. It is published in Gaza.

SEE ALSO Bayt al-Maqdis.

ITTAHAD WATANI ISLAMI

SEE Islamic National Union.

ITTIHAD, AL- (Union): For a long time Israel's only Arabic-language daily newspaper. Founded as a weekly in 1944 by activists close to the Arab Workers Congress, the paper fully supported the 1948 United Nations decision to partition Palestine, which led to the creation of the State of Israel. Historian Emil Toma was its first editor, followed by Israeli Arab writer Emil Habibi, who ran the paper until 1990. *Al-Ittihad* became a daily in 1983. It is published in Haifa and has a daily circulation of twelve thousand.

ITTIJAH, AL- (Direction): The Union of Arab Community-Based Organizations, an umbrella group of Palestinian nongovernmental organizations in Israel, based in Haifa. Founded in 1995, Ittijah fosters cooperation among Palestinian Israeli organizations that provide social support services, advocate for change, and promote the development of Palestinian civil society and cultural autonomy within Israel. These organizations are more important to Palestinian Israelis than to Jewish Israelis because of the government's discrimination against its Palestinian citizens and its lack of funding for the institutions that serve them. Ittijah focuses on three principal areas: advocacy (making the status of Palestinian Israelis known to the Palestinian and Israeli publics and to the Arab and international publics, nongovernmental organizations, and governments); "capacity building" (increasing the resources of its member organizations through staffing, technical help, education, and fundraising); and networking (bringing together organizations with similar agendas and expertise locally, regionally, and internationally). Among its dozens of member organizations are groups focused on civil and human rights, women's advocacy, children's welfare, theater, history, scholarly research, library support, and religious charity. It maintains links with Palestinian nongovernmental organizations in the West Bank, Gaza Strip, and Lebanon, as well as with foreign nongovernmental organizations and international organizations, including the United Nations. Its funding comes from voluntary contributions, mainly from foreign nonprofits and the European Union.

Ittijah also takes public stands against policies and acts of the Israeli government that injure Palestinian Israelis, as well as those directed against Palestinians in the occupied territories. The government has harassed Ittijah, as well as other Palestinian civil agencies and institutions, through legal, illegal, and extralegal means: it has proposed legislation forbidding Palestinian Israeli nongovernmental organizations from accepting funding from foreign governments; it has broken into offices and stolen files and computers; it has intimated to donors and potential donors that such organizations "support terrorism." Ittijah maintains a web site at www.ittijah.org.

SEE ALSO Gaza Strip; Palestinian Israelis; West Bank.

IUM

SEE Islamic Unification Movement.

IVRIT: The modern Hebrew language.

IYAR (*Yhiar, Ityar*): Name of the eighth month of the Hebrew calendar, corresponding to late April and early May. The festival of Yom ha-Atzma'ut is celebrated on 5 Iyar and that of Lag B'Omer on 18 Iyar.

SEE ALSO Hebrew Calendar; Yom ha-Atzma'ut.

IZZ AL-DIN AL-

SEE Qassam, Izz al-Din al-.

IZZ AL-DIN AL-QASSAM

SEE Qassam, Izz al-Din al-.

IZZ AL-DIN AL-QASSAM BRIGADE

SEE HAMAS.

J

Jaafari: A word derived from the name of the Shiʿite imam Jaafar, used to designate the twelver juridical school.

SEE ALSO Shiʿite.

Jabal: Arabic word meaning "mountain."

Jabal Musa: "Mount Moses," "Mountain of Moses"; the Arabic name for Mount Sinai.

Jabara, Hussniya (1958–): Israeli Arab, professor of Middle East studies at Beit Berl College. A member of the lay Meretz Party, she won a seat in the general elections of 18 May 1999, becoming the first Arab woman elected to the Knesset.

SEE ALSO Knesset; Meretz Party.

Jabhat al-Dimuqrati al-Tahrir al Filastin

SEE Democratic Front for the Liberation of Palestine.

Jabhat al-Inqadh

SEE Palestinian National Salvation Front.

Jabhat al-Islamiyya al Alamiyya Li-Jihad al Yahud was al-Salibiyyin

SEE World Islamic Front for Holy War against Jews and Crusaders.

Jabhat al-Khalas al-Islami al-Filastin

SEE Islamic Front for the Salvation of Palestine.

Jabhat al-Tahrir al Arabiyya

SEE Arab Liberation Front.

Jabotinsky, Vladimir Ze'ev (1880–1940): Zionist ideologist, born in Odessa. Vladimir Jabotinsky studied in Switzerland and Italy, where he was influenced by romantic nationalism. Advocating a radical Zionism, he had begun propounding his concept of a Jewish state by 1903. In 1918, during World War I, he helped create a Jewish battalion that was integrated into the British army and fought the Ottoman army. He made a name for himself there. In 1923 students supporting Jabotinsky's ideas founded the Betar movement, which was transformed into a paramilitary force. In 1925 he created the Union of Revisionist Zionists, an independent branch of the Zionist movement. Between 1928 and 1929 he lived in Jerusalem, where he directed an insurance company and published a daily, *Do'ar ha-Yom*. Confrontations on 1 May 1928 between young Betar members and communist militants were evidence of a scission, which over time grew larger, between the revisionists and the socialist majority of the Zionists. From that time on, Betar found itself spearheading the fight for the "liberation of Palestine."

VLADIMIR JABOTINSKY. THE RADICAL ZIONIST INSPIRED THE CREATION OF THE BETAR MOVEMENT, AND HE ESTABLISHED THE UNION OF REVISIONIST ZIONISTS IN THE 1920S. JABOTINSKY ADVOCATED THE CREATION OF A JEWISH STATE IN ALL OF PALESTINE, REJECTING MORE CAUTIOUS ZIONIST PROPOSALS AND BRITISH ADVOCACY OF PARTITIONING PALESTINE. *(© Government Press Office [GPO] of Israel)*

In 1930, when Jabotinsky was visiting South Africa, British authorities prevented him from returning to Palestine by refusing to renew his visa, obliging him to live in Paris. In 1931 he broke with the leadership of the Zionist Congress, which refused to pronounce itself openly in favor of creating a Jewish state in all of Palestine. In 1935, at the time of the Vienna Zionist Congress, he announced the creation of a new movement, of which he was the president, the New Zionist Organization, whose headquarters were in London. He rejected the British plan to partition Palestine and made numerous attempts to further his cause with any government that approved of creating a Jewish national homeland, obtaining financial and material help from Poland. In 1937 Betar and the Irgun coordinated their actions against British forces in Palestine. In September 1938, at the Betar conference in Warsaw, he was strongly criticized by party members, in particular by Menachem Begin, who favored passing to the "military phase." After the start of World War II, he recommended the creation of a Jewish brigade, which would participate in combat against Germany. Jabotinsky died of a heart attack during a visit to a Betar youth camp in New York State. His ashes were long barred from entry into Israel by the Zionist Labor leadership but were finally transferred to Mount Herzl, in Jerusalem, in 1964.

SEE ALSO Begin, Menachem; Betar; Ottomans; Zionism.

JACOB (Yaakob, "held by the heel," in Hebrew; Yaqub, in Arabic): According to Biblical tradition, Jacob was the son of Isaac and Rebecca, and the father of the twelve sons who became the eponymous ancestors of the tribes of Israel. In most of the prophetic writings he was designated by the name *Israel,* which became the ethnic name of the people of Israel.

SEE ALSO Isaac.

JACOBITE CHURCH: Name of a Syrian religious community of Christians who in 451 refused to adhere to the decisions of the Council of Chalcedon and who do not recognize the authority of the Pope. The Syrian Orthodox patriarch sits in Antioch, Turkey. The Jacobite Church is one of the many Christian denominations that share rights to the Holy Sepulcher.

SEE ALSO Christianity.

JAFFA: Ancient port on the eastern Mediterranean, south of present-day Tel Aviv, Israel. Known as Joffa in biblical times, Jaffa prospered under Egyptian, then Ottoman, rule in the nineteenth century as a thriving port city. The population, 5,000 in the mid-nineteenth century, expanded to 40,000 by 1914; 15,000 of that number were Jews. The city was virtually deserted during World War I, but under the subsequent British Mandate, Jaffa revived, reaching a population of 30,000 by 1922 and continuing to grow thereafter. After the United Nations decision to partition Palestine in 1947, riots broke out in Jaffa. Following the fighting, Jewish forces took the city, and most of its 65,000 Arabs fled. In 1950 Jaffa was incorporated into the Tel Aviv municipality and remains a mixed Jewish and Arab section of the metropolitan area.

JAHBAZ: ("Cashier" or "banker," in Arabic.) For many centuries in the Muslim world, this work was the exclusive province of Jews and Christians, as it was for Jews in Christian societies.

JAHILIYYA: ("Ignorance" or "barbarism," in Arabic.) In Islam *jahiliyya* traditionally has referred to Arabia in the period before Islam, when the predominant religions were animistic or pantheistic. Among contemporary extremist Islamist thinkers, however, the term has been applied to all non-Islamic societies and belief systems, and indeed to "un-Islamic" elements incorporated into modern Muslim societies. According to Sayyid Qutb (1906–1966), the Egyptian theorist of the Muslim Brotherhood, only two cultures exist in the world, Islam and jahiliyya.

SEE ALSO Muslim Brotherhood.

JAI

SEE Jewish Agency for Israel.

JAMIʿ: Arab word used to designate a main mosque.

SEE ALSO Mosque.

JAMIʿA AL-ISLAMIYYA, AL- (al-Gamaʿa al-Islamiya, "Islamic group"): Islamic militant movement that surfaced in Egypt in the late 1970s. In the early 1970s the regime of President Anwar al-Sadat released many of the Islamic militants who had been jailed by President Gamal Abdel Nasser, particularly those of the Muslim Brotherhood. Sadat encouraged and aided the spread of the Brotherhood and of new Islamic groups (*al-gamaʿat al-Islamiya*), some of which had been created in prison, to counteract the influence of leftists in universities and the labor movement. All fundamentalist tendencies were represented in these groups, and they had various affiliations and influences in and out of Egypt. Their success soon put them beyond the government's control, particularly in the period after the Arab-Israel War of 1973 when Sadat was following a policy of rapprochement with Israel and the United States and opposition to the regime was rising.

In 1978, representatives of the *jamiʿa* won a landslide victory in the university student union elections. The following year, their increasing opposition to the policies of President Sadat forced the government to ban their activities in the universities. But, encouraged by the success of the Iranian revolution, the Islamic movement become more radical, demanding, among other things, the cessation of negotiations with Israel. Small extremist splinter groups appeared, among which the most radical was one called simply al-Jamiʿa al-Islamiyya, the Islamic Group. Its principal initiators, Karam Zuhdiand Najeh Ibrahim, advocated resorting to violence in order to gain power and establish an Islamic state in Egypt. In 1980, the Egyptian Islamic Jihad made efforts to convince Karam Zudhi of the desirability of an alliance between their two movements. The following year, the latter was arrested and accused of complicity in the murder of President Anwar al-Sadat, carried out by a commando of the Jihad.

In 1985, one of the principal leaders of the Jamiʿa, Muhammad Shawqi, quit the movement to found his own group, Al-Shawqiyun, inspired by Ahmad Shukri Mustafa, former head of Al-Takfir wa al-Hijra. The Jamiʿa al-Islamiyya was made up of small cells, coordinated by leaders either in Egypt or abroad (Pakistan, Europe). In liaison with Islamic Jihad, the terrorist actions of the Jamiʿa al-Islamiyya targeted Egyptian political personalities, heads of security services, and sometimes tourists. On 5 July 1997, at the opening of a trial of ninety-seven Islamists before the military court of Cairo, six founders of the movement, condemned to hard labor for the assassination of Anwar al-Sadat, launched an appeal to end the violence. In February 1998, the Jamiʿa al-Islamiyya and the Jihad joined the World Islamic Front for Holy War against Jews and Crusaders, of which Osama Bin Ladin was one of the principal leaders.

On 26 April 1999, the Egyptian government decided to liberate one thousand militants of the movement, after a number of al-Jamiʿa leaders announced that they were renouncing violence. The main leaders of the movement are Jamal Ferghali Haridi, Mustafa Hamza, Rifaʿi Ahmad Taha, and Muhammad Shawqi Islambuli. The spiritual head of al-Jamiʿa al-Islamiyya was Shaykh Omar Abd al-Rahman, who had emigrated to the United States in 1989. He was convicted in 1995 of being involved in the February 1993 bomb attack on the World Trade Center in New York, and is currently serving a life sentence.

SEE ALSO Egyptian Islamic Jihad; Muslim Brotherhood; Nasser, Gamal Abdel; Sadat, Anwar al-; Takfir wa al-Hijra, al-; World Islamic Front for Holy War Against Jews and Crusaders.

JAMIʿA AL-ISLAMIYYA AL-LIBNANIYA, AL-: Lebanese Islamic movement (the Lebanese Islamic Group, in Arabic), which surfaced in 1962 under the impetus of Fathi Yakan. Originating from the Jamaʿa 'Ibad al-Rahman (Group of Servants of the Merciful), this organization, which advocated struggle against Israel, was a branch of the Muslim Brotherhood. In 1972, one of its members, Said Shabaan, quit the movement in order to form the Islamic Unification Movement (IUM). In 1990, at the time of the Gulf War, the Jamiʿa al-Islamiyya decided to support Iraq, which led to an interruption in the Saudi aid it had been receiving. In 1992, so as to participate in legislative elections, the movement changed into a party and won several deputy seats. The following year, Faysal al-Mawlawi, leader of the branch of the northern part of the country, replaced Fathi Yakan as leader of the movement. In 1996, a split appeared in the movement, caused by a power struggle for the leadership between Fathi Yakan and Faysal al-Mawlawi, which Mawlawi won.

SEE ALSO Islamic Unification Movement; Muslim Brotherhood.

JAPANESE RED ARMY (JRA): Japanese terrorist movement formed in 1971 to support the Palestinian cause. Originating from the Armed Faction of the Communist League (AFCL), this small group became known as "Red Army Faction" in 1971.

Established in Lebanon, in the Baqaa Valley, the group participated in many attacks in the West and the Middle East from 1972 to 1988, including airplane hijackings, in concert with the Popular Front for the Liberation of Palestine (PFLP), in particular.

On 30 May 1972, a JRA commando exploded a bomb in the Tel Aviv Airport, killing twenty-seven and wounding seventy. Twenty-five years later, the Lebanese authorities arrested a number of Japanese citizens in the south of the country whom they suspected of belonging to the JRA. In 2000, Lebanon deported to Japan four members it arrested in 1997, but granted a fifth political asylum. Longtime leader Fusako Shigenobu was arrested in November 2000 and faces charges of terrorism and passport fraud.

SEE ALSO Popular Front for the Liberation of Palestine.

JARRING MISSION: A United Nations-sponsored mission to negotiate an Arab-Israel peace settlement. In November 1967, UN Secretary-General U Thant appointed Gunnar Jarring, a Swedish diplomat who had served as Sweden's ambassador to the United Nations (1956–1958) and ambassador to the United States (1958–1964), as special envoy to promote a peace settlement based on UN Security Council Resolution 242. Jarring began his mission in 1968, but the parties demonstrated little interest in his initiatives. His mission was suspended when UN representatives of the countries began direct talks, then resumed briefly in 1970, after the August cease-fire agreement between Israel and Egypt ended the war of attrition along the Suez Canal. It was again suspended because of Egyptian violations of that agreement, then resumed again in December 1970. In February 1971, Jarring presented proposals to Israel and Egypt, but no agreement could be reached. The mission lapsed, though it was not formally ended until 1990.

SEE ALSO Resolution 242.

JCS (JOINT COMMITTEE FOR SECURITY)

SEE Joint Coordination and Cooperation Committee for Mutual Security Purposes.

JDPP

SEE Jordanian Progressive Party.

JEDDAH, TREATY OF: Signed on 20 May 1927 by King Abd al-Aziz ibn Abd al-Rahman al-Sa'ud—known as ibn Sa'ud—and the British, this treaty established the frontiers of the newly established Saudi Arabia with the British protectorates of Transjordan, Iraq, and Kuwait. With the Treaty of Jeddah, Great Britain recognized ibn Sa'ud as "King of Hijaz, Nejd, and its dependencies."

SEE ALSO Jordan.

JERICHO: City in the West Bank, situated at the northern end of the Dead Sea. Considered to be the oldest city in the world, Jericho (Ariha, in Arabic) is 825 feet below sea level. According to Biblical tradition, the city was conquered by the Hebrews under Joshua in the twelfth century B.C.E., through the power of a *shofar* sounded by priests. After the signature in Washington on 13 September 1993 of the Israeli-Palestinian Declaration of Principles, Jericho became the first "autonomous" Palestinian city.

SEE ALSO West Bank.

JERUSALEM (in Arabic, Beit al-Maqdis, "holy house,"or al-Quds al-Sharif, "the holy"; in Hebrew, Yerushalayim): Venerated by each of the three great monotheistic religions, the city of Jerusalem has always been a battleground. Its name, Yerushalayim, in Hebrew means, according to some, "city of peace"; according to others, it means "foundation of Shalem," and has thus been identified with the city of Shalem (Salem) mentioned in Genesis. Therefore, according to Jewish tradition, the name of Jerusalem would come from the association of two places, Shalem and Yeru, the latter being where Abraham prepared to sacrifice his son Isaac. The city of Salem was supposed to have been built by the Canaanite goddess Anet in honor of her brother, Salem, the god of peace. In the twelfth century B.C.E., Jerusalem was already considered a holy city because of the presence of the Gihon spring, reputed to be miraculous. It became the Jewish religious and national center after it was conquered by David (c. 1000 B.C.E.); it remained so until the destruction of the second Jewish Temple by the Romans (70 C.E.) and the subsequent rebellions against Roman occupation, which resulted in the Jewish exile from Jerusalem.

Practically forgotten for five centuries, during which a number of Christian churches were built in the city, Jerusalem began to be more prominent with the birth of Islam. According to the Qur'an, the prophet Muhammad spent time there, during which he ascended to heaven (*miraj*). In 634 the Arabs took the city and gave it the name of Ilia, from the Latin appellation of Aelia Capitolina. After Muhammad established Mecca as the premier holy site of Islam, the Umayyads decided to make Jerusalem a sacred city, naming it Bayt al-Maqdis or al-Quds. In 688–691 the Umayyads built the first great edifice of Islam, the Cupola of the Rock (Dome of the Rock), on the ruins of the Temple of Solomon, and on the spot where the prophet Muhammad was believed to have begun his ascension to the heavens. In 715 a second mosque was built in Jerusalem, again on the Temple Mount, which the Umayyads called Al-Masjid al-Aqsa (the furthest Mosque).

After the fall of the Umayyad dynasty, Jerusalem was forgotten once more, allowing the Christian community to develop there, until 1077, when the city was conquered by Seljuk troops. On 15 July 1099, the Crusaders, led by Godfrey de Bouillon, took the city by assault. The conquest of the Holy City gave birth to the Latin states of the east, and Baudouin de Flandre became the first king of Jerusalem. The Kingdom of Jerusalem comprised at the time all of Palestine, which name was dropped, in favor of "Holy Land." In 1149 the Crusaders rebuilt the Holy Sepulchre, destroyed by the Arabs fifty years before. On 4 July 1187, at Hittin, the troops of Saladin crushed those of the Franks and three months later the Muslims retook Jerusalem. In 1229 one of the grandsons of Saladin yielded control of the city to the emperor Frederick II, but in 1244 the Muslims reconquered it. In 1291 the fall of Acre marked the end of the Latin states of the east. Palestine was divided by the Mamluks into six districts and was joined with Syria. In 1516, Jerusalem was easily conquered by the Ottomans, and two centuries later, in 1757, the Sultanate decided to divide the guardianship of the holy places among Christians of every obedience.

In 1831, Ibrahim Pasha, son of the vice-king of Egypt, Mehemet Ali, backed by France, took control of Palestine. In 1850, Louis Napoleon Bonaparte reclaimed the right of protection over the holy sites of Jerusalem, retained by Russia since 1808. This claim was one of the causes of the Crimean War (1854–1856). In 1860, taking advantage of the decline of the Ottoman Empire, England expanded its sphere of influence in Palestine. In 1878 an accord was signed at the Berlin congress, which confirmed the rights of France over the holy sites of Palestine. In 1885 the treaty of Berlin specified "that there shall be no alteration of the status quo of the holy sites." In 1889 the Jerusalem region passed out of Syrian control, for the first time in six hundred years, to be governed by Constantinople. In 1898, as a counterweight to the French, Russian, and British influence, Germany began building religious edifices in Jerusalem. On 9 December 1917, during World War I, in which the Ottoman Empire backed Germany, British troops entered the city and immediately declared martial law.

On 29 September 1923, the British Mandate over Palestine went into effect, and Jerusalem became the capital of the country. Under the British Mandate, Jerusalem became the center of both Zionist and nationalist movements. Arab Palestinian fears of displacement and of continued Zionist immigration led to violence in 1929 (the Western Wall Disturbances) and to the Palestine Arab Revolt of 1936–1939. Both were suppressed by British military force. On 29 November 1947, in the context of United Nations Resolution 181 on the partition of Palestine, it was proposed that the city be accorded a special status as a separate entity (*corpus separatum*), overseen by an advisory council, in order to guarantee the rights of the three religious communities. On 15 May 1948, a few hours before the end of the British Mandate, David Ben-Gurion proclaimed the creation of the State of Israel, which led to the first Arab-Israel war. On 28 May, when Israel took over the western part of Jerusalem, Transjordanian troops occupied the Old City, where the Muslim holy places were located. On 3 April 1949, an armistice was signed between Transjordan and Israel. While the Arab camp emerged defeated from the conflict, Transjordan found itself aggrandized, by the West Bank and the control of the Arab part of Jerusalem. The Israeli government then launched into an intense program of development of the New City of Jerusalem, where its administrative offices were transferred. On 19 December 1949, the UN passed a resolution demanding the internationalization of the Holy City, but the resolution was ignored by both Israel and Jordan. In

1950 Israel proclaimed Jerusalem its capital, even though most governments did not relocate their embassies from Tel Aviv.

On 28 May 1964, at the first congress of the Palestine National Council (PNC), held in East Jerusalem, the Arab countries decided to create the Palestine Liberation Organization (PLO), whose goal was the liberation of "all of occupied Palestine." In June 1967, during the Arab-Israel War, the Israeli army occupied the West Bank and East Jerusalem. On the following 4 and 14 July, the UN passed Resolutions 2253 and 2254, declaring the annexation of Jerusalem by Israel illegal, and demanding that the latter refrain from any decision that would change the status of the city. From that time, as Israel ignored these resolutions, Jerusalem became one of the principal subjects of dispute in the Israeli-Palestinian conflict. An accord was reached between the Waqf and the Israeli authorities, stipulating that only the Muslim religion would be practiced in al-Haram al-Sharif (Temple Mount). In September 1969, after a fire at the al-Aqsa Mosque, the leaders of the Muslim states decided to create the Islamic Conference Organization (ICO), to oversee the safeguarding of the holy sites of Jerusalem.

The Israeli occupation gave rise to a new Palestinian nationalism, whose watchwords were the "right of return" and the creation of a state, with Jerusalem as its capital. On 30 July 1980, the Israeli Knesset passed a law proclaiming Jerusalem "one and entire, eternal capital of Israel," which provoked an international outcry. On 20 August, the UN Security Council adopted Resolution 478, rejecting the decision of the Israeli government. In September 1981, at the Third Islamic Summit, which took place in Ta'if (Saudi Arabia), the Arab states decided to create the al-Quds Committee, in charge of protecting Muslim interests in the city of Jerusalem. On 9 September 1982, at the Twelfth Arab summit in Fez, the member states adopted a plan for resolving the Israeli-Arab conflict, which provided, notably, for a Palestinian state, with Jerusalem (al-Quds) as its capital. The Israeli authorities undertook a campaign, vainly, to have Jerusalem recognized as the "capital of Israel" by the international community. On 15 November 1988, at a meeting of the Palestine National Council (PNC), the leader of the PLO, Yasir Arafat, proclaimed the "independence of the Palestinian state," with Jerusalem as its capital.

In March 1990, the U.S. Senate passed a resolution in favor of recognizing Jerusalem as "capital of Israel," which caused a wave of protest in much of the international community. When U.S. president George Bush, in March 1991, launched the idea of a peace plan for the Middle East, the subject of the internationalization of the status of Jerusalem came up again, prompting Israeli prime minister Yitzhak Shamir to reiterate that Jerusalem would forever remain the capital of Israel. On 19 May 1993, on the occasion of the twenty-sixth anniversary of the Israeli occupation of the eastern part of the city, Israeli prime minister Yitzhak Rabin declared that the "question of Jerusalem is not part of the agenda in negotiations for a temporary accord" concerning the occupied territories. On 4 September 1995, the Israeli administration of the city announced a celebration, to last fifteen months, to commemorate the third-millennium anniversary of the declaration of King David, proclaiming Jerusalem as capital of the Jewish people. The European Union and the Palestinians decided to boycott these events, so as not to support Israeli claims on the Arab part of the city. At the opening of these festivities, other than the absence of European diplomats, that of the ambassador of the United States was also noticeable. On 24 October 1995, the U.S. Senate voted (93 for and 5 against) to move the embassy of the United States from Tel Aviv to Jerusalem, a decision approved by Congress (374 in favor and 37 against), notwithstanding the opposition of the Clinton administration, which was wary of harming the peace process. Implicitly recognizing Jerusalem as the capital of Israel, this U.S. initiative prompted much anger and protest in Arab countries.

On 4 December 1996, referring to the Israeli decision of 1980 to extend its laws, jurisdiction, and administration over Jerusalem, the United Nations General Assembly declared the takeover of the Holy City to be illegal. This resolution was passed by a massive majority, with 148 voices for, one against (Israel) and 13 abstentions, including the United States. The municipal elections of 10 November 1998, in which the abstention rate was almost 60 percent, allowed the ultra-orthodox SHAS Party to win 15 seats of the 31, while the lay party of the left, Meretz, won only 7 seats. In July 2000, at the Israeli-Palestinian summit hosted by the United States at Camp David, Israeli prime minister Ehud Barak said he was willing to accord administrative powers to the Palestinians over the Arab part of Jerusalem, provoking the anger of the Israeli right and the ultra-orthodox. In September, a visit by the head of Likud, Ariel Sharon, to al-Haram al-Sharif (Temple Mount) sparked a violent outbreak of the al-Aqsa Intifada, which prompted Israeli authorities to restrict Palestinians who did not reside in Jerusalem from entering the city. HAMAS and the Islamic Jihad carried out more suicide bombings, and Israeli authorities began constructing a barrier to cut off Palestinian areas from Jewish areas. In January 2004 the wall was extended to cut off the Palestinian suburb of Abu Dis from the city. Jerusalem remained at the heart of the Israeli-Palestinian conflict.

SEE ALSO Aqsa Intifada, al-; Arab-Israel War (1948); Arab-Israel War (1967); British Mandate; Haram al-Sharif; Palestine National Council; Resolution 181; Resolution 2253; Sharon, Ariel.

JERUSALEM POST: Israeli weekly, founded in 1932 under the name *Palestine Post,* becoming the *Jerusalem Post* in 1950. Openly Labor until the middle of the 1980s, this publication was bought by a Canadian group in 1989 and has been transformed into a daily newspaper of the center-right. Its owners control also 49 percent of the shares of the biweekly *Jerusalem Report.*

SEE ALSO Israel Labor Party.

JESUS (Jesus Christ; Isa, in Arabic; Joshua, in Hebrew): The founder of Christianity, Jesus is considered by Christians to be the Messiah, son of God, and redeemer of humanity. According to many historians, the effect of Jesus' preaching was to annoy the great Jewish priests, Pharisees and Sadducees, who saw in his discourse the ferment of unrest in the Jewish community of Palestine. After he went to Jerusalem for Passover, Jesus was arrested, condemned to death, and crucified on the order of the Roman procurator, Pontius Pilate. After his death, his apostles claimed that Jesus had been resurrected, thereby giving birth to the first generation of Christians, whose faith was based on the preaching of Jesus. The year in which Jesus is believed to have been born marks the beginning of the common era. However, many historians think Jesus was actually born in Galilee six or seven years earlier.

SEE ALSO Christianity; Galilee; Isa; Messiah.

JEW (yehudi, in Hebrew): Name accorded since the Exile (4th century B.C.E.) to the descendants of Abraham, a monotheistic Semitic people who lived in Palestine. The word *Jew* was used for the first time in 332 B.C.E. to designate the inhabitants of Judea at the moment when Alexander the Great conquered the Middle East. Judea was a province of the Persian Empire that issued from the Kingdom of Judah, one of the sons of Jacob. After the creation of the State of Israel in 1948, many political, intellectual, and religious leaders launched a public debate about who exactly was a Jew. Lay people and most political figures favored a separation between religion and politics, and between religion and nationality, but the ultra-Orthodox favored the creation of a religious state and connected ethnic origin with religion, as the Israeli government eventually did and continues to do. The Law of Return (Hoq ha-Shvut), passed by the Knesset on 5 July 1950, provides that any Jew is entitled to immigrate to Israel and become a citizen. A 1970 amendment extended citizenship rights to non-Jewish spouses and the children of Jews. Some Orthodox leaders have called for an amendment narrowly defining a Jew as a person born of a Jewish mother or converted according to Orthodox tradition. This has sparked considerable debate among the Jewish Reform, Orthodox, and Conservative movements.

SEE ALSO Abraham; Jacob; Knesset; Law of Return.

JEWISH AGENCY FOR ISRAEL (JAI): The Jewish Agency for Palestine was officially created in 1929. Its name comes from the text of the 1922 British mandate calling for "a Jewish agency." It became the Jewish Agency for Israel after 1948. In 1929, the organization was opened to non-Zionist Jewish groups and also became the executive arm of the World Zionist Organization. Numerous non-Zionist personalities, including Albert Einstein and Leon Blum, belonged to the Jewish Agency. Created while Palestine was under British mandate, the JAI cooperated with the British administration to find solutions to the problems of Jewish immigration.

In the 1930s the agency supervised the transfer of Jewish capital from Germany to Palestine, as well as the immigration—both legal and illegal—of thousands of European Jews. But faced with restrictive measures regarding the immigration of the Jews into Palestine, the executive committee of the Jewish Agency decided, in 1939, to harden its position regarding British authority. In May 1941, in the context of the war against Nazi Germany, the Jewish Agency and Haganah decided to create the PALMACH (Hebrew acronym for "shock brigades"), some of which would be merged into the Jewish Brigade of the British Army and would participate in combat against the German Army. At the end of January 1943, faced with the persecutions of the European Jews of Central Europe, the Jewish Agency created a "Rescue Committee," directed by Yitzhak Gruenbaum, to help Jews leave their country to go to a neutral one or to Palestine.

In December 1946, approving the positions of the Jewish Agency, the Twenty-Second Zionist Congress designated David Ben-Gurion to head a defense committee. After the creation of the State of Israel in May 1948, the Jewish Agency concentrated its activities on immigration and the integration of the masses of new immigrants. In 1954 the Israeli government and the executive committee of the World Zionist Organization confirmed the role of the Jewish Agency for immigration into Israel. The Jewish Agency also organizes the rescue of Diaspora Jews in danger and retains some authority regarding agricultural resettlement. It spends a large portion of its budget on educational and cultural activities related to its mission of increasing the commitment of world Jewry to the State of Israel.

SEE ALSO Ben-Gurion, David; Haganah.

JEWISH RELIGIOUS HOLIDAYS: Yom Kippur (Day of Atonement; falls on 10 Tishri); Rosh Hashana (New Year's Day; falls on 1 and 2 Tishri); Sukkoth (Feast of the Tabernacles; falls between 15 and 21 Tishri); Pesach (Passover; falls between 15 and 21 Nisan); Purim (Feast of the Drawing of Lots; falls on 13 or 14 Adar); Shavuoth (Pentecost; falls on 6 and 7 Sivan).

SEE ALSO Yom Kippur.

JIBRIL, AHMAD (1935–2002): Palestinian political figure born in 1935, near Ramla, in Palestine. Having taken refuge in Syria in 1948, at the time of the first Israeli-Arab conflict, Ahmad Jibril joined the Syrian army in 1952, becoming a captain. He was expelled from the army in 1958 at the time of the creation of the United Arab Republic. He briefly worked with Fatah in 1965 and then created a *fida'iyyun* group, the Palestine Liberation Front (PLF).

In 1967, after the Arab defeat in the Arab-Israel War of 1967, he participated in the creation of the Popular Front for the Liberation of Palestine (PFLP), headed by George Habash and Nayif Hawatma, and born of a merging of the PLF and the Arab Nationalist Movement (ANM). The following year, in disagreement with George Habash, he quit the PFLP to found the Popular Front for the Liberation of Palestine-General Command (PFLP-GC), which put armed struggle before political action. The PFLP-GC, whose headquarters was in Syria, made itself known on 21 February 1970 by blowing up, in flight, a Swissair plane directed toward Tel Aviv. In the following year, the PFLP-GC carried out many attacks on Israeli soil. In March 1974, three of Jibril's closest collaborators died in an automobile accident, causing wavering in the movement. During the year, in spite of his opposition to the policies of Yasir Arafat, the PFLP-GC joined the PLO, with Jibril becoming a member of the central committee of the organization.

AHMAD JIBRIL. THE PRO-SYRIAN—AND LATER PRO-IRANIAN—RADICAL, WHO LONG OPPOSED THE POLICIES AND RULE OF YASIR ARAFAT, FOUNDED THE BREAKAWAY POPULAR FRONT FOR THE LIBERATION OF PALESTINE—GENERAL COMMAND IN 1968 AND COMMITTED MANY TERRORIST ACTS IN ISRAEL AND ELSEWHERE BEGINNING IN 1970. *(© Reza/Webistan/Corbis)*

Bolstered by aid from Syria and Libya, the PFLP-GC launched into a series of terrorist actions against Israel, which impaired the diplomatic initiative that had been undertaken by the PLO. In 1977, the pro-Syrian policy advocated by Jibril prompted Muhammad ʿAbbas Zaydan (Abu al-Abbas) to resign from the PFLP-GC, to found his own movement, which retook the name of the Palestine Liberation Front. In 1983, a new opposition surfaced in the PFLP-GC, giving birth to the PFLP-GC-Temporary Command. In 1984, expelled from the PLO, the PFLP-GC joined the Palestinian opposition, by adhering to the Palestinian National Salvation Front (PNSF). Certain opponents of Yasir Arafat began regarding Jibril as a possible successor to the head of the PLO. Between

1985 and 1989, the PFLP-GC planned and carried out many terrorist actions. In 1990, Jibril became closer to Iran, making efforts also to back an Islamic current that had surfaced in his movement, one which participated regularly in joint actions with Hizbullah.

In September 1993, opposing the Israeli-Palestinian Declaration of Principles, signed in Washington, he made a death threat against Arafat, whom he accused of treason, and he decided to join the Palestinian opposition, the Alliance of Palestinian Forces (APF). As the Israeli-Palestinian peace process evolved, Jibril found himself becoming more irrelevant to Palestinian movements. Two currents surfaced in the PFLP-GC: the radical current, which he advocated, along with his son, Muhammad Jihad Jibril; and the moderate current, advocated by the assistant secretary general, Talal Naji, in favor of supporting the policies of the Palestinian Authority (PA). Muhammad Jihad Jibril was assassinated by car bomb in Beirut in May 2002.

SEE ALSO Alliance of Palestinian Forces (APF); Arab-Israel War (1967); Arab National Movement; Arafat, Yasir; Fatah, al-; Habash, George; Hawatma, Nayif; Hizbullah; Palestinian Authority; Popular Front for the Liberation of Palestine; Zaydan, Muhammad ʿAbbas.

JIHAD: (Arabic word meaning "struggle" or "effort.") According to the Qurʾan, jihad is a duty for each Muslim, to achieve the "wisdom and perfection" necessary to deserve the blessing of Allah. This is the "greater jihad," the personal struggle with the self to improve the character, to be a better Muslim. The "lesser jihad" is the collective struggle to create a more just social order, or the necessary struggle to protect the Muslim community when it is threatened by external danger. In this case, jihad may include or consist of "holy war," an armed struggle undertaken in the name of God, with the promise of spiritual rewards. This concept was reborn among extremists of the modern Islamist movement, subsequent to the creation of the State of Israel (considered by the Muslim community as an amputation of a part of the land of Islam). The spread of this movement owes a great deal to the ineffectiveness of secular Arab governments in dealing with the Israeli-Palestinian issue, and also to their failure to serve the needs of their people, their corruption, and their suppression of democratic political alternatives. In current Western political discourse, "jihad" is often taken to have the meaning of "holy war" exclusively.

SEE ALSO Allah.

JIHAD AL-BINA: Organization (Effort for Construction, in Arabic) subsidiary to the Lebanese Hizbullah, in charge of reconstruction, in the Shiʿite sections of Lebanon, of homes destroyed by Israeli bombardments.

SEE ALSO Hizbullah.

JOINT COORDINATION AND COOPERATION COMMITTEE FOR MUTUAL SECURITY PURPOSES (JSC) : Organization created in May 1994, within the framework of the Israeli-Palestinian accord on the application of Palestinian autonomy (Oslo Accords II), for the purpose of coordinating the actions of Palestinian and Israeli police in the West Bank and Gaza. After the coming to power in Israel of Benjamin Netanyahu in June 1996, the Israeli government secured the presence of the American CIA on this committee to advise the Palestinian police on combating terrorism and also to serve as an arbiter in case of disagreement.

SEE ALSO Gaza; Netanyahu, Benjamin; Oslo Accords II; West Bank.

JOINT LIAISON COMMITTEE (JLC)

SEE Local Aid Coordination Committee (LACC).

JORDAN: The territory that is now Jordan was, like most of the Arab East, under Ottoman rule until World War I. During the war, the British encouraged the Arabs, under the leadership of Husayn ibn Ali al-Hashim, sharif of Mecca and amir (after 1917, king) of the Hijaz (western Arabia), to rebel against the Ottomans.

In 1920, his son Faysal, who had been chosen by local notables to be king of Syria, was expelled by the French, who held a League of Nations mandate over that country. The next year Faysal's older brother Abdullah led an army into Transjordan and established himself at Amman, with the intention of moving to restore Faysal in Syria. The British, who held a mandate over Palestine and Transjordan, persuaded him to remain in Amman and agreed to recognize him as ruler there (at the same time they installed Faysal as king of Iraq). By treaty in 1923, Abdullah agreed to accept this arrangement and became Emir Abdullah I of an autonomous emirate of Transjordan (in which the British controlled finance, the military, and foreign relations). In 1946 the country became nominally independent, and declared itself the Hashimite Kingdom of Jordan, and Abdullah king. A treaty of 1948, however, preserved Britain's dominating presence in the country. It supplied financial aid and stationed troops there; in addition, Jordan's army, known as the Arab Legion (al-Jaysh al-Arabi), continued to be commanded and largely run by British officers.

Abdullah also wished to rule Palestine, or as much of it as possible. This put him in conflict with the rising Palestinian nationalist movement, particularly the Arab Higher Committee headed by the mufti of Jerusalem, Hajj Amin al-Husayni, and from the early 1920s he maintained a secret relationship with the Zionist leadership designed to further their mutual interest in thwarting Palestinian aspirations. In November 1947, shortly before the United Nations adopted a resolution partitioning Palestine between Jewish and Palestinian states, the king and the Jewish Agency reached an agreement to divide Palestine between them—the Zionists would establish their state, Abdullah would recongnize it and annex the "Arab part of Palestine" to Jordan, and there would be no Palestinian state. Although matters did not go as Abdullah expected—he did not wish to fight a war against the Zionists, but he was subject to Arab pressures—the truce lines at the end of the Arab-Israel War of 1948—1949 left Jordanian forces in control of a substantial portion of Palestine. On 3 April 1949, the Rhodes armistice agreement ratified this control, and a year later Jordan officially annexed East Jerusalem and the West Bank by an Act of Union. Abdullah wanted to negotiate a peace agreement with Israel, but Arab pressure prevented him from doing so.

On 20 July 1951, the king was assassinated by a Palestinian at the Haram al-Sharif in Jerusalem. His son Talal succeeded him but abdicated in favor of his own son, Hussein, on 11 August 1952. Resentment of Britain; anti-Hashimite and Nasserist-Arab nationalist sentiment (the Egyptian revolution had overthrown a British-associated monarchy in 1952, and its leader was idolized in the Arab world); the presence of Palestinians in the kingdom (half to two-thirds of the population was Palestinian, including more than 800,000 refugees from the 1948 war); and the continuing Palestine crisis—including frequent Israeli incursions into the West Bank—shaped the political situation at the time Hussein came to power. In 1954 there was major public unrest when general elections were rigged by the Hashimite government. In 1955, under public pressure, the king could not sign on to the Baghdad Pact, initiated by Britain and the United States. On 14 December 1955, Jordan was admitted to the UN. In March 1956, also under public pressure, the king dismissed Sir John Glubb, the British commander of the Arab Legion (and changed its name), and announced new elections. These took place in October 1956, shortly before the Suez War, and resulted in the installation of a left-leaning nationalist government.

British collaboration with Israel in the attack on Egypt inspired the end of Jordan's subordinate relationship with Britain. In January 1957, Jordan entered the Arab Solidarity Agreement with Egypt, Saudi Arabia, and Syria, which provided for military cooperation as well as financial assistance to Jordan. In March the government cancelled the 1948 treaty with Britain and negotiated a new one, under which Britain ended its subsidies, turned over its bases, and withdrew its troops. Believing that his Nasserist government was planning to abolish the monarchy, however, Hussein dismissed it in April 1957. After a coup d'etat by the Nasserist army commander was squelched, the newly appointed conservative government dissolved parliament and banned political parties. From this time Hussein took the lead in governing the country himself. The Arab Solidarity Pact having fallen apart almost immediately, the king, claiming to be menaced by Communism, requested and received aid from the United States, which aroused fierce opposition to him in the country. In return for the aid he allowed American and British intelligence agencies to operate freely in Jordan, and they helped him against his foreign and domestic opposition, which included Palestinians, nationalist Jordanians, Nasserists, and pan-Arabists.

At the beginning of February 1958, following the creation of the United Arab Republic (UAR) by Syria and Egypt, Hussein decided, with his cousin Faysal II of Iraq, to form the Arab Union, which ended the following July when the Iraqi monarchy was overthrown and Faysal was assassinated. Fearing similar events in Jordan, Hussein's government declared martial law; the United States began supplying Jordan with oil, and Britain sent in troops. On 10 November 1958 Hussein himself escaped an assassination attempt while flying to Switzerland, when a Syrian plane tried to force his down. In August 1960 Hussein's prime minister was assassinated in his office; on 29 August the king escaped from an attack directed against him. The plot was traced to Syria. On 30 May 1967, with regional tension rising, Jordan signed a military defense accord with Egypt and Syria, leading to the 1967 war with Israel, resulting in the loss of the West Bank including East Jerusalem, and the arrival of almost 350,000 newly uprooted Palestinian refugees in the kingdom.

While favoring a peaceful resolution of the conflict with Israel, King Hussein was blocked by the refusal of Arab countries, which, by way of compensation, accorded him significant financial aid, principally from Saudi Arabia and Kuwait. On 16 February 1968, following new reprisals by the Israeli army in Jordanian territory, he condemned armed actions by the Palestinian resistance, but after the Battle of Karama in March 1968, activities by Palestinian guerrillas (*fida'iyyun*) in Jordan increased. There was fighting between the Jordanian army and Palestinian organizations, who by then were trying to bring down the Hashimite regime. The situation culminated in what has come to be known as Black September 1970. Hussein installed a military government and the army launched a massive attack on the Palestinian fighters, killing about four thousand of them in ten days—and defeating a Syrian force that had been sent to help them—until a truce was negotiated by Egyptian president Gamal Abdel Nasser at the behest of the League of Arab States. After renewed fighting in July 1971 the Palestinian Liberation Organization (PLO) and other groups were expelled to Lebanon, and all the Palestinian civil organizations that had made up the Palestinian state-within-a-state were shut down. In November 1971, Jordan's prime minister, visiting Cairo, was assassinated by the Palestinian group Black September. Jordan became even more isolated in the Arab world because of an economic crisis caused by the halting of Arab financial help, as well as because of the king's proposed project for a Jordanian-Palestinian federation with the West Bank, to be called the United Arab Kingdom, which he announced on 15 March 1972. This was rejected the next month by the Palestine National Council (PNC). In November, Jordanian security services uncovered a conspiracy organized by Jordanian officers to overthrow the king.

During the October 1973 war against Israel, under the influence of the United States, Jordan remained neutral when the conflict started, although it did send two armored brigades to reinforce the Syrian front. On 26 October 1974, King Hussein opposed the decision of the Arab League summit meeting in Rabat recognizing the PLO as "sole and legitimate representative of the Palestinian people" and supporting an independent Palestinian state in liberated territory. He accepted the decision, however, and dissolved parliament, half of whose constituencies were in the West Bank. He also maintained Jordanian civil and administrative ties to the West Bank. In 1977, the trip by the Egyptian president, Anwar al-Sadat, to Jerusalem led to a reconciliation between King Hussein and Yasir Arafat. Both opposed the establishment of autonomous regimes under Israeli control for the inhabitants of the West Bank and the Gaza Strip, and both wanted Israel to withdraw from the territories it had occupied since 1967. In 1978 Hussein declined to participate in the Camp David negotiations between Israel and Egypt or endorse the 1979 peace treaty, in spite of the secret meetings that he had been conducting for years with Israeli leaders. Consequently, at the Arab summit in Baghdad in September 1980 the Gulf states decided to accord some significant financial help to Jordan. From 1980 through 1988, Hussein supported Baghdad in the Iran-Iraq War, which allowed his kingdom to benefit from trade with Iraq. In 1981 he negotiated an arms deal with the Soviet Union, which was also supplying Iraq. In 1984 Hussein allowed parliament to reopen, and Jordan began dealing with Egypt again despite the Arab League ban that had been imposed after the 1979 treaty. At the summit of the Organization of the Islamic Conference (OIC) in Casablanca in January 1984, Jordan supported the return of Egypt to the Arab community.

In 1985 Hussein allowed the PNC to meet in Amman. He came to an agreement with the PLO regarding a coordinated approach to a Palestinian-Israeli settlement, but differences developed—partly over the loyalties of expatriate Palestinians with Jordanian citizenship—and it was abandoned by 1987. In December 1987 the Intifada began in the occupied territories and in July 1988, fearing the violence would spill across the Jordan River, Hussein renounced all legal and administrative claims and responsibilities in the West Bank (this included the cancellation of the payment of salaries of public officials and of the Jordanian citizenship of all West Bank Palestinians). This move gave the PLO complete responsibility for Palestinian interests. During the Gulf Crisis in 1990, Hussein did not support the Iraqi invasion of Kuwait, but refused to join the anti-Iraq coalition. At the Arab League on 3 August 1990, Jordan abstained from voting on the resolution condemning Iraq, but Hussein did support the League's position that the crisis should be resolved by negotiation under Arab auspices, and rejecting foreign intervention. When the Arab League modified this position a week later, approving the Gulf states' right to self-defense and implicitly approving their use of outside forces, Jordan voted in favor but expressed "reservations"—in effect, chose to remain neutral.

The end of the Gulf War in 1991 led to the organization of the Madrid Conference on Middle East peace, which opened on 30 October 1991. Hussein agreed to the PLO's inclusion in the Jordanian delegation, since the Israelis refused to deal with it directly. On 14 September 1993, following the signature of the Oslo Accords between Israelis and Palestinians, Israel and Jordan signed an agreement in Washington on future peace negotiations. On 18 July 1994, the first formal peace parley took place, and on 26 October 1994, Jordan and Israel signed a peace treaty. This accord aroused strong opposition in Jordan, as did the accords between Israel and the PLO. Some Jordanians felt that Palestinians with Jordanian citizenship, who presumably would be leaving for a projected Palestinian state, should not be allowed to vote; some Jordanians still favored annexation of the West Bank to Jordan. Many Palestinians still suspected Hashimite friendliness with Israel. In the context of the Israeli-Palestinian peace process, however, Jordan since 1988 has been an advocate of Palestinian statehood, as well as a necessary intermediary.

In February 1996, there was a change in Jordan's previously friendly relations with Iraq when the king authorized the opening of the office of an Iraqi opposition group in the Jordanian capital. On 5 June 1996, after the coming to power in Israel of a Likud government opposed to the Oslo Accords, Hussein organized, with Yasir Arafat and Husni Mubarak, a mini summit to reaffirm his support for the Israeli-Palestinian peace process. On 3 August, Jordan resumed diplomatic relations with Syria, which had been interrupted by the Israeli-Jordanian peace accord. On 6 August, Hussein met with the new Israeli prime minister, Benjamin Netanyahu, and five days later, he was in Saudi Arabia for the resumption of Jordanian-Saudi relations, interrupted since the Gulf War. On 15 October, he met Yasir Arafat in Jericho, to show his support in the current negotiations with Israel over Hebron, which were at a stalemate. On 12 January 1997, he helped break the stalemate when he mediated an accord on the redeployment of Israeli troops. In August 1998, his health failing, Hussein delegated most of his power to his brother Hassan, and left for the United States for medical treatment. While there, he lent his assistance to the U.S.-sponsored Israeli-Palestinian talks at Wye River Plantation in October. Returning to Amman in January 1999, he settled the succession on his son Abdullah. He died on 7 February 1999.

The new king, Abdullah II, spent his first months traveling extensively and making himself known on the international political scene. On 5 September Abdullah signed onto an accord developed at Sharm el-Sheikh, Egypt, between Yasir Arafat and Israeli prime minister Ehud Barak, that was thought to open the way to negotiations for a final Israeli-Palestinian peace settlement. A few days later Jordan resumed relations with Kuwait, broken off since the Gulf War. Domestically, Abdullah issued a warning to Jordanian Islamists opposed to peace with Israel and announced his intention of continuing the process of democratization begun ten years previously. On 25 November, he declared that Israel should renounce its territorial ambitions in the eastern sector of Jerusalem and accept the return of Palestinian refugees in order to attain a durable peace in the Middle East. On 22 August 2000, he made his first official visit to Tel Aviv, where he was received by Prime Minister Ehud Barak. Before his trip Abdullah had talked with Yasir Arafat and had reaffirmed to him Jordanian support for the Palestinian cause. The al-Aqsa Intifada, however, which began in September 2000, has reduced Jordan's ability to mediate, as well as threatened the peace within Jordan. The king implicitly supported the U.S. campaign to disarm the regime of Saddam Hussein in 2002–2003, but opposed the war, refusing U.S. forces the use of Jordanian airspace.

In June 2003 Abdullah hosted the Aqaba Summit, which was intended to work out the means of implementing the Road Map plan put forth that April by the so-called Quartet. The king met privately with Ariel Sharon in Israel in March 2004 to discuss the "separation wall" Israel was building around Palestinian areas in the West Bank; aside from his opposition to the wall as inflammatory, he was concerned that it would eventually cause a mass movement of new Palestinian refugees into Jordan, resulting in economic stress and upsetting the demographic balance between Palestinians and East Bank Jordanians that already threatens the political stability of the country. The international context of Jordanian politics in 2004 is largely shaped by the al-Aqsa Intifada in the Palestinian territories and by the American "war on terror." The king, concerned mainly with the survival of the Hashimite regime and heavily dependent on aid from the West, remains active in his attempts to encourage a political settlement for the Palestine-Israel issue while cooperating with the United States.

SEE ALSO Abdullah I ibn Hussein; Abdullah II ibn Hussein; Aqaba Summit; Aqsa Intifada, al-; Arab Higher Committee; Arab-Israel War (1967); Arab-Israel War (1973); Arafat, Yasir; Baghdad Pact; Black September 1970; Black

LEADERS FOR PEACE. ISRAELI PRIME MINISTER YITZHAK RABIN (LEFT) AND KING HUSSEIN OF JORDAN TALK ALONG THE SEA OF GALILEE AFTER SIGNING A HISTORIC PEACE TREATY BETWEEN THE TWO NATIONS ON 26 OCTOBER 1994. THIS ENDED FORTY-SIX YEARS OF HOSTILE RELATIONS BETWEEN ISRAEL AND JORDAN. *(© Photograph by Ya'acov Sa'ar. Government Press Office [GPO] of Israel)*

September Organization; Camp David; Haram al-Sharif; Hashim, al-; Hebron; Husayni, Hajj Amin al-; Hussein ibn Talal; Intifada (1987–1993); Iran-Iraq War; League of Arab States; Madrid Conference; Mubarak, Husni; Occupied Territories; Nasser, Gamal Abdel; Organization of the Islamic Conference; Oslo Accords; Palestine Liberation Organization; Palestine National Council; Road Map (2002); Sharon, Ariel; Suez Crisis; West Bank.

JORDANIAN-ISRAELI PEACE TREATY: Signed on 26 October 1994 by Jordan's King Hussein and Israel's prime minister Yitzhak Rabin at a ceremony on the Israel-Jordan border, attended by U.S. president Bill Clinton. This treaty, the second signed by the Jewish state with an Arab country, put an official end to the state of war existing between Israel and Jordan since 1948.

The principal elements of the accord were an agreement to fix the international border at the 1922 Mandate frontier between Palestine and Transjordan, with minor adjustments; an agreement regarding Jordan River water sharing; an agreement that Palestinian refugees in Jordan would be settled in that country (for which purpose Jordan would receive American aid); an agreement that the Muslim holy sites of Jerusalem would be controlled and maintained by Jordan; and an agreement regarding cross-border trade and economic exchanges. A salient feature of these agreements, to which the Palestinians were not a party, was that in each case the claims of the Palestinians were ignored. The Jordanians had undermined their claims to a share of Jordan River water, to custodianship of the holy sites, and above all to the refugees' right of return. These points were to have been part of the negotiations between the Israelis and the Palestinians that were to have taken place under the terms of the Oslo Accords and subsequent Declaration of Principles that had been signed the previous year. The Israeli-Jordanian Peace Treaty was condemned by the Palestine Liberation Organization (PLO) and other Palestinian organizations, by Syria, and by Lebanon, and it was extremely unpopular with ordinary Palestinians and other Arabs as well.

SEE ALSO Hussein ibn Talal; Oslo Accords; Rabin, Yitzhak.

JORDANIAN LABOR PARTY (JLP): Jordanian socialist political party, created in February 1998. Most of its founding members, with close ties to the Israel Labor Party, were from the Irbid region, a Jordanian-Israeli industrial area. Favoring a normalization of relations with Israel, this group benefited from official support of the Jordanian government. The current secretary general is Muhammad al-Khataibah.

JORDANIAN-PALESTINIAN ACCORD: Signed 11 February 1985 in Amman between King Hussein of Jordan and the leader of the Palestine Liberation Organization (PLO), Yasir Arafat, this accord envisioned a common action meant to conclude in a peaceful solution to the Middle East conflict. The accord stipulated 1) the application of the principle "land in exchange for peace," according to United Nations resolutions, including those of the Security Council; 2) the right of the Palestinian people to self-determination; 3) a solution of the problem of Palestinian refugees, according to the UN resolutions; 4) a solution to the Palestinian question in all its aspects; 5) that peace negotiations will take place at an international conference, participants to include the five states that are permanent members of the Security Council and all the parties involved in the conflict, including the PLO, as the sole legitimate representative of the Palestinian people, in the framework of a common (Jordanian-Palestinian) delegation.

On 25 February 1985, Egyptian President Husni Mubarak asked the United States to organize direct Israeli-Jordanian-Palestinian negotiations. In the course of the autumn, discussions between the different parties were suspended after the failure of a

Jordanian-Palestinian meeting that had taken place in London on 14 October. In February 1986, because of a lack of full support of the PLO for United Nations Security Council Resolutions 242 and 338, King Hussein of Jordan halted the application of the accord. A year later, on 22 April 1987, the Executive Committee of the PLO, meeting in Algiers, abrogated the Amman Accord.

SEE ALSO Arafat, Yasir; Mubarak, Husni; Resolution 242; Resolution 338.

JORDANIAN PALESTINIAN CONFEDERATION: Proposed solution to the Palestinian issue, associating an autonomous Palestinian territory with Jordan. Since the 1930s a number of proposals have been made for uniting Palestinian territory with Jordan, but until 1977 they involved the merger of such territory into the Jordanian state (as actually happened when Abdullah I incorporated the West Bank into Jordan after the 1948 War), rather than a confederation between sovereign political entities. In 1972 King Hussein proposed that the West Bank be merged with Jordan as the United Arab Kingdom, but the idea was rejected by the Palestine Liberation Organization (PLO). In 1977 he revived the idea as a federation between an autonomous Palestinian West Bank and Jordan. This too was rejected. In 1982, the Reagan Plan proposed by the United States provided for Palestinian autonomy in association with Jordan, and Hussein again offered the PLO a confederation. This time the Palestine National Council approved the federation in principle, but only when both parties were sovereign. In 1985 Hussein and the PLO agreed to make a joint proposal for a settlement that included a Palestinian-Jordanian confederation, based on United Nations resolutions, to be negotiated at an international conference including the permanent members of the UN Security Council, Israel, and a joint Jordanian-PLO delegation. It was opposed by the United States and Israel; both refused to settle the matter in an international conference or to negotiate with the PLO, and Israel claimed the right to approve the Palestinian negotiators. Hussein and the PLO also had disagreements over UN Security Council Resolution 242. This proposal was given up in February 1986.

In March 1992, during the Madrid Conference talks, which were then stalled, Yasir Arafat proposed to King Hussein that the PLO and Jordan form a confederation in order to get the talks moving and to strengthen both their hands in the negotiations. It is not clear how far the proposal went toward being realized; Hussein was agreeable and even discussed the matter with his contacts in the US government. Many Palestinian leaders were opposed, including Saib Erekat, the chief Palestinian negotiator in Madrid, who believed it was premature given that the negotiations were over interim arrangements only. Others believed it was mainly a way for Arafat to regain some control over the Palestinian negotiators. In any case, before anything concrete resulted, Arafat, without informing Hussein or the Madrid negotiators, started an entirely new set of negotiations directly with Israel, in Oslo; King Hussein is known to have felt betrayed by Arafat, and the confederation proposal, as well as the Madrid talks, became moot. Thereafter when the issue was raised with the king he took the position that confederation might be discussed when there was a sovereign Palestine for Jordan to deal with, but not until then.

SEE ALSO Abdullah I ibn Hussein; Arafat, Yasir; Erekat, Saib Muhammad; Hussein ibn Talal; Madrid Conference; Oslo Accords; Palestine Liberation Organization; Palestine National Council; Reagan Plan; Resolution 242; West Bank.

JORDANIAN PEOPLE'S DEMOCRATIC PARTY (HASHD): Palestinian-Jordanian left-wing political party (Hizb al-Sha'b al-Dimuqrati al-Urduni, known by the acronym HASHD) created in October 1989 by the leadership of the Democratic Front for the Liberation of Palestine (DFLP). Jordanian authorities opposed the constitution of Jordanian parties with foreign ties. Nayif Hawatma, head of the DFLP, hoped to integrate his movement into the Jordanian political scene. In 1990, a split in HASHD led to the creation of the Jordanian Progressive Party (al-Hizb al-Taqaddumi al-Urduni), headed by Ali Amr.

At the beginning of the 1994, following the Israeli-Palestinian Oslo Accords and Declaration of Principles of 13 September 1993, a new rift surfaced in HASHD, resulting in divergent tendencies. The first tendency was called the "democratic current," under the leadership of Bassam Haddadin and Nurad Abu Ghoush; the second, called the "historical current," headed by Taysir al-Zeiri and Salim al-Nahas; and a third tendency, under the impetus of Azmi al-Khawaja. All three of these tendencies were opposed to the policies of the DFLP. In 1994, Azmi al-Khawaja became secretary general of his own movement, the Jordanian United Democratic Popular Party. The principal figures in HASHD are Taysir al-Zeiri, Bassam Haddadin, Hussein Abu Rahman, and Jamal Toumari. The secretary general is Salim al-Nahhas.

SEE ALSO Democratic Front for the Liberation of Palestine; Hawatma, Nayif; Jordanian Progressive Party.

JORDANIAN PROGRESSIVE PARTY: Palestinian-Jordanian socialist political party (al-Hizb al-Taqaddumi al-Urduni), founded in 1990 following a split in the Jordanian People's Democratic Party, or HASHD. Its leading figures were Ali Amr, Salah Raafat, and Yussef Hurani. The secretary general in 2004 is Fawaz al-Zubi.

JORDAN RIVER: River roughly 200 miles or 320 kilometers long, flowing from northernmost Israel to the Dead Sea. The Jordan is formed from the confluence of three streams just south of the Israel-Lebanon border: the Hasibani and the Dan Rivers, originating on the Lebanese side of Mount Hermon (Jabal al-Shaykh), and the Baniyas, arising on the Syrian side of Mount Hermon. It flows into Lake Tiberias (the Sea of Galilee) at the point where the Syria-Israel border meets the lake; it flows from the lake south within Israel until it is joined by the Yarmuk River. From there to the Green Line east of Jenin it forms the border between Jordan and Israel; from the Green Line to the Dead Sea, it forms the border between Jordan and the West Bank.

An overall plan for cooperative use and development of the Jordan's water by Lebanon, Syria, Jordan, and Israel was negotiated in 1953–1955 by an American mediator, Eric Johnston, but its final acceptance by the Arab states was conditional on the resolution of the Palestinian issue. The plan was therefore never ratified, although until 1967 both Israel and Jordan adhered to its terms. In 1964, however, Israel began pumping water from Lake Tiberias for use on the coastal plain and in the Negev. The Arab states objected to this unilateral diversion and planned to counter it with their own diversion project on the Jordan's tributaries inside Lebanon and Syria. Israel destroyed the project by bombardment. Currently Israel controls all use of Jordan River water; it is partially regulated by the 1994 Jordanian-Israeli peace treaty, but Israel has no such agreements with Lebanon or Syria. Israel now pumps far more than was contemplated under the Johnston Plan. Israel's use of water per capita is the highest in the Middle East. According to B'Tselem, the Israeli human rights organization, Israeli consumption (from all sources, and for all purposes) is 128 cubic meters per person per year (350 liters per day); Palestinian consumption is 26 cubic meters per person per year (70 liters per day). Approximately one-third of the water used by Israel comes from the Jordan River and its tributaries; none of it goes to the Palestinians.

SEE ALSO B'Tselem; Green Line; Jordanian-Israeli Peace Treaty.

JRA

SEE Japanese Red Army.

JTIC

SEE Palestine Development and Investment Company.

JUDAISM: Religion, philosophy, and lifestyle of the Jewish people. In its modern meaning, this word designates the teaching dispensed by the Torah. This word was first utilized by the Hellenized Jews of the first century B.C.E. Its Hebrew equivalent, *yahadut*, was not employed until modern times. Judaism is based on the belief in a single god, and on the covenant God made with a people whose history dates from the period of Abraham, 4000 years ago. At the demand of God, Abraham left his native region of Ur, in Chaldea, to go to Canaan, where he was to found a great nation. His descendants became known as "Israelites" or "Hebrews." Judaism came into its own after the destruction of the Kingdom of Judah, in 586 B.C.E., and the exile of its population to Babylon. Making no distinction between the temporal and the spiritual, Judaism is at once a religion and a philosophy that concerns every aspect of daily life, including food, rest, sexuality, medicine, and holidays. Presently there exists, parallel to the traditionalist or orthodox currents of Judaism, two other tendencies: liberal or Reform Judaism, mainly centered in the United States; and Conservative Judaism.

The Jewish diaspora has led to some differences in the traditions of Judaism, particularly among the Sephardic Jews—who were exiled from the Middle East, North Africa, and the Iberian Peninsula—and the Ashkenazic Jews—whose origins are from France and German-speaking countries, but who spread throughout Europe and the Americas. Both traditions are based on the Torah, though each has distinct rituals and customs based on ethnic experiences as well as their different chief rabbis and interpretations of the Torah that have guided them over the years. Even so, Rashi, an eleventh-century Ashkenazic exegete, and Maimonides, a twelfth-century Sephardic rabbinic codifier, are recognized by all Jewish traditions to be authoritative interpreters of Judaism.

Besides the religious convictions specified in some Knesset parties (particularly notable among them: SHAS and the National Religious Party), politics and religion also have strong ties in the rulings of the rabbinate of Israel. The chief rabbis of Israel—representing the Sepharadic and Ashkenazic traditions—preside over the Rabbinical Supreme Court (*bet din gadol*), which primarily hears appeals, while a rabbinical council of judges (*dayanim*) delivers regular rulings. The council of the chief rabbinate typically makes decisions on matters of religious law and supervises *Kashrut*—the strict observance of dietary laws, including how foods must be prepared in order to be deemed kosher—in addition to overseeing the activities of ritual circumcisers (*mohalim*) and Torah scribes in Israel. Among other responsibilities, the council maintains contacts with Orthodox rabbis in the diaspora and links Jewish communities around the world with spiritual leaders.

In relation to the Israel-Palestine conflict,, the chief rabbinate has expressed definitive political opinions, such as "Eretz Yisrael ha-Shelema" (the Individual Land of Israel) and "no return of territories for peace." Recently, however, the standing of the chief rabbinate has declined as non-official rabbinic institutions, such as the ultra-Orthodox Eda Haredit, compete for a larger Orthodox following. Some decisions made by the Supreme Court of Israel—overruling decisions of the chief rabbinate on the grounds that they exceeded their jurisdiction—have also hindered the rabbinate's standing.

Generally, Judaism defines a Jew as someone born of a Jewish mother or someone who has submitted to religious conversion. Although debate abounds around what constitutes the minimal requirements of conversion, the *halakhic* (Judeo-legal) minimum requirement consists of male circumcision, immersion in a ritual bath (*mikveh*), a period of Torah study, and a commitment to be bound by all the laws of Judaism. During the twentieth century, some non-Orthodox Jews expanded the definition of a Jew to include children of a Jewish parent and they do not require all of the aforementioned laws to be kept. Yet, the debate over what constitutes a Jew is a controversial one in Israel, which guarantees full citizenship rights to all Jews under the "Law of Return." The Law of Return defines Israel as a Jewish state and grants automatic citizenship to Jewish immigrants who settle in Israel.. Non-Jewish spouses and children of Jews were granted similar rights in 1970, although the Orthodox and Conservative movements in particular do not accept this amended law.

Within Israel, the generic term for non-Jews is "minorities." This group includes mainly Muslim Arabs, but also Christians who are primarily Arabs, as well as Druze, Bahai, Circassians, and Samaritians. "Jewishness" tends to hold religious and political meaning to the majority of Israeli Jews, who recognize Israel as a "Jewish State" and who seek a reflection of this in the state's conduct.

In 1948, with the founding of the state of Israel, the Jewish Sabbath—25 hours, from sundown on Friday to sundown on Saturday, each week—was branded the official day of rest for the Jewish population. An allowance was made for Muslims to have a day of rest on Friday, and for Christians to rest on Sunday.The Work and Rest Hours Law of 1951 legislated that Jews be given days off on the Sabbath and festival holidays. Businesses that aim to stay open on the Sabbath must obtain a license from the Israeli Ministry of Labor. In the biblical account of creation, this seventh day marks God's rest after his work and is intended to be a day of spiritual refreshment and joy. Thus, on Saturdays, observant Jews wear special clothes, enjoy festive meals, and attend synagogue. For non-Orthodox Jews, the Sabbath is largely a day of leisure, perhaps a time to spend at a sporting event, café, or the beach. Traditional festivals (Rosh ha-Shana, Yom Kippur, Sukkot, Simhat Torah, Shavuot, and the first and last days of Passover) are also days of rest, as is Independence Day (5 Iyer), though the extreme Orthodox do not typically observe the latter.Yom Kippur, the Day of Atonement, in particular, is respected by all Israeli Jews. On that day, broadcasting is suspended and the streets are open only to pedestrians.

SEE ALSO Abraham; Ashkenazi; Covenant; Diaspora; Halakhah; Jewish Religious Holidays; Knesset; Law of Return; National Religious Party; Sephardi; SHAS; Torah.

JUDEA AND SAMARIA: Biblical names for the territory known in the twentieth century as the West Bank of the Jordan River.

SEE ALSO West Bank.

JULAN, AL-

SEE Golan Heights.

JULIAN CALENDAR: Established by Julius Caesar and used in the West until the Gregorian reform of 1582, this calendar is still in use in the Greek Orthodox Patriarchate of Jerusalem and in some Orthodox churches.

SEE ALSO Eastern Orthodox Church.

AMIN JUMAYYIL. A SON OF ONE OF THE FOUNDERS OF THE CHRISTIAN PHALANGE PARTY, HE WAS CHOSEN TO BE PRESIDENT OF LEBANON AFTER THE ASSASSINATION OF THE PRESIDENT-ELECT, HIS BROTHER, IN 1982. NEAR THE END OF A TERM MARKED BY FACTIONAL FIGHTING AND PRESSURE FROM SYRIA, ISRAEL, AND THE UNITED STATES, JUMAYYIL WENT INTO EXILE FOR TWELVE YEARS. *(© Corbis)*

JUMAYYIL, AMIN (1942–): Lebanese Maronite political figure, born on 22 January 1942 at Bikfaya, in a politically active family. His father, Pierre Jumayyil, was the founder of the right-wing nationalist Christian Phalange (Kata'ib) Party, and his younger brother, Bashir, was president-elect of the republic (but did not take office) in 1982.

A lawyer by training, Amin Jumayyil went into politics early on, encouraged by his family. He joined the Phalange in 1961, and nine years later became a deputy, taking the seat of his uncle Maurice, who had recently died. He was reelected in 1972, but ceded his place as the head of Phalange to his younger brother, Bashir, leader of the Phalangist militia. During the Lebanese Civil War (1975–1990), his public image was that of a "politico," while Bashir, who commanded the Lebanese Forces (LF), an alliance of Maronite Christian militias formed in 1976, was an active, enthusiastic participant in the war. In 1981, Amin Jumayyil was elected secretary general of the Phalange. In June 1982 Lebanon was invaded by Israel, which bombarded Beirut, where the Palestine Liberation Organization (PLO) was headquartered, for weeks. After a ceasefire negotiated by the United States, the PLO left Lebanon for Tunis, the withdrawal supervised by a Multinational Force (MF) composed of American, French, and some Italian troops, and the Israelis and Syrians withdrew from the city. On 23 August 1982, Bashir Jumayyil, an asset of both the CIA and the Mossad, was elected president of the republic. On 10 September, the last MF troops departed.

On 14 September, a week before he was to take office, Bashir Jumayyil was assassinated. The next day Israeli forces, violating the ceasefire agreement, moved into Beirut to help the Lebanese Forces secure the city. With the help of the Israelis, the LF moved into the Palestinian refugee camps of Sabra and Shatila and murdered an estimated 1500–3000 civilians, ostensibly in reprisal for the assassination of Bashir Jumayyil (who had actually been killed by Syrian nationalists who wanted to annex Lebanon). On 21 September 1982, parliament elected Amin Jumayyil president in place of his brother. After the massacres, the United States and France returned the Multinational Force to Beirut. In May 1983, under pressure from the United States, Jumayyil agreed to sign a peace treaty with Israel, which was actually ratified by parliament. Opposition to this treaty among Lebanese—and by the Syrians—was so great, however, that Jumayyil felt obliged to refuse to sign it. The Syrians would not negotiate, and the Israelis, who had been protecting Jumayyil's government from its factional enemies, withdrew their forces from the Shuf district southeast of Beirut to South Lebanon. Fighting among the factions then broke out again. The "peacekeepers" became involved in the fighting on the Christian side—American warships shelled Syrian positions in the mountains (killing many civilians in the process)—which provoked retaliation on the ground. In October, suicide bombings, probably carried out by Hizbullah, killed 241 American and 56 French soldiers. The Multinational Force troops were kept in their barracks and eventually left Lebanon in the spring of 1984.

By February 1984 so many Muslim and Druze soldiers had deserted the army, many to factional militias, rather than fight on behalf of a sectarian Christian government, that the army disintegrated. Jumayyil repudiated the agreement with Israel in March 1984. However, opposition to him increased, while the death of his father in August 1984 further accentuated his isolation in the Christian camp, resulting in bloody confrontations between his supporters and members of the militia that was led by Elie Hobeika and Samir Geagea. On 12 March 1985, these two took over the command of the Lebanese Forces. A year later, he backed Samir Geagea, who, on 15 January 1985, expelled Elie Hobeika from the leadership of the LF. In the following month, he refused to resign the presidency of the republic, in spite of intense pressure from the opposition. The latter reproached him for not having ratified the accord between the militias that was signed on 14 January by the leaders of the Shiʿite AMAL, the Druze Progressive Socialist Party (PSP), and the Maronite LF, and which was thought amenable to bringing back peace. In spite of the opposition of Christian leaders, whose chief he was supposed to be, he made overtures to Syria, which led to a schism in the Christian camp.

On 17 January 1987 he took part in the "Christian summit" of Smar Jubayl, with former presidents Camille Chamoun, Charles Hilu, and Sulayman Franjiyya, to try reunifying their movement. On 12 February 1988, he narrowly escaped death when a bomb was discovered in an airplane that was about to take him from Cyprus to Sanaa, Yemen. On 22 September, just before the end of his presidential term and without a successor having been elected, in order to maintain the Christian camp in power, he formed a provisional government led by the Maronite general Michel Aoun, while the official prime minister, Selim al-Hoss, was refusing to resign. At the beginning of October, after receiving death threats from the Lebanese Forces of Samir Geagea, he left Lebanon to go to Paris. In June 1991, he met with Shimon Peres in Brussels and discussed the situation in South Lebanon. In 1992, after returning home to attempt to persuade the Phalangist party to boycott the legislative elections, he was obliged, under government pressure, to cut his stay short.

In July 2000, after twelve years as an exile, he returned to Lebanon, where the situation had changed, due to the death of Syrian president Hafiz al-Asad and the withdrawal of the Israeli army from South Lebanon. He made an attempt to regain the leadership of Phalange, but was frustrated, and later formed a splinter group called Kataʾib al-Qaʿida (the Phalange Base). In 2002 he was expelled from the party, and sued, for insulting the leadership (he used the term "prostitution" in reference to the leadership of current secretary general Karim Pakraduni).

SEE ALSO AMAL; Aoun, Michel; Asad, Hafiz al-; Chamoun, Camille; Druze; Franjiyya, Sulayman; Geagea, Samir; Hizbullah; Hobeika, Elie; Jumayyil, Bashir; Peres, Shimon; Phalange; Sabra and Shatila.

JUMAYYIL, BASHIR (1947–): Lebanese political figure, born on 10 November 1947 in Beirut, Bashir Jumayyil was the son of Pierre Jumayyil, founder of the Phalange (Kataʾib), and the younger brother of Amin Jumayyil. A lawyer by training, he worked for a law firm in Washington, D.C., in the early 1970s and was recruited by the CIA.

He launched his political career in 1972, becoming the head of the Phalange for the Ashrafiah sector. His brother Amin, who had just been elected deputy, yielded his place to Bashir as the leader of the party. In 1974 Bashir became the head of the Phalange militias. When the civil war broke out in Lebanon, in 1975, he became totally involved in the fighting. On 13 July 1976, he became commander-in-chief of the military council of the Phalange. A few days later he became head of the Lebanese Forces (LF), the militia of the Lebanese Front, an alliance of several right-wing Christian parties, dominated by the Phalange. Under his guidance, and with substantial military and financial assistance from Israel and from the CIA, the LF became the largest Maronite paramilitary force in Lebanon.

Bashir Jumayyil wanted to be president of Lebanon, and worked to eliminate potential rivals. In June 1978 he had a Phalangist commando attack the home of Tony Franjiyya, son of former president Sulayman Franjiyya, killing him and his family. On 23 February 1980 Bashir escaped an assassination attempt in the course of which eight people died, including his daughter. In the same year his Phalangist forces engaged in a series of battles with the Tigers, the militia of the National Liberal Party, led by Dany Chamoun, culminating in the "Day of the Long Knives," 7 July 1980, in which the Tigers were effectively wiped out. Chamoun was the son of former president Camille Chamoun, who was the political head of the Lebanese Front. In June 1982, Israel invaded Lebanon, partly to go after the Palestine Liberation Organizatin (PLO), which was headquartered there, and partly to help support Bashir Jumayyil, a client through whom they hoped to impose control over Palestinian and Muslim forces. The PLO was defeated, and in August and September, after an American-sponsored truce, the PLO leadership and about 14,000 fighters were evacuated from Beirut. On 23 August 1982, parliament elected him president of Lebanon. On 14 September he was assassinated when the Phalange headquarters was bombed. The PLO was blamed, although the real assassins were Syrian nationalists. This led the IDF to return to Beirut to assist the LF in controlling the situation, as well as letting the LF into the Palestinian refugee camps of Sabra and Shatila, where they perpetrated a horrifying massacre. On 21 September, Amin Jumayyil was elected president in his brother's place.

SEE ALSO Franjiyya, Sulayman; Jamayyil, Amin; Lebanese Forces; Lebanese Front; Phalange; Sabra and Shatila.

JUMBLATT, KAMAL (1917–1977): Lebanese political figure, belonging to the important Druze clan of Jumblattis, Kamal Jumblatt studied law, obtaining a degree in 1942. The next year, he was elected deputy, and in 1946 became minister of economy and agriculture. Three years later he founded the Progressive Socialist Party (PSP). After having pushed for the resignation of President Beshara al-Khuri, then broken with the new president, Camille Chamoun, Jumblatt joined the opposition. After the accession to the presidency of Fu'ad Chehad in 1958, he assumed various governmental functions: minister of national education (1958), public works and planning (1961), interior (1961, 1964). In 1964, with Rashid Karame, he played an important role in the election of Charles Hilu to the presidency of the republic.

After the Arab-Israel War of June 1967, he drew progressively closer to Palestinian organizations and formed a radical front of the left. In 1969, he was named minister of the interior, responsible mainly for the application of the Cairo accords granting the PLO operational independence in areas of Lebanon with large Palestinian refugee populations. He denounced the involvement of the army in Lebanese political life, which was growing ever greater. In the following month of August he decided to back the candidacy of Sulayman Franjiyya for the presidency. But in May 1973, following Lebanese-Palestinian confrontations, he took a position against the chief of state. At the time of the Lebanese civil war of 1975, he became the leader of the Lebanese left and one of the principal supporters of the Palestinian resistance. He became president of the political council of the Lebanese National Movement, which allied parties and organizations of the left and made common cause with the Palestine Liberation Organization (PLO) against the right-wing Christian Lebanese Front (LF), dominated by the Phalange. The success of this alliance, particularly in the "Battle of the Mountain" against the Christian militias in March 1976, provoked Syrian intervention in June on the side of the LF. On 16 March 1977, he was assassinated in his car on the road to Moukhtara by pro-Syrian factions of the Lebanese Syrian Socialist Nationalist Party (SSNP). Awarded the Lenin Prize in 1972, Kamal Jumblatt was the author of a number of works about Lebanon. His son, Walid, succeeded him as head of the PSP and the Lebanese National Movement.

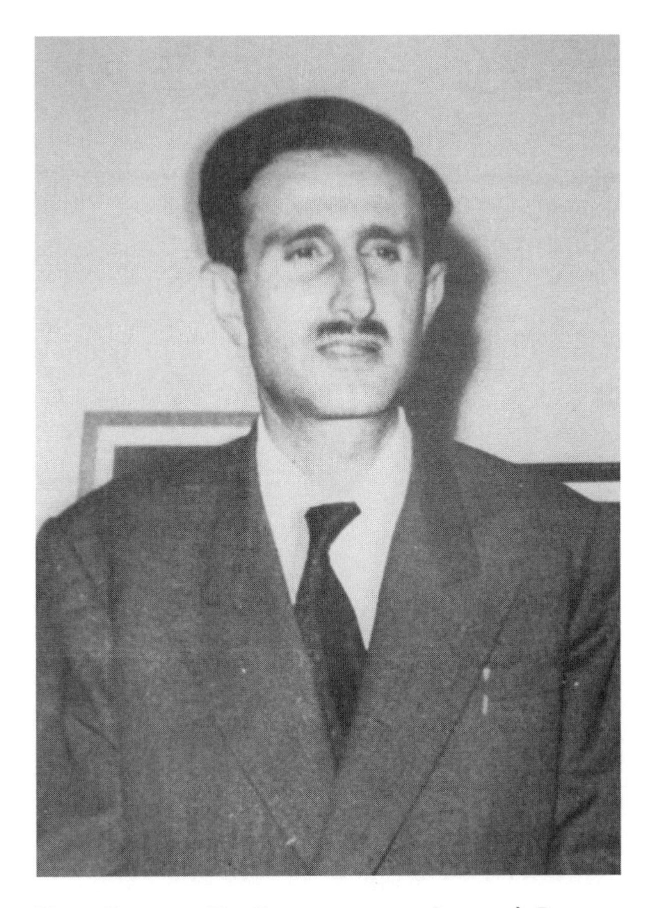

KAMAL JUMBLATT. THE DRUZE FOUNDER OF LEBANON'S PROGRESSIVE SOCIALIST PARTY IN 1949, JUMBLATT SERVED IN VARIOUS MINISTERIAL POSTS BEGINNING IN THE 1940S AND LATER SUPPORTED OPERATIONS BY THE PALESTINE LIBERATION ORGANIZATION IN HIS COUNTRY, BEFORE HIS ASSASSINATION IN 1977.

SEE ALSO Arab-Israel War (1967); Jumblatt, Walid Kamal; Lebanese Front; Lebanese National Movement; Palestine Liberation Organization.

JUMBLATT, WALID KAMAL (1949–): Lebanese political figure, born in 1949 in Moukhtara, in the Lebanese Shuf, Walid Jumblatt belonged to one of the most important Druze clans in Lebanon, the Jumblattis. During his youth, drawn to Arab nationalism, Nasserist in inspiration, he met Gamal Abdel Nasser a number of times. In 1973, he obtained a degree in political science from the American University of

WALID KAMAL JUMBLATT. A DRUZE LEADER AND HEAD OF LEBANON'S PROGRESSIVE SOCIALIST PARTY AFTER HIS FATHER'S ASSASSINATION IN 1977, HE SUPPORTED THE PALESTINE LIBERATION ORGANIZATION AND BATTLED RIGHT-WING MARONITE MILITIAS. JUMBLATT LATER HELD VARIOUS CABINET POSTS AND WORKED FOR LEBANESE UNITY AND INDEPENDENCE FROM SYRIAN CONTROL. *(AP/Wide World Photos)*

Beirut. In 1975, when the Lebanese war started, he participated in recruitment for the militia of the Progressive Socialist Party (PSP) led by his father, Kamal Jumblatt.

In April 1977, after Kamal's assassination, Walid Jumblatt became the head of the PSP and of the Lebanese National Movement (LNM), a federation of parties of the left opposed to the confessional system and favorable to the Palestinian cause. Although a supporter of the PLO, he opposed settling Palestinian groups in his fief of the Shuf. As his father's son, he also became an important leader of the Druze, in spite of the reservations of religious leaders, and he tried, vainly, to unify the different Druze currents. In June 1982, at the time of the Israeli invasion, he advocated "passive resistance." In September of the following year, backed by Syrian artillery and Palestinian fighters, he emerged victorious in combats in the Shuf district lasting several months, between Druze and Maronite militias, thereby consolidating his position as head of the Druze community.

After Lebanese president Ilyas Sarkis constituted a committee of national salvation, he participated in the work of this group, upholding at once Lebanese unity and the Palestinian cause. From April 1984, when he entered the government of Rashid Karame, until December 1998 (with only a four-month hiatus in 1991), he held various cabinet posts in several governments. From then on, Jumblatt become one of the leaders of the opposition to the new president, Emile Lahhud. After the Israeli withdrawal from South Lebanon, he demanded that the Syrians also withdraw from the country. For the 2000 parliamentary elections, he joined with the Christian anti-Syrian faction, the National Bloc. As a result of this election, Jumblatt consolidated his position as opposition leader, most of his party's candidates defeating those backed by President Lahhud or by Damascus. He then refused an invitation to join the new government of Rafiq Hariri, to emphasize his opposition to the presence of Damascus in Lebanese affairs. He became persona non grata to the Syrians for some months after this.

On 4 August 2001, he received Msgr. Nasrallah Sfeir, patriarch of the Maronite Church, thereby sealing the reconciliation of the Druze and Maronite communities. On 16 August, he participated in the national congress for the defense of liberty and democracy, held at Beirut, in the course of which he reaffirmed his desire to unite opponents to the Syrian presence in Lebanon. Since the attacks on the United States of 11 September 2001, he has made a number of public statements explicitly critical of American policies, and has grown friendly once again with the Syrians, although still advocating Lebanese independence of them. He has also parted ways with Msgr. Sfeir by advocating the reelection of Emile Lahhud as president.

SEE ALSO Jumblatt, Kamal; Karame, Rashid; Lahhud, Emile; Lebanese National Movement; Sfeir, Nasrallah; South Lebanon.

JUSTICE IS DONE OPERATION: Code name of the Israeli military operation, launched on 25 July 1993, against Hizbullah bases in Lebanon.

SEE ALSO Hizbullah.

TIMELINE OF MODERN ARAB-ISRAELI HISTORY

1878 First Jewish settlement in Palestine. Petah Tikvah, several miles outside Tel Aviv, is founded by a group of religious Jews from Jerusalem. By 1882, the Jewish population in Palestine is about 24,000.

1881 Russian czar Alexander II assassinated by revolutionaries. Hundreds of thousands of Jews flee the pogroms (1881–1884) in Russia and Eastern Europe. The Russian Zionist movement, Hibbat Zion (Love of Zion), establishes the first European Jewish farming colonies in Palestine. Because the settlers speak many different languages, Hebrew is revived and used as a common tongue.

1881–1903 First *Aliyah.* About 30,000 to 40,000 Jews, mostly Eastern European fleeing the pogroms, settle in Palestine during this first wave of immigration.

1896 Publication of *Der Judenstaat* (The Jewish State). Book written by Theodor Herzl, primarily as a response to European anti-Semitism, claiming that both the world and Jews need a Jewish state. At the First Zionist Congress, the author establishes the Zionist Organization (later known as the World Zionist Organization), which forms the foundation of the Zionist movement.

1897 First Zionist Congress, Basel, Switzerland. Meeting of Jewish leaders to discuss the ideas in *Der Judenstaat* of establishing a Jewish state. Issues the Basel Programme, which calls for a "home for the Jewish people in Palestine secured by public law."

1901 Fifth Zionist Congress. Establishes the Jewish National Fund (JNF) to raise funds and buy land in Palestine for Jewish settlers. By the early 2000s, the JNF owns about 14% of the land in Israel.

1903 Sixth Zionist Congress, Uganda proposal. A Zionist homeland is proposed in Uganda in East Africa by Herzl and Great Britain. The suggestion bitterly divides the congress because many Jews trace their homeland back to biblical territories (Palestine) and want to establish a state there.

1903–1914 Second *Aliyah.* About 35,000 to 40,000 Jews, mostly socialist-Zionists, immigrate to Palestine and establish the kibbutz and Zionist labor movements.

1905 Failed revolution in Russia. Pogroms (1903–1906) force thousands of Jews to flee Eastern Europe. Tens of thousands settle in Palestine.

1914–1918 World War I. As a result of the Allies' victory, lands previously under Ottoman rule are divided between France and England; Palestine lands under British rule.

1915–1916 Husayn-McMahon correspondence. Series of ten letters between Sharif Husayn ibn Ali, a leader of the Arab nationalist movement and king of the Hijaz, and Sir Henry McMahon, Britain's high commissioner in Egypt. British pledge support for Arab independence in exchange for an Arab revolt against the Ottomans and an alliance between the sharif and Britain.

1915 Sykes-Picot Agreement. Secret agreement between the French and British that divides Middle Eastern lands between the two countries after World War I. Formally known as the Anglo–Franco–Russian agreement, Britain receives common-day Iraq, Jordan, Israel, and Palestine; France receives commonday Syria and Lebanon.

1916 Balfour Declaration. Letter drafted by Zionist leaders of the British government calling for the establishment of a Jewish homeland in Palestine. This declaration is in direct conflict with the Husayn-McMahon correspondence (1915–1916), which called for an independent Arab state.

1916–1919 Arab revolt against Ottomans. Arab nationalist movement against Turkish rule of what is now Syria, Lebanon, Iraq, and most of the Arabian Peninsula. Backed by British supplies and led by Husayn ibn Ali and his four sons, the Arabs gain control of Mecca and other Ottoman garrisons, thus proclaiming their independence.

1917–1918 British troops occupy Palestine to secure a sea and land route to India.

1917–1922 Russian revolution and civil war. Pogroms (1919–1921) force many Jews to flee Russia, and thousands settle in Palestine.

1918 Muslim-Christian Association formed. Palestinian nationalist organization opposed to Zionism.

1919 Paris (Versailles) Peace Conference. Produces the Treaty of Versailles (1920), which ends World War I and establishes the League of Nations and the mandate system of lands surrendered by Germany. The Treaty of Sèvres (1920) virtually dismantles the Ottoman Empire. Britain gains control of Palestine.

1919 King-Crane Commission. U.S. president Woodrow Wilson sends two representatives, Henry C. King and Charles R. Crane, to Palestine and Syria to gather local reactions to rule under Britain and France. They find that the Palestinians and Syrians are opposed to the mandate system, perceiving it as a form of colonial rule, and want national independence for their countries. Zionists also oppose. British and French disregard the report.

1919–1924 Third *Aliyah*. About 35,000 Jews, mostly from Poland and Russia, immigrate to Palestine in response to the Russian Revolution.

1920 San Remo (Italy) Conference. Palestine and Iraq are assigned to Britain and Syria and Lebanon are assigned to France as Class A mandates, or trusteeships. Independence is promised only when the British or French determine that political systems are developed enough to be admitted to the League of Nations.

1921 Faisal I ibn Hussein—Amir Faisal—expelled from Syria by the French. A leader of the Arab revolt for nationalism from the Ottomans and king of Syria (1920) and Iraq (1921–1933), Faisal is forced to leave Syria shortly after he is appointed constitutional monarch by a congress of Arab nationalists.

1921 British accept Emir Abdullah as client ruler of Transjordan, install Faysal in Iraq. Britain grants the Palestinian Mandate east of the Jordan River to Abdullah II, who forms the Hashemite Kingdom of Transjordan. Jewish settlement is outlawed.

1922 Churchill White Paper. Policy paper by British government on the tensions between Arab and Jewish communities in Palestine. The statement claims equal protection and rights to both groups: Jewish immigrants should continue to settle in Palestine and have the right to do so; Arabs should not be subordinated by the immigration; and immigration should be economically sustainable by the region.

1922 British and French Mandates confirmed. League of Nations confirms British Mandate in Palestine, Transjordan, and Iraq. Syria and Lebanon are given to French Mandate.

1924–1930 Fourth *Aliyah.* Due to tough economic conditions, about 80,000 Jews from Poland immigrate to Palestine.

1929 Zionist demonstrations over prayer rights at Western (Wailing) Wall; Palestinian attacks on Jews. At the Western (Wailing) Wall, a holy site to both Jews and Muslims, Zionists protest when the British tear down a partition they had built to separate men and women. Palestinians attack religious Jewish communities, and Jews riot, killing Palestinians. British and police open fire in an attempt to stop the violence. About 250 people die that year.

1930 Passfield White Paper. Policy paper by British government on tensions between Arab and Jewish communities in Palestine finds that Arabs fear their economic, political, and national future is obstructed by Jewish immigration and land ownership, which results in violence against the Jews. Recommends clear policy statements protecting Arab rights and regulating Jewish immigration and land purchase.

1930 Shaw Commission. Commission of inquiry by British government on the violence between Arabs and Jews at the Western (Wailing) Wall in Palestine, 1929. Finds that Arabs are hostile toward immigrating and land-owning Jews because they pose a threat to the future of their economic and political stability and control. Calls for a policy that limits Jewish immigration.

1930 Sir John Hope-Simpson White Paper. Policy paper by British government on the tensions between Arab and Jewish communities in Palestine. Calls for drastic reduction in the number of Jewish immigrants and restrictions on land purchase because of widespread Arab unemployment and lack of farmable land.

1931 MacDonald Letter. Written by British prime minister Ramsay MacDonald (1924, 1929–35) to Zionist leader and future president of Israel, Chaim Weizmann. The letter reaffirms British support for Arab and non-Arab people in Palestine while expressing a responsibility to establish Jewish homeland in the region.

1931–1939 Fifth *Aliyah.* About 225,000 Jews, mostly educated and professional, immigrate to Palestine to flee the Nazis's increasing hold over Germany.

1933 Nazi accession to power in Germany. Anti-Semitic policies lead many Jews to flee Eastern Europe. At first, Nazis support the immigration to Palestine, as it helps their ethnic cleansing policies. However, once the Jewish population seeks statehood, Hitler sees a possible threat in the eastern European refugees.

1933–1945 Holocaust in Europe. Anti-Jewish policies of the Third Reich (Nazi Germany, 1933–1945) that include land and rights seizures; forced migrations into ghettos, work camps, and concentration camps; and the systematic genocide of six million Jews. Hundreds of thousands of Jews flee Europe to Palestine, as both legal immigrants and refugees.

1936 General strike and formation of the Arab Higher Committee. Palestinians strike against the British and the Jewish economy, determined to continue until Jewish immigration ceases, land sales are prohibited to Jews, and a national government and elected assembly are established. Five days into the strike, Palestinians form the Arab Higher Committee to present Arab demands to the British government.

1936–1939 Palestinian insurrection ("Arab Revolt"). Revolt against British support for a Jewish homeland in Palestine. Beginning with the general strike in 1936, the revolt escalates to full combat with the British and Jewish population from 1937–1938. About 10% of the adult male Palestinian population is killed, injured, or detained; the revolt has disastrous consequences for the Palestinian economy and leadership.

1937 Peel Commission Report. British Royal Commission Report that outlines solutions to tensions and unrest between the Arab Palestinians and Jewish immigrants. It concludes that the mandate system cannot work without repressing the Arab population and recommends that Palestine be divided into two nations, one Jewish and one Arab. The Jewish Agency accepts the plan, but opposes the borders and insists that the Palestinian population be deported from the Jewish state. The Palestinians' Arab Higher Committee denounces the plan, arguing that they have 70% of the population and 90% of the land and that Palestine should remain a unified state.

1937 Bludan Conference. Meeting of delegates from Syria, Palestine, Lebanon, Transjordan, Iraq, Egypt, and Saudi Arabia to discuss the Peel Commission. They reject the recommendation of splitting Palestine into Jewish and Arab states and call for a boycott of Jewish goods and British goods if the commission is carried out.

1938 Publication of *The Arab Awakening*. Book written by George Antonius, an Egyptian-born Christian and member of the British Palestine Administration. Discusses, from an Arab point of view, the origins of Arab nationalism, the significance of the Arab Revolt (1916), and the consequences of the British mandate system of dividing the Arab world after World War I.

1938 Woodhead Partition Commission. British report that retracts the Peel Commission's suggestion to partition Palestine.

1939 London (St. James/Roundtable) Conference. British host discussions between Arabs and Jews of Palestine on the future political situation in the Mandate. Talks held through British intermediaries, as the Arabs and Jews will not meet face-to-face. The Arabs call for the end of the mandate system, the creation of an independent Arab state, an end to Jewish immigration and land sales to Jews, and minority rights for Jews. The Jews call for an increased immigration to Palestine, especially with Hitler's rise to power and growing anti-Semitism in Europe.

1939 MacDonald White Paper. Policy paper issued by the British government outlining Britain's proposals from the London Conference on the post-Mandate government of Palestine. It calls for Jewish immigration to be limited to 75,000 over five years, after which Arab approval will be needed, limited land purchase by Jews, and promised self-government for Palestinians within ten years. Jews will have minority rights. Because of the outbreak of World War II, this policy is largely unimplemented.

1939–1945 World War II. British and French fight to secure their interests in the Middle East from the Germans. At the end of the war, Britain and France maintain control of the region.

1942 Biltmore Conference. New York City conference of about 600 American Zionists, plus many from around the world. They demand implementation of the Balfour Declaration (1916), which calls for a Jewish homeland, denounce the 1939 MacDonald White Paper as "cruel" in its quota of Jewish immigration to Palestine during a time of persecution and genocide in Hitler's Germany, and declare that there will never be peace in the world without a Jewish homeland. Sponsorship for Jewish immigration to Palestine shifts from Britain to the United States.

1943 National Pact in Lebanon, effective independence established. Christian and Muslim leaders come together to negotiate terms of a government independent of French influence in Lebanon.

1945 Arab League (League of Arab States) established. Formed to express the economic and security needs of Arab states. First founded with 7 Arab states; In 2004, it has 22 members.

1946 Anglo-American Committee of Inquiry. American and British collaboration formed to address the Arab-Israel conflict and Jewish refugees and survivors of the Holocaust.

1946 Morrison-Grady Plan for Palestine. Report by Britain's Herbert Morrison and United States' Henry Grady calling for a semi-autonomous Palestine divided into Jewish and Arab regions. Limits Jewish immigration to 100,000 in the first year, then to be determined by Britain, with Britain controlling the military, foreign relations, immigration, and customs. Rejected by both the Jews and Arabs.

1946 Anglo-American Conference (second Bludan Conference). Arab League meets to discuss Anglo-American Committee of Inquiry report. They criticize American interference in Palestine, suggest a boycott of Jewish goods, and vow to help the Palestinian Arabs.

1946 France leaves Syria and Lebanon; British end Mandate over Transjordan.

1947 United Nations votes partition plan (Resolution 181). Award Jews a homeland in Palestine. With one-third of the population and 7% of the land ownership, Jews are awarded 55% of Palestine. The plan is violently rejected by Arab Palestinians.

1948 Dayr Yasin (Deir Yasin) massacre. Surprise attack and massacre on Palestinian village outside Jerusalem kills 105 to 205 people and leaves the village in ruins. Conducted by Jewish paramilitary units, National Military Organization (led by Menachem Begin) and Fighters for the Freedom of Israel.

1948 British Mandate on Palestine expires on 14 May. British relinquish Mandate. Next day Jews proclaim the independent State of Israel. David Ben-Gurion, the Zionist leader, becomes Israel's first prime minister. Neighboring Arab countries send in troops to combat the Jews as British depart.

1948–1949 Arab-Israel war; known as *Nakba* to the Arabs and the War of Independence to the Jews. In Arabic, *Nakba* means "disaster" or "catastrophe." This war over the establishment of an Israeli state in Palestine results in the displacement of 700,000 to 750,000 Arabs (more than half the Arab population in the Mandate), confiscation of property, massacres, and the loss of a Palestinian homeland and society. Neighboring Arab countries (Lebanon, Syria, Jordan, Egypt, and Iraq) come to the aid of the Palestinians. Israel extends its boundaries by about 2,500 square miles.

1948 Count Folke Bernadotte assassinated; UN General Assembly passes Resolution 194. Bernadotte, a United Nations mediator in Israel and Palestine, proposes a truce between Arabs and Jews, which is broken and restored several times. In the two versions of the Bernadotte Plan for Arab-Israeli Settlement, boundaries are proposed in which Jerusalem goes to Transjordan (version 1) or is placed under United Nations control (version 2). Displaced Palestinians are offered repatriation or compensation for resettlement. Israel is to be recognized as an independent state. Both Arabs and Israelis reject his plan. On September 17, Bernadotte is gunned down by the Israeli group LEHI in Jerusalem.

1948 All-Palestine government; Palestine declaration of independence. In response to the formation of the Israeli state, the Palestinians declare the need for an Arab government to represent and defend their interests. It is backed by surrounding Arab countries, but ultimately is ineffective.

1949 General armistice agreements between Israel and Egypt, Jordan, Syria, and Lebanon. Peace agreements, sponsored by the United Nations and mediated by Ralphe Bunche, put an end to the 1948 Arab-Israel War.

1951 King Abdullah I is assassinated by a group of disgruntled Palestinians thought to have been working for Egypt's intelligence agency. In 1950, Abdullah I had held a conference in which it was proposed that the East and West Banks of Palestine were to be part of Jordan with parliamentary representation. The proposition was adopted unanimously and Abdullah became king of Palestine.

1953 Revolution in Egypt. Led by Nasser and the Free Officers, the coup overthrows the monarchy of King Farouk installed by the British. A republic is formed.

1954 Lavon Affair. Also known as the "mishap." Israeli-trained espionage group of Egyptian Jews are caught in mid-sabotage. They claim orders came from the head of the Intelligence Division of the Israeli Defense Forces, Colonel Benjamin Gibli, who in turn cites orders from Pinchas Lavon, the minister of defense. Lavon's involvement cannot be proven. The scandal extends into the 1960s and ultimately leads to the temporary withdrawal of David Ben-Gurion from politics in 1963.

1954 Moshe Sharett becomes prime minister of Israel when Ben-Gurion resigns.

1955 David Ben-Gurion elected prime minister of Israel for the second time.

1956 Arab-Israel War; Suez Crisis and War. The United States, Britain, and the World Bank pull out support for loans to Egypt after ties between Egypt and the Soviet Union grow closer. Egypt retaliates by nationalizing the Suez Canal Company, of which Britain is the largest shareholder. In response, Britain and France declare war on Egypt with support and troops from Israel. Under pressure by the United States, Britain, France, and Israel accept a cease-fire after about ten days of fighting.

1958 Founding of United Arab Republic (UAR). The UAR combines Syria and Egypt from 1958–1961 and poses a threat to the West with Nasser's pan-Arab mission and anti-Western stance.

1958 Civil war in Lebanon, U.S. intervention. Sparked by the killing of a journalist, but rooted in grievances of political access, corrupt elections, elitist politics, and representation in government. Lebanon's president, Camille Chamoun, blames the UAR for inciting the violence and requests military intervention by the United States on his behalf.

1958 Revolution in Iraq. Hashemite monarchy, installed by British in 1921, violently overthrown in military coup led by the Free Officers. The revolution's goals are to rid the region of imperialistic forces and promote social and cultural reform. It results in a republican government and a foreign policy of nonalignment.

1959 Al-Fatah (Palestinian Liberation Movement) founded. Palestinian nationalist movement founded by Yasir Arafat. Its mission is to liberate Palestine by Palestinians, not by outside Arab assistance, through methods of armed struggle, not negotiation.

1961 Dissolution of UAR. Syria becomes increasingly dissatisfied with its diminishing role in the government; the Baʿthist party is dismissed and Nasser's policies seem more like an occupation than a collaboration. Syria's contingency in the army mounts a coup, which is met by little resistance from Nasser.

1963 Levi Eshkol becomes prime minister of Israel upon Ben-Gurion's resignation.

1964 Palestine Liberation Organization (PLO) and Palestine National Council (PNC) founded; Palestine National Covenant approved. Formed as a result of the first Arab Summit in Cairo, the PLO's mission is to be an organized representative body of Palestinian nationalism and liberation. The PNC is its parliamentary branch. The Covenant calls for a liberation of Palestine by the Palestinians and the end of Israel.

1967 Arab-Israel War, also known as the Six-Day War. Issues left simmering from the British Mandate period—Palestinian refugees, water rights, and border with Arab States, arms race, growing Arab nationalism, and Israel's right to exist—lead to war between Israel and Syria, Jordan, Iraq, and Egypt. As a result of the war, Israel increases its land mass by almost three times and includes Egypt's Gaza Strip and Sinai Peninsula, Jordan's West Bank and East Jerusalem, and the Golan Heights from Syria.

1967 UN Security Council Resolution 242. The "land for peace resolution" calls for peace in the region based on Israel's withdrawal from lands won during the 1967 war and a recognition of secure boundaries. Little progress is made on the resolution.

1967 Popular Front for the Liberation of Palestine (PFLP) founded. Unites three groups: Heroes of the Return, the National Front for the Liberation of Palestine, and the Independent Palestine Liberation Front. Mission based on Palestinian national sovereignty, Arab unity, opposition to the State of Israel, and Marxist-Leninist ideology, borrowing some of Fidel Castro's methods. Second in importance and influence to al-Fatah.

1968 Palestine National Charter revised. After the Arab defeat in the 1967 war, the charter is revised to emphasize an Arab Palestinian homeland, national sovereignty, and self-determination. Calls for armed struggle to gain liberation.

1969 Democratic Front for the Liberation of Palestine (DFLP) founded. Marxist-Leninist group organized to liberate Palestine.

1969 Golda Meir becomes prime minister of Israel upon Eshkol's death.

1970 "Black September." Term used by some Palestinians (PLO and PFLP) to describe their defeat in the Jordanian Civil War. They had staged attacks against Israel from the Jordanian border since 1967, which provoked Israeli counter-attacks. The Jordanian army wins after ten days and thousands of casualties, many of which are civilian Palestinian refugees. A radical Palestinian terrorist group founded by members of al-Fatah takes this name.

1970 Gamal Abdel Nasser dies. President of Egypt from 1956–1970 and figurehead of pan-Arab nationalism, Arab socialism, and anti-Israel policies dies of a heart attack.

1971 PLO expelled from Jordan. At the end of the Jordanian Civil War (1970–1971), the Jordanian army ousts the PLO from the country, pushing them into southern Lebanon.

1973 Arab-Israel War, also known as the October War, Yom Kippur War, or Ramadan War. Caused by failure to resolve territorial disputes from the 1967 war. After diplomatic efforts fail, Egypt and Syria, backed by Soviet Union arms, plan a secret two-front attack on Israel, which is supported by United States weapons. A cease-fire is called when the United States proclaims a military alert in response to the Soviet Union's offer to send troops to Egypt. The war results in thousands of dead and injured and a dependence on the Soviet Union (Egypt) and the United States (Israel) for military support.

1973 UN Security Council Resolution 338. Passed during the cease-fire of the 1973 war. Calls for an immediate end to military operations, implementation of Resolution 242 (from 1967), and a start to peace negotiations.

1974 Yitzhak Rabin elected prime minister of Israel. First native-born prime minister. Makes major strides in diplomacy with Jordan and Palestine. Shimon Peres succeeds him in 1977 after a financial scandal.

1974 PLO implicitly accepts two-state solution. At the PNC in 1974, the PLO modifies its goal of liberating all of Palestine and focuses on creating a Palestinian state in the West Bank and Gaza.

1974 UN and Arab League accept PLO as sole legitimate representative of Palestinians. Yasir Arafat makes first appearance at the UN proposing peace.

1974 Suez I, or Sinai I, agreement between Israel and Egypt. Cease-fire agreement ending the 1973 war; moderated by U.S. Secretary of State Kissinger. Israeli troops pull back west from the Suez Canal and east on the Sinai front of the canal. Three buffer security zones are created for Israel, Egypt, and the UN.

1975 Suez II, or Sinai II, agreement between Israel and Egypt. Cease-fire agreement ending the 1973 war moderated by U.S. secretary of state Kissinger. Israel withdraws troops an additional 12 to 26 miles and the UN occupies buffer zone.

1975 UN General Assembly Resolution 3379. Equates Zionism with racism.

1975–1990 Lebanese Civil War. Series of domestic disruptions in southern Lebanon where the PLO is based and many Palestinian refugees live. Much fighting occurs in the region between Israelis and Palestinians.

1977 Menachem Begin elected prime minister of Israel. First right-wing prime minister. His term is marked by diplomacy with Egypt.

1978 First Israeli invasion of Lebanon. Israel backs the Lebanese Forces, a coalition of right-wing militias, and Syria backs the Palestinians. Israel invades to rid the region of pro-Palestinian groups and PLO training camps and occupies a strip of land called "the security zone."

1978 Camp David Accords. Peace negotiations between Israel and Egypt, mediated and hosted by the United States. Calls for the implementation of UN Security Council Resolution 242 "land for peace" principle whereby Israel will return the Sinai to Egypt (pre-1967 borders) in exchange for peace. Palestine and Lebanon oppose the accords. The establishment of an autonomous Palestinian state in the West Bank and Gaza is not achieved. The accords mark the first time an Arab nation officially recognizes the statehood of Israel.

1979 Egypt-Israel peace treaty. Treaty signed by Egypt and Israel as a result of the Camp David Accords. The two agreements include "A Framework for Peace in the Middle East" and "A Framework for the Conclusion of a Peace Treaty between Egypt and Israel."

1979 Revolution in Iran. Overthrow of Mohammad Reza Shah Pahlavi, the last monarch of the 450-year old Safavid dynasty. The shah had used the secret police to repress dissident voices during a period of social, economic, and cultural change. Its leader, Ayatollah Khomeini, opposed the shah's alliance with the United States and his support of Israel. A religious Islamist state replaces the monarchy.

1980–1988 Iran-Iraq War (First Gulf War). Iraq launches a surprise attack on Iran in 1980 because, according to Iraq, Iran was plotting raids across the border. Missile attacks and raids last for eight years, mostly on Iraqi soil, taking hundreds of thousands of lives. The UN Security Council intervenes in 1987 when international ships are threatened in the Gulf.

1981 Anwar al-Sadat assassinated. President of Egypt and successor to Nasser killed by three Egyptian soldiers discontented that Sadat did not ensure a liberated Palestine at the Camp David Accords and by Egypt's deteriorating economic condition.

1982 Second Israeli invasion of Lebanon ("Operation Peace for Galilee"). A PLO rocket attack on Israel prompts Israel to invade Lebanon and rid the area of PLO forces and Syrian troops. Israeli forces reach Beirut and the conflict takes over 20,000 lives. The U.S. mediates and expels PLO and Syrian troops from Beirut.

1982 Sabra and Shatila massacre. From 800 to 2000 Palestinian refugees, mostly women, children, and the elderly, are massacred at the Sabra and Shatila refugee camps by the Phalange (Lebanese Christian militias). Israeli troops, which had invaded West Beirut and surrounded the camps, stand back while the massacres take place. Defense Minister Ariel Sharon is found indirectly responsible for the killings.

1982 PLO expelled from Lebanon. Although the mission of the Israeli invasion is to wipe out the PLO in Beirut, they succeed in transplanting the PLO to Tunis, Tunisia.

1983 Yitzhak Shamir becomes prime minister of Israel.

1984 Shimon Peres becomes prime minister of Israel.

1986 Yitzhak Shamir becomes prime minister of Israel for second time.

1987–1994 First Intifada. Palestinian uprisings in the West Bank and Gaza against Israeli policies of land and property seizure and demolition, censorship, restricted travel and construction, and military tribunals instead of civilian courts. The uprisings escalate from labor strikes, boycotts against Israeli goods, demonstrations, and Palestinian youths throwing stones at Israeli troops in 1987 to riots and violence in 1994. More than 20,000 people die.

1987 HAMAS founded. Palestinian liberation group with the mission of establishing an Islamic Palestinian state. Employs methods of terror and violence.

1988 Algiers Declaration. Palestinian statehood proclaimed at PNC meeting.

1990 Iraq occupies Kuwait. After eight years of fighting with Iran, Iraq is left in severe debt. Accuses Kuwait of overproduction of oil to lower the price per barrel, which is seen as an act of war. U.S. forces are sent to protect Gulf states, particularly Saudi Arabia, under the operation Desert Shield.

1990 Ta'if Accord ends Lebanese Civil War. Morocco, Saudi Arabia, and Algeria make recommendations to Lebanon and Syria to end the war and establish Syria and Lebanon's relationship with Israel.

1991 Multinational war against Iraq ("Operation Desert Storm," Second Gulf War). A major five-week air offensive and 100-hour ground campaign, led by the United States, drives the Iraqis out of Kuwait.

1991 UN General Assembly Resolution 4686. Revokes Resolution 3379, which equates Zionism with racism.

1991–1993 Madrid Peace Conference. U.S.-led and -mediated talks between Israel, Syria, Jordan, Egypt, and Palestine. First time Israeli, Palestinian, and Arab diplomats (except Egypt) meet for public peace talks. Arab states recognize Israel as a nation.

1992 Yitzhak Rabin elected prime minister of Israel for second time.

1993 Oslo Accords I; Palestinian-Israeli "Declaration of Principles." Secret talks between PLO and Israel resulting in a land-for-peace agreement. PLO and Israel agree to recognize each other and sign the "Declaration of Principles," which outlines sovereignty for

Palestinians in Gaza and the West Bank for five years. PLO gives up claims to territory won by Israel in the 1967 war.

1994 Hebron massacre. U.S.-born Israeli settler opens fire on Palestinian worshippers at the al-Haram al-Ibrahimi mosque, killing 29.

1994 Cairo Agreement. Outlines Israel's withdrawal from parts of the West Bank and Gaza. A five-year plan is laid out for further Israeli withdrawals, negotiations on Jerusalem, settlements, refugees, and Palestinian sovereignty.

1994 Institution of Palestinian Authority. Autonomous Palestinian government set up in the West Bank and Gaza, chaired by Yasir Arafat and comprised of other PLO ministers.

1995 Oslo Accords II (Taba Accord). Set the stage for Palestinian elections, security, economic relations, and legal and civil matters. The accords do not lead to peace. Instead, escalating violence and terrorism rack the area in the late 1990s and into the 2000s.

1995 Prime Minister Yitzhak Rabin assassinated. Israeli prime minister killed by Jewish extremists who are opposed to his peace negotiations with Palestine. Shimon Peres succeeds him.

1996 First Palestinian elections for PLO president and Palestinian National Congress. Arafat wins election for president.

1996 Benjamin Netanyahu elected prime minister of Israel. Netanyahu's Likud Party campaigns against the Olso Accords and Peres and Rabin's peace process with Palestine.

1998 Wye River Memorandum. Document produced by talks between Israel and the United States after an 18-month stagnation of the peace process. Calls for Israel to hand over 80% of Hebron and outlines further withdrawals from the West Bank.

1999 Ehud Barak runs on a Labor platform and is elected prime minister of Israel. Barak, running on a platform of bringing peace between Israel and Syria, Lebanon, and Palestine, wins the election and resumes peace talks with Palestine.

2000 Israel withdraws from Lebanon. Barak calls the army out of the region, except for the area of the Shab'a Farms, which Israel maintains is Syrian territory and therefore can occupy with troops.

2000– Second Intifada (al-Aqsa Intifada). In reaction to Ariel Sharon's tour of the al-Aqsa mosque (Islam's third holiest shrine) with 1000 riot police, Palestinians take to the streets in demonstration. Israeli police shoot live ammunition and rubber bullets at the crowd, killing six. Fundamentally, the Palestinians rise up against the dead-end peace process. They are against the Israeli occupation of the West Bank and Gaza, the growing number of settlements in the area, land seizures, home and property destruction, and restricted travel.

2001 Israeli-Palestinian negotiations at Taba. U.S.-mediated talks that lay the final plans for Israeli withdrawals and Palestinian refugees. Time runs out on the accords before the details can be agreed upon and the proposals are not followed through.

2001 Ariel Sharon elected prime minister of Israel. Sharon advocates harsh punishments for Palestinian terror groups and campaigns against the Oslo peace accords. He wants a Greater Israel and encourages the settlements in the West Bank and Gaza. Violence escalates and Israel re-occupies almost all of the West Bank during Sharon's time in office.

2001 Palestinians claim Zionism is racist. At the World National Conference Against Racism, Palestinians claim that they are victims of crimes against humanity and the Zionist movement is racist.

2003– U.S.-UK war against, and occupation of, Iraq. Without UN support, the United States, Britain, and a coalition of countries send troops into Iraq to depose Saddam Hussein. Although the stated mission is to remove weapons of mass destruction from Iraq, none are found.

2004– Israel to withdraw unilaterally from Gaza Strip. Announcement made by Israeli prime minister Ariel Sharon in February seen as source of clashes with settlers, bitter disagreements in Israel, and potential split within Likud. On 26 October, the Knesset approves Sharon's plan, which calls for Gaza's complete evacuation by end of 2005.

2004 In mid-October, Yasir Arafat grows increasingly weak with an unknown illness. On 29 October he is allowed to leave his compound in Ramallah to seek medical help. He is taken to a military hospital outside Paris for diagnosis and treatment.

2004– Yasir Arafat dies 11 November from an unknown illness. Mahmud Abbas sworn in as PLO chairman. Rawhi Fattuh sworn in as interim president of the Palestinian Authority. Faruq Qaddumi named al-Fatah leader.

TIMELINE OF THE ARAB-ISRAELI CONFLICT

1897 First Zionist Congress discusses plans to establish a Jewish state in Palestine.

1914–1918 World War I; the Ottoman Empire is defeated.

1916 Sykes-Picot Agreement divides Ottoman Arab lands into zones controlled by either the French or the British.

1917–1918 Palestine comes under British control, as British troops move northward from their bases in Egypt.

1917 Britain issues the Balfour Declaration, supporting "the establishment in Palestine of a national home for the Jewish people, . . .it being clearly understood that nothing shall be done which may prejudice the civil and religious rights of existing non-Jewish communities in Palestine. . ."

1920 League of Nations at San Remo divides Arab lands into mandates, which are supposed to eventually create nation states for the indigenous peoples. Britain holds the Mandate for Palestine.

1922 British create the Amirate of Transjordan out of Mandatory Palestine east of the River Jordan. The Jewish national home provisions of the Balfour Declaration will be applied only west of the Jordan.

1933 Adolf Hitler begins his rise to power in Germany. Jewish immigration to Palestine increases.

1936–1939 The Arab Revolt against British pro-Zionist policy and in a quest for an independent Arab state in Palestine.

1946 Hostilities in Palestine escalate and include Jewish terrorism against Britain. U.S. president Harry S. Truman expresses support for partition and a "viable Jewish state in an adequate area of Palestine."

1947 The United Nations General Assembly Resolution 181 recommends the partition of Palestine into Jewish and Arab states, with greater Jerusalem to be an international city. The resolution is adopted by a vote of 33-13-10, but rejected by Arab and Muslim delegates.

1948 Israel declares statehood as the British Mandate over Palestine ends. Arab armies attack Israel. The resulting war leaves Jerusalem divided and 650,000 Palestinians refugees. UN Resolution 194 declares that refugees should be allowed to return to their homes, and establishes a commission to facilitate their repatriation or compensation.

1949 An armistice is signed at Rhodes between Israel and Egypt. Similar agreements with Lebanon, Jordan, and Syria follow. U.N. conference at Lausanne produces no agreement between Israeli and Arab delegations.

1949–1950 Israel holds 77 percent of the former Palestine. Jordan annexes East Jerusalem and the West Bank. Egypt controls the Gaza Strip. The United Nations Relief and Work Agency is established. Jews from several Arab countries begin migration into Israel.

1956–1957 Egyptian president Gamal Abdel Nasser's nationalization of the Suez Canal leads to military action by Israel, Britain, and France. U.S. President Dwight D. Eisenhower threatens economic sanctions against Israel and succeeds in forcing Israel's withdrawal from Sinai and Gaza. United Nations puts UNEF [Emergency Force] along the Egyptian-Israeli frontier.

1964 The Palestinian Liberation Organization (PLO) is established.

1967 Israel captures the Golan Heights, the Gaza Strip, the West Bank, and East Jerusalem from Syria, Egypt, and Jordan. As many as 600,000 Palestinians become refugees. UN Resolution 242 calls for Israeli withdrawal and establishes the "land for peace" principle.

1969–1970 Israel begins establishing settlements in disputed areas. Egypt's War of Attrition against Israel, with Soviet aid, leads to the Rogers Plan, which uses UN Resolution 242 as the basis for negotiations.

1973 Egypt and Syria attack Israel. No territorial changes result. UN Resolution 338 calls for negotiations between the parties. Minor border changes result as U.S. helps to broker disengagement agreements.

1977 Menachem Begin and the Likud coalition win Israeli elections. Settlements in Occupied Territories increase. Egypt's president Anwar al-Sadat goes to Israeli Knesset in the first efforts toward an Arab-Israeli peace treaty.

1978 Negotiations between Sadat and Begin are brokered by U.S. president Jimmy Carter at Camp David, Maryland, and result in the Camp David Accords, followed in 1979 by the first peace treaty between Israel and one of its Arab neighbors. The Arab League expels Egypt. Israel invades Lebanon in response to terror attacks and in an attempt to clear out Palestinian fighters along the border.

1980 The Israeli government declares Jerusalem its capital. Ambassadors are exchanged between Israel and Egypt.

1981 Israel annexes the Golan Heights, captured from Syria in 1967. Sadat is assassinated by Islamic fundamentalists.

1982 Israel invades Lebanon a second time, laying siege to Beirut. The PLO moves its headquarters from Beirut to Tunis. The Reagan Peace Initiative and the Fez Summit Peace Proposal are launched.

1987 Palestinian uprising, known as the Intifada, begin in Gaza and spread to the West Bank. Over the next several years, several thousand Palestinians and hundreds of Israelis are killed in the fighting.

1988 The Palestinian National Council (PNC) accepts UN Resolutions 242 and 338, tacitly recognizing Israel, and declares a Palestinian state. The United States government begins dialogue with the PLO.

1991 The Gulf War begins in January. Later that year, a Middle East peace conference opens in Madrid between Israel and Arab nations, including, Jordan, Lebanon, and Syria. Palestinian representative participate, for the first time, in such an international forum as part of the Jordanian delegation.

1992 The administration of U.S. president George H. W. Bush stops $10 billion in U.S. loan guarantees to Israel in an attempt to curtail the spread of Israeli settlements into disputed areas.

1993 The Oslo Process begins during the administration of U.S. president Bill Clinton. Palestinian leader Yasir Arafat and Israeli prime minister Yitzhak Rabin meet at the White House. The PLO and Israel sign the Declaration of Principles, outlining a plan for Palestinian self-rule in the Occupied Territories.

1994 The Cairo Accords between the PLO and Israel establish Palestinian self-rule in Gaza and Jericho but allow Israeli settlements to remain in place. Jordan and Israel sign a peace treaty with Clinton in attendance. Arafat, Shimon Peres, and Rabin receive the Nobel Peace Prize.

1995 The Interim Agreement on the West Bank and the Gaza Strip, known as Oslo II, establishes three areas in the West Bank, one under direct Palestinian control, one under both Palestinian civilian control and Israeli security, and one under Israeli control. Rabin is assassinated in Tel Aviv.

1996 Benjamin Netanyahu is elected Israel's prime minister. Israel launches Operation Grapes of Wrath in southern Lebanon. Arafat, Jordan's King Hussein, Netanyahu, and Clinton participate in a political summit in Washington, DC to negotiate for peace.

1997 The Hebron Protocol divides the city of Hebron. Palestinians protest the building of an Israeli settlement, Har Homa, on a hill overlooking East Jerusalem.

1998 The Wye River Memorandum is signed but not implemented.

1999 The PLO postpones a declaration of statehood. Ehud Barak, newly elected prime minister of Israel, pledges to work for peace. The Sharm al-Shaykh memorandum is signed between Israel and the PLO. Clinton attends a PNC meeting in Gaza to witness the elimination of Palestine National Covenant clauses calling for the destruction of Israel.

2000 Israeli Army withdraws from South Lebanon. At the Camp David II meetings in July, Clinton chairs negotiations between Arafat and Barak. Negotiations break down. The al-Aqsa Intifada begins, fueled by Ariel Sharon's visit to the Temple Mount/Haram al–Sharif.

2001 Sharon is elected prime minister of Israel.

2002 Israeli troops reoccupy Palestinian areas in response to a terrorist suicide bombing of elderly people celebrating Passover at a resort hotel. Arafat is placed under house arrest in his Ramallah compound. The Church of the Nativity in Bethlehem is stormed by armed Arab Palestinians. A Saudi peace plan, endorsed by the Arab League, promises recognition of Israel in exchange for ending occupation of all Arab lands. UN Resolution 1397 affirms a two-state vision for Israel. U.S. president George W. Bush announces a plan for a "viable Palestinian state next to a secure Israel." Israel begins construction of a highly controversial "security fence" around the West Bank in response to suicide bombing inside Jewish civilian population areas.

2003 The United States invades and begins its occupation of Iraq. The Road Map for Peace, sponsored by the "Quartet" (U.S., U.N., Russia, and the European Union), is released.

2004 Ariel Sharon's government promotes a plan that involves Israeli evacuation of the Gaza Strip and the abandonment of the settlements there. In October the Knesset votes to back Sharon's plan to remove Israeli troops, as well as twenty-one settlements from Gaza and four small settlements from the northern part of the West Bank. The vote—sixty-seven for, forty-five against, and seven abstentions—marks the first time in twenty years that the parliament had favored the withdrawal of Jewish settlers from the region. Sharon rejects a call for a referendum by the Likud which creates turmoil in the Knesset.

2004 In mid-October, Yasir Arafat, suffering from an unknown illness, is allowed to leave his compound in Ramallah to seek diagnosis and treatment in France. Israeli prime minister Ariel Sharon states that if Arafat dies, he will not allow Arafat to be buried in Jerusalem.

2004– Yasir Arafat dies 11 November from an unknown illness. Mahmud Abbas sworn in as PLO chairman. Rawhi Fattuh sworn in as interim president of the Palestinian Authority. Faruq Qaddumi named al-Fatah leader.

GLOSSARY

Adar: Name of the sixth month of the Hebrew calendar, corresponding to the period between the end of the month of February and the beginning of the month of March. A second month of Adar is added every 3rd, 6th, 8th, 11th, 14th, 17th and 19th years of the calendar's nineteen-year cycle to align with the lunar calendar.

Agha: Socio-political title of authority. Agha ("chief," "master") was associated with certain administrators in the Ottoman empire. It is also used in other settings, such as among Kurds.

Almenor: Name of the central platform in a synagogue, from which the rabbi officiates. Also called a bima.

Amir: Political title. See dictionary entry "Emir."

Ashur: Islamic tithe. Also called zakah or zakat, ashur (from the Arabic word for "ten") is a charitable tithe prescribed in Islam. In North Africa, ashur also denotes the tenth month of the Islamic calendar, Muharram.

Av: Eleventh month of the Hebrew calendar, corresponding to the period between the end of July and the beginning of August. The destruction of the Temple of Solomon is commemorated on the 9th of Av (*Tish'a b-Av*).

Bar-mitzva: "Son of the commandment," in Hebrew. Jewish religious ceremony celebrating the passage from adolescence to majority and one's admission into the adult community. During the ceremony the 13-year old "mitzva" reads from the Torah and puts on phylacteries, symbolic of the commandments to which he will henceforward submit. The equivalent of bar-mitzva for young women is the bas-mitzva, which is celebrated at the age of 12.

Beit midrash: School of rabbinical studies, generally attached to a synagogue.

Beth: Also "beir, bait, bayt, beit." Hebrew word meaning "house," often figuring in composite names such as Bethel (house of God), Bethlehem (house of bread) or Beth Din (house of the law).

Bey: Political title. Bey is a Turkish term often translated as "prince." In the Ottoman empire's administration and military, it was given to mid-level officers. In modern Turkey, it is often used as a suffix to a man's first name as a polite form of address.

Bint: Arabic, "girl." Female children in the Arab world sometimes are referred to by making reference to their father. Thus, "so-and-so, bint [daughter] so-and-so."

Casbah: Old quarters of an Arabic city. From the Arabic *qasaba* ("divide," "cut up"; also, "citadel" or "capital"), it is a term often used by Europeans to denote the older, native quarters of a town, as distinct from the newer areas in which foreigners lived.

Darb: Street or path. Has come to refer to a neighborhood, especially in Morocco.

Dey: Political title. The Turkish word for maternal uncle, the position of dey originally was military, but came to denote administrative power as well. Deys were found in North Africa, especially Tunisia and Algeria, from the late seventeenth through the early nineteenth centuries.

Dhu al-Hijjah: Name of the twelfth month of the Islamic calendar.

Dhu al-Qiʿdah: Name of the eleventh month of the Islamic calendar.

Dinar: Monetary unit. Dinar is derived from the Greek "dinarion" and the Latin "denarius." During the early Islamic period, it was a type of gold coin. Currently it serves as the currency of Algeria, Bahrain, Iraq, Jordan, Kuwait, Libya, and Tunisia.

Dirham: Monetary unit. During the early Islamic period, the dirham was a type of silver coin. Currently it is used in Morocco, Libya, the United Arab Emirates, and Jordan.

Effendi: Honorific title. The origins of this title are Greek, and refer to a man of property or education. During the late Ottoman period, it was used as a sign of respect for middle class males as well as for some bureaucratic positions. Another form of the word, effendum, is still used in Egypt to mean "mister" or "sir."

Exilarch: "Leader of the exile" (rosh ha-gola, in Hebrew; resh galonta, in Aramaic). Lay head of some Jewish communities settled outside of Israel.

Feddan: Unit of surface area. Deriving from an Arabic term for a yoke of oxen, it referred to the amount of land such animals could farm. Thus the actual surface area called a feddan varied from region to region. In Egypt, where it remains the standard unit of surface area today, it equals 4,200.883 square meters, slightly more than one acre.

Fellah: Peasant. Fellah (also fallah; plural: fallahun, but more commonly fallahin following colloquial usage) derives from the Arabic verb *falaha* ("cultivate"). It refers to small scale, subsistence level cultivators in Arab countries, but can be used, often derisively, by urbanites to refer to the rural population generally.

Gentile: Word used by Jews, from the time of the end of the Second Temple (between 19 and 70 C.E.) to designate non-Jews, then used by Christians to designate pagans.

Ghazel: Type of poetic form. The word is Arabic (ghazal; "flirtation" or "love poem"), and is also seen as gazel or ghazal. A lyrical poetic mode often expressing romantic love or eroticism, the form passed into Turkish, Persian, and Urdu poetry as well.

Goy: (*Goi*, pl. *goyim*) "Nation or people" in Hebrew. Word used by Jews currently to designate "gentiles", that is, non-Jews.

Hazan: Hebrew word used to designate the performer of a Jewish religious office, especially having to do with chanting prayers and teaching children.

Heshvan: Name of the second month of the Hebrew calendar, corresponding to the end of October and the beginning of November.

Hoca: Honorific title. Hoca is a Turkish word derived from the Persian *khwaja.* In the Turkish speaking parts of the Ottoman empire, it denoted religious scholars and certain administrative bureacrats. It is still used in modern Turkey to refer to teachers and religious scholars. See also "khawaja."

Hofshi: Hebrew word meaning "free." By extension designates a secular Jew.

Hosainiyeh: Place of a certain type of religious ceremony. In Iran, it is a place where the martyrdom of the Imam Husayn ibn Ali is commemorated, especially on Ashura, the tenth day of the Islamic month of Muharram. It refers to the death of Husayn, grandson of the prophet Muhammad, in 680 at the hands of the Umayyads at Karbala, in Iraq. Traditionally, a hosainiyeh was a different structure than a mosque, and was a populist institution rather than one under the control of the Islamic clerics.

Inqilab: Revolution or uprising. In modern Arabic political usage, the term inqilab is usually used to connote a sudden seizure of political power, often via a military coup d'état. In Persian, the term means "revolution," such as the 1979 revolution in Iran.

Iyar: Name of the eighth month of the Hebrew calendar, corresponding to late April and early May.

Jumada al-awwal: Name of the fifth month of the Islamic calendar.

Jumada al-thani: Name of the sixth month of the Islamic calendar.

Kaddish: Hebrew word, from Aramaic, meaning "sanctification." Prayer of praise, addressed to

God and recited periodically in the course of a synagogue service, by men in mourning. Also called the prayer of the dead.

Kara: Hebrew term designating someone who reads and interprets sacred writings without the help of commentaries.

Kaza: Ottoman administrative unit. Kaza is a Turkish word derived from the Arabic *qada.* By the late Ottoman empire, a province (*vilayet*; Arabic: *wilaya*) was divided into governorates called *sanjaks* (Arabic singular: *sanjaq*) or *livas* (Arabic singular: *liwa*). These in turn were divided into smaller units called kazas. Kaza can also refer to the judgment of a *qadi,* or judge. See also "liwa," "qa'immaqam," and "vilayet."

Khan: Highway inn for travelers, or a warehouse for merchandise. Khans were built as rest stops for travelers and caravans. A khan was also an urban complex for storing merchandise and hosting merchants.

Khanjar: Type of Arabic dagger. A khanjar usually refers to a slightly curved, double edged dagger that tapers to a point. The hilt is often decorated.

Khatib: Islamic preacher. A khatib is the religious official who delivers the sermon during Friday prayers in a mosque, usually from a raised pulpit called a minbar. See also "minbar."

Khawaja: Honorific title of Persian origin. In Egypt and parts of the Fertile Crescent, khawaja was a title used to denote a non-Muslim, both foreigners as well as native Christians and Jews. The term comes from the Persian *khwaja.* See also "hoca."

Khawr: Natural harbor; also part of place names. The term is used in the Persian/Arabian Gulf region.

Khedive: High-level title used in Egypt from 1867–1914. Khedive is a Persian word for a high prince that was used by the governors of Ottoman Egypt from 1867–1914 to replace the title "pasha" carried by other governors in the empire. It was first used by Isma'il Pasha, grandson of Muhammad Ali, who secured this right from the Ottoman sultan in order to differentiate and elevate himself from other provincial governors. The term was replaced with "sultan" by the British, who occupied Egypt starting in 1882. See also "pasha."

Kiddush: Blessing pronounced at a meal, or during Jewish religious holidays.

Kiddush ha-Shem: Hebrew word for Jewish martyrs in general.

Kippah: ("yarmulka" in Yiddish) Skullcap worn by observant Jews, as a sign of submission to God.

Kislev: Word for the third month of the Hebrew calendar, corresponding to the period between the end of November and the beginning of December. On 25 Kislev, the holiday of Hanukkah is celebrated.

Koran: See dictionary entry "Qur'an."

Lailat al-Qadr: Muslim holiday, celebrated on 27 Ramadan, commemorating the night of Qur'anic revelation.

Lira: Ottoman monetary unit. The lira, or pound, was named after an Italian silver coin, and was the currency used in the Ottoman empire. Modern Turkey, Syria, and Lebanon continue to use the lira as their national currencies.

Liwa: Ottoman administrative unit. During the late Ottoman empire, a province (*vilayet*; Arabic: *wilaya*) was divided into liwas (called liva in Turkish). A liwa was also called a *sanjak* (Arabic: *sanjaq*). These in turn were divided into smaller units called qadas or kazas.

Luti: Term implying deviation from moral standards. In Iran during the late nineteenth and early twentieth centuries, the term originally referred to a member of a chivalrous brotherhood. It later assumed more negative connotations implying drunkenness and moral deviation. In parts of the modern Arab world, luti is a term used for a homosexual. Some surmise that the term derives from the biblical figure Lot, son of Noah.

Majles: Legislature or parliament. Majles is the Persian form of the Arabic *majlis* (in Turkish, *meclis*), which is derived from the verb *jalasa* ("to sit"). It can mean a meeting, or sitting, in a number of senses, both private and public. In the public realm, it became the term used for legislatures in the Middle East and North Africa once these began to emerge in the nineteenth century. It can also refer to an appointed consultative body.

Malik: "King" in Arabic. Malik derives from the Arabic verb *malaka* ("to own"). It has been used in the modern Arab world to mean king.

Ma'palim: Illegal Jewish immigrants to Palestine. Ma'palim (Hebrew, "the daring ones") were Jewish immigrants who entered Palestine in violation of immigration quotas established by the British Mandate in Palestine, especially after the 1939 White Paper. The Zionist community in Palestine established the clandestine organization Mossad le-Aliyah Bet in 1938 to assist Jews fleeing Nazi persecution in Europe in reaching Palestine. British forces intercepted many maʿpalim and interned them in camps in Cyprus, including the 4,515 passengers aboard the ship *Exodus,* whose detainment in 1947 helped turn international sentiment against British rule in Palestine.

Menorah: Hebrew word for the seven-branch candelabra, principal object of worship in the Jewish temple. Its shape was inspired by a plant known in antiquity under the name of moriah. When the first temple of Jerusalem was destroyed, the candelabra disappeared with all the other sacred objects.

Mezuzah: Little case in wood or metal, containing a verse of the Torah, attached to the frame of the door to a house.

Mikvah: Purifying bath, a practice of Orthodox Jews.

Minbar: Pulpit in a mosque. In a mosque, the sermon (*khitab*) is delivered by the preacher (*khatib*) from a raised pulpit called a minbar, derived from the Arabic *nabara* ("to raise the voice"). See also "khatib."

Minha: Hebrew word for "offering." Name of the Jewish afternoon prayer.

Minyan: Hebrew word meaning "number." A quorum of ten adult males is required for Jewish public prayer.

Mitnagdi: Hebrew word used to designate a Jew who is opposed to the Hasidic movement.

Mitzva: Practical commandments of Judaism. According to tradition, the Torah contains 613 commandments, of which 248 are "positive" (obligations) and 365 are "negative" (interdictions).

Moslem See the dictionary entry "Muslim."

Muezzin: The one who calls Muslims to pray. A muezzin (Arabic: *muʾadhdhin*) calls the Muslim faithful to pray, usually from a minaret. The call to prayer must be in Arabic, even though most of the world's Muslims do not speak Arabic.

Muharram: Name of the first month in the Islamic calendar. The first of Muharram is New Year's Day; the tenth of Muharram, the Feast of Ashura, commemorates at once the meeting of Adam and Eve, the end of the deluge, and the death of Husayn. Among the Shiʿa, Ashura is celebrated in distress, since they commemorate on this day only the death of Husayn. Before the Islamic epoch, the month of Muharram corresponded to a period of sacred repose. Concerning New Year's Day, the Iranians continue to celebrate the "Naw Rouz" (new light), the Sassanid New Year's Day, having survived the coming of Islam, which falls after the spring equinox, 21 March.

Mukhtar: Chief or headman. Deriving from the Arabic word *khatara* ("to choose" or "select"), a mukhtar ("selected one") was an official appointed by the Ottoman authorities to serve as a go-between between the government and a tribe, village, or urban quarter. The function was part of the Ottomans' centralization efforts, efforts that included attempts to undercut traditional religious figures who had maintained levels of local influence. The position is still found in parts of the Arab world.

Mulai: Title and form of address. In Arabic, "my lord." Also mawlai, mawlay. A form of address formerly used when speaking to a king, sultan, or caliph. It is still used in Morocco when referring to the crown prince.

Mutasarrif: Ottoman provincial official. A mutasarrif was the recipient of taxes from sub-provincial governorates in the Ottoman empire. By the late Ottoman era, the term denoted the government-appointed head of a governorate, or sanjak (also liwa). See also "liwa."

Narghila: Water pipe. A narghila (also called *arghila, qalyan,* and *shisha*) is a water pipe used in the Middle East and North Africa to smoke tobacco, usually flavored tobacco called *tombac.* They are commonly seen in all-male coffee houses.

Nissan: Month of the Hebrew calendar, occurring between late March and early April. The holiday of Pesach (Passover) is celebrated from 15 to 21 Nissan. Yom ha-Shoah (Holocaust Remembrance Day), observed on 27 Nissan, is a national day of mourning in memory of Jews who died in the Holocaust during World War II.

Oasis: Watered area surrounded by desert. An oasis is a fertile area, watered by wells, that is found in the midst of a desert. They can be small or large.

Pesh Merga: Kurdish, "those who face death." Modern term used to denote armed Kurdish fighters. It first appeared during the Kurdish war against the Iraqi government that began in 1962.

Qaʾid: Arabic for "leader." Arabic term denoting political leadership.

Qaʾimmaqam: Ottoman provincial official. The term itself is Arabic, and was the title given by Ottoman authorities to the official appointed to head a subgovernorate called a kaza (also qada). See also "kaza," "liwa," and "vilayet." It was also used to denote a low ranking military officer.

Qanat: Canal. A qanat (also qana) can mean an underground water channel for irrigating fields, but can also denote a surface level canal, both small and large (such as the Suez Canal).

Qat: Plant with mildly stimulant effect. The leaves of the qat (also khat) plant, Catha edulis, are chewed in southwestern Arabia and eastern Africa for their mildly stimulant effect. Similar to the stimulant qualities of caffeine, qat is chewed in the company of others as an important form of social gathering. In this regard, gathering together to chew qat is akin to gathering in a coffee house to drink coffee or tea.

Qibla: Direction of Islamic prayer. The qibla is the direction in which Muslims must pray. The first qibla was Jerusalem, but this was quickly changed in the seventh century to the direction of Mecca. Muslims around the globe all pray in the direction of Mecca.

Qirsh: Monetary unit. The Arabic word qirsh, and Turkish word ghurush or kuruş, is translated as piastre, itself the Italian name for the medieval peso duro. The qirsh was introduced into the Middle East in the early seventeenth century and became a unit of Ottoman currency equivalent to one-hundredth of a lira. It is still used as a small unit of currency in parts of the Middle East.

Rabi al-awwal: Name of the third month of the Muslim calendar. The 12th of this month is celebrated as the anniversary of the birth of the prophet Muhammad. In the Maghreb, this holiday is called *al-Mawled* (*Muled, Mulud*).

Rabi al-thani: Name of the fourth month in the Muslim calendar.

Rajab: Name of the seventh month of the Muslim calendar, during which, on the 27th, the Muslims commemorate the ascension of the prophet Muhammad. During this month, some believers also celebrate the birth of Zaynab, eldest daughter of the Prophet.

Ramadan: Ninth month of the Islamic calendar, lasting twenty-nine or thirty days. Ramadan is a month of fasting, which is one of the five obligations of Islam, and so between sunrise and sunset the believer abstains from smoking; partaking of food or drink; telling lies, gossiping and engaging in other unethical behavior; and engaging in sex. At sunset everyone breaks the fast, usually in a large meal with family and friends (*iftar*). The end of the month of Ramadan is celebrated with a feast, the *ʿId al-Fitr*. Between the 27 and 28 Ramadan falls the Night of Destiny (*lailat al-qadr*), when according to a widespread belief everyone's fate is decided. For some this date marks the first revelation of the Qurʾan to Muhammad.

Rosh ha-Shanah: (*Rosh Hashana*; head of the year, in Hebrew) Jewish New Year's Day, celebrated on the first and second days of the month of Tishri (September-October). This holiday, after which, for a period of ten days, every Jew shows penitence, is extended by the additional day of *Yom Kippur*. On the afternoon of the first day the *tashlih* occurs, a purification ceremony. In the Old Testament, Rosh ha-Shanah was called *Yom Teruʿah* (Day of the Trumpet), since the new moon on that day was announced by the sound of the shofar.

Safar: Name of the second month of the Islamic calendar.

Sayyid: Arabic word for "master," "lord," "chief," or "mister." Prior to the coming of Islam, sayyid (plural: sada or asyad) was used in Arabia to denote a tribal chief. After the coming of Islam, it assumed a particular meaning: descendants and certain relatives of the prophet Muhammad. The term sayyid thereafter came to denote the direct descendants of the Prophet through his two grandsons, Hasan and Husayn, the sons of the union of the Prophet's daughter, Fatima, and his son-in-law (and cousin), Ali. In some part of the Arab world, notably in the Hijaz region of Arabia and parts of the Fertile Crescent, sayyid came to denote those who were part of the lineage of Husayn, while the term *sharif* denoted those descendant from Hasan. Sayyids were held in high social esteem. However, the terms sayyid or sid (also, "sidi": "my lord") have also been used in a variety of Islamic societies as a form of address for holy men and religious figures. It also is the modern Arabic equivalent of "mister."

Seven Sisters: Group of Western oil companies in the Middle East. The Seven Sisters were a cartel of Western oil companies that dominated the Middle Eastern oil industry from 1930–1970. They were: Standard Oil of New Jersey (Exxon), British Petroleum, Royal Dutch Shell, Chevron, Texaco, Mobil, and Gulf Oil. They increasingly lost power starting in the 1950s and 1960s as Middle Eastern countries began nationalizing their oil industries. With the merger of Chevron and Gulf in 1986, the number of "sisters" dropped to six, which remain important companies in the fields of oil refining and distribution.

Sha'aban: Name of the eighth month of the Islamic calendar. According to a belief dating back to the 10th century, for every Muslim, the night of 14–15 of this month is considered as the "night of destiny," in the course of which everyone finds out what the year to come has in store. Others think this "revelation" occurs on the night of 27–28 Ramadan.

Shawal: Tenth month of the Islamic calendar, following the month of Ramadan. On the 1st of this month Muslims celebrate the end of the fast (*Id el-Fitr*).

Shevat: Name of the fifth month of the Hebrew calendar, corresponding to the period between the end of January and the beginning of February.

Shuttle Diplomacy: Term denoting a diplomatic intermediary shuttling back and forth between countries in an effort to arrange an agreement among contending countries. The term was first raised to the level of public discourse to describe the efforts of American secretary of state Henry Kissinger to bring about a disengagement of forces after the October 1973 Arab–Israeli war. Kissinger had to shuttle back and forth between the capitals of Egypt, Syria, and Israel, carrying his proposals, because the parties could not agree to meet together.

Sitt: Arabic for "lady." Sitt is often used in female royal titles.

Sivan: Nine month of the Hebrew calendar, corresponding to the period between the end of May and the beginning of June. On 6 Sivan the holiday of the first fruits takes place (Shavuot).

Tammuz: Name of the tenth month of the Hebrew calendar, corresponding to the period between the end of June and the beginning of July.

Taqlid: Islamic legal term. In Sunni Islam, the term taqlid came to mean "deference" or "imitation," in the sense that religious jurisprudents were obliged to defer to the doctrinal precedents of their respective schools of law (the Shafi'i, Hanbali, Hanafi, and Maliki schools). This, then, reduces the realm of individual interpretation (*ijtihad*). In Shi'ite Islam, however, the position of marja al-taqlid is quite different, and denotes an elite jurist who is spiritually empowered to employ *ijtihad.*

Tariqa: Sufi order or brotherhood. Tariqa is an Arabic word derived from the term meaning "the way." It is used to denote sufi mystical orders.

Tell: Hill or mound. The Arabic word *tall* means a hill, and is used to describe such geographical features. In archeological parlance, however, it refers to a mound containing ancient archeological remains. Finally, it also refers to a large region of North Africa from Morocco to Tunisia.

Tevet: Name of the fourth month of the Hebrew calendar, corresponding to the period between the end of December and the beginning of January.

Thalweg Line: Maritime boundary. The thalweg principle of international law, whereby a river or some other body of water constitutes an international border, was most notably used in the Middle East in the case of the border between Iraq and Iran.

Tishri: Name of the first month in the Hebrew calendar, corresponding to the period between the end of September and the beginning of October. On 1 and 2 Tishri the holiday of Rosh ha-Shana falls, on the 10th that of Yom Kippur, and on the 21st, Simhat Torah.

Tishrin: Arabic term for the tenth and eleventh months of the Gregorian calendar. In the modern Arab world, Tishrin al-Awwal ("First Tishrin") refers to the Gregorian (Western) month of October, while Tishrin al-Thani ("Second Tishrin") refers to November. Some Arab countries, notably Saudi Arabia, do not use the Gregorian calendar but only the Islamic (hijri) calendar. It is also the name of a newspaper in Syria, named after the initial Arab victories in the October 1973 Arab-Israeli war.

Tu B'Shvat: Name of the Jewish holiday, called "of the trees," celebrated on 15 Shevat, month corresponding to the period between the end of January and the beginning of February.

Turkmen: Turkic peoples in Turkmenistan, Iran, and Afghanistan. The Turkmen are speakers of Western Oghuz Turkic, and were originally pastoral nomads. They lived east of the Caspian Sea and west of the Amu Darya (Oxus) River. In addition, Turkmen minorities today reside in Iraq, Syria, and Turkey.

Urf: Arabic customary law. Urf refers to largely unwritten tribal or customary codes that govern social relations, in contradistinction to Islamic law (*shari'a*) or state legal codes (qanun).

Ustadh: Arabic for "teacher" or "master." This term (also ostad or ustaz) is used to denote a teacher or professor, but can also be used as a polite form of address for any educated person.

Uzi: Type of Israeli firearm. The uzi is a short submachine gun designed by the Israeli army office Maj. Uziel Gal, after whom it is named.

Vali: Ottoman provincial governor. The term vali is the Turkish and Persian rendition of the Arabic *wali,* referring to someone who has been deputized to exercise authority. It meant "governor." The Mamluks assigned valis to their smallest administrative units, whereas in Iran and later in the Ottoman empire, a vali was the governor of the largest type of administrative unit. In the Ottoman empire, a vali was head of a *vilayet,* or province. See also "kaza," "liwa," and "vilayet."

Vilayet: Ottoman Turkish term for province. A vilayet, from the Arabic word *wilaya,* was the largest administrative unit within the Ottoman empire. See also "vali."

Vizier: Type of government official; "minister." Under the Ottomans, the vizier (Arabic: *wazir;* Turkish: *vezir*) served as a government minister. The vezir-i azam, or grand vizier, was the functional equivalent of a prime minister under the sultan. The Ottomans replaced the term with *vekil* (Arabic: *wakil*) in the 1830s, although *wazir* is still in use to denote a government minister in the Arab world.

Za'im: Arabic for "boss" or "leader." Usually used in an informal manner to denote a strong leader. It is also used as a military rank in some Arab countries.

BIBLIOGRAPHY

Abbas, Mahmoud. *Through Secret Channels: The Road to Oslo.* Readings. Reading, UK: Garnet, 1995.

Abed, George T. *The Economic Viability of a Palestinian State.* Washington, DC: Institute for Palestine Studies, 1990.

Abu-Amr, Ziad. *Islamic Fundamentalism in the West Bank and Gaza: Muslim Brotherhood and Islamic Jihad.* Bloomington: University of Indiana Press, 1994.

AbuKhalil, As'ad. *Bin Laden, Islam, and America's New "War on Terrorism."* New York: Seven Stories, 2002.

———. *Historical Dictionary of Lebanon.* Lanham, MD: Scarecrow Press, 1998.

———. "Lebanon." *Political Parties of the Middle East and North Africa,* edited by Frank Tachau. Westport, CT: Greenwood, 1994.

Aburish, Said K. *Arafat: From Defender to Dictator.* New York: Bloomsbury, 1998.

———. *Saddam Hussein: The Politics of Revenge.* New York: Bloomsbury, 2000.

Adelson, Roger. *London and the Invention of the Middle East: Money, Power, and War, 1902–1922.* New Haven, CT: Yale University Press, 1995.

Ahmed, Leila. *Women and Gender in Islam: Historical Roots of a Modern Debate.* New Haven, CT: Yale University Press, 1992.

Alexander, Yonah. "Popular Front for the Liberation of Palestine." *Palestinian Secular Terrorism.* Ardsley, NY: Transnational Publishers, 2003.

Algar, Hamid. "A Brief History of the Naqshbandi Order." In *Naqshbandis: Cheminements et situation actuelle d'un ordre mystique musulman,* edited by Marc Gaborieau, Alexandre Popovic, and Thierry Zarcone. Istanbul and Paris: Editions Isis, 1990.

Almog, Oz. *The Sabra: The Creation of the New Jew,* translated by Haim Watzman. Berkeley: University of California Press, 2000.

Alterman, Jon. *New Media, New Politics?: From Satellite Television to the Internet in the Arab World.* Washington, DC: Washington Institute for Near East Policy, 1998.

Amery, Hussein A., and Aaron T. Wolf, eds. *Water in the Middle East: A Geography of Peace.* Austin: University of Texas Press, 2000.

Anderson, Benedict. *Imagined Communities: Reflections on the Origin and Spread of Nationalism,* revised edition. London and New York: Verso, 1991.

Arian, Alan, and Michal Shamir. *The Elections in Israel, 1996.* Albany: State University of New York Press, 1999.

Arian, Asher. *The Second Republic: Politics in Israel.* Chatham, NJ: Chatham House, 1998.

Armstrong, Karen. *Jerusalem: One City, Three Faiths.* New York: Ballantine, 1997.

Arnow, David. "The Holocaust and the Birth of Israel: Reassessing the Causal Relationship." *Journal of Israeli History* 15, no. 3 (autumn 1994): 257–281.

Aronoff, Myron. *Israeli Visions and Division: Cultural Change and Political Conflict.* New Brunswick, NJ: Transaction Books, 1990.

Aronson, Geoffrey. *Israel, Palestinians, and the Intifada: Creating Facts in the West Bank.* London and New York: Kegan Paul, 1990.

Aronson, Shlomo. *The Politics and Strategy of Nuclear Weapons in the Middle East.* Albany: State University of New York Press, 1992.

Aruri, Naseer H. *The Obstruction of Peace: The United States, Israel, and the Palestinians.* Monroe, Maine: Common Courage, 1995.

Arzt, Donna E. *Refugees Into Citizens: Palestinians and the End of the Arab-Israeli Conflict.* New York: Council on Foreign Relations, 1997.

Ashrari, Hanan. *This Side of Peace: A Personal Account.* New York: Simon and Schuster, 1995.

Avruch, Kevin, and Walter P. Zenner, eds. *Critical Essays on Israeli Society, Religion and Government.* Albany: State University of New York Press, 1997.

Awaisi, Abdal-Fattyah Muhammad al-. *The Muslim Brothers and the Palestine Question, 1928–1947.* New York: I. B. Tauris, 1998.

Baker, Raymond William. *Sadat and After: Struggles for Egypt's Political Soul.* Cambridge, MA: Harvard University Press, 1990.

Bar-On, Mordechai. *The Gates of Gaza: Israel's Road to Suez and Back, 1955–1957.* New York: St. Martin's Press, 1994.

———. *In Pursuit of Peace: A History of the Israeli Peace Movement.* Washington, DC: U.S. Institute of Peace, 1996.

Bar-Siman-Tov, Yaacov. *Israel and the Peace Process, 1977–1982: In Search of Legitimacy for Peace.* Albany: State University of New York Press, 1994.

Bass, Warren. *Support Any Friend: Kennedy's Middle East and the Making of the U.S.-Israel Alliance.* Oxford and New York: Oxford University Press, 2004.

Beaumont, Peter. "Water Policies for the Middle East in the Twenty-first Century: The New Economic Realities." *International Journal of Water Resources Development* 18, no. 2 (2002): 315–334.

Beinin, Joel, and Joe Stork. *Political Islam: Essays from Middle East Report.* Berkeley: University of California Press, 1997.

Ben-Eliezer, Uri. *The Making of Israeli Militarism.* Bloomington: Indiana University Press, 1998.

Ben-Rafael, Eliezer, and S. Sharot. *Ethnicity, Religion and Class in Israeli Society.* Cambridge and New York: Cambridge University Press, 1991.

Ben-Rafael, Eliezer. *Crisis and Transformation: The Kibbutz at Century's End.* Albany: State University of New York Press, 1997.

———. *Jewish Identities: Fifty Intellectuals Answer Ben-Gurion.* Leiden, Netherlands: Brill, 2002.

Benvenisti, Meron. *City of Stone: The Hidden History of Jerusalem.* Berkeley: University of California Press, 1997.

Ben-Yehuda, Nachman. *The Masada Myth: Collective Memory and Mythmaking in Israel.* Madison: The University of Wisconsin Press, 1995.

Berg, Nancy E. "Transit Camp Literature: Literature of Transition." In *Critical Essay on Israeli Society, Religion, and Government: Books on Israel,* Vol. 4, edited by Kevin Avruch and Walter P. Zenner. Albany: State University of New York Press, 1997.

Berkowitz, Michael. *Western Jewry and the Zionist Project, 1914–1933.* New York: Cambridge University Press, 1997.

Bickerton, Ian J., and Carla L. Klauser. *A Concise History of the Arab-Israeli Conflict.* 2d ed. Englewood Cliffs, NJ: Prentice-Hall, 1995.

Binur, Yoram. *My Enemy, My Self.* New York: Penguin, 1990.

Black, Ian, and Benny Morris. *Israel's Secret Wars: A History of Israel's Intelligence Services.* New York: Grove Press, 1991.

Bohn, Michael K. *The Achille Lauro Hijacking: Lessons in the Politics and Prejudice of Terrorism.* Dulles, VA: Brassey's, 1999.

Bose, Meena, and Rosanna Perotti, eds. *From Cold War to New World Order: The Foreign Policy of George H. W. Bush.* Westport, CT: Greenwood, 2002.

Boyd, Douglas A. *Broadcasting in the Arab World: A Survey of the Electronic Media in the Middle East,* 3d edition. Ames: Iowa State University Press, 1999.

Brentjes, Burchard. *The Armenians, Assyrians, and Kurds: Three Nations, One Fate?* Campbell, CA: Rishi, 1997.

Brom, Shlomo, and Yiftah Shapir, eds. *The Middle East Military Balance, 2001–2002.* Cambridge, MA, and London.: MIT Press, 2002.

Brooks, David B., and Ozay Mehmet, eds. *Water Balances in the Eastern Mediterranean.* Ottawa: International Development Research Centre, 2000.

Brown, Nathan. *Palestinian Politics after the Oslo Accords: Resuming Arab Palestine.* Berkeley: University of California Press, 2003.

Brynen, Rex. *Sanctuary and Survival: The PLO in Lebanon.* Boulder, CO.: Westview Press, 1990.

Brynen, Rex; Bahgat Korany; and Paul Noble, eds. *Political Liberalization and Democratization in the Arab World,* 2 volumes. Boulder, CO: Lynne Rienner, 1995.

Burdett, Anita, ed. *The Arab League: British Documentary Sources, 1943–1963.* Slough, UK: Archive Editions, 1995.

Burrows, William E., and Robert Windrem. *Critical Mass: The Dangerous Race for Superweapons in a Fragmenting World.* New York: Simon and Schuster, 1994.

Caplan, Neil. *Futile Diplomacy,* Vol. 4: *Operation Alpha and the Failure of Anglo-American Coercive Diplomacy in the Arab-Israeli conflict, 1954–1956.* Totowa, NJ; London: Frank Cass, 1997.

Carey, Roane. *The New Intifada: Resisting Israel's Apartheid.* London: Verso, 2001.

Carroll, James. *Constantine's Sword: The Church and the Jews, a History.* Boston: Houghton Mifflin, 2002.

Caspi, Dan, and Yehiel Limor. *The In/Outsiders: The Mass Media in Israel.* Cresskill, NJ: Hampton Press, 1999.

Cassese, Antonio. *Terrorism, Politics, and Law: The Achille Lauro Affair.* Princeton, NJ: Princeton Univ. Press, 1989.

Chomsky, Noam. *The Fateful Triangle: The U.S., Israel and the Palestinians.* 2d ed. Boston: South End, 1999.

Choueiri, Youssef M. *Arab Nationalism: A History: Nation and State in the Arab World.* Oxford and Malden, MA: Blackwell, 2000.

Christison, Kathleen. *Perceptions of Palestine: Their Influence on U.S. Middle East Policy.* Berkeley: University of California Press, 1999.

Ciment, James. *Palestine/Israel: The Long Conflict.* New York: Facts on File, 1997.

Cobban, Helena. *The Israeli-Syrian Peace Talks, 1991–1996 and Beyond.* Washington, DC: Institute of Peace Press, 1999.

———. *The Palestinian Liberation Organisation: People, Power, and Politics.* Cambridge and New York: Cambridge University Press, 1984.

Cohen, Avner. *Israel and the Bomb.* New York: Columbia University Press, 1998.

Corbin, Jane. *The Norway Channel: The Secret Talks that Led to the Middle East Peace Accord.* New York: Atlantic Monthly Press, 1994.

Cubert, Harold. *The PFLP's Changing Role in the Middle East.* London: Frank Cass, 1997.

Davila, James R., ed. *The Dead Sea Scrolls as Background to Postbiblical Judaism and Early Christianity: Papers from an International Conference at St. Andrews in 2001.* Boston, MA: Brill, 2003.

Davis, Joyce M. *Martyrs: Innocence, Vengeance, and Despair in the Middle East.* New York: Palgrave, 2003.

Dawisha, Adeed. *Arab Nationalism in the Twentieth Century: From Triumph to Despair.* Princeton, NJ: Princeton University Press, 2003.

Deeb, Marius. *Syria's Terrorist War on Lebanon and the Peace Process.* New York: Palgrave Macmillan, 2003.

Diskin, Abraham. *The Last Days in Israel: Understanding the New Israeli Democracy.* London: Frank Cass, 2003.

Divine, Donna Robinson. *Politics and Society in Ottoman Palestine: The Arab Struggle for Survival.* Boulder, CO: Rienner, 1994.

Doumain, Beshara. *Rediscovering Palestine: Merchants and Peasants in Jabal Nablus, 1700–1900.* Berkeley: University of California Press, 1995.

Dowty, Alan. *The Jewish State: A Century Later.* Berkeley: University of California Press, 2001.

Drezon-Tepler, Marcia. *Interest Groups and Political Change in Israel.* Albany: State University of New York Press, 1990.

Dumper, Michael. *Islam and Israel: Muslim Religious Endowments and the Jewish State.* Washington, DC: Institute for Palestine Studies, 1994.

———. *The Politics of Sacred Space: The Old City of Jerusalem in the Middle East Conflict.* Boulder, CO: Lynne Rienner Publishers, 2002.

Dupuy, Trevor N. *Elusive Victory: The Arab-Israeli Wars, 1947–1974,* 3d edition. Dubuque, IA: Kendall/Hunt, 1992.

Eban, Abba. *Personal Witness: Israel through My Eyes.* New York: Putnam, 1992.

Eisenberg, Laura Zittrain, and Neil Caplan. *Negotiating Arab–Israeli Peace: Patterns, Problems, and Possibilities.* Bloomington: Indiana University Press, 1998.

Elad-Bouskila. *Modern Palestinian Literature and Culture.* London: Frank Cass, 1999.

Elmusa, Sharif S. *Water Conflict: Economics, Politics, Law, and the Palestinian-Israeli Water Resources.* Washington, DC: Institute for Palestine Studies, 1997.

El-Nawawy, Mohammed, and Adel Iskander. *Al Jazeera: How the Free Arab News Network Scooped the World and Changed the Middle East.* Cambridge, MA: Westview Press, 2002.

Elon, Amos. *Herzl.* New York: Holt, Rinehart, 1975.

Enderlin, Charles. *Shamir.* Paris: Orban, 1991.

———. *Shattered Dreams: The Failure of the Peace Process in the Middle East, 1995–2002.* New York: Other Press, 2003.

Eshed, Haggai. *Reuven Shiloah: The Man behind the Mossad,* translated by David and Leah Zinder. London: Frank Cass, 1997.

Fahmy, Ninette. *The Politics of Egypt: State-Society Relationship.* New York; Routledge, 2002.

Falk, Richard. "Azmi Bishara, the Right of Resistance, and the Palestinian Ordeal." *Journal of Palestine Studies* 31, no. 2 (winter 2002): 19–33.

Farsoun, Samih K., and Christina Zachharia. *Palestine and the Palestinians.* Boulder, CO.: Westview Press, 1996.

Feiler, Gil. *From Boycott to Economic Cooperation: The Political Economy of the Arab Boycott of Israel.* London: Frank Cass, 1998.

Fernea, Elizabeth Warnock, and Hocking, Mary Evelyn, eds. *The Struggle for Peace: Israelis and Palestinians.* Austin: University of Texas Press, 1992.

Finlan, Alistair. *The Gulf War 1991.* New York: Routledge, 2003.

Firro, Kais. *The Druzes in the Jewish State.* Leiden, Neth.: Brill, 2001.

Fleischmann, Ellen L. "Selective Memory, Gender and Nationalism: Palestinian Women Leaders in the British Mandate Period," *History Workshop Journal* 47 (1999): 141–158.

Fraser, T. G. *The Arab-Israeli Conflict.* New York: St. Martin's, 1995.

Freedman, Lawrence, and Efraim Karsh. *The Gulf Conflict, 1990–1991: Diplomacy and War in the New World Order.* Princeton, NJ: Princeton University Press, 1993.

Friedland, Roger, and Richard Hecht. *To Rule Jerusalem.* Cambridge: Cambridge University Press, 1996.

Friedman, Robert I. *Zealots for Zion: Inside Israel's West Bank Settlement Movement.* New York: Random House, 1992; New Brunswick, NJ: Rutgers University Press, 1994.

Friedman, Thomas L. *From Beirut to Jerusalem.* New York: Farrar, Straus & Giroux, 1991.

Fry, Michael, and Miles Hochstein. "The Forgotten Middle East Crisis of 1957: Gaza and Sharm el Sheikh." *International History Review* 15 (1993): 46–83.

Gal, Allon. *David Ben-Gurion and the American Alignment for a Jewish State.* Bloomington: Indiana University Press, 1991.

Gawyrch, George W. *The Albatross of Decisive Victory: War and Policy Between Egypt and Israel in the 1967 and 1973 Arab-Israeli Wars.* Westport, CT: Greenwood Press, 2000.

Geddes, Charles L., ed. *A Documentary History of the Arab-Israeli Conflict.* New York: Praeger, 1991.

Gerner, Deborah J. *One Land, Two Peoples: The Conflict over Palestine,* 2d edition. Boulder, CO: Westview Press, 1994.

Gilbert, Martin, ed. *The Illustrated Atlas of Jewish Civilization: 4,000 Years of Jewish History.* New York: Macmillan, 1990.

———. *Israel: A History.* New York: Morrow, 1998.

Glock, Albert. "Archaeology." In *Encyclopedia of the Palestinians,* edited by Philip Mattar. New York: Facts On File, 2000.

Glubb, John Bagot. *The Changing Scenes of Life: An Autobiography.* London: Quartet, 1983.

Golani, Motti. *Israel in Search of A War: The Sinai Campaign, 1955–1956.* Brighton and Portland, OR: Sussex Academic Press, 1998.

Goldberg, Harvey E., ed. *Sephardi and Middle Eastern Jewries: History and Culture in the Modern Era.* Bloomington: Indiana University Press, 1996.

Goldschmidt, Arthur, Jr. *A Concise History of the Middle East,* 4th edition. Boulder, CO: Westview Press, 1991.

Gollaher, David L. *Circumcision: A History of the World's Most Controversial Surgery.* New York: Basic Books, 2000.

Gordon, Haim, ed. *Looking Back at the June 1967 War.* Westport, CT: Praeger, 1999.

Gorman, Anthony. *Historians, State and Politics in Twentieth Century Egypt: Contesting the Nation.* London and New York: Routledge Curzon, 2003.

Government of Palestine. *A Survey of Palestine for the Information of the Anglo-American Committee of Inquiry* (1946), 2 vols. Washington, DC: Institute for Palestine Studies, 1991.

Gowers, Andrew, and Tony Walker. *Behind the Myth: Yasser Arafat and the Palestinian Revolution.* London: W. H. Allen, 1990.

Greilsammer, Ilan. "The Religious Parties." In *Israel's Odd Couple: The 1984 Knesset Elections and the National Unity Government,* edited by Daniel J. Elazar and Shmuel Sandler. Detroit: Wayne State University Press, 1990.

Grossman, David. *Sleeping on a Wire: Conversations with Palestinians in Israel.* New York: Farrar, Straus & Giroux, 1993.

Haddadin, Munther J. *Diplomacy on the Jordan: International Conflict and Negotiated Resolution.* Boston: Kluwer Academic Publishers, 2001.

Haidar, Aziz. *Education, Empowerment and Control: The Case of the Arabs in Israel.* Albany: State University of New York Press, 1994.

Halamish, Aviva. *The Exodus Affair: Holocaust Survivors and the Struggle for Palestine,* translated by Ora Cummings. Syracuse, NY: Syracuse University Press, 1998.

Halper, Jeff. *Between Redemption and Revival: The Jewish Yishuv of Jerusalem in the Nineteenth Century.* Boulder, CO: Westview Press, 1991.

Halpern, Ben, and Reinharz, Jehuda. *Zionism and the Creation of a New Society.* New York: Oxford University Press, 1998.

Hart, Alan. *Arafat: A Political Biography.* Bloomington: Indiana University Press, 1989.

Hatina, Meir. *Islam and Salvation in Palestine: The Islamic Jihad Movement.* Tel Aviv: Tel Aviv University, 2001.

Hazan, Reuven. *Reforming Parliamentary Committees: Israel in Comparative Perspective.* Columbus, OH: Ohio State University, 2001.

Heiberg, Marianne, and Geir Ovensen. *Palestinian Society in Gaza, West Bank and Arab Jerusalem: A Survey of Living Conditions.* Oslo, Norway: FAFO Institute for Applied Social Science), 1993.

Heilman, Samuel C. *Defenders of the Faith: Inside Ultra-Orthodox Jewry.* New York: Schocken, 1992.

Heller, Joseph. *The Birth of Israel, 1945–1949: Ben-Gurion and His Critics.* Gainesville: University Press of Florida, 2000.

———. *The Stern Gang: Ideology, Politics, and Terror, 1940–1949.* Portland, OR, and London: Frank Cass, 1995.

Herb, Michael. *All in the Family: Absolutism, Revolution, and Monarchy in the Middle Eastern Monarchies.* Albany: State University of New York Press, 1999.

Hersh, Seymour. *The Samson Option: Israel's Nuclear Arsenal and American Foreign Policy.* New York: Random House, 1991.

Hertzberg, Arthur, ed. *The Zionist Idea: A Historical Analysis and Reader.* Philadelphia: Jewish Publication Society, 1997.

Herzog, Chaim. *Living History: A Memoir.* London: Weidenfeld and Nicolson, 1997.

Hetzron, Robert, ed. *The Semitic Languages.* New York: Routledge, 1998.

Hilal, Jamil. "PLO Institutions: The Challenge Ahead." *Journal of Palestine Studies* 89 (1993): 46–60.

Hiro, Dilip. *Sharing the Promised Land: A Tale of the Israelis and Palestinians.* New York: Olive Branch, 1999.

Hitti, Philip K. *History of the Arabs: From the Earliest Times to the Present,* revised 10th edition. New York: Palgrave Macmillan, 2002.

Hourani, Albert. *History of the Arab Peoples.* Cambridge, MA: Belknap Press of Harvard University, 2002.

Hroub, Khaled. *Hamas: Political Thought and Practice.* Washington, DC: Institute for Palestine Studies, 2000.

Ilan, Amitzur. *Bernadotte in Palestine: A Study in Contemporary Humanitarian Knight-Errantry.* London: Macmillan, 1989.

———. *The Origin of the Arab-Israeli Arms Race: Arms, Embargo, Military Power and Decision in the 1948 Palestine War.* New York: New York University Press; London: Macmillan, 1996.

Inbar, Efraim. *Rabin and Israel's National Security.* Washington, DC: Woodrow Wilson Center

Press; Baltimore, MD: Johns Hopkins University Press, 1999.

Institute for Palestine Studies. *The Palestinian-Israeli Peace Agreement: A Documentary Record.* Washington, DC: Institute for Palestine Studies, 1994.

———. *United Nations Resolutions on Palestine and the Arab-Israeli Conflict, 1947–1998.* 4 vols. Washington, DC: Institute for Palestine Studies, 1988-99.

Jaimoukha, Amjad. *The Circassians: A Handbook.* New York: Palgrave, 2001.

Jankowski, James. *Nasser's Egypt, Arab Nationalism, and the United Arab Republic.* Boulder, CO: Lynne Rienner Publishers, 2002.

Jayyusi, Salma Khadra, ed. *Anthology of Modern Palestinian Literature.* New York: Columbia University Press, 1992.

Jumayyil, Amin. *Rebuilding Lebanon's Future.* Lanham, MD: University Press of America, 1992.

Kaikobad, Kaiyan Homi. *The Shatt-al-Arab Boundary Question: A Legal Reappraisal.* New York: Oxford University Press; Oxford: Clarendon Press, 1988.

Kamali, Mohammad Hashim. *Principles of Islamic Jurisprudence.* Cambridge: Islamic Texts Society, 1991.

Kamalipour, Yahya R, and Hamid Mowlana, eds. *Mass Media in the Middle East: A Comprehensive Handbook.* Westport, CT: Greenwood Press, 1994.

———. *Mass Media in the Middle East.* Westport, CT: Greenwood Press, 1994.

Kaminer, Reuven. *The Politics of Protest: The Israeli Peace Movement and the Palestinian Intifada.* Brighton, UK: Sussex Academic Press, 1996.

Kark, Ruth. *Jaffa: A City in Evolution, 1799–1917,* translated by Gila Brand. Jerusalem: Yad Izhak Ben-Zvi Press, 1990.

Katz, Yossi. *Partner to Partition: The Jewish Agency's Partition Plan in the Mandate Era.* London and Portland, OR: Frank Cass, 1998.

Kawar, Amal. *Daughters of Palestine: Leading Women of the Palestinian National Movement.* Albany: State University of New York Press, 1996.

Kennedy, Valerie. *Edward Said: A Critical Introduction.* Malden, MA: Blackwell; Cambridge: Polity Press, 2000.

Khalaf, Issa. *Politics in Palestine: Arab Factionalism and Social Disintegration, 1939–1948.* Albany: State University of New York Press, 1991.

Khalidi, Rashid. *Palestinian Identity: The Construction of Modern National Consciousness.* New York: Columbia University Press, 1997.

Khalidi, Rashid; Lisa Anderson; Muhammad Muslih; et al., eds. *The Origins of Arab Nationalism.* New York: Columbia University Press, 1991.

Khan, Saira. *Nuclear Proliferation Dynamics in Protracted Conflict Regions: A Comparative Study of South Asia and the Middle East.* Aldershot, UK, and Burlington, VT: Ashgate, 2002.

Kimche, David. *The Last Option: After Nasser, Arafat, and Saddam Hussein—The Quest for Peace in the Middle East.* New York: Charles Scribner's Sons; Maxwell Macmillan International, 1991.

Kimmerling, Baruch, and Joel S. Migdal. *Palestinians: The Making of a People.* New York: Free Press, 1993.

———. *The Palestinian People: A History.* Cambridge, MA: Harvard University Press, 2003.

Kolars, John. "The Spatial Attributes of Water Negotiation: The Need for a River Ethic and River Advocacy in the Middle East." In *Water in the Middle East: A Geography of Peace,* edited by Hussein A. Amery and Aaron T. Wolf. Austin: University of Texas Press, 2000.

Kurzman, Dan. *Soldier of Peace: The Life of Yitzhak Rabin, 1922–1995.* New York: HarperCollins, 1998.

Kyle, Keith. *Suez.* London: Weidenfeld and Nicolson, 1991.

Landau, David. *Who Is a Jew? A Case Study of American Jewish Influence on Israeli Policy.* New York: American Jewish Committee, Institute on American Jewish-Israel Relations, 1996.

Lahav, Pnina. *Judgment in Jerusalem: Chief Justice Simon Agranat and the Zionist Century.* Berkeley: University of California Press, 1997.

Lapidus, Ira M. *A History of Islamic Societies,* 2d edition. Cambridge and New York: Cambridge University Press, 2002.

Laqueur, Walter, and Barry Rubin, eds. *The Israel-Arab Reader: A Documentary History of the Middle East Conflict,* 6th revised edition. New York and London, Penguin Books, 2001.

Laqueur, Walter, and Judith Tydor Baumel, eds. *The Holocaust Encyclopedia.* New Haven: Yale University Press, 2001.

Laskier, Michael M. *Israel and the Maghreb: From Statehood to Oslo.* Gainesville: University Press of Florida, 2004.

Lesch, Ann Mosely. *Transition to Palestinian Self-Government: Practical Steps toward Israeli-Palestinian Peace.* Bloomington: Indiana University Press, 1992.

Lesch, Ann Mosley, and Dan Tschirgi. *Origins and Development of the Arab-Israeli Conflict.* Westport, CT: Greenwoood Press, 1998.

Lesch, David W., ed. *The Middle East and the United States: A Historical and Political Reassessment,* 3d edition. Boulder, CO: Westview, 2003.

Livingstone, Neil C., and David Halevy. *Inside the PLO: Covert Units, Secret Funds, and the War against Israel and the United States.* New York: Morrow, 1990.

Lorch, Netanel. *Shield of Zion: The Israeli Defense Forces.* Charlottesville, VA: Howell Press, 1991.

Lockman, Zachary. *Comrades and Enemies: Arab and Jewish Workers in Palestine, 1906–1948.* Berkeley: University of California Press, 1996.

Lowi, Miriam. *Water and Power: The Politics of a Scarce Resource in the Jordan River Basin.* Cambridge and New York: Cambridge University Press, 1993.

Lucas, W. Scott. *Divided We Stand: Britain, the US, and the Suez Crisis.* London: Hodder & Stoughton, 1991.

Lukacs, Yehuda, ed. *The Israeli-Palestinian Conflict: A Documentary Record, 1967–1990.* Cambridge: Cambridge University Press, 1992.

Lunt, James. *Glubb Pasha: A Biography.* London: Harvill, 1984.

Lustick, Ian S. *For the Land and the Lord: Jewish Fundamentalism in Israel.* New York: Council on Foreign Relations, 1988.

———. *Arab-Israeli Relations: A Collection of Contending Perspectives and Recent Research.* 10 vols. Hamden, Conn.: Garland, 1994.

Luz, Ehud. *Parallels Meet: Religion and Nationalism in the Early Zionist Movement, 1882–1904,* translated by Lenn J. Schramm. Philadelphia: Jewish Publication Society, 1988.

Maʾoz, Moshe, and Gabriel Sheffer, eds. *Middle Eastern Minorities and Diasporas.* Brighton, UK: Sussex Academic Press, 2002.

MacDonald, Eileen. *Shoot the Women First.* New York: Random House, 1991.

Magnes, Judah Leon. *The Magnes-Philby Negotiations, 1929: The Historical Record.* Jerusalem: Magnes Press, Hebrew University, 1998.

Mahler, Gregory S. *Politics and Government in Israel: The Maturation of a Modern State.* Boulder, CO: Rowman and Littlefield, 2004.

Makovsky, David. *Making Peace with the PLO: The Rabin Government's Road to the Oslo Accord.* Boulder, CO: Westview Press, 1996.

Marr, Phebe. "The Iran-Iraq War: The View from Iraq." In *The Persian Gulf War: Lessons for Strategy, Law, and Diplomacy,* edited by Christopher C. Joyner. Westport, CT: Greenwood Press, 1990.

Massad, Joseph A. *Colonial Effects: The Making of National Identity in Jordan.* New York: Columbia University Press, 2001.

Masud, Muhammad Khalid; Brinkley Messick; and David S. Powers, eds. *Islamic Legal Interpretation: Muftis and Their Fatwas.* Cambridge, MA: Harvard University Press, 1996.

Mattar, Philip. "The PLO and the Gulf Crisis." *Middle East Journal* 48, no. 1 (winter 1994): 31–46.

The Mufti of Jerusalem: Al-Hajj Amin al-Husayni and the Palestinian National Movement, revised edition. New York: Columbia University Press, 1992.

McCarthy, Justin. *The Population of Palestine: Population History and Statistics of the Late Ottoman Period and the Mandate.* New York: Columbia University Press, 1990.

McGowan, Daniel, and Marc H. Ellis, eds. *Remembering Deir Yassin: The Future of Israel and Palestine.* Brooklyn, NY: Olive Branch Press, 1998.

Medoff, Rafael, and Chaim I. Waxman. *Historical Dictionary of Zionism.* Lanham, MD: Scarecrow Press, 2000.

Mernissi, Fatima. *The Veil and the Male Elite: A Feminist Interpretation of Women's Rights in Islam.* Reading, MA: Addison-Wesley, 1991.

Meyers, Eric M., ed. *Galilee through the Centuries: Confluence of Cultures.* Duke Judaic Studies Series, vol. 1. Winona Lake, IN: Eisenbrauns, 1999.

Miller, Anita; Jordan Miller; and Sigalit Zetouni. *Sharon: Israel's Warrior-Politician.* Chicago: Academy Chicago, Olive, 2002.

Mintz, Jerome R. *Hasidic People: A Place in the New World.* Cambridge, MA: Harvard University Press, 1992.

Mishal, Shaul, and Avraham Sela. *The Palestinian Hamas: Vision, Violence, and Coexistence.* New York: Columbia University Press, 2000.

Mitchell, John, et al. *The New Economy of Oil: Impacts on Business, Geopolitics, and Society.* London: Earthscan, 2001.

Momen, Moojan. *An Introduction to Shi'i Islam: The History and Doctrines of Twelver Shi'ism.* New Haven, CT: Yale University Press, 1985.

Moosa, Matti. *The Maronites in History.* Syracuse, NY: Syracuse University Press, 1986.

Morris, Benny. *Israel's Border Wars, 1949–1956: Arab Infiltration, Israeli Retaliation, and the Countdown to the Suez War.* Oxford: Clarendon Press, 1993.

———. *Righteous Victims: A History of the Zionist–Arab Conflict, 1881–1999.* New York: Alfred A. Knopf, 1999.

Moussalli, Ahmad. *Historical Dictionary of Islamic Fundamentalist Movements in the Arab World, Iran, and Turkey.* Lanham, MD: Scarecrow Press, 1999.

Moderate and Radical Islamic Fundamentalism: The Quest for Modernity, Legitimacy, and the Islamic State. Gainesville: University of Florida Press, 1999.

Munthe, Turi, ed. *The Saddam Hussein Reader.* New York: Thunder's Mouth Press, 2002.

Muslih, Muhammad Y. *The Origins of Palestinian Nationalism.* New York: Columbia University Press, 1988.

Mutahhari, Morteza. *Jihad: the Holy War in Islam and the Legitimacy in the Qur'an,* translated by Mohammad Salman Tawhidi. Tehran, Iran: Islamic Propagation Organization, 1998.

Nashashibi, Nasser Eddin. *Jerusalem's Other Voice: Ragheb Nashashibi and Moderation in Palestinian Politics, 1920–1948.* Exeter, UK: Ithaca, 1990.

Nassar, Jamal R. *The Palestine Liberation Organization: From Armed Struggle to the Declaration of Independence.* New York: Praeger Publishers, 1991.

Neff, Donald. *Fallen Pillars: U.S. Policy towards Palestine and Israel.* Washington, DC: Institute for Palestine Studies, 1995.

Netanyahu, Benjamin. *A Place Among the Nations: Israel and the World.* New York: Bantam Books, 1993.

Newman, D. "Boundaries in Flux: The Green Line Boundary between Israel and the West Bank." *Boundary and Territory Briefing* 1, no. 7 (1995).

Newman, David, ed. *The Impact of Gush Emunim: Politics and Settlement in the West Bank.* New York: St. Martin's Press, 1985.

Newman, David. *Population, Settlement and Conflict: Israel and the West Bank.* Update Series in Contemporary Geographical Issues. New York: Cambridge University Press, 1991.

Oren, Michael B. *Six Days of War: June 1967 and the Making of the Modern Middle East.* New York: Ballantine, 2003.

Pappé, Illan. *The Israel-Palestine Question.* London: Routledge, 1999.

Parker, Richard B., ed. *The Six-Day War: A Retrospective.* Gainesville: University Press of Florida, 1996.

Peres, Shimon. *Battling for Peace: A Memoir.* New York: Random House, 1995.

Peres, Shimon, and Robert Littell. *For the Future of Israel.* Baltimore, MD: Johns Hopkins University Press, 1998.

Peretz, Don. *Intifada: The Palestinian Uprising.* Boulder, CO: Westview Press, 1990.

———. *Palestinians, Refugees, and the Middle East Peace Process.* Washington, DC: United States Institute of Peace Press, 1993.

Peters, F. E. *Mecca: A Literary History of the Muslim Holy City.* Princeton, NJ: Princeton University Press, 1994.

———. *The Hajj: The Muslim Pilgrimage to Mecca and the Holy Places.* Princeton, NJ: Princeton University Press, 1994.

Peterson, Erik R. *The Gulf Cooperation Council: Search for Unity in a Dynamic Region.* Boulder, CO: Westview Press, 1988.

Postel, Sandra. *Pillar of Sand: Can the Irrigation Miracle Last?* New York: Norton, 1999.

Quandt, William B. *Peace Process: American Diplomacy and the Arab-Israeli Conflict Since 1967,* revised edition. Berkeley, CA: Brookings Institution Press, 2001.

Rabin, Leah. *Rabin: Our Life, His Legacy.* New York: Putnam, 1997.

Rabinovich, Itamar. *The Brink of Peace: Israel and Syria, 1992–1996.* Princeton, NJ: Princeton University Press, 1998.

Ranstorp, Magnus. *Hizb'allah in Lebanon: The Politics of the Western Hostage Crisis.* New York: Palgrave Macmillan, 1997.

Raswamy, P. R. Kuma, ed. *Revisiting the Yom Kippur War.* London and Portland, OR: Frank Cass, 2000.

Raviv, Dan, and Yossi Melman. *Every Spy a Prince: The Complete History of Israel's Intelligence Community.* Boston: Houghton Mifflin, 1990.

Rebhun, Uzi, and Chaim I. Waxman, eds. *Jews in Israel: Contemporary Social and Cultural Patterns.* Hanover, NH: University Press of New England/ Brandeis University Press, 2004.

Reeve, Simon. *One Day in September: The Full Story of the 1972 Munich Olympics Massacre and the Israeli Revenge Operation "Wrath of God."* New York: Arcade Books, 2001.

Reinhart, Tanya. *Israel/Palestine: How to End the War of 1948.* New York: Seven Stories Press, 2002.

Reiter, Yitzhak. *Islamic Endowments in Jerusalem under British Mandate.* London: Frank Cass, 1996.

Rogan, Eugene L., and Avi Shlaim, eds. *The War for Palestine: Rewriting the History of 1948.* New York: Cambridge University Press, 2001.

Rogers, Peter, and Peter Lydon, eds. *Water in the Arab World: Perspectives and Prognoses.* Cambridge, MA: Division of Applied Sciences, Harvard University, 1994.

Rolef, Susan Hattis, ed. *Political Dictionary of the State of Israel,* 2d edition. New York: Macmillan, 1993.

Ron, James. *Frontiers and Ghettos: State Violence in Serbia and Israel.* Berkeley: University of California Press, 2003.

Ross, Dennis. *The Missing Peace: The Inside Story of the Fight for Middle East Peace.* New York: Farrar, Straus & Giroux, 2004.

Rossoff, Dovid. *Safed: The Mystical City.* Spring Valley, NY, 1991.

Rouhana, Nadim. *Palestinian Citizens in an Ethnic Jewish State.* New Haven, Conn.: Yale University Press, 1997.

Rouyer, Alwyn R. *Turning Water into Politics: The Water Issue in the Palestinian-Israeli Conflict.* New York: St. Martin's Press, 1999.

Roy, Sara. *The Gaza Strip: The Political Economy of De-Development,* 2d edition. Washington, DC: Institute for Palestine Studies, 2001.

Rubin, Barry. *Revolution until Victory? The Politics and History of the PLO.* Cambridge, MA: Harvard University Press, 1994.

Rubinstein, Amnon. *From Herzl to Rabin: The Changing Image of Zionism.* New York: Holmes and Meier, 2000.

Rubenstein, Danny. *The People of Nowhere: The Palestinian Vision of Home.* New York: Times Books, 1991.

Saad-Ghorayeb, Amal. *Hizbullah: Politics and Religion.* London: Pluto Press, 2002.

Sachar, Howard M. *A History of Israel: From the Rise of Zionism to Our Time,* 2d edition. New York: Knopf, 1996.

Said, Edward. *Edward Said: A Critical Reader,* edited by Michael Sprinker. Cambridge, MA, and Oxford, UK: Blackwell, 1992.

———. *End of the Peace Process: Oslo and After.* New York: Pantheon, 2000.

Sakr, Naomi. *Satellite Realms: Transnational Television, Globalization and the Middle East.* New York and London: I. B. Taurus, 2001.

Savir, Uri. *The Process: 1,100 Days that Changed the Middle East.* New York: Vintage, 1999.

Sayigh, Yezid. *Armed Struggle and the Search for State: The Palestinian National Movement, 1949–1993.* Oxford: Clarendon Press, 1997.

Schiff, Benjamin N. *Refugees unto the Third Generation: UN Aid to Palestinians.* Syracuse, NY: Syracuse University Press, 1995.

Schiff, Ze>ev, and Ehud Ya'ari. *Intifada: The Palestinian Uprising—Israel's Third Front.* New York: Simon and Schuster, 1990.

Schumacher, Gottlieb. *The Golan: Survey, Description and Mapping.* Jerusalem, 1998.

Seale, Patrick. *Abu Nidal: A Gun for Hire.* New York: Random House, 1992.

———. *Asad: The Struggle for the Middle East.* Berkeley: University of California Press, 1995.

Segev, Tom. *One Palestine, Complete: Jews and Arabs under the Mandate,* translated by Haim Watzman. New York: Metropolitan Books, 2000.

Seikaly, May. *Transformation of an Arab Society, 1918–1939.* New York: St. Martin's Press, 1995.

Selim, Mohammad El Sayed, ed. *The Organization of the Islamic Conference in a Changing World.* Giza, Egypt: Center for Political Research and Studies, Cairo University, 1994.

Shafir, Gershon. *Land, Labor and the Origins of the Israeli–Palestinian Conflict, 1882–1914,* revised edition. Berkeley: University of California Press, 1996.

Shafir, Gershon, and Yoav Peled. *Being Israeli: The Dynamics of Multiple Citizenship.* Cambridge, UK, and New York: Cambridge University Press, 2002.

Shapira, Anita. *Land and Power: The Zionist Resort to Force, 1881–1948.* Stanford, CA: Stanford University Press, 1999.

Shapland, Greg. *Rivers of Discord: International Water Disputes in the Middle East.* New York: St. Martin's Press; London: Hurst, 1997.

Sharkansky, Ira. *The Politics of Religion and the Religion of Politics: Looking at Israel.* Lanham, MD: Lexington Books, 2000.

Sharon, Ariel (with David Chanoff). *Warrior: The Autobiography of Ariel Sharon,* 2d Touchstone edition. New York: Simon & Schuster, 2001.

Sharoni, Simona. *Gender and the Israel-Palestinian Conflict: The Politics of Women's Resistance.* Syracuse, N.Y.: Syracuse University Press, 1995.

Shavit, Yaacov. *Jabotinsky and the Revisionist Movement, 1925–1948.* Totowa, NJ; London: Frank Cass, 1988.

Shemess, Moshe. *The Palestinian Entity, 1959–1974: Arab Politics and the PLO.* 2d ed. London: Frank Cass, 1996.

Shimoni, Gideon. *The Zionist Ideology.* Hanover, NH: Brandeis University Press/University Press of New England, 1995.

Shlaim, Avi. *Collusion across the Jordan: King Abdullah, the Zionist Movement, and the Partition of Palestine.* New York: Columbia University Press, 1988.

———. "The Rise and Fall of the All-Palestine Government in Gaza." *Journal of Palestine Studies* 20, no. 1 (autumn 1990).

———. *The Iron Wall: Israel and the Arab World since 1948.* New York: W. W. Norton, 1999.

Shlonsky, Ur. *Clause Structure and Word Order in Hebrew and Arabic: An Essay in Comparative Semitic Syntax.* New York: Oxford University Press, 1997.

Shultz, George P. *Turmoil and Triumph: My Years As Secretary of State.* New York: Scribner's, 1993.

Sifry, Micah L., and Christopher Cerf, eds. *The Gulf War Reader: History, Documents, Opinions.* New York: Times Books, 1991.

Silberstein, Laurence J., ed. *New Perspectives on Israeli History: The Early Years of the State.* New York: New York University Press, 1991.

Simon, Reeva S.; Michael M.Laskier; and Sara Reguer, eds. *The Jews of the Middle East and North Africa in Modern Times.* New York: Columbia University Press, 2002.

Slater, Robert. *Warrior Statesman: The Life of Moshe Dayan.* New York: St. Martin's, 1991.

Smith, Barbara J. *The Roots of Separatism in Palestine: British Economic Policy, 1920-1929.* Syracuse, N.Y.: Syracuse University Press, 1993.

Smith, Charles D. *Palestine and the Arab-Israeli Conflict.* New York: St. Martin's Press, 2004.

Smith, Pamela Ann. *Palestine and the Palestinians, 1876–1983.* New York: St. Martin's, 1984.

Smith, Peter. *The Babi and Baha'i Religions: From Messianic Shi'ism to a World Religion.* Cambridge and New York: Cambridge University Press, 1987.

Sofer, Sasson. *Begin: An Anatomy of Leadership.* New York and Oxford, UK: Blackwell, 1988.

Sprinzak, Ehud. *Brother against Brother: Violence and Extremism in Israeli Politics from Altalena to the Rabin Assassination.* New York: Free Press, 1999.

Stern, Jessica. *Terror in the Name of God: Why Religious Militants Kill.* New York: Ecco, 2003.

Sternhell, Ze'ev. *The Founding Myths of Israel: Nationalism, Socialism, and the Making of the Jewish State.* Princeton, NJ: Princeton University Press, 1998.

Stillman, Norman A. *The Jews of Arab Lands in Modern Times.* Philadelphia: Jewish Publication Society, 1991.

Swedenburg, Theodore. *Memories of Revolt: The 1936–1939 Rebellion and the Palestinian National Past.* Fayetteville: University of Arkansas Press, 2003.

Takkenberg, Lex. *The Status of Palestinian Refugees in International Law.* Oxford, UK: Clarendon, 1998.

Tejirian, Eleanor H., and Reeva Simon. *Altruism and Imperialism: Western Cultural and Religious Missions in the Middle East.* New York: Columbia University Press, 2002.

Telhami, Shibley. *Power and Leadership in International Bargaining: The Path to the Camp David Accords.* New York: Columbia University Press, 1990.

Tessler, Mark. *A History of the Israeli-Palestinian Conflict.* Bloomington: Indiana University Press, 1994.

Teveth, Shabtai. *Ben-Gurion's Spy: The Story of the Political Scandal that Shaped Modern Israel.* New York: Columbia University Press, 1996.

Touval, Saadia. *The Peace Brokers: Mediators in the Arab-Israeli Conflict, 1948–1979.* Princeton, NJ: Princeton University Press, 1982.

Troen, Selwyn Ilan. *Imagining Zion: Dreams, Designs, and Realities in a Century of Jewish Settlement.* New Haven, CT: Yale University Press, 2003.

Troen, Selwyn Ilan, and Moshe Shemesh. *The Suez-Sinai Crisis, 1956: Retrospective and Reappraisal.* New York: Columbia University Press; London: Frank Cass, 1990.

Victor, Barbara. *Army of Roses: Inside the World of Palestinian Women Suicide Bombers.* Emmaus, PA: Rodale, 2003.

———. *A Voice of Reason: Hanan Ashrawi and Peace in the Middle East.* New York; Harcourt Brace, 1994.

Wallach, Janet, and John Wallach. *Arafat: In the Eyes of the Beholder.* New York: Lyle Stuart, 1990.

Wasserstein, Bernard. *The British in Palestine: The Mandatory Government and the Arab-Jewish Conflict, 1917–1929,* 2d edition. Oxford, UK, and Cambridge, MA: B. Blackwell, 1991.

Waterbury, John. *The Nile Basin: National Determinants of Collective Action.* New Haven, CT: Yale University Press, 2002.

Weaver, Many Anne. *A Portrait of Egypt: A Journey through the World of Militant Islam.* New York: Farrar Straus Giroux, 1999.

Wiktorowicz, Quintan. *The Management of Islamic Activism: Salafis, the Muslim Brotherhood, and State Power in Jordan.* Albany: State University of New York Press, 2000.

Wilson, Jeremy. *Lawrence of Arabia.* Stroud, UK: Sutton, 1998.

Wilson, Mary C. *King Abdullah, Britain, and the Making of Jordan.* Cambridge and New York: Cambridge University Press, 1987.

Wistrich, Robert S. *Antisemitism: The Longest Hatred.* New York: Pantheon, 1991.

Wolfe, Michael, ed. *One Thousand Roads to Mecca: Ten Centuries of Travelers Writing About the Muslim Pilgrimage.* New York: Grove Press, 1997.

Wright, Richard. *The Color Curtain: A Report on the Bandung Conference.* Jackson: University Press of Mississippi, 1995.

Yahil, Leni. *The Holocaust: The Fate of European Jewry, 1932–1945.* New York: Oxford University Press, 1990.

Yaqub, Salim. *Containing Arab Nationalism: The Eisenhower Doctrine and the Middle East.* Chapel Hill: University of North Carolina Press, 2004.

Yergin, Daniel. *The Prize: The Epic Quest for Oil, Money and Power.* New York: Simon and Schuster, 1991.

Zerubavel, Yael. "The Historic, the Legendary, and the Incredible: Invented Tradition and Collective Memory in Israel." In *Commemorations: The Politics of National Identity,* edited by John R. Gillis. Princeton, NJ: Princeton University Press, 1994.

———. *Recovered Roots: Collective Memory and the Making of Israeli National Tradition.* Chicago: University of Chicago Press, 1995.

Zipperstein, Steven J. *Elusive Prophet: Ahad Ha'am and the Origins of Zionism.* Berkeley: University of California Press, 1993.